Child Analysis and Therapy

edited by

JULES GLENN, M.D.

with the assistance of

Melvin A. Scharfman, M.D.

JASON ARONSON INC.
Northvale, New Jersey
London

ISBN: 0-87668-356-1
Library of Congress Catalog Number: 78-65122

Manufactured in the United States of America. Jason Aronson Inc. offers books and cassettes. For information and catalog write to Jason Aronson Inc., 230 Livingston Street, Northvale, New Jersey 07647.

CONTENTS

Part Four

CHILD ANALYSIS

AT DIFFERENT DEVELOPMENTAL STAGES

Part Five

ASPECTS OF THE

ANALYTIC PROCESS

Part Six

ADJUNCTS TO CHILD ANALYSIS

Part Seven

A SPECIAL SITUATION

Part Eight

APPLICATIONS OF THE PRINCIPLES
OF CHILD ANALYSIS

PREFACE

This volume originated as part of an encyclopedia of psychoanalysis which was never completed. When the editors decided to dismantle the encyclopedia, the many excellent authors who had agreed to contribute articles on child analysis felt it would be wise to produce an autonomous volume. We are indebted to Drs. Mark Kanzer and George H. Pollock, the editors of the defunct encyclopedia, for encouraging this project.

We decided that a new and updated book on the technique of child analysis was needed. In contrast to previous works, we would emphasize two approaches to the subject. In one section we would describe children of different levels of maturity—prelatency, latency, and preadolescence—and demonstrate in detail how the developmental point of view influences technique. Then, pursuing a second approach, we would cut across developmental lines and discuss the analytic process from the consultation procedure through the termination of treatment.

The book that emerged does not employ a series of recipes or formulae. At the very start, we discuss general principles and theoretical underpinnings. Thereafter, each author reviews specific topics in a theoretical context. The contributors provide us a wealth of clinical data to illustrate the issues under consideration and bring them to life. We hope that we have achieved a proper balance of the theoretical and the clinical.

In contrast to previous books in the field, we have not restricted ourselves to child analysis per se. We discuss at length various adjuncts to psychoanalysis—the nursery, tutoring, and simultaneous analysis of parent and child—as well as the applications of child analysis to prevention and treatment in infancy, to psychotherapy, and to psychoanalytic training.

In addition to thanking Drs. Kanzer and Pollock for their initial encouragement—and the former in particular for his continued support—I wish to express my appreciation to my wife, Sylvia, who has actively aided in the production of this book. Her editorial suggestions have led to more explicit pinpointing of ideas. She has been extremely tolerant of the time I have spent on this book—for much of the work had to be done in relative isolation.

Dr. Melvin A. Scharfman has been both encouraging and helpful in lessening the burden of editorial work. Others to whom I am indebted for their suggestions include Drs. Samuel Abrams, Isidor Bernstein, Alan J. Eisnitz, Milton E. Jucovy, and Marianne Kris. I am particularly appreciative of the supervisors who taught me child analysis when I was a student at the New York Psychoanalytic Institute—Mrs. Berta Bornstein, Dr. Marianne Kris, and Dr. Mary O'Neil Hawkins—and to other teachers including Dr. Grace M. Abbate and Dr. Margaret S. Mahler. Patients too can be teachers; I am grateful to all I learned from them as we worked together.

Since we planned this book the Association for Child Psychoanalysis has held meetings in which a number of the topics covered here were considered—confirming the need for an organized up-to-date exposition. Participating in these meetings has enriched the book. So, too, have I been stimulated by my students in the child analysis program at the Downstate Medical Center Division of Psychoanalytic Education. Their astute observations and searching questions have pressed me to seek clarification of the many issues they raised. I also want to thank my colleagues at Downstate who have helped me through the spirit of encouragement typical of that fine psychoanalytic institute.

Deborah Tax and Doris Main have been extremely helpful in providing secretarial services. Mrs. Tax often went out of her way to help me meet deadlines.

Irene Sax and Muriel Spanier Marcuvitz made valuable editorial suggestions regarding some of the chapters. Dr. Jason Aronson has backed this project from the time I first proposed that a volume on child analytic technique was needed. Finally, I want to thank the many authors whose hard work and expertise have made this book possible.

Jules Glenn, M.D.

PREFACE TO THE SECOND PRINTING

The response to the publication of *Child Analysis and Therapy* has been gratifying. Many training programs in child psychoanalysis and psychotherapy have found the volume helpful as a guide to understanding normal children and their families as well as unhappy or disturbed children. It has aided mental health professionals to help children with neuroses, borderline conditions, and psychoses. I am delighted that this volume is once more available.

The text has held up very well because we anticipated many of the advances in psychoanalytic knowledge. We anticipated the insight that comes from studies of children with learning disabilities[1] and the integration of educational approaches with psychoanalysis and therapy. We foresaw the importance of infant observations in the understanding and treatment of prelatency and latency boys and girls.[2, 3] (At the same time, we did not go overboard and misapply the excellent research in the field.) We anticipated the fact that more and more psychoanalytic knowledge and theory would be applied to the techniques of therapy other than analysis. The chapter on the treatment of psychotic children contains principles that can be and have been applied to the treatment of borderline children. Indeed, that chapter should have been titled "Psychoanalytically Oriented Psychotherapy of Borderline and Psychotic Children," a title similar to the one Dr. Rudolf Ekstein originally proposed.

The insights in the chapter on the child analyst's emotional reactions to his patients were extended in the book to include reactions to parents as well. Since then these insights have proved valuable in understanding nonanalytic therapists' emotional responses as well as counterreactions to adult patients.

Child Analysis and Therapy is still up to date. Books on the subject published since 1978 (and before that) do not include the variety of issues it deals with, I say with pride. The authors of the individual chapters are farsighted, experienced, humane psychoanalysts who provided expertise in weaving their complex knowledge into a neat, accurate pattern.

Our aim was to present the intricacies of our knowledge in clear and simple language, with emphasis on clinical descriptions. Theory, we hoped, would come to life through the descriptions of actual events and treatments. The popularity of the book indicates that we have succeeded.

We welcome new readers who will enter the exciting world in which children, parents, and analysts (and therapists) join together to understand and help children with their inner conflicts.

We have one deep regret. Since the publication of *Child Analysis and Therapy,* we lost one of our contributors. Dr. John Sours' death is a loss not only to his family, friends, colleagues, and patients; our science lost a vibrant and poetic contributor. His work on anorexia nervosa, for instance, was scientifically rigorous and emotionally sensitive.[4] Knowing of the pleasure he would have experienced in the second printing, I dedicate it to him.

Jules Glenn, M.D.

1. Rothstein, A. et al. (1988). *Learning Disorders*. Madison, CT: International Universities Press.
2. Stern, D. N. (1985). *The Interpersonal World of the Infant*. New York: Basic Books.
3. Dowling, S., and Rothstein, A., eds. (1989). *The Significance of Infant Observational Research for Clinical Work with Children, Adolescents, and Adults*. Madison, CT: International Universities Press.
4. Sours, J. A. (1980). *Starving to Death in a Sea of Objects. The Anorexia Nervosa Syndrome*. New York: Jason Aronson.

PART ONE

INTRODUCTION

Chapter 1

AN OVERVIEW OF CHILD ANALYTIC TECHNIQUE

Jules Glenn, M.D.

Sigmund Freud, the man who initiated the sexual revolution of our time and whose work adumbrated the liberation of women, also propelled what can be called the children's revolution. He perceived women and children, as well as men, as individuals with deep personal feelings and strivings that Victorian society pretended did not exist and, worse, squelched.

During an era in which the sufferings of the emotionally disturbed were scorned or treated with repressive or punitive measures, Freud developed a therapy that permitted patients to reveal their inner turmoil and the anguish embedded in the black lava of their past. He encouraged his adult patients to talk freely and found that their associations drove them back to significant childhood events. The child in the family setting, far from playing an insignificant role, became the central figure in the drama of adult conflict. When Freud (1909b) was initiating the Rat Man into treatment in 1907, he told his patient that the unconscious mind was like a tomb in which objects from the past were preserved. In what he acknowledged to be an oversimplification, Freud then explained that "the unconscious . . . *was* the infantile" (p. 177). Eventually, Freud reconstructed the Rat Man's childhood responses to his father's ob-

jections to his sexual life—reactions which persisted to the present
and influenced his obsessional neurosis.

Freud, in addition to discovering the significance of childhood for
others, bravely analyzed himself and uncovered the repressed experiences of his own early life. He described his joyous reactions to the
death of his eight-month-old brother, Julius, when he was nineteen
months of age, as engendering the seed of self-reproach within him. He
described his nurse, who remained with the family until he was two and
a half years old, as the "prime originator of [his] neurosis" and recalled
seeing his "mater nuda," a memory of his oedipal years.[1]

Having reconstructed many of the significant events of childhood
from the analyses of adults, Freud turned to children themselves to
confirm and extend his findings. He asked his colleagues to make observations of their youngsters—and also studied his own.

Then, in 1908, the importance of the child in psychoanalysis increased. In addition to childhood being a source of adult difficulty, the
child himself became important. In that year, Freud (1909a) treated
(through the father) the son of one of the members of his Wednesday
evening group—five-year-old Hans who had developed a phobia of
horses. Freud's touching and empathic description of the frightened
little patient from his initial restricted anxious state to his final "trium-
phant phantasy" and recovery reflects the new conception of the child
as an individual. Freud insisted that the child's curiosity and suffering
should not be swept aside, but dealt with forthrightly by the parents in
accordance with the child's own wishes for information and help.

Freud's personal analysis, his remarkable ability to reveal to himself
his past traumata and face, even revel in, their implications, aided him
in championing the child as a human being in his own right. He knew
from his personal as well as clinical experiences that the presence of
infantile libidinal impulses was normal and did not signify degeneracy,
as was then (1909) commonly believed.

We must pause here to say that Freud did not totally appreciate the
child. In some ways he viewed his young patient, Hans, as a small adult.
Freud did not fully appreciate the subtle differences between the five-
year-old's cognitive capacities and the grown-up's; for example, he
somehow overlooked the little boy's reaction to a tonsillectomy. Nevertheless, his recognition of the child as an individual went far beyond the
knowledge of the day—the difference can be compared to the state of

physics before and after Newton. Whereas his colleague, Ferenczi, decided that a patient was unanalyzable because he could not free associate, Freud realized the child was incapable of sustained free association. He and Hans's father let the boy communicate in an age-appropriate way.

Freud did not adopt the Platonic view that the child can be fully molded or the Rousseauean belief in the primitive's complete innocence. He rejected Locke's contention that the mind is a tabula rasa and the contrary belief that all knowledge is a priori. Under Lamarck's influence, Freud contended that there exists unconscious knowledge—for example, of the primal scene, the primal horde, or even the threat of castration. At the same time, he recognized the potent influence of the environment. Freud saw that there is an innate timetable of development which can be affected by external circumstances. At the time he wrote about Little Hans, the details of the interaction had not been established and, in fact, we are still attempting to achieve a full appreciation of the complex unfolding of childhood. (Today we reject the Lamarkian hypothesis without discarding the importance of biology.) Freud's descriptions of the libidinal stages and the development of the ego and superego have been supplemented by studies of affective and cognitive development in infancy (Spitz 1965, Weil 1970, Inhelder and Piaget 1958), new concepts of latency (Bornstein 1951, Inhelder and Piaget 1958) and adolescence (A. Freud 1958, Blos 1962, Erikson 1963, Inhelder and Piaget 1958). Mahler's studies of separation-individuation have broadened the scope of psychoanalytic research (Mahler, Pine, & Bergman 1975).

Despite Freud's deficiencies in 1909, we can hardly fault him for not seeing the entire picture at once. In science, slow and tortuous advances are based on a few huge leaps, like Freud's discoveries of the importance of the dynamic unconscious and the impact of childhood.

Freud's interest in children per se rather than children as seen through the adult's eyes led in several directions. He asked whether his study of Little Hans "can be made to shed any light upon the mental life of children or to afford any criticism of our educational aims" (p. 101, Freud 1909a). Indeed, the Wednesday evening study group, which had already discussed the sexual enlightenment of children in January, 1907, once again turned to this thorny topic. These pioneering meetings were stimulants to modern beliefs in honesty in parent-child relations and the child's right to obtain the knowledge necessary for his optimal development (Glenn, Bezahler, and Glenn, in press).

Freud's interest in direct observation and the application of psychoanalytic findings to child rearing practices also stirred future analysts (and others) to study the importance of parents in infancy and childhood. The work of Spitz (1945, 1965) has revealed that children reared without constant parents or parent substitutes will suffer developmental arrests which, if the deprivation is sufficient, will be extremely severe. Those attempting to prevent such failures in growth and maturity have rightly proposed adoption as a most important prophylactic measure. We continue to search for the optimal means of promoting mental health in infancy and childhood, as Dr. Sally Provence outlines in chapter 21. For instance, we try to refine procedures for preventing adoption from creating difficulties. Dr. Herbert Wieder has undertaken the important job of investigating the complications of adoption and the special problems that arise in the analyses of adoptees in chapter 20. His work is but one attempt to determine the effects of child-rearing practices and the methods most suited to raise children equipped to adapt to and improve our society.

The treatment of Little Hans in 1908 was, as we have seen, the first application of the technical principles of adult analysis to a child. Child analysis, a new therapeutic discipline, was soon to develop and, indeed, continues to evolve.

The essential feature of child analysis, as with adult analysis, is interpretation of the patient's conflicting drives and defenses—a premise stated by Dr. Jules Glenn in chapter 2, below, and confirmed by authors throughout this book. As the analytic process gets under way, interpretation of defenses leads to the revelation of drive derivatives which in turn can be understood. The patient sees not only the nature of his unconscious drives, but also learns how he grapples with his forbidden urges. As a result of the analytic work, the ego comes to function more adaptively. Interpretations lead to alteration of defenses, superego modification, and greater drive gratification. Regressive tendencies diminish. The child overcomes inhibitions and developmental arrests. The energies released and neutralized become available for sublimated activity.

Two approaches to the practice of child analysis appeared. Anna Freud's method (1922–1970) involved an initial "preparatory" phase in which the analyst won the child over to analysis. Following this, the patient was treated by careful interpretation of the defenses and then, as the repressed became conscious, of the drives.[2] Melanie Klein (1932), on the other hand, eschewed any acts that might be considered seductive. She interpreted the child's behavior diligently from the start. Her interventions often bypassed the defenses and struck directly at the unconscious symbolic meanings of the patient's play and talk during his sessions. While the ego was not completely ignored, the defenses which were most focused on were the primitive ones. Projective-identification implies extreme vagueness of boundaries between the patient's self-representation and object-representation. Mrs. Irma Pick and Dr. Hanna Segal describe the Kleinian approach in chapter 15.

Whereas Anna Freud found the transference to be weak in child analysis because the child still maintained his ties to his parents, Melanie Klein interpreted the child's feelings toward the therapist from the start. Adherents to the Kleinian point of view generally try to minimize contact with parents and thus avoid the resultant interference with the development of the transference. The followers of Anna Freud usually see parents regularly to obtain information about the child.

In recent years, the Freudians have drawn closer to the Kleinian approach in maintaining a stance of abstinence. Whereas previously it had been common to give the children food or gifts as well as to actively try to win them over, the present trend is to avoid such gratifications whenever possible. Paradoxically, the insights of an ego psychology which the Kleinians reject have convinced many Freudians that analysis can best be carried out in an atmosphere of relative abstinence.

Berta Bornstein (1949) used defense analysis rather than seductiveness to establish a working relationship in which the child benefited from the analyst's interpretations. The terms *therapeutic alliance* and *working alliance* appeared years later, but we can apply them in retrospect to her procedure. Interpretations of defenses and attention to affects will enable the child to seek help through the analytic process. When the initial "preparatory" period is avoided, the transference can be observed with greater clarity and then analyzed. Although we may salute Melanie Klein for her insistence on abstinence, we must also recognize that the analysis of transference by present-day Freudians is not quite the same as that of the Kleinians. Kleinians focus on primitive fantasies and defenses while Freudians emphasize reality factors and more mature defenses as well.

The increased knowledge of child development, which has grown out of direct observation of children and findings in the analytic consultation room itself, has enabled us to decide more accurately who is best suited for psychoanalytic treatment. The developmental point of view is essential to the evaluation of patients—a fact that permeates the three chapters on assessment and a later chapter in which Dr. John A. Sours describes diagnostic consultation procedures (chapter 22). Drs. Isidor Bernstein and Albert M. Sax (chapter 3) clearly demonstrate that the consultant must not only take symptoms into account; he must also examine the child's developmental achievements and setbacks. A major indication for treatment is the failure to reach or maintain age-appropriate levels of development, and symptoms themselves—phobias, obsessions, or sadness, for instance—must be evaluated in a developmental context.

There are a host of possible configurations. Transient symptoms may be normal expressions of developmental stress. Neurotic symptoms requiring analysis may appear as a result of unconscious conflict in children whose immaturity makes them vulnerable to conflict, as well as in patients without developmental delay. Regression secondary to conflict may produce developmental deficits.

We can best understand diagnostic categories when we consider developmental issues. Psychoneurotic children have achieved relatively stable oedipal object relationships which are enmeshed in conflict. In schizophrenia or borderline states, there is extensive arrest in all areas of functioning—libidinal as well as ego. Learning disabilities, which may occur in a number of diagnostic categories, involve at least partial arrests. They may result from difficulties of a functional nature that are primarily constitutional, or be caused by an organic brain disorder, stem from environmental factors (such as overstimulation which delays latency), or combinations of these factors. Inhibition secondary to psychic conflict can cause a learning disability.

Once a diagnostic assessment has been made, the consultant must decide on the proper therapy. Analysis succeeds best when the child has achieved stable oedipal object relations and when the drives involved have become embroiled in unconscious conflict to produce serious symptoms or inhibitions. Reality testing should be relatively intact and ego deficiencies minimal. This configuration is the basis for psychoneuroses as differentiated from psychoses or borderline states in which preoedipal factors prevail (often seriously distorting the oedipal phase), assessment of reality is poor and ego functioning markedly distorted. Frankly psychotic patients require treatment other than analysis. The decision as to which borderline (and other) patients are analyzable can be reached only after determining which ego functions are intact, which are impaired, and to what degree. Dr. Martin A. Silverman calls our attention, in chapter 4, to the fact that the developmental profile constructed by Anna Freud demands careful attention to the details of the balance of drives, ego, and superego.

Other factors which Bernstein and Sax stress are the patient's intelligence and psychological mindedness. If these are not well developed, the patient will not be able to understand and profit from the analyst's interpretations. Finally, the parents' traits must be considered to determine, among other things, whether they can sustain the analysis through periods of stress.

The analytic consultant usually reaches a decision about analyzability after interviewing the child and his parents and informally assessing the child's developmental level and capabilities as well as the parents' characteristics. Anna Freud has conceived a rigorous format for assessment at the start of analysis and thereafter—one of tremendous research value. Silverman provides us a lucid description of the Developmental Profile.

Psychological tests, information from teachers, and physical examinations will supplement the information acquired from the patient and his family. A special source of information is available for very young children. Nursery school teachers, especially from superb facilities such as the Hanna Perkins School described by Erna Furman in chapter 5, possess a unique expertise. The teachers' detailed observations of their pupils as they engage in creative play and in their interaction with teachers and other children can cast light on areas not visible in the ordinary analytic consultation. A nursery can provide an ideal setting in which the consultant himself can observe the child in action. Since teachers know the entire family, they can aid in the decision as to which treatment is most appropriate and help prepare parents and children for analysis or other therapy. Certain forms of treatment probably should be done only in a nursery setting in which the therapist can objectively ascertain the child's reaction to interventions, and hence the appropriateness of the intervention. Kestenberg (Olch 1971) has suggested that treatment through parents can succeed at the Hanna Perkins school because this type of information is available; in other settings such a procedure may be hazardous.

Knowledge of normal and pathological development has also enabled us to refine our technique and to construct interpretations appropriate to each developmental stage. Both the form and content of interventions will vary in different periods of the child's life. (Of course, the patient's individual traits based on other factors will affect the analyst's modes of interpretation.)

The prelatency child, the latency child, and the preadolescent (described respectively in chapters 6–8 by Glenn, Kramer and Byerly, and Wieder) differ in both drive and ego organization. The prelatency period is characterized by intense and relatively unrestrained impulse expression. Depending on the child's level of development, oral, anal, or phallic and oedipal urges will predominate. The drive organization and the cognitive state of these small children—the prominence of primary process thinking tempered by growing secondary process thought, narcissism, and egocentricity—intertwine to produce an exciting creative child who can easily charm the analyst by revealing a colorful fantasy life.

The cognitive style changes with the advent of latency. At that time superego functions restrain impulse discharge, thus permitting the innate capacity for secondary process thinking to come to the fore. Impulses are tamed and utilized for sublimated pursuits. Hartmann (1964) has emphasized that neutralized libidinal or aggressive energy complements the original neutral energy used for these purposes. The child becomes interested in school work, hobbies, and organized games as he identifies with parents and teachers. These children, who typically are compulsive, would be boring to work with in an uncovering therapy were it not for sparks of "interrupted" latency that produce periods of exciting revelation.

Things change once more with preadolescence, which is characterized by the paradoxical coincidence of an increased cognitive capacity —the child enters the stage of formal operations (Inhelder and Piaget 1958)—and ego regression. The intellect of some children at this age blossoms, but for the most part teachers complain that the child entering junior high is unruly and undisciplined—restless and distracted from serious study. The heightened intensity of drives disrupts ego functions.

The analysis of children of these different stages will vary. The play of the prelatency child will often reveal his conflicts in more or less transparent form, allowing for relatively rapid interpretation. The analyst of the latency child will have to be more cautious, lest he interfere with sublimations, and more patient as he waits for those sessions that permit palpable interpretation. The preadolescent's therapist will also have to be patient but for different reasons. The preadolescent's restless, provocative behavior and silences will try the analyst's stability. Eventually, however, his patience will often be rewarded. The preadolescent, finding the therapist steady, stalwart and sincere, will come to trust him with secrets he had previously kept even from himself.

Despite the vast differences between patients of different developmental stages there is an essential identity to the analytic process at any age. Hence, in one section of this book, we are able to describe a chronological development characteristic of analysis. In the opening phase, described by Dr. Peter B. Neubauer (chapter 9), the therapeutic alliance is established. As Neubauer emphasizes, however, this alliance wanes and must be refueled periodically throughout the analysis. In the opening phase the analyst must be especially astute. He must evaluate the seriousness of the patient's pathology and determine if the child requires a preparatory period in which to attain the maturity necessary for analysis. The analysand must be mature enough to adequately differentiate himself from his environment, thus permitting transferences to develop and be analyzed.

Although the stages of analysis cannot be separated completely, the middle period is characterized by the appearance of analyzable transferences, and the achievement of a relatively stable therapeutic alliance between the patient and analyst. This stage of analysis is elucidated by Dr. Melvin A. Scharfman in chapter 10. In the ideal adult analysis, transference manifestations coalesce and the patient experiences a transference neurosis—an organized structure that replaces (or at least mirrors) the neurosis that brought the patient to treatment; the patient experiences his conflicts in relation to his analyst. In children, however, a transference neurosis rarely appears. When it does, it is usually short-lived.

Scharfman distinguishes the child's transference reactions, which are disguised repetitions of emotions originally experienced toward parents and other significant persons of the patient's past, from displacements from the parents as they presently are, and from the analyst as realistically represented in the child's mind. When the child advances to a new developmental stage, he may conceive of the analyst as a new object appropriate to that stage before he develops a new representation of the parent. Then, in an extensive discussion of the essential requirements for the ability to develop a utilizable transference, Scharfman expands on previous analytic formulations.

In chapter 11, Dr. Paul Kay carefully examines the balance of frustration and gratification in child analysis and its affect on both the transference and the therapeutic alliance. One of his patients, frustrated when Dr. Kay would not accept a gift, benefited from the therapist's abstinent attitude. The emotions this incident evoked led the patient to insights into his feelings about his mother's death, and his intense desire for gratification.

Both Kay and Scharfman note that a proper balance of frustration and gratification can further the developmental achievements of distinguishing self-representation from object representation, reality testing, and secondary process thinking, all of which are requirements for transference formation. An abstinent attitude and reliance on internalization can also help convince the patient of the analyst's sincerity and his devotion to the therapeutic process.

Dr. Ted E. Becker in chapter 12 demonstrates how the analyst can encourage dream analysis, and thus enhance the working alliance and therapeutic achievement. He emphasizes that dream analysis in children and adults is essentially the same, and points to the numerous cues available to the child analyst in understanding his patient's dreams. Although children frequently cannot associate to the elements of the manifest dream, the child analyst may ascertain the day residues from the child or his parent. The therapist also relies on the flow of material during the session, his knowledge of the current state of the analysis and, perhaps more than in adult analysis, on a knowledge of symbolism. The analyst can help a patient understand his dreams and integrate dream interpretation into the rest of the analytic work.

Kay takes a courageous step when he alerts the reader to his personal reactions while attempting to determine the optimal balance of frustration and gratification in any particular analysis. He describes his own uncertainties, an essential part of the analysis. Drs. Isidor Bernstein and Jules Glenn, in chapter 13, "The Child Analyst's Emotional Reactions to His Patients," carry the matter further. They note that not only countertransferences, but other responses to the patient as well, comprise the analyst's reactions. These include: transferences to the patient; identifications and counteridentifications; experiencing the patient as an extension of the analyst's self; and reactions to the patient as a real person. The latter include empathic responses which can generate insight, and signal affects which can also be used to further the analysis.

Here again we find ourselves in an important arena first entered by Freud. He alerted analysts to the importance of self-analysis to avoid irrational interferences with the therapeutic process. Child analysts have special difficulties to cope with. Grown-ups have surrendered childlike modes of thought to behave adaptively in the adult world, but the child analyst must conjure these up once more if he is to empathize with his patients. In addition, the child analyst, finding himself in the midst of his patient's actual family conflict may discover that his own childhood conflicts are reappearing.

Present-day educational arrangements in the United States require that training as a child analyst follows adult analytic training. The embryo child analyst may have completed or be in the process of terminating his personal analysis when he starts working with children. This circumstance may at times interfere with the optimal development of the student unless he returns to analysis.

In chapter 14 Dr. Lawrence M. Sabot, along with Glenn and Bernstein, notes that the analyst reacts emotionally to his patient's parents as well as to the patient himself. Frequently the therapist identifies with the child and develops transference reactions to the patient's parents as if they were his own father and mother. Matters are more complicated when the analyst concurrently identifies with the parents, and becomes antagonistic to the child who, he imagines, refuses to recover and become a perfect extension of the grown-ups.

It is generally agreed that the patient's parents are in a difficult position. They must act as their child's alter ego and support the treatment, while at the same time they find themselves locked out of the analysis itself—unable to learn the details of the interplay between child and analyst. Controversy regarding the analyst's relationship with his patient's parents centers around whether to see the parent and whether to advise him or even offer him interpretations. The position of Glenn, Bernstein, and Sabot is that an "information alliance," in which the parents alert the analyst to the present circumstances of the child's life and the past reality, is most important. Sufficient knowledge of the reality of the patient's life usually cannot be obtained from the child himself, but is necessary for a proper balance of interpretation. Fantasies and reality, past and present, should be taken into account when formulating interpretations.

Dr. Samuel Abrams describes the new forms that the interactions of child, parent and analyst take in the terminal phase of analysis (chapter 16). The therapist must be cognizant of the parents' as well as the patient's wishes and worries, happiness and mourning, when the parties involved—the patient, the parents, and the doctor—make the decision to end the analysis. The analysis often is enriched as the issue of losing the person who has played such an important role in the patient's life takes center stage. Although the child still has his parents at home, and thus can tolerate the relinquishment of his analyst better than most adults, he nevertheless reacts to the loss. The transference may be muted, but the attachment is still present and to be contended with. As had been true throughout the analysis, the therapist relies on interpretation as his chief instrument to the very end.

A child does not live in isolation. The analyst is keenly aware of the reality of his patient's life circumstances as he engages in the treatment. Interpretations include references to his external, as well as his internal world. The analyst perceives his patient's parents, teachers and peers as the child represents them, and also as they are in actuality. The analyst also sees the child's distorted view of his parents in the transference.

The child continues to be affected by his parents throughout treatment. At times, when parental behavior is detrimental, the analyst finds it necessary to attempt to alter it. When the parents are both motivated and analyzable, change is best accomplished if they enter analysis themselves. Skillful psychotherapy or guidance may be the preferred course in many cases.

Dr. Ilse Hellman, in chapter 17 on "Simultaneous Analysis of Parent and Child," demonstrates the value of this approach. She is also cognizant of the research value of simultaneous analysis. When the child's therapist and the therapist of the father or mother report to a single coordinator, contamination is avoided, and the mutual interaction of parents and child can be evaluated.

Dr. Hellman clarifies the means by which a child reads and reacts to his parents' unconscious. The pathways of unconscious communication can be verbal, preverbal and nonverbal. The child may identify with his father or mother and acquire defenses typical of his family. When the balance of defenses is proper, the child will benefit, but excessive use of pathological defense mechanisms will interfere with his adaptive capacity.

Parents influence their children in other ways as well. Some mothers discourage separation-individuation by keeping the infant excessively close to them, while others cannot tolerate contact. Some evoke anxiety and interfere with oedipal development by premature or continuing sexual stimulation, or by deprecating the other parent. There are mothers who use their children to fulfill their own ambitions, and thus diminish their youngsters' pleasure in achievement.

Of course, a parent cannot completely mold his son or daughter. The child possesses an innate psychic apparatus with a degree of autonomous functioning which can be altered by the environment. Glenn, Sabot, and Bernstein emphasize the complex mutual interaction of parent and child and the effect of extra-familial influences. Hellman notes that when pathological parental influence reinforces the child's propensities, the influence is greatest. Similarly, when the adult's unconscious fantasies express themselves in actual behavior, the pathogenic effect is greatest.

Tutoring, another important adjunct to child analysis, can help the child overcome learning difficulties which are based on innate perceptual disturbances (disturbances that may have contributed to the neurosis) or are secondary to unconscious conflict. Even in the latter case, special instruction may help the child with his school work and prevent years of academic difficulty during the period prior to the resolution of the basic unconscious inhibitions through the analysis.

Joseph Opperman, in chapter 18 ("Tutoring: The Remediation of Cognitive and Academic Defects by Individual Instruction"), describes the importance of the child's relationship to the educator if tutoring is to succeed. He also alerts the reader to the dangers of a split transference, especially if the tutor makes interpretations to the child.

We have already discussed the use of the nursery school as an aid to assessment during the initial evaluation of the child. Elizabeth Daunton, in a later section (chapter 19), discusses the help that the nursery can be during the analysis. The nursery school teacher can complement information received from the parents by describing her observations to the analyst. She may also help the child with sublimations and mastery of tasks, especially when the analysis frees inhibitions and enables the child to use his energies more adaptively. Help with reality testing and inner control may increase the child's analyzability. In addition, the teacher may aid the parents to sustain the analysis.

I have never given tranquilizers, psychic energizers or sedatives to a child in analysis, and I have not heard of such a practice. In general, one may say that analyzable children do not need medicine. When drugs are required, the psychosis, borderline condition, or organic brain disorder is usually so severe as to preclude analysis as the treatment of choice.

The adjuncts to analysis that we have described may be the major—or even the sole—mode of help for the child where analysis is not indicated. Nonneurotic children with learning disabilities not due to conflict but maturational lags or perceptual disorders, require tutoring, not analysis. Nursery schools help children socially as well as educationally. Analyses of parents may improve the atmosphere of the home and thus help the child.

Child psychoanalysis, which appeared as an adaptation of adult analysis, has stimulated many other forms of child therapy, some of which Dr. John A. Sours discusses in chapter 23.[3]

Some forms of child psychotherapy have evolved as modifications of child analysis. Other forms developed relatively independently of analysis but were later influenced by it. Still other forms of treatment, psychopharmacology, or conditioning for instance, do not rely on analytic principles, but analytic understanding may help us comprehend their effectiveness or limitations.

The mental hygiene movement was growing at the time that child analysis was taking form.[4] Child guidance clinics, which were springing up in the United States, developed a team approach in the treatment of children. Psychiatrists, social workers, and psychologists worked together. One member of the team treated the child, while others guided —or treated—his father or mother. Soon group therapy supplemented individual efforts. In addition, these clinics started to utilize analytic insights. They adopted interpretive methods of therapy, and principles of guidance based on psychoanalytic knowledge.

Later, studies of family dynamics, based on the analytic finding that family members profoundly influence one another, emerged.

Methods of altering family structure to alleviate individual pathology developed. Freud's vivid description (1905) of his adolescent patient trapped in a web of family intrigue (Dora) is a remarkable example of pathological interaction.

A spreading movement to encourage the treatment of delinquents spawned such men as August Aichhorn. Aichhorn, who possessed an uncanny talent for influencing antisocial adolescents, later became an analyst and applied his new understanding to his patients (1935, 1964). By demonstrating to his delinquent charges the inadequacy of their methods, Aichhorn converted them into neurotics, and then used interpretive psychotherapy to help them recover.

Other therapists also conceived of using aspects of the psychoanalytic method for therapeutic purposes. Adapting the use of free play in child analysis, Levy encouraged children to enact what he determined were their core conflicts, and thus find relief—even without the therapist's using interpretation. Children who had undergone discrete traumata, such as surgery, could master their anxiety through play. Lauretta Bender used a specific type of play material—puppets—and was far less restrictive of the type of fantasy the child chose to enact, but also refrained from interpretation. Supposedly, abreaction was the means of recovery. Others decided that the relationship alone could bring about a cure.

These noninterpretive modes of treatment contrast with analysis in which interpretation is the chief vehicle of psychoanalytic change. However, as Anna Freud (1965) pointed out, even in analysis the child may select what he needs from the analytic situation and bring about the therapeutic relief he requires. Some children need to identify with the analyst to achieve a sense of wholeness, while others build inner structure from this identification or use this mechanism to achieve object constancy. Some children use repetitive play for working through or to achieve a degree of mourning, while others make use of it for mastery. The child may learn from the analyst how to use defenses adaptively or to modulate his demands and compromise.

These methods, while not the core of analysis, can be important factors in recovery. While psychoanalysis is so structured that the child can choose what he needs from the smorgasbord before him, specific therapies may restrict the menu.

Another important development involves the use of interpretation in analytically oriented child psychotherapy. Children who cannot participate in psychoanalysis per se may benefit from a limited form of interpretive treatment. Certain children who are not sufficiently psychological-minded to engage in analysis, can nevertheless understand interpretations of minor impact. Other children with fragile defenses, who would deteriorate if rigorous analysis were instituted, can tolerate and benefit from a modicum of interpretation carefully selected for their needs. Often, this same type of patient requires more emphasis on reality testing and environmental manipulation than occurs in analysis.

Rudolf Ekstein and his colleagues apply the principles of psychoanalysis to the treatment of borderline and psychotic children in chapter 24. While acknowledging that the constitutional factor is of much greater importance in the etiology of schizophrenia than in neurosis, they state that the complex interplay of the psychotic child and his family is so important that one cannot point to a discrete etiology. The psychotic child affects his family profoundly, and they in turn influence him. In a circular interchange, each encourages the primitive autistic and symbiotic retreats, advances, and anxiety typical of the disorder.

The child's family is so intimately involved in the disturbance that each individual family member must be treated to disrupt the pathological interplay. Often even individual therapy is insufficient, and ancillary help is needed. These "support systems" include special schools or a therapeutic milieu away from home.

Utilizing Mahler's (Mahler and Furer 1968, Mahler, Pine and Bergman 1975) work to enrich their own, Ekstein and his colleagues observe the primitive personality structure of the psychotic or borderline child. Autistic and symbiotic fixations dominate the picture. The symbiotic patient attempting to separate from his parents becomes panicky and retreats to autism, which, according to them, also affords progressive potential. Repeated regressions and progressions between autism, symbiosis, and more mature functioning are typical. These vacillations prevail as psychoanalytically oriented intensive therapy proceeds.

The characteristics and needs of borderline and psychotic children impel them to seek help through features of the treatment situation which other patients use to a lesser extent. The therapist must modify his approach to meet those needs. He is available—may even offer himself—for contact and identifications which may afford temporary relief when the patient feels himself completed by the therapist's presence. These identifications may eventually lead to more permanent structural changes within the patient. The child may acquire a greater degree of reality testing, secondary process thinking, and the use of more mature defensive and adaptive mechanisms, including impulse control. Preoedipal features may become less prominent, and the oedipal more stable and less distorted.

In order to help the psychotic or borderline child, the therapist must empathize with, and understand his patient. He must learn his patient's primitive way of thinking with its confusing use of metaphor, simile and indirect expression. He will then be able to talk to the child in his own language and provide a relatively safe base from which the frightening advances and retreats can be interpreted and progression encouraged.

The therapy Ekstein et al. describe is daring indeed. They treat severely ill patients and their parents with great skill. In one example, a psychotic mother, although seen only once a week, benefits from insight therapy. Usually people that ill require more frequent therapy if it is to be interpretive, or simply support if the patient is available only once a week. The importance of the well trained and experienced team is intrinsic to this type of work, and it should not be attempted by inexperienced therapists working in relative isolation.

Other methods of working with psychotic children have developed. Manuel Furer has used a tripartite treatment design in which child, mother and therapist frequently work together. In this setting, the mother hears many of the interpretations—based on analytic understanding of psychosis—made to the child. In addition, the therapist observes when the patient's mother fails to understand the child's cues, and then teaches the significance of these cues to the parent. The work is slow and plodding, but eventually can be rewarding. Anni Bergman's treatment of Violet serves as an illustration of the difficulties and rewards. (See Mahler and Furer 1968.)

We have included a section on the application of the principles of child analysis to psychotherapy, but must emphasize that the main focus of this book has been on child analysis itself.

The rigors of the training for this specialty are described by Dr. John J. Francis in his outline of the teaching of child psychoanalysis in the United States in chapter 25. In this country, psychoanalytic institutes accredited by the American Psychoanalytic Association require that one be a student of adult analysis prior to starting child analytic training. There are a number of justifications for this position. Historically and conceptually, adult analysis preceded child analysis. As child analysis was adapted from techniques with adults, it makes sense to learn the original model first. Further, work with parents, and the evaluation of the child's family so essential to child analysis requires an understanding of grown-ups best acquired through analysis of adults.

On the other hand, it may be argued that this requirement may thwart many potential child analysts who are simply not talented in adult work. Just as most adult analysts do not possess the capacity to analyze children—special types of empathy and tolerance are required—so too there are those who do best with children and eschew adult analysis.

Recently the Dutch Psychoanalytic Society has instituted a training program for child analysts who are not adult analysts. Even before that skillful child analysts—sometimes labeled child therapists—have succeeded in acquiring training without analyzing adults.

A committee of the American Psychoanalytic Association, under the chairmanship of Dr. Morton Shane, is studying the feasibility of constructing a core curriculum leading to training in child or adult analysis, depending on the proclivities of the student. A core curriculum would also underline the contributions that child analysis has made to adult analysis.

The interaction of child and adult analytic theories is so great that their contributions often intertwine. Although the authors most concerned with the treatment of borderline and narcissistic patients (Kernberg 1975, Kohut 1971) are not child analysts, the observations of child analysts, particularly Mahler (Mahler, Pine, and Bergman 1975), have clarified their constructions and stimulated further refinement of their concepts. Observation of infant and child can extend the knowledge of narcissism gained from adult analysis.

On an immediately practical level, the flexibility necessary for analyzing children has stimulated adult therapists, who recognize the infantile in their disturbed patients, to deal with them in a similarly flexible manner. That methods of communication other than free association can be utilized for understanding and interpretation has long been known. However, the child analyst relies almost completely on modes other than free association as he listens to the child's relatively controlled speech and watches his play which can be nonverbal. He develops an expertise that can be taught to analysts of adults.

The developmental point of view is related to, but subtly different from, the genetic point of view (Abrams 1977, Settlage et al. 1974, Shane 1977). The latter arose as one of the metapsychological approaches to clinical data (Rapaport and Gill 1959) obtained in adult analysis. The analyst uses the patient's childhood recollections and distorted "memories," in the form of dreams, acting out, transference reactions and screen memories, to reconstruct childhood experiences. The method is *retrospective;* the adult neurosis is explained as a modified repetition of the infantile neurosis.

When Freud urged his colleagues to observe their children, he laid the groundwork for another means of understanding children and adults which was to culminate in the appearance of the developmental point of view. Longitudinal studies—observations from childhood on —(Kris 1957), allow us to learn the sequence of events in an individual's life *prospectively.* Fries (1977) has recently reported the development of a child from infancy to adulthood. Direct observation was the means of collecting data, not analysis. The case of Frankie afforded another opportunity to study a pathological epigenesis. This patient was first analyzed when he was five years old, was analyzed a second time by Ritvo (1966) when he attended college.

The organization of data gathered prospectively comprises the developmental point of view. Development, of course, continues throughout life (Erikson 1963). It does not come to a halt when a person reaches adolescence or becomes an adult. As Abrams (1977) noted, the older person does not simply repeat infantile conflicts. New elements enter at later stages, creating a new gestalt. For instance, the teenager's new cognitive capacities and new forms of narcissism make idealism and adaptive planned action possible (Glenn and Urbach, in press).

Child analysts, who are constantly aware of the forward sweep of movement—Anna Freud (1965) has referred to a drive to complete development—can alert adult analysts to the continuing development of grown-ups, and to developmental arrests that remain from childhood or start in adulthood.

Child analysis and direct observation permit one to know what children are really like and what they experience with an accuracy not easily attained in reconstructions. Armed with the knowledge and empathy derived from work with children, the analyst can offer reconstructions to his adults patients that are more accurate and therefore more helpful. To induce vivid impressions of childhood, the child analyst can describe analyses, or direct observations of youngsters, or he can show his students movies of children. In addition, students of adult analysis can make direct observations themselves or treat at least one child, preferably with supervision. More exact reconstructions of both external events as seen through the child's eyes and his emotional reactions will then be possible.

Child analysts have influenced techniques with adults in other ways as well. Anna Freud's (1936) momentous study of the ego and the defense mechanism is replete with examples of children in conflict, and lays the basis for the theory of technique of adult as well as child analysis. The analyst, "when he sets about his work of enlightenment . . . takes his stand at a point equidistant from the id, the ego and the superego" (p. 28). The therapist must avoid a one-sided analysis. He must help his patients understand ego as well as id, defenses as well as drives, and means of dealing with reality as well as inner urges. Certainly this approach to analysis did not stem from child analytic findings alone. However, the child analyst's careful study of the ego's management of drives as the child matures fortifies this technique.

Similarly, the fact that the patient perceives the analyst as a real person as well as a transference object did not arise from observations in child analysis alone, but in the child analytic situation, a patient's representation of the analyst as he really is stands out in relief.

The concept of the therapeutic or working alliance—which rests on the premise that the patient is aware that the analyst intends to help him through analysis—was developed by adult analysts (Zetzel 1956, Greenson 1967) under the influence of observations by child analysts. Anna Freud (1962) brought perspective to the theories of those who emphasized the symbiotic base upon which the therapeutic alliance rests. She stated:

> The therapeutic alliance between analyst and patient is *not* carried by any of these earlier stages of object relationship although all of these stages are "material" . . . [It] is based . . . on ego attitudes that go with later stages, namely, on self-observation, insight, give-and-take in object relationships, the willingness to make sacrifices. It is the oedipal relationship which offers those advantages; thus it serves as material for interpretation, as well as for cementing the alliance between analyst and patient. [p. 192]

We have come full circle. We started with the historical fact that adult analysis gave birth to child analysis. Now we see that the child has grown and influenced the parent who, at times, resists his off-spring's suggestions. The mutual enrichment of child and adult analysis is not a primitive symbiosis, but depends on mature and rational cooperations.

NOTES

1. A full exposition of Freud's self-analysis is impossible here. The reader is referred to Jones (1953–1957), Schur (1972), Freud (1887–1902), and Kanzer and Glenn (1979).

2. Sigmund Freud used a preparatory maneuver with some of his adult patients. As he initiated the Rat Man "into the nature of the treatment" in 1907, Freud praised him, thus making analysis more attractive. In the first session of A. Kardiner's analysis in 1921, Freud also complimented his analysand, spurring him to enthusiastic work (Kardiner 1977). Today, however, we generally avoid this approach.

3. The reader is referred to Alexander and Selesnick (1966) for a fuller discussion of history.

4. 1909, the year that Freud published the case of Little Hans, was also the year that the National Committee for Mental Hygiene was formed (Lief 1948) and the first child guidance clinic opened in the United States (Witmer 1946).

REFERENCES

Abrams, S. (1977). The genetic point of view: antecedents and transformations. *Journal of the American Psychoanalytic Association* 25: 417–25

Aichhorn, A. (1935). *Wayward Youth.* New York: Viking.

────── (1964). *Delinquency and Child Guidance: Selected Papers,* ed. O. Fleischmann, P. Kramer, and H. Ross. New York: International Universities Press.

Alexander, F. G., and Selesnick, S. T. (1966). *The History of Psychiatry.* New York: Harper and Row.

Blos, P. (1962). *On Adolescence: A Psychoanalytic Interpretation.* New York: Free Press of Glencoe.

Bornstein, B. (1949). "The analysis of a phobic child: some problems of theory and technique in child analysis. *Psychoanalytic Study of the Child* 3/4:181–226.

────── (1951). On latency. *Psychoanalytic Study of the Child* 6:279–285.

Erikson, E. H. (1963). *Childhood and Society.* Revised Edition. New York: W. W. Norton.

Freud, A. (1922–1970). *The Writings of Anna Freud,* volumes 1–7. New York: International Universities Press.

────── (1936). The ego and the mechanisms of defense. *The Writings of Anna Freud,* vol. 2. New York: International Universities Press.

────── (1958). Adolescence. *The Writings of Anna Freud,* vol. 5, pp. 136–166. New York: International Universities Press.

────── (1962). The theory of the parent-infant relationship. *The Writings of Anna Freud,* vol. 5, pp. 187–193. New York: International Universities Press.

────── (1965). Normality and pathology in childhood: assessment of development. *The Writings of Anna Freud,* vol. 6. New York: International Universities Press.

Freud, S. (1887–1902). *The Origins of Psychoanalysis: Letters to W. Fliess.* New York: Basic Books, 1954.

────── (1905). Fragment of the analysis of a case of hysteria. *Standard Edition* 7:3–122.

────── (1909a). Analysis of a phobia in a five-year-old boy. *Standard Edition* 10:3–149.

———— (1909b). Notes upon a case of obsessional neurosis. *Standard Edition* 10:153–318.

Fries, M. E. (1977). Longitudinal study: prenatal period to parenthood. *Journal of the American Psychoanalytic Association* 25:115–132.

Glenn, J., Bezahler, H., and Glenn, S. (In press). Sex education and its psychological implications. In *Sexuality and Contemporary Psychiatry,* ed. T. Karasu and C. Socarides. New York: International Universities Press.

Glenn, J., and Urbach, H. (In press). Adaptive and non-adaptive action in adolescence. In *Explorations in Psychoanalysis* [tentative title], ed. S. Orgel and B. Fine. New York: Jason Aronson.

Greenson, R. R. (1967). *The Technique and Practice of Psychoanalysis.* New York: International Universities Press.

Hartmann, H. (1964). *Essays on Ego Psychology.* New York: International Universities Press.

Inhelder, B., and Piaget, J. (1958). *The Growth of Logical Thinking from Childhood to Adolescence.* New York: Basic Books.

Jones, E. (1953–57). *The Life and Work of Sigmund Freud,* 3 vols. New York: Basic Books.

Kanzer, M., and Glenn, J. (1979). *Freud and His Self-Analysis.* New York: Jason Aronson.

Kardiner, A. (1977). *My Analysis with Freud. Reminiscences.* New York: W. W. Norton.

Kernberg, O. F. (1975). *Borderline Conditions and Pathological Narcissism.* New York: Jason Aronson.

Klein, M. (1932). *The Psycho-Analysis of Children.* London: Hogarth.

Kohut, H. (1971). *The Analysis of the Self.* New York: International Universities Press.

Kris, M. (1957). The use of prediction in a longitudinal study. *Psychoanalytic Study of the Child* 12:175–189.

Lief, A. (1948). *The Commonsense Psychiatry of Dr. Adolf Meyer.* New York: McGraw-Hill.

Mahler, M. S., and Furer, M. (1968). *On Human Symbiosis and the Vicissitudes of Individuation. vol.1: Infantile Psychosis.* New York: International Universities Press.

Mahler, M. S., Pine, F., and Bergman, A. (1975). *The Psychological Birth of the Human Infant. Symbiosis and Individuation.* New York: Basic Books.

Olch, G. B., reporter (1971). Panel: Technical problems in the analysis of the preoedipal and preschool child. *Journal of the American Psychoanalytic Association* 19:543–551.

Rapaport, D., and Gill, M. M. (1959). The points of view and assumptions of metapsychology. *International Journal of Psycho-Analysis* 40:153–162.

Ritvo, S. (1966). Correlation of a childhood and adult neurosis: based on the adult analysis of a reported childhood case. *International Journal of Psycho-Analysis* 47:130–131.

Schur, M. (1972). *Freud: Living and Dying.* New York: International Universities Press.

Settlage, C. F. et al. (1974). Conference on Psychoanalytic Education and Research Commission IX. Child Analysis. Position Paper.

Shane, M. (1977). A rationale for teaching analytic technique based on a developmental orientation and approach. *International Journal of Psycho-Analysis* 58:95–108.

Spitz, R. A. (1945). Hospitalism: an inquiry into the genesis of psychiatric conditions in early childhood. *Psychoanalytic Study of the Child* 1:53–74.

———— (1965). *The First Year of Life.* New York: International Universities Press.

Weil, A. P. (1970). The basic core. *Psychoanalytic Study of the Child* 25:442–460.

Witmer, H. L. (1946). *Psychiatric Interviews with Children.* London: Oxford Unviersity Press.

Zetzel, E. R. (1956). Current concepts of transference. *International Journal of Psycho-Analysis* 37:369–376.

PART TWO

GENERAL PRINCIPLES

Chapter 2

GENERAL PRINCIPLES OF CHILD ANALYSIS

Jules Glenn, M.D.

When Freud (1909) boldly decided to supervise the first child analysis in 1908, he did not realize the enormity of the enterprise he had initiated. He believed at the time that only a parent could act as a young patient's analyst because a child could not sufficiently trust a stranger to permit therapeutic interchange. Although delighted that Little Hans confirmed reconstructions of childhood that analyses of adults had permitted, Freud did not predict that child analysis, limited as he thought it to be, would make original contributions to analytic technique.

As the case of Little Hans demonstrates, children are more capable of analytic understanding than one might expect. Freud successfully applied the tenets of adult analysis[1] to his five-year-old patient, but wisely did not insist on free association. He noted that the analyst had to supply words for the child's concepts to a greater extent than was necessary for adults.

After other children were analyzed, Freud revised his opinion and recognized that physicians other than family members were perfectly capable of carrying out the treatment. Although originally child analysis was based on principles derived from analyses of adults, since then mutual enrichment has prevailed. Theoretical and technical issues that appeared in the analysis of adults were both broadened and resolved as more children were analyzed. Hence it is not surprising that the basic principles emerging from child analysis apply to the treatment of all age groups. Of course the means of implementing those principles will vary with the nature of each patient, whatever his age.

Children differ from adults and from each other in the structures of their personality, and in the degree of developmental flux. Therefore, they must be treated differently from adults. Children of different ages vary so greatly that we will consider the treatment of prelatency, latency and preadolescent children in separate chapters. Children of different developmental levels perceive differently, think differently, communicate differently, and respond differently to interpretations. Nevertheless, the basic principles of analysis remain the same. The analyst helps the patient to understand himself through interpreting the patient's communications, thus allowing changes in the personality structure, and a dissolution of symptoms and maladaptive behavior.

In this chapter we will describe the fundamentals on which adult and child analyses are based, and will emphasize adaptations required for work with children.[2] We will supplement elementary exposition with excursions into areas of greater complexity, and hint at difficulties in implementing the basic tenets.

We will note the syncretic nature of the general principles, which do not comprise a completely consistent system. The analyst, for instance, must be neutral and objective and, at the same time, compassionate and empathetic. He must be a "mirror" in which the patient can perceive his own characteristics, while also revealing himself as a human and helpful therapist. It is not always easy to be at once the reality-bound interpreter, and the active participant in the child's games.

This introductory chapter will provide the basis on which later chapters will be structured. Most of the issues outlined here will be discussed in greater detail in later chapters.

THE SETTING

Before going into detail about the basic principles of psychoanalysis, it would be useful to say a few words regarding the setting in which the treatment is carried out. I will start by describing those aspects common to child and adult analyses, and then show specific arrangements characteristic of the treatment of children.

Psychoanalysis requires that the therapist possess a detailed and intimate awareness of his patient's inner urges and his means of dealing with his drives, of his emotional conflicts and his attempts at their resolution, and of his autonomous ego functioning. In order to obtain this knowledge, the therapist must see his patient frequently. The doctor and patient meet four or five times a week, each session lasting forty-five to fifty minutes. Not only does this provide an opportunity for observation of the patient's functioning, and for the development of the empathy so essential for the analyst to understand and interpret properly; it also helps the patient develop an optimal intensity of emotional reaction to the analyst.

The child analyst obtains additional information about the patient's present environment, and acquires knowledge about his past and present reactions to the world about him, by seeing the patient's parents (usually primarily the mother) frequently, once a week at the start of the analysis and for a considerable period thereafter. In this way, the original history that the analyst gets from the parents is expanded and corrected as the treatment proceeds.

Although the analyst may tell the child what his parents have related, strict confidentiality is maintained about the patient's communications. This may cause grief and resentment in parents who are eager to know the details of their child's feelings and attitudes, but confidentiality is essential if the patient is to reveal his inner secrets. How can a child reveal his antagonism and sexual love for his parents if there is danger that the analyst will expose his secrets to the people involved?

While an adult analysis takes place in the consultation room, a child is seen either in a consultation room or playroom. At present, there is a greater attempt to encourage verbalization than in earlier days, and hence the playroom sees service less often. Some child analysts have no playroom at all. Nevertheless, provision must be made for younger children to use toys or artistic materials such as crayons, paints, or clay in the office if he wishes to express himself with these age-appropriate tools. It is best for this purpose to have toys like blocks, dolls, and cars that enable the child to depict his own fantasies rather than make use of organized games which restrict expression. Although a playroom is not a necessity, the analyst with such facilities is less likely to be personally concerned about the child's messiness and destructiveness than the doctor who sees child patients in his consultation room. The analyst is then able to make interpretations and permit or restrict untoward behavior in accordance with the patient's needs, rather than his own.

THE PATIENT'S MEANS OF COMMUNICATION

The setting, then, must provide opportunities for the patient to communicate to the analyst in ways that are appropriate for the patient. Although free association is encouraged in adults, children are incapable of it. They express themselves in speech of other sorts, and by nonverbal methods like play, drawing and painting. As with adults, bodily movements are important clues to children's thoughts and feelings.

Empirically, if you ask a child to free associate, that is, to say everything that comes to mind, you learn that he cannot do it. Perhaps this is because the child, in his struggle to be mature and to control his thoughts, is too vulnerable to regression. The ego ideal of the latency child requires that he attempt to be rational in his speech and thoughts, and he cannot systematically disregard inner dicta to that effect. In fact, many *grown-ups* cannot allow themselves to attempt free association and participate in analysis. For them, permitting primitive thoughts and disorganized modes of speech produces too much anxiety, and must be avoided. Nevertheless, a child may, for brief periods, do something akin to free association when the analyst asks him occasionally to play "The What Pops into Your Mind Game" (Fraiberg 1962). In addition, there may be brief periods of spontaneous associations.

Ideally the patient's communications should encompass a balance of primary and secondary process thinking. There should be enough organization for the analyst to understand what he is being told, and sufficient loosening of control of thoughts to allow usually hidden aspects of the personality to emerge. Optimally, the patient will reveal his drive derivatives, fantasies, wishes, defenses, and conflicts so that he and the doctor can discuss them. He will recall significant recent and remote experiences. Such openness of expression may produce anxiety, and there should be sufficient control of what is said so that the patient does not experience excessive fear. Extreme anxiety may result in the patient's refusal to reveal more lest he be overwhelmed again. The analyst's comments must be gauged to help overcome resistances without provoking panic.

INTERPRETATION, THE PRIME INSTRUMENT OF ANALYSIS

As the patient conveys aspects of his inner strife, the analyst must help him to understand himself. Interpretation is the primary instrument of therapeutic change in analysis. Although a great deal of flexibility is essential, interpretations are generally made in an orderly and systematic fashion. The following generalizations can be offered.

1. Defenses are interpreted before drives.

2. The surface is interpreted rather than deeper unconscious material. Comments are directed to the affect, especially anxiety. As defenses alter, and the patient becomes more aware of thoughts that were previously unconscious or otherwise defended against, the analyst will be able to interpret further. Sudden confrontation with ego-dystonic aspects mobilize defenses and stymie the analysis.

3. As a corollary of this second tenet: external influences are taken into account in making interpretations. The analysis should not be carried out as though the external environment did not exist. Similarly, as the analyst is an important object whose presence is palpable, the patient's feelings toward him serve as a guide to interpretation. (See Kanzer 1953.)

4. Interpretations of the patient's conflicts must be offered. When conflicting aspects of the patient's personality are kept in focus, the patient attains a balanced picture of himself. Feeling that the analyst is urging him to carry out forbidden wishes may thus be avoided.

Excessive emphasis on drive interpretation may lead to acting out, resulting from the patient's feeling that he is being egged on. On the other hand, repeated discussion of defenses, without indicating what is being defended against, can lead to a stalemate.

A shift in emphasis has developed in the psychoanalytic theory of technique. At first, the patient's resistances were seen simply as obstacles preventing him from engaging in treatment, and revealing his unconscious thoughts. The analyst sought to get rid of these resistances.

After it was recognized that resistance consisted largely of defenses mobilized to protect the patient from the impact of his forbidden drives, the aim remained the same. The defenses had to be pushed aside. Reich (1933) even spoke of piercing the character armor.

The publication of *The Ego and the Mechanisms of Defense* (A. Freud 1936) marked a turning point in the theory of technique. The ego was seen as an important part of the personality, mediating between the outside world, the drives, and the superego. The defenses, an essential part of the ego, had to be analyzed in their own right along with the drives. It became important to understand how the ego dealt with the outer world and the inner struggle. Analysis truly became a study of the entire personality.

Nevertheless, the therapist must be aware of the patient's struggles against the analytic process. Often the most rewarding paths of investigation lie in those areas in which the patient's resistance is greatest. The interpretation of defenses where the battle is most heated may lead to emotion-laden, meaningful insights.

A word of caution is necessary. The analyst's experience and judgment should warn him against blunt, premature, and tactless interpretations of ego-dystonic conflicts before the patient is prepared to deal with them.

5. The analyst must talk to the patient in a human and empathic way, taking the patient's affect into account. He should avoid technical jargon and adhere to speech that the patient understands. Although this is essential at any age, it is especially important in the case of children. The analyst must know his patient's personal language as well as the extent of his vocabulary. He cannot be ponderous. He must temper his serious intent with a light touch.

Again we must emphasize the importance of flexibility. Although I have mentioned specific sequences of interpretation, these cannot be followed rigidly. For instance, sometimes a drive may plague a patient so much that it is wise to discuss it before the defenses are fully elucidated.

Bornstein (1949) has applied these basic tenets of interpretation with the utmost care and thought. In "The Analysis of a Phobic Child," she described a game that Frankie, her five-and-a-half-year-old patient, played repeatedly. In the game, a boy of four sat alone on a chair which was placed in an elevated position, while his father visited a lady in the hospital. This woman may have given birth. The boy, who played the roles of doctor and nurse, cared for the babies lovingly. A fire erupted and killed all the infants, and the frightened boy became a fireman. He rescued most of the women, but failed to save the one he called "Mommy."

Although the analyst recognized Frankie's fury against his mother and younger sister, she also perceived the defense against loneliness and sadness that the play dramatized. Feelings of omnipotence and games of destruction warded off the child's sadness. Addressing herself to the affect, the analyst "expressed sympathy for the lonely child [in the game] who is barred from his mother's sickroom, and who is too little to understand why his father is admitted" (p. 188). Only after Frankie became sad could the defenses be explained to him. He could then gradually discuss the specific situations in his life that led to his distress, and appreciate his rage at his parents for abandoning him when his sister was born.

The analyst's aim was not simply to get to the unconscious material, but rather to bring about an ego change through a thorough analysis of all aspects of the personality. Bornstein pointed out that interpreting the child's motives for his aggression first would cause quick suppression of the phobic symptoms, or strengthen the phobia. The child would have been forced to face unconscious impulses too quickly.

Encouraging catharsis, Bornstein stated, would alleviate symptoms by the temporary discharge of tension, but would leave the child's conflicts intact. Nevertheless, this example illustrates the importance of affect. The analyst must make comments that lead to the patient's emotional involvement and understanding, not solely to an intellectual process.

As his analysis proceeded, Frankie saw connections between his *present* phobia and his *past* experiences. His fear that he would not find his way home from school "corresponded to his unconscious, revengeful wish that his mother, who had abandoned him, would never return" (p. 189).

A patient of mine, Al, was an eight-year-old enuretic boy who came to analysis reluctantly. Early in the treatment he proclaimed his slogan: "An apple a day keeps the doctor away." He was not timid in stating that the doctor he wanted to avoid was the analyst. The analyst joined him as a play ally in his campaign. Patient and doctor made signs conveying the slogan which they exhibited as they marched about the playroom. In this way the analyst acknowledged his patient's affect and strengthened the therapeutic alliance. Soon Al announced that there was a second doctor, his father, whom he wanted to avoid. His father had angered him by giving him shots which he did not like. He cut up a clay figure of a doctor who represented both his father and, in the transference, the analyst, baked it in the oven, and then ate it.

During the month that these themes developed, the analyst emphasized how difficult it was for Al to be critical of his father, whom he loved. As a result, Al criticized his analyst rather than his father. When the patient revealed that he wanted to avoid his father, and he then cut up the clay doctor, his play was interpreted as showing that he wanted to do to the doctor what he felt his father had done to him. Al wanted to be a big and powerful person rather than a small and weak victim. This was pointed out when he engaged in a mock baseball game in which the analyst was beaten by fantastic scores such as 100,000,000 to 0. The defensive reversal, the identification with the aggressor, was interpreted before the aggressive drive. The patient's conscious fears of the injections his father gave him guided the analyst's interpretations. As the analysis proceeded, deeper conflicts emerged. It was not until a year later that Al's desire to get rid of his father as an oedipal rival appeared. Here, too, the conflict between his love and hatred was underlined.

THE PSYCHOANALYTIC PROCESS

Interpretations further the psychoanalytic process (Greenacre 1968, Feigelson 1976). The psychoanalytic process is difficult to define because it refers not to a single configuration, but to an endless variety. Optimally, an inexorable momentum develops in the course of the treatment. One insight leads to the patient's revelation of further material, and to further insights. An understanding of defenses leads to the discovery and interpretation of drive derivatives. This is accomplished through a gradual emergence and working through of data regarding the reality of the patient's life—the transference, his fantasies, dreams, behavior, etc. Interpretations activate a change in the configuration of forces and structures within the patient. Insights strengthen the therapeutic alliance which is necessary for further un-covering, interpretation, insight, and realignment.

This description does not imply that all analytic hours are "good" (Kris 1956b) in the sense that they produce dramatic, overt insight. The therapeutic process continues quietly and without fanfare during hours that seem uneventful.

ALTERATIONS IN PSYCHIC STRUCTURE AS A RESULT OF INTERPRETATION

Interpretations lead to changes in psychic structure and economy. As defenses alter, there is greater flexibility in their use and they function more adaptively.

In many cases the patient becomes more tolerant of his drives, result-ing in a diminution of repression and other defenses. To accomplish this, superego restrictions ease, and the ego is better able to master and tame urges. With a decreased need for defense, energy previously used for countercathexis is released for more adaptive activities, and greater satisfaction and pleasure.

In other cases, more efficient and constructive use of defenses may exert a similar effect. Energy is neutralized and made available for sublimation and other adaptive purposes. Primitive defenses like pro-jection and regression, which are relatively ineffective in preventing anxiety, lose prominence. Defenses acquire a more adaptive nature and attain the status of secondary autonomous ego functions. For instance, reaction formations which originally defended against unacceptable anal urges, assume the new function of maintaining order and neatness in nonconflictual areas (Hartmann 1964).

With greater tolerance of drives, increased efficiency of defenses, and diminution of tendencies to regression, age-appropriate levels of libidi-nal development become stabilized. As developmental arrests are over-come, ego and superego functions mature. The patient also becomes able to achieve more mature id satisfaction. A child of oedipal age who had previously gained gratification chiefly from oral and anal stimula-tion will find pleasure in his genitals.

Concomitant with changes in the area of gratification, there are changes in object relations. Arrest in or regression to the oral stage will produce a clinging, demanding child who becomes outraged when he is not immediately satisfied. A patient fixated in the anal stage will find himself battling his mother or her surrogates about possessions and the hostility may intensify his separation anxiety. When the child progresses to the oedipal stage, cathexis of his genitals will increase, his attitude toward the opposite sex parent will become more loving, and hostility toward the parent of the same sex will appear.

AREAS OF INTERPRETATION: TRANSFERENCES AND DISPLACEMENTS

The analysand invariably develops irrational ideas and feelings about the analyst. In adults, these can be explained as transferring to the analyst feelings that were originally experienced toward parents and other significant persons during childhood. The understanding of these transferences is so valuable that often this becomes the central issue in the analysis. Defenses associated with feelings displaced from parents are important parts of the transference.

Because children are intimately involved with their parents at the time of analysis, the issue of transference is more complicated. Often true transferences appear and the patient experiences emotions and defenses in relation to his analyst that occurred *in the past* in relation to his parents. But frequently we see not transferences from the past, but displacements of present attitudes from the parent to the analyst. In other words, the analyst can either come to represent a parent imago from the past, or can acquire in the patient's mind the present characteristics of the parents.

Most often a transference neurosis occurs during the analysis of adults. The frequency with which this occurs in child analysis—if it occurs at all—is a matter for debate. In any case, the transferences, the transference neuroses (when they appear), and the displacements all call for interpretation. I refer the reader to the section entitled Interpretation, The Prime Instrument of Analysis for an illustration of transference. Al pictured the analyst as being dangerous like his father, a physician, who had given him injections. The child wanted to avoid both doctors, and become the active aggressor rather than the passive victim. Transference involved defenses as well as drives.

Eventually Al expressed a desire to get rid of his father and become "the man of the house." But since this involved the death of his beloved father, who was then ill in the hospital, Al tried to avoid recognition of the wish. Hatred was displaced to his sister and mother who tried to keep him from taking his father's place, and to the analyst who reminded him of his father and who, he felt, was depriving him of his masculine prerogatives.

It is important to distinguish between the patient's picture of the analyst as a transference or displacement object, and other representations of the analyst. When the patient projects aspects of his own self-representation[3] onto the analyst, an unrealistic image of the therapist appears. In addition, the child may perceive the analyst's characteristics correctly, i.e. conceive of him as a *real object*. When he recognizes the analyst as a sympathetic person who would like to help him with his difficulties, the child can engage in a therapeutic alliance with his analyst (see below). Again recognizing the analyst as a *real object* the patient may react to actual seductive behavior, antagonism or errors. The analyst's evaluation of his patient's view of him is complicated by the fact that the patient may unconsciously select real aspects of the analyst's personality to construct a representation that fits his transference expectation.

Another representation of the analyst is that of a *new object*. This occurs when a child attains a new stage of development. As we have observed in the portion of this chapter on changes in the psychic structure, different types of object representations emerge at different libidinal stages. For instance, as a patient enters the oedipal stage, his image of the analyst changes to one appropriate to that period. Because the patient spends so much time with his analyst, and develops such an intense relationship with him, a new representation of the analyst may appear before the child changes his view of his parents!

The term *new object-representation* refers to the change in the image of the object that occurs with developmental advance. The analyst is also a new object because he is different from the child's parents and other adults the child has known. A new object relationship involves a change in self-representation as well as object-representation.

GENETIC INTERPRETATIONS AND RECONSTRUCTIONS

The analyst interprets the child's present conflicts and their origins in the past. Children are less interested in the past and the future than they are in the present. Consequently they tend to be less impressed with explanations of the development of symptoms or character than are adults.

Ordinarily many gaps in the patient's memory remain in the course of the analysis and the patient describes his past incompletely. However, disguised memory forms provide hints of what occurred. Although inexact and unconventional, the patient's dreams, fantasies, symptomatology, transference reactions, and acting out are forms of memory. What the patient remembers as a solitary event may turn out to be many episodes condensed into one (see Kris 1956a). The analyst and patient sift through clues and fill in the lacunae. In this way they make *reconstructions* of the patient's earlier life. They reconstruct both external events and the patient's inner reactions. They discover patterns of behavior and emotional reaction. They provide connections between experiences that had appeared to be isolated events. Object-relations, libidinal and aggressive urges, and defenses can gradually be reconstructed. Analyst and patient, working together, correct, clarify, and breathe life into the past. A sense of conviction develops about events not conventionally remembered.

The analyst depends on his knowledge of the usual types of integration and experiences at different developmental levels. Therefore an accurate concept of child development is essential for both the child and adult analyst.

In addition, the child analyst has the opportunity to utilize information provided by his patient's parents in making reconstructions of past significant events. This source carries all the jeopardies of a double-edged sword—for although the parents may be accurate in assessing the child's past experiences, it is possible that they may not gauge the child's state of mind properly. The analyst must therefore guard against failing to properly empathize and making false reconstructions based solely on information from the parents. He must follow the patient's thinking in presenting the correct construction, and not bide by parental recollections alone. The child analyst must not use his extra-analytic knowledge carelessly and make premature interpretations. He must respect the rhythm and timing that emanates from the patient's needs in the analysis.

AREAS OF INTERPRETATION: DREAMS. FANTASIES. BODILY SENSATIONS.

Dreams do not usually occupy the same prominent place in the analyses of children as they do with adults. However, in many instances the child is quite capable of telling and discussing his dreams.

The child describes his fantasies verbally as well as in drawings and play. Delicacy and tact are required in dealing with sublimated fantasy formations. The analyst can be very astute in recognizing the latent content of manifest dreams, stories, artistic work, and play. This is especially true when the patient helps with associations. However, the analyst must be careful not to explain unconscious thoughts in a way that inhibits the child's future play or creative activity. This would cause an important source of analytic material to dry up and might adversely influence the child's future development.

Some analysts have suggested that interpretations of sublimations be avoided altogether, except when the sublimation breaks down. They recommend that knowledge gained from play be kept in mind and utilized later for interpretations of other types of communication. They believe that interpretation, especially if drive oriented, may force the patient to recognize tabooed aspects of his creative work, which he will then cease to perform. Ego regression may occur in which neutralized cathexes are instinctualized; then conflicts reappear between the ego and forbidden thoughts and feelings.

Other analysts have stated that the patient's communication must be interpreted, whatever its form, to successfully analyze the child. The truth probably lies between these two extremes. It is a matter of judgment whether, in specific instances, one should explain the meaning of play or avoid it. Some children communicate through play or creative work and thrive on its analysis. Their understanding of the therapeutic alliance is that all means of expression are to be dealt with in the treatment. In any case, a sublimation should not be interpreted solely as a drive derivative. When the patient makes a development advance it would be an error to treat it as a regressive expression.

Bodily sensations are important at all ages, but particularly in childhood. Children are often confused about their physiological functions, and have trouble understanding and controlling them. Explanations of vague and fleeting feelings may enable a child to organize his body image, and develop a more stable self-representation. He may become more tolerant of his drives after he comprehends the complexities of the perceptions of his inner urges. The use of primitive defenses like denial and projection to combat inner feelings may become less prominent after the child is aware of the origins and meanings of his "queer feelings." Often such awareness is a step toward an understanding of the conflicts involved.

> Eddie spent months drawing pictures of the body. He and the analyst produced books showing how the body functioned in illness and health. One day the patient, then nine, became braver. "I have a question to ask about the nervous system. Does the penis have nerves in it?" When the analyst said yes, and added that Eddie must know this because of feelings in his penis, Eddie admitted he masturbated. When the patient then denied masturbating, the analyst suggested that Eddie was reluctant to talk about masturbation because his mother opposed it, and he feared the analyst would be against it too. The patient then described his masturbatory conflicts in detail. It turned out that Eddie wanted a circumcision as a birthday present to feel more manly. But, because he feared the operation as a punishment, Eddie tried to avoid penile masturbation and stimulated his testicles instead. Squeezing his testicles would create pain while gently touching his scrotum was clearly pleasant. Eventually the significance of these forms of masturbation were analyzed. (see Glenn 1969)

WORKING THROUGH

Interpretations and insights rarely appear as single bursts. The analyst must make the same dynamic and genetic interventions over and over in forms appropriate to the many ways in which the conflict is presented. In this way the patient repeatedly sees patterns of behavior and defenses typical of him, his fantasies and other drive derivatives, his means of dealing with the environment, and so forth. The emotional viewing and re-viewing of the same problem in protean forms in many situations comprises "working through."

Jim, a nine-year-old enuretic boy, knew that he wet when the pressure of urine grew within his bladder. Jim became aware that he also felt a growing pressure inside himself as he became angry. He imagined fury as a kind of fluid that had to be released. At first Jim thought his theory of anger was an obvious fact. Gradually he came to see that when he was angry, he felt like urinating on people.

After realizing this aspect of his angry, uncontrolled outbursts, Jim described many situations in which his fury resulted in someone becoming angry with him, and attacking him. When Jim broke his bedroom window, his mother hit him, and then made him pay for its replacement. When he attacked his brother as the family rode into the city, his father hurt him by becoming silent and sullen. After seeing this sequence over and over again, Jim came to realize that he required punishment for his forbidden anger.

The same sequence occurs in this process as we have seen for interpretations in general. Surface observations precede deeper interpretations. As the patient works through his defenses, and drives appear more clearly, then drive derivatives are worked through.

We must distinguish the repetitions of working through, and those that occur in attempts at mastery, even though an overlap of function can emerge. Only when the repetitive attempts at mastery are accompanied by insight can they be called working through.

Betty, at four years of age, was still grappling with desires to thwart her mother's attempts to toilet train her. She wanted to control the situation actively, rather than be her mother's passive victim. Betty played games in which she pretended to soil, while the analyst, acting the mother, insisted that she wait until she reached the toilet. At other times Betty reversed roles: she acted the mother, and ordered the analyst-child to be clean.

In this clinical vignette we find repetitious attempts at mastery. As these were explained to the child, working through occurred. The child recognized her typical defenses, wishes and patterns of behavior. Eventually, wishes to find pleasure in retention became clear.

Working through serves many interrelated purposes. Material discovered during analysis is often forbidden and painful, and is defended against. Rediscovery is necessary to achieve a prolonged lifting of repression, denial, isolation, and other defenses. The patient eventually develops a sustained sense of conviction as he repeatedly recalls and integrates what had been hidden from him. This increased ability to remember earlier experiences helps integrate past and present. Different facets of the personality become more harmonious, fostering the therapeutic aim: where id was, there shall ego be. In addition, as the patient grows more mature, and decathects archaic object-representations, working through becomes a vehicle for mourning lost objects.

Eventually Jim started to observe that his parents fought with each other. Through repeated juxtaposition of his own provocative and attacking behavior with that of his battling parents, Jim gradually accepted interpretations that he acted the way his parents did. It was difficult for him to identify with the more mature aspects of his parents, because this involved surrendering his attachment to important primitive parts of them, parts that implied intense emotions, both love and hatred.

Working through helped Jim to decathect these aspects of his parents. As he repeatedly experienced attachment to them, and a desire to provoke and fight them and their substitutes, these wishes gradually lost their power.

The process is similar to what Freud (1917) described in "Mourning and Melancholia." Hypercathexis precedes decathexis. Incidentally, it would have been immensely more difficult for Jim to give up the archaic imagos of his parents if had they not changed. Fortunately they grew more mature, laying the path for their son.

COMMUNICATIONS OF THE ANALYST OTHER THAN INTERPRETATIONS: PREPARATION FOR INTERPRETATION

Although we have been emphasizing the importance of interpretations, we have inevitably touched on other types of communications by the analyst. These include preparations for interpretations, and "running comments." We will discuss explanations of the treatment and comments intended to maintain the neutrality of the analyst in other sections of this chapter.

We have mentioned explanations of bodily sensations as preparations for later interpretation of conflicts between the ego and the drives. Confrontations may serve the same purpose. A child who is dishonest, provokes others, or is prone to self-injury, for instance, may not be aware of these characteristics in himself. Pointing them out may prepare him to later realize how and why he punishes himself, and to see his behavior as part of a huge jigsaw puzzle which involves inner conflicts.

Observing how patterns of behavior repeat themselves under similar circumstances may also lead to later explanations of unconscious motives.

Although adults may object to the analyst's silence, they can usually tolerate it better than a child can. Therefore, the analyst may have to make remarks about a child's play—"running comments," as Kramer (1960) has called them—to sustain the child's activity. This type of analytic communication also helps the child to become aware of the nature of his play and fantasy, and leads to future interpretive work.

PARAMETERS AND ADAPTATIONS

In a classic article, Eissler (1953) has suggested that many of the technical interventions that are not interpretations be called *parameters.* When an analysis is in danger of reaching a stalemate, the analyst often has to make a suggestion that will enable resumption of progress. For instance, he may recommend that a phobic patient enter the situation which he feels is dangerous. In this way material related to the symptom will appear in the analysis and be subject to interpretation. This maneuver is a *parameter,* "a deviation both quantitative and qualitative from the basic model technique, that is to say, from a technique that requires interpretation as the exclusive tool" (p. 110). These procedures are essential to the proper outcome of therapy, and must be sharply differentiated from errors, whims of the analyst, and preparations for interpretation. The analyst must at some point analyze the meaning of the parameter to the patient.

A parameter, Eissler observed, is properly applied in cases of ego deviation, in which the usual characteristics of the patient, those which allow him to benefit from interpretations alone, are absent or distorted. Commonly, the interventions of child analysts, because they are different in quality from those of adult analysts, are erroneously labeled *parameters*. Kris (Maenchen 1970) and Maenchen (1970) have correctly emphasized that child analytic procedures that are not appropriate for adults, but are suitable for children, are more properly called *adaptations* of technique. Telling a child to free associate would be an error, not standard procedure. Explaining that talk, play, and drawings will help the analyst understand his patient's troubles, and hence bring relief, is the appropriate procedure for this developmental stage. It is an adaptation of the analytic procedure, not a parameter, and it would be foolish to try to interpret the influence of this procedure on the child patient. Similarly, providing the child with toys or paints and paper to enable him to communicate in the child's equivalent of adult free association, is an adaptation.

Offering or accepting presents would most often be an error in adult analysis, but at times constitutes a parameter in the analysis of a child. Such activity on the part of the child analyst can be an error, a parameter, or an adaptation. If the aim of gift giving or receiving is to get a faltering analysis back on track, or to anticipate and forestall difficulty by eliciting a hidden problem, then the term *parameter* would apply. If the doctor gives a present to his patient on a whim, it may cause complications in the analysis or camouflage some of the patient's problems. In either case, this would be an error. When gift giving is done to maintain the analyst's neutral position, it is an adaptation. (We will discuss the analyst's "neutrality" in a later section.)

THE PRINCIPLE OF ABSTINENCE

A basic principle of analysis holds that if too much gratification is attained from the analyst, the patient will not be able to discuss his difficulties. Wishes, conflict, and anxiety may be hidden when drives are fulfilled in the analysis. This is in accordance with the fact that analysis works best when the patient expresses his wishes, their derivatives, and his defenses against them in words, rather than action. When the patient acts out his transference desires rather than verbalizes them, it becomes more difficult to understand his conflicts. Acting out can take place in the analytic setting itself (in which case it is called "acting in" [Eidelberg 1957]) or outside of the consultation room. Acting out is inevitable and requires analysis. There is a value in keeping acting out to a minimum, and because it is often incorrectly equated with antisocial behavior, some have erroneously used the term in a pejorative manner.

In child analysis it is not always easy to differentiate dramatic action intended as communication, acting in as a form of remembering and reliving, and behavior aimed at discharging tension. Children often express themselves in games and other activities. Question arises as to when behavior comprises a communication, and is therefore helpful to the analysis, and when it is the type of acting out that obfuscates the material. We must recognize that most types of communication in analysis represent conflict. Hence the patient usually expresses and disguises what he is communicating simultaneously. The analyst must be a master at translation to sort out these aspects.

Since action is so prominent a feature of many child analyses, there is danger that the treatment will be impeded. Not only does the child act, the analyst does too. He carries out roles assigned to him by the child as part of the play communication. The analyst may go beyond the child's best interests, and gratify the child excessively. On the other hand, it is impossible to carry out any analysis without gratifying the patient to some degree. The analyst spends a great deal of time with the patient, listening carefully to his every word and understanding him as no other human being can. This in itself provides tremendous satisfaction. Several illustrations will help us evaluate the extent to which the analyst may go in his gratifying activity.

Four-year-old Betty imagined that babies were BMs born from the anus following oral impregnation. Because of her age, she could not explain this to the analyst. Rather, she played a game in which the analyst, pretending to be her servant, poisoned her. Then, lying in the lithotomy position, she asked the therapist, now taking on the role of an obstetrician, to remove the BMs, which were equated with babies, from her anus. The analyst played the assigned roles, pretending to feed her poison and later delivering the BM-babies. He interpreted the play, and refrained from bodily contact.

The patient certainly enjoyed the game, but its main function was communication. The analyst's role-playing enabled the patient to tell her fantasy in her own way. The analyst's avoidance of touching the patient kept the gratification to a minimal level, and avoided a degree of excitement that would have been both overly-gratifying and frightening. She considered the analyst's behavior appropriate and in accordance with the therapeutic alliance, not seductive and dangerous.

Five-year-old Andy wanted to play games with his analyst because his father was not home a great deal, and was not playful when he was there. Andy also wanted to tell his analyst about the types of sexual pleasure he wished to engage in. The game Andy selected for this double purpose was leap frog. In great excitement he had the analyst leap over him, the doctor's genitals perilously close to his head. At another time Andy was allowed to sit on his therapist's lap and hug him. This excessive contact interfered with the flow of material. The patient became too excited and frightened. Soon the patient left the office, climbed over a barrier outside the room, and kept the analyst away from him.

In Betty's case communication prevailed. In Andy's, the mutual acting out by patient and doctor interfered with the analytic process. It should be noted that in the case of Betty, the existence of emotion along with the play facilitated treatment. Just as an adult's isolated verbalization carries little conviction, play without feeling has limited benefits.

Excessive gratification outside of the analytic situation may impede treatment as well. Parents may encourage developmental arrest through excessive indulgence of immature behavior. Whenever Betty held her fist up to her father, he repeatedly responded by hitting her, thus maintaining a sadomasochistic relationship. Once Betty's father decided to stop this game, the child brought her masochistic wishes into the analysis where it could be understood.

Although engaging in child analyses affords the therapist gratification, and indeed can be fun, this too must be kept at a reasonable level. The analyst may enjoy himself so much that his powers of observation decline, and he neglects his interpretative work. In addition, he may find himself unknowingly indulging his patient along with himself.

THE ANALYST'S NEUTRALITY

It is frequently correctly stated that analysis works best when the analyst is "neutral," but the meaning of this term is difficult to conceptualize. Basically, neutrality means that the analyst limits himself to interpretations, and preparations for interpretations. He avoids excessive gratification of the patient's needs—both libidinal and aggressive wishes, and desires for punishment. He does not attempt to manipulate the patient into relinquishing symptoms that he finds annoying. He is there to help the patient through interpretation, but does not have specific goals for the patient. Although he realizes and points out deleterious unadaptive behavior, he does not disapprove of the patient. Rather, he tries to understand and help the analysand.

The analyst maintains a benevolent neutrality, a helpful and protective attitude which aims at relief of suffering. Neutrality does not imply indifference or inactivity. As a result of the analyst's benign attitude, the patient can express himself freely, and with impunity.

If the analyst can maintain his neutrality—it is not an easy task, particularly with children—then the patient's misconceptions of the analyst and his wishes can be interpreted. On the other hand, if the analyst behaves like a parent, and attempts to impose his goals on the child, then when the patient thinks the doctor is like his father or mother, the analysis of these transferences or displacements will be impossible.

Ideally, when the patient gets angry at the analyst, the causes of the anger lie within the patient and the analyst has not provided a stimulus or justification for the hostility. If the analyst contributes in such a way as to make it impossible for the patient to recognize the inner origins of his anger, the analysis may fail. The analyst must not be a provoking agent.

The child's restricted cognitive capacities, his limited tolerance for frustration, and consequently, his limited understanding of analytic abstinence make the child's criteria for neutrality different from that of most adults. The analyst must gauge the patient's expectations of him as an adult, and estimate what the child can tolerate without becoming so furious that he cannot participate in the treatment.

When the analyst refrains from answering questions early in treatment, most adult analytic patients are able to understand the reason for the doctor's behavior. They come to see that the treatment is best served by the analyst's silence, and to contrast their rational decision not to expect an answer with the irrational fury that wells up in them. This juxtaposition of feelings leads to the analysis of the transference expectations.

Most children, however, expect the analyst to answer questions, and would not understand explanations of the therapeutic purposes of silence. To a child, the analyst who refrains from replying is not a neutral person, but a nasty adult. The child does not contrast his inner anger and his sensible thoughts. His rage appears perfectly reasonable. In such a situation, then, the analyst must answer the child's questions. He must wait until the child has a better grasp of the principles of analysis before he can refrain from replying. At later time he can further the analysis by learning the child's feelings and fantasies while concealing his own thoughts. Early in treatment the analyst often cannot remain totally anonymous.

Telling the child certain facts about his personal life—such as whether he is married and has children—may interfere with the clarity of the child's transference, but refusing to reply to the child's early inquiries may interfere with the treatment even more. The child becomes angry at what is, to him, the unnatural restraint of the adult. He may take the analyst's reticence to signify that frankness is not required—if the doctor is secretive, the child may be also. Obviously, it is a matter of judgment as to how much the analyst reveals about himself.

Similarly, many children expect gifts from adult friends on important occasions like birthdays. In many cases it is best to comply rather than risk the child's unanalyzable fury.

An unanalyzable resentment can occur if the therapist fails to protect the child. The child needs and expects the adults in his life to offer adequate protection and care. The protecting analyst is, paradoxically, the neutral analyst. If such aid is absent, the patient will be justifiably furious.

On several occasions Betty's mother forgot to appear in time to take the four-year-old patient home at the end of her session. Instead the mother sat on a park bench across the street from the office. Betty, eager to see her mother, rushed out of the door to greet her. This incurred the danger of being hit by a car, and so the analyst helped Betty cross the street.

Failure to do this would have made Betty feel that the analyst was a nonprotective adult and consequently interfere with the therapeutic alliance. A neutral position could be maintained only through protecting the patient. Of course, there are other considerations—the analyst could not in good conscience allow the patient to run in front of an auto! Another issue is the patient's need for protection from injuring himself, or the analyst, or the office. In the permissive atmosphere of the analysis, the temptation to do anything, even injurious acts, is tremendous. However, the analyst who permits such dangerous behavior will be viewed by his patient as a dangerous, untrustworthy, and even seductive person.

THE THERAPEUTIC ALLIANCES

For interpretations to exert their beneficial effects, it is important that an alliance be established between patient and doctor (Zetzel 1956, Greenson 1967, Kanzer 1975). This involves a number of factors. The patient recognizes the analyst as a *real person* who intends to help him with his difficulties. The patient finds the interpretations useful in overcoming symptoms and creating understanding. The patient identifies with the analyst and his methods, and thus is able to participate in the analytic process. The patient must be able to differentiate transferences, and other irrational and unrealistic representations of the analyst from the realistic representations, and utilize these differences for the analysis.

This involves a capacity to observe oneself while undergoing the analytic experience (Sterba 1934). The patient experiences irrational emotions and thoughts which he takes note of, recognizes as inappropriate, and, with the analyst's help, comes to understand.

The patient must be psychologically minded and reality bound at the same time. He must also be able to tolerate the frustration that inevitably develops when transferences become intense. For the analyst cannot gratify his patient's growing wishes for satisfaction. The patient must be able to understand the nature of the analytic situation and the therapeutic process. Early in analysis, the analyst explains this to the patient in terms the child can understand. Throughout the treatment, further explanations may be required.

It is surprising how many children can grasp the idea of the unconscious, and the basic principles of treatment. I often provide the child with a simple analogy of how analysis works based on Freud's topographical approach of 1911. The mind consists of two rooms, the conscious room which is very small, and an unconscious room which is very large. The conscious part of the mind contains all the thoughts that you know about, and the other room encompasses forbidden thoughts and feelings that one would rather not know of. A door between the two chambers keeps unconscious room thoughts from entering the conscious room. However, at night the door opens a bit, and unconscious room thoughts, *in disguise,* enter the conscious part of the mind. Symptoms are explained to the patient as disguised unconscious room thoughts that have entered the conscious part of the mind during the day. Treatment consists of finding out what these unconscious thoughts are. To accomplish this the patient must be as frank as possible, and tell the analyst about his thoughts through speech, play, talking of dreams, and any other method he can use.

In many analyses, at some point I explain that although the patient can *say* anything that occurs to him, he cannot *do* anything he wishes. This clarifies that dangerous or destructive action is not advantageous.

The therapeutic alliance is impossible if the patient does not trust and like the analyst. The patient must react to the real character of the therapist as a kind, empathic, and helpful person. It is impossible for the patient to perceive these traits unless he has attained a degree of maturity that enables him to experience basic trust (Erikson 1950) or confident expectation (Benedek 1938). The patient's capacity to rely

sufficiently on the analyst to engage in the therapeutic endeavor ultimately rests on a displacement of the warmth and confidence the child
felt with his mother or mother surrogate in early childhood.

Every infant experiences both frustration and gratification in relation
to the person who cares for him. Hating and loving feelings alternate,
for instance, as the child awaits feeding and then is fed. When a parent
fails to protect the child from excessive stimuli or otherwise fails to care
for the child, the balance may be tipped toward a conviction that he
will not be looked after properly. If the balance lies in the direction of
hatred and the anticipation of lack of care, then the child may find
himself unable to depend on any adult when he gets older. As a patient,
he may be unable to mobilize the basic trust needed for the therapeutic
alliance.

Another crucial period for the establishment of trusting relationships
is the rapprochement subphase of the separation-individuation period
(Mahler, Pine, and Bergman 1975). At about fifteen months the previously confident toddler begins to recognize more fully that he is not
really part of his protecting, omnipotent mother. His progressive developmental desires to get away from his mother run counter to his fears
of being unprotected in her absence. The child reacts by clinging to his
mother, at whom he becomes angry for seemingly deserting him.[4] The
ambivalence and the splitting of the representation of his mother into
"good" and "bad" imagos that characterize this period eventually recede. The toddler becomes more confident in himself and the adults
about him. However, if the child does not weather this stormy period,
he may remain a sullen, angry person unsure of the grown-ups he
depends on. Analysis may evoke the ambivalence characteristic of the
rapprochement subphase.

In addition to these preoedipal displacements, transferences from
later periods play an important part in determining the establishment
of the therapeutic alliance. A predominantly negative transference may
lead the patient to refuse to engage in the treatment. An erotic transference may lead the patient to concentrate on seducing the analyst rather
than engaging in a search for understanding. (Erotic transferences often
conceal potent preoedipal wishes and intense defenses against primitive
hatred.)

Before the concept of the therapeutic (Zetzel 1956) or working
(Greenson 1967) alliance was clarified, it was thought that all analyses

required a predominantly positive transference. The therapeutic alliance was the equivalent of the positive transference. We now differentiate between the two states. If the therapeutic alliance is firm, the patient can experience and profit from the analysis of an intense and prolonged hatred for the therapist.

In child analysis, however, this is less likely to occur, because the impact of a long period of hatred of the analyst may shatter the alliance. The doctor is unlikely to be able to convince the child that these negative feelings require understanding, and should be kept in perspective. The ego of the child may be too immature, and his cognitive powers insufficient to maintain the split we have described as essential to the therapeutic alliance.

Therefore, the child analyst should analyze negative transference early, and avoid actions which the child views as unhelpful. In the past, child analysts have offered gifts of candy or food in an attempt to keep the transference positive. Such gifts may indeed encourage the child to like the therapist on the basis of present reality, but they can not produce a positive *transference,* which is by definition a displacement of affectionate feelings from the parents onto the therapist. Although such seductive behavior may make the child eager to engage in the treatment, it will also camouflage the transference, and make analysis of it difficult or impossible. Most analysts, therefore, avoid this type of seductive approach. When it is truly necessary, it is a parameter.

A special characteristic of the child who is brought to analysis is that he often does not desire treatment at all, at least at its inception. This cannot be the case with an adult patient, for if he doesn't want treatment, he is free to refuse to attend.

The parent brings the child to the doctor because of a problem the grown-up sees. The child rarely initiates analytic contact by asking for treatment. Often it is the parent, not the child, who suffers from the child's symptoms. In such cases, there is no therapeutic alliance with the child at the start. In the initial phase of treatment, the analyst can help the child engage in therapy through his interest and concern, through his astute perceptions of the child's attempts to avoid suffering, and through his apt interpretations.

Initially, then, the parent must insist that the child attend the treatment. Later, the child will periodically become upset by what he is discovering or by the transferences that emerge, and will wish to avoid analysis. Or the child may find himself "cured" after a period of analysis and not wish to continue. An adult in such circumstances will generally survey the situation and decide to persist in the analysis despite pain or early relief; he will keep the long-range goals in mind. But a child generally possesses no such vision.

The treatment, then, will depend on the parents who act as auxiliary egos to the child and insist he continue the analysis even when the child is frightened or reluctant. Clearly, a therapeutic alliance must exist with the parent as well as with the patient. The parents must be willing to bring the child to the doctor's office, to pay the bills, and provide the information that the analyst needs. They must also tolerate the frustrations that are inherent in the procedure. They do not know what the child tells the analyst, the therapy requires a prolonged period of time, and a child pictures his analyst as a surrogate parent. Ideally parents will allow the work to continue after the child's external appearance has changed, but optimal resolution of inner problems has not yet occurred.

The alliance with the parents is largely an *information alliance.* Whether the analyst should offer advice to the father and mother will be pursued in more detail in chapter 14. Here let me only state two general principles: (1) Advice to parents should be kept to a minimum and should, if possible, be restricted to suggestions relating to the parents' conduct regarding the analysis itself; (2) At times, advice is necessary to establish the sufficiently stable home environment required for an analysis to proceed.

ADDITIONAL THERAPEUTIC ASPECTS OF THE ANALYTIC SITUATION

Although interpretation is the primary therapeutic instrument in analysis, the patient may respond to other aspects of the analytic situation as well. Anna Freud (1965) has said that each patient makes use of the analytic situation in ways that satisfy his individual needs. "The nature of the child's disturbance reveals itself via the specific therapeutic elements which he selects for therapeutic use when he is offered the full range of possibilities that are contained in child analysis" (p. 229). In addition to furthering the analytic process, the patient's identification with the analyst may be therapeutic in itself. The patient may develop inner structures based on this identification. His ego may become sturdier, more capable of sublimation and the use of neutralized energy, or more flexible in its use of defenses. His superego may either become more lenient, or stronger, as the patient's needs require. Introjecting the analyst in fantasy may lead to feelings of completeness where there was a sense of emptiness before.

Through perceiving the analyst at work and aspiring to be like him, the patient may learn to modulate the intensity of his emotional responses, better tolerate frustration, and restrain his tendencies to impulsivity (see Settlage and Spielman 1975). He may learn to organize his drives, and the means of gratification. In achieving these aims the patient may use the analyst as an auxiliary ego, as the child ordinarily uses his parents. At times the analyst may consciously teach the patient adaptive behavior or methods of work and thought, but more often the patient learns from the therapist without conscious intent on the analyst's part. Learning can occur without teaching (Olch 1971). The use of the analyst as an auxiliary ego is likely to occur when the child's parents have not been available for this function.

Interpretations may alter personality structure and enable the patient to constructively use adults when he had previously been unable to do so. When a developmental arrest of this type is overcome, the patient may be able to learn better from his teachers, his parents, and his analyst.

Although the deficiencies of function that create learning inadequacies may be neurotic in nature—that is, due to inner conflict—they are often due to faults in the child's ego apparatuses as well. In such cases, analysis can be of help for secondary or concomitant neurotic disturbances or inhibitions, but the primary deficiency is best dealt with by other means such as tutoring.

Some patients may attain a transference cure—out of love for the analyst, the patient may surrender his symptoms. Although this may be very gratifying to all, such improvement is usually short-lived. Unfortunately, it occasionally results in the parents' terminating the analysis prematurely, before a true analytic process can be instituted or completed.

ANALYTIC TACT

The analyst's interventions require the utmost tact. Although the therapist's words may be eagerly sought, their actual appearance may provoke opposition and produce antagonism. Indeed, frequently patients feel attacked by the analyst's interpretations. Although an occasional aggressive response to intervention is inevitable, the analyst can take pains to avoid encouraging such reactions. When they occur, further interpretations may be indicated.

Hartmann (1964) offered the most abstract explanation of the eruption of hostility after interpretation. He suggested that the defenses utilized neutralized aggressive energy; when countercathexis is diminished or eliminated, aggressive energy is liberated.

It is also true that patients become angry when they are suddenly confronted with drives that have been hidden from consciousness. The patient feels traumatized by the sudden burst of affect when defenses diminish and drive derivatives spring forth. He becomes angry at the analyst who seems to have deprived him of protection and appears to have caused pain instead. Such defensive fury is often seen in children, who possess fragile egos and cannot easily master their drives. The analyst can avoid an unmanageable hostile reaction by careful "dosage," by attempting to make interpretations to limit the release of drive derivatives to manageable proportions.

Patients often feel attacked because of masochistic predispositions or, in a related way, because they project their superegos onto the analyst and imagine that his comments are critical. Here we find that transference from parents plays a significant role.

Finally, interpretations sometimes evoke hostility because they offend the patient's narcissism. Patients wish that they were perfect, and the analyst inevitably points out an imperfection when he describes a conflict, a defense, or a drive that causes difficulty. It is developmentally appropriate for a child's narcissism to be greater than an adult's. This makes it especially necessary for the child analyst to exert caution. Analysis may diminish narcissism, but it cannot eliminate it.

In addition, the child's narcissistic equilibrium is more precarious than the adult's because of less stable self-representation. The analyst's words may thus challenge the child's sense of identity, or lead the child to misinterpret the analyst's comments to mean that the patient is bad or babyish.

It is neither possible nor desirable to bypass completely the problems I have outlined. The analyst must eventually deal with these problems by interpretation, and use them to help understand the patient. Care must be taken to couch comments in terms that will not cause excessive disruption of the analysis. This is particularly true in work with children, whose fragile and immature egos cannot immediately cope with the hostility that emerges.

Of all the special measures that child analysts often use to soften interpretations, only a few can be mentioned. Sometimes the analyst interprets the behavior of a character in the child's play. The reader will recall Mrs. Bornstein (1949) told Frankie that the *child* in Frankie's game was sad and lonely. Only later, when her patient experienced this affect, was she able to talk of Frankie's feelings.

At other times the analyst may talk about how children in general react, for example, "sometimes when a child knocks something down, and feels bad about it, he says that someone else has done it."

The interpretation may be made in the form of a story based on the child's own tale: "Once upon a time there was a baby deer who was very sad because he had been left by his parents. He felt so bad that he tried to get other deer to pay attention to him by annoying them."

Singing an interpretation to a very young child or saying it with humor and a light touch will also make it easier for the child to listen to and accept what the doctor says.

These measures cannot, and optimally should not, succeed in totally avoiding the narcissistic and other insults the child will imagine. The analyst must not be discouraged when the child covers his ears to block out distasteful interpretations. Rather, he should realize that this means he has hit the spot, but that the child is perfectly entitled to employ denial and thus regulate his inner tension. Eventually the patient will grow to tolerate what was once intolerable.

PSYCHOANALYSIS AND OTHER FORMS OF PSYCHOTHERAPY

Strictly speaking, analysis depends on correct interpretations for its therapeutic effect, but, as we have seen, other factors may contribute to the patient's improvement. In other forms of treatment, the therapeutic result rests on a different foundation. Those therapeutic factors that we have found to be incidental in analysis become the primary cause of improvement in other forms of treatment: identification with the therapist, feeling more complete because of contact with the therapist, surrendering symptoms out of love for the therapist, educational interventions by the therapist, and alterations in the patient's environment.

The fact that the analyst sees the patient very frequently makes for a profound difference between analysis and other forms of therapy where the contact is less. The analyst is in a better position to make correct interpretations, whereas a psychotherapist is more likely to make incomplete, incorrect or inexact interpretations which may, nevertheless, be helpful. The patient may conceive of the analyst's words as magical and this in itself may alleviate symptoms. He may feel he is united with a powerful person who says remarkable things; in such a case, the accuracy of interpretations may be less significant than the fact that the patient imagines that the therapist is transferring his power to him.

The greater frequency of sessions in analysis as compared to psychotherapy also makes for a more intense transference, and perhaps the appearance of a transference neurosis which can be analyzed, giving a more stable result. In psychotherapy of other sorts, the transference may be used, but it cannot be analyzed adequately.

It is important that the correct form of treatment be determined before embarking on a therapeutic voyage. We will proceed therefore to several chapters in which the authors discuss the indications and counterindications for child analysis and the diagnostic measures that may be utilized for the determination of the optimal technical approach.

NOTES

1. Freud's early papers on psychoanalytic technique were published from 1911 to 1914, but many tenets had been established before Hans' analysis (Freud 1905, 1911, 1912a, 1912b, 1913, 1914).

2. In addition to specific articles referred to throughout this chapter, I wish to alert the reader to the many articles and books on child and

adult analytic technique that form a basis for this chapter. These include articles by S. Freud cited above (see note 1) and the following: Abbate (1964), Bernstein (1957, 1975), Bornstein (1949), Casuso (1965), Eissler (1953), Feigelson (1974), Fenichel (1941), A. Freud (1927–1970), S. Freud (1915, 1917, 1919, 1937a, 1937b, 1940), Furman et al. (1976), Glover (1955), Greenson (1967), Harley (1961), Kestenberg (1969), Kohrman (1969), Loewald (1960), Maenchen (1970), Menninger and Holzman (1975), Pearson (1968), Stone (1961), Van Dam (1966), Wolman (1972). Brenner (1976) was published after this chapter was written.

3. In this book we are using the term *object* to refer to an actual person that the subject loves or hates. The *object-representation* is the individual's conscious or unconscious mental representation of the object, and differs from the characteristics of the real object. Similarly the *self* comprises an actual person in all his complexity, his physical being and psychic structure. The *self-representation* is the individual's conscious and unconscious mental representation of himself. (See Hartmann 1964, Jacobson 1964, Eisnitz 1969)

4. See chapter 6 for a discussion of other factors determining the ambivalence of this period.

REFERENCES

Abbate, G. M., Reporter (1964). Panel: child analysis at different developmental stages. *Journal American Psychoanalytic Association* 12: 135–150.

Benedek, T. (1938). Adaptation to reality in early infancy. *Psychoanalytic Quarterly* 7:200–214.

Bernstein, I. (1975). On the technique of child and adolescent analysis. *Journal American Psychoanalytic Association* 23:190–232.

———, Reporter (1957). Panel: indications and goals of child analysis as compared with child psychotherapy. *Journal American Psychoanalytic Association* 5:158–163.

Bornstein, B. (1949). The analysis of a phobic child. Some problems of theory and technique in child analysis. *Psychoanalytic Study of the Child* 3/4:181–226.

Brenner, C. (1976). *Psychoanalytic Technique and Psychic Conflict.* New York: International Universities Press.

Casuso, G., Reporter (1965). Panel: the relationship between child analysis and the theory and practice of adult analysis. *Journal American Psychoanalytic Association* 13:159–171.

Eidelberg, L. (1957). Quoted by H. Kohut, Reporter (1957), Panel: clinical and theoretical aspects of resistance. *Journal American Psychoanalytic Association* 5:548–555.

Eisnitz, A. (1969). Narcissistic object choice, self representation. *International Journal of Psycho-Analysis* 50:15–25.

Eissler, K. (1953). The effect of the structure of the ego on psychoanalytic technique. *Journal American Psychoanalytic Association* 1:104-143.

Erikson, E. H. (1963). *Childhood and Society.* 2nd ed. New York: Norton.

Feigelson, C., Reporter (1974). Panel: a comparison between adult and child analysis. *Journal American Psychoanalytic Association* 22:603–611.

———— (1976). Panel: The Essential Components of the Child Analytic Situation. Presented at the Association for Child Psychoanalysis, March 1976.

Fenichel, O. (1941). *Problems of Psychoanalytic Technique.* Albany, New York: Psychoanalytic Quarterly.

Fraiberg, S. (1962). Technical aspects of the analysis of a child with a severe behavior disorder. *Journal American Psychoanalytic Association* 10:338–367.

Freud, A. (1936). *The Ego and the Mechanisms of Defense.* New York: International Universities Press.

———— (1965). *Normality and Pathology in Childhood.* New York: International Universities Press.

———— (1922–1970). *The Writings of Anna Freud.* Vol. 1–7. New York: International Universities Press.

Freud, S. (1905). On psychotherapy. *Standard Edition* 7:257–268.

———— (1909). Analysis of a phobia in a five-year-old boy. *Standard Edition* 10:5–149.

———— (1910). Five lectures on psycho-analysis. *Standard Edition* 11:9–55.

———— (1911). The handling of dream-interpretation in psycho-analysis. *Standard Edition* 12:91–96.

_____ (1912a). The dynamics of transference. *Standard Edition* 12: 99–108.

_____ (1912b). Recommendations to physicians practicing psychoanalysis. *Standard Edition* 12:111–120.

_____ (1913). On the beginning of treatment. *Standard Edition* 12: 123–144.

_____ (1914). Remembering, repeating and working-through. *Standard Edition* 12:147–156.

_____ (1915). Observations on transference-love. *Standard Edition* 12:159–171.

_____ (1917a). Mourning and melancholia. *Standard Edition* 14: 243–258.

_____ (1917b). Introductory lectures on psycho-analysis. *Standard Edition* 15 and 16.

_____ (1919). Lines of advance in psycho-analytic therapy. *Standard Edition* 17:159–168.

_____ (1937a). Analysis terminable and interminable. *Standard Edition* 23:216–53.

_____ (1937b). Constructions in analysis. *Standard Edition* 23:257–269.

_____ (1940). An outline of psycho-analysis. *Standard Edition* 23: 144–207.

Furman, R., Chairman; V. Calef, A. Eisnitz, C. Feigelson, S. Weiss, panelists (1976). Panel: The Essential Components of the Child Analytic Situation. At the Association of Child Psycho-analysis Meeting, March 1976.

Geleerd, E. (1967). *The Child Analyst at Work.* New York: International Universities Press.

Glenn, J. (1969). Testicular and scrotal masturbation. *International Journal of Psycho-Analysis* 50:353–362.

Glover, E. (1955). *The Technique of Psychoanalysis.* New York: International Universities Press.

Greenacre, P. (1968). The psychoanalytic process, transference and acting out. In P. Greenacre, *Emotional Growth,* Vol. 2, pp. 762–775. New York: International Universities Press, 1971. Originally published in *International Journal of Psycho-Analysis* 49:211–218.

Greenson, R. R. (1967). *The Technique and Practice of Psychoanalysis.* New York: International Universities Press.

Harley, M., Reporter (1961). Panel: resistances in child analysis. *Journal American Psychoanalytic Association* 9:548–561.

Hartmann, H. (1964). *Essays on Ego Psychology.* New York: International Universities Press.

Jacobson, E. (1964). *The Self and the Object World.* New York: International Universities Press.

Kanzer, M. (1975). The therapeutic and working alliances. *International Journal of Psychoanalytic Psychotherapy* 4:48–73.

———— (1953). Past and present in the transference. *Journal American Psychoanalytic Association* 1:144–154.

Kestenberg, J. S. (1969). Problems of technique in child analysis in relation to the various developmental stages: prelatency. *Psychoanalytic Study of the Child* 24:358–383.

Kohrman, R., Reporter (1969). Panel: problems of termination in child analysis. *Journal of the American Psychoanalytic Association* 17:191–205.

Kramer, S. (1960). Running Comments, Confrontation and Interpretation. Presented at the Philadelphia Psychoanalytic Institute Child Analysis Study Group. (Unpublished)

Kris, E. (1956a). The recovery of childhood memories. *Psychoanalytic Study of the Child* 11:54–88.

———— (1956b). On some vicissitudes of insight in psychoanalysis. *International Journal of Psycho-Analysis* 37:445–455.

Loewald, H. W. (1960). On the therapeutic action of psychoanalysis. *International Journal of Psycho-Analysis* 41:16–33.

Lorand, S. (1946). *Technique of Psychoanalytic Therapy.* New York: International Universities Press.

Maenchen, A. (1970). On the technique of child analysis in relation to stages of development. *Psychoanalytic Study of the Child* 25:175–208.

Mahler, M. S., Pine, F., and Bergman, A. (1975). *The Psychological Birth of the Human Infant.* New York: Basic Books.

Menninger, K. A., and Holzman, P. S. (1975). *Theory of Psychoanalytic Technique,* 2nd ed. New York: Basic Books.

Olch, G. B., Reporter (1971). Panel: technical problems in the analysis of the preoedipal and preschool child. *Journal American Psychoanalytic Association* 19:543–551.

Pearson, G. H. J., ed. (1968). *A Handbook of Child Analysis.* New York: Basic Books.

Reich, W. (1933). *Character-Analysis.* 3rd ed. New York: Orgone Institute Press (1945).

Settlage, C. F., and Spielman, P. N. (1975). On the Psychogenesis and Psychoanalytic Treatment of Primary Faulty Structural Development. Reported in the Association for Child Psychoanalysis Summaries of Scientific Papers and Workshops. Second Series.

Smirnoff, V. (1971). *The Scope of Child Analysis.* New York: International Universities Press.

Sterba, R. F. (1934). The fate of the ego in analytic therapy. *International Journal of Psycho-Analysis* 15:117–126.

Stone, L. (1961). *The Psychoanalytic Situation.* New York: International Universities Press.

Van Dam, H., Reporter (1966). Panel: problems of transference in child analysis. *Journal American Psychoanalysis* 14:528–537.

Wolman, B.B., ed. (1972). *Handbook of Child Psychoanalysis.* New York: Van Nostrand Reinhold.

Zetzel, E. (1956). Current concepts of transference. *International Journal of Psycho-Analysis* 37:369–76.

PART THREE

THE ASSESSMENT OF PATIENTS

Chapter 3

INDICATIONS AND CONTRAINDICATIONS FOR

CHILD ANALYSIS

Isidor Bernstein, M.D.
Albert M. Sax, M.D.

The decision as to whether a particular child should be analyzed depends on the consultant's understanding of both the patient and the analytic process. Child analysis as a treatment has undergone marked changes since its origin in 1908; as a result there have been changes in the type of patient selected for treatment. We will start this chapter with a brief description of historical developments in child analysis. We will then present an outline of the consultation procedure, and a statement of the factors that must be balanced in determining the indications and contraindications for child analysis without major modifications, as it is generally practiced today.

The bulk of this chapter will consist of six case presentations—three prelatency and three latency patients—which illustrate the complexities involved in deciding the treatment best suited for a particular child. We will discuss clinical and metapsychological considerations.

In the final section, we will state the general principles that have emerged from these six consultations. We note the importance of the following overlapping factors in a dynamic evaluation:

1. the child's endowment
2. the child's developmental level (including an assessment of each

of the structural components of the personality)
3. the symptomatology
4. the diagnosis
5. the parents and other aspects of the child's past and present environment
6. the degree of internalized conflict

CHANGING CONCEPTS AND CHANGING INDICATIONS

The choice of psychoanalysis as the appropriate form of treatment for a child is based not only on the need of the patient, but also on his capacity to make use of this form of treatment. For both the child and the adult in analysis, the process of interpreting defenses will lead to the uncovering of unresolved conflicts. Through the process of working through using the transference, the goal of structural change will be reached. There, however, the similarities between child and adult analysis diminish greatly. While the general goal of each is the same, it is important to realize that the child has an immature personality in an ongoing state of development. Structural change therefore has to be redefined in accordance with this process of development and further growth. For this same reason the technique of child analysis is not merely a modification of adult analysis, but exists as a treatment method with its own rationale. Thus, although the indications and contraindications for the use of analysis as a treatment modality are dependent on the diagnostic assessment of the child (just as one would assess the analyzability of an adult), there are other factors involved which must be taken into account.

With adults, the task is somewhat easier in spite of the fact that the psychoanalytic literature at times tends to be somewhat ambiguous as to the criteria for selection. The widening scope of analysis has resulted in the proliferation of studies and application of modified classical analytic techniques to the analysis of other than neurotic conditions. Nonetheless, we can comfortably say that in the ideal adult analysand we have a self-motivated individual who experiences suffering as a goad to seeking treatment, whose neurotic structures are generally fixed, who can free associate, and who can simultaneously observe his reactions to inner and outer stimuli while assessing his transference to the analyst.

In contrast, the child is usually not aware of internal suffering, but instead sees his problems as environmentally determined. The child is in a state of flux, and even though he displays a discernable neurotic constellation, he often does so in a shifting and changeable form. In addition, the child cannot be expected to free associate. His whole life is bound up with his environment in such a way that it is still being used for developmental purposes. This same child is brought for evaluation by his parents, rather than coming volitionally, and his treatment can only be instituted and helped to make progress with the active participation and involvement of the parents. Although there is major disagreement about this fact, it seems self-evident that even those analysts who do not involve the parents in the treatment as informants, do at least rely on them for support in payment, in keeping appointments, and in the establishing of a certain degree of good will towards the process.

When child analysis began, it was believed that neuroses in childhood had the same features as neuroses in adults, and were treatable by the methods of adult analysis. But even in its beginnings, it was recognized that child analysis required different techniques, although what they must be was only slowly delineated. Thus, the analytic understanding of Hans was achieved through the agency of his father.

In 1913 Ferenczi reported that his attempts to analyze a child were unsuccessful because the child wanted only to play. There was soon a growing awareness that child neuroses held only an incomplete resemblance to adult neuroses. In 1920 Hug Helmuth wrote that an analysis similar to the analysis of adults was not possible with children. The problem of child analysis was confused because a technique suitable for the child had not been developed to any degree. Children in need of help were only considered to be analyzable if they showed a rather clear-cut set of symptoms which could be dealt with by modifications of usual analytic techniques. Interestingly, though, the aim then, as now, was to get the child to verbalize his conflicts. An understanding of how to do this, had yet to be elaborated. Melanie Klein began to apply analytic understanding to the play of the child. She declared that play was the free association of the child, and should be interpreted. She evolved a theoretical schema according to which all young children could be analyzed in this way, since all play with the analyst would be expressed as transference. A. Freud wrote that play in children, although valuable as a passageway to the unconscious, was not routinely available for interpretation. She also stated that because the original objects were still real, and available for libidinal and aggressive discharge, they too needed to be involved in the analytic process. Although they paid increasing attention to developmental progress and arrest, both Klein and A. Freud were primarily concerned with symptoms. Miss Freud eventually came to look on evaluating ego, superego, and drive development as the major factor in the assessment of indications for analytic treatment. Berta Bornstein persuasively stated that children need not be seduced into an analytic process, but could be approached by the forthright interpretation of defenses as expressed in their behavior. Offering an early interpretation can be used as a diagnostic aid, especially because it may reveal something about the child's capacity to develop a conceptualization of inner psychic processes.

The problem of the evaluation of children for analysis seemed insurmountable so long as they were viewed only from the standpoint of libidinal development and the oral, anal, and phallic stages. However, coinciding with the elaboration of ego psychology were changes in the theory of aggression, and in the ideas associated with object relations and separation-individuation. Gradually there came to be an increasingly systematic way of viewing a disturbed child. It was no longer necessary to be convinced that a fixed neurotic structure existed before a child was considered suitable for analysis. In fact, many children who appeared to have crystallized neuroses were found to be not analyzable because major aspects of their development were faulty, and the symptoms masked more serious pathology. Thus consideration of developmental lines gradually became the more systematic and satisfactory method for the diagnostic assessment of children. This in turn led to a greater clarity in the formulation of the disturbances of childhood. This gradual burgeoning of knowledge aided in the growth of the understanding of the child, and was found to be useful in interpreting conflicts based on development. This has not been the only salutory effect, however. With the increase of knowledge about the earliest stages of development, analytic understanding has permitted development of techniques other than psychoanalysis for the treatment of more disturbed children. Some of these techniques include Mahler's tripartite approach and corrective symbiotic relationship, or Alpert's technique of corrective object relationship. Similarly, Weil has proposed an "educational" period prior to analysis. Its aim is to help the deviational child over the obstacles of arrested development so that they might engage in the analytic process.

This chapter will deal with the process used to decide which cases are appropriate for child analysis. This selection process is in accordance with what is generally considered current child analytic technique without major modifications. The clinical, metapsychological, and environmental factors that must be considered as we decide whether analysis or some other form of treatment is required will be examined.

THE STRUCTURE OF THE CONSULTATION

First, we will describe the form of the initial contacts: the structure of a well-run consultation. It is the rare child who is brought for consultation because he asked his parents for help with his problems. Those children who do so are usually children of families which have a significant connection with analysis either with parents as practitioners, or because the parents have been analyzed themselves. Most often a child is brought for consultation because of parental concern or a recommendation from the child's school.

Generally there has been some observation of significantly deviant behavior, or symptoms which have not improved with the passage of time as those accustomed to the fluctuation of childhood behavior would have expected.

In consultations for young children it is generally advisable that the therapist see the parents, together and separately, as many times as he feels will be productive in obtaining material about the child's difficulties. In this way the consultant will be able to evaluate the history of the disturbance, as seen through the eyes of the child's parents. Also, he will be able to assess the nature of the parental interaction through observing the way both parents view the child while talking to the consultant separately and together. A history of the child's development should be obtained, although one has to be aware that parents, for reasons both conscious and unconscious, may withhold information that the consultant would consider significant. At the very outset it is the task of the consultant to convey the analytic attitude that it is important to understand as much as possible about the child so an appropriate judgment can be made.

Most parents will be grateful for the concern that is shown in a careful, deliberate evaluation and the consultant will be able to gain as much material as possible. During the consultation period a child may be seen more than one time, interspersed, if necessary, with visits of his parents. Here one has to be somewhat cautious. If the consultant decides that analysis is the treatment of choice, but does not himself have time to see the child, transference phenomena may occur which will prove troublesome for the eventual analyst. Thus, during this period, early interpretations to the child should be kept at a minimum, occurring only as a test of how readily the child can use such interpretations. Data from the school may be of great help in determining the locus of the child's difficulty. When a very young child is being evaluated, a visit to the nursery school often proves invaluable if the school is set up so that observation is possible. Finally, psychological testing may be a helpful tool in those cases where not only is there a question about the development of the ego and its ability to deal with reality, id, and superego demands, but also a need to assess cognitive and motor deficits that may be based on organic difficulties. This includes an evaluation of the child's intelligence. It may also be of help in further persuading the parents that treatment, especially analytic treatment, is required.

When the final evaluation is made, it is important to balance a number of factors: the child's endowment; where the child is and has been developmentally; the nature of the child's symptomatology; the diagnosis; the degree of internalization of conflict; and an evaluation of the parents and their emotional capacity to facilitate treatment.

CLINICAL ILLUSTRATION: JEFF

Jeff, age eight and a half, was in great need of help. Jeff's school, which he had attended for only four months, had been increasingly concerned about him because of his concocting fantastic tales, his inattention in class, his infrequent attendance, his inability to write in spite of a high IQ and excellent reading ability, and the discovery that he carried a knife with which he periodically threatened other children. In addition, Jeff was precociously interested in sex, and looked eagerly at pictures in girlie magazines. He was repeating third grade, ostensibly because his class in another state had not covered the material required by his new school. Jeff lived with his mother and younger brother, age six. His parents were separated. His mother reluctantly agreed to the consultation because of the school's urging, and found to her surprise that Jeff was eager to talk to someone. He said he had no friends, and was unhappy. Jeff also told his mother that he carried a knife to protect himself from other children and from dangerous situations. His mother was seen by the consultant three times, he was seen twice, and his father, after frequent broken appointments, was seen once. Psychological testing was obtained.

At the time of the consultation, Jeff's mother was forty-seven and his father was forty-two. After nine years of marriage, his mother's second, Jeff's parents had decided to adopt a child, because his mother was infertile. She felt a child could bring more meaning to the marriage which had been characterized by an infantile hedonism. The baby was obtained through illegal channels, but as far as the mother knew, the pregnancy and birth were normal. Jeff was a docile baby who seemed to tolerate the succession of housekeepers that cared for him. In addition he did not seem troubled when taken to parties, treated as a toy, and put to sleep in an extra room. This happened often. In fact Jeff was quite lovable until he began to walk at age thirteen months. At this time he began to refuse to let his mother cuddle him. Up to this point Jeff had been taken with his parents everywhere. Now he was left at home and frequently there were arguments about whether to stay home with him. Often his father left and his mother waited until Jeff was asleep before joining her husband. During this time Jeff sucked his thumb, clung to a favorite blanket which he didn't give up till age five and a half and began to have frequent temper tantrums with breath-holding.

Jeff was an extremely articulate child. He said words before he could walk, and could speak in sentences before age two. He was toilet trained overnight at age two. From then on Jeff was once again taken with his parents wherever they went. He was given everything he wanted, often to prevent an outburst of rage. Jeff developed pavor nocturnus at age two and a half. This would occur nightly until age five and at the time of the consultation would still occur occasionally. At four Jeff began to have monster dreams which still occurred at the time of the consultation. He seemed happiest when with his parents at late-night parties and included in all of their activities. Jeff was frequently taken to his parents' bed at night but his mother insisted there was no primal scene exposure. Both parents slept in the nude. Beginning at age five the family moved frequently either as part of a new money making enterprise or as part of his parents impulsive and exuberantly lavish life style. At one point the family lived in a forty room mansion for eight months. Jeff grew closer to his father, and idolized his grandiosity, his overindulgence. He was party to many of his father's activities including, as it turned out, extramarital affairs.

When Jeff was four, his mother prevailed on his father to adopt Carl. She thought a second child would provide Jeff with a needed companion, and recalled that her marriage seemed more intact after Jeff's adoption. Shortly after the adoption of the younger child, Jeff's father, feeling that family life was excessively restraining, left home, and got a divorce. He saw Jeff frequently, spent a great deal of time with the family, but didn't feel hampered by responsibility. In fact, after each of his affairs he would return briefly to his wife. After one and a half years his parents remarried, but by this time Jeff's mother had become increasingly intolerant of her husband's immature excesses, and there were frequent and stormy arguments. These led to separations which lasted several months and which were followed by reconciliation of a few months.

At age five, because of the night terrors, the nightmares, the attachment to his blanket, and excessively aggressive behavior in kindergarten (this aggression towards other children had been the hallmark of his relations with other children since age three in nursery school) Jeff was seen in a "conjoint" therapy for a few months with his mother. Jeff's mother felt this therapy helped her to deal with her own problems and with Jeff. When she stopped treatment, she ended Jeff's as well.

When Jeff was six and a half the family moved to another state where they continued their sybaritic existence. Jeff's adjustment in school was very difficult. After a medical evaluation which included a neurological examination, Jeff was diagnosed as having dyslexia and hyperactivity. He was treated with amphetamines which had only a minimally salutory effect. Jeff abruptly stopped taking the amphetamines after the family once again moved. His mother had a hysterectomy and stated that she was then treated for cancer of the uterus and of the kidney with cobalt and radiation prior to this move. This, of course, further disrupted the family, and both children were exposed to the mother's illness.

In the meantime, Jeff's greatest pleasures occurred accompanying his father on luxurious outings where marijuana, cocaine, and alcohol were used excessively. During this time it was noted that Jeff began to read omnivorously, but was unable to write. He and his brother spent a good deal of time together cared for by a succession of housekeepers. Apparently they clung together, rarely fought, and provided some measure of stability for each other.

Jeff's mother, although concerned about him, was strangely detached in pursuing the investigation of her child's difficulties. She apparently did so only in the hope that if serious difficulties were discovered, Jeff's father, out of affection for the child, would be compelled to forego his impulsive life style, and once again settle down with the family. On the other hand, her husband, an immature, brilliant, but paranoid man, was suspicious of the whole consultation. He was reluctant to be involved, and felt that the child's difficulties were based on his wife's self-indulgences. He claimed that her illnesses were fabricated to keep him and the children in line. At the time of the consultation, the couple was once again separated, and Jeff's father was angrily refusing to support his wife.

Jeff was a handsome child with a sad, masklike expression. He discussed his problem with adult gravity. He claimed that he wanted to be helped because he couldn't keep friends, and felt it was necessary to carry a knife to protect himself from bullies. When asked about the tall tales he told to other children about the princely luxury of his life, Jeff repeated some of them, and acknowledged that he exaggerated so the other children would like and respect him. Jeff also said he wanted his father to return home so he could see him more often. Jeff then stared at the consultant before asking whether the latter could help him achieve that. He went on to say that his only other problem was difficulty in writing and printing. Jeff spoke of his nightmares, which had recently diminished, with an air of unconcern. There was no indication that Jeff saw any of his difficulties as being other than externally derived. Throughout the consultation Jeff maintained an ingratiating, superficially cooperative attitude coupled with a peculiarly intense stare. He was constantly involved with the details of realistic situations and solutions. He was uncomfortable talking about fantasies, and only in the second interview would he play a game. Jeff's game was extremely sophisticated, and made use of puppets as if they were in a play that would be produced on stage. The play had to do with a man and a woman who visited a strange city where they became ill. They consulted a doctor and a nurse who turned out to have the same name as the sick couple. Eventually it was revealed that the doctor was the man's long-lost brother, and the nurse was the woman's long-lost sister. The two couples were happy and would try to find out how they had been separated.

While there were no blatant distortions of reality or demonstrable thought disorder, Jeff's careful control in his play indicated extreme concern about impulse control. His relationships pointed to poor judgment and a paranoid orientation, coupled with attempts at manipulation to achieve security and self-gratification. If Jeff didn't get what he wanted, he calmly advocated violence to achieve his ends.

Psychological testing revealed a child who was brilliant, extremely manipulative, and whose aggressive and sexual impulses were in variable control often only by threat of external punishment. The testing confirmed that his anti-social behavior, which was covered by ingratiating charm, produced little remorse. An ego deviational pattern was discerned in which there was an underlying identity confusion, and a tendency toward personality disorganization due to excessive rage. The use of projection as a defense was greatly in evidence, and a paranoid development was predicted. Jeff's attachment to his father masked an intense disparagement of men as drunk, unemployed thieves who will attack others when provoked. His mother was seen as weak, seductive, and easily manipulable.

After the month-long consultation was complete, it was felt that Jeff showed evidence of a marked ego deviation with antisocial and paranoid trends, coupled with serious problems in impulse control. Definite cognitive lags existed in addition to a deficit in finer motor movements. Both of these difficulties were intensified by his emotional conflicts. Therapy was considered necessary. It was thought that analysis was not only not feasible, but also contraindicated at this time.

Jeff was referred to a therapist who saw him three times weekly for approximately two months. His mother was seen once weekly. His father refused to be seen, and in anger rejected the therapeutic process. At the end of two months, the family moved out of state without warning. Jeff's school tuition, the consultant's fee, and the therapist's fee were all unpaid. Attempts to contact them were to no avail.

Discussion. Jeff was a latency child who was having considerable difficulty in coping with the constant eruption of both libidinal and aggressive drive elements. This was in great part due to the excessive overstimulation that he had experienced throughout his life and continued to experience. Consequently, Jeff's object relations had a marked narcissistic and anaclitic tinge, and he had been able to utilize precocious ego functions to insure gratifications. Memory, speech, and secondary thought processes were highly developed, but his reality testing was shaky. When Jeff was not achieving narcissistic or dependency gratification from the outside, he reacted with poorly controlled rage which was defended against mostly by projection.

Jeff's exaggerations, although reflecting some truth, seem to have been woven into a complex, grandiose view of himself which served as a protection from repeated narcissistic blows. His defective self-image was constantly threatened, particularly in the area of his innate deficit in fine motor coordination; hence his particular distress about his defective writing. Superego functioning was markedly deficient, giving way to the pressures for self-gratification and an ego-syntonic view of violently and criminally achieving his ends. Furthermore, controls on his behavior were primarily seen as coming from external forces. Nevertheless, this identification with his impulse-ridden, paranoid father did provide some stability to his personality structure. However, the pressure for drive fulfillment was so great, as was the fear of punishment, that Jeff suffered severe anxiety, manifested in his persistent dreams of monsters.

Jeff's excellent intelligence, coupled with his search for more stable and reliable objects (as portrayed in his fantasy play), indicated a dim awareness of the deficiencies in his primary objects, and were progressive forces for continuing development. Nevertheless, drive regressions, and ego and superego defects would militate against starting an analytic process. The analysis would necessarily be colored by the likelihood that Jeff would cathect the analyst as a new object who, he would insist, should supply all gratifications, and provide the stable environment he sought. A period of extensive therapy oriented to the exploration of the demands of reality and his reactions to narcissistic injury would be most in order as a prelude to the actual analytic work. However, for even this to be considered it would have been necessary to have the cooperation of his parents, coupled with their awareness of their own need for treatment. It could be predicted that the instability of the family would preclude the long term commitment necessary for analysis. As was demonstrated both by their life styles and their inability to maintain even the initial contacts, neither therapy, nor analysis, could be instituted.

CLINICAL ILLUSTRATION: DOLORES

Dolores, age nine and a half, was seen once. Her mother was seen on three separate occasions, her father was seen one time, and her parents were seen together twice. Psychological testing was obtained.

Dolores was a tall, beautiful blond youngster whose mother had been concerned about her since she was an infant. Her mother's major worry had been that Dolores never seemed to eat properly and would react with intense aversion to some of the foods the family ate. Dolores would eat roast beef, steak, and cereal, and would drink milk. In addition, at the time of the consultation she ate an assortment of junk foods. There was never any evidence of malnutrition, and in fact Dolores was always in excellent health. Her aversion to other foods was intense, and when her parents would try to force her to eat some of these foods, she would stubbornly refuse and occasionally retch with nausea. Her mother's anxiety about her led her to consult many physicians, and she even had psychological tests done. Her concern for Dolores' well being extended to other areas, and she was always surprised when she found that the child was functioning well both socially and academically. Dolores's mother harbored the nagging doubt that somehow Dolores would not be able to function, and that she would be unhappy because of her stubborn and self-contained manner. The mother feared that Dolores would be disliked and shunned by other children and adults because of her cheerful ebullience and take-charge attitude. Her husband was pleased with the child, but periodically felt great concern when his wife pointed to what she conceived of as Dolores's flaws. Feeling that it was her mission to protect Dolores from future difficulties, her mother constantly hovered over her, questioned her closely on all of her activities, assiduously did her homework with her, and cooked special foods for her, which the rest of the family then ate also. Dolores's mother's attitude towards her daughter was in sharp contrast to that towards her six-and-a-half-year-old son. He was felt to be quite adequate, and faced none of the disasters that were predicted for Dolores. Throughout Dolores's life, her mother had an awareness that such excessive concern was somehow her own problem, yet she couldn't help being obsessed with Dolores's performance and functioning.

The history of Dolores's development shows that, in spite of a constant thread of oral conflict, she mastered all developmental steps quite adequately. Dolores was breast fed as a baby. Her mother's concern about adequate food intake led her to supplement feedings with a bottle which the infant often refused. Dolores was a thumb sucker, and used a crib blanket as a transitional object until age three. As a toddler she was excessively demanding, and most of her wishes were gratified. At no time however did Dolores have a separation problem. When her younger brother was born there was a brief flurry of aggression and Dolores stated her wish that her brother would die. This was soon replaced by affection, and the relationship smoothed out to its current lordly domination. Even though the struggle to control Dolores's food intake continued, toilet training was achieved with ease in the space of two months when she was two years old. At age four and a half, while negotiating phallic-oedipal conflicts, there was an increasing demanding quality, and an increased insistent stubborness. Associated with this was a heightened awareness of nudity, and attempts to see her father naked through intruding on him in the bathroom and bedroom. At age five and a half this behavior was replaced by a coquettish attitude, and an intense interest in acting and ballet. Dolores began to ignore her mother's commands, and idolized her father, who enjoyed the theater. The conflict about the quality and quantity of Dolores's food intake heightened, and it was then that mother sought psychiatric advice. She was told that therapy was indicated for Dolores, but after a discussion with her husband, in which it was pointed out that Dolores's only problem was in resisting eating certain foods, and that her nourishment and general well-being were perfectly satisfactory, Dolores' mother decided against any treatment for the child.

When the consultant interviewed Dolores he found her a relaxed, confident, flirtatious youngster who eagerly discussed her ballet lessons, and easily described her friendships with many children. When the problem of food was discussed Dolores became somewhat embarrassed, and said she was ashamed of her strong likes and dislikes about food. She felt there was something wrong, but couldn't arrive at any reason for her aversion. Dolores spoke freely about the fact that her mother was more concerned about her food problems than she was, but also implied that this was her mother's difficulty, not hers. She confessed shamefacedly that she still occasionally sucks her thumb at night before going to sleep, but that no one else knows it. When asked if she felt that she needed help for her food problem, Dolores indicated she wouldn't mind talking about it, but felt it wasn't that serious a problem. It is interesting to note that Dolores's father, a kindly and insightful man, felt her difficulties were exaggerated by her mother. He said if the consultant felt it necessary, he would surely support treatment, but he himself couldn't view it as serious.

Psychological testing, done with the expectation that the mother would be able to use the information, revealed a child who was in the main well adjusted and competent, with good academic skills and a marked social and esthetic sensitivity. Reality testing and thought processes were intact. There was a quality of self-centered expansive narcissism and a somewhat excessive sensitivity to criticism. Men were seen as strong and powerful and women were perceived as weak and inadequate. There was some concern that the sexual and aggressive pressures of adolescence may cause some difficulty.

As the mother was seen more frequently, it was apparent that her obsession about Dolores was covering an underlying depression and dissatisfaction with her own life. She became increasingly aware of this, and when it was advised that she enter analysis for herself and that Dolores didn't need therapy at that time she gratefully accepted the suggestion.

Three years later, when deciding on another consultation for Dolores, the mother revealed that she had herself been in analysis. She had discovered a great deal about her ambivalent relationship with the child and during this time had gradually loosened her hold on Dolores and was able to act less as a servile flunky to her. She stopped doing Dolores's homework with her on a nightly basis. As Dolores entered puberty her school work, which had previously been excellent, began to falter. She rarely studied, but her excellent mind permitted her to pass. Dolores devoted more and more of her energies to the theater and to ballet. Although she still avoided some foods, the variety of those she would eat had increased.

Discussion. Dolores was a child who was firmly in latency and occupied with the growth, accomplishments, and ego development that diminished and neutralized drive pressures provide. Her only symptom was a somewhat limited diet, which created no difficulty for her physically, and was sufficiently varied so that the foods she rejected, although clearly having symbolic meaning, could not be associated with any available fantasy. Dolores was an independent child whose self-regard was somewhat excessive. She had clearly negotiated the oedipal conflict and maintained a firm feminine identity. Disparagement of her mother was exaggerated and, while indicating anger at the latter's intrusiveness, it was also used defensively. Ego functions were intact and adaptive. Dolores's intelligence was in the very superior range, but she tended to deal with academic exercises too hastily, and complete assignments sloppily. Her major focus was on dramatic activities which she pursued with excellent performance, and was the vehicle for neutralized gratification of phallic wishes.

Dolores's tendency to have her mother help with homework was another reflection of the conflict with her mother. It revealed the negative oedipal wish as expressed in oral terms—she would be "fed" in academic areas, but would not allow herself actually to be fed. Psychological testing predicted that there might be academic difficulties in puberty. Socialization was achieved with ease, even though her tendency to lead and dominate would occasionally lead to losing friends who didn't wish to be dominated. This tendency possibly indicated a certain degree of anxiety, associated with her conflicts about independence and phallic wishes. However, this independent attitude was a progressive force in Dolores's development, even though it had some conflicted roots. Although there were evidences of early character problems based on orality, dependence, and castration anxiety, at the time of the evaluation, Dolores was coping quite well with all demands made on her, both internally and externally. Possible future difficulty was postulated, but both Dolores's and her parents' motivation for therapeutic intervention at this time was minimal. Instead the mother saw her obsessive concern as a reflection of her own problems. Therefore, her entering analysis and her eventual understanding of herself caused a shift in the nature of her relationship with her daughter. Entering puberty intensified Dolores's anxiety, and led to a regression to greater dependency on her mother. Dolores's seeming academic failure is a return to a state which symbolically invites her mother to be reinvolved. It is possible that the present may be a more suitable time for Dolores to enter analysis. With her own concern about academic failure, she and her parents are more amenable to analytic intervention, especially since she has not been able to understand the failure of her narcissistic character defense.

CLINICAL ILLUSTRATION: MARK

Mark was eight and a half when his parents sought consultation. He was seen three times, his mother twice, his father twice, and the two together twice. Psychological testing was obtained.

Mark had experienced frequent and prolonged crying spells at home for the previous six months, usually as the result of a minor reprimand. At the time of the consultation these spells had increased in frequency, and for the previous three months Mark had complained of abdominal pains or upper respiratory tract symptoms, especially in the mornings. Often these symptoms would disappear when he was permitted to stay home from school or when he was forced to attend. In addition, Mark was extremely competitive with his brother, two years his senior, whom he idolized. He was also accident prone. Finally, Mark was fearful that his father would die while on one of his frequent trips. His parents were loving and considerate of him, but they often differed about how to handle him, especially regarding his school attendance. His father insisted that he go, and his mother indulgently allowed him to stay home. It was his father's perception that Mark's crying spells arose out of rage. His mother felt they were based on inconsolable grief. Mark's father was a man with a violent temper who, though never physically abusive, frightened his children by his frequent verbal outbursts. Mark's mother was chronically depressed, felt burdened by her role as a mother, and would frequently drink quietly to cope with her own distress. There were many altercations between the parents, but they were consistent about their concern for Mark.

Mark was born after a normal pregnancy and was described as an active baby who was easily held. He slept and ate well, and was weaned from breast to bottle at four months. Mark kept his bottle at night until he was four, and used the satin edge of a blanket as a transitional object which he gave up with his bottle. He walked at twelve months and was speaking in sentences at fourteen months. The only complication in Mark's infancy was a mild case of coeliac disease which lasted from his ninth month to his twentieth. This required special diet, but didn't mar his sunny disposition. However, during this time his older brother had a severe case of coeliac syndrome, and as a result, Mark suffered some deprivation of his mother's attention. At twenty months Mark was toilet trained in his characteristic way—he decided it was time and quite rapidly implemented his own toileting. When Mark was three years old the family moved and he no longer shared a room with his brother. From then on he was a frequent night time visitor to the parents' bedroom with complaints of night time fears. Shortly thereafter his parents installed a cot in their room on which he would sleep. This night time visiting, a result of frequent nightmares, waxed and waned over the next few years, and was quite persistent at the time of the consultation. From age three to five Mark had temper tantrums when frustrated, but by age six he had developed a tight control on himself, and his only angry outburst would be revealed by occasionally slamming his door. From an early age Mark's remarkable intelligence was manifest, and he did quite well in school. In contrast to his older brother, he was an early and avid reader. However, his main concern was to excel in sports which was his brother's metier. Older and larger than Mark, his brother was the wonder and delight of their father because of his exceptional athletic ability. Mark, on the other hand, while well-coordinated, tended to be incautious and even reckless in his attempts to outdo his brother, revealing his underlying guilt. Just prior to his consultation Mark had beaten his brother in a ski race. Shortly thereafter he fell and hurt himself. Then, to his dismay, he lost the medal that he had won. He had many friends and was well-liked by his teachers and classmates.

Mark's mother had been in analysis for six years prior to her marriage, and felt that she had a successful experience. Her husband, because of his irascible behavior and anxieties about work, was currently in therapy. He was a business man who had educated his children when they were quite young in all facets of sexual knowledge. This included diagrams and pictures of sexual activity and the physiology of spermatogenesis, ovulation, fertility, and birth.

Mark easily and confidently spoke of his need for help with his problems. He described his crying spells and added that they were accompanied by "funny feelings" in his stomach. These were the same feelings he would sometimes get in the morning before school. Mark cooperatively drew pictures of his dreams, and spontaneously volunteered that something was making him feel bad, but he didn't know what. He spoke of his difficulties with his brother, and said he was sad that his brother didn't include him in some of his activities. He chose not to play with toys, but rather talked and drew stories of some of his fantasies about being a star athlete, an Indian Chief, or a king, who was injured in conflict with antagonists.

Psychological testing verified his excellent endowments — Mark had a very high intelligence quotient—and focussed on the intensity of his hidden rage. Phobic and obsessional features were present and, along with a high degree of separation anxiety, considerable castration fears were in evidence.

When Mark was presented with the idea of getting help he welcomed it, and immediately began to discuss the hours that he would come. Both parents were relieved that analysis was recommended. His analysis lasted five years during which Mark developed considerable awareness of his positive oedipal rivalry, his castration fears, and an understanding of his ambivalent relationship with his brother. He chose to terminate when he did, which coincided with his entry into puberty, because of a reactivation in the transference of some of his dependency conflicts. These were similar to those he had experienced with his mother. Mark clearly stated that he chose to work out his problems alone. It was likely that he wished to avoid exploration of the negative oedipal relationship in the transference, and the new and confusing bodily experiences that appear at puberty.

Discussion. Mark can best be characterized as a latency child who developed a crystallized neurosis which was threatening to interfere with his progressive development. His ever-increasing successful rivalry with his brother in the academic area produced anxiety. In addition, Mark's success actually stimulated his brother's and father's hostility, and made him even more frightened. This drove him closer to his mother. There was a reawakening of castration fears at the hands of his father, both as a result of fears of retaliation and his own wish to submit to father. This led to regression to a dependent, clinging involvement with his mother, and also gave rise to his school phobia and conversion symptoms. The alternating rivalry and love for his brother was the vehicle by which he expressed his positive and negative oedipal conflict. Mark's conscious fantasy life had to do with phallic themes. Most of his ego functioning was on a very high level. In part, this was due to his constitutional endowment. Also, his ego development had not been seriously impeded. The major autonomous area drawn into conflict was in the sphere of motility. His recklessness that led to accidents was an unconscious masochistic reaction to the guilt Mark felt about phallic achievements. Thus there was a well-developed superego, and his conflicts were primarily internalized and expressed in some acting out of masochistic fantasies.

There was some indication that there was also conflict between activity and passivity. Although his capacity to sublimate was quite well developed, it, too, had been drawn into his conflicts and his regressive tendencies toward passive clinging to his mother threatened to interfere with his previously intact area of functioning. His regression to conflicts about dependency also prevented him from handling his intense anger for fear of losing both primary objects. Hence there was also observable depressive symptomatology. Mark showed many of the characteristics of an adult neurosis. The adequate structuralization of the personality and the psychological acceptance by his parents of the process permitted a relatively uncomplicated analysis. In Mark's case, we were considering not only his immediate symptomatology, but also the prediction that if analytic intervention were not instituted, we would undoubtedly see significant developmental interferences.

CLINICAL ILLUSTRATION: PETE

Pete, age four and a half, was seen in consultation as an emergency. A few weeks after his manic-depressive mother was hit by a truck and killed, Pete began to develop fears of death, a morbid preoccupation with accidental injury, and frequent crying spells. While crying he verbalized missing his mother. Coupled with this was a sudden increase in accidental injuries. Pete seemed to exercise no caution or judgment in his running and playing. On a few occasions he dashed into the street heedless of oncoming traffic. Often while playing at crashing cars— Pete's favorite game—he would seemingly inadvertently hurt his hands, leg, or bang his head against the furniture. His father had deserted the family when Pete was two and a half. He was cared for by his mother under the careful and watchful eye of his youthful and loving maternal grandparents. They now assumed his total care and upbringing. Pete attended nursery school and was easily integrated into the group because of an exceptionally sensitive teacher. She was able to tolerate his wild and exuberant play, and contain him for group activities. Pete played well with other children, and exhibited little aggression towards them. He had walked and talked early, and had been an appealing, alert, and bright child. He sucked his thumb and used a toy rabbit as a transitional object, which he still took to bed with him. Although Pete always had a voracious appetite, he was not an obese child. Occasionally he would have temper tantrums when he wanted something to eat that wasn't immediately forthcoming. Toilet training was effected easily at two and a half, but after his mother's death there was some enuresis. The grandparents indicated that there was evidence that Pete had periodically been beaten by his mother when she was dissatisfied with him, but this had never been observed. In fact, in spite of her chronic depression and three hospitalizations during his life (the first for three months post-partum), she was described as a devoted, dedicated, albeit inconsistent mother. During his mother's absences his grandparents had cared for him.

Pete was a bright, appealing, and articulate child who loved to draw. He immediately accepted the idea that the consultant would help him with his problem about hurting himself, and with his sad feelings about his mother's death. While playing Pete banged his head on a shelf and with tears in his eyes smiled bravely, saying, "I'm not hurt, it's just nothing." When it was pointed out that in fact it had hurt him and it was serious, Pete immediately began to play his car crash game. He described in detail how cars were hurt and how they could be fixed. He was reluctant to leave at the end of the session, but welcomed the fact that he would return. In subsequent sessions Pete spoke of dreaming about his mother and of how much he missed her. When it was pointed out to Pete that he was testing to make sure he wouldn't really get hurt when he had a "crash," he smiled beatifically. Within three weeks Pete had stopped hurting himself. He calmed down considerably in school, his disposition was sunny, and his night time fears had abated. Frequent sessions with the grandparents were devoted to helping them understand his sorrow and rage at the loss of his mother. This was coupled with guidance in aiding them to deal openly with his acute guilt, plus his identification with his mother. It was decided to continue the therapy with an eye to eventual analysis if his conflicts interfered with further development.

Discussion. At the time of his mother's death, Pete had been primarily involved with phallic oedipal concerns potentiated by the absence of his father. Before the sudden death of his mother these wishes were often expressed in an oral dependent fashion which gave rise to outbursts of rage. However, his close tie to his grandparents, who were consistent figures, had enabled Pete to achieve a state of object constancy in spite of the separations and inconsistent cruelty he had experienced at the hands of his mother. Aggression was primarily directed against himself and not other children, although sometimes they would be involved in his wild and exuberant play. Identification with his mother, and fear for his own body (castration fear potentiated) led to a counter-phobic defense. He attempted to master body-threatening situations by reckless endangerment, hurting himself, and experiencing relief that he escaped relatively unscathed. Pete's play at car crashes and his preoccupation with the intactness of the car revealed both his identification with the instrument of his mother's death, and his fear of retaliation by her.

Ego functions were fairly intact: In fact, there was a tendency toward a heightened sense of reality in Pete's insistence that all games he played were "only pretend." Because of the massive trauma at the time of the consultation, it was difficult to evaluate the full extent of his conflicts.

Nevertheless, Pete's ego functions appeared remarkably intact. His ability to understand and use the early interpretation of his counter-phobic trend spoke well for the future consideration of analysis if it appeared that his frustration tolerance, his ability to concentrate (tolerate anxiety) and his handling of aggression had not resumed its normal course.

CLINICAL ILLUSTRATION: EMILY

Emily, a six-year-old first grader, was seen only one time. Her four-year-old sister was in nursery school and she had a two-year-old brother. Both parents were seen on a number of occasions during the month of the consultation, and Emily's kindergarten teacher was consulted. Her parents, both in analysis, had become increasingly disturbed by Emily's behavior during the previous two months. She exaggerated dramatically to them about her activities in school; had again started to suck her finger publicly, and she was distraught when they went out at night and left her with a baby sitter. The final event that had them seek a consultation occurred one evening when Emily informed the nursery school bus driver not to bring her sister home, saying that the latter was sleeping at a friend's house. Her parents found out about the lie when the school called to verify this.

Emily's mother, an anxious woman, had been in therapy since her marriage of ten years, and in analysis for the previous four and a half years. She spoke of how well she had done in analysis, understanding a great deal about herself, including the solution to a number of phobias. She stated she wanted Emily evaluated to make sure her daughter wouldn't have similar problems. She was particularly concerned about the exaggerations and lying because she too, in adolescence, had indulged in the same dramatic exaggeration with her friends, ostensibly in order to improve their opinion of her. Her deep shame about this led her to discover some of the determinants of feeling degraded and demeaned as a woman, and also led to a profound concern about honesty. A loving and concerned mother with deep affection for her children, she was especially attached to this oldest child. In her narcissistic identification with the child, she wanted Emily to be seen as a well-adjusted and competent child. Emily's public finger sucking was therefore quite painful to her. She stated she was dealing with this narcissistic identification in her analysis.

Emily's public display of pathology was also of concern to her father. Like his wife, Emily's father was devoted to his children and had a firm yet loving relationship with them. His relationship with Emily, whom he called "princess," was somewhat seductive. While less disturbed about Emily's behavior, he cooperated fully in the evaluation because of his wife's concern. It soon became apparent that Emily's father was also concerned about the appearance of pathology. He was most distressed about the public finger sucking. He felt that the lying and night time fears were somehow transitory since everything else in Emily's life was going quite well. Both parents reported that, having started first grade, Emily was doing well in reading and arithmetic. She had many friends, and had recently begun to ask to sleep at her friends' houses and to have them sleep at hers. During the day Emily was generally independent of her mother, involving herself in satisfactory play and school. Her mother acknowledged ruefully that at times she felt Emily had become too independent of her. In her relationship with her sister, Emily was domineering. The two would sometimes fight but for the most part they got along quite well. Toward her brother, Emily was both maternal and dominating. Generally she was kind to him, but sometimes she hit him impatiently.

Emily had smiled early, was a cuddly baby, and was always a good eater. She walked at eleven months, said her first word at thirteen months, and was speaking in sentences at one and a half. She was easily toilet trained at two and a half. When Emily was four years old she had a two-month period of sleep difficulty associated with nightmares and fears of monsters. Her parents dealt with this and the attendant clinging with gentleness and kindness. Her finger sucking, which recently recurred, had been given up in public at four after the nightmares disappeared. This was also due to her parents' constant remarks on the matter. Emily still sucked her fingers at night before going to sleep, although she had given up her special diaper which she had used as a transitional object. Her nursery school teacher said she was a bright, charming, and articulate child. Emily was also said to be eager for new experiences, friendly with other children, and sought after by them because of her happy and imaginative play. Seductive behavior had been noted in the past year with boys and with her father.

When Emily was seen by the consultant he initially found her shy, but bright and appealing. She industriously set about drawing a house with a family living in it. There were three children in her drawing. The middle child, a girl (her sister), was at some distance from the family group. When asked if she knew why she was seeing the consultant, Emily immediately replied it was because she had lied about her sister's sleep-over date. When asked why she had done that, Emily said she thought it would be fun for her sister to sleep-over at a friend's, just as it had been fun for her. She added that she knew it had been wrong because her Mommy didn't know about it. When asked if anything worried her, Emily said sometimes when Mommy and Daddy went out at night she was afraid, but that the last two times it happened (after the episode of lying) she had not been afraid. Emily also talked about how her sister sometimes annoyed her by taking her things, and wanting to play with her and her friends. She acknowledged, however, that she played with her sister, when she wasn't playing with her friends.

During the next two months all of Emily's regressive symptoms disappeared and with the exception of some occasional finger sucking before bed time there was no recurrence. It was felt that this was a temporary regression, and required no further intervention.

Discussion. Emily's regressive behavior seems to have been based on a number of factors which potentiated each other. Primarily, it represents a temporary reaction to anxieties having to do with progressive development. Although Emily negotiated libidinal phase development quite well and without any interference with ego development, there seems to have been certain oral fixation elements which persisted as development proceeded. One of the reasons for the continued finger sucking appears to have been her parents' excessive concern about it. This was interpreted by Emily as pushing her toward premature independence. However, in her life she had been able to incorporate this aspect without undue developmental interference. Thus, as Emily entered first grade she embraced her new independence enthusiastically. However, this was coupled with her mother's increasing independence from her as the result of her own analysis. Rivalrous feelings toward her sister surfaced, and were handled with reaction formation. Periodically the aggression broke through. Identification with her mother led Emily to adopt a caricature of a maternal attitude toward her siblings. It also gave rise to exaggerations about her role in class—taking the teacher's place. She related to her classmates with a somewhat feigned superiority, based on the assumption of adult responsibilities. This seems also to have temporarily reactivated the positive oedipal relationship with her father, who responded to her seductiveness. A temporary reactivation of these conflicts led to a regressive reappearance of orality and her oedipal fears. As time progressed, the symptom disappeared due to the progressive developmental forces which allowed Emily to enter firmly into latency. The appearance of her symptoms can be postulated as due to developmental strain.

CLINICAL ILLUSTRATION: ALLEN

Allen, age five years, two months, was first discussed with the consultant at age four. At this time he showed great anxiety about his bowel movements, and was fearful of having diarrhea. This was accompanied by considerable disgust, and occasional vomiting and screaming "Mommy, Mommy" upon looking at his feces. At the time of the first consultation, Allen's mother was six months pregnant, and Allen was very interested in the pregnancy. His mother had allowed him to examine her abdomen with his toy doctor's kit, at times when she was in the bath tub. (She covered her genitals with a washcloth.) Allen had been adopted six years after the parents' marriage because his adoptive mother had been unable to carry her pregnancies to term, and had had numerous spontaneous abortions. When Allen was one and a half his mother had an uncomplicated spontaneous abortion. When he was three his mother was put to bed for six weeks with a nurse in attendance because of a threatened abortion. At that time Allen spent a great deal of time with his mother in her room and saw her brown-stained menstrual pads. According to his mother, he had no immediate reaction to them. It was at this time, however, that the first instances of vomiting and disgust about his own bowel movements occurred. After his mother was hospitalized for three days in order to complete the abortion, Allen no longer was disgusted with his bowel movements. He did have a brief period of fear of heights, which gradually disappeared.

A few months prior to this spontaneous abortion, Allen's mother had begun his toilet training. This proved to be extremely difficult partly because of the systematic and concrete way in which she approached the problem. She sat with him for long periods while he was on the potty, singing and reading to him, and urging him to produce. Periodically she erupted in anger and abuse when he didn't comply. After many months Allen was finally trained, and when he started school at three years, nine months, he was free of accidents. It was apparent at the time of the first consultation that Allen's mother was inordinately concerned about his growing up "all right." She was preoccupied with the idea that he was somehow defective, "his penis was too small, his circumcision had not been performed properly." She felt that the fact of Allen's adoption put an extreme burden on him. To ameliorate this, she tried to make him into a child with no problems. At times she was overindulgent and seductive, and at other times harsh and rejecting. Her feelings alternated between love and admiration, on the one hand, and fury and loathing on the other. Allen's father, an intelligent but passive man, would be drawn into her excessive concerns. After the persistence of Allen's fears and disgust about his bowel movements his father was also distressed about Allen. As the pregnancy progressed to term, Allen became more and more interested in the baby, and the process of birth. He asked many questions but particularly wanted to know if the baby was in the same place as the "poo-poo." Allen also wanted to know if he had been in the "tummy with the poo-poo" of his natural mother. The fact of his adoption was well known to him because, following the guidelines of the adoption agency, Allen's mother talked with him frequently about adoption. When Allen was an infant she had crooned a song to him with the words, "My lovely adopted baby."

Allen's parents' concern about him and the health of the fetus had been intensified as soon as they were aware that Allen's mother was pregnant. They had been assured the pregnancy was normal, and Allen's brother, Jimmy, was born when Allen was five years old. In the meantime, Allen's symptoms had waned and his adaptation to nursery school was age-adequate. His parents had been advised to contact the analyst if his previous reactions returned. They consulted the analyst in the fall of the year Allen began kindergarten, when he was age five years, two months. His nausea and disgust had returned, he showed an ambivalent attitude toward his brother, and at times reacted to him as if he were dirty like feces. In addition, Allen had begun to soil and occasionally wet his pants. He had been called "stinky-poo" by his new classmates in kindergarten. An increasing stubborness appeared along with passive-aggressive obstructionism, refusal to take no for an answer, and an obstinate defiance of direct commands. Allen was unwilling to talk to his mother, and expressed his ambivalent love for his brother by squeezing him too hard. His behavior in kindergarten was described as immature and aggressive. He persisted in wrestling and fighting with the other boys, even though they didn't want to constantly indulge in this immature play. Allen was more responsive to his teacher than to his parents, but she felt his behavior was not dissimilar from other infantile boys in her class. Allen's mother had clearly begun to compare her two boys when she again complained of the size of Allen's penis. She said Jimmy's was considerably larger than Allen's. Though Jimmy was a cranky baby, it was clear she was more at ease with him, and demonstrated greater affection for him than she did for Allen, about whom she spoke with dislike and guilt.

Allen's mother was an extremely angry woman with many compulsive traits. Her father and two brothers had died in the years since Allen was adopted. She dealt with her chronic depression and guilt by an intensification of obsessional defenses, which she brought to the care of her children. Periodically, when these defenses broke down, she erupted in rage, and threatened to leave her husband and take the children, or to commit suicide. She had been in analysis for five years prior to Allen's adoption, but viewed the experience as unsuccessful. While she desperately wanted help for Allen, she contemplated the possibility of therapy for him with alarm. She feared the stigma of therapy would taint any future career Allen chose as an adult. Allen's father was an obsessional character who had had a long but successful analysis which had enabled him to marry. He was kind and gentle with Allen, although somewhat distant. Often he was unable to discipline his son, and was prone to long discussions in which he attempted to find out why Allen was afraid of his bowel movements, or why he behaved in a stubborn manner. He was by far the more consistent figure in Allen's life.

Allen's adoption was postponed until he was two months old because he was being evaluated for a possible congenital hip displacement, which diagnostic studies revealed he did not have. The foster mother who cared for him during this period reported he was afraid of water.

Allen's adoptive mother, however, did not note this, and described him as quiet, happy, placid, and easily satisfied.

Allen's maturation was normal. He stood at nine months and walked at one year. He spoke early and in complete sentences by the time he was two years old. Allen always slept and ate well. He never suffered physical symptoms, had no nightmares, and was unafraid except for the presenting fear of feces. Allen took stuffed animals to bed with him, and continued to do so at the time of his evaluation. He never sucked his thumb or fingers.

The analyst did not see Allen at the time of the first consultation, but did meet with him one year later when Allen was age five years, two months. Allen was dressed in an army uniform, and told the consultant he had lots of costumes, such as Superman, cowboy, fireman. He wore them all periodically, a fact which his mother had related. Initially, Allen was apprehensive, but gradually began to play with the materials. First he played an army game. Then he played with a truck which he labeled a garbage truck, and which dumped "waste" into the river. Allen became somewhat excited as he played this game, and clutched his penis. He spoke of all of the waste polluting the river, and then left the playroom to urinate. In the second session, playing the same game, Allen was clearly physically uncomfortable. He crossed his legs and writhed and, when the consultant asked him about it, he said that when he was playing he didn't like to stop to go to the bathroom. The analyst asked, "Did this cause you to sometimes have accidents?" Allen answered yes as he left the room to go to the toilet to have a bowel movement. When Allen returned he stated that he didn't like to have accidents, and it worried him when he did. He also worried about losing his teeth as another older child had. Allen seemed quite interested when presented with the idea that it was possible to find out more about how accidents happened, and how to control them.

Psychological testing was obtained, and revealed a bright normal child with a propensity for stubborn withholding and withdrawal under pressure. There were strong feelings of sibling rivalry, anger related to frustrated dependency needs, and jealousy. Reality testing and thinking were intact. Allen's stubbornness about performance prevented the adequate evaluation of a possible perceptual difficulty.

It was recommended Allen begin analysis, and that his mother concommitantly begin psychotherapy with another analyst. Because of her serious depression, it was suggested she reconsider returning to analysis. Allen's analysis has proved to be difficult because of his stubborn, often silent, reactions. His mother is in therapy with only minimally positive results.

Discussion. There was considerable anxiety about the pregnancy in the family at the time of the initial consultation. Allen was preoccupied with the new baby's arrival. Age and phase appropriate oedipal conflicts had resulted in what seemed to be a temporary regression to the intense reaction formations of anal preoccupation. Therefore, the analyst postponed a complete evaluation until after the birth of the baby. In fact, Allen's symptoms had abated somewhat, and development appeared to progress although lagging behind that of his peers. Entering kindergarten, a new school, combined with separation from his mother, and his preoccupation with his brother, seems to have triggered an intensification of Allen's rivalrous feelings toward his brother, and a regression to anal sadistic modes of interacting. Thus Allen's relationships with his parents were characterized by stubborn negativism. With his peers, an aggressive excitement dominated. Sadistic behavior towards his brother alternated with excessive concern. One evidence of phallic interest was his penchant for dressing up as one of a number of powerful figures. Even this strongly suggested the anal component of control. Castration anxiety was seen in his fear of bodily injury. This too had an anal tinge, especially as expressed by his preoccupation with the disposal of waste matter. Faced with being controlled in school, Allen had a tendency to withdraw and resist. This interfered with learning. Superego functioning was immature—many controls still had to be imposed from outside. Mastery of anxiety was achieved primarily by regression to the anal sadistic phase. Allen was without adequate defenses to deal with this regression. Drive, ego, and superego regressions led to a picture of a clear developmental lag with considerable immaturity. Memory, speech, motility, and reality testing were intact. In spite of the disordered relationship with his mother, object constancy had been achieved, though with a quality of nagging demandingness. Analysis was considered the appropriate form of treatment to deal with the internalized obstructions to Allen's development.

GENERAL PRINCIPLES

Although the six cases presented do not cover the wide variety of clinical problems presented to the consulting child analyst, they do lend themselves to illustrating the theoretical and clinical considerations in recommending psychoanalysis as the treatment of choice. There is sufficient distinction between the prelatency and the latency child to have presented three clinical examples of each, illustrating for each phase children chosen for analysis, children who needed no therapy at the time of consultation, and children for whom therapy but not analysis was indicated. Even though there is a difference between the early latency child and the later latency child, developmentally, the hallmarks of latency are the same. These include cognitive growth, socialization, and adaptation to and mastery of the environment, while appropriately defending against the drives and their regressive expressions. The partial resolution of the conflicts of the phallic-oedipal period, its concomitant identifications, and superego formation have led to more or less sufficiently neutralized energy to facilitate the above tasks. However, the prelatency child not only has immature ego functioning, but he is still dealing with the pressing issues of his instinctual demands as related to the primary incestuous objects. Since internalizations are in the process of occurring, psychic structures are less clearly defined, and the clinical picture is therefore much more in a state of flux. This requires a different perspective in evaluating the degree of psychopathology in prelatency children. Although we have not presented any prepubertal children, a major difference between them and the earlier latency child is their greater degree of autonomy. Greater emphasis is placed on their own motivation for treatment because their cooperation in analysis cannot be so easily dictated by the insistence of their parents (see chapters on prelatency, latency, and preadolescence—6, 7, and 8).

Case material of children with severe congenital defects was not presented, because in these cases the question of analyzability is decided not on the basis of the presence or absence of a defect, but rather on the total clinical picture in which the defect is only one factor. In fact, when evaluating whether a child needs psychoanalysis or another mode of treatment, the governing principle is the need to assess as much of the total clinical picture as is available to the consultant. Therefore it is necessary to evaluate (1) the child's endowment, (2) his environment,

(3) the rate of development of id, ego, and superego, both in the past and present, (4) the diagnosis, (5) symptomatology, and (6) the degree of internal conflict. The principles that guide the eventual choice of psychoanalysis, psychotherapy, or no treatment can be grouped under these six rubrics. A fixed neurosis interfering with development constitutes, of course, the prime indication for psychoanalysis. A psychosis in a child is a contraindication for psychoanalysis, and most analysts feel such children require other treatment approaches. Regressive symptomatology may be only an expression of a temporary developmental disturbance requiring no therapeutic intervention.

From the standpoint of the child's environment, the characteristics of the parents have to be evaluated in terms of their ability to allow their child to begin and maintain psychoanalytic treatment. In addition, the current environment has to be assessed in terms of the stability of the home, and the degree of trauma the child is or has been subjected to. In this regard, an evaluation of the child's past environmental conditions is also necessary. Unstable parents who provide a threatening or excessively stimulating or depriving environment, constitute a contraindication to psychoanalysis. Also, parents' statements about their children must be evaluated in the light of their own psychopathology. Parents may unconsciously propagate their child's symptoms, or they may mislead the consultant, especially if they view their child as an extension of themselves.

From the standpoint of the child's endowment, it is important to state that intelligence and psychological mindedness are necessary factors for analysis. A retarded child or even a rigidly defended, intelligent child constitutes contraindications to the psychoanalytic process. Also, a degree of object constancy needs to have been attained so that transference reactions and neurosis can develop and be interpreted as the analysis proceeds.

A history of evenness of development, prior to the onset of neurosis, is a positive indication for psychoanalytic treatment. If a child has had difficulties negotiating earlier developmental phases, a more serious psychological disturbance may be present. Furthermore, a degree of frustration tolerance, impulse control, and intact reality testing are necessary requirements for an analytic process. Children who are overwhelmed by the strength of their instincts should not be analyzed until it is determined that the interpretation of their defenses would not lead to overwhelming panic. These are the general principles which guide the evaluation of whether or not a child should be analyzed. Each of the cases presented above will be discussed in these terms.

Neither Emily nor Dolores needed treatment at the time of consultation. In their development both had shown signs of mild to moderate fixation having to do with orality and dependency on their mothers. However, in spite of this coloring they had met and mastered the tasks of each succeeding developmental phase, albeit with the inevitable difficulties that accompany such mastery. In Emily's case, a temporary regression was experienced which lasted somewhat longer than usual. She was dealing with the dual phenomena of her mother's decreased neurotic involvement with her, and her own impetus for emancipation which was partially stimulated by the new and exciting demands made on her. The flurry of regressive behavior and Emily's preoccupation with assuming the maternal role diminished as she became more comfortable with her increased independence, with mastery of school, and with social requirements. This phenomenon could be viewed as a developmental conflict.

In Dolores's case it became clear that as long as her mother was obsessed with her food intake and performance, it would be difficult to arrive at an accurate assessment of Dolores's psychopathology. In spite of all worries and dire predictions about her future, Dolores showed little evidence that her mild oral fixation, her seductiveness, and her exhibitionism was interfering in a significant way with her latency. Thus, although internalized conflicts were present in her, at the time of the consultation it was Dolores's mother, not Dolores, who was in need of analysis. These two cases illustrate that, in and of itself, regressive symptomatology, either acute or chronic, is not a prime consideration in recommending that a child be analyzed or otherwise treated. It is the total picture of the child, including endowment, environment, and current state and rate of development of id, ego, and superego that must be assessed before any decision is made.

All the other cases presented led to a clear decision that a therapeutic intervention of some sort was indicated. The basis for the decisions to analyze Mark (school phobia) and Allen (encopresis), and not to analyze Pete (self-destructive behavior) and Jeff (borderline) will be discussed under the following three rubrics: endowment, environment, and psychic structure and diagnosis.

Endowment. In none of the cases presented was there question of any degree of mental retardation. In fact, all of the children were quite intelligent, and possessed the capacity to conceptualize and verbally express some derivatives of their conflicts. Even Jeff's writing block was a symptom of neurotic conflict, and not evidence of intellectual deficit. Since the analytic process requires not only the capacity to express and verbalize affects, but also the potential to understand and utilize interpretations, it would follow that a child who lacked this innate intellectual foundation would not be suitable for analysis. Retarded children do suffer the broad range of psychopathology, and can be helped in a more limited way by other therapeutic modalities. Severe physical handicaps, on the other hand, are not a contraindication to psychoanalysis, since the understanding of these defects can be integrated into conflict resolution.

Environment. Two major factors need to be considered in deciding whether or not a child should be analyzed—the external condition of the child's life at the time of the consultation, and the characteristics of his parents. If there is considerable and persistent external chaos without much evidence that some stability can be introduced, efforts must be directed towards bringing about a certain amount of order before analysis can begin. Otherwise, the child will be preoccupied with the traumatic uncertainty of his daily life rather than the internalized psychopathologic structures that are amenable to change. In Pete's case, the decision to analyze him had to be postponed until some measure of order could be established in his life after his mother's death and a structured environment in his new home could be established. So too with Allen, the need for analysis was initially unknown since his symptoms could have been temporary. Until some reordering of the family dynamics took place after his brother's birth, it could not be determined that Allen's pathological responses were not constantly aggravated by outside factors. For Jeff, the chaotic life style of his parents and the immutable neurotic and psychotic factors in their personalities led to chronic and persistent damage to him, making psychoanalysis contraindicated.

As Bernstein (1958) pointed out, for a child to be analyzed his parents need to have the capacity to recognize the suffering of their child, and have the desire that he be well, independent of their own neurotic gratifications. In this regard parents must be able to cooperate with the analyst about practical matters, and participate by conveying important information, while at the same time being able to tolerate the narcissistic injury occasioned by the child's illness and subsequent improvement. Furthermore, the parents have to be able to relinquish some involvement with the child, thus granting the privacy necessary for ongoing analytic work. They have to cope with changes in the child to the point where the analysis is not destroyed. In this regard, it may be necessary to recommend to some parents that they be analyzed, so that the child can be treated. The importance of the parents to a successful child analysis cannot be minimized.

Psychic Structure and Diagnosis. Assessing a child for psychoanalysis is also simultaneously to evaluate his capacity to adapt to, and to utilize the analytic process. As with adults, the prime indication for analysis is a serious neurosis. However, it is not enough to label various symptoms complexes, call them neuroses, and say that they constitute indications for child psychoanalysis. Further clarification is needed. Similar symptoms and groups of symptoms may be seen in disorders which are fundamentally quite different. Anna Freud in 1970 wrote that "manifest symptoms may be identical so far as their appearance is concerned but may differ widely in respect to latent meanings and pathological significance" (p. 163). Diagnosis, symptomatology, and a dynamic evaluation of the psychic structure and its developmental history are inseparable, and will be considered jointly in discussing the four children who needed treatment.

Pete was subjected to the major traumas of losing his father at age two and a half, the inconsistency of psychotic mothering, and his mother's death when he was four and a half. Self-destructive behavior suddenly appeared, and he was brought in for a consultation. Emergency intervention was required along with careful counseling of his grandparents to enable them to deal with his overwhelming fears. The interpretation of Pete's counterphobic defense, and the warmth and stability of his new home led to an amelioration of the dangerous symptom. Still, it was not possible to determine whether an analysis was indicated. Even though there was sufficient evidence of neurotic conflict, it could not be determined whether this had been internalized in a fixed manner which would interfere with his further development, or was merely a temporary reaction to massive trauma. Pete was capable of verbalizing his fears, tolerating the intense grief of his loss, and appreciating that he could be helped by understanding. These characteristics, coupled with his ability to utilize interpretations, all pointed to the fact that Pete had achieved object constancy, and a certain stability of ego functioning. In addition, the evenness of his previous development and his contact with reality pointed to the capacity to undergo psychoanalysis if a childhood neurosis appeared when phallic oedipal concerns came to the fore. In 1946 Buxbaum stated: "Analysis is the instrument we use in cases of permanent neurosis which entails disturbances in developmental processes. Psychotherapy can be used in cases of recent disturbances which temporarily impair further normal development" (p. 126).

Before discussing Allen, the other prelatency child for whom analysis was indicated, it may be worthwhile to review some of the characteristics of the prelatency period. Children brought for consultation are usually involved in oral, anal, or phallic-oedipal conflicts as ongoing developmental concerns. As Furman (1960) suggested, there is a special sensitivity between these young children and their mothers. This relationship is undoubtedly representative of how close in time the child is to achieving object constancy. M. Kris, in 1944, pointed out that neurotic symptoms before the oedipal phase's resolution often represent a conflict between the id and ego, and the external environment. Often these disturbances are only partially internalized. Drive elements are much more intense and pressing. Accompanying this is often a willingness to verbalize fantasies in a more rich, vivid, and imaginative fashion than is present in the older child. Finally, both impulse control and superego development have yet to achieve the stability of the post oedipal (latency) child. This produces much more activity on the part of the child even while he is expressing his fantasies verbally. When children enter latency, there is often an increased ability to form a therapeutic alliance, but there is also a tendency to want no contact at all with the analyst. Also, the richness of the child's available fantasy life is most often dulled upon entry into latency.

Allen's reaction to his brother's birth superimposed itself upon the serious developmental interferences of his anal phase. His struggles with phallic oedipal conflicts and enormous castration anxiety led to a serious childhood neurosis manifested by encopresis, a regression to anal sadistic modes of relating, and oral demandingness. Immature social reactions, interference with learning, and a trend toward withdrawal due to some repression of expression were also noted. Yet in spite of this, Allen's capacity for imaginative play, his intact reality testing, relatedness, superior intellectual endowment, and remarkable articulateness were all indications that he could be involved in an analytic process and its attendant frustrations of gratification. A prediction could be made that not only transference reactions, but also a transference neurosis would develop.

For Mark, analysis was clearly the treatment of choice. While dealing with an activation of oedipal rivalries, both positive and negative, Mark's relation to his brother demonstrated regression to oral and phallic concerns, and a masochistic trend. Not only did Mark demonstrate his superior intelligence, his history showed an evenness in development marred only by a mild case of coeliac disease during infancy. His social development was good, as was his academic performance. There was no evidence of narcissistic regression, and he showed considerable frustration tolerance. In addition, he was aware of his suffering, and easily acknowledged that his difficulties were derived from inner forces, which is an unusual phenomenon in a child. In fact, early in Mark's analysis, he was able to understand the relationship between symptoms, dreams, behavior, and his conflicts. It was possible to predict from his initial manner of relating to the analyst that a transference neurosis would develop and could be analyzed.

The decision not to analyze Jeff was based on two separate factors. First was the marked instability of the parents, and their alternating overindulgence and rejection of him which created constant turmoil in his life. If Jeff's parents had been more stable, it is possible that an analytic process could have been instituted, with the awareness that we would be dealing with a child who although not psychotic, showed considerable disturbance of ego-functioning, marked superego deficiencies, and difficulty in coping with both aggressive and libidinal drive elements. Thus, in spite of his superior intellectual functioning, he showed an unevenness in development manifested early in his life by hypermotility. Frustration tolerance was deficient and impulse control was tenuous. Jeff's object relatedness had a narcissistic demanding quality. His self-esteem was quite low, and he dealt with this by a reactive self-aggrandizement. These factors were coupled with a withdrawal into fantasy and a hungering for external forces to solve all problems. As a consequence, Jeff's social development was superficially sophisticated, but geared to narcissistic gratification. Although in contact with reality, this too suffered under the impact of his anxiety and massive use of projection as a defense. Treatment for Jeff would have to include providing a new, stable figure on whom he could depend and upon whom he could demand the reordering of his environment that he sought so desperately. Too great a frustration of these demands would lead to outbursts of disappointed rage which would militate against self-understanding. A considerable period of time would be needed in which cautious frustration of gratifications might lead to a tolerance of their frustration. Possibly, this would enable Jeff to internalize more of his conflicts, and thus be analyzed.

A final word must be said about the use of the developmental profile as adumbrated for children by Anna Freud in her 1965 work *Normality and Pathology in Childhood: Assessments of Development.* This work is a major contribution to the diagnostic assessment of children in the continuum from normality through pathology. Every child analyst has come to understand children clinically with this profile in mind. However, it is a cumbersome task to laboriously fill in the outline, and rigidly adhere to every subheading. Often, all of the information is not available, and frequently will not be until after treatment has begun. It is suggested that the profile be used as an important guide to understanding the child, and that decisions usually must be made without complete information. The concept of a trial analysis may be considered in some uncertain cases.

SUMMARY

Three prelatency and three latency children were presented as examples of relatively common clinical situations in which the child analyst has to evaluate the indications and contraindications for psychoanalysis. Consideration was given to environmental factors, constitution, diagnosis, and psychic structure as the areas under scrutiny. Indication for analysis include sufficient internalized neurotic constellations whose fixed, nontransitory effects will interfere with the child's further development. Contraindications include insufficient intellectual endowment, emotional incapacity of the parents to maintain the analysis, and a deviational or retarded development in the child of sufficient magnitude to show major disruptions of ego-functioning.

REFERENCES

Alpert, A. (1954). Observations on the treatment of emotionally disturbed children in a therapeutic center. *Psychoanalytic Study of the Child* 9:334–343.

Arthur, H. (1952). A comparison of the technique employed in psychotherapy and psychoanalysis of children. *American Journal of Orthopsychiatry* 22:484–498.

Becker, T.E. (1974). On latency. *Psychoanalytic Study of the Child* 29:3–11.

Bernstein, I. (1957). Panel report: indications and goals of child analysis as compared with child psychotherapy. *Journal of the American Psychoanalytic Association* 5:158–163.

———(1958). The importance of characteristics of the parents in deciding on child analysis. *Journal of the American Psychoanalytic Association* 6:71–78.

———(1975). On the technique of child and adolescent analysis. *Journal of the American Psychoanalytic Association* 23:190–232.

Bick, E. (1962). Symposium on child analysis I: child analysis today. *International Journal of Psycho-Analysis* 43:328–332.

Bornstein, B. (1951). On latency. *Psychoanalytic Study of the Child* 6:279–285.

———(1949). The analysis of a phobic child: some problems of theory and technique in child analysis. *Psychoanalytic Study of the Child* 3/4:181–226.

Buxbaum, E. (1946). Psychotherapy and psychoanalysis in the treatment of children. *Nervous Child* 5:115–126.

———(1954). Technique of child therapy: a critical evaluation. *Psychoanalytic Study of the Child* 9:297–333.

Casuso, G. (1965). Panel report: the relationship between child analysis and the theory and practice of adult analysis. *Journal of the American Psychoanalytic Association* 13:159–171.

Ferenczi, S. (1913). A little chanticleer. In *Sex in Psychoanalysis,* pp. 240–252. New York: Basic Books, 1950.

Finch, S. M. and Cain, A. C. (1968). Psychoanalysis of children: problems of etiology and treatment. In *Modern Psychoanalysis: New Directions and Perspectives,* ed. J. Marmor, pp. 424–453. New York: Basic Books.

Freud, A. (1927). Four lectures on child analysis, I: preparation for child analysis. *The Writings of Anna Freud* 1:3–18. New York: International Universities Press.

———(1928). The theory of child analysis. *The Writings of Anna Freud* 1:162–175. New York: International Universities Press.

———(1945). Indications for child analysis. *The Writings of Anna Freud* 4:3–38. New York: International Universities Press.

———(1954). Problems of infantile neurosis: contribution to the discussion. *The Writings of Anna Freud* 4:327–355. New York: International Universities Press.

———(1954). The widening scope of indications for analysis: discussion. *The Writings of Anna Freud* 4:356–376. New York: International Universities Press.

———(1957). The contribution of direct child observation to psychoanalysis. *The Writings of Anna Freud* 5:95–101. New York: International Universities Press.

———(1962, 1964). Assessment of pathology in childhood, parts 1 and 2. *The Writings of Anna Freud* 5:26–52. New York: International Universities Press.

———(1965). Diagnostic skills and their growth in psychoanalysis. *International Journal of Psycho-Analysis* 46:31–38.

———(1965). Normality and pathology in childhood assessments of development. *The Writings of Anna Freud,* Vol. 6. New York: International Universities Press.

———(1968). Indications and contraindications for child analysis. *The Writings of Anna Freud* 7:110–123. New York: International Universities Press.

———(1970). The symptomatology of childhood: a preliminary attempt at classification. *The Writings of Anna Freud* 7:157–188. New York: International Universities Press.

Furman, E. (1957). Treatment of under-fives by way of parents. *Psychoanalytic Study of the Child* 12:250–262.

Galenson, E. (1964). Panel report: prepuberty and child analysis. *Journal of the American Psychoanalytic Association* 12:600–609.

Geleerd, E. R. (1962). Symposium on child analysis: contributions to discussion. *International Journal of Psycho-Analysis* 43:338–341.

_____(1967). *The Child Analyst at Work.* New York: International Universities Press.

Goldblatt, M. (1972). Psychoanalysis of the schoolchild. In *Handbook of Child Psychoanalysis,* ed. Benjamin B. Wolman, pp. 253–296. New York: Van Nostrand Reinhold.

Hawkins, M.O. (1940). Psychoanalysis of children. *Bulletin of the Menninger Clinic* 4:181–186.

Hug-Hellmuth, H. (1921). On the technique of child-analysis. *International Journal of Psycho-Analysis* 2:287–305.

Kaplan, E.B. (1962). Panel report: classical forms of neurosis in infancy and early childhood. *Journal of the American Psychoanalytic Association* 10:571–578.

Karol, C. (1967). Panel report: adult and child analysis: mutual influences. *Psychoanalytic Quarterly* 37:168–171.

Klein, M. (1960). *The Psychoanalysis of Children.* New York: Grove Press.

Kramer, S., and Settlage, C.F. (1962). On the concepts and techniques of child analysis. *Journal of the American Academy of Child Psychiatry* 1:509–535.

Kris, M. (1957). The use of prediction in longitudinal study. *Psychoanalytic Study of the Child* 12:175–189.

Lippman, H. (1939). Trends in therapy—child analysis. *American Journal of Orthopsychiatry* 9:707–712.

Maenchen, A. (1970). On the technique of child analysis in relation to stages of development. *Psychoanalytic Study of the Child* 25:175–208.

Mahler, M.S. (1968). *On Human Symbiosis and the Vicissitudes of Individuation.* New York: International Universities Press.

Nagera, H. (1966). *Early Childhood Disturbances, The Infantile Neurosis, and the Adulthood Disturbances.* New York: International Universities Press.

Neubauer, P.B. (1963). Panel report: psychoanalytic contributions to the nosology of childhood psychic disorders. *Journal of the American Psychoanalytic Association* 11:595–604.

_____(1972). Psychoanalysis of the preschool child. In *Handbook of*

Child Psychoanalysis, ed. Benjamin B. Wolman, pp. 221–252. New York: Van Nostrand Reinhold.

Oberndorf, C. (1930). Technical procedure in the analytic treatment of children. *International Journal of Psycho-Analysis* 11:79–82.

Olch, G. B. (1971). Panel report: technical problems in the analysis of the pre-oedipal and pre-school child. *Journal of the American Psychoanalytic Association* 19:543–551.

Pearson, G. H. J. (1948). Panel report: indications and criteria for the psychoanalysis of children and adolescents. *Bulletin of the American Psychoanalytic Association* 4:20–28.

———, ed. (1968). *A Handbook of Child Psychoanalysis.* New York: Basic Books.

Pieper, W. J. (1973). Panel report: indications and contraindications for child analysis: current views. *Journal of the American Psychoanalytic Association* 21:603–616.

Pine, F. (1974). On one concept of "borderline" in children: a clinical essay. *Psychoanalytic Study of the Child* 29:341–367.

Rexford, E. (1962). Child psychiatry and child analysis in the U.S. *Journal of the American Academy of Child Psychiatry* 1:365–384.

Ritvo, S. (1974). Current status of the concept of infantile neurosis: implications for diagnosis and technique. *Psychoanalytic Study of the Child* 29:159–181.

Segal, H. (1964). *Introduction to the Works of Melanie Klein,* New York: Basic Books.

Settlage, C. F. (1964). Psychoanalytic theory in relation to the nosology of childhood psychic disorders. *Journal of the American Psychoanalytic Association* 12:776–801.

Silverman, M. A. (1979). The developmental profile (chapter 4, this volume).

Silverman, M. A., Rees, K., and Neubauer, P. B. (1975). On a central psychic constellation. *Psychoanalytic Study of the Child* 30:127–157.

Smirnoff, V. (1971). *The Scope of Child Analysis.* New York: International Universities Press.

Waldhorn, H. F., ed. (1967). Indications for psychoanalysis. *Monograph Series of the Kris Study Group of the New York Psychoanalytic Institute* 2:3–51. New York: International Universities Press.

Weil, A. P. (1973). Ego strengthening prior to analysis. *Psychoanalytic Study of the Child* 28:287–301.

Weiss, S. (1964). Parameters in child analysis. *Journal of the American Psychoanalytic Association* 12:587–599.

Weiss, S., Fineberg, H., Gilman, R.L., and Kohrman, R.. (1968). Technique of child analysis, problems of the opening phase. *Journal of the American Academy of Child Psychiatry* 7:639–662.

Chapter 4

THE DEVELOPMENTAL PROFILE

Martin A. Silverman, M. D.

A BRIEF HISTORY OF THE PROFILE

The Developmental Profile was proposed by Anna Freud as a guide to the organization and diagnostic consideration of clinical material. It grew out of her work with children and adults, and reflects a psychoanalytic viewpoint that pays careful heed to the developmental process. It emphasizes the value of a thorough, multifaceted approach that considers clinical data from multiple, metapsychological points of view. As such, it is both a clinical tool, and perhaps even more important, a special way of thinking about the development and functioning of human beings.

The basic elements of The Profile were contained in a series of lectures delivered by Anna Freud in New York City in 1960 with the title "Four Contributions to the Psychoanalytic Study of the Child." She subsequently introduced The Profile to the Diagnostic Research Group of the Hampstead Child Therapy Clinic in London. There it was used as a diagnostic scheme designed to yield a cross-sectional picture of a child's personality organization at any point in time. She published an outline of The Profile (A. Freud 1962) in 1962, and a year later, Nagera (1963) described its practical use in the diagnostic evaluation of an eleven-and-a-half year old boy. Since then, there have been a number of reports describing ongoing modifications and adaptations of The Profile. Its design makes it suitable for the diagnostic assessment not only of children at different developmental levels, but also of adolescents and adults (A. Freud, Nagera, and W. E. Freud 1965, Laufer 1965, Meers 1966, Silverman and Neubauer 1971).

THE USE OF THE PROFILE IN CHILDHOOD

Diagnostic evaluation is more complex and uncertain in childhood than it is with adults. Since the child has not yet completed his course of development, signs of possible pathology can best be understood when they are projected upon a backdrop of the normal developmental process with its numerous variations. As Anna Freud (1965) has pointed out, it is often difficult to know whether seemingly pathological phenomena represent serious disturbances for which therapeutic intervention is indicated, temporary difficulties which the child can be expected to overcome spontaneously in the course of further development, or reactions that are normal at certain developmental stages. This is especially marked early in prelatency (Silverman and Neubauer 1971), and again in adolescence (A. Freud 1958).

The Profile seeks to solve this problem by combining a developmental approach with a thorough mapping out of the *total* personality organization, including both its strengths and weaknesses, at the time clinical data are collected. It's aim is to examine the data in terms of the observable trends within the structure of the developing personality, rather than viewing them in isolation. This is accomplished by systematically approaching the data from multiple points of view. Care is taken to examine all the major components of the developing personality, and an assessment is made of those characteristics which appear to be key indicators of the degree of overall developmental success or failure.

AN OUTLINE OF THE PROFILE

Before proceeding to a detailed description of The Profile, an outline of its overall organization and the items it encompasses will be presented:

Identifying Data
Sources of Information
   I. Reasons (and circumstances) for referral
  II. Description of the individual
 III. Family background (past and present) and personal history
  IV. Possibly significant environmental circumstances (positive as well as negative)
   V. Assessment of development
      A. Drive development
         1. Libido
            (a) With regard to phase development
            (b) With regard to libido distribution
               (1) Cathexis of the self
               (2) Cathexis of objects
         2. Aggression
            (a) According to the quantity
            (b) According to the quality
            (c) According to the direction of expression
      B. Ego and superego development
         1. The Ego:
            (a) Ego apparatuses
            (b) Ego functions
            (c) Ego reactions to danger situations
            (d) Defense organization
            (e) Secondary interference of defenses with ego functions
         2. Superego development and functioning
  VI. Assessment of fixation points and regressions
 VII. Assessment of conflicts
      A. External conflicts
      B. Internalized conflicts
      C. Internal conflicts

THE DETAILS OF THE PROFILE

The Profile starts out by inquiring about the reasons, both conscious
and unconscious, for the diagnostic assessment. It then calls for a
description of the individual's appearance, characteristic moods, general attitudes, behavioral qualities, etc. There is a section for family
background, and personal history, and one for possibly significant, past
and present, environmental influences, positive as well as negative.

An assessment is then made of the development of the drives, the ego,
and the superego. Libidinal and aggressive drive development are considered separately. Libidinal trends are considered according to phase
progression, and distribution of libidinal cathexis. As to the former, a
description of the degree and quality of drive activity, and its intercon-
nection with ego development and performance is requested. An emphasis is placed upon determining how far the individual has progressed, especially whether the phallic level has been attained, whether
phase dominance has been achieved at that level, and whether the
highest level is being maintained at the time of assessment or there has
been significant regression to an earlier one. The sources of information
will vary, of course, with the developmental level of the individual being
profiled. In latency, for example, generally much more reliance will
have to be made upon fantasies and other indirect expressions of drive
activity than at other times of life, because of the suppression of direct
drive expression characteristic of that period. A record of the sources
of the information that was utilized in preparing The Profile is called
for at the beginning of The Profile. Depending upon the age and life
stage of the individual involved, this might include interviews with the
patient and other family members, observations, physical examinations,
psychological tests, interviews of teachers, examination of school or
health records, etc.

The subsections on libido distribution are concerned with (1) the
mechanisms and success of self-esteem regulation, for example,

whether there is sufficient narcissistic cathexis of the self to ensure self-esteem and self-regard without leading either to over-investment in, or over-estimation of the self on the one hand, or to excessive dependence upon outside objects for an adequate sense of well-being on the other; and (2) the level and quality of object relationships, past and present, and their correspondence with the level(s) of phase development which have been attained, and at which the individual is currently functioning.

Since much less is known about the phase development of aggressive drives, aggression is considered according to its expression, rather than to the issue of developmental sequencing. The Profile calls for a description of aggressive expression quantitatively—the presence or absence of overt and covert aggression in the individual's behavior, qualitatively —the correspondence of the aggressive expression with the level of libidinal development, and directionally—whether, and the ways in which aggression is expressed toward the object world and/or toward the self. Whenever possible, the profiler is expected to distinguish between defensive and primary expressions of aggression.

Ego development is assessed in terms of the intactness or defectiveness of ego apparatuses and ego functions, the details of defense organization, and the extent to which defense activity is interfering with ego functioning. The developmental dimension comes into play prominently with regard to the drives, but structural considerations now become equally important. An attempt is made to identify and distinguish between *primary disturbances* of ego functioning arising from congenital or acquired defects in any of the various ego apparatuses and *developmental disturbances* stemming from the environment's failure to facilitate or actual interference with the ego's intrinsic potential for growth and development. The extent of the injury, the degree to which it can be reversed, and the manner in which the disturbance contributes to the development of conflicts, and to the structure and organization of the defense system constitute important diagnostic and prognostic considerations to which The Profile specifically addresses itself. Since the psychoanalytic clinician finds himself overwhelmingly preoccupied with the effects of internalized conflict, the tendency is to seek causal explanations of psychopathology exclusively in that direction. The Profile insists on scrutinizing the details of ego development and functioning. This helps draw attention to the possibility of arrests or faults in the ego's development which otherwise might be overlooked. Attention is also called to the role of variations in endowment, and the effect of early structuralizing experience in shaping personality organization, choice of defenses, and so on.

The ego's attitude toward danger situations and details of the defense organization are to be fully outlined. The Profile asks whether defenses are employed specifically against individual drives, or against drive activity in general, if they are age-adequate, too primitive or precocious, and whether they are well balanced or restricted to the excessive use of only a few. It also asks whether and to what extent the defenses are effective against anxiety, contribute to or mitigate overall ego strength and mobility, and are able to function without assistance from the object world. Stress is placed upon assessing whether and in what ways defense activity exacts a price for its effectiveness by interfering with significant ego achievements. Allowance also is made for the possibility that the individual's defense organization provides secondary gains to the personality. This needs to be taken into consideration in deciding whether or not treatment should be undertaken, and what the individual's response might be to the initiation of a course of treatment. Subsections on affects and on identifications have been added in The Adolescence Profile (Laufer 1965) because of the special significance of these factors during that period.

The Profile examines the superego in terms of the degree of its development; its sources, functions, effectiveness, and stability; and the degree of secondary sexualization or aggressivization that might have taken place. In each instance the age and stage of the individual being evaluated is taken into consideration. The vicissitudes of ego ideal formation are stressed in the adolescent.

One section calls for the assessment of fixation points and regressive shifts, as indicated by the individual's object relationships, manifest behavior, fantasy elaborations, and by the presence of certain characteristic symptoms and character traits. The genetic origin of fixations and regressions, and their effect upon and significance within the developmental process are to be recorded. Fixations do not impede developmental progress equally or in the same way in all individuals. Temporary regressions are so frequent in childhood that the presence of a regressive movement is meaningful only to the extent that important functions are involved. A regressive movement becomes noteworthy if internal and/or external factors prevent it from being reversed, and/or it ties up such quantities of instinctual energy that it interferes with overall developmental progression (A. Freud 1965, Frijling-Schreuder 1966, Nagera 1963, Silverman and Neubauer 1971). Since there are variations among different children in their style of developmental progression and regression, the developmental style becomes an additional factor in assessing regressions in children.

Libidinal regression and reaggressivization of certain functions also takes place regularly in the transition between the oedipal period and latency. Normal adolescence, too, is characterized by temporary, but often sweeping, drive and ego regressions. The developmental orientation of The Profile helps to hold these factors in perspective.

Another section seeks to assess, in structural, dynamic, and economic terms, the presence of conflicts. These might include external conflicts between id-ego agencies and external objects, internalized conflicts between ego-superego agencies and the id (as well as conflicts between different ego-ideals), and/or internal conflicts between competing, incompatible, or insufficiently fused drive representatives (for example, masculinity vs. feminity, activity vs. passivity, libido vs. aggression, etc.). The relative importance of each of these subsections will, of course, vary with the age and stage of the individual being profiled. To a certain extent, what is recorded in this section will be a summarization and synthesis of material recorded earlier in The Profile.

The eighth and last heading prior to integrating the material into a diagnostic statement is the "Assessment of Some General Characteristics." This contains items of particular significance as indicators of overall development, long term prognosis, and treatability via psychoanalytic or other methods. These indicators are frustration tolerance (in general and with respect to specific types of frustration), overall attitude and type of response to anxiety (with particular attention to whether the basic mode is avoidance and warding off, or an attempt at active mastery), sublimation potential, and the balance between progressive forces and regressive tendencies.

A subsection on "Development of the Total Personality (Lines of Development and Mastery of Tasks) or Age-Adequate Responses," which was included in the section on Assessment of Development in the early days of The Profile, has been shifted to an appendix to Section 8, as The Profile is currently is at The Hampstead Clinic. This was done because lines of development (A. Freud 1963) differ greatly as a conceptual category from the remainder of The Profile. They were introduced as a means of evaluating, on a practical basis, whether very young children have adequately progressed along certain behavioral and interactional lines of development to be ready for such steps as entry into nursery school. Laufer (1965) has revised the content of this category to make it a useful component of The Adolescence Profile and it has been modified for The Adult Profile.

The final, diagnostic statement aims at an integration of the material into a meaningful statement that formulates the type of disturbance in broad terms. A conclusion is requested that distinguishes among normal development, despite the presence of transitory behavioral disturbances or manifestations of developmental strain; more or less irreversible regressions that are leading to permanent, neurotic symptoms or character disturbances; arrested or distorted development and structuralization causing atypical personality formation; and malignant processes of fixation, regression, and ego damage leading to disorders of a psychotic, borderline, or delinquent nature.

THE PROFILE AS A DIAGNOSTIC TOOL

The value of The Developmental Profile as a diagnostic tool is obvious when it is employed in the evaluation of children, whose development is still incomplete and for whom, therefore, the diagnostic process has to be fitted into a developmental frame of reference. A modification of The Profile making it suitable for use with adults has also been prepared. Its initial purpose was to serve in studies of children and their parents, but it soon became apparent that The Profile could offer enough advantages to the assessment of adults to make it worthwhile in its own right. Although a developmental orientation is less important for adults than it is for children, its stress on ongoing development and epigenetic reorganization provides a perspective of surging life and movement. The Profile's emphasis on a metapsychologically balanced, cross-sectional picture of the *total* personality structure helps assure diagnostic accuracy. It is a particularly good instrument for assessing and studying the analyzability of prospective patients. In this regard it is notable that Freud never abandoned any of the various metapsychological points of view as new data propelled him on to new vantage points from which to observe and comprehend the workings of the human mind. As Rapaport and Gill (1959) have pointed out, human psychology is so complex that its accurate comprehension is ensured only by approaching it from multiple points of view.

It is obvious that The Developmental Profile is no more than a conceptual tool, varying in its usefulness according to the experience and skillfulness of the diagnostician employing it. It is not to be filled out like a questionnaire. The Profile embodies a particular way of looking at psychological data. It certainly cannot be expected to solve the problems of differential diagnosis.

AN EXAMPLE OF THE DIAGNOSTIC USE OF THE PROFILE

A condensed summary of The Profile's employment in the diagnostic process with a young child can serve to illustrate its use, as well as its usefulness.

Identifying data: Frank was three years six months old at the time of The Initial Profile. He came from a middle class family, with parents in their early thirties and had one brother, three years eight months older than the patient.

Sources of information: The Profile was based upon review of infant study, prenursery, and nursery school records; nursery school observations over a two month period; interviews with each parent; and a play interview with the child. Psychological testing was not done yet because of research design.

I. Reasons for Referral: Frank was brought at age two and one half years to a child guidance center which focussed on preschoolers because his mother considered herself inadequate and in need of assistance in childrearing. She listed her son's problems as low frustration tolerance, stubbornness, refusal to cooperate with her, and a quick temper that contributed to much fighting both with his brother and her. The center staff noted labile mood swings and a lack of animation or sustained pleasure.

II. Description of Child: Frank at three and one half years was tall, sturdy, masculine, handsome (but less so than his brother). Despite his almost continuous smiling, he had a sad look. He was exuberant, active, and always busy. He sought and usually attained the limelight in his nursery school group by exhibiting his strength, loud voice, and an excellent physical ability of which he clearly was very proud. Frank was socially adept and quickly became the leader among his peers. With his teachers, he varied between flexible cooperation and cranky irritability. He would pout and sulk when unable to get his way, and become angry and defiant when "given orders." Frank was particularly intolerant of frustration of his attempts to communicate his wishes, or to demonstrate independent proficiency with educational materials. He courted the (female) teachers with gallantry and charm, and the girls in the group vied to be his favorite. Frank's affects were somewhat labile. He might cry in misery or rage, and fume when frustrated, but he would not maintain his distress for long. He preferred to snap himself out of his unhappiness and cheer up.

III. Family Background and Personal History: Frank's mother was a very attractive, likeable woman who had had a very difficult, severely traumatized childhood. This left her with certain immaturities, and a fear of close relationships and either being depended upon or depending upon anyone. She had fears of being aroused by her infant sons, and she tended to push them away from her by distancing maneuvers that included intermittent failure to meet their requests for need satisfaction. As infants they often had been left to cry alone in their room. From eight months on, Frank often was cared for by babysitters. The father, a writer, was an anxious, intermittently depressed, somewhat immature man who alternated between being unavailable to the children, and devoting himself tenderly to them. He enjoyed cooking for them, and actively encouraged the development of both athletic prowess and facility with words. There was continual marital strife, and the couple was contemplating divorce. The older brother was close to Frank, but continually and mercilessly teased, bullied, and hit him.

Frank's birth was unremarkable, as was the pregnancy. He was turned over to a series of short-term maids for care, and received erratic, shifting stimulation. He was constantly rocked and held in the early months to prevent him from crying. However, after one month, the cessation of the flow of breast milk led to a period of discomfort and crying. Although Frank wanted to give up his bottle at a year, his mother encouraged him to retain it to make certain he would sleep through the night. He finally gave up his night bottle by hiding it in his mother's drawer when he was three years old. Teething was painful. Very early Frank was noted to be perceptually alert and interested in his environment. He quickly became attuned to his mother's comings and goings. Motor development was adequate except that independent observers (he was the subject of an infant study) noticed "low frustration-tolerance, perseveration, and toeing outward" during the first year. He was very outgoing by the age of two years and was rather aggressive until he settled down at two and one half. Toilet training was "easy" and unhurried. Frank developed full control within a month after a potty seat was made available to him at age two. Until Frank was two, his mother had to clean his penis twice a week and periodically apply salve because of an incomplete circumcision. He became fearful of having his hair and nails cut after he observed his father urinating when he was one year eight months old. Frank became concerned about broken things after he "discovered" and began to occasionally play with his penis at two years two months. He became anxious about his penis after he was bathed with a female cousin, and his brother began to tease him by telling him that his penis would fall off.

IV. Possibly Significant Environmental Circumstances: Frank's mother sought assistance at a time when he was approaching nursery school age, his older brother was approaching termination of analytic treatment at the child guidance center (for unhappiness and fury at his mother), and her marital problems were reaching crisis proportions. Probable deleterious environmental factors have been described in the above section. Possible favorable influences include the parents' genuine affection and concern for their children, and the influence of the child guidance center personnel while conducting the infant study in which Frank had been included.

V. Assessment of Development:

A. Drive Development:

1. Libido: (a) Regarding phase development, there was evidence of early phallic ascendancy and phallic dominance in Frank's relations with his teachers and peers, his play themes, his struggle against masturbatory urges at naptime, and his intermittent castration fears. Persistent anal-sadistic conflicts were revealed in his avoidance of the sand box, discomfort with messy materials, and occasional excessive hand washing. More prominent oral fixations were suggested by an apparent need to control and regulate people to make certain that they remained

available for need satisfaction, an intensive struggle against the emergence of powerful yearnings for passive care and nurturance (in which his father seemed to be the object rather than his mother), and erratic eating patterns. Frank's strong quest for attention seemed to have roots in all libidinal phases.

(b) Regarding libido distribution, Frank seemed to depend excessively on obtaining admiration and attention from the outside to maintain adequate, positive cathexis of his self-representation. His relationship with objects was uneven, with oscillation between cheerfully and optimistically seeking friendship and attention, and defiantly pushing people away in favor of an insistent show of self-sufficiency. This seeming paradox became clearer when viewed in terms of the fact that Frank learned early in his life that his parents were erratically available, and often needed to be entertained or cheered up. His mother was more likely to stay with him when he fought with her, than when he wooed her, either affectionately or anaclitically.

2. Aggression: Frank was noted from the beginning to be quite aggressive, with angry impulses tending to interfere with neutralization. However there was an increasing modulation, taming, and channeling of aggressive energies into relating to others, learning, and play activities using large muscles. At the time of profiling, these modes were well-developed, with intermittent regression into short-lived, but intense temper tantrums, successfully but barely controlled impulses to bite, and episodes of defiance and rebelliousness. Aggressive impulses were almost always directed outward.

B. Ego and Superego Development:

1. Ego Development: There were indications from early on of the possibility of minor, intrinsic defects in ego apparatuses implicating motor control and cognition. Observation in infancy had led to the conclusion that there were mild neurological irregularities as evidenced by perseveration, low frustration tolerance, toeing outward, and poor manipulation of objects. His parents reported that between two and two and one half years of age, Frank had fallen a lot, tripped over his feet, and walked into walls when tired and irritable. Neurological examination when he was two and a half revealed no abnormalities except for "excessive accessory movements to maintain balance during balancing tricks." Classroom observation during the profiling period revealed that Frank at times tended to lose his balance, fall, or trip over himself. Most

of the time, however, he was a superb, unusually supple, and graceful athlete. The profiler concluded that although interference with motor control by emotional conflict might have explained the occasional lapses, the possibility of a neurological defect affecting perceptual-motor or motor coordination needed to be assessed further. Ego functions were well developed except for certain areas. Although language functions were highly developed, Frank at times tended to use words that he did not truly understand, and to reverse syntactical order. In addition to the intermittent impairment of large motor control, there was some constriction of the range of affective responses, and a tendency to a stubborn inflexibility in cognitive operations. Frank's intermittently impaired frustration tolerance and excessive aggressivity were considered to reflect defective and/or delayed drive synthesis and neutralization, and hence, a general ego weakness of an as yet undetermined severity. The ego's reaction to danger situations was difficult to clearly identify. However, there seemed to be a combination of fear of loss of the object's love, fear of loss of the object, and castration anxiety, all perceived as emanating from the outside world. Frank's more basic fear seemed to be of ego passivity. His defense organization seemed to center around complex introjective/projective mechanisms to exteriorize internal and internalized conflicts. This was followed by alloplastic mechanisms to control external objects to ensure their availability, and the likelihood of favorable responses, and to provide an illusion of active mastery. Only if this failed was there a tendency to give in to a regressive pull to an infantile, anaclictic state in which he might feel protected and nurtured. Otherwise regression was warded off vigorously. The major price paid for the upkeep of this defensive organization was restriction of affective experience, a degree of superficiality and shallowness of object relations, and a tendency toward phobic avoidance of situations threatening him either with failure of ego mastery or with the danger of passive libidinal temptation.

2. Superego Development: For so young a child superego development is approachable largely in a predictive fashion. Superego precursers, in the form of reaction-formations and internalized parental guidelines about behavior, seemed to operate relatively well. There were, however, intermittent eruption of aggressive defiance or attack directed mainly against his mother and female teachers. The relative insufficiency of neutralization of aggressive drive impetus indicated the dan-

ger of eventual harsh superego functioning, and obsessive struggles for self-control. The alloplastic defensive organization, in which externalization was playing a significant role, suggested possible problems later on in moving beyond fear of external punishment to true internalization of behavioral guidelines. Precociously developed ego ideals encouraged Frank to be charming and pleasing to people. These ideals could be seen as serving to help offset the tendency to attack the objects of erupting aggressive derivatives. The need for a continual show of strength and competence to maintain adequate self-esteem, it was apparent, could present problems when the inevitable defeats of the oedipal period and beyond were encountered.

VI. Fixation Points and Regressions needed to be assessed in a somewhat fluid manner in a child only three and one half years old. As described in Section V. A. 1, and 2, there was evidence of persistent oral-dependent and oral-aggressive tendencies in Frank's behavior, fantasies, and object relations. This did not, however, prevent advance into phallic ascendancy and even dominance.

VII. Assessment of Conflicts revealed external conflicts in the form of struggles with maternal figures who threatened to take over and dominate him. Internalized conflicts existed between conflicting ego ideals and between phallic-exhibitionistic, rivalrous ambitions and castration anxiety. Internal conflicts involved active vs. passive strivings (with the very beginnings of a masculinity-femininity conflict) and ambivalence in object relations.

VIII. Assessment of Some General Characteristics: All informants reported that frustration tolerance was low. Observation indicated a relative intolerance to frustration of both libidinal and aggressive drives that was much less severe than had been reported by others. Inability to communicate his wishes led to the most intense frustration. The overall attitude to anxiety seemed to center around an urge to active mastery, but with a tendency to denial and externalization that could have indicated inadequate tolerance of anxiety. Although Frank's striving for achievement and the social value of the aims and directions provided by his ideals indicated a good sublimation potential, a surprising lack of creativity and avoidance of certain classroom activities were observed. There were indications of strong progressive tendencies that seemed to counterbalance a regressive pull to oral-dependent inclinations.

IX. Diagnosis: Despite early deprivations and possible minor organic defects, Frank was showing progressive development. His current symptomatic expressions could be viewed as being partly transitory and related to current environmental stresses, and partly permanent, in the form of ego distortions which were relatively ego-syntonic. It could be expected that there might be characterological deformities in the form of persistent phallic character traits. Associated with this is a diminished range of possible affective experiences resulting from the introjective-projective and alloplastic processes. These appeared to be deeply ingrained into Frank's ego structure. The balance of progressive versus regressive forces, and the intensity of his castration anxiety were not entirely clear. Frank would need to be watched carefully as he went through the turmoil of the oedipal phase. There was the real danger, because of his intense ambivalence towards his mother, his regressive tendency, his insistent passive strivings, and turning to his father as the most important love object, of the development of a latent homosexuality and an obsessive tendency. The intense reaction-formations against anal erotic impulses, indicative, perhaps, of inadequate resolution of anal erotic trends, indicated a possible weak point in any future, major, regressive shift. Sublimation of drive energies into learning seemed inadequate, and required further assessment.

As a result of the findings of this Profile, the decision was made not to intervene psychotherapeutically, but to investigate further into the indications of a possible, mild, neurological defect, and to follow Frank's ongoing progress. Intervention in the form of parent counselling did appear to be indicated, and was carried out. The expectation was that depending upon the neurological assessment, there was a strong possibility that psychoeducational intervention would be required. Depending upon the way Frank negotiated the oedipal period, psychotherapy of one form or another might prove necessary.

A second Profile, drawn up six months later, revealed the presence of a physiologically mild, but developmentally significant neurological disorder. It consisted of a mild perceptual-motor, motor, and aphasic disorder that interdigitated with other emotional-developmental factors to produce a significant learning disturbance, and a skewing of personality development. Highly successful assistance was provided for Frank (for further details, see Silverman, 1976).

AN EVALUATION OF THE PROFILE

The Profile itself is an imperfect tool, and it has been undergoing continual modification and refinement since its introduction. As Nagera (1963) has pointed out, the various items of The Profile belong to different levels of conceptualization, and the process of integration is far from simple. The degree to which the different dimensions of the personality are investigated, and the depth to which they are explored also varies from one section of the Profile to another. For example, affects, cognitive functioning, and the role of identifications in the period prior to adolescence receive relatively little attention. The Profile and the way of thinking which it represents have been applied to more and more individuals since its introduction, and have especially been applied to the study of groups of people at different levels and with different kinds of problems. The knowledge that has been gained about various aspects of human development and functioning has been integrated back into The Profile and has furthered its development as a diagnostic and conceptual instrument. This readiness to make continual changes and improvements is reflected in its instructions for use. The Profile-Maker is advised to use the various headings to facilitate a thorough thinking-through of clinical material, rather than as a questionnaire to be filled out. He is asked to look for inconsistencies and contradictions, and to use these observations to point to areas in which further investigation and clarification are necessary, rather than expecting to come to a definitive and certain diagnostic statement.

FUNCTIONS OF THE PROFILE IN CLINICAL AND INVESTIGATIVE WORK

At the Hampstead Clinic, The Profile has been utilized not only at the beginning of treatment, but at various points in the process, as well as at the end of treatment. It is not expected that a complete or entirely accurate diagnostic picture can be attained at the initial diagnostic stage. Data gathered during an ongoing analysis can be used both to improve and enhance diagnostic understanding of a case, and to assess the accuracy of the initial diagnostic process. The Terminal Profile can be used to objectively appraise the effects of treatment.

The Profile's function as a research tool is a central aspect of its use. It is hoped that by systematically collecting and comparing data from many cases, knowledge can be gained that can be used to validate and refine many of our theoretical propositions. It is also hoped this knowledge can contribute to the eventual elaboration of a psychoanalytic classification of childhood and adult disorders. The Profile has been employed to study the development of blind children (see A. Freud, Nagera, and E. W. Freud 1965) and to investigate the functioning of atypical and borderline children (Thomas et al. 1966). Michaels and Stiver (1965) have used it to draw up a composite picture of the personality organization of "the impulsive, psychopathic character." It also lends itself very well to use in investigations of the developmental process (Silverman, Rees, and Neubauer 1975). W. E. Freud (1967, 1968, 1971) has developed a Baby Profile for recording baseline observations with predictive value for use as an initial tool in longitudinal studies of development. Heinicke (1965) has used The Profile to compare the effectiveness and results of different forms of psychotherapy in childhood.

The Developmental Profile, in other words, is more than a clinical, diagnostic tool. It is an encapsulation of Anna Freud's thorough, open-minded, developmentally oriented, metapsychologically balanced, investigative approach to psychoanalysis. While its use is too time-consuming and tedious to make it suitable for general use with all patients, it is greatly useful for selected purposes, and can serve as an invaluable guide to the organization and integration of data. As a metapsychological outline it can be kept in mind and mentally filled out for all patients.

REFERENCES

Freud, A. (1958). Adolescence. *Psychoanalytic Study of The Child* 13:255–278.

———— (1960). Four Contributions to the Psychoanalytic Study of the Child, Lectures delivered in New York City.

———— (1962). Assessment of childhood disturbances. *Psychoanalytic Study of The Child* 17:149–158.

———— (1963). The concept of developmental lines. *Psychoanalytic Study of The Child* 18:245–265.

_____ (1965). *Normality and Pathology in Childhood, Assessments in Development.* New York: International Universities Press.

Freud, A., Nagera, H., and Freud, W. E. (1965). Metapsychological assessment of the adult personality: the adult profile. *Psychoanalytic Study of The Child* 20:9–41.

Freud, W. E. (1967). Assessment of early infancy: problems and considerations. *Psychoanalytic Study of The Child* 22:216–238.

_____ (1968). Some general reflections on the metapsychological profile. *International Journal of Psycho-Analysis* 49:498–501.

_____ (1971). The baby profile, part II. *Psychoanalytic Study of The Child* 26:172–194.

Frijling-Schreuder, E. C. M. (1966). The adaptive use of aggression. *International Journal of Psycho-Analysis* 47:364–369.

Heinicke, C. M. et al. (1965). Frequency of psychotherapeutic session as a factor affecting the child's developmental status. *Psychoanalytic Study of The Child* 20:42–98.

Laufer, M. (1965). Assessment of adolescent disturbances: the application of Anna Freud's diagnostic profile. *Psychoanalytic Study of The Child* 20:99–123.

Meers, D. R. (1966). A diagnostic profile of psychopathology in a latency child. *Psychoanalytic Study of the Child* 21:483–526.

Michaels, J. J. and Stiver, I. P. (1965). The impulsive psychopathic character according to the diagnostic profile. *Psychoanalytic Study of The Child* 20:124–141.

Nagera, H. (1963). The developmental profile: notes on some practical considerations regarding its use. *Psychoanalytic Study of The Child* 18:511–540.

Rapaport, D., and Gill, M. M. (1959). The points of view and assumptions of metapsychology. *International Journal of Psycho-Analysis* 40:153–162.

Silverman, M. A., and Neubauer, P. B. (1971). The use of the developmental profile for the prelatency child. In *The Unconscious Today,* ed. M. Kanzer, pp. 363–380. New York: International Universities Press.

Silverman, M. A., Rees, K., and Neubauer, P. B. (1975). On a central psychic constellation. *Psychoanalytic Study of The Child* 30:127–157.

Silverman, M.A. (1976). The diagnosis of minimal brain dysfunction in the preschool child. In *Mental Health in Children,* vol. II, ed. D. V. Siva Sankar, pp. 221-301. Westbury: PJD Publications.

Thomas, R. et al. (1966) Comments on some aspects of self and object representation in a group of psychotic children: an application of Anna Freud's diagnostic profile. *Psychoanalytic Study of the Child* 221:527–580.

Chapter 5

USE OF THE NURSERY SCHOOL FOR EVALUATION

Erna Furman

ASSOCIATION OF PRESCHOOL EDUCATION
AND CHILD ANALYSIS

Historical survey. In chapter 19 Daunton traces the beginnings of S. Freud's interest in early childhood education, and describes his first contacts with prominent pedagogues of his time in an attempt to forge a closer link between psychoanalysis and education. A. Freud (1974), in her introduction to the first volume of her collected papers recalls the first flourishing of child analysis in Vienna in the late twenties and, coincident with it, the analysts' keen interest in educational matters.

In Vienna, from 1927 onward, a group of analysts, later joined by colleagues from Budapest and Prague, held regular meetings with me to discuss the child-analytic technique I had suggested, . . . Apart from these therapeutic developments, Vienna had at that time also become a fertile ground for the analytic study of normal child development and for the application of these new findings to education. Many of us had for years been listening to the inspiring lectures for teachers and youth leaders given by Siegfried Bernfeld, and many young and enthusiastic workers had joined his educational experiment in "Kinderheim Baumgarten," a camp school for children made homeless by World War I. (1974, p. viii)

The child analysts were interested in the education of all age groups of childhood and adolescence, and, in the fruitful years of 1927–1938, found numerous ways of establishing ongoing contact with educators and parents. A child guidance clinic for young children was directed by E. Sterba, one for adolescents by A. Aichhorn, and a three-year post-graduate training course for teachers by W. Hoffer. A. Freud and Burlingham focused especially on working with nursery school teachers, and through them, on understanding and helping preschoolers.

> Thus, the Four Lectures for Teachers and Parents . . . were not an independent venture of mine but were commissioned by the Board of Education of the City of Vienna and were furthermore followed by a regular seminar for nursery school teachers conducted by Dorothy Burlingham and myself . . . in 1937[1] an experimental day nursery for toddlers was founded and maintained by Dr. Edith Jackson, and administered by myself in conjunction with Dorothy Burlingham and the pediatrician Dr. Josephine Stross. (A. Freud 1974, pp. viii–ix)

Fuchs Wertheim (1974) recalls this period from her point of view as a nursery school teacher in the day care centers of the City of Vienna from 1928 to 1934.

> In about 1928 or 1930 I helped "history" by interesting the Director of Preschool Education, Philipp Frankowsky, in the work of Anna Freud. It all started with an article I wrote for the Journal of Psychoanalytic Education in about 1930. That article created a furor among my immediate superiors since I had mentioned the City Kindergartens in connection with some naughty sexual behavior of their students. However, the real chief, Mr. Frankowsky, was delighted. I brought him one evening to Berggasse 19 and he was deeply impressed by Anna Freud. He then helped me to establish the Special Group in the demonstration kindergarten, connected with the Training School for Kindergarten Teachers, and a seminar for teachers interested in special groups headed by Anna Freud. Anna Freud

frequently mentioned that she was the first member of her family in an official position in Vienna.

Fuchs Wertheim attended weekly "control sessions" with A. Freud for years. Her colleagues, A. Poertl and K. Pensimus, worked similarly with Burlingham. Poertl later took over Fuchs Wertheim's position as director of work with problem children in the city nurseries, and the latter became educational director of the Edith Jackson *Krippe*.

For the most part, the children in these nurseries lived in abject poverty with emotionally deprived, seriously disturbed, and disrupted families. They shared all the hallmarks of what we now know as the slum or ghetto milieu. Their pathologies were often severe, longstanding, and engulfed much, if not all, of their personality functioning. Fuchs Wertheim's article (1932) conveys a vivid picture of the varied nature of the difficulties of the children in her special group. More recently, she recalls, "At that early time the nursery schools and kindergartens of the City of Vienna were for the very poorest of the poor. I remember that at one point A. Freud said . . . 'You can't give any advice to a mother whose child has to go barefoot,' and she provided money that I could buy shoes" (Fuchs Wertheim 1974). Even later, when some private nursery schools with children of middle class background participated in the analytic consultation program, there were youngsters who in addition to phase-appropriate conflicts, coped with special stresses such as divorce and separation (Minor-Záruba 1937).

In her introduction to a series of translated articles which originally appeared in the *Journal of Psychoanalytic Education,* A. Freud described the work of Poertl and Pensimus in the public kindergartens of Vienna as a "practical demonstration of the symbiosis" (1935, p. 1) between analytic theory and educational work. Let us look a little more closely at the nature of this mutually dependent and beneficial relationship.

Bernfeld (1934) summarized what psychoanalysis can contribute to education: (1) a nonjudgmental viewpoint allowing objective observation of all aspects of a child's behavior; (2) a genetic approach focusing on processes rather than static facts, and on how behavioral manifestations come about (thereby understanding the child who, by definition, is in a transitional stage); and (3) a recognition of, and respect for, the forces of nature (drives) which underlie behavior. This, in turn, generates appreciation for the difficult task the educator faces in his attempts to influence children.

In their early work with nursery school teachers A. Freud and Burlingham pursued these aims. In Fuchs Wertheim's (1974) words, "The stress then was to develop the teacher's awareness of individual psychological needs, and to provide the knowledge of how to deal with them." These goals were extended to include diagnostic and therapeutic elements. A. Freud (1974) recalls, "When we worked with Nursery School teachers in Vienna and in the *Pädagogenkurs* initiated by Dr. Hoffer, our emphasis was [more] on the signs of disturbance and the clues given by the child to underlying conflicts which could be seen in his Nursery School behavior." In a number of excellent articles (Fuchs 1932, 1933, Pensimus 1933, Poertl 1933, Fischer 1933, Schmaus 1933, Fischer and Peller 1934, Landau 1936, Braun 1936, Minor-Záruba 1937) gifted teachers described how they were helped to use psychoanalytic understanding with their students. They adapted their educational handling to the children's needs, and aided them in recognizing and verbalizing affects; they clarified misconceptions resulting from factors within and without the child's mind. Sometimes they were able to influence parents in the direction of alleviating the children's external conflicts. Also, they judiciously interpreted some defenses and some preconscious aspects of developmental conflicts. Each article bears witness to the considerable benefits both the teachers and their young pupils derived from the application of psychoanalytic understanding to the educational process.

How much did education contribute to psychoanalysis? First and foremost opportunity was provided to observe large numbers of children who exhibited a wide variation of normal growth processes. In his work with a few disturbed young patients, the child analyst cannot gain the necessary detailed knowledge of normal development, and cannot adequately assess the incidence and nature of individual pathology in general terms. The analyst of adults lives in an adult world which readily provides him with a framework of the vicissitudes of normal personality functioning. The child analyst, by contrast, has to make a special effort to acquaint himself with children in their own setting. Experiences within families are always limited to a small number of children, and the school or daycare center provides a welcome opportunity to observe groups of children. Those child analysts who come to the profession from medicine or other fields in which children are seen rarely, or only in circumscribed situations, are particularly aware of a lack of knowledge about normal childhood life, and find this handicaps their work with patients and parents. For example, in observations at the nursery school even candidates who were pediatricians often learned for the first time about a child's mastery of such tasks as putting on his coat, tying his shoes, dressing and undressing for independent toileting, painting a representational picture, and so on (R.A. Furman 1966, Schiff 1969, Archer and Barnes 1975).[2] Some of the early Viennese child analysts no doubt utilized their observations in a similar way. Fuchs Wertheim (1974) speaks of "many now famous visitors" to her nursery group, and A. Katan (1974) vividly recalls what she learned from her participation in the care of the toddlers at the Edith Jackson Krippe.

Beyond this immediate professional need, however, a detailed knowledge of normal growth processes as well as pathological ones is essential for developing an understanding of mental functioning, and for formulating theoretical principles of psychoanalytic child psychology. The observation of many children in nonanalytic settings also contributes toward delineating the variations of normal, and distinguishing these from signs of pathology. A. Freud's and Burlingham's observations in nursery schools, and their work with teachers, were particularly rewarding because an opportunity was provided for longterm study. Using the children's verbalizations and behavior as clues, they were able to gain knowledge about the children's underlying conflicts. They learned about the manifestations and course of phase-appropriate conflicts, and could compare these with pathology caused by arrests at earlier levels. Also, internal conflicts could be separated from external ones; it was possible to study how analytically oriented educational handling facilitated normal growth processes. This brought about a broader and more detailed understanding of early personality development, and added much to data derived from the analytic treatment of children and from reconstructions in the analyses of adults.

Education thus contributed significantly to establishing concepts of normality in childhood, as well as to developing diagnostic criteria, and evaluating the need for different kinds of therapeutic intervention. As early as 1937, Burlingham stated that one of the tasks of the nursery school teacher was to educate both children and parents about the need for psychoanalytic treatment whenever indicated. In later papers, A. Freud (1951, 1953, 1958), Burlingham (1974), and others discussed the contribution of direct observation of children to the study of specific areas, and to analytic psychology in general.

The growth of the mutually beneficial relationship between education and psychoanalysis in Vienna was tragically interrupted by the Nazi Anschluss in 1938. The analysts who had participated in the early endeavors dispersed. Only gradually did some of them establish new links with teachers in different countries, or set up centers with new colleagues in which educators and analysts could work together.

Recent trends in cooperation between preschool education and child analysis. A. Freud and Burlingham continued their work in the Hampstead Nurseries during World War II, and later, in the facilities of the Hampstead Clinic in London. These facilities included a therapeutic nursery school, which originally was geared to children with developmental conflicts. More recently, the nursery served children from economically and culturally deprived families (Edgcumbe 1975). A special nursery school for the blind (Wills 1965, 1968, Nagera and Colonna 1965, Burlingham 1974) is also part of the Hampstead Clinic facilities.

In the U.S.A., the ties between psychoanalysis and education have taken various forms and encompassed work with all age groups of children. In the context of this paper it seems pertinent to remind ourselves especially of psychoanalytic contact with nursery school aged children and their teachers.

In some instances the joint efforts of education and psychoanalysis have taken forms modeled on A. Freud's earlier work in Vienna. Some analysts regularly consult with teachers in selected nursery schools, more or less along the lines of A. Freud's and Burlingham's work in Vienna. Ruben's (1960) work with the School for Nursery Years, and the Cleveland Center for Research in Child Development (R.A. Furman 1966, Redmond 1975) consultation service for nursery schools exemplify this approach. In a less systematic and long-term manner this type of consultation has been practiced in several areas. Following the example of A. Freud, Bernfeld, and other analysts from the twenties and thirties, there are now many analysts who, individually or in connection with centers, give lectures, workshops, and full-length courses for preschool teachers. The Reiss-Davis Child Study Center, and the Cleveland Center for Research in Child Development are examples.

Another approach has been to establish centers for preschoolers which are specially designed to combine the work of analysts and educators. These nursery schools are primarily geared to children with developmental and neurotic disturbances, but to a limited extent these schools also admit youngsters with atypical symptoms and/or mild organic handicaps. The educational settings and the methods of analytic and educational cooperation reflect the individuality of each center (Archer and Hosley 1969). The aims, with varying emphasis, include research, service, and teaching. In "therapeutic nursery schools" at some of these centers the psychoanalysts participate not only through their work with the teachers and through regular direct observation, but they also undertake various forms of analytic psychotherapy and child analysis. Longitudinal studies complement the focus on depth of understanding. Among these are the Yale Child Study Center in New Haven, the Child Development Center of the Jewish Board of Guardians in New York, the Hanna Perkins Nursery and Kindergarten operated by the Cleveland Center for Research in Child Development and the Center for Human Services, the Cornerstone Project Nursery of the Center for Preventive Psychiatry in White Plains, and the Preschool Day Treatment Center of the Menninger Clinic.

Other centers are similarly oriented, but the child analyst is involved in a supervisory capacity, and does not, as a rule, act as therapist. Teaching of allied professionals, especially in the fields of psychiatry, social work, and psychology, is a main focus. Examples of such settings are the nursery schools of the Michigan Child Study Center and the Hillcrest Children's Center.

In still other instances, analytically oriented nursery schools cooperate closely with analysts on specific research projects over a one or two year period, for example at the Reiss-Davis Child Study Center (Heinecke et al. 1973a, 1973b, 1974).[3]

A number of centers for preschoolers focus especially on work with certain types of disturbances. Here the methods of the educator, as well as of the child analyst, are adapted to the specific needs of these children. However, analytically oriented research, service, and teaching remain the basic goals. Centers for children with atypical disturbances have included Master's Children's Center in New York (Mahler 1963, Roiphe 1973) and the James Jackson Putnam Center (Rexford 1949, Putnam, Rank, and Kaplan 1951, Pavenstedt 1973) and the Chapel Hill Nursery for Psychotic Children (Speers and Lansing 1965). The Mental Development Center's Preschool in Cleveland (Kessler, Ablon, Smith 1969, Kessler 1974) works with retarded children.

Although analysts have worked with older children and their teachers in educational settings, association with children under five in nursery schools has been particularly fruitful. Numerous publications by analysts, individually and in collaboration with colleagues and educators, attest to the many findings gained through such cooperative efforts. Some of these articles will be referred to in the context of this discussion. In the area of diagnosis, access to the direct observation of children in nursery schools has proved invaluable to psychoanalysis.

CONSIDERATIONS ON THE ASSESSMENT OF YOUNG CHILDREN

The personality of the prelatency child is immature and unstable. Processes of relatively rapid change are the norm, and mental equilibrium is rare and short lived. Waves of partial drives succeed one another, reach a crest, overlap, and frequently backwash as their intensity and timing fluctuate in response to internal forces and external stimulation. The young child's ego, still close to the id, and dependent on its energies, is in the process of developing and struggles to bring its various functions under autonomous control. Selective gratifications, control of impulses, and establishment of basic defensive measures vis-a-vis the drives (such as reaction formations) are as limited and labile as the ego's ability to interact adaptively with the world of reality. Superego precursors vary in nature and harshness. They are inadequately integrated, and tend to hinder as well as help the immature ego's attempts at mastery. Unable to function independently, the young child's personality relies on its closest object ties for inner and outer safety. At the same time, he involves his loved ones in the satisfaction of drives. The child's parents, especially his mother, become targets for instinctual discharge, participants in infantile gratifications as well as the source of external conflict. By serving as educators and models, parents contribute to the emergence of internalized conflict. This state of mental affairs poses special diagnostic problems that are considerably different from those of older children.

As a rule the child analyst is not called upon to identify definite neurotic illness or circumscribed disorders of the personality, but rather to assess the process of change itself. Indeed, experience has shown that it is essential to conceive of special diagnostic categories in work with prelatency children (Daunton 1969). Are all or some areas of the personality developing phase-appropriately or at an uneven pace? Do the pathological phenomena impede progression? Do regressive trends predominate, have rigid defenses produced a deadlock, or is the resolution of the Oedipus complex endangered? What are the chances of spontaneous reversibility? To what extent are the existing difficulties indicative of external or internalized conflict? The child's personality extends into that of his parent, and his parent's attitude and handling directly bear on the child's past, current, and future growth potential. Our assessment, therefore, must also include the child's "facilitating environment" (Winnicott 1965). It is necessary to determine whether the child's parenting has caused interferences at some or all levels of development and in which areas. Usually, an attempt is made to gauge whether the parent is capable of making changes in child-rearing practices. Not infrequently the nature of a developmental lag or behavior problem can be assessed only after some changes have been made (Daunton 1969).

This is a difficult task even when utilization is made of the diagnostic profile especially adapted to the assessment of the prelatency child (Nagera 1963, 1966, A. Freud 1965, Daunton 1969). It requires a wealth of accurate data, including repeated observations of the mother-child relationship, as well as of the child himself in a familiar setting so that stress reactions do not unduly skew the picture. Most authors agree that the diagnosis of the young child is a prolonged or even an ongoing process, and needs to encompass an assessment of the parents and the parent-child relationship (Rexford 1949, Kris 1950, Neubauer, Alpert, and Bank 1958, Katan 1959, Daunton 1969, E. Furman 1969a, c, Ferlemann 1973, Edgcumbe 1975, Ware 1975).

The usual method of diagnostic interviews has serious limitations

(Kris 1950, Neubauer, Alpert, and Bank 1958, Katan 1959). A personal history given by the child's parents can be very misleading. While the special intimacy of the early mother-child relationship may enable the mother to be particularly perceptive in some areas, in others it necessarily contains blind spots or makes differentiation between the parent's problems and the child's difficult. In addition, it is often impossible for a parent to know or understand how his child functions in his absence (Benkendorf 1969, Oppenheimer 1969, E. Furman 1969b). When attempting to supplement the parents' report by interviewing the child, data of dubious validity is often gained. Office interviews of the child with his mother present minimize the stress factor for the child, and provide material on the parent-child relationship. However, it is difficult to assess how much is distorted by the mother's anxiety and by the artificial nature of the situation.

When the child is interviewed alone, the data collected may be considerably expanded. It is possible to discover personality weaknesses, such as lack of impulse control or poor narcissistic investment of the self; unsuspected strengths, for example an ability to master bodily care which had been obscured by the mother's ministrations; or advanced super ego elements which had been masked by a defensive externalized struggle with the mother. Indications of internalized conflicts may be seen, or the interview may bring to the fore traumatic events, particularly those which had occurred during previous parental absences, for example, hospitalizations. Unfortunately, when data are gained in such a limited time period and in an unfamiliar setting, the child's labile, immature personality makes it impossible to evaluate them correctly, to weigh adequately their significance, and to differentiate temporary from habitual responses. Moreover, persons outside the child's family are not fully cathected so that the interviewer may be variously, and to an undeterminable extent, invested with aspects of the parent-child relationship, with parts of the child's inner conflicts, or with facets of specific past experiences, for example with the physician. This differs markedly from interviews with older children whose personality is structured and stabilized, and whose ego can grasp and adapt to the interview framework in a more or less expectable manner. Even instinctual derivatives, often close to the surface and readily recognizable in the under-five's behavior, play, and fantasy, may be deceptive. Although they provide insight into the developmental level of the drives and their vicissitudes, interview data do not enable us to gauge the effect of overlapping of phases, temporary regressions, current upsets, or responses to precocious stimulation. At best, diagnostic interviews give status quo information rather than the essential understanding of ongoing processes.

For children beyond the toddler phase, the most feasible solution to these diagnostic impediments is an opportunity for observation in the nursery school. There both parent and child can adapt to a natural setting and the child and mother can be observed in interaction. Also, the child can be viewed functioning independently in a variety of familiar and unfamiliar activities, as well as in relationships with peers and adults outside the family. In contrast to the older child, the pre-schooler's instinctual derivatives are often as open to view at school as they are at home because of his fluid defenses, and relative lack of differentiation between settings and relationships. Several authors have described their experiences with nursery school observations (Rexford 1949, Alpert 1954, Kris 1955, 1962, Neubauer, Alpert, and Bank 1958, Neubauer and Beller 1958, Katan 1959, R.A. Furman 1966, R.A. Furman and Katan 1969, E. Furman 1969a, Ronald and Kliman 1970, Heinecke et al. 1973a, 1973b, Edgcumbe 1975). In some instances these authors have included detailed clinical examples and/or stressed areas in which nursery school observation has proved especially fruitful: ego functioning and social relationships, differentiation of internalized and external conflicts, assessment of arrests versus regression or inhibition, observations of responses to stress and handling of developmental steps, achievements along developmental lines, evidence of earlier forms of functioning which help trace the child's personal history, the nature and development of the mother-child relationship. Usually there are symptoms or difficulties which have escaped parental notice, or were not recognized as indicative of pathology. Depending on the period of nursery school attendance and accompanying work, it also becomes possible to assess the maturational potential of the child's personality and the parents' flexibility in altering their educational approaches. Whether and to what extent nursery school data is valid and available depends on many factors.

FACTORS INFLUENCING THE AVAILABILITY AND VALIDITY OF OBSERVATIONAL DATA FROM THE NURSERY SCHOOL

A full and detailed discussion of all determining factors would constitute a separate study. For our present purpose it seems sufficient to highlight a few factors that are most commonly encountered. They fall into the broad categories of what is observed, by whom, how, and in which setting. Let us begin with the latter.

THE INDIVIDUAL NURSERY SCHOOL SETTING

The educational orientation and aims of the nursery school. There is currently a wide variety of centers that undertake the care of preschool children. In terms of attendance, they range from daily, twelve-hour care to twice weekly two-hour sessions. Some centers accept babies and toddlers, while others limit themselves to the three to five year old age group. The primary purpose of some centers is to babysit. Others, such as Montessori schools, specialize in specific educational techniques, and some have special therapeutic goals. Each school setting selects its teaching staff and designs its program to meet its specific needs, and in turn, attracts parents who find its program particularly suitable for their children.

To gain pertinent diagnostic observations, a nursery school has to be geared to the age-appropriate needs of a young child, and aim at facilitating the development of all aspects of his personality. For example, a child accepted for a two to five hour daily nursery school program should be at the point where he has mastered the tasks necessary for entry to nursery school (A. Freud 1963, 1965). If pathology is present, concomitant therapeutic measures should be instituted to help the child achieve these masteries. Children under the age of two and a half or three years are not ready to cope with these tasks. Even a "ready" three-year-old finds his resources stretched to the extreme if he remains at school for a whole day. In such situations entry to nursery school may become a developmental interference, affect the child's handling of his current conflicts, and distort his subsequent development. On the other hand, if a "ready" child attends nursery school for only two brief weekly sessions, many areas and aspects of the child's functioning will not manifest themselves at school. In the former case, observational data may be distorted by the stress of the school; in the latter, their availability will be curtailed.

Let us take another example from the educational program. An analytically oriented nursery school respects the three-year-old's recently acquired or still developing reaction formations of cleanliness by introducing potentially messy media sparingly, by stressing their creative use, and by providing the opportunity to clean up. Similarly, reaction formation and sublimation at the phallic level are helped by bathroom privacy, by encouraging exhibition of skills and achievements, and by satisfying curiosity in displaced, potentially neutral areas. By contrast, if a nursery school "seduces" their three-year-olds to mess with paints and clay, and provides no privacy for toileting, it may create a variety of developmental interferences. Children who are not permitted such instinctual gratifications at home may experience a loyalty conflict, or a serious shock if they encounter sexual differences for the first time during an initial separation from their mother. For children who have only recently acquired reaction formations to dirt, and are still struggling with impulses to look and be looked at, the nursery school's opportunities for direct satisfaction may lead to an undoing of necessary defenses, or promote an adherence to instinctual outlets to the detriment of sublimatory interests. In a setting geared to the age-appropriate needs of a young child, observations can be meaningful. In a "seductive" setting, the distortions produced by the school invalidate observations, and often makes it impossible to distinguish internalized from added external conflicts.

The nursery school's understanding of the mother-child relationship. The opportunity to observe the mother-child relationship depends on the amount of time the mother spends in the nursery school, and on the capacity in which she does so. If a mother regularly brings and picks up her child, and lingers to settle him in in the morning or to admire something he has done at the end of the day, or pays occasional longer visits, we can note the mother-child interaction specifically. When she comes to the nursery to work, for example as an assistant to the teacher, her role with her child is more obscured. Observation of the mother-child relationship, however, includes other opportunities: what she shares with the teacher about home, how she reacts to the teacher's daily comments on her child's successes and difficulties, and what transpires in regular longer conferences. In a therapeutic nursery school, these observations are greatly augmented by the mother's weekly meetings about her child with the therapist. When all or some of these casual and formal opportunities are lacking, observations are not available; for example when children are bused to school, when parents hurriedly "drop" them off, when there are no regular meetings with the teaching staff, and therapeutic work is not a part of the setting. However, it is not merely a question of opportunity for observation, but also the use a mother makes of her time in the nursery, and whether her attitude to the school encourages unstilted behavior and promotes genuine information. This depends on the school's understanding of the mother-child relationship, on recognizing its ongoing importance for both mother and child, and realizing that without the mother's emotional support for the school, the child's adjustment and progress there will be seriously limited. Such understanding shows itself concretely at once in a nursery school's appreciation that entry to school constitutes a difficult developmental step for the "ready" youngster, as well as for his mother (R.A. Furman 1966, R.A. Furman and Katan 1969, E. Furman 1969a). For the first time the child learns to relate to a teacher, rather than to a mother substitute, and to function relatively independently in a peer group. This requires a new and different integration within the child's mental structure. The mother not only experiences a few hours separation from her child, but also the loss of their early relationship as he moves into a stage in which verbal communication succeeds bodily intimacy. At the same time, the mother exposes her child for the first time to the critical eye of public authority which, she feels, judges her competence as a mother on the basis of her child's behavior. Unless the school's approach is based on a sympathetic understanding of the feelings of both mother and child in this period of stress it is easy for mother and child to defensively end up at cross purposes with one another, and with the school. Time and help are necessary for a gradual physical separation, and subsequent mastery of the mental separation.

When Ellen entered our nursery school, her mother was quite concerned that Ellen make a good impression. She extolled the school to Ellen and encouraged her to enjoy all it had to offer. Ellen was obviously unhappy and disinterested at school at first. However, she refused to visit her mother in the waiting room, sent her away abruptly, and dallied when she was picked up. At one point Ellen carried her defense of passive into active a step further. She told her mother that her teacher kissed and hugged her, although this was not true. All this time the mother made a considerable effort to remain available to Ellen only to find herself persistently "rejected." She felt sure Ellen did not need her. She started to "pay Ellen back" by leaving her, and becoming impatient with Ellen's increasingly pro-vocative behavior at home. The teachers now made a special effort to describe to the mother Ellen's indirect ways of missing her mommy, and the therapist pointed out Ellen was doing to her mother what she felt mommy had done to her. This helped the mother empathize with Ellen. Ellen and her mother discussed missing one another. Ellen began to ask questions about separation and the school which the mother could answer helpfully and reassuringly. This enabled both mother and child to continue their task of adjusting without the added burden of a defensive interference. [E. Furman 1969a, pp. 150–151]

In many similar circumstances sufficient understanding of mother and child is not available. Teachers may really "woo" the child away from his mother under the guise of effecting a good adjustment. The mother rarely protests openly, but may suddenly act defensively and announce that from now on the father will bring the child, or that she needs to go on a trip, or has made a commitment which necessitates her absence from home. In these ways the mother anticipates, or uncon-sciously repays, the child's rejection. Intensive study has shown that even under optimum circumstances,

the period of stress and of experimental adaptation lasted for several weeks and the child achieved relative mastery by the end of two months of school attendance. For purposes of personality assessment it seems therefore necessary not only to study the child's adjustment reactions throughout his first weeks at school, but to evaluate their significance when at least partial mastery has been achieved, and the personality once again becomes relatively stabilized. Assessments prior to the child's entry lack much of the vital information which the school observations provide. Assessment during the stress period does not provide a valid picture of the child's habitual functioning. In cases where the child has not been able to effect healthy mastery of the developmental task of entry, his personality assessment will be complicated by the pathological consequences of his entry. In such a case, the developmental step may have become a developmental interference (H. Nagera 1966) and a source of conflict. [E. Furman 1969a, pp. 151–152]

This applies equally to the "normal" mother whose relationship with her child is not especially burdened by neurotic conflicts. Only if the school can sufficiently assist her during this crucial first period, will her relationship to the staff enable her to share many valid aspects of the parent-child relationship. In addition, a child who senses his mother's distance from and distrust of the school may refrain from bringing into the school his home experiences and feelings, or he may experience a loyalty conflict when he does share them. In either case, observations of the child's inner life become limited and/or distorted.

Recognition of stressful elements within the nursery school. Every nursery school expects a child to cope with numerous events that arise within its setting. As long as these experiences are recognized by the staff, as well as the child's responses to them, and sufficient effort is made to help him with mastery, they present excellent opportunities for obtaining observational data. If, however, the experiences themselves, or the child's reactions to them are not appreciated, and if appropriate help with mastery is not offered, they can become interferences for the child, and affect the availability and validity of observations.

Some such experiences are a more or less permanent part of the school, for example, racial differences, physical handicaps, or pathological behavior on the part of peers and their parents.

In one nursery group a little girl had a minor anomaly of her left hand which did not interfere with her use of it. Until the teacher openly discussed this with the children, and alerted their parents to possible questions and concerns, each child's behavior showed non-verbal responses that could have easily been misinterpreted. For example, Jimmy began to avoid art activities, Sharon showed hostility to the little girl, and Bob refused to allow others to touch his toys and productions.

Other stresses are temporary and unexpected. They may range from the simplest, and in adult eyes, benign occurrence, to the most serious tragedy: the appearance of a fireman to check the safety of the building, the absence of a teacher due to illness, a peer getting hurt, a house being demolished in the vicinity of the school, or a dead bird in the playground.[4]

Of equal importance are events to which the child is not directly exposed, but of which he hears from his peers: a new baby, a burglary, or divorced, sick, or dead parents. Through the nursery school, a child inevitably comes in contact with many new aspects of life which, because of his immaturity and lack of self-differentiation, affect him deeply. The school needs to be aware of their impact on child and parent, and assist them with mastery. When parents complain of the many colds or bad habits their children acquire at nursery school, they are often indirectly alluding to these other stressful experiences. Sometimes a child's behavioral difficulties are really caused or augmented by conflicts in school, rather than home.

These are but some of the characteristics of a school setting which contribute to making observations more or less available and valid. Some nursery schools approach an ideal in these respects, while others fall far short of it. This does not mean that observations should only be made in some schools, but rather that data are prolific in some and scarce in others, and all observations have to be sifted and evaluated in light of a school's individual circumstances.

Some inevitable limitations of nursery school observations. Given all or many of the favorable circumstances outlined above, observation at the nursery school yields such a wealth of valid diagnostic data that it is sometimes easy to overlook certain limitations. Usually these are not great enough to falsify the broad diagnostic category in a given case, but rather to obscure, or fail to elucidate, some areas of the personality or its interaction with the environment.

Certain symptoms or behavioral adaptations only occur outside the nursery school, either because the school setting provides little or no opportunity for them, or because the child defensively isolates or controls them. Among these are sleep difficulties, reactions to physical illness, relationships with older siblings and men, and certain toileting troubles in which the child soils or wets only at home, or manages not to use the school bathroom. Such home behaviors may be due to internal or external conflicts. Sometimes it is possible to pick up traces of them at school, or with the help of mother and teachers, to enable the child to "bring" them to school. However, at times such efforts fail. In certain circumstances it may not be advisable to encourage the manifestation of difficulties in the school setting lest they interfere with neutral functioning or progressive trends. In some instances, differences between school and home functioning show separate aspects of the same symptom complex. For example, A. Katan (1959) described the excessive talking of a little girl at home, and her total silence at school. This reflected her earlier constipation and diarrhea during her struggle over toileting.

Many aspects of the parent-child relationship may also not be accessible. The full impact of phase-appropriate phallic and oedipal relationships, for example, can never show itself at school. Fathers' and mothers' visits are too short, as a rule, do not occur together and never involve the most highly cathected times, such as sharing a family meal or preparing for sleep. In addition, some facets of the parent-child relationship, or their intensity or pervasiveness, are consciously or unconsciously hidden from view. Parents readily sense or assume what is acceptable in the eyes of the school and other parents. As a result, they may deal with their child differently in front of others, or show an interaction in a much milder form. In many instances school situations do not provoke some forms of reaction or handling, but evoke others. Home visits do not necessarily help, as the same factors interfere with the parents' spontaneity. Unfortunately, it is not always the same facets that elude observation. For example, a mother's periodic withdrawal of cathexis from her child may play an important part in their relationship, and may profoundly affect the child's personality in such areas as integration, self-regard, object relationships, and ability to concentrate on tasks. This quality of the mother-child relationship can be traced in some cases, but not in others.

In spite of adequate endowment, Charlie[5] showed very immature ego functioning and infantile dependency in his relationships. At the nursery school, his mother was always overly attentive to his needs and failed to encourage mastery. It seemed her "babying" of him related in part to certain earlier stressful events, and provided an undue gratification of Charlie's prephallic impulses. It was only later, during the boy's analysis, that his dependency and some aspects of his learning difficulty could be seen to stem from the mother's intermittent cathexis of him.

Tim showed many similar characteristics. His mother too consistently dressed him, held him, and anticipated his needs. There were also similar past traumata in the family that seemed to have paved the way toward this particular mother-child interaction. When Tim's inattentiveness to the teacher's words and his short attention span at tasks were reported to his mother, she recognized he behaved similarly at home. In her work with the therapist, the mother focused on specific incidents and became aware that they related to her periodic emotional withdrawal from her child. She had not previously realized this aspect of her relationship to Tim, much less appreciated its effect on him.

In some families, there are specific secrets, past or present, which the parents do not share, and which the child knows or senses, but also does not discuss. Certain forms of parental pathology are among these, such as alcoholism, extra-marital relationships, and severe temper outbursts. While some of these secrets can eventually be surmised by the school, or are confessed by the parent, others remain excluded.

Stressful past events sometimes come to light at the very start of the child's school attendance, for example, experiences with a sadistic adult (Benkendorf 1969), or unusual circumstances of exposure to sexual differences (E. Furman 1969b). In other instances, however, they cannot be detected, and remain unrecognized as the cause of the child's symptomatology.

THE OBSERVER AND HIS METHODS

In the nursery school, it is the teacher in charge of the child who is the obvious observer. She was the sole source of observational data during A. Freud's work with nursery schools in Vienna, and a number of authors have recently underlined the teacher's special contribution to the diagnosis of the preschooler (Neubauer, Alpert, and Bank 1958, Neubauer and Beller 1958, Katan 1959, R.A. Furman 1966, R.A. Furman and Katan 1969, Ronald and Kliman 1970). If the teacher is a skilled and experienced educator, she is especially able to assess many areas of ego functioning and social relationships. She can readily pinpoint the stage a child has reached along developmental lines, and how this affects his mastery of tasks. When a teacher is particularly interested in emotional development, naturally gifted, and insightful, her observational ability is deepened and extended to the areas of drive derivatives, affects, and the parent-child relationship. Ongoing special training with an analyst and a teacher's personal analysis further enhance her skill and reliability as an observer. Her continuous presence and close relationship with the child afford her a most advantageous opportunity for the kind of long-term observation that is so essential for the diagnosis of the young child.

Parents are also important observers in the nursery school. Sometimes they helpfully supplement the teacher's observations, but more essentially, they provide the framework for evaluating school observations. We need to learn from the mother whether certain forms of her child's behavior are the same or different at home or in other settings, whether changes can be related to events outside the school, and whether different forms of handling or school experiences affect the child's responses at home and his relationships with members of his family. Sometimes a parent gives this kind of information in response to the teacher's observations. However, quite often a parent needs to observe the child at school before she is able to put his behavior or verbalizations into context, and recognize aspects of her own relationship with her child. In spite of blind spots, parents' longstanding and uniquely intimate relationship with the young child usually makes their observations particularly pertinent.

The child analyst brings his special professional skills to the task of observing the child and the parent-child relationship, but the extent of his opportunity for gaining data and for correctly assessing them depends on many factors. The analyst's familiarity with all aspects of the nursery school, the quality of his relationship with the teachers, children, and parents and the frequency and length of his visits all affect his observations. In addition, the analyst's personal ease with young children, and his understanding of educational principles and practice are important factors. It is usually not possible for an analyst to observe the entire nursery period on a daily basis during the ongoing diagnostic process. However, if the child analyst maintains a close working relationship with the teaching staff and with the parents, as is the case in therapeutic nursery schools, his regular observation periods serve several purposes. He gains many valid observations and uses them to understand and supplement teachers' and parents' observations. He can also point out areas in which further observations are needed. By sharing some of his own data with teachers and parents, he demonstrates how to observe, and in this respect serves as a model for identification.

Often many others observe children in a nursery school—the cook, the caretaker, or visiting professionals, such as psychologists, pediatricians, and psychiatric residents. All observations should be taken into account, as they may add a significant element, or clarify a particular aspect of functioning. However, their relative value can only be assessed in the total context. The most complete and reliable diagnostic picture emerges from the integration of all observers' data by the analyst who knows the child, the observers, and the setting. E. Kris (1957) and others have pointed out that observations for analytic assessment are best gained in the context of a relationship oriented to serving the client. Observers who do not maintain a relationship with the child and his parents, and are outsiders to the nursery school, do not gain more objective data, however detailed and lengthy their records may be.

Several authors have described their particular methods of observation (Kris 1957, Neubauer, Alpert, and Bank 1958, Katan 1959, R.A. Furman 1966, R.A. Furman and Katan 1969, E. Furman 1969a, Ronald and Kliman 1970, Heinecke 1973b, Ware 1975). Some use very structured techniques, including films, tape recordings, ratings, and statistical analysis of data. Since in psychoanalysis, objectivity depends on internal, rather than external factors, the majority of authors rely on the human instrument of the analyzed and/or especially skilled and gifted observer. Studies at the Hanna Perkins Nursery School indicate that two months of concentrated observation usually provide sufficient data for a diagnostic profile (R.A. Furman and Katan 1969, E. Furman 1969a). In some instances, however, special considerations make it necessary to observe for many months (Daunton 1969, Oppenheimer 1969). For example, longer observations may be needed for assessing the effect of changes in handling, or of reaching the crest of oedipal phase development. However, some workers have utilized a much shorter period to gain an initial picture (Neubauer, Alpert, and Bank 1948).

When diagnosing preschoolers, we concentrate more on processes, than on pieces of behavior, and on flexibility and modulation, rather than on crystallized entities. For this reason, data can only assume the necessary internal coherence through meaningful integration by the coordinating child analyst. As mentioned earlier, the developmental profile adapted for children under five (Daunton 1969) is a most useful tool in this task, especially when the profile is utilized repeatedly for comparative purposes (E. Furman 1969a). In many instances, circumstances that are less than ideal can still produce quite reliable diagnostic information. For example, even if an analyst has no direct contact with the child and parents (R.A. Furman 1966), he can regularly consult with a nursery school, know its setting, and coordinate and guide the observations of competent teachers.

SOME RECIPROCAL BENEFITS BETWEEN NURSERY SCHOOL OBSERVATIONS AND DIAGNOSTIC ACCURACY

Repeated opportunity to validate diagnostic nursery school observations against subsequent material from a child's analytic treatment, makes it possible to pinpoint with increasing exactness areas which tend to escape observation at school, or are inadequately elucidated. In addition, such comparison helps, in retrospect, to find those clues in the child's or parent's school behavior which could have been utilized more successfully. This process has been used for many years at the Hanna Perkins Nursery School in Cleveland, and has enabled teachers and therapists to refine their observational skill. At the same time, many long-term nursery school observations have shed new light on different facets of normal and pathological development in early childhood. Special aspects of the parent-child relationship, the nature of interferences at the preoedipal and phallic-oedipal levels, and their effect on further maturation have been elucidated by such studies. This has contributed to a deeper and wider understanding of the young child's personality functioning, the variations of normality, and the danger signals of pathology. Diagnostic criteria for this age group have become increasingly refined and accurate as a result (R.A. Furman and Katan 1969).

RECOMMENDATIONS FOR TREATMENT

When evaluation of a prelatency child indicates the need for therapeutic intervention, the form and timing of treatment will depend on several factors. Among these are the nature of the child's disturbance, the availability of therapeutic facilities, and the parents' ability to follow through and support the recommended therapy.

In our discussions of the structure and functions of nursery schools, it has become apparent that many observations are made that can help determine whether a child needs treatment, and, if so, whether psychoanalysis is the treatment of choice, or if other forms of therapy are preferred.

The nursery school staff can discover symptoms and other disturbances that parents either minimize or do not describe. The staff can provide raw data about the child's development on which one can formally and informally construct a diagnostic profile (A. Freud 1965, Nagera 1963, M. Silverman Chapter 4). In this way the child's normal or pathological progression, arrests, and regressions can be clarified. The staff can help evaluate parental characteristics and family interaction. They can see the effect of specific situations on the child, and determine whether the child's reactions are usual and transient, or abnormal. They can also assess whether the child's conflicts are external or internal.

The parents of young children usually find it especially difficult to accept a recommendation for intensive treatment such as psychoanalysis and to cooperate sufficiently for the necessary, long years. Parents find this step much easier and are more able to support the child's analysis when their child attends a nursery school where, through their own observations and work with the teacher and/or analyst (E. Furman 1969c, Oppenheimer 1969), they have been a part of the ongoing diagnostic process.

In the nursery school age group most disturbances are not clearly demarcated diagnostically. However, many children require intervention when their disturbances interfere with maturational progression and endanger the healthy resolution of the oedipus complex. Pathology may be related to exaggerated phase-appropriate conflicts, or to the impact of unusual recent or ongoing stresses. In other instances, neurotic symtomatology may be the product of interferences at prephallic levels. Lags in ego functions may be caused by omissions in the educational environment of the home. Timely intervention may forestall the formation of a full-scale neurosis, or of serious unevenness in personality structure.

The nature and combination of educational and therapeutic measures vary considerably. They depend on the specific needs of the case, the approach of the individual analyst or center, and the facilities available. Archer and Hosley (1969) and Edgcumbe (1975) discussed the teacher's educational methods of furthering the child's ego maturation within the therapeutic nursery school. This is especially helpful in cases where lags in the development of various functions are of main concern, and appear to have been caused by earlier or current educational omissions, for example, motor skills, speech, recognition and verbalization of affects, mastery of internal and external stresses, autonomy of activities as a source of self-esteem, and pleasure in achievement. Parent guidance (Ruben 1960) is conducted by the teacher and/ or psychoanalytic consultant in the form of occasional or regular interviews with the parents. It focuses on educational changes within the home to correct omissions or inadequacies, and to facilitate the resolution of external conflicts. In treatment-via-the parent (E. Furman 1957, 1969c), the child analyst meets in weekly sessions with the nursery school child's mother, and sometimes, with the father. While this method includes work on educational measures, it aims more specifically at bringing about appropriate changes in the parent-child relationship, and at utilizing the parent in a therapeutic role. The child is made aware of his defenses and underlying conflicts to afford him an opportunity for conscious reassessment and healthy resolution. Kliman (1970) described a method by which the analyst does some direct interpretive work with individual children during his daily visits with the nursery school group. Alpert and Krown (1953) used a particular method of guided regression to alleviate libidinal fixation points in certain cases. Undoubtedly there are other approaches, all linked to the child's attendance in the nursery school.

The efficacy of any one or combination of methods depends on many factors. In each case, however, it is important that the work not only aim at alleviating difficulties and facilitating progress, but it should also be utilized for further diagnostic study. This makes it possible to assess whether, to what extent, and in which areas the therapeutic measures are proving helpful, and which new or previously unseen factors influence the course of the child's development. This ongoing evaluation helps to gauge whether and when individual child analysis is indicated and feasible. When the possibility of taking a child into analytic treatment is readily available, as is the case in a number of therapeutic nursery school centers, other forms of intervention are not unduly burdened with having to succeed or "make do." Instead these other forms can be given a fair chance, serve as an additional diagnostic tool, and if necessary, serve as a preparation for analysis. When therapeutic methods involve the parent as an active participant, such as in parent guidance or treatment-via-the parent, they prove especially valuable in developing the parent's understanding of his child's need for analysis and his ability to support it. Work with the parents can also be geared to other aims. For example, sometimes the young child's disturbance requires analytic treatment, but observations have shown his parents are unable to provide the kind of home milieu necessary for the child to successfully utilize analysis. In such cases, the analysis has to be postponed until the child is less emotionally dependent on his parents. However, work with parents can help them see their child's need for treatment in the future.

In cases of severe ego disturbances, special forms of preparatory treatment are used specifically to pave the way for analysis. Such therapeutic measures may take the form of assisting the development of certain ego functions (A. Katan 1961), or of working with the mother to help her develop empathy with her child and appropriately alter her educational methods (E. Furman 1956). Alpert (1959) in this connection described the special method of "corrective object relationship." Each of these methods requires the specialized setting of the therapeutic nursery school as a means to the goal of intensive individual treatment.

The use of the nursery school in preparing parents and children for treatment, and in assisting them during the analytic work is described in greater detail by Daunton in chapter 19.

NOTES

1. A. Katan questions this date as she recalls working at the Krippe in 1936.

2. As these example show, observation of children in an educational setting provides much opportunity for studying ego and drives in interaction. Although this was not the main focus during the years of A. Freud's and Burlingham's work with the Viennese teachers, it seems likely that these early experiences contributed to A. Freud's much later significant work on the lines of development and mastery of tasks (A. Freud 1963, 1965.)

3. Unfortunately the Reiss-Davis child Study Center has recently changed its character as well as much of its personnel.

4. McDonald (1963) showed how the teacher's unconscious avoidance of the subject of death was sensed by the children and how numerous and open their ideas and feelings became once the teacher's taboo was lifted.

5. I am indebted to R. A. Furman, Charlie's analyst, for this vignette.

REFERENCES

Alpert, A. (1954). Observations on the treatment of emotionally disturbed children in a therapeutic center. *Psychoanalytic Study of the Child* 9:334–343.

———— (1959). Reversibility of pathological fixations associated with maternal deprivation in infancy. *Psychoanalytic Study of the Child* 14:169–185.

Alpert, A., and Krown, S. (1953). Treatment of a child with severe ego restriction in a therapeutic nursery school. *Psychoanalytic Study of the Child* 8:333–354.

Archer, L. and Barnes, M. (1975). The Special Contribution of the Therapeutic Nursery School in the Training Curriculum of a Child-psychiatry Clinic. Paper presented at the Annual Meeting of the American Association of Psychiatric Services to Children, New Orleans, La., Nov.

Archer, L., and Hosley, E. (1969), Educational program. In *The Therapeutic Nursery School,* ed. R.A. Furman, and A. Katan, pp. 21–63. New York: International Universities Press.

Benkendorf, J. (1969). Martin. In *The Therapeutic Nursery School,* ed.

R.A. Furman, and A. Katan, pp. 156–180. New York: International Universities Press.

Bernfeld, S. (1934). Psychoanalytic psychology of the young child. *Psychoanalytic Quarterly* 4:3–14, 1935.

Braun, E. (1936). Eine Kinderfreundschaft (A friendship between two children). *Zeitschrift für Psychoanalytische Pädagogik* 10, no. 2: 84–92.

Burlingham, D.T. (1937). Probleme des Psychoanalytischen Erziehers. *Zeitschrift für Psychoanalytische Pädagogik* 11:91–97.

―――― (1972). Problems confronting the psychoanalytic educator. In *Psychoanalytic Studies of the Sighted and the Blind,* pp. 71–79. New York: International Universities Press.

―――― (1974). Letter of March 29 to Elizabeth Daunton.

Daunton, E. (1969). Diagnosis. In *The Therapeutic Nursery School,* ed. Furman, R.A. and Katan, A., pp. 204–214. New York: International Universities Press.

Edgcumbe, R. (1975). The border between therapy and education. In *Studies in Child Psychoanalysis: Pure and Applied,* Monograph Series of the Psychoanalytic Study of the Child, no. 5, pp. 133–147. New Haven: Yale University Press.

Ferlemann, M. (1973). Wednesday's child is full of woe. *Menninger Perspective* Winter: 9–14.

Fischer, H. (1933). Sehnsucht und Selbstbefriedigung (Longing and autoerotic satisfaction). *Zeitschrift für Psychoanalytische Pädagogik* 7:140–144.

Fischer, H., and Peller, L. (1934). Eingewöhnungsschwierigkeiten im Kindergarten (Adjustment difficulties in the nursery school). *Zeitschrift für Psychoanalytische Pädagogik* 8:33 – 36.

Freud, A. (1935). Introductory notes. *Psychoanalytic Quarterly* 4:1–2.

―――― (1951). Observations on child development. *Psychoanalytic Study of the Child* 6:18–30.

―――― (1953). Some remarks on infant observation. *Psychoanalytic Study of the Child* 8:9–19.

―――― (1958). Child observation and prediction of development. *Psychoanalytic Study of the Child* 13:92–116.

―――― (1963). The concept of developmental lines. *Psychoanalytic Study of the Child* 18:245–265.

_____ (1965). *Normality and Pathology in Childhood.* New York: International Universities Press.

_____ (1974). Introduction. In *The Writings of Anna Freud,* vol. 1. New York: International Universities Press.

_____ (1974). Letter of March 18 to Erna Furman.

Fuchs Wertheim, H. (1932). Psychoanalytische Heilpädagogik im Kindergarten (Psychoanalytic education in the nursery school). *Zeitschrift für Psychoanalytische Pädagogik* 9(6):349—391.

_____ (1933). Probleme der heilpädagogischen kindergartengruppe (Problems of the therapeutic nursery school group). *Zeitschrift für Psychoanalytische Pädagogik* 7, no. 5/6:243-250.

_____ (1974). Letter of March 2 to Erna Furman.

Furman, E. (1956). Preparation for Analysis of a Four-Year-Old Boy with a Severe Ego Disturbance. Paper Presented at the Hampstead Clinic Scientific Meeting. London, July.

_____ (1957). Treatment of under-fives by way of parents. *Psychoanalytic Study of the Child* 12:250–262.

_____ (1969a). Observations on entry to nursery school. *Bulletin of the Philadelphia Association for Psychoanalysis* 19, no.3:133–152.

_____ (1969b). Janie. In *The Therapeutic Nursery School,* ed. R.A. Furman, and A. Katan. pp. 180–203. New York: International Universities Press.

_____ (1969c). Treatment via the mother. In *The Therapeutic Nursery School,* ed. R.A. Furman, and A. Katan, pp. 64–123. New York: International Universities Press.

Furman, R.A. (1966). Experiences in nursery school consultations. In *Ideas That Work with Young Children,* ed. K. Baker. pp. 225–236. Washington, D.C.: National Association for the Education of Young Children, 1972.

Furman, R.A., and Katan, A. (1969). *The Therapeutic Nursery School.* New York: International Universities Press.

Heinecke, C.M. (1973a). Parent-child relations, adaptation to nursery school and the child's task orientation: a contrast in the development of two girls. In *Individual Differences in Children,* ed. J. Westman, pp. 159–198. New York: John Wiley and Sons.

Heinecke, C.M., Busch, F., Click, P., and Kramer, E. (1973b). A methodology for the intensive observation of the preschool child. In

Individual Differences In Children, ed. J. Westman, pp. 243-264. New York: John Wiley and Sons.

Heinecke, C.M., et al. (1974). Relationship Opportunities in Day Care: Changes in Child and Parent Functioning. University of California and Reiss-Davis Child Study Center. Unpublished manuscript.

Katan, A. (1959). The nursery school as a diagnostic help to the child guidance clinic. *Psychoanalytic Study of the Child* 14:250–264.

———— (1961). Some thoughts about the role of verbalization in early childhood. *Psychoanalytic Study of the Child* 16:184–188.

———— (1974). Personal communication.

Kessler, J. (1974). The preschool child: dilemmas of diagnostic labeling. *Canadian Psychiatric Association Journal* 19(2):136–141.

Kessler, J., Ablon, G., and Smith, E. (1969). Separation reactions in young, mildly retarded children. *Children* 16(1):2–7.

Kliman, G. (no date). Application of Psychoanalytic Technique in Nursery and Kindergarten Classes. White Plains, New York: The Center for Preventive Psychiatry. Unpublished manuscript.

Kris, E. (1950). Notes on the development and on some current problems of psychoanalytic child psychology. *Psychoanalytic Study of the Child* 5:24–46.

———— (1955). Neutralization and sublimation: observations on young children. *Psychoanalytic Study of the Child* 10:30–46.

———— (1962). Decline and recovery in the life of a three-year-old: or: data in psychoanalytic perspective on the mother-child relationship. *Psychoanalytic Study of the Child* 17:175–215.

Landau, A. (1936). Angsterlebnisse eines Dreijährigen (A three-year-old's experiences of anxiety). *Zeitschrift für Psychoanalytische Pädagogik* 10:366–378.

Mahler, M. (1963), Thoughts about development and individuation. *Psychoanalytic Study of the Child* 18:307–323.

McDonald, M. (1963). Helping children to understand death: an experience with death in a nursery school. *Journal of Nursery Education* 19(1):19–25.

Minor-Záruba, E. (1937). Die fünfjährige Nora im Kindergarten (Five-year-old Nora in the nursery school). *Zeitschrift für Psychoanalytische Pädagogik* 11(3/4):253–261.

Nagera, H. (1963). The developmental profile: notes on some practical considerations regarding its use. *Psychoanalytic Study of the Child* 18:511–540.

––––––– (1966). *Early Childhood Disturbances, the Infantile Neurosis and the Adulthood Disturbances.* New York: International Universities Press.

––––––– and Colonna, A.B. (1965). Aspects of the contribution of sight to ego and drive development. *Psychoanalytic Study of the Child* 20:267–287.

Neubauer, P.B., Alpert, A., and Bank, B. (1958). The nursery group experience as part of a diagnostic study of a preschool child. In *New Frontiers in Child Guidance,* A.H. Esman, ed., pp. 124–138. New York: International Universities Press.

Neubauer, P., and Beller, E. (1958). Differential contributions of the educator and clinician in diagnosis. In *Orthopsychiatry and the School,* ed. M. Krugman, pp. 36-45. New York: American Orthopsychiatric Association.

Oppenheimer, R. (1969). The role of the nursery school with the children who received direct treatment. In *The Therapeutic Nursery School,* ed. R.A. Furman, and A. Katan, pp. 274-292. New York: International Universities Press.

Pavenstedt, E. (1973). Marian Cabot Putnam. *Psychoanalytic Study of the Child* 28:17–20.

Pensimus, K. (1933). Folgen der Entrechtung. *Zeitschrift für Psychoanalytische Pädagogik* 7:233–242.

––––––– (1935). A rejected child. *Psychoanalytic Quarterly* 4:37–49.

Poertl, A. (1933). Verspätete Reinlichkeitsgewöhnung. *Zeitschrift für Psychoanalytische Pädagogik* 7:224–232.

––––––– (1935). Profound disturbances in the nutritional and excretory habits of a four and one half year old boy: their analytic treatment in a school setting. *Psychoanalytic Quarterly* 4:25–36.

Putnam, M.C., Rank, B., and Kaplan, S. (1951). Notes on John I.: a case of primal depression in an infant. *Psychoanalytic Study of the Child* 6:38–58.

Redmond, S. (1975). Evaluating the Child Study Group: Psychoanalytic Consultation with Preschool Teachers, Doctoral Thesis. Cleveland: Department of Education, Case Western Reserve University.

Rexford, E. (1949). The role of the nursery school in a child guidance clinic. *American Journal of Orthopsychiatry* 19: 517–524.

Roiphe, H. (1973). Some thoughts on childhood psychosis, self and object. *Psychoanalytic Study of the Child* 28: 131–145.

Ronald, D. and Kliman, G. (1970). The Unique Function of the Teacher in an Experimental Therapeutic Nursery School. Paper presented at the Meeting of the American Association of Psychiatric Services to Children. Philadelphia, Nov. 6.

Ruben, M. (1960). *Parent Guidance in the Nursery School.* New York: International Universities Press.

Schiff, E. (1969). Role of the nursery school in relation to total child analytic program. In *The Therapeutic Nursery School,* ed. R.A. Furman, and A. Katan, pp. 293–297. New York: International Universities Press.

Schmaus, M. (1933). Bravheit und neurotische Hemmung (On being good and neurotic inhibition). *Zeitschrift für Psychoanalytische Pädagogik* 7:129–139.

Speers, R.W. and Lansing, C. (1965). *Group Therapy in Childhood Psychosis.* Chapel Hill: University of North Carolina Press.

Ware, L. (1975). Psychotherapy in Conjunction with a Therapeutic Pre-School. Children's Division, The Menninger Foundation. Unpublished manuscript.

Wills, D.M. (1965). Some observations on blind nursery school children's understanding of their world. *Psychoanalytic Study of the Child* 20:344–364.

————— (1968). Problems of play and mastery in the blind child. *British Journal of Medical Psychology* 41:213–222.

Winnicott, D.W. (1965). *The Maturational Processes and the Facilitating Environment.* New York: International Universities Press.

PART FOUR

CHILD ANALYSIS AT DIFFERENT DEVELOPMENTAL STAGES

Chapter 6

THE PSYCHOANALYSIS OF PRELATENCY CHILDREN

by Jules Glenn, M.D.

THE AGE OF THE CHILDREN UNDER CONSIDERATION

Strictly speaking, prelatency children comprise all children, no matter what their age, who have not entered the psychosexual stage of latency. In accordance with custom, in this chapter we will restrict ourselves to children under the age of six. Older children who have failed to attain the characteristics of latency because of psychological disturbances will not be discussed here.

The children we will discuss will be three, four, or five years of age, and will occupy the oral, anal, or oedipal stages of development. Because their cognitive and verbal capacities are extremely limited, children under the age of three are rarely analyzed. Nevertheless, skillful psychotherapy with these very small children has been helpful.

The author wishes to thank Dr. Marianne Kris for her many helpful suggestions.

CHARACTERISTICS OF PRELATENCY CHILDREN

Although the name given to the children under consideration, prelatency, emphasizes libidinal aspects, the complexities of their ego, as well as their id development must be examined. The changing cognition of children under six will be discussed as well as the nature of their self- and object-representations, and the libidinal and aggressive aspects of their attachments to their parents and others.

LIBIDINAL DEVELOPMENT: AN OVERVIEW

Freud's observations and reconstructions of the libidinal characteristics of prelatency have for the most part been remarkably accurate. (See Freud 1905, 1908, 1909, 1913, 1923, 1924.) The observations of Mahler (Mahler and Furer 1968, Mahler, Pine and Bergman 1975), Spitz (1957, 1965), Erikson (1963), Anna Freud (1922–70) and others have supplemented Freud's. In this section we will limit ourselves to a sketch of these complexities.

The shift of cathexis from the oral to the anal and to the genital areas has been repeatedly confirmed. The infant is most occupied with his mouth. During the oral phase, not only is there satisfaction during feeding and sucking of the hands or other objects, there is also the gratification of looking, of incorporating the mother with one's eyes as one feeds. The oral satisfaction continues in a diminished form as the child, in the second year of life, becomes more interested in his "anal" zone, an area that includes the lower gastrointestinal tract and even the abdomen. Then cathexis shifts to the genital area, mainly the penis in the boy and clitoris in the girl. Significant awareness of the testicles and vagina appears to help determine self-representations as well. Although the exact time tables for certain of the subtleties of the balance of cathexis are not yet settled, it is known that by the age of three, the child normally experiences interest in and pleasure from all of the areas described, and that the genital desires have become more dominant (Freud 1923). Marked genital cathexis will continue throughout the period prior to latency. In the children we analyze, however, a disproportionate degree of pregenital (oral and anal) interest often persists or reappears.

DEVELOPMENT FROM AUTISM TO OBJECT CONSTANCY

Changes in the child's perception, conception, and interaction with his parents occur concomitant with shifting libidinal interests. The newborn infant's perception of the inner and outer world is hazy and inaccurate. Although some degree of focusing on external objects occurs, for the most part the infant fails to distinguish himself from the outer world. By the time the child reaches three, his perceptions have increased so markedly that such distinctions are possible. Some orally fixated children retain to an immense degree the inaccuracy of perception characteristic of infants. If this is excessive, the children cannot be analyzed. More commonly, a libidinal fixation at the oral stage occurs in a child who has, to a considerable degree, attained a more mature cognitive state.

As the child gets older, his perceptual ability increases and he is able to distinguish himself from those around him with greater accuracy. Mahler, Pine, and Bergman (1975) have outlined the stages in this development. During the autistic stage (from birth to one or two months) the child is largely unaware of the external world. At about two months he enters the symbiotic stage, in which he is aware of his mother, but feels as if she is part of him. This stage persists until five months, but significant residua of symbiosis persist into the second year of life and even beyond that. As the child comes to unconsciously recognize some degree of differentiation between his parents and himself, he maintains a degree of illusion of oneness with his mother and of omnipotence in conjunction with this fantasy of unity. This separation-individuation stage starts at five months and can be divided into a number of substages: (1) differentiation (5–10 months); (2) practicing (10–15 months); (3) rapprochement (15–22 months); and (4) the last subphase, which leads to the achievement of object constancy at three years.[1]

The reader should be aware that there are children past three who have been arrested in earlier phases or who have regressed. A child of four who is arrested in the autistic state or retains an overwhelming symbiotic relationship is not analyzable. However, it is possible to successfully analyze many prelatency children who have not achieved object constancy, or are engaged in intense rapprochement conflicts. A period of preparation or considerable modification of technique may be required when the child is extremely ill.

According to Spitz, the beginning of differentiation, of the I and non-I, begins at about two months. At that time the social smile first appears in reaction to seeing the gestalt of a face. According to Hoffer (1949), further separation-individuation starts at about five months, when the child knowingly sucks his thumb. During differentiation, the first separation-individuation subphase (5–10 months), there is further evidence of the process of differentiation. At 4–8 months, for instance, the existence of stranger reactions indicates an increased awareness of objects.

The practicing subphase (10–15 months) is most clearly epitomized by the child's new ability to walk. The child, still feeling one with his mother, happily scoots towards and away from her. He suffers the inevitable injury of falls with little diminution of confidence, and with renewed and optimistic efforts to continue his motility. A degree of periodic contact with mother for "emotional refueling" is required to maintain the proper balance of symbiotic confidence and adventure-some separation.

This balance changes when the child enters the rapprochement sub-phase (15–22 months). The waning of the illusion of unity with an all powerful adult results in decreased confidence and increased anxiety. There is anger at the parent, who is felt by the child to be less close. This is due in part to an inner need on the part of the child to leave his mother, and leads to a fear that his destructive wishes may come true. Separation anxiety leads to hostility, which in turn frightens the child. Irritation also appears toward the mother as an opponent and depriver during the anal stage. This is not simply because she tries to toilet train the child, but also because of other restrictive, educative activity and the child's fantasies about loss of autonomy. This is a period of anxiety. The child wishes to get away from his mother, but clings to her. The lure of passive satisfaction from mother often leads to a defensive and adaptive activity.

A genital element complicates this phase. At about eighteen months the child develops a panicky awareness of the difference between the sexes (Roiphe and Galenson 1972).

At the end of this turbulent period, things calm down, and the child gradually becomes more independent during the fourth and final sub-phase. Through identifying with adults, engaging in symbolic play, and playing roles, the child gradually masters the dangers of being deserted.

Eventually he can tolerate his mother's absence for longer periods of time. He achieves libidinal object constancy at three and can retain the loving image of a good mother even when she is not present. Prior to this, hostile reactions to her absence produced anxiety.

As the child is more and more able to tolerate his mother's absence, he becomes able to attend nursery school, and eventually kindergarten and elementary school which require even more time away from home.

CHANGING OBJECT-REPRESENTATIONS AND OBJECT RELATIONS

I have mentioned that parent-child interactions change as the child progresses through the libidinal stages and the subphases of separation-individuation. The child of the oral stage normally finds his mouth extremely important to him. He also tends to cling to his parents or parent surrogates, and finds it difficult to tolerate frustration, becoming furious when he is not gratified. Anxiety about destruction of lost objects emerges. Oral gratification, such as thumb sucking, biting, and feeding, provides pleasure and prevents rage.

Frequently, when a child is fixated in the oral stage, these very same infantile traits persist or return. We may see a clinging, angry child who is sad or anxious, and who may seek oral gratification to prevent these unpleasant affects.

Another "oral" configuration involves the passive expectation that the environment will provide satisfaction, that the mother is and will continue to be good and gratifying. Failure to achieve this may lead to rage and a reversal of the object representations; the mother becomes pictured as bad and frustrating.

One would surmise that different types of oral children have had different early experiences. In one case, frustration predominated in infancy and led to a lack of basic trust or confident expectation. In the second, gratification prevailed. It is a truism that an optimal balance of gratification and frustration is required for optimal personality development. Only then will the child be able to separate himself properly from his mother, eventually develop a firm self-representation, and achieve an integrated picture of his mother with both good and bad qualities.

Ordinarily the types of object representation typical of the oral stage recede as the child enters the anal stage, and new types of object relations emerge. At this stage the mother is pictured as an opponent who deprives the child of the pleasures involved in the stimulating effects of defecation, urination and retention. The mother, insisting that her child surrender bodily products on demand, may be pictured as a villainous depriver of bodily *parts*. To the small child, stool and urine are parts of the self. However, as the mother succeeds in supporting the child's ego autonomy and helps him master control of bodily functions, his image of her will reflect her helpfulness.

A certain degree of conflict between mother and child over toilet training often occurs. This may be accentuated by excessive strictness, cleanliness, or punitiveness on the part of the parent. Or, the difficulty may arise from within the child. Unusual libidinal interest in excretory functions may cause the battle to be especially bitter. Constitutional factors or early experiences, such as severe diarrhea—as a result of coeliac syndrome for instance—may lead to a fixation. The mother may unconsciously urge her child to retain stool or to mess, repeating her own early experiences. This struggle between parent and child is not entirely based on hatred. The child can attain sadistic or masochistic libidinal pleasure by withholding or soiling. Torturing mother or being attacked by her can be fun.

The child also enjoys pleasing his mother who gratifies his wishes, cares for him, feeds him, and protects him. Typically an intense ambivalence develops in which the child both loves and hates his mother. The child wishes to comply, but resists surrender. The child's image of his mother is split; he separates her "good" and "bad" aspects.

This ambivalence contributes to the stubbornness characteristic of the rapprochement subphase, which, as we have noted, occurs during the anal libidinal stage.

Eventually the child allows toilet training to take place. He is often pleased by his mastery, and happy that his parents have assisted him. Nevertheless, the victory may be of love over hatred; fear of loss of mother's love and of other punitive measures contribute. Initially, the child surrenders to external pressure, but soon he incorporates the representation of his mother, and superego precursors begin to be established.

The child develops defenses that have an important adaptive value.

Particularly through reaction formation, he comes to value cleanliness over messiness, orderliness over immediate anal gratification, and love over hatred. Secondary processes are thus enhanced, and there is an advance in ego functioning. Hartmann (1964) has emphasized the significance of the change of function that occurs when the defenses, originally used to combat anxiety and inner conflict, become autonomous in a conflict-free sphere. For instance, orderliness and cleanliness, at first mere reaction formations that ward off anxiety and libidinal urges, become important adaptive mechanisms which ordinarily will maintain themselves through life. If these mechanisms again become enmeshed in conflict, their value diminishes, and symptoms develop.

By the age of three, oral and anal cathexes normally have diminished, and cathexis of the genital area increases. The child at this age is normally well on his way to object constancy.

Our patients, however, are often not so fortunate. Oedipal involvements may be delayed or distorted by preoedipal influences on ego and id development (Silverman, Rees, and Neubauer 1975). The child may still cling to his mother in a pathological way. Freeing the child from such developmental arrest or delay is often the chief task of analysis.

Normally, the child of three experiences increased genital sensations and seeks pleasure from genital stimulation. Boys generally stimulate their penises and girls' masturbation centers on the clitoris. Some boys stroke their testicles or scrotal sac and some girls penetrate their vaginas. Certain authors have suggested that all children go through periods of marked testicular (Bell 1964, Glenn 1965, Kestenberg 1968) or vaginal cathexis (Kestenberg 1968) prior to the phallic stage, but this has not been proved. Although girls do not generally directly penetrate their vaginas, it is likely that they experience vaginal sensations when spontaneously sexually excited or when they masturbate their vulvas.

At about the time that genital sensations become dominant, oedipal fantasies appear. (Early oedipal wishes may not be predominantly genital in nature.) The boy wishes genital intimacy with his mother, and comes to fear his father whom he hates as an antagonist. The girl comes to love her father and considers her mother her rival. The opposite configuration, the negative oedipus complex, appears in both sexes, and enhances conflict and complicates development. Normally the positive oedipus complex exceeds the negative in intensity.

The development of gender identity is presently being reevaluated (Galenson 1976, Stoller 1968, Glenn 1977b). Freud's (1933) statement that until the age of three boys and girls are identical has rightfully been challenged. Children develop a relatively firm gender identity by two years of age. This early, frequently nonconflictual development, appears to be based on learned gender role, identification with the parent of the same sex, and biological factors. However, conscious conviction of one's gender does not preclude the presence of conflicting wishes to be of the opposite sex. Penis envy in girls appears as early as one and a half years, and according to Freud, is an important motive for the establishment of the female Oedipus complex. Identification with mother, wishes to obtain a baby from father, and responses to father's interest in his daughter constitute other motives. Biological factors are again important here. The oedipal child's urges to thrust and penetrate give way in the girl to receptive wishes as well. Early in the phallic phase a little girl may harbor the same desires to push and enter her mother as oedipal boys do. Passive desires to be entered may appear, quite possibly biologically based on vaginal sensations. Along with these receptive tendencies, the girl may retain active wishes to mother, feed, and care for a baby through identification with her mother. In our society, a boy's nurturing attitudes are frequently subdued.

THE SUPEREGO

The emergence of the Oedipus complex incurs the hazard that the child will fear punishment for his forbidden wishes. Castration, other types of genital or bodily injury, and desertion are all possibilities to the little child. Perhaps the most maladaptive defense against these dangers is regression. When irreversible, its pathological consequences bring many children to analysis. In a more constructive vein, the oedipus complex leads to the development of a firm superego. Children identify with their directing and prohibiting parents, and similar preoedipal identifications are reinforced. Superego formation enables the child to further restrain himself from immediate impulsive satisfaction, and lays the groundwork for adaptive sublimation in latency.

COGNITIVE DEVELOPMENT

The child analyst must recognize two interrelated phenomena described by Freud and elaborated on by Piaget (Inhelder and Piaget 1958, Piaget and Inhelder 1969): (1) the gradual diminution of narcissism and the emergence of increased object relations (Freud 1914); (2) the gradual change from primary process to secondary process thinking (Freud 1900).

The prelatency child, while still devoted to himself and his family, can develop a sufficiently strong attachment to his analyst to work with him. The egocentricity (in Piaget's sense) of the child may make it difficult for him to accept the analyst's point of view, and understand the analyst's interpretations, but often the child can accomplish these difficult feats. However, the analyst must be careful to recognize the child's limitations, and not offer interpretations that are too complex or out of the child's range of experience.

An appreciation of the child's mode of thought is equally important. The language of the child of three or more displays sufficient grammatic structure and enough range of vocabulary for the analyst to understand the child's communications, and for the child to understand the therapist. At the same time, imaginative displacements and condensations, and manifestations of primary processes, are sufficiently in evidence in speech and play to reveal the child's rich fantasy life. There is often an optimal balance between primary and secondary process thinking in prelatency for the complex tasks of analysis.

Piaget's studies of the child's modes of thought add to Freud's schematization. The first one and a half to two years of life comprise the *sensory-motor stage* of development. The child starts by performing only simple reflexes, and ends this period with a capacity for symbolism. Along the way, he gradually coordinates reflexes, starts pleasurable activity, and is able to recognize that objects (things) have permanence.

From the second year on certain behavior patterns reveal a semiotic (symbolic) function in which one thing stands for another. (1) Using *deferred imitation* the child will repeat the acts of an absent person. (2) *Symbolic play* will appear in which a child pretends to carry out a previously experienced activity such as lying down and taking a nap. (3) Such play may come to include or be replaced by *verbal evocation* of events, for example, when a child says "good bye, daddy" some time after the father has left. (4) After the child is two or two and a half he becomes able to draw a graphic image which is an intermediate stage between play and autonomous *mental image formation.*

The semiotic function enables the child to speak. Although the child's vocabulary increases by leaps and bounds throughout the prelatency period, it remains limited. The incautious analyst may easily use words the child has not learned, or make use of concepts the child cannot comprehend. Increasingly complex forms of play emerge. *Play for pleasure's sake* gives rise to *symbolic play* which reaches its apogee between two and six. Later, complicated *games of construction,* in which problem solving occurs, appear. In symbolic play the child may act and think like a thing (for example, a church) or like a person. In the latter instance, the role playing described by Mahler as part of the final stage of separation-individuation is evident. This serves adaptively to strengthen the ego and allows greater tolerance for separation. It also acts as an early preparation, through the identification with grown-ups, for eventual adult identity formation.

Piaget and Inhelder (1969) add that "symbolic play frequently deals with unconscious conflict: sexual interests, defenses against anxiety, phobias, aggression or identification with aggressors, withdrawal from fear of risk or competition, etc. Here the symbolism of play resembles the symbolism of the dream, to such a degree that child psychoanalysts make frequent use of play material" (p. 62).

During the second year then the child develops a new capacity, the semiotic function. At six or seven he enters a new stage, one prepared for by the cognitive accomplishments that occur between one and a half and six or seven. Piaget calls this new phase the *operative stage,* or *stage of concrete operations.* The operative stage is ushered in by the appearance of the ability for *conservation.* At about seven the child becomes aware of conservation of substances. When water is poured from one container to another of different shape, the child, for the first time, realizes that it is the same water, and that nothing has been added or taken away.

During the time between the beginning of the semiotic function and the appearance of the operative stage, the child gradually becomes less egocentric and more capable of seeing things from the point of view of others. In psychoanalytic terms, his narcissism decreases and his object orientation increases.

According to Piaget the speech of children between four and six often consists of monologues or "collective monologues" in which each child in a group talks to himself. However, according to some observers, in certain situations, as when talking to adults, children make less egocentric remarks. The child analyst can verify that the analysand of this age will be egocentric, but will also be able to direct speech and play toward the analyst who is interested in the child and his difficulties. Egocentricity (or narcissism) is satisfied by directed speech organized and made comprehensible by secondary process thinking.

Prior to the stage of concrete operations, the egocentricity of the child limits his point of view. The analyst's comments may be interpreted by the child in accordance with his own wishes, and the child will speak or play without an awareness that the analyst may not be able to understand him. Reciprocal communication is strained, but is nevertheless possible because of the mutual wish to help the child, and the analyst's careful evaluation of the situation.

Piaget and Inhelder observe that for the child of under seven, everything is centered on his own body and actions. Objective evaluation of inter-object relationships is difficult. For instance, a child of four or six can identify his right and left hand, but is not able to comprehend that the right hand of a person facing him is to his own left.

In the analysis of small children we must recognize the egocentricity, the self and body orientation of the child, but not underestimate the child's growing cathexis of object representations. The more he is immersed in the oedipal complex, the more will the child be able to realistically discuss issues with the analyst. Narcissistic children whose development is markedly delayed will test the analyst's empathy and skill.

All in all, prelatency children are delightful. They are imaginative, driven, enthusiastic, and frank. With the appearance of latency their superegos demand more restraint. Defenses become firmer and more stable; repression, reaction formations, and isolation become more prominent. Drives are less apparent and more neutralized as the child devotes himself to the rigors of a new and more formal type of learning both in school and at home.

TECHNICAL ISSUES[2]

Indications for analysis. Prelatency is an excellent time for analysis. The intensity of drives provides a pressure which impels the child to express himself in speech and play. During prelatency the superego and its precursors are relatively weak and the defenses are fluid and less fixed than later, so that impediments to expression are minimal. Prelatency children are more willing to expose their desires and reveal their fantasies than are latency children. In addition, the balance of primary and secondary process thinking favors psychoanalytic treatment. The secondary processes of children over three are sufficiently established that the child can clarify his thinking through speech and structured play. At the same time, primary processes are powerful enough to form imaginative fantasy which is so helpful to analysis.

When deciding whether to treat a prelatency child or to delay, the consultant should recognize that once the child enters latency, analysis often proceeds at a slower pace and is more tedious.

Superior intelligence and verbal ability are favorable to analysis. On the other hand, extreme narcissism or panicky clinging to mother prevents communication with the therapist, and the child may not be able to participate in the analytic process. However, often such children can be won over to analysis.

Transient symptoms are characteristic of the preoedipal and oedipal periods, and the analyst must ascertain whether these disturbances persist before starting treatment. Simple reactions to external stress do not require analysis. If symptoms such as stuttering, fears, phobias, or sleep disturbances occur in a pathological personality structure, analysis may be called for. Developmental arrests or severe inner conflicts which appear likely to be unresolved by time would suggest analytic intervention. The child's difficulties must be sufficiently serious to warrant the expenditure of time and human resources that analysis requires. Severe pathology such as schizophrenia, borderline conditions, or organic brain pathology are contraindications for analysis.

Evaluation of the child's family is extremely important. The child of three, four, or five cannot attain sufficient autonomy to surrender his symptoms when his environment is in turmoil, or when societal or parental pathology causes or supports his symptomatology or developmental arrest. The family must be able to tolerate changes in the child.

The child's parents must be capable of cooperating sufficiently to bring the child to his sessions regularly, even in the face of resistance, and to supply required information for the doctor and patient to do their work.

Formal arrangements. In child analysis, the analyst usually sees his patient four times a week, and one or both parents once a week.

Small children require a playroom or at least a play area in the analyst's consultation room. While all analysts do not offer their patients similar toys, a number of items are frequently used. A doll house with miniature furniture and a doll family enables the child to dramatize his fantasies about family life. A larger doll and bottle, toy kitchen utensils, guns, toy cars, blocks, paper, crayons, and clay provide further material for expression. I prefer omitting paints and darts because they may lead the child into activities that have to be prohibited. Formal games, like cards, checkers, chess, and board games discourage spontaneous inventiveness. If an individual patient has need of one of these games it can be made of paper during the analytic session.

The child is encouraged to express himself verbally as well as in play. The analyst's questions about the child's game will often help clarify what is going on. The child's spontaneous conversation with the analyst will also be very helpful.

The parents or a substitute provide information about the child's present activities and past life not only during meetings with the analyst, but also through telephone communication or notes sent to the doctor. A parent's description shortly before an analytic hour of an important occurrence which took place will often clarify the otherwise mysterious play of the child. Children, especially very small ones, are prone to reveal their fantasies rather than the reality that produces them and gives them form.

BASIC PRINCIPLES

A brief review of the basic principles of child analysis will place the next sections in perspective. The prime tool of analysis is interpretation. The patient lets the therapist know as much as possible about himself, and the analyst, in turn, offers interpretations to the patient. The analyst tends to make comments about surface matters first.

Later, unconscious fantasies or thoughts that are defended against become the center of discussion. The analyst generally points out defenses before content or drive. As the treatment proceeds, the patient's conflicts and fantasies become clearer and clearer; his defensive structure changes so that defenses are used in a more adaptive manner. A patient who uses denial or projection almost exclusively will be able to use them less, and employ other defenses as well. Eventually, many of the defenses will change their function and become adaptive mechanisms.

With the change in defensive configuration, the patient will allow himself greater drive satisfaction in more adaptive ways. As regression diminishes and certain developmental arrests are dispelled the child achieves more advanced libidinal stages. A child of four may emerge belatedly from the oral or anal stage, and enjoy discrete genital gratification. Sublimation becomes more prevalent as psychic energy from previously repressed drives becomes available and neutralized. Greater ego maturity occurs and the child uses secondary process thinking to a greater degree. He becomes able to restrain discharge and delay gratification until it is appropriate. The reality principle attains greater dominance over the pleasure principle. Prelatency children cannot be expected to become so mature that they are adults in miniature. Instead, an age-appropriate maturation is the ideal.

A therapeutic alliance must prevail if these goals are to be achieved. The child must realistically recognize the analyst as a person who wants to help him overcome his difficulties. In addition, parents must ally themselves with the analyst, and supplement the child's ego by their support of treatment and encourage the child to engage in it.

The therapeutic alliance is based in part on the child's realistic appreciation of the analyst as a helpful person, and partly on positive transferences and displacements. The child, as in the case of the adult, often identifies with his analyst and attempts to understand himself.

Transferences are in themselves displacements to the analyst of emotions and defenses that appeared toward the parents in earlier periods of life. The child, especially the prelatency child, in addition to developing transferences, displaces, i.e., he experiences feelings and uses defenses in the analytic situation that are currently operative at home. Such displacements appear prominently, and, along with transferences, provide fertile soil for understanding and interpretation.

When a child who has experienced libidinal developmental arrest proceeds, as a result of the analytic work, to a more advanced stage, his object-representations change. We have seen that a little girl in the anal period conceives of her mother as a grasping and depriving enemy whom she must stubbornly oppose in order to preserve her bodily products. In the oedipal stage this same child will view her mother as the woman who deprives her of her father. The father, who was dimly represented in the anal stage, becomes a strongly cathected love object in the oedipal period.

Not only does the representation of the parents change with developmental advance. The representation of the analyst is altered concomitantly or even before the parental image. Put succinctly, the analyst becomes a *new object.*

THE CHILD'S MEANS OF COMMUNICATION

Children behave in accordance with their developmental level. In the review of libidinal and ego development of prelatency children, it became clear that their interests, fears, and styles of relationship organize their patterns of communication.

As we have explained in chapter 2, children are incapable of sustained free association. Attempts to encourage such age-inappropriate behavior will end in a stalemate. Prelatency children express themselves by direct conversation with the analyst and by playing games, and using toys, clay, drawings, and paintings. The analyst should allow the child's fantasies to emerge without contamination, but this may be difficult. Often a child requires the analyst's activity, and wants him to participate in games. Frequently, following the doctor's suggestion, the patient will direct the analyst, tell him exactly what he is to do and say during dramatic play. By cooperating in this way, the analyst's participation expresses the child's fantasy life rather than his own.

To clarify technical issues that will be discussed, I will make liberal use of illustrations from the analysis of several prelatency children. Treatment of one of these children, Betty, will be described in more detail in the last section of this chapter. However, it may be helpful to the reader at this point to know that Betty entered analysis at the age of three for extremely severe obstipation, and that she emerged from the analysis at four asymptomatic, and firmly involved in age-appropriate oedipal conflicts.

Betty invented a game in which she played Captain Jack and the analyst played his assistant, Bosco Bear. At other times the analyst was assigned the role of a doctor. In one session Bosco Bear fed Captain Jack candy. When Captain Jack became ill, the doctor was called. At Betty's direction the doctor examined her. The analyst followed Betty's orders to a point, but was careful not to touch her lest the intimate contact both gratify and frighten her. In this safe and reassuring atmosphere Betty became more and more capable of communicating forbidden fantasies in play. Eventually she dramatized a fantasy of childbirth. She, as Captain Jack, lay on her back in the lithotomy position, while the doctor, played by the analyst, removed stool from her anus— again without actual body contact.

The prelatency child will frequently draw, but his lack of skill will often prevent accurate representation. The analyst, following the child's orders, may produce the picture the patient intends, and thus help him express his fantasies.

Play may proceed without the analyst being part of it. The child may use dolls to dramatize actual or fantasied events.

Betty at three and Andy at five both played a game that children often engage in. The child neatly put the play house in order, and then created a hurricane or tornado. Imitating a whirlwind, the child tossed everything—people and furniture—about, and created a mess.

For Andy this scene represented his wish to be masculine. Betty's creation of pandemonium portrayed her inner bodily sensations, the rigors of peristalsis when she prevented defecation.

Children tell their fantasies, dreams, and experiences, both recent and past. The child may describe what he thinks about his parents, his teachers, his friends, or his analyst. He may do this in simple conversation or while engaged in play.

After almost a year of analysis four-year-old Sarah, who refused to eat or drink because she might be poisoned, directly told her analyst that her grandfather had been poisoned while in the hospital. The revelation of the event that precipitated her illness was clarified by her parents. Her grandfather had died of serum hepatitis following a blood transfusion. The family had called this a "poisoning."

Children reveal a great deal about their physical sensations and bodily image to the perceptive analyst through direct statements, play, and drawings.

> Betty, who retained her bowel movements, would playfully toss Tinkertoys out of their box, and then stand in the corner of the room, as she tightened her anal sphincter and attempted to prevent herself from impending defecation. The "big throw," as she called her game, expressed her bodily need to evacuate. After the analyst explained that this act depicted her conflict over retention of stool, Betty said, "My body says, 'go out.' I say 'stay in.' "

The analyst's explanation of the child's bodily sensations may help the child organize his perceptions and enable him to exert more control. Additionally, this helps the child recognize his unconscious conflicts (and his means of defense), and eventually resolve them.

Play and speech discharge emotions and provide gratification as well as communicate. The analytic situation makes use of the pleasure seeking aspects to further understand the child. The analyst's calm approach and objective attitude encourages the child to modulate his excitement, but not to the degree that treatment is an emotionless experience. Play without emotion can hardly lead to analytic insights into the patient's struggles with intense drives and feelings.

At times, however, the playing child loses control. Aggression may be expressed to a degree and in a form that is dangerous to the child or the analyst.

> When Betty's mother left the office with the child's younger brother, the patient became sad and angry. The analyst's interpretation of this led Betty to attack him, a substitute for her mother. Initially, Betty's emotions were under control and could be discussed. Suddenly she became furious at the analyst and threw dishes at him. Betty was no longer using play for communication. She was now only dimly aware that her therapist was a helpful person distinguishable from her mother who was now hated. When the analyst

offered Betty a clay figure, the patient turned her loathing to that surrogate and she ripped it up. At this point Betty realized the analyst was *not* her mother, but a person to whom she was telling things in order to obtain relief. The therapeutic alliance was reestablished.

Libidinal pleasures may become intense and frightening. In accordance with the principle of abstinence, a minimum of gratification is essential for insight to be achieved. In addition, excessive gratification will frighten the child and stifle the expression so necessary for analysis. Or the child may be so happy with the pleasure he attains he may sacrifice treatment to maintain it. Children usually can tolerate less tension than adults, and must be afforded more gratification.

THE ANALYST'S COMMUNICATIONS

The child tells his analyst about himself through play and speech, and the therapist uses this information to help his patient. The analyst's prime function is interpretation. Additionally he helps facilitate insight through preparatory remarks.

Interpretations may be classified as:

1. Defense interpretations
2. Descriptions of conflict
3. Interpretation of drive derivatives and the content of fantasy
4. Reconstructions
5. Transference interpretations
6. Interpretations of displacements

Sometimes early interpretation can foster the analysis.

In her first session Betty accused the analyst of knocking down a tower she had constructed when in fact she had toppled it herself. The therapist explained the projection involved by saying, "Sometimes when children knock something down and feel they shouldn't have, they say someone else did it." Betty opened her eyes wide with surprise and said, "I didn't know that!" Later in the session, when the blocks fell again Betty started to cast blame, and then said that she had been responsible.

An early intervention, if it impresses the patient, shows the child how she uses a defense; it also is an introductory elucidation of the analytic process.

More frequently the analyst must help the child lay the groundwork for the eventual interpreting. He will make *running comments* (Kramer and Byerly, chapter 7) about the child's play. Often, this takes the form of describing the child's activity. Providing descriptive words helps the child become more aware of what he is doing, and gives him a sense that the analyst is attentive and interested. When empathic statements supplement the running comments, the child's appreciation will be enhanced; the child's narcissism will be gratified in a useful way.

Eventually the analyst describes patterns of behavior to the child and this leads to or blends into interpretations.

The analyst remarked on Betty's repeated activity of tossing tinker toys from their box. He then observed that she did this when she had to have a bowel movement. Later he added that she must make the "big throw" when her body wants to push the BM out, and she wants to keep it in.

To facilitate communication the analyst may ask questions to clarify the nature of an event and how the child experiences it. On occasion he will judiciously introduce information that the child's parents have given to clarify a situation which the child does not understand. This must be done infrequently and cautiously, or the child will come to rely too heavily on externally provided data, and expend less effort himself. Great care must be taken or the patient will resent the analyst's contact with his parents, their revelation of his secrets, or coming between him and his therapist. The child may become bitter over a loss of autonomy.

Examples have been provided of the analyst acting roles at the patient's request, and drawing pictures at his patient's direction.

At times the excitement engendered during the analytic situation snowballs and the patient loses control and perspective. The analyst must then help the child regain control. Otherwise the ensuing panic may make the child reluctant to continue the analytic procedure. While interpretation is the method of choice, it frequently does not stem the child's wild, dangerous, or distracting behavior. In the excitement of the moment, the analyst may be unable to decide on a correct interpretation. Interpretation must frequently be accompanied by suggesting that a substitute object be used or that speech replace action, and in this way stop or diminish the child's excitement.

Toward the end of her analysis Betty told her analyst that she "scratched" herself, i.e. masturbated. When the therapist, through drawing pictures, tried to ascertain the location of the genital stimulation, Betty suddenly lunged head first at his genitals so that her mouth was close to his penis. The therapist suggested Betty use puppets to show what was happening, and she engaged two male puppets in a fight. After Betty (and the analyst) achieved relative composure, further interpretations could be made.

At times, interpretation fails. The analyst may then appeal to the patient to desist from throwing blocks at him, and explain that such behavior distracts him from his task of helping the patient. Or the analyst may have to restrain the patient forcefully. This latter course will reassure the patient that the therapist will prevent actual damage to either of them and this furthers treatment. On the other hand, the patient may well derive satisfaction from the bodily contact and possible pain of physical restraint. If the analyst inadvertently gratifies the patient he restrains, interpretation of the patient's acting out, the analyst's response and the patient's libidinal, aggressive or rudimentary superego gratification may save the day and turn an unhappy situation into a productive one. Similarly, if the patient becomes furious about being restricted, interpretation of the patient's modes of attack and fears of aggression may be rewarding.

Obviously the analyst must address his patient in language the child can understand. He must learn the child's range of vocabulary, and often with the help of the child's parent, become familiar with family jargon for sexual and excretory acts and organs. The therapist's style of speech must fit the child's, and complicated sentence structure should be avoided.

The analyst frequently refers to the patient directly when making interpretations. When describing a patient's conflict, he may say, "You're worried about being angry at your brother," or "A part of you loves your mommy, but another part is very angry at her." When interpreting a defense he may say, "When you are angry at Mommy and don't want to be, you hit the doll instead."

As discussed in chapter 2, the child often cannot tolerate such a direct confrontation. This is especially true of prelatency children whose age-appropriate narcissism is prominent. The child may not be able to tolerate thoughts of injury to his parents as they are experienced as extensions of himself; damage to one symbiotic partner means harm to the other.

Prelatency patients who have flexible defenses and a relatively gentle morality which permits expression of drives will be more tolerant of direct interpretations. But even with these children, the analyst must be cautious and alter his mode of speech in accordance with the changing balance of defense and drive.

The reader will recall Betty's analyst pointed out her projection indirectly. He talked of "some children" blaming others for their misdeeds. Later in the session, Betty applied this generalization to herself. At times interpretation of *other* children may serve the same purpose.

Interpretations given in story form may bypass the child's narcissism and guilt (these must then be more fully discussed at later time in the analysis). This style tends to have a soothing effect on the child. He associates adult kindness and approval with story telling, and is therefore less likely to take offense or feel criticized.

Five-year-old Andy asked the analyst to draw a rhinoceros with a horn, but soon lost interest. Seeing an opportunity to make an interpretation, the analyst persisted, and drew a deer even though the child had not asked him to. He then told a story based on certain experiences which lay at the core of Andy's neurosis. The analyst said the deer liked to annoy the rhinoceros until the animal stuck him. When Andy asked why, the therapist said the deer was so upset and puzzled he had come to a psychiatrist to find an answer to that question. In analysis the deer remembered that when he was young, his parents left him and he became lonely. After that he wanted to be stuck because it made him feel that somebody liked him.

The story fascinated Andy and made sense to him. He had the

analyst draw several rhinoceroses and deer. A mother deer protected her child from the attacker.

The story-interpretation was based on Andy's history. When he was three, his parents and two siblings went on a week-long trip while Andy remained in the care of a maid. He recalled that week with agony. He waited and waited, uncertain that his parents would return. Since that time Andy had been a terrible tease, and provoked his brother to hit him, and his younger sister to squeeze his penis.

Singing an interpretation to a small child provides the same calming reassurance that story-telling does. The intolerable anxiety an interpretation ordinarily provokes may be alleviated by the light touch of a song. Betty, adumbrating her passage from the anal to the phallic stage, sang "I am sixteen going on seventeen." Her analyst picked up the tune and reiterated her wish to be a big girl, a wish that she considered dangerous and forbidden.

Children can tolerate ponderous comments to a very limited degree. A witty remark, a smile, a story, or an interpretation with a light touch furthers the analysis, and reinforces the child's recognition of the therapist's benign intentions.

The analyst may intentionally make an error during his commentary to the child, and in that way deepen an interpretation.

Betty frequently enacted stories about Captain Jack and Bosco Bear. It became clear that Captain Jack represented Betty's mother, and Bosco Bear was her child, Betty. After a while, another character appeared—Jules Bear, a new sibling. Bosco Bear (played by the analyst) became angry at Jules Bear for hurting Captain Jack (mother) and hit him. Instead of saying "I'm angry at Jules Bear who hurt Captain Jack," as the patient requested, the therapist "accidentally" said, "I'm angry at Phil [her younger brother] who hurt mother." When Betty objected, her analyst explained he had erred because the situation "reminded me of your trouble when Phil was born."

The analyst may make an interpretation by introducing a purely nonverbal element into the child's play. Acting the patient, the analyst may cry and scream at being deprived of food. In this way he can indicate how sad and angry the child feels in such a situation.

THE ROLE OF THE PARENT

Although parental therapeutic and information alliances are essential for any child analysis, participation by the parents of prelatency children is often of special importance. Many little patients have either not achieved object constancy, or have attained a tenuous hold. Their difficulty in separating from mother, a pathological problem in itself, manifests itself in a particular technical issue: the child may engage in treatment with the mother present.

Frequently the patient who cannot leave his mother failed to complete the rapprochement subphase of separation-individuation. When he enters the final subphase, remnants of the rapprochement struggle remain. Often anal libidinal stage conflicts with mother, which prevail in the rapprochement period, are supplemented by oedipal fears. Failure to achieve object constancy may result from constitutional factors, but the influence of the child's parents is important as well.

Before turning to the analytic means of dispelling this developmental arrest, we will discuss how the mother's presence during the analysis influences the treatment.

It is not surprising that the patients described in articles about mothers in consultation rooms (Schwarz 1950, McDevitt 1967) are prelatency children. A close tie between a prelatency child and his mother is age-appropriate. Commonly young children seek their mother's presence during periods of anxiety. When the child regularly *panics* about separation or will not tolerate separation at all, the situation is pathological.

The presence of a patient's mother in the consultation room would appear to be a drawback to treatment. However, it has been seen that a small child is often able to tolerate his mother hearing the analyst's comments, and even interpretations, without dismay. The patient himself may engage in treatment with little or no inhibition about his mother's presence. He may even have his mother play roles in play-communication. Instead of playing with a doll or a puppet, the child plays with his mother, and an indelible portrait of how the mother and child interact is created. The mother follows her child's cues and her own inclinations and will often spontaneously join the game.

Andy B., age five, was gathering courage to become more manly and give up feminine traits and infantile fixations. In a number of sessions Andy made quite a mess in the playroom by knocking down toys. He created a tornado and destroyed a house and its inhabitants. This activity was alternated with shooting a gun vigorously. On the basis of these activities and other material, the analyst remarked that Andy felt it was manly to hurt and shoot, and that to be hurt was to be like a girl. Andy was told that part of him wants to be a boy and part of him wants to be a girl.

While in the waiting room with his mother before the next session, Andy told his analyst he had seen a picture of his mother naked. After a pause, he added in a joking manner that his mother was a baby in the picture. Andy said he likes to see her naked. He added mischievously that his older brother had seen her naked under a towel. As his mother listened, she blushed. Andy noticed the blushing, approached her, and made loving sounds. She cooed back. Andy then sat in another chair, and cuddled and stroked his mother's fox fur coat. The analyst asked him whether this reminded him of anything, and Andy recalled having had a blanket with which he used to go to sleep. The analyst said that when Andy gets worried about being a grownup, he acts like a baby instead.

This episode increased Mrs. B.'s awareness of her son's conflict, but I am not sure it increased her self-confidence as a mother. The experience which bordered on play, clearly demonstrated the mother-child relationship. The vividness of the experience and the analyst's interpretation of it were helpful to Andy. Using his mother to illustrate his wishes and conflicts added to the intensity of the playful behavior, and made the interpretation more meaningful.

A few sessions later, Mrs. B. reported in her weekly session with me that Andy had acted "like Oedipus." He had fantasied that Santa Claus died. Andy then removed Santa's beard and mustache. He then started to rub his eyes as if they hurt. The mother is an important source of information about home life. This is necessary to achieve proper empathy with the child, and to understand his fantasies during sessions in the total context.

For several sessions thereafter, Andy made gifts for his mother and for the family's pregnant housekeeper. He gave paper bracelets and necklaces to his mother in the waiting room, and kissed and hugged her elaborately. His mother blushed at his strong display of affection. She was pleased, but embarrassed. Afterward, in the consultation room, the therapist said Mrs. B. was Andy's best girlfriend. Andy became furious, and said the analyst was prohibiting him from making and giving presents to his mother. He refused to make any more. The next day, after Andy had calmed down, he said he had known his therapist would not be angry with him—as his mother had thought. Andy said his expression of anger would help his analyst to understand him. The analyst told Andy that boys sometimes worry when a man objects to their love for their mother and their desire to give her presents.

We have concentrated on the analysis of the child's inner conflicts, but there are times when the child's parents can help the process if they are able to alter their own behavior. The analytic sequence I have described was possible because Mrs. B, following the analyst's advice, no longer allowed Andy to touch her breasts. While his mother had not noticed this behavior, the analyst had seen a great deal of it in the waiting room. When Mrs. B. frustrated Andy's attempts at direct libidinal gratification, his wishes appeared in play, and could be analyzed. Prior to that, gratification led to anxiety and regression, but could not be verbalized. His mother had to be prepared for the open discussion that followed.

It is preferable for a parent to alter his behavior spontaneously, out of an appreciation of the pathological nature of his interaction with the child, or as a result of the parent's diminished need for the behavior. Indeed this does occur and can be very helpful in furthering the analysis. The advantage of spontaneous alteration of parental behavior is that it is then less probable that a subtle substitute for the original pathological interaction will appear.

Betty's analyst became puzzled by a game she played after she had been in analysis for about six months. Betty shook her fist at the analyst and then looked at him with joyful defiance. The analyst had been unable to learn anything about the meaning of this game from Betty's mother. However, in a meeting with Betty's father, the analyst was told that she played a similar game with him. Her father responded to Betty's gesture by playfully hitting her. Without any suggestion from the therapist, Betty's father stopped this behavior. As a result, sadomasochistic fantasies regarding pregnancy and birth became more prominent in the analysis. This led to a game (described above in my opening statement) in which the analyst delivered BMs from Betty anally, and then babies from her vagina.

Parents must be able to tolerate the child's developmental advances if optimum results are to be achieved. Betty began to masturbate genitally when she gave up BM retention. Her mother recognized this as a step forward and did not interfere. Betty's grandmother did warn Betty of injury, but her influence was not sufficient to lead to permanent regression.

FURTHERING SEPARATION-INDIVIDUATION

It has been emphasized that analysis can help the child proceed from one libidinal stage to the next. Analysis can also help the child overcome arrests in the separation-individuation process (Mahler, Pine, and Bergman 1975). The resolution of libidinal conflicts facilitates increased separation-individuation. Severe anal conflicts provoke intense hatred for mother; consequent defensive attachment to the mother characterizes the rapprochement subphase. A child who adheres to the anal stage either because of developmental delay or due to regression from oedipal involvements will be prone to rapprochement conflicts. Changes in the hierarchy of defenses accompany libidinal change due to analysis, and a more adaptive use of defenses prevents anxiety and clinging.

The analytic situation can help a child achieve object constancy in another related way. Role playing in the last subphase of separation-individuation facilitates that achievement. Repeated identification with adults, and mastery of separation trauma through the repetition in play of anxiety-producing situations helps the child to be relatively independent without fear. Interpretation of the child's fears can further this process.

Parents' fear of losing their child may complement the child's anxiety. Sometimes the mother's growing confidence in the analyst whom she sees weekly and his support of her wish for the child's independence permits her to encourage the child's autonomy. The mother may use the analyst as a new object to cling to. When the mother changes as a result of her own individual treatment, the result will be more stable. However, many relatively healthy mothers can succeed in encouraging their child's autonomy without therapy.

For the child to start analysis is a step toward permitting him to break away from mother. An analyst who respects the child's autonomy will, as a new object, foster further separation from adults. Through identifying with the analyst, the child will often learn adaptive means of independence.

I must emphasize that I am referring to *relative* independence. The child of five or six still depends on his parents for sustenance, love, and protection. Without them, he cannot develop properly.

CLINICAL ILLUSTRATION

Throughout this chapter I have offered examples from several pre-latency analyses, particularly that of a little girl named Betty. In this section I will summarize Betty's analysis so as to provide the reader with a knowledge of the sequence of events.

History. Betty started her analysis when she was three and a half. It lasted a little more than a year. For seven months Betty had been retaining stool for as long as nine days at a time when her mother brought her to me. When Betty's vigorous attempts to prevent defecation failed, she would produce a bowel movement the size of a baseball. Betty would then not sit on the toilet, but would soil her pants for several days before retaining once more.

Betty had suffered from coeliac syndrome from the age of one year two months to two years two months. Her mother had tried to toilet train her without success after this severe diarrhea had started. A special diet failed to alleviate her illness. Betty was weaned from the bottle at two, shortly before the coeliac syndrome subsided.

Mrs. G., Betty's mother, became pregnant when Betty was two years two months, and gave birth to a baby boy, Phil, when Betty was two years eleven months of age. Her constipation started in the last trimester of her mother's pregnancy, not long after Mrs. G. said she had a baby in her "stomach." At the time the analysis started, Betty still wet her bed at night.

Betty's constipation was an expression of her identification with her pregnant mother, whom she feared losing. The stool within her symbolized the baby she wished to keep within her. It also represented the penis she wished to possess. This latter meaning grew in importance after her brother was born. Betty envied his favored position in the family and his genitals. The family admiringly called him a "ballbuster."

Betty's diarrhea influenced her symptomatology. She was fixated at the anal level by early intestinal stimulation, and her mother's vain and premature attempts at toilet training. Betty expressed her wishes in a very concrete manner. She did not merely fantasize pregnancy; she created the illusion of pregnancy and the possession of male genitals through actually having something (the stool) grow within her.

Although Mrs. G.'s inappropriately early toilet training of her daughter would indicate an anal fixation of her own, I found no other evidence of that. She seemed to be a flexible and empathic woman. She was devoted to her children whom she loved. Mr. G., a banker, was an orderly, pecunious man who enjoyed teasing, sadomasochistic play, and possessed certain "anal" character traits. Despite his skepticism about analysis, he was devoted to his daughter's cure and was cooperative and helpful. Mrs. G., upset and depressed about her child's ordeal, began to smoke excessively, but Mr. G., a calm man who encouraged his wife, maintained his composure.

The start of the analysis. Betty was a delight. She was a bright and friendly girl, a leader among her peers, and she enjoyed being with adults as well as children. She responded quickly to my remarks and rapidly caught on to the *modus operandi* of analysis. As noted above, in the very first session during the consultation, Betty applied my explanation of projection to herself when she took responsibility for toppling a tower of blocks.

A diagnosis of developmental arrest was established. I recommended analysis, and Mr. and Mrs. G. accepted the suggestion. Arrangements were made for Betty to have four analytic sessions a week. Her mother (and occasionally her father) came to see me once a week to keep me informed about Betty's present life and to add to her past history. They also telephoned to let me know of important recent events.

The developmental arrest was a partial one, involving fixation in the anal stage. For the most part, Betty's autonomous ego functions and object relations had been invaded by conflict only insofar as her symptom was involved. A moderate degree of separation anxiety indicated some arrest in separation-individuation.

Early in the analysis several interrelated themes appeared. Betty became upset when her mother left her; she played games in which a baby was deprived of food; and envy of her brother emerged.

Adhering to the psychoanalytic principles of interpretation, I commented on her play, paying particular attention to the emotions involved; and I limited my remarks to surface material. I made statements that I thought Betty could accept with ease. In later sessions these running comments would lead to interpretations of her defenses and drives as the situation demanded.

In one session, Betty sobbed as she said she wanted her mother to remain with her. I said that she loved her mother very much and wanted her to be with her. Betty was delighted when she saw a gun in the playroom. She picked it up and shot pellets at her mother and the therapist. When I suggested she use a clay figure or a puppet instead of people, she complied. Betty ripped up a clay Dr. Glenn, and then re-formed the clay into a snake. She shot a figure she first called mother and then Dr. Glenn. After that, Betty shot the gun aimlessly while saying that boys had penises and girls have vaginas. She added that she had a *little* gun at home. Noting her joyful play, I said that it's nice to have a big gun here. She responded by saying that her brother was at her grandmother's house.

In a short time, following a suggestion of mine, Betty started to assign me roles. She and I could then play games which expressed her wishes, defenses, and conflicts. She fed a baby, played by me, and then refused to feed him until he cried. After she played this game several times, I told Betty that she was sometimes angry because the baby gets so much, a drive interpretation. Once, after her anger at the baby-analyst led her to throw and break dishes, Betty ran into the waiting room to kiss her mother. I pointed out the reassuring defensive nature of this behavior: worried that her mother would object to her anger, Betty kissed her.

Toward the end of the first month of analysis, Betty felt free enough to talk of "BMs" and of her "behind." She said her nighttime defecation didn't hurt, but her daytime BMs did. Later she said she wanted to "have BMs like other people."

A therapeutic alliance was now established! Aware of why her parents had brought her for treatment, she too wanted to rid herself of her symptom. Through play she expressed her troubles and revealed her conflicts. She accepted interpretations as friendly comments intended to help her. Betty's eagerness for relief, encouraged by her parents, led her to use her excellent intelligence to realistically appraise the analytic situation. Positive transferences and displacements supplemented her recognition of the analyst as a reliable and decent person who liked her and could help her. Betty enjoyed the games which permitted her to give vent to her antagonism and jealousy with impunity. Many of these games were also gratifying because they provided active mastery.

Preoedipal themes: morality, sibling rivalry, orality. The motifs I have mentioned continued. Betty's food-deprivation game helped her to actively master her fears that she would be deprived. They also expressed her wish to frustrate and destroy her brother, Phil, whom she wished to replace.

Mother brought Phil to a session and then left with him. Betty looked for her mother's return throughout the hour. She had me, as the baby, cry for mother and then refused me food. Addressing the defense, I told Betty that she wishes mother were here so she wouldn't have to be angry at her for going away with Phil. When Mrs. G. returned Betty crawled on the floor like a baby. I said she wished to be like Phil so she can be with mother.

Messiness invaded the sessions. Soon a pattern emerged. Betty collected Tinkertoys and other toys in a large cylindrical container. When the box was full she threw or poured the contents out. This "big throw," which was patterned after her own retention-defecation sequence, appeared when Betty was angry.

Reactions to the birth of a cousin. During the third month of treatment, Betty reacted to the birth of a male baby cousin. This reactivated memories, which I reconstructed for Betty, of her brother's birth, her anger at him and her mother, and her envious desire to hurt her brother.

In one session, Betty, after frank irritation at Phil, became angry at a baby doll, which she felt like pushing and kissing roughly. She wanted to know why she felt that way (the therapeutic alliance again), and I suggested we find out through play. Betty placed a baby doll and a girl doll in a bathtub. Then the two children went to the doctor's in a doctor's car that was soon to become an ambulance. Betty then repaired cracked cars by hammering them. Then mother left and the baby, played by the analyst, emptied a Tinkertoy box.

In this session primary processes ran rampant. There were rapid shifts from one type of play to another. The same idea appeared in different forms, challenging the analyst's skill. It was only after I learned about the birth of Betty's cousin that the session made sense to me. Her associations had gone from irritation with her brother to irritation with the doll to symbolic representations of birth (first as an experience in the bath, then as a trip to the doctor's) to a dramatization of the harm that pregnancy and birth can entail. At the end of the session Betty once more revealed her anger at her mother. This was expressed through a displaced defecation.

This rapid shifting was a manifestation of primary process thinking; cathexis shifted rapidly from one representation to another. Despite the many confusing displacements, secondary processes were present to a sufficient degree to enable the analyst to eventually understand Betty's communications.

In the next session, Betty reported the birth of her cousin (which Mrs. G. had already told me about). I was able to offer Betty a reconstruction. I said that the birth of her cousin had reminded her of how she felt when her brother was born. The incomplete reconstruction that Betty felt angry at the time and tried to contain her fury, hinted at other aspects of Betty's rich fantasy life.

In that session Betty's wishes appeared in franker form. She wanted to throw the new baby and his mother out. In an undisguised expression of penis envy, she first struck me in the genitals and then broke the penis off a clay substitute figure. She agreed when I said that she doesn't want the new baby, and wants to be the only one with mommy and daddy.

Mrs. G. now reported that Betty was saying her mother's abdomen had been big when Phil was in it and she, Betty, had a baby inside of her when retention made her abdomen large. Betty had become aware of a prime purpose for her obstipation.

In one session, when asked how babies were born, Betty responded by throwing clay around the room. In another session, Betty "squeezed" —made a concerted effort to keep from defecating despite obvious cramps—after first messing by throwing clay, marbles, and cards. I told her that her body feels like pushing things out, but that she doesn't want to, and so throws things.

The equation of baby, bowel movements, and the toys she tossed about was apparent. Peristalsis, which had multiple meanings, was resisted, but bodily demands were externalized in her play.

Captain Jack and Bosco Bear. Betty now introduced several characters who were to help us clarify her preoccupations. She played Captain Jack and the analyst acted the role of Bosco Bear, his assistant or servant. Rather consistently the games could be understood by recognizing that Captain Jack was mother and Bosco Bear was Betty. Of course, as Betty identified with her mother, things were not always clear cut.

Betty embellished and altered the game as she became more capable of revealing her secrets. In an early version of the game, Bosco Bear fed Captain Jack chocolate. Then the pair went hunting for a baby or a nose. They shot Mrs. G. as she sat in the waiting room. Betty, as Betty, wanted to remove her mother's shoe.

Several months later, Betty changed the story. Captain Jack, after being fed by Bosco Bear, became ill and was examined by a doctor (played by the analyst). The illness turned out to be a pregnancy. The doctor removed BM-babies from Captain Jack's anus. Toward the end of the analysis, after Betty was firmly entrenched in the phallic phase, the doctor delivered babies from Captain Jack's genitals.

During the fourth month of analysis, when Betty started the Captain Jack–Bosco Bear game, fantasies of oral conception and anal birth were well disguised. Her play at that time evolved so that battles for possession of bodily parts were frequent. Penis envy, already prominent, appeared alongside confrontations over toilet training. As in a tug of war, Popeye and Bluto each pulled Olive whom they wished to possess. In these games, mother (Bluto) pulled stool (Olive) from the child (Popeye). After Betty expressed concern over her parents' wish that she cease retaining and soiling, Betty asked me to tell her what happens to children. My reply was an interpretation. I said that children younger than she like to have BMs but sometimes don't like it when their parents try to make them have a BM on the toilet. After an initial outburst in which Betty threw things, she played a game in which Captain Jack (this time an alter ego for Betty) was stuck onto the seat or onto the floor. Popeye (the analyst) rescued him. In games played at the same time, Betty, after a Tinkertoy broke, said that *she* felt broken. She also played games in which someone or something was stuffed and then emptied. After Christmas Betty played that she received many presents as she slept. She then threw these presents into the garbage with delight. (At home her large BMs were placed in the garbage to prevent them from clogging the toilet.)

Betty was entranced by the analyst's interpretation via stories he invented about a teacher who takes clay from a child. She replied that her teacher (she had just started nursery school) had said that she shouldn't touch clay. Soon Betty played a game in which she tells the analyst to have a BM and he refuses. In a variation of this game, Betty and I order each other to sit, but refuse to comply. Soon thereafter, she tried to pull my finger off. I responded with an interpretation: "Don't pull the part I want and love away from me." At other times Betty wanted to knock my penis off and said she was a boy.

Conflicts over toilet training. Betty's preoccupation with toilet training continued for several months and appeared in more direct form. During the sixth month of analysis, Betty, as a giant, pushed me into the bathroom and made me remain there until I urinated. This was an active mastery of her feelings that she was forced to do things by her parents. Betty then interviewed Jimmy (the analyst) who, at her direction, tells how the teacher took his BM, not his papers, away. On my own initiative I then said that I retain stool because defecation hurts. Betty then became a doctor who reassured her patient that he could have BMs without pain.

In a new and surprising development, Betty disclosed she thought adults didn't defecate. I eventually contradicted this notion after analyzing it to a degree. Betty thought since grownups were clean and didn't smell, they didn't have BMs. Betty wanted very much to grow up, and learning that adults *do* defecate strengthened her desire to overcome her retention.

Betty continued to play games in which someone violates the rules, but at this point the forbidden wetting or soiling take place in bed. At home, Betty's struggle to control nocturnal enuresis manifested itself by a mild insomnia.

Seductiveness. Betty soon became rather seductive. She sang "I'm getting married in the morning" as she tried to engage me in body contact with her. She exposed herself by walking out of the toilet with her pants down.

Betty's desire for me to see her, touch her, and even exhibit myself to her could be connected with her wish that I be like her mother, who had dressed her. It was also associated with wishes as a woman, to bite men. Betty felt she had been castrated by her mother. This was expressed when she dramatized her version of "Three Blind Mice"— Mother, played by Betty, cuts off the mouse's tail. In another game, a rat's tail became both a penis which was eaten, and stool which could be taken away. After singing "Three Blind Mice" Betty shot her mother, and tried to cut me. I offered the interpretation that she felt like cutting mother because mother had cut her tail.

Betty's obstipation could be understood not only as a means of identification with her mother to keep mother with her, but was also an expression of her battle with mother over the time and place of defecation. Betty wanted to obey her mother and defecate properly like other children, but she did not want to surrender parts of her body. Betty identified her stool with her penis. She thought her mother had castrated her, and wanted to re-acquire a penis. In her struggle, Betty tried to master the situation by being active rather than passive. She tried to restrain her hatred toward her mother and brother, whom she also loved, by the use of repression, displacement, and reaction formation.

Sadomasochistic games. Mr. G. provided me with information which extended my understanding of Betty. For months Betty and her father had played a game in which she would shake her fist at him—as she often did with me during sessions—and he would hit her hand. After this revelation Mr. G. spontaneously decided to discontinue the game, and Betty was deprived of sadomasochistic gratification at home.

Betty raised her fist in a subsequent session. I told her what her father had said, and suggested she wanted to be hit by her father or me. Betty's eyes gleamed with agreement. The games she played could now be understood in terms of seeking pleasure through injury and pain. For instance, when Captain Jack went to the hospital, he *liked* the operations performed there. When Betty and the therapist chased each other about the room playing "Three Blind Mice," the fun she had could be discussed. However, Betty's enjoyment involved denial and this defense was not ignored by me. Through picturing injury and pain as pleasant Betty could avoid anxiety.

I connected her masochistic pleasure and her retention. Betty loved a game in which mother and daughter hit one another. After discussing the game, I told Betty she tries to have her BMs taken from her and hence holds onto them. It should be noted that when Betty was frustrated by her father discontinuing hitting her, the analysis profited. However, even if Betty's father had continued this activity, the new insight derived from his description of the hitting game would have furthered the analytic work.

Pregnancy wishes. Having worked through her masochistic fantasies repeatedly, Betty added a new character to the Captain Jack–Bosco Bear game during the eighth month of the analysis. Jules Bear was introduced as Captain Jack's new baby. At first Betty's play emphasized her resentment of the new baby; she beat him mercilessly. Soon her desire to enter a hospital where she could conceive and deliver a baby emerged.

The Chief, another new personage played by Betty, became ill. A BM within his abdomen "acts like a baby." At the hospital, the "hospital man takes the baby out of the mother" but, Betty added, he also puts the baby into her.

Masturbation replaces retention. At the end of the ninth month of analysis Betty started to produce bowel movements regularly while on the toilet. As her symptom disappeared, masturbation began, sometimes following urination. A shift of cathexis from the "anal" area, which included the lower intestine, to the genital area was occurring.[3]

The Captain Jack–Bosco Bear game acquired new significance. Once again Captain Jack became ill; this time the doctor diagnosed a "virus in his stomach." It was "one yard big." It was like a "flower design on the shirt." When I said it sounded like a baby, Betty enthusiastically agreed. Betty (as Captain Jack) lay on her back in the lithotomy position as I, at her direction, played removing babies from her vagina. The position she lay in was identical with the position she had previously assumed to enable the therapist to remove stool from her anus in play. Body contact was avoided.

Demonstrating the equation of baby and stool, Betty called the baby a BM. When the analyst in turn called it a BM-baby, she did not demur.

Oedipal motives and fears of injury. In the next session an oedipal theme appeared. Betty told me her nose itches and added that my nose itched too. This projection revealed her wish that I would be as excited as she was. After urinating in the toilet Betty washed her hands a great deal, enjoying it. Referring to the sink, she said the bottom was missing, and was delighted when it reappeared. Then she told me that she dislikes her mother, who is dead, and likes the man across the street—her father.

When Betty started to masturbate, both her mother and grandmother issued warnings. Her mother told her to "try not to scratch or it will get worse." Her grandmother suggested that an ointment be used to prevent itching.

Consciously, Mrs. G. approved of Betty's masturbation and recognized it as a sign of progress. In other analyses, parental opposition to a developmental advance may impede the analytic work and therapeutic accomplishment. In these cases, the analyst may need to explain the progress involved, and urge the parent not to interfere. In this case, Mrs. G. was aware, either autonomously or through careful observation of my demeanor, that the masturbation was a welcome sign, so explanation and advice were unnecessary.

Despite her mother's conscious approval, and the mildness of her warnings against masturbation, Betty concluded that scratching oneself could result in hospitalization. As indicated in her play, the bottom could disappear.

I tried to ascertain the area in which Betty stimulated herself. Through her pointing I learned the area was located in the anterior part of her vulva. When I asked for further details, and started to draw a picture to help with the localization, Betty paid no attention at first. She then lunged head first at my genital area, so that her mouth was near my penis. I suggested she use puppets to show what had occurred. Betty engaged two male puppets in a fight. I asked about her head being near my penis and Betty started to rip a coloring book apart. She stopped when a bright red page shocked her. I asked Betty what her tearing was like. She did not reply, but continued to rip at the book. I then suggested that ripping was like biting, and maybe she felt like doing that to me.

By the next session Betty had forgotten much of what had occurred the previous time, and wanted to see the coloring book. I reminded Betty that after she told me about her itching, she had lunged at my genitals (pointing), and then had ripped the book. It looked, I said, as though she wanted to rip something. She replied, "Your penis. Then it would be inside me." Why? I asked. "Because I don't like you. You would not be able to make." Make what? I asked. "BM." Jokingly, she now said that BM comes from the penis, urine from the head and behind, and BM from the vagina.

The dangers of sexual involvement appeared in a different form when, two days later, Betty invited me into the toilet after she entered it. She became alarmed when I tried the door, but then opened it. The toilet became a spaceship and we were off on a trip to Pleasure Island, the land to which Pinocchio had traveled. At Pleasure Island I became a donkey and had to say "Hee-haw" as I knelt on my hands and knees. At Pleasure Island I could do anything I pleased, good or bad; I could tickle myself. When I asked where I could tickle myself, she said, "Under your chin. No, you can't." Later she said I could tickle my tush, penis, or vagina. Betty became Gideon the Fox who prohibited acts which she then permitted. The analyst had to say, "I don't want to be a donkey; I do want to be a donkey." Becoming a donkey was punishment for doing bad things during the several trips to Pleasure Island.

In another session, I had the opportunity to interpret to Betty her fear that something would happen to her, some punishment—like losing part of herself, becoming a donkey, or becoming stupid—because she scratched herself. She therefore, I said, was tempted to go back and become a little girl who made BMs on the floor or retained BMs.

By the tenth month of treatment Betty had progressed from the anal libidinal to the phallic-oedipal stage. She no longer expressed her wish to be pregnant like her mother by retaining feces. She had dramatized this, and other unconscious desires in play, and they had become acceptable wishes.

Separation and termination. In the next few weeks Betty became preoccupied with separating from the analyst during the summer vacation. She attempted to reverse the situation and become the deserter rather than the deserted. Betty became so furious at me that she slammed the door in my face. She tried to lock me in prison so I could not leave her.

As so often happens in child analysis, the patient's parents decided on termination, not the analyst. I wanted to continue treatment in the fall, so the therapeutic result would be stabilized. A compromise permitted an abbreviated, terminal stage in which Betty was seen once a week for several months.

As it turned out, Mr. and Mrs. G.'s judgment was correct; the treatment's excellent outcome sustained itself. A follow-up phone call five years later revealed Betty remained a happy, asymptomatic girl.

NOTES

1. The ages mentioned in this section are approximate. There is considerable variation from child to child. And, of course, the different stages do not start suddenly, but blend into one another.

2. The reader is referred to the following articles and panel reports on the technique of prelatency analysis: Abbate (1964), Neubauer (1972), Olch (1971), Maenchen (1970), Kestenberg (1969), Bornstein (1949). Geleerd (1967) contains several chapters on the topic.

3. For convenience I have written about cathexis of parts of the body rather than their representations. This shorthand evades the controversial theoretical question as to whether the body itself is cathected. Whether it is cathected or not, the representation certainly is.

REFERENCES

Abbate, G. M. Reporter (1964). Panel: child analysis at different developmental stages. *Journal American Psychoanalytic Association.* 12: 135–150.

Bell, A. P. (1964). Bowel training difficulties in boys. *Journal of the American Academy of Child Psychiatry* 3:577–590.

Bornstein, B. (1949). The analysis of a phobic child: some problems of theory and technique in child analysis. *Psychoanalytic Study of the Child* 3/4:181–226.

Erikson, E. H. (1963). *Childhood and Society.* Revised Edition. New York: Norton.

Freud, A. (1922–1970). *The Writings of Anna Freud.* 7 vols. New York: International Universities Press.

Freud, S. (1900). The interpretation of dreams. Standard Edition 4/5.

_____ (1905). Three essays on the theory of sexuality. *Standard Edition* 7:130–243.

_____ (1908). Character and anal eroticism. *Standard Edition* 9:169–175.

_____ (1909). Analysis of a phobia in a five-year-old boy. *Standard Edition* 10:5–149.

_____ (1913). The disposition to obsessional neurosis. *Standard Edition* 12:317–326.

_____ (1914). On narcissism: an introduction. Standard Edition 14:73–102.

_____ (1923). The infantile genital organization. *Standard Edition* 19:141–145.

_____ (1924). The dissolution of the Oedipus complex. *Standard Edition* 19:173–179.

_____ (1933). New introductory lectures on psycho-analysis. *Standard Edition* 22:5–182.

Galenson, E., Reporter (1976). Panel: psychology of women. *Journal American Psychoanalytic Association.* 24:141–160.

Geleerd, E. R. (1967). *The Child Analyst at Work.* New York: International Universities Press.

Glenn, J. (1965). Sensory determinants of the symbol three. *Journal American Psychoanalytic Association* 13:422–34.

_____ (1977). Child Psychoanalysis: Prelatency Children. In *International Encyclopedia of Psychiatry, Psychology, Psychoanalysis and Neurology* 3:123–128, ed. B. B. Wolman. New York: Aesculapius Publishers.

_____ (1977b). Psychoanalysis of a constipated girl; clinical observations during the fourth and fifth years. *Journal American Psychoanalytic Association* 25:141–161.

Hartmann, H. (1964). *Essays on Ego Psychology.* New York: International Universities Press.

Hoffer, W. (1949). Hand, mouth and ego-integration. *Psychoanalytic Study of the Child* 3/4:49–56.

Inhelder, B. and Piaget, J. (1958). *The Growth of Logical Thinking from Childhood to Adolescence.* New York: Basic Books; London: Routledge and Kegan Paul.

Kestenberg, J. S. (1968). Outside and inside, male and female. *Journal American Psychoanalytic Association* 16:457–520.

————— (1969). Problems of technique of child analysis in relation to the various developmental stages: prelatency. *Psychoanalytic Study of the Child* 24:358–383.

Kramer, S. (1960). Running Comments, Confrontation and Interpretation. Presented at the Philadelphia Psychoanalytic Institute Child Analysis Study Group. Unpublished.

Maenchen, A. (1970). On the technique of child analysis in relation to stages of development. *Psychoanalytic Study of the Child* 25:175–208.

Mahler, M. S. and Furer, M. (1968). *On Symbiosis and the Vicissitudes of Individuation.* New York: International Universities Press.

Mahler, M.S., Pine, F., and Bergman, A. (1975). *The Psychological Birth of the Human Infant.* New York: Basic Books.

McDevitt, J. B. (1967). A separation problem in a three-year-old girl. In *The Child Analyst at Work,* ed. E. R. Geleerd. New York: International Universities Press.

Neubauer, P. B. (1972). Psychoanalysis of the preschool child. In *Handbook of Child Psychoanalysis,* ed. B. B. Wolman. New York: Van Nostrand Reinhold.

Olch, G., Reporter (1971). Panel: technical problems in the analysis of the preoedipal and preschool child. *Journal American Psychoanalytic Association* 19:543–551.

Piaget, J., and Inhelder, B. (1969). *The Psychology of the Child.* New York: Basic Books.

Roiphe, H., and Galenson, E. (1972). Early genital activity and the castration complex. *Psychoanalytic Quarterly* 41:334–347.

Schwarz, H. (1950). The mother in the consulting room: notes on the psychoanalytic treatment of two young children. *Psychoanalytic Study of the Child* 5:343–357.

Silverman, M. A., Rees, K., and Neubauer, P. B. (1975). On a central psychic constellation. *Psychoanalytic Study of the Child* 30:127–157.

Spitz, R. A. (1957). *No and Yes—On the Genesis of Human Communication.* New York: International Universities Press.

———— (1965). *The First Year of Life.* New York: International Universities Press.

Stoller, R. J. (1968). *Sex and Gender.* New York: Jason Aronson.

Chapter 7

TECHNIQUE OF PSYCHOANALYSIS OF THE
LATENCY CHILD

Selma Kramer, M.D.

L. J. Byerly, M.D.

Psychoanalysis as a therapeutic method was instituted by Freud for the treatment of neurosis in adults, and has been successfully extended, adapted, and established as a treatment method for children. In considering general aspects of child analysis and their application to the analysis of the latency child, it is of interest to note that many significant contributions of child analysts were made as a result of their work with latency children (see Mahler 1945, Bornstein 1949, Fraiberg 1967). In conjunction with recent child observational research, contributions from the analytic work with prelatency and preoedipal children have become increasingly important in working with and understanding the latency child.

The developmental phase of latency is regarded by many child analysts as the optimal time to conduct child analysis. By the time the child has advanced to the latency period, his psychic structure is much more complete than formerly. The consolidation of the superego, and the organizing capacity of the Oedipus complex, permit the technique of analyzing the latency child to move closer to the technique of adult analysis (Fraiberg 1964). During latency we may expect the child analysand to gradually diminish his need to communicate via play, and to increase his use of verbalizations. It is important to note, however, that the latency child still experiences free association as a "particular threat to his ego organization," because "the use of free association is actually a regression to the primary process" (Bornstein 1951, p. 279). Therefore, the analyst's basic task with the latency child is to understand the child's affects and to use them, together with his play and verbalizations, as a substitute for the verbal free associations of the adult.

The advance of the developmental lines of separation-individuation permits the latency child to experience a broader range of independent behavior. There is an age-appropriate broadening of cathexes to include object representations other than parent representations. The latency child's ability to relate to teachers, other adults, and friends, while he distances himself from his parents, provides the potential for transference in analysis. There is, in addition, an increase of the ego's capacity to deal with reality during latency, resulting from the continued development of such ego functions as cognition, and the capacity to delay gratification. This has the effect of stabilizing the ego, which then has an increased ability to limit regression, and to rebound more quickly from regressive positions to more mature ego and libidinal levels.

Another reason that latency is an optimal time for child analysis is that neurosis decreases in intensity during this period (A. Freud 1945). Conflicts between the ego and the id, which form the basis of symptom formation, are relatively decreased. Bornstein (1951) feels that this is especially true in the second period of latency (8–10 years). However, she finds that neurotic symptom formation and behavioral difficulties occur more frequently in the first period of latency (5½–8 years) than is usually noted. Bornstein regards this first period of latency as "one of the best times for analysis. In early latency the defenses are not yet consolidated, reaction formation and character formation have not become crystallized. The child suffers. The psychic structure is modifiable" (Becker 1974, pp. 4–5).

The latency child has his own characteristic resistances to analysis. The "openness" or "naiveté" with which the prelatency child expresses libidinal and aggressive material is no longer present. The increase in superego functions accounts for the characteristic defenses against libidinal and aggressive material in the latency child. Equally defended against is the latency child's tendency to regress. Sporadic regressions become a particular problem for technique when it becomes necessary to utilize the regressive material in the analysis.

AIMS OF CHILD ANALYSIS

The aims in child analysis are the same as those in adult analysis: to bring to consciousness the unconscious content of psychic material, no matter to which psychic institution the unconscious material belongs. Psychoanalysis as a therapeutic method in the child and the adult is based on the process of interpretation, as outlined by Freud. Mahler (1945) describes the aims of psychoanalytic technique in both the child and the adult as

> effected through interpretation of those pathological formations of the ego with which it wards off the instinctual impulses or its derivatives. By confronting the sound, mature portions of the ego through interpretation with these pathological formations, we gradually enable the ego to dispose of these defenses, so that the deep or unconscious conflicts in its ramifications can be brought within the searchlight of the conscious. By repeating this procedure and working through all the ramifications of the conflict, the more mature part of the ego may correct the pathological attitudes and symptoms and solve the conflict more successfully. [p. 271]

Although the aims and principles of psychoanalysis are identical in child and adult analysis, the means by which we achieve these aims and utilize these principles are adapted to the child's developmental position. Technique, not basic psychoanalytic precepts, is adapted to enable the child to become a partner in the analytic process, to be "reached" by the analyst, and to communicate with him.

Historically, the evolution of technique in child analysis can be divided into two phases (Brody 1974, p. 13). These phases reflect the evolution of technique as it developed in relation to increased application of the analytic method, and to an increased understanding of child development. From 1920 child analysis was characterized by the use of play as a therapeutic medium (Hug-Hellmuth 1921). The inability of the child to verbally free associate in any sustained manner resulted in a reliance on play as the predominate means of communication. In 1926 Anna Freud described the main tasks of child analysis as developing the child's insight into his illness, working within the limitations of transference as it appears in child analysis, and working with the parents. It was during this period that A. Freud (1926) formulated her concept of an "introductory phase." With the advent of defense analysis she (1966) no longer considers an "introductory phase" necessary in child analysis except with certain deviational children (see Weil 1973).

The second period of child analysis began about 1945. "Defense analysis" emerged from Freud's (1923) formulation of the structural theory, an understanding of adaptation (Hartmann 1939), and the introduction of ego psychology (A. Freud 1936). Defense analysis is particularly well suited for use with children, for, as Mahler (1945) noted, the child lives closer to his instinctual wishes than does the adult. Further, because of the instability of the secondary process, the child's age-appropriate defenses are not completely reliable in warding off instinctual conflicts. His affects are particularly transparent and are available to the analyst. Analysis of the defenses against affect leads the analyst to the unconscious instinctual conflict. Bornstein (1951) states that "since defense and affect are closer to the ego than impulse, we are able, through them, to make interpretations which the child can recognize and accept without undue resistance" (p. 284).

No longer relying mainly upon play, child analysts make use of all the child's productions as substitutes for verbal free associations, specifically those related to the analysis—drawings, actions, fantasies, and, especially, his affects. To understand the analytic meaning of the child's productions and communications requires an extensive knowledge of child development, that is, of age-adequate and phase-specific affects and behavior which arise not only from conflict and pathology, but also from normal development and adaptation.

CHARACTERISTICS OF THE LATENCY CHILD

Freud's earliest reference to the concept of latency was in a letter (number 46) to Fliess. The term *latency* was borrowed from Fliess (Freud 1896). In 1905 Freud described latency in "Three Essays on the

Theory of Sexuality." During this period in the development of psychoanalysis major emphasis was placed on the sexual drive or libido theory. Latency began with the ending of the oedipal relationship and infantile sexuality, and was thought to be the result of the blockade of the libidinal drives because of the dangers of the Oedipus complex. It is during

> this period [latency] of total or, at least partial latency that the psychic forces develop which later act as inhibitions of the sexual life, and narrows its direction like dams. These psychic forces are loathing, shame and moral and esthetic ideal demands. [Freud 1905, p. 583]

In essence, "libidinal energies are repressed and aggressive energies are redirected into elaborating a more effective web of defenses" (Hinsie and Campbell 1970). "It is important to note, however, that the influx of this (infantile) sexuality does not stop even in this latency period, but its energy is deflected whether wholly or partially from sexual utilizations and conducted to other aims" (Freud 1905, p. 584). In this regard latency is typically interrupted by the breaking through of primitive drive derivatives. During regressive pulls towards oedipal and preoedipal conflicts and solutions, the ego is overwhelmed by the id and superego. The ideal of latency described by Freud (1905), "the successful warding off of instinctual demands," is a relative, idealized developmental state that is only sporadically achieved during the progression of latency. Freud (1905) titles his section on this developmental phase, Latency and Its Interruptions. In the normal latency child, relatively undisguised drive-derivatives appear periodically, but not excessively. An optimum balance between "ideal" latency and "interruptions" allows the child to obtain libidinal satisfaction directly (as through masturbation), as well as to achieve pleasure through sublimated activity.

The progression through the separation-individuation process, the frustration of the oedipal phase, the "organically determined inhibitions," as well as cultural and educational influences (Freud 1905) establish the latency period. The interaction of these factors determine the characteristics of latency, and set the developmental task of warding off drives and their numerous regressive expressions (Becker 1974, p. 5).

Bornstein's classic paper "On Latency" (1951), focuses on latency as a developmental stage, dividing it into two phases:

1. A first period (approximately from five to eight years of age) characterized by the "emergence of the superego and the intermingling of the different sets of defenses: those against pre-genital impulses and genital impulses." Reaction formation represents the first character change in early latency.

2. A second period (approximately eight to ten years of age) characterized by a lessening of sexual demands and a less rigid superego structure, allowing the child to have a greater interest in, and ability to cope with reality.

The Oedipus complex and its preoedipal antecedents have a dominant influence on the latency period, particularly in the implications they hold for the vicissitudes of the infantile neurosis. (Here we are using the concept of the infantile neurosis in a developmental sense.) Every normal latency child, in the course of the inevitable neurosis, must ward off incestuous fantasies and masturbation temptations by partial regression. Masturbation becomes the repository of conflicts between pregenital and genital drive and ego derivitives and its significance as such has been emphasized by Bornstein (1951). Optimally the latency child's ego deflects these drive energies from pregenital aims, and uses them in sublimation and reaction formation (Bornstein 1951). Where the infantile neurosis has been strongly influenced by problems arising from within the separation-individuation process, the characteristic regression of latency is manifested by the "need to cling to the primary object" (Bernstein 1975). In such instances, it is not unusual to find latency ushered in with manifest clinical symptoms, such as "school phobias."

Bornstein (1951), in describing two developmental subphases of latency, amplified Freud's concepts of normal latency ("ideal latency") and provided an outline of the deviations (psychopathology) common to latency. In addition she provided the means to understanding latency in terms of object relation theory, and the reverberations of the separation-individuation process. The interrelated aspects of object-relations and the separation-individuation process has been well described by Mahler and others (Mahler 1966, 1967, 1972, Mahler and Furer 1963, Mahler and La Perrierre 1965, Mahler, Pine, and Bergman 1975).

In defining the developmental characteristics of the separation-individuation process, Mahler (Mahler, Pine, and Bergman 1975) describes this intrapsychic process as consisting of two interwined developmental lines which are not "always commensurate or proportionately progressing" (Mahler, Pine, and Bergman 1975, p. 63). Either developmental line may be out of phase with the other during the normal separation-individuation process (the first three years of life), and more markedly in certain pathological states and during later developmental stages. It is the intrapsychic progression of the developmental lines of separation and individuation through the succeeding developmental stages beyond the first three years of life (normal separation-individuation process) that accounts for the "reverberation [of the] the separation-individuation process throughout the life cycle."

Bornstein (1951) systematically organizes the early phase of latency (5½–8 years) around the predominant manifestations and intrapsychic consequences of the developmental line of *separation*. More specifically, it is the resurgence of separation, and its characteristic change, that delineates this early phase of latency from other developmental stages. "Early animal phobias are replaced by a new wave of separation anxiety and open castration fear is substituted by fear of death" (p. 281).

The developmental task of latency as stated by A. Freud (1965, p. 154) is the "step from the triangular oedipal situation into a community of peers." It is this "step from the triangular oedipal situation" that accounts for the characteristic upsurge of separation anxiety, and the predominance of the developmental line of separation during the early phase of latency. In the later stage of latency, the step "into a community of peers" will be manifested by an upsurge in the developmental line of individuation.

The child in early latency, in his attempts to separate from the triangular oedipal situation, and faced with regression to the oedipal conflict, retreats to a pregenital level as a defense against the pressure of his genital impulses. Reaction formation against these pregenital drives develops as the "first character changes in early latency" (Bornstein 1951, p. 280). Reaction formation gives the latency child his characteristic obsessive-compulsive features. The two most commonly observed reaction formations are *disgust,* a defense of the ego against oral sexual impulses (and often a reaction to anal impulses or stimuli as well), and *shame,* a defense against exhibitionism (Hinsie and Campbell 1970). The resultant strain between the consolidating superego and the id is experienced in the obsessional picture as heightened ambivalence.

We have stated that it is the normal progression of the developmental lines of separation and individuation through the subsequent phases of development that accounts for the "reverberations of the separation-individuation process throughout the life-cycle." We must also add that it is the specific manner in which the "intertwining of the developmental lines of separation and individuation" occurs during the normal separation-individuation process that accounts for the manner in which the "reverberations of the separation-individuation process" will occur throughout the life cycle. From the normal separation-individuation process (the first three years of life), we know that the affectual implications of the disillusion of the child with the dyadic (mother-child) configuration and the shared-omnipotence is an important implication of separation (Mahler 1966). The latency child's separation from the triadic oedipal situation produces similar consequences, and in many aspects parallels his initial separation from the original dyadic situation. In normal development there is a capitulation toward *individuation.* The reverberations of the "rapprochment crisis," his ambivalence and ambitendencies experienced during the normal separation-individuation process *will* condition the manifest way he progresses through latency and his separation from the triadic oedipal situation.

Bornstein uses this criterion to define the second subphase of latency. It is the heightening state of ambivalence that separates the two subphases. In the latency child this heightened state of ambivalence, that is, his intrapsychic state of disillusionment with the parental aspect of the triadic relationship (oedipal situation), and the resultant obsessional defenses is "experienced in the child's behavior by an alternation between obedience and rebellion" (Bornstein 1951, p. 280). The upsurge of the developmental line of individuation is manifested during this later subphase of latency by the stabilization of the superego and a balance between defense and instinct. The resolution of the child's ambivalence and the stabilization of his psychic structures is described by Bornstein as the result of "the child's increased self-sufficiency and a shift from the belief in the omnipotence of his parents to greater reliance on his peer group and on other adults" (1951, p. 281).

The child in the later subphase of latency, "stepping into a community of peers," makes friends at first with both sexes, but soon limits friendships to his own sex. Initially his friendships are tentative and do not serve the child's need to free himself from parental ties, nor to contribute significantly to psychic structure. By mid-latency, children love to form clubs which are usually maintained long enough to elect officers, and to make stringent rules before disbanding them. By late latency clubs such as Boy Scouts or Girl Scouts furnish organization by means of adult supervision, strict rules, prohibitions, and rewards. Less controlled play with peers permits expression both of sadism and defense against it (for example, "step on a crack, break your mother's back"). The peer group offers late latency boys and girls the chance to exchange secrets of sexual information, often incorrect, often quite sadistic with abhorrence and fear of forthcoming menses in late latency girls.

Although the tendency to regress and the resultant need to maintain rigid defenses are common to all developmental stages, the necessity of establishing equilibrium between impulses and still newly established defenses is of particular importance to the latency child. As a consequence, he reacts with intense pride to his accomplishments and with shame to his failures (Bernstein 1973).

It is in the later subphase of latency that the developmental consequences of latency can be seen in terms of sublimation, neutralization and related specific defenses. Anna Freud (1936) states: "Sublimation, i.e. the displacement of the instinctual aims in conformity with higher social values, presupposes the acceptance or at least the knowledge of such values, that is to say, presupposes the existence of the superego" (p. 52). With early latency the consolidation of the super-ego "the acceptance or at least the knowledge of (social) values" is enhanced by the increase in intellectual development and the socializing process of elementary school. The latency child devotes much time and energy to learning. The latency child's ability, as described by Piaget (Flavell 1963), to perform more complex concrete operations, structures his thinking and strengthens his secondary process.

Kris (1955) defines sublimation as the ability to set, define and achieve goals, that is goal-displacement. The transformation of energy necessary for this task is drawn from the interrelated aspect of noninstinctual energy and the maturational process; as well as from the neutralization of instinctual energy and its connection with the organization of action and problem solving.

Of all the specific related defenses of latency that deal with sublimation and the neutralization of instinctual energy, identification retains most clearly the object libidinal core (Peller 1956). The important identification process of the oedipal phase, with its resolution and increasing availability of neutralized energy, is enhanced by the "distancing" forms of identification the latency child establishes with his teacher and peer group. This disentanglement from the oedipal complex allows increasing neutralization of instinctual drives. In Freud's words: "in latency the Oedipus complex is receding and the defenses and sublimations take the upper hand in the child's development as a transformation of the dissolution of the Oedipus complex" (Freud 1924). Particularly in late latency the defenses of isolation, reaction formation and displacement create an aura of obsessive-compulsive behavior. These defenses serve well the function of balancing the intra-psychic forces of the id, ego and superego and permit sublimation to develop unimpeded. For, as Hartmann (1955) has noted, in sublimation the functions of the psychic structures are synergistic and not antagonistic.

One of the remaining consequences of latency which needs to be noted is the fact that the latency child is action oriented. As Kaplan (1965) notes, "libidinal aggressive gratification in latency is released normally through the perceptual-motor system. . . . in latency the transition is from the unrepressed, freer affect to motor expressions to the repressed, purposeful activities, such as the sedentary actions of writing and reading, which utilize the new capacity of fine muscle organization." Mahler (1949) has called our attention to the ease with which the motor system in the latency child can become involved in neurotic formation.

The transition from action orientation to "acting out," also assumes significance in latency. A. Freud (1968), commenting on acting out, states that neurotic latency children are "no different from adults, becom[ing] more inclined under analysis to act on impulse; equally, that impulsive latency children do so as part of their pathology and that this habitual behavior needs to be drawn into the transference before it becomes useful therapeutically" (pp. 105–106). In viewing the technique of child analysis from the aspect of acting out, she notes that latency as a developmental stage separates the age-appropriateness of prelatency children's normal need for action, from the significant and therapeutic importance we attach to acting out during and after latency.

The major characteristics of latency that shape technique in the analysis of the latency child include the following:

the instability of the superego (resulting in superego rigidity and reaction formation or in the swamping of the ego by the id)

the tendency to regress with a predilection for primary process expression

the need to maintain and guard newly acquired defenses (including sublimation) so that the analysis itself threatens the child by threatening these defenses

the idealization of action and the inability of the latency child to be inactive both in and outside of the analysis

The analyst must recognize the latency child's readiness to regress and to express himself in primary process terms, which threaten the child's new autonomy. He must understand the latency child's idealization of action, his driven tendency toward activity, and the implications that acting out holds from this developmental stage forward. The analyst must respect the child's resistances and his defenses. Bornstein (1951) has emphasized as the primary adaptation of technique in latency the "analysis of defense against drives." For "the latency child presents us with defense rather than impulse" (Becker 1974, p. 5).

INITIATING THE ANALYTIC PROCESS: INVOLVEMENT
WITH THE PARENTS

Harley (1974) notes that a "special condition distinguishing child from adult analysis is the child analyst's contact with the parents, through which information is obtained from sources other than the patient" (p. 605). Contact with the parents of the latency child provides a history and other information before the analysis gets under way, and serves to guarantee the continuity of the analysis.

The initial interviews with the parents serve multiple functions:

1. To obtain the history of the child. One hopes to elicit the immediate concerns which bring the parents to consult the analyst, as well as a relatively complete developmental and family history (this history will of course be supplemented and corrected during the course of the analysis). This information should help the child analyst evaluate what the child and his problems mean to the parents, and how they see themselves and their problems reflected in the child. We should attempt to formulate the genesis of the problem and its ramifications.

2. To estimate the parents' commitment to the analysis, and their ability to cooperate with the analytic process. This can be done only incompletely. Experience has made us distinguish between the parents' conscious commitment, and their unconscious ambivalence or hostility to the analysis. For this reason, we can not expect parents to understand their impulse to terminate the analysis when symptoms improve, or when regression occurs in the child, or when they feel threatened by the analysis or the analyst. It is the child analyst's task to guide and aid the parents during these periods.

3. To help the parents prepare the child for analysis. We should not assume that the latency child needs less preparation for analysis than a younger child. The parents must prepare the child, and it is the analyst's responsibility to discuss with them how to explain to the child his need for analysis in terms of the child's suffering or his symptoms. It is often advisable and necessary for the analyst to supply parents with words, ideas, and concepts to use in talking with the child, for example, "worry doctor," and to help them introduce analysis in a nonpunitive way, and to describe the analyst's function as realistically as possible. The child's first visit to the analyst should be discussed with the parents in the preparatory interviews. It is by no means unusual for the young latency child to be timid about entering the treatment room with a

stranger, and it is not necessarily a sign of mental health for a child to leave his parents without reluctance.

4. To explain to the parents such things as fees, missed appointments and vacations. It is important to convey to them the reasons for regularity of appointments. These issues are not superfluous, but an integral part of the analytic process, and in child analysis, remain primarily the responsibility of the parents.

Although a great deal can be accomplished in the initial interviews with the parents, in many instances parental resistances will inevitably occur. In this regard we differ with Weiss et al. (1973), for our experience has been that neither preparation of the parents nor their proper motivation can supersede their pathology. We have found that it is not always possible in initial interviews to "expand the parents' awareness of his analytic reality" (Weiss 1964). Resistances will arise in the parents in response to factors which may occur in the course of their child's analysis:

The parent's narcissism may be injured when the analyst is able to alleviate the child's suffering and provide relief which the parent could not do.

A parent with too great a need for closeness to his child may respond with anxiety, depression or anger when the child begins to be more independent.

A parent may respond negatively to an increase in the child's assertiveness, or to his acting out of analytic material in the home or school situation.

A parent may feel left out and hurt that his child and not *he* is receiving therapy.

However, it is important to note that resistances of the parents are not entirely responsible for the child's missed or late appointments. The child analyst must be aware of the likelihood that interferences are caused by the child in unconscious collusion with parental resistances, or quite independent of them, because of the child's own resistances.

No matter how well the parents are helped to prepare the child for treatment and for meeting the analyst, the analyst should find out during the child's early sessions how the child consciously or, more importantly, unconsciously, perceives the analysis and the analyst. *It is the work with the child which is the integral part of the analysis.* The initial interviews with the parents are extra-analytic. Although we attempt to "prepare" the parents before the child's analysis starts, and we may anticipate their excellent cooperation, we must recognize there is a great difference between their manifest declaration of cooperation and unconscious resistance.

The main reason for seeing parents once the analysis is underway is to keep the analysis going. Harley (1974) feels that, "with the exception of the very young pre-latency child, the child can provide the necessary material for the analysis: a stronger reason for contact with the parents is the child's need to feel that his parents are in accord with the analysis. To exclude them from the treatment would be tantamount to a neglect of the child's developmental needs" (p. 605). We consider the *informative alliance* (with the parents) necessary for the latency child's analysis; however, we regard material from this informative alliance as secondary to the child's own material.

THE ANALYTIC PROCESS: THE OPENING PHASE

The opening phase of the analysis includes the period during which the child is introduced to the *analytic process;* it extends over the time during which the child joins the analyst in the *therapeutic alliance.*

In early sessions, as the child becomes familiar with the analyst, it is helpful to find out why the child thinks he has been sent for analysis. In addition to understanding the child's view of the analysis and the analyst, early sessions offer a unique opportunity to explore related fantasies which are at this time relatively undefended.

As noted above, in spite of thorough and well-intentioned preparation, in the early part of the analysis many children tend to see their analysis as punishment. At this time the child has no reason to trust the analyst, nor does he have the experience to enable him to anticipate that he will feel better as the outcome of treatment.

As with patients of any age, the opening phase in the analysis of the latency child serves to help him become an analysand. The use of defense analysis permits the analyst, without using educational methods or intellectualization, to convey to the patient an understanding of what the analysis is, and what the process requires of him and the analyst. Gradually the patient will come to "work" within the context of the analytic process.

Unless the child is extremely troubled, very anxious, or overly aggressive, it is best if the analyst does not intrude during the early sessions, but follows the child's leads. The child analyst will reveal his role as he gradually involves himself with his patient. The analyst's position should be neither one of passivity nor overactivity, but should maintain the delicate balance between activity and passivity that allows the child to direct and lead the analysis.

As child analysis has become more sophisticated, and child analysts better experienced, their equipment has become simpler, their toys fewer. Increased reliance on the analytic process is reflected even in the choice of office furniture. Many child analysts find that an office table used for adults is quite satisfactory to their child patients. The complicated paraphernalia earlier used in child analysis may be reduced to crayons, pencil and paper, a ball, a deck of cards and plasticene. The latency child will reveal his fantasies quite well using the things around the office—scotch tape, paper clips, tissues, etc. Latency children often use the office telephone, typewriter, dictaphone, or calculators to obtain a needed distance while they express their conflicts. An abundance of toys may serve to excite, distract and, indeed, overwhelm a child. The choice of toys is also important. Early in our child analytic experience, we eliminated cumbersome, time-consuming games since they afforded a too-ready opportunity for resistance.

The material of the early hours of a child's analysis has been compared to the first dream of the adult in analysis. There is much richness, for the child is quite naive and unguarded. This early openness is often followed by a period of increased tension when the child may become guarded, somewhat resistant, and complain that the analyst "makes a big deal of what I say." To minimize resistance it is important to engage the child in the analysis so that he feels he is a responsible part of it, and that he and the analyst are partners in the analytic endeavor.

We repeat that the aim of the opening phase should be the formation of the therapeutic alliance, a milestone which may be recognized in the child's grudging admission that he "knows what is going on." Frequently he reveals his involvement with the analysis by saying "You (the analyst) would probably say this, so I may as well say it first." When the child's own insights begin to contribute to the analytic work we feel that "the child is *in* analysis." Now the child's productions, carefully represented to him by the analyst, begin to show the impact of the integrating functions of his ego (A. Freud 1962). At the same time the analyst's demeanor—his seriousness of purpose (with a light touch), his understanding of the child and the child's problems, his sharing this understanding with the child—are the analyst's contribution to the developing therapeutic alliance.

MAINTAINING THE ANALYTIC PROCESS

The therapeutic alliance will support the analytic process, and enable the child to tolerate any dystonicity stirred up by the analysis. Our principles of technique reflect the belief in the basis of the therapeutic alliance—the "dialogue" between analyst and child—which becomes the work of analysis.

As the analysis of the latency child proceeds, play becomes less and less important as a means of communication, often persisting as the background music to an increasing verbal dialogue. The importance of establishing verbal expression can not be overemphasized. Katan (1961) has noted that verbalization of the content of the inner world makes reality testing possible (Goldblatt 1973). In latency, a phase of transition from primary process to secondary process ("verbalization" in the context used by Katan) becomes a significant aid in stabilizing the new structure formation.

The following case (Matt) illustrates the progression from play to verbalization in the analysis of a latency-age boy.

Matt came to analysis at age eight because of a very severe learning disorder, and serious behavior problems. He was the only child of a rather cold and controlling mother and an elderly father. They imposed rigid standards of behavior on him and at the same time treated him as if he were much younger than his actual age.

Early in analysis, Matt insisted on playing cards, which he did rather badly—cheating, changing the rules, and seeking every advantage. In spite of these attempts, he became so confused that he would often lose anyway. When I attempted to comment on his behavior, I would be ordered to "shut up and deal."

In these early months of analysis, Matt's use of card games revealed:

1. His need to control the analysis out of fear of what I might discover.

2. His "forgetting of rules" resulting from his ego's inability to handle impulses. This made him "forget" even when he had a great need to win. At times during the early phases of the analysis, failure of his defenses resulted in temper outbursts, much more frightening (to him) breakthroughs of his id impulses than his inability to play the card game honestly.

3. The alternation between effectiveness and ineptness.

4. His intolerance of frustration.

During the early months, when appropriate to do so, I expressed all of the above mentioned aspects of his problems which the card games were revealing. Matt's usual response was, "It is just a game. Don't make anything out of it." He listened to my words, although it was obvious that he did not always like them. The continuing card games began to be interspersed with hide-and-seek games, the most significant characteristic of which was the fact that Matt peered through his widely spread fingers.

Later, Matt played Concentration and demonstrated an amazing ability to remember what cards he had turned up. When I commented on this, Matt listened with interest, and added that he remembered the underneath side of the cards better than I did.

Matt continued to play cards with pleasure, but with less imperativeness. He also played a "peeking" game with a great deal of excitement, as once more his id erupted. I stopped him from running around while commenting on his increased excitement. I reviewed with him the fact that he knew and remembered what he saw on the underneath side of the cards, that he wanted me to know about the peeking which excited and worried him, and connected this with the learning problem which was one of the reasons he came to analysis.

Matt seemed embarrassed by this, and told me that his cousins had visited last Sunday. I waited, and Matt asked shyly, "Do any of your other patients play 'naked'?" Matt could not go on verbally, and started to play Concentration. I summarized the session, saying that he felt pleased when he remembered the cards "underneath," but he felt naughty and bad after playing 'naked' when he and his cousins looked at each other. Matt said that his cousins made him angry because they teased him and called him a baby because he still believed in Santa Claus, the Easter Bunny, and the Tooth Fairy. This material led to a long discussion about what Matt really knew but pretended not to know because he felt his parents did not want him to know so many things —from the fact that there was no Santa Claus to the differences between the sexes.

Although for a long time card games remained "background music" to our verbal exchanges, more and more verbal communications replaced the earlier insistence on play.

The "dialogue" of child analysis can be effected by (1) running comments, (2) confrontation, and (3) interpretations.

Running Comments are a summing up procedure—repeating aloud what the patient has said (through his word, or actions, or what he does not do or say) in an effort to familiarize the patient and the analyst with his productions. This lays the groundwork for later confrontations or interpretations by conveying to the patient an awareness that there is a significance to his speech and actions, without yet interpreting them. The use of running comments makes the patient accustomed to the analyst's role from the start; it also serves the purpose of enabling the analyst to enter into the play or fantasy of the child while remaining the observant therapist, not the playmate. Running comments provide the chance to acquaint the patient with the analytic process, and gives the analyst more knowledge of the configuration of the material.

Confrontations are closely related to running comments. In a confrontation one uses not only immediate material, but draws on previous material and observations. There is now an opportunity to interject more of the analyst's own ego functions. For example, the analyst may show wonderment, or puzzlement, or comment on inconsistencies, or point out how things "hang together." By using his own reality testing, the analyst begins to make the patient aware that a defense is being used. Making the patient aware of the existence of a defense is a significant step towards the eventual interpretation of it. In running comments the analyst verbalizes what he sees so the patient can see it too. In confrontations the analyst acquaints the patient with patterns and configurations which are characteristic of his material and, very likely, of himself. The analyst and child patient have to "dig" deeper in confrontations, and begin the process of integration. The analyst must make the connections necessary to allow further understanding.

Interpretations. By the time an interpretation is made the patient should be prepared for it since he has been acquainted with the concept of defense through a critical awareness that more than one meaning may exist for his material. The patient is now ready to proceed to the next step—to know the purpose of the defense, and what is being defended against. To judge when the patient is ready for the interpretation, the analyst must be guided by the child's material, on the basis of the affectual content of the material as well as the ideational content. The patient is now conversant with the analytic process. He is part of the process, because the analyst has shared his knowledge with the patient. On an ego level, it is no longer necessary for the patient to maintain the pathological defense. The analysis has made it possible for the patient to face previously defended against unconscious material. This is the major difference between confrontation and interpretation. By repeatedly, and with the child's growing participation, communicating to the child the configurations the analysis discloses, the child's observing ego is strengthened in alliance with the analyst. Interpretation puts the pathological configuration into the position of being less ego-syntonic and less necessary for the already stronger ego.

TYPICAL DEFENSES AND THEIR ANALYSIS

The following excerpts from the analysis of Bonnie and Michael are presented to illustrate typical defenses used by latency aged children in analysis, and to illustrate the concepts of *running comments, confrontations,* and *interpretations.* Bonnie is representative of the early latency age child; *Michael* of the older latency child.

Bonnie, seven years old, had come to analysis because of severe separation problems, obsessive-compulsive symptoms, and intense fear of body damage. After several months during which separation problems were most important, the material of the analysis centered on the fear that her wild and uncontrolled excitement would result in injury and death.

Bonnie came in for her hour under great pressure. She was very eager to play, and avoided speaking to me except to say hello in a too-cheerful fashion. She played with the dollhouse toys, and made them go through wild and unpredictable antics, laughing all the time. There was no red thread to the play except for the unpredictability and her laughter.

My *running comments* focused on the unpredictability of her play and her inappropriate affect. I said, "The mother doll starts to cook and then does gymnastics. The children look at TV and suddenly start to run around. And the father begins to mow the lawn and stops. They all do unexpected, puzzling things. You look worried but you laugh."

Bonnie continued laughing, but more hollowly, and she settled down somewhat. The doll play continued, but now there was a theme. After the dolls played in an excited and erotic manner, they became ill and were taken to the hospital to be operated on. Once more Bonnie laughed frantically.

I *confronted* Bonnie with her attempt to hide her worries from herself and from me by laughing them off, adding that they must be big worries to cause so much laughing.

Bonnie became more pensive and serious and continued with the game of hospitalizing the dolls. The following hour, Bonnie said as she entered, "My uncle had his operation. He's okay now." In response to my questions, Bonnie said that the day before her uncle had become very sick after playing with her brothers and her, and had to be rushed to the hospital. "It was so sudden after all the fun. Everyone at home acted mean and worried. I couldn't go with them to the hospital because I had to come here. I don't want to talk any more about it, so shut up." Bonnie started to be silly and giggly once more. I interrupted, saying, "Now I understand what happened yesterday. You were so worried about your uncle's sudden illness, you couldn't even talk to me about it." I *confronted* her with the defensive denial she had used, and added that her attempt to "laugh her worries away" had not worked. I said that something about it bothered her very, very much. Bonnie said that she didn't know what was wrong with him. She showed me that he had clutched his genitals with sudden pain. She then went to the light switch and began turning the light on and off. Previously we had spoken about Bonnie's attempt to control masturbation by turning the switch on and off.

I finally *interpreted* to her that her uncle's sudden illness and hospitalization after rather active play, had reminded her of her worries that wild play and touching her bottom might make her sick, and that she had been so very worried that she tried to laugh it off.

Bonnie ended the session expressing her fear that operations, blood, and the separation that hospitalization entailed, were all punishment for being bad.

Michael, age nine, came to analysis because of deep depressions, marked temper outbursts in school and at home, poor school achievement in spite of his high intelligence, and severe stuttering. He was the eldest of six children, all of whom he detested and browbeat. During the early phase of analysis Michael dealt with his fear of instinct liberation by the analyst—that it would unleash badness such as no one had ever seen before. As he developed a positive, trusting, relationship with the analyst, he began to try to see other patients, and ridiculed to the analyst a disturbed boy he encountered on leaving. Michael told the analyst that it must be awful to have to see such a "retard," and he wondered whether such patients were given less time than he.

Michael had always expressed his love for animals, and now proclaimed that there should be a "be kind to animals week." He told me of the ugly black dog he had picked up, starving and cold, during the winter. While telling me this, he played a game with toy soldiers, and engaged them in an aggressive, erotic play in which it was impossible to distinguish winners from losers. All ended in a chaotic heap. As he played the wild, hostile game, and spoke tenderly of his dog, I *commented* on the differences in his affect—the warmth toward the dog, and the excitement and enmity expressed in the game which ended up with all of the soldiers dead. Michael continued to avow his concern about animals with increasing fervor, and stammered once more (a problem which had not been present for about ten months). In his play Michael tested limits. He set up the soldiers near lamps, and other breakable furniture that he knew were off limits. I *confronted* Michael with his need to have me help him with controls by saying that it seemed he felt he couldn't stop himself and wanted me to stop him.

Michael's soldier play now changed. Instead of two sets of nameless enemies the soldiers became factions in his own family. Finally, Michael was pitted against his five younger siblings. The "Michael" toy was bigger, stronger, trickier, and fiercer than the five sibling toys together. His hostility to his siblings in play was paramount. I commented on his wild play and how uncomfortable it seemed to make him. Michael had felt similarly when he had told me how he beat up his brother, James, tricked him, and either stole his brother's allowance or schemed to get it from him.

Interpretation of Michael's reaction formation followed rather soon. He told me of his newest club, a "Be Kind to Animals Club" of which he was president and treasurer. Every member was a ten-year-old boy, all had pets, and, interestingly, all had pesky younger siblings. No younger siblings were allowed to join the club. After a few weeks, Michael (as treasurer) decided to permit younger siblings to join the club and pay dues, but their participation was severely limitated.

Michael began to be aware of the hostility of his friends to *their* siblings. He told me how mean Jed was to his seven-year-old brother, David, and how cruel Marvin was to little Harry. We spent a lot of time approaching Michael's own anger through discussing the anger of his alter egos, his best friends. By focussing on his friends' problems with anger we were able to get to the reasons they were so uncomfortable with their siblings—they were so stupid, so indulged, they got away with so much, etc. Michael said to me, "I guess you're going to say I feel that way about the kids in my family." After a pause he said, "I do sometimes, but I'd never be that mean to them." I pointed out to Michael that, nevertheless, he was very afraid that he might be as mean to them as his friends in the "Be Kind to Animals Club" were to their younger siblings. Michael said "I guess we should have called it 'Be Kind to Little Brats Club,' instead of 'Animals.' Following up on this, I interpreted that people may control their frightening impulses by bending over backwards to do the opposite. Michael must be very worried about wanting to be mean to animals or "brats" and that he tried to hide from himself and me how he really felt. Now Michael was able to face his fury with his siblings for being born, and handle his fears of starvation and emotional deprivation based on the certainty that he would never again get the emotional supplies he needed. He proceeded to the real object of his anger, his beloved mother, who had cheated him by having so many kids.

TRANSFERENCE

As with the adult patient, the child patient transfers to his analyst both positive and negative concepts and emotions. Transference manifestations are included in the child's total relationship to the analyst. The total relationship to the analyst includes use by the child of the analyst—as a new object, as an object of libidinal and aggressive transference, and as an object for externalization (A. Freud 1965). (For a discussion of the difference between transference and externalization see W. Brodey 1965.)

There is a continuing discussion among child analysts about transference neurosis. Important papers by Harley (1967, 1971) and Fraiberg (1964) report analyses of children in which a full-blown transference neurosis existed for at least part of the child's analysis. Fraiberg (1966) felt that the term *transference neurosis* "should apply to repressed conflicts revived in the course of the analysis, transferred to the person of the analyst and worked through in the analytic situation" (p. 536). Harley (1971) would restrict the use of the term to "a neurotic symptom formation arising from repressed conflict, [which] is activated by the analytic situation and centered around the analyst" (p. 39). However, transference in both adult and child analysis is commonly described in broader terms: "cognitive, affective and behavior manifestations directed towards the analyst, which express infantile relationships without developing a more cohesive structure and expression in the form of a symptom neurosis centering around the analyst" (Bernstein 1975, p. 203).

The intrapsychic structure of the neurotic latency child should permit the possibility of a transference neurosis. Brody (1961) states that "the development of a transference neurosis at any age begins to become possible at the point where the patient identifies with the analyst and his purposes. After that, it depends not only on maturational factors but on the patient's readiness to seek gratification from objects other than the original infantile ones, and in the degree of abstinence that the analyst can maintain and still keep the patient in at least a minimally positive analytic relationship" (p. 272). Full transference neuroses have been reported in child analytic cases for periods of the analysis (Fraiberg 1951, Harley 1967). Anna Freud (1965) has recently modified her view that a transference reaction in child analysis does not develop into a complete transference neurosis.

Most child analysts with whom we have communicated report that they have seen transient transference neuroses in latency children which are less sustained than in adolescents or adults. A part of the revived conflicts in the latency child is likely to be directed to the original love object, the parents. For example:

Steven, nine and a half years of age, was the eldest of five children and had been in analysis since eight years of age because of a severe learning problem and marked hostility toward his mother. He insisted that he wanted to go to Boy Scout Camp for two weeks—a decision with which his harrassed parents were happy to comply. When his parents went to fetch him home after his stay at camp Steven seemed surprised to see his mother. He then became increasingly angry with her and complained that she had not packed one essential possession, a blue flashlight. His mother had, in fact, packed his new red flashlight. She remonstrated that she had done so, but his anger did not abate.

On his visit to the analyst Steven was still angry as he repeated his complaint—no blue flashlight. The analyst spoke to him about the color and commented that he was angry because he didn't have the *blue* flashlight, and felt as if his mother had denied him something that would have made him feel much better.

The patient glowered at the analyst and said, "You're not helping me either." The analyst commented, "So it wasn't bad enough to go away from home and from your analyst; missing a blue flashlight made it worse."

The patient picked up the word *miss.* He said, "Of course I missed the flashlight because she promised it to me and I didn't get it, ever."

The analyst asked *when* that had happened. The patient said, "She was supposed to get me a blue flashlight and instead she went away for two weeks." The analyst said, "Two weeks, just the amount of time you were away at camp." Steven said, "But I was at my grandmother's house because Sandra (his sister, born when he was three years old) was born. And she didn't give it to me and she didn't come for me afterwards."

It was later verified by his parents that when Steven was three his mother had indeed promised him a blue flashlight, and was about to purchase it when active labor started. Instead of being separated from Steven for four or five days, as she had anticipated, she had to be in the hospital for two weeks. During this time a sad Steven remained with his grandmother. Contrary to the original plan, Steven's mother was unable to accompany her husband when he fetched Steven after her return home.

When the conflict was activated by the analysis, Steven reexperienced anger and disappointment. Although he expressed anger toward his analyst about the camp experience, and said that she hadn't helped him either, the revived fury was expressed toward his mother, as Steven later said, "in living color."

For the latency aged child to tolerate tensions which an analysis stirs up, he must be in an at least moderately positive transference. The achievement of the positive transference is aided by the child's growing awareness that his anxiety has diminished because of the analysis, as well as by the analyst's handling of painful situations with empathy and delicacy.

Conversely, the child cannot tolerate prolonged negative transference. When it occurs, as inevitably it must, it is important to analyze the negative transference as soon as possible. If negative transference is sustained, and the basis for it not analyzed, the child may refuse outright to come to his analytic sessions, or he may provide his parents with myriad excuses to skip sessions. At times of negative transference, the parents' cooperation in getting the child to the analysis is of great importance.

COUNTERTRANSFERENCE

Our experience reveals that the practice of child analysis may set the stage for countertransference reactions which are quite specific to the child analytic situation. The involvement of the parents creates characteristic stresses in the child analyst which we feel to be most important in stirring up countertransference reactions. Other factors include the analyst's rescue fantasies, his continuing identification with the authority of his own analyst or of his parents, the revival of traumata from his own childhood by the child analytic experience, his reactions to the patient's aggression and seduction, and his guilt feeling because he is very occupied with child patients when he has young children of his own.

We are in general agreement with the restricted sense of the term *countertransference,* by which it is used to refer only to those instances in which "the child analyst uses his child patient as a transference object" (Maenchen 1970, p. 194). However, there is considerable value in regarding countertransference in a broader sense to include the child analyst's reaction to the parents, and to some elements characteristic of the child analysis situation. Most young child analysts experience some of these reactions, if only transiently. These reactions are usually modified, and worked through in the process of the candidate's training in child analysis. Serious handicaps which cause unyielding countertransference reactions militate against one's becoming a capable child analyst (Kramer 1970).

Kohrman and his associates (1971) stress the intensity of countertransference reactions in child analysis, and the frequency with which they occur. They feel that the analyst's unacceptable sexual or aggressive feelings towards his child patient increase tension in the analyst, possibly more tension than would be stirred by such reactions in the analysis of adults.

A factor which helps the child analysis candidate with his approach to the patient's parents, and with his counterreaction to the child's material, is his own increased experience in child analysis. As he develops the conviction that child analysis is the best available treatment where indicated, and therefore, feels that he is offering the parents the ideal treatment for their child, his discomfort and defensiveness with the parents diminishes and ultimately disappears.

Tension caused by conflict over authority, or fear of the parents' jealousy, or by the analyst's need to prove that he is better than the child's own parents, may make the child analyst misunderstand the parents' needs. By misreading their cues, he may contribute to a crisis which threatens the analysis.

Solomon H., nine years old and adopted, was in analysis with Dr. C., a candidate in child analysis. Solomon had serious behavior problems and refused to adhere to any diet for his uncontrollable diabetes. He administered insulin to himself.

Mrs. H. was angry when she learned (from an outsider) that Dr. C. had not yet graduated from the child analytic program. Dr. C. was uneasy with Mrs. H., angry at her, and afraid of her hostility. At my suggestion (S.K.) he asked her to come in for an interview.

After some preliminary skirmishes, Mrs. H. began to cry about her failures in raising Solomon, who she considered a "sacred trust to her." She thought that as an adoptive mother she was similar to the Egyptian maiden who rescued Moses from the bullrushes, and raised the future "King of the Jews." Solomon, adopted at eight days, was given the name of a Jewish King by the H.'s. His need for analysis, as well as his diabetes, proved to her that she was inadequate. Her dismay over the fact that the analyst was still a candidate was a projection of her own poor self-concept. As well, this was a blow to her determination to obtain the best for Solomon, often at sacrifice to herself.

This meeting cleared the air between Mrs. H. and Dr. C. It provided Dr. C. with an understanding of Mrs. H. and made a marked change in Dr. C.'s attitude toward, and ability to cope with, Mrs. H.'s interferences.

TERMINATION

In the presence of a true transference neurosis, termination encompasses the analysis of the transference. In latency child analysis, without the consistent appearance of true transference neurosis, issues around transference become less clearly defined. We think of termination in child analysis in terms of "the removing of obstacles in the path of normal development" (Maenchen 1970, p. 195).

Most child analysts would agree that an analysis is terminated when the neurotic conflict that interferes with functioning and development is resolved (Bernstein 1975). It is the resolution of the internalized conflict, described by Mahler (1945), that permits the child's ego to resume its developmental progress. As such, careful developmental evaluation and appraisal of the child's functioning, the stability of structural changes, and the child's ability to progress become important considerations relating to termination.

The criteria as to when to terminate a child's analysis will depend on treatment goals. E. Ticho (1975), using a developmental approach to termination, states that there are life goals and termination goals. Failure to make this distinction "can lead to perfectionistic expectations and to prolongation of analysis" (p. 167). This concept is a critical issue in child analysis where an intermittent analysis frequently becomes the prudent choice. Mahler (1974) notes that "after a good piece of analytic work has been accomplished, it is best to judge the crossroads" (p. 610). If by the analysis we have secured the best possible position for the ego, we should consider interrupting the analysis—"to let the child go"—for too prolonged analysis may interfere with the synthetic function of the ego. Maenchen (1970) says "further analysis [prolonged analysis], it is believed, might drain the ego of the energies needed for mastery [outside of analysis], *especially during latency*" (p. 195, italics ours). The decision to terminate must be based on the resolution of internal conflicts, and not on the child's wish to avoid analyzing painful conflicts. Nor should termination be based on symptomatic improvement alone.

In the analysis of some children we should consider the possibility of *intermittent analysis,* or the similar concept of "re-entry" (Maenchen 1970, p. 196). In child analysis "the door to the analyst's office remains relatively open" after termination. It is not unusual for a child to "re-enter" analysis in a later stage of development. He may now be ready to face a new developmental challenge or to handle conflicts which previously he could not.

There is also a distinction between analytic termination and termination which results from nonanalytic circumstances. At times, the painful decision to terminate a child's analysis is beyond the control of the analyst, child, or parents, (for example, when the family must move). At such times it is necessary to help the child with the enforced termination, assess the analytic work that has been completed, and delineate the unresolved conflicts.

Among the many issues that appear during the terminal phase of analysis are those which deal with loss and separation. The relative emergence of the analyst as a real object rather than a transference object takes place, and a possible exacerbation of symptoms. Most of these issues will be handled around the therapeutic alliance and its resolution. Novick (1970) reminds us that despite the additional progressive forces present in the treatment alliance during termination, it does not remain "stable nor autonomous but require[s] technical intervention for its re-establishment" (p. 252). His comments are directed toward resistances common to termination. Resistances and issues revolving around the terminal phase will take on regressive characteristics, but will be neither unfamiliar nor unique. Instead they repeat analytic material already uncovered or dealt with in previous phases. Therefore, the technical interventions required in the terminal phase will be found in the admonition to continue to analyze to the very end.

REFERENCES

Becker, T.E. (1974). On latency. *Psychoanalytic Study of the Child* 29:3–11; New Haven: Yale University Press.

Bernstein, I. (1973). Discussion of "The opening phase, treatment of an adopted child with symptoms of encopresis" by E. Daunton; Panel: the opening phase in the analysis of the pre-latency child. *Papers of The Meetings of The Association for Child Psychoanalysis (April, 1973),* 1975.

––––––– (1975). On the technique of child and adolescent analysis. *Journal of the American Psychoanalytic Association* 23:190–232.

Bornstein, B. (1949). The analysis of a phobic child: some problems of theory and technique in child analysis *Psychoanalytic Study of the Child* 3/4:181–226.

––––––– (1951). On latency. *Psychoanalytic Study of the Child* 6:279–285.

Brodey, W. (1965). On the dynamics of narcissism, 1. externalization and early ego development. *Psychoanalytic Study of the Child* 20:-165–193.

Brody, S. (1974). Contributions to child analysis. *Psychoanalytic Study of the Child* 29:13–20.

––––––– (1961). Some aspects of transference resistance in prepuberty. *Psychoanalytic Study of the Child* 16:251–274.

Flavell, J.H. (1963). *The Developmental Psychology of Jean Piaget.* New York: Van Nostrand Reinhold.

Fraiberg, S. (1951). Clinical notes on the nature of transference in child analysis. *Psychoanalytic Study of the Child* 6:286–306.

––––––– (1964). Panel discussion: child analysis at different developmental stages, G. Abbate, reporter. *Journal of the American Psychoanalytic Association* 12:135–150 (p. 143).

_____ (1966). Transference in child analysis. Reported in: Panel: Problems of transference in child analysis, H. Van Dam, reporter. *Journal of the American Psychoanalytic Association* 14:528–537.

_____ (1967). The analysis of an eight-year-old girl with epilepsy. In *The Child Analyst at Work,* ed. E. Geleerd, pp. 229–287. New York: International Universities Press.

Freud, A. (1926). Introduction to the technique of child analysis. *Nervous and Mental Disease* Monograph Series, No. 48, 1929.

_____ (1936). The ego and the mechanism of defense. *The Writings of Anna Freud* 2. New York: International Universities Press.

_____ (1945). Indications for child analysis. *The Writings of Anna Freud* 4:3–38. New York: International Universities Press.

_____ (1962). Assessment of childhood disturbances. *Psychoanalytic Study of the Child* 17:149–158.

_____ (1965). Normality and pathology in childhood. *The Writings of Anna Freud* 6. New York: International Universities Press.

_____ (1966). A short history of child analysis. *Psychoanalytic Study of the Child* 21:7–14.

_____ (1968). Acting out. *The Writings of Anna Freud* 7:94–109. New York: International Universities Press.

Freud, S. (1896). Letter No. 46. In *The Origins of Psychoanalysis.* New York: Basic Books, 1954.

_____ (1905). Three contributions to the theory of sex. In *The Basic Writings of Sigmund Freud.* New York: Random House, 1938.

_____ (1923). *The Ego and the Id.* London: Hogarth Press and the Institute of Psychoanalysis, 1927.

_____ (1924). The dissolution of the Oedipus complex. *Standard Edition* 19:173–179.

Goldblatt, M. (1972). Psychoanalysis of the schoolchild. In *Handbook of Child Psychoanalysis,* ed. B. Wolman, pp. 253–296. New York: Van Nostrand Reinhold.

Harley, M. (1967). Transference developments in a five year old child. In *The Child Analyst at Work,* ed. E. Geleerd, pp. 115–141. New York: International Universities Press.

_____ (1971). The current status of transference neurosis in children. *Journal of the American Psychoanalytic Association* 19:26–40.

_____ (1974). Some comparison of adult analysis with child analysis. Reported in Panel: a comparison between adult and child analysts,

C. Feigelson, reporter. *Journal of the American Psychoanalytic Association* 22:603–611.

Hartmann, H. (1939). Ego psychology and the problem of adaptation. In *Organization and Pathology of Thought,* ed. D. Rapaport, pp. 362–396. New York: Columbia University Press, 1951.

———— (1955). Notes on the theory of sublimation. *Psychoanalytic Study of the Child* 10:9–29.

Hinsie, L., and Campbell R. (1970). *Psychiatric Dictionary.* 4th ed. London: Oxford University Press.

Hug-Hellmuth, H. (1921). On the technique of child analysis. *International Journal of Psycho-Analysis* 2:287–305.

Katan, A. (1961). Some thoughts about the role of verbalization in early childhood. *Psychoanalytic Study of the Child* 16:184–188.

Kaplan, E.B. (1965). Reflections regarding psychomotor activities during the latency period. *Psychoanalytic Study of the Child* 20:220–238.

Kohrman, R. et al. (1971). Technique of child analysis: problems of countertransference. *International Journal of Psycho-Analysis* 52: 487–497.

Kramer, S. (1960). Running comments, confrontation and interpretation. Paper presented at The Philadelphia Psychoanalytic Institute, Child Analysis Study Group.

———— (1970). Countertransference. Paper presented at The Philadelphia Psychoanalytic Society, Scientific Session, September 16, 1970.

Kris, E. (1955). Neutralization and sublimation: observations in young children. *Psychoanalytic Study of the Child* 10:30–46.

Maenchen, A. (1970). On the technique of child analysis in relation to stages of development. *Psychoanalytic Study of the Child* 25:175–208.

Mahler, M.S. (1945). Child analysis. In *Modern Trends in Child Psychiatry,* ed. N.D.C. Lewis and B.L. Pacella, pp. 265–289. New York: International Universities Press.

———— (1949). A psychoanalytic evaluation of tics: a sign and a symptom in psychopathology of childhood (symptomatic tic and tic syndrome). *Psychoanalytic Study of the Child* 3/4:279–310.

———— (1966). Notes on the development of basic moods: the depressive affect. In *Psychoanalysis—A General Psychology: Essays in Honor of Heinz Hartmann,* ed. R. Lowenstein, L. Newman, M. Schur, and A. Solnit, pp. 152–168. New York: International Universities Press.

———— (1972). On the first three subphases of the separation-individuation process. *International Journal of Psycho-Analysis* 53:333–338.

———— (1974). Panel discussion: a comparison between adult and child analysis, C. Feigelson, reporter. *Journal of the American Psychoanalytic Association* 22:603–611.

————, and Furer, M. (1963). Certain aspects of the separation-individuation phase. *Psychoanalytic Quarterly* 32:1–14.

————, and LaPerriere, K. (1965). Mother-child interaction during separation-individuation. *Psychoanalytic Quarterly* 34:483–498.

————, Pine, F., and Bergman, A. (1975). *The Psychological Birth of the Human Infant: Symbiosis and Individuation.* New York: Basic Books.

Novick, J. (1970). The vicissitudes of the "working alliance" in the analysis of a latency girl. *Psychoanalytic Study of the Child* 25: 231–235.

Peller, L. (1956). The school's role in promoting sublimation. *Psychoanalytic Study of the Child* 11:437–449.

Ticho, E. (1975). Panel: termination: problems and technique, W.S. Robbins, (reporter.) *Journal of the American Psychoanalytic Association* 23:166–176.

Weil, A. P. (1956). Some evidences of deviational development in infancy and early childhood. *Psychoanalytic Study of the Child* 11: 292–299.

———— (1973). Ego strengthening prior to analysis. *Psychoanalytic Study of the Child* 28:287–301.

Weiss, S. (1964). Parameters in child analysis. *Journal of the American Psychoanalytic Association* 12:587–599.

———— et al. (1973). Panel: the opening phase in the analysis of the pre-latency child, S. Weiss, reporter. *Papers of the Meetings of the Association for Child Psychoanalysis (April 1973),* 1975.

Chapter 8

THE PSYCHOANALYTIC TREATMENT OF

PREADOLESCENTS

Herbert Wieder, M.D.

While charting the developmental phases from early childhood through adolescence, psychoanalysts have applied their observations and theoretical conclusions towards adapting psychoanalytic technique to each phase (Maenchen 1970). These adaptations have been most successful for prelatency and latency children, and for adolescents over fifteen or sixteen years of age. However, controversy over therapeutic technique with preadolescents still prevails.

Some analysts do not believe that preadolescents can engage in an analytic alliance. Others maintain that adapting analytic technique to the psychological requirements of these patients permits an alliance. Still others insist that only piecemeal, discontinuous periods of work are possible. Actually, all of these opinions are justifiable, and characterize different periods in treatment. However, even the most optimistic analysts are cautious. As Geleerd (1957) aptly stated: "All analysts will agree that the treatment of the late latency and the early, almost preadolescent child, is one of the hardest tasks to undertake" (p. 263).

DEFINITION OF PREADOLESCENCE

We believe that preadolescence is best defined as the transitional, developmental stage between late latency and early adolescence. It holds an ambiguous relationship to other developmental phases. Some analysts consider preadolescence the final period of latency. Sarnoff (1976), for example, discusses preadolescence in his book on latency. Others maintain it is an early subphase of adolescence (Bornstein 1951, Blos 1958, Harley 1970, A. Freud 1958). To place preadolescence in proper relation to these other phases, and to draw its boundaries, a few remarks about latency and adolescence are in order.

Latency, starting at about five or six years of age, eventuates from the child's relative mastery of the oedipal conflict and the development of the superego. To a great extent, the sexual and aggressive drives become neutralized and controlled by defensive-adaptive mechanisms, for example, sublimation, isolation, reaction formation, and identification. Consequently, the child is able to direct his energies into socializing and intellectual functions, and thereby expands the ego's domain (for the details of this process, see chapter 7). The strict and severe superego controls characteristic of the first or early subphase of latency (Bornstein 1951) are fragile and unstable. Interruptions of the overt calm occur, as relatively undisguised id derivatives erupt or escape defense and dominate the behavioral picture for periods of time.

The later phase of latency, approximately from eight to ten years of age, is the period of most harmony between the psychic systems, and the peak of the latency child's defensive force. The stability of defense, however, will waver under the impact of the drive increment that characterizes the onset of preadolescence.

At about the age of ten, an increase in hormonal levels has a crucial influence on the child's physical and psychological state. The period in which these physical changes appear has been labelled prepuberty, while the related psychological state is called preadolescence. Although prepuberty and preadolescence are clearly interrelated, to conceive of preadolescence as simply a psychological response to hormonal changes is misleading.

Problems in the definition of preadolescence are similar to those regarding adolescence. Although now generally accepted as a psychological state of change, adolescence at times had been equated and synonymous with puberty, a physical state of change. Dated by the physical signs of the first ejaculation in boys, and menstruation in girls, the appearance of puberty traditionally signified the attainment of biological maturity. Actual, observable changes in growth, body configuration, physiology, and endocrine effects are visible and measurable long before ejaculation or menarche appear (Wilkins 1965). Additionally, refinements of observation have revealed that first menstruations generally are anovulatory, and first ejaculations aspermic. Therefore, even if reproductive maturity is the essential characteristic of puberty, these "firsts" are not conclusive evidence of it.

Some controversy developed among purists over what observable changes should be considered the initial herald of puberty. Ultimately, the decision is an arbitrary one, depending on the observer's criteria. Consensus or tradition still retains menarche and ejaculation as the hallmarks of the onset of puberty. In turn, they stimulate society to practice pubertal rites of passage into adulthood.

The constellation of physical maturational and the physiological changes which antedate ejaculation and menarche has been designated "prepuberty" for descriptive, chronological purposes. Prepuberty begins and is recognizable biochemically and physically between the ages of ten and twelve. Girls' breasts develop, boys' testicles and penises enlarge, nipples of both sexes may become sensitive, and pubic hair appears. On the average, girls tend to show maturational signs earlier than do boys. However, both sexes undergo growth spurts, and internal organs mature. On the average menarche occurs soon after the thirteenth birthday. The mean age of boys' first ejaculation is shortly before he becomes fourteen (Tanner 1962).

Although a relationship exists between the genetic, biological timetable and chronologically related psychological adaptations, adolescence is defined in terms of psychological maturation and development. Blos (1965) states that "each adolescent phase can be described along three lines, namely, in terms of typical drive and ego modifications, an integral conflict to be solved, and of developmental tasks to be fulfilled" (pp. 146–147). This description avoids strict chronological age limits or biological prerequisites, and is applicable to preadolescence as well as other phases of life.

Adolescence possesses psychological characteristics which distinguish it from childhood on the one hand, and adulthood on the other (A. Freud 1936, Spiegel 1951, Jacobson 1961). Preadolescence, the psychological state of change resonating with prepubertal factors, has characteristics which set it apart from latency and adolescence.

CHARACTERISTICS OF PREADOLESCENCE

The preadolescent manifestations, the psychological prelude to adolescence, are more readily observable and sensitive indicators of developmental and maturational changes than the frequently non-visible, prepubertal changes.

Drive modifications. Prepuberty initiates a period of increments in drive energy. The increase, probably based on small changes in quantities, rates of increase, and ratios of sex hormone, although at first not sufficient to produce substantial physical changes, may nevertheless produce interrelated psychic changes (Kestenberg 1967, 1968). This alteration in milieu disturbs the equilibrium that had slowly been established between the psychic systems during the latency years.

Phallic, anal, and oral drive manifestations increase at this age, signifying either a loosening of repressive forces, an increment in the drive, or both. Anal and oral derivatives attain even greater intensity because of a defensive regression initiated by a quickened oedipal conflict. The relative strength of the id over the ego recapitulates the balance of forces of early childhood (A. Freud 1936).

The drive increment accentuates the passive as well as active yearnings of sexuality and aggression. The conflict of active and passive aims, typical of the preadolescent, eventually develop into the early adolescent's characteristic conscious bisexual conflict.

Ego modifications. The restlessness of these children exemplifies the influence of the drive increase on the ego. Since they are expressed through the ego, drive aspects of preadolescence cannot be totally distinguished from ego aspects.

Geleerd (1957) described many of the complex interactions of the two systems.

This is the period . . . in which the group identification is intense, and the attachment to parental figures has been pushed altogether into the background. In this period the repression of the oedipal conflict has become most successful. At the same time, preadolescent regression has set in (it is a matter of discussion whether one is dealing here with a partial regression or just an increase in id energies) so that many of the learned reaction formations seem to fall apart. The boys look sloppy and they have numerous conflicts with the adult environment and parent substitutes about washing hands, taking baths, haircuts, etc. They are defiant and provocative in their behavior, and among themselves conversations center around destruction, physical prowess and dirty stories. The girls show an increased interest in clothes; they use quantities of lipstick and powder and talk constantly about boys. The interest in boys and in clothes is not a satisfaction of their real feminine needs but reflects their competitiveness and penis envy. The application of powder and lipstick is a reaction formation against anal satisfactions as well as a substitute for it. The girls also have many conflicts with the adult environment, about messy rooms and closets, or schoolwork. They make increased demands on the mother for material possessions and become more violent in their reproaches and criticism of her. In both sexes the defiance and provocativeness reflect an increase in sadomasochistic tendencies. [pp. 263–264]

The onset of fidgetiness, touching compulsions, sleep disturbances, hypochondriacal concerns, interest in the body, and the altered relationship between boys and girls signify the end of latency's psychic organization. A behavioral passivity in boys may alternate with greater motoric activity as responses to the intensifying sexual and aggressive urges. In addition, boys become aware of testicular size and motility (Bell 1965) and penile changes. In girls, tomboyishness represents a turning of feared, passive yearnings to activity (Deutsch 1967) as a defense against increased and anxiety-laden feminine sexual and body preoccupations.

Maenchen (1970) emphasizes that "with the genital drives increasing at a time when the auxiliary ego is weakening, the integrity of the self can be maintained by defensive regression of the drives" (p. 182). According to her, the normal pregenitality (anality expressed through "dirty talk" or orality through greedy acquisitiveness) is more a token than a direct expression of the undisguised drive (pathologically discharged, as in encopresis or biting).

Schoolwork often undergoes a transient but turbulent phase of decline. This underscores seventh graders' reputation for creating difficulties for teachers. Illogic, daydreaming, and difficulty in concentrating on learning tasks interfere with academic achievement. Paradoxically, the preadolescent's cognitive capacity advances as he becomes capable of greater abstraction (Inhelder and Piaget 1958). Intellectual functions receive a heightened cathexis leading to constructive intellectual adaptation in some children, and intellectualization as a defense (A. Freud 1936, Wieder 1966).

A particularly interesting characteristic of preadolescence is the change in relationships between boys and girls. Open warfare between the sexes replaces the peaceful coexistence and the relative freedom to tolerate sexual feelings and fantasies of latency. The preadolescent finds himself in the throes of hateful feelings of aversion and sadistic tendencies toward children of the opposite sex.

DEVELOPMENTAL TASK AND INTEGRAL CONFLICT

Preadolescence stimulates tentative thrusts towards new goals which the child will only achieve later, in adolescence. It is a phase of starts and stops, progressions and regressions.

The overt clash between child and parent masks the beginning of the emotional detachment on the road to maturity. The child's defiance serves two ends: it creates an illusion of emancipation and self-sufficiency, and it defends against the intensified sensual life. Sexual urges directed at the parents are now, more than ever, taboo, because sexuality acquires a more genital, adult quality. Oedipal fantasies involving parents lead to marked anxiety and guilt. The child's need to detach himself from the parents becomes urgent, and the anxiety will initiate regressive trends. Therefore, conscious and recognizable sexual feelings towards grown-ups are short lived: regression quickly prevails.

As a result of regression to anality (as well as an increase in the pregenital drives at this age) the child displays a primitive sloppiness which provokes adults, and furthers alienation from them. Battles over preoedipal anal issues may then camouflage and replace oedipal encounters.

Preadolescents are in an unenviable position. They are overtly hostile, angry, and defiant toward parents and adults. Old, useful, and needed identifications are being relinquished, and new ones become necessary. The children require new objects for ego and superego identifications. As a further complication, anxiety spurs the regressive revival of preoedipal identifications with and attachments to the mother.

In both boys and girls, the regressive pull revives closeness to the mother. The girl feels this as a threat to her femininity, and the increased passive sexual yearnings are felt as a threat to her bodily integrity. She may defensively become sexually promiscuous. Boys do not fear the regressive pull as much as girls in terms of the object, which is heterosexual. Their major concern is over passivity and submission to women, who are viewed as phallic and castrating. Blos (1965) has observed that the fantasy of the phallic mother threatens the boy of this age. The fact that girls may be taller seems to confirm the boy's belief that women are towering and overpowering creatures. Passive yearnings with the mother as object lead to a defensive, exaggerated sadism. Preadolescent boys frequently attempt to prove their strength and masculinity daringly and aggressively.

Nuances of enjoyable relationships between the sexes mark the entrance into early adolescence and beyond. Blos (1965) describes this development in his discussion of the narcissistic object choice of the early adolescent boy:

After the regressive position of male preadolescence the forward movement of object libido leads in its first step to a narcissistic object choice. That this choice remains within the confines of the same sex should be no surprise to us. [This is] the time of friendships with unmistakably erotic overtones, either attenuated or more or less consciously experienced. Mutual masturbation, transient homosexual practices (i.e. fellatio), mutually granted scoptophilic gratifications, shared transgressions or crimes, idealizations, feelings of bliss and elation in the presence of the friend—these are the experiences in which the narcissistic object choice is manifested. Furthermore, these are the experiences which bring about the sudden termination of friendships whenever the intensity of the instinctual drive arouses homosexual panic or, to be more specific, mobilizes passive wishes. [p. 161]

Puberty may contribute to the forward movement of object libido, transforming the preadolescent active-passive conflict into the homosexual-heterosexual content of the early adolescent. However, this transformation often occurs prior to puberty. Toward the end of preadolescence, the child frequently develops heterosexual and homosexual fantasies which will appear in a more definitive form after puberty starts. The anticipation of ejaculation may itself function as an effective organizer of the conflict and task characteristic of early adolescence, as in the vignette below.

When Tom was thirteen, increasing restlessness and unverbalized excitement dominated many of his sessions. He repeatedly imagined chemical experiments and explosions. In discussing his interest in girls, Tom revealed that his shyness with them troubled him. Masturbation experiences particularly worried him. He had not yet experienced "jerking off with sperm shooting out." Try as he might to "get something out of his penis," success eluded him. His penis would hurt from his urgent, masturbatory attempts to produce sperm. Believing that failure meant he was feminine, Tom feared if his friends knew, they would think him "queer" or homosexual, and girls would despise him.

The absence of puberty, therefore, need not delay the transition from preadolescence into early adolescence. Furthermore, the appearance of puberty early in preadolescence may even aggravate the preadolescent's regressive reactions. Deutsch (1944) has observed menarche at the early age of ten to have such an effect. If preadolescence is not traversed optimally, a developmental lag or fixation may occur, and its features may then dominate the adolescence even after puberty (see Blos 1967).

MASTURBATION

Masturbation may be as important as the advent of pubescence in furthering the development of object relationships and ego functions. Bernstein (1974) demonstrated "specific integrative aspects of masturbation—how it enters into the formation of self-concepts including body ego, how it operates in fusing pregenital and genital and aggressive drives, and how it is involved in object choice and relations" (p. 53).

A complete orgasm certainly does not occur in boys, and probably not in girls prior to puberty. Orgastic-like experiences or isolated components may occur in girls (Clower 1976). Lichtenstein (1961) and Eissler (1958) discuss the far reaching effects of the orgastic experience on the sense of reality, sexual identity, and ego functions.

A gradual line of development proceeds from the infant's autoerotic activity that occurs without fantasies, conscious aim, or orgasm, to the complex adolescent aim-related, masturbation experiences with their accompanying fantasies and orgasm. As neither Masters and Johnson (1966) nor other physiologists have studied prepubertal sexual reactions, we cannot be certain of the actual bodily changes during sexual activity at this age.

Genital primacy is tentative and subject to lapses in the preadolescent. Not until mid or late adolescence will masturbation, and then sexual intercourse, unite in one act the genital sexual urges and strivings directed at some person. As his pregenital drives increase, or as he regresses defensively, the preadolescent will often seek oral or anal rather than genital satisfactions. When they engage in sexual intercourse, preadolescents may utilize fantasies of a pregenital nature. Eventually, when genital primacy prevails, pregenital urges will be incorporated and blended into sexual foreplay and intercourse.

Latency children need only mask the expression of sexual urges which are directed primarily at their parents. In preadolescence the process of displacement onto new representations and the search for new objects is accelerated. New objects serve as adaptive replacements for incestuous ones. Although displacement to other objects does occur, it is much less prominent in preadolescence than in adolescence, when even a hidden expression involving the parent is felt as an incest breach.

THE PSYCHOANALYSIS OF PREADOLESCENTS

When the preadolescent enters analysis his perception of the analyst as a new object may enable him to participate in treatment with enthusiasm. Nevertheless, the developmental conflicts of this age frequently produce obstacles in establishing or maintaining a working alliance. Hostility toward and rejection of adults, derived from conflicts over attachment, dependency, and passivity, act as forceful resistances. Many preadolescent patients who are in distress welcome the prospect of its relief, and therefore accept the analyst at first. However, after a period of alliance based on this distress, a preadolescent may turn against his therapist.

This reaction may express a developmentally appropriate desire for autonomy. Simultaneously, it also defends against feared active and passive yearnings. Through the hostile interactions generated with parents, it also gratifies incestuous wishes in a disguised form. Adults often turn away in anger and frustration from such an antagonistic youngster. In fact, the child's hostile stance is the major reason offered for not analyzing preadolescents. We may wonder whether the consultant's emotional reactions to the preadolescent play a role in such a decision.

A parent who responds with healthy external opposition to his youngster's attempts at revolt and defiance acts as an auxiliary ego moderating regressive trends. We view this confrontation as necessary for developmental adaptations in both the preadolescent and the parents. Many parents, unable to achieve their own adaptive changes, react to the youngster's hostility as if a realistic separation or removal were threatened. Analytic perception underscores the fact that these children are not simply hostile. They are beginning a process that will eventually lead to the achievement of the second individuation (Blos 1967). Conflicted, they overtly reject what they covertly need, want, and will for the most part retain.

Child analyses that have extended into preadolescence illuminate the covert side of this conflict (Brody 1961). Frequently, the change from late latency to preadolescence is heralded in analysis by increasing silences and motoric restlessness in sessions. These mark the beginnings of libidinal detachment from the parents and rejection of adults. Susan is representative of many preadolescents who have been in analysis since latency.

Susan's analysis started when she was eight years old, and extended through her twelfth year, terminating about eight months after her menarche. Difficulties in school performance, peer relations, and an inability to find pleasure in activities originally led to the consultation and analysis. Her treatment revealed that her reactions to a severe somatic illness at age twenty months had adversely affected her developing object relationships, self-representation, and contributed to her feelings of loneliness.

Cooperative, articulate, and intelligent, Susan had willingly accepted the possibility of finding out "why she had so much trouble making friends." During the first three years of analysis, many of her difficulties improved and her academic, social, and home relationships became more satisfying to her and her parents.

At about the time she had turned eleven, I became aware that she was talking less than was her style. Using drawing paper, crayons, sticky tape, and scissors, Susan was now quietly absorbed in herself.

In the past, silence yielded to interpretations of its defensive intent. But now the silences were different. Susan thwarted any attempt to discuss her changed behavior by hostilely yelling at me, and calling me "farter" or "stink hole."

These new additions to her vocabulary were manifestations of her changing ego. Often she would finish her drawing or paper work ten or fifteen minutes before the end of her hour. Noting the time, she would defiantly leave. Sessions were unpredictable as to content or style. Only at rare moments would Susan permit an exchange of ideas, or accept an invitation to discuss her behavior.

During our weekly conference, Susan's mother stated that the child was hostile to her also. Arguments, name calling, and rude defiance were new facets of Susan's behavior at home. Sleep patterns were changing, and Susan used her objections to going to bed to provoke sadomasochistic arguments. Later in the analysis, we understood the bedtime conflict as due to a phobic avoidance of distressing dreams with latent masochistic content.

Vocally hostile and argumentative about most things, Susan tried to coerce her mother to stop analysis. Significantly, she did *not* defiantly refuse to come. The mother's strong belief and unwavering insistence that Susan's treatment must continue were important features in the maintenance of the analysis.

Although her sessions were often silent, Susan revealed her preoccupying thought content indirectly. For example, she would cut paper into three sizes and arrange them into three piles. Each pile would be taped into a package and labeled "pads for mommy," "pads for Susan," or "pads for Agnes" (her sister). Ostensibly, these pads were for homework or shopping notes. After a while, Susan labelled them "Maxi, Regular, and Mini" corresponding to advertisements for menstrual pads. She then initiated a protracted, often nonverbally communicated, revelation of concern and fears about menstruation and body changes. Her mother reported that Susan had started asking questions and requested a book to read about "periods" or "it."

Superficially, Susan appeared hostile, disinterested in me or what I had to say, had difficulty expressing herself verbally, and could not attend to analytic work. I viewed her hostility as a developmental reaction, not as a real bid to leave analysis. Her non-verbal and verbal communication of concerns, and her exchange of thoughts, although infrequent, expressed her covert wish to retain her relationship with me. Many months later Susan was able to discuss the safety she felt in being physically present with the analyst while having feelings in her body she couldn't understand.

Patients of all ages may react defensively in such an overtly rejecting manner. Had I terminated Susan's analysis because of her antagonistic withdrawal, I would have been behaving as a frustrated adult, misjudging or ignoring her unhappiness. One frequently learns from adolescents who had been in analysis during preadolescence that the analyst's unintrusive yet firm presence, like that of the dedicated parent's, had been experienced as a reassuring strength. Contrary to parental reactions, the analyst allows the sullen, silent behavior in an atmosphere of tolerance.

The developmental manifestations of motoric restlessness, hostility to adults, and reluctance to talk permit neither the analytic techniques of mid or late adolescence, which are closer to the adult model, nor the talking, drawing, or dramatizing techniques of latency. Modifications are needed, paralleling the need for parental adaptation, which accommodate the limitations of the ego at this stage.

Critics of analysis for preadolescents claim the technique is nonanalytic because at times developmental factors prevent analyzing defenses or content. This is a weak argument indeed.

There are times in all analyses, adult as well as child, when content and defense cannot be interpreted, because the analyst's remarks will fall on deaf or antagonistic ears. The analyst then uses his knowledge of his patient and developmental phase patterning to guide therapeutic interventions. He may concentrate on preparations for interpretations rather than on interpretations themselves. As is true of all analysis, the analyst will not make interpretations that will interfere with adaptive mechanisms (Settlage 1974). He will continue to make astute observations that will help him when the patient is ready to accept interpretations in the future.

"Technique," according to Maenchen (1970), "is dictated not by symptomatology alone or the developmental stage, but by the actual and particular state of ego functioning in its connection with psychopathology. One could say that it is this causal relation between the state of ego functions and the symptomology which dictates technique" (p. 185).

The issue of modification of technique immediately raises the questions of parameters and adaptations. I quote in full Settlage's (1974) remarks.

Marianne Kris (Casuso 1965) proposed that the term *adaptations* be used for modifications in technique required by the developmental level of the child and by the need to create an analytic therapeutic climate. Maenchen (1970) also discusses the differences between adaptation of analytic technique in keeping with the child's level of development and the use of technical parameters. She offers the following clarifying statement, which she credits to Philip M. Spielman.

[The term] "parameter" should be used to designate deviations in technique necessitated by the patient's psychopathology (ego strength, nature of anxiety, extent of regression), and "adaptations" should be reserved for modifications in the approach appropriate to different developmental levels (with no pathology implied) and to technical shifts in relation to new developmental phases in the same patient. . . . both terms should be distinguished from "errors in technique" which are based on the analyst's incorrect assessment of the child and his needs. [p. 4–5]

ADAPTATIONS OF TECHNIQUE

Preadolescence is a particularly difficult developmental phase during which analysis may falter. At times, acute distress facilitates a working alliance at the start, but when the patient finds relief, the alliance often dissolves. Seemingly unproductive sessions, non-compliance with working rules or aims, hostile attitudes, and silences all require technical adaptations.

Verbal communication. Almost all prelatency and many latency children express themselves through play as well as speech (see chapters 7 and 8). The analyst of these patients views this communication through action as age-appropriate. The therapist's running comments encourage and assist the patient's verbal conceptualization, and afford necessary narcissistic supplies for the patient. These children would not be able to continue their play and discussion without the analyst talking.

Although the analyst's speaking to the patient seems natural when a child is quite young, the preadolescent's need for the therapist's verbalization may be less apparant. Rather than play, these children usually choose to sit facing the doctor and talk intermittently. If the analyst views them as little adults, he may tend to remain silent, expecting free association. A strained atmosphere will develop when the patient doesn't talk, and the analyst feels obliged to be silent. The tension can frequently be broken if the analyst says even a few words after some period of silence.

Alec,[1] an eleven-year-old boy who provoked his parents until they viciously attacked him, remained silent at the start of most of his analytic sessions. After a few minutes, the analyst would start the session by saying, "What's new?" or "You look very pensive today," or, when he knew the patient had been to a party, "How was the party Saturday night?" The boy would then engage in discussions. Before the analyst had decided to make introductory remarks, long periods of silent antagonism had prevailed and the therapeutic alliance became weak. After a few months, Alec informed the analyst of one reason for his previous silence. He said that he had been looking at a lamp that hung over the analyst's chair, and had thought the lamp was an instrument for reading patients' minds. He therefore had tried not to think, so his secrets would not be known, and he would be safe from retaliation.

Even with the analyst's verbal encouragement, many periods of silence occur. Not talking to adults is an expression of the adaptive detachment process frequently encountered in social and therapeutic situations. It also results from the child's confusion about his strange, new bodily sensations. Unable to describe these feelings to himself, he cannot tell the analyst what he experiences. Frightened by these eerie stirrings, he also worries that their revelation will provoke criticism. Often, the analyst cannot help the child by using language as a vehicle for mastering and organizing bodily feelings until much later in treatment. Since silence does not yield to interpretation, the analyst may as well tolerate the situation gracefully. To attempt to change this condition early through interpretation is to convey a parental attitude of intolerance or frustration, and may even frighten the child. It is more important to maintain the relationship until some later date when the symptom can be analyzed.

Many adolescents reveal that their experiences during the preadolescent silence contained the implicit reassurance that the analyst protected them. Many recall attributing the value of the sessions to a magic absorption in the omniscient, benevolent analyst.

Motility. Allowances must be made for the youngster's restlessness, and the consequent relative inability to engage in continuous, quiet, and contemplative discussion. The defensive quality of certain behavior should not be interpreted as such until the working alliance is well established. Preadolescents in particular are prone to misunderstand the analyst's observations regarding their motility as criticisms or restrictions, and to then react in a hostile manner.

Roy, who was thirteen at the start of his analysis, would often spin in a swivel chair while he talked. An inexperienced therapist might find this annoying and distracting, but one used to the behavior of preadolescents would take it for granted. Not until the analysis had been in progress for a year did the doctor point out that as Roy spun, he often banged his foot against the furniture.

Roy then revealed he had knowingly done this from the beginning, and had tried to keep the analyst from seeing it. Eventually, the hostility inherent in the restlessness could be understood. Although Roy displayed the restlessness characteristic of his age, he could also engage in long periods of verbal analytic work.

Frequency. The therapeutic alliance is intimately interwoven with issues regarding frequency of sessions. Because of the preadolescent need to develop a more autonomous position, the immediate imposition of a four or five time per week schedule often seems like an entrapment to the youngster. When the child knows he is participating in the decisions about procedure, he is less likely to feel infantalized than when adults impose treatment on him.

As the child and analyst discuss the optimal frequency, the therapeutic alliance starts to develop. In those cases where it is necessary for the parents to insist that the child attend frequent sessions because of the severity of the illness or the indecisiveness of the child, for instance, the alliance may be adversely influenced. On the other hand, such children often feel protected by parental firmness. Optimally, the analyst and child decide between themselves.

Frequency of sessions will be influenced by the analyst's assessment of the youngster's reactions. Infrequent sessions may be precarious, because the child may think that his underlying, covert wishes are not being taken seriously or recognized. In addition, too few sessions will preclude the continuity necessary for effective analytic work.

In discussions of frequency, the analyst and youngster will clarify the conflict between the child's need to grow up, and his reliance on an adult to help him do just that. There are times in the course of an analysis when the child's striving for autonomy clashes with his need for four or five sessions per week. He may feel so threatened by his attachment to the analyst that he becomes unable to talk freely. In such circumstances, prudence may dictate a temporary decrease in the frequency. Such a reduction may become permanent, and even phase out the analysis. Flexibility in the service of the patient's needs must be the guideline.

Use of the couch. When a patient suspends critical judgment, and lies motionless on a couch, archaic imagery, illogical thoughts, and intense feelings enter consciousness. Verbalization of disjointed syntax both reflects and enhances regressive tendencies, while reality testing momentarily wavers. These aspects of free association often frighten young people.

The capacity to free associate in the service of analysis develops from childhood, where it is minimal, to adulthood, where it is maximal. The preadolescent's capability to utilize the couch for free association is restricted by his intolerance of its anxiety-producing effects. Fearing loss of control over impulses, and questioning his sanity, he may describe reverie as a disorganization of his mind. Youngsters who display particular disturbances in reality testing, or blur the distinction between self and object, or use regression as a prominent mode of defense should not be invited to use the couch. In addition, the passive position may mobilize a boy's fears of homosexual submission to a male analyst, or a girl's rape fantasies. In most cases, however, the patient may be allowed the choice of either using or not using the couch.

Whether used or not, the couch conjures up fantasies that are always valuable for discussion. When a youngster raises questions about its role, or refers to stereotyped jokes about it, the analyst explains its function. The youngster is then free to try it, if he wishes. Characteristically, as anxiety vacillates with courage, the youngster is off and on the couch. Until convinced that the patient's regressive loss of reality testing is resilient and rapidly recoverable, we stay visible as a reality landmark and do not sit out of the youngster's line of vision.

Contact with parents. Bernstein (1958) discussed the qualities that parents should ideally possess to successfully maintain their child's analysis. The perseverance and dedication of the parents are essential to successful analysis of preadolescents, perhaps even more so than in the analysis of younger children. The older child's vocal resistance and modes of opposition are formidable; his independent mobility affords him many opportunities to evade his sessions physically. Defiant, he may miss sessions and taunt his parents over a wasted fee. He may be secretly testing the steadfastness of both the analyst and his parents.

A firm, not overly punitive parent may prevent or control such enactments which, if chronic, would sabotage the treatment. At the beginning of the analysis, we often alert parents to the possibility the child will, at times, miss his sessions, and explain that this is a common occurrence at this age. The analyst must keep his neutrality, and not inform on his patient's occasional infractions. For the most part, parents accept this troublesome possibility.

In general we consult with the parents of preadolescents less frequently than with the fathers and mothers of younger children, and more frequently than with those of adolescents. Contact with parents diminishes as the patient takes over his own autonomous functioning. Sometimes, when antagonism to adults is at a peak, preadolescents react suspiciously if the analyst confers with their parents. At such moments, it is better to refrain from seeing parents than alienate the youngster.

It is useful to see the parents two or three times before seeing the child. In addition to learning as much as possible about the child, we can also obtain the parent's permission to make all time and frequency arrangements with the youngster himself. The need for privacy and the possibility that they will have only occasional contact with the analyst is explained. When the youngster is seen, we tell him about the arrangements that have been made, and add that his parents are entitled to know of our decisions. All permission or prohibition resides with the parents. Although we may not be in regular contact with them, parents are advised to feel free to call about anything they believe the analyst should know.

CLINICAL EXAMPLE

Allen suddenly developed a fear of going to school, which could not be eased by parental reassurances. After a week of absence from classes, he was brought for consultation. This eleven-year-old boy had recently changed in both his attitude and achievements, indicating the advent of preadolescence. A hostile attitude to his mother now alternated with a need to be close to her. His academic work declined, and there were changes in his sleep and eating habits. Both parents had been analyzed, and they were prepared to offer analysis to Allen if this were recommended. When told of their intention to seek consultation, he defiantly said, "I won't tell him anything, then I won't have to go!" His parents rejoined, "We can't make you talk, but we do insist you go." Allen's reluctance to go to the consultation paralleled his fear of going to school. However, his willingness to participate under parental pressure indicated that he did wish for help. In fact, Allen was more communicative than his statement to his parents would have indicated. He told me his fear of school developed after two months of difficulty falling asleep at night. "I would get these awful thoughts and feelings, like I was going to die. Then I'd have bad dreams about dead people."

His apparent distress, and the relative ease with which he accepted me, characterized the opening phase of an analysis that extended for four years. Knowing about analysis from his parents, Allen readily accepted my suggestion that we arrange visits at a frequency sufficient to insure continuity of thoughts. I did not, at first, insist on a four or five time per week schedule, but left that open as an option for a later date. Nor did I insist Allen use the couch or freely associate. He was told that whatever arrangement made it easier for him to let me know his thoughts would be acceptable. I told him that he could even paint or draw if he chose. Allen decided to come twice a week, and to "use the couch like a grown-up" to "try to find out why I can't go to school."

Although he had elected to use the couch, I did not sit behind him. Instead, I sat across the room, within his view, for reasons mentioned above.

Within a few weeks, Allen understood that his fear "wasn't about school at all, but about a lot of other ideas." Much relieved, he returned to school, and continued to analyze his anxiety about dying, being away from home, and not doing well in school. When Allen recognized that two sessions a week weren't sufficient, he agreed to a four time per week schedule.

During the first six months, we learned that the death of a loved housekeeper, almost a year earlier, had made Allen feel lonely and sad. Fear of sleep resulted from a frightening, unconscious wish to die, and thus be with her. As he equated sleep with death, he found sleep dangerous. Additional material pointed to the displacement of oedipal wishes from his mother to the housekeeper, so that desires to "sleep with" a woman were heavily tinged with incest guilt.

Allen informed me his trouble really didn't start when Nanny died, but rather a "bad feeling" had become worse at that time. His fear of sleeping started about six months before Nanny's death, when he learned with great trepidation about rules and regulations concerning dog breeding. Allen's dog had been spayed to prevent her from passing on a hip-displasia defect to her whelps. "Dogs with defects can't breed." This disclosure introduced a whole area of concern about his reading defect, a speech defect, and a muscular defect that Allen had as a little boy. He had even been considered a learning disabled child in first grade, and was told that he had "cognitive defects."

Allen's identification with a defective animal who shouldn't be allowed to breed, his yearning to be close to his mother, and his guilt and anxiety were approachable through interpretation. As his symptom diminished and his behavior at home improved, Allen stopped talking in his sessions for long periods of time. He brought homework and books to read, thereby isolating himself from me. To some extent, Allen's silence reflected his identification with his tacitern father who had difficulty relating in an affectionate manner with his son. His silence was also a defense against passive yearnings to be loved by me, a new version of his father, and protected him from revealing forbidden oedipal fantasies.

In addition, we learned that the most dangerous threat in Allen's mind emanated from his mother and other females. After Allen heard about abortion, he spoke to his mother who confirmed that some women do have them. Allen concluded that abortion, like spaying, was a way "women can kill babies." He intermittently spoke of his fear of his mother's rages during a two year period of relatively silent sessions.

SOME FURTHER REMARKS

Although relatively silent analytic sessions extending over long periods of time may appear to be unproductive and of little influence, material from patients contradicts this idea. Unquestionably, the process is erratic for a while, and not always to the analyst's expectation or liking. A major problem in analyzing preadolescents is their capacity to evoke negative countertransferences and other emotional reactions in the therapist (see chapter 13). When the analyst is not frustrated by long periods of waiting, and is not irritated by the youngster's hostile, repudiating attitudes, he becomes responsive to the intermittent fruitful moments of talkativeness. The analysis of preadolescents is less formidible when the analyst understands and tolerates his patient's state of mind.

Geleerd's (1957) summary on the treatment of adolescents is applicable to preadolescents as well. "In adolescence," she wrote, "1. a greater effort has to be made to increase the tolerance of the ego to pathogenic conflicts. 2. A greater amount of help in learning to test reality is necessary. 3. The analyst fulfills the need of a parent substitute, although in a reserved, restrained and most natural way. 4. A consistent and systematic analysis of all defense mechanisms is not possible, and in some instances is contra-indicated. 5. The working-through process is only possible to a limited degree. 6. The handling of the transference is different . . ." (p. 282).

Maenchen (1970) offers a succinct statement of technique: "it seems advisable to gear technique . . . to the functioning of the ego as we find it. Stated simply, I would say that we analyze the child on whatever level we find him: on whatever level the fixation left him or the regression pulled him back to" (p. 206).

NOTE

1. I wish to thank Dr. Miguel Brzostovski for this clinical vignette.

REFERENCES

Abbate, G. M. (1964). Panel report: child analysis at different developmental stages. *Journal of the American Psychoanalytic Association* 12:135–150.

Bell, A. I. (1965). The significance of the scrotal sac and testicles for the prepuberty male. *Psychoanalytic Quarterly* 34:182–206.

Bernstein, I. (1958). The importance of characteristics of the parent in deciding on child analysis. *Journal of the American Psychoanalytic Association* 6:71–78.

—————— (1974). Integrative aspects of masturbation. In *Masturbation from Infancy to Senescence,* ed. I.M. Marcus and J.J. Francis, pp. 53–76 New York: International Universities Press.

—————— (1975). On the technique of child and adolescent analysis. *Journal of the American Psychoanalytic Association* 23:190–232.

Blos, P. (1958). Preadolescent drive organization. *Journal of the American Psychoanalytic Association* 6:47–56.

—————— (1965). The initial stage of male adolescence. *Psychoanalytic Study of the Child* 20:145–164.

—————— (1967). The second individuation process of adolescence. *Psychoanalytic Study of The Child* 22:162–186.

Bornstein, B. (1951). On latency. *Psychoanalytic Study of the Child* 6:279–285.

Brody, S. (1961). Some aspects of transference resistance in prepuberty. *Psychoanalytic Study of the Child* 16:251–274.

Clower, V.L. (1976). Theoretical implications in current views of masturbation in latency girls. *Journal of the American Psychoanalytic Association* 24:109–125.

Deutsch, H. (1967). *Selected Problems of Adolescence.* New York: International Universities Press.

———— (1944). *The Psychology of Women,* Vol 1. New York: Grune and Stratton.

Eissler, K. R. (1958). Notes on problems of technique in the psychoanalytic treatment of adolescents: with some remarks on perversions. *Psychoanalytic Study of the Child* 13:223–254.

———— (1953). The effect of the structure of the ego on psychoanalytic technique. *Journal of the American Psychoanalytic Association* 1: 104–143.

Fraiberg, S. (1951). Clinical notes on the nature of transference in child analysis. *Psychoanalytic Study of the Child* 6:286–306.

———— (1965). A comparison of the analytic method in two stages of a child analysis. *Journal of the American Academy of Child Psychiatry* 4:387–400.

Freud, A. (1936). *The Ego and the Mechanisms of Defense.* New York: International Universities Press.

———— (1949). On certain difficulties in the preadolescent's relation to his parents. In *The Writings of Anna Freud 4.* pp 95–106. New York: International Universities Press, 1968.

———— (1958). Adolescence. *Psychoanalytic Study of the Child* 13: 255–278.

Galenson, E. (1964). Panel report: pre-puberty and child analysis. *Journal of the American Psychoanalytic Association* 12:600–609.

Geleerd, E. (1957). Some aspects of psychoanalytic technique in adolescence. *Psychoanalytic Study of the Child* 12:263–283.

Harley, M. (1974). *The Analyst and the Adolescent at Work,* ed. M. Harley. New York: Quadrangle.

———— (1970). On some problems of technique in the analysis of early adolescents. *Psychoanalytic Study of the Child* 25:99–121.

Inhelder, B., and Piaget, J. (1958). *The Growth of Logical Thinking from Childhood to Adolescence.* New York: Basic Books.

Jacobson, E. (1957). On normal and pathologic moods: their nature and function. *Psychoanalytic Study of the Child* 12:73–113.

————— (1961). Adolescent moods and the remodelling of psychic structure in adolescence. *Psychoanalytic Study of the Child* 16:164–183.

Kestenberg, J.S. (1967 and 1968). Phases of adolescence. *Journal of the American Academy of Child Psychiatry* 6:426–463; 7:577–614.

Kut, S. (1953). The changing pattern of transference in the analysis of an eleven-year-old girl. *Psychoanalytic Study of the Child* 8:355–378.

Lampl–deGroot, J. (1960). On adolescence. *Psychoanalytic Study of the Child* 15:95–103.

Laufer, M. (1965). Assessment of adolescent disturbances: The application of Anna Freud's diagnostic profile. *Psychoanalytic Study of the Child* 20:99–123.

————— (1968). The body image, the function of masturbation, and adolescence: problems of the ownership of the body. *Psychoanalytic Study of the Child* 23:114–137.

Lichtenstein, H. (1961). Identity and sexuality. A study of their interrelationship in man. *Journal of the American Psychoanalytic Association* 9:179–260.

Maenchen, A. (1970). On the technique of child analysis in relation to stages of development. *Psychoanalytic Study of the Child* 25:175–208

Masters, W.H., and Johnson, V.E. (1966). *Human Sexual Response.* Boston: Little, Brown.

Sarnoff, C. (1976). *Latency.* New York: Jason Aronson.

Settlage, C.F. (1974). The technique of defense analysis in the psychoanalysis of the early adolescent. In *The Analyst and Adolescent at Work,* ed. M. Harley, pp. 3–39. New York: Quadrangle.

Spiegel, L.A. (1951). A review of contributions to a psychoanalytic theory of adolescence: individual aspects. *Psychoanalytic Study of the Child* 6:375–393.

Tanner, J.M. (1962). *Growth at Adolescence.* 2nd ed. Oxford: Blackwell.

Wieder, H. (1966). Intellectuality: aspects of its development from the analysis of a precocious four-and-a-half-year-old boy. *Psychoanalytic Study of The Child* 22:294–323.

Wilkins, L. (1965). *The Diagnosis and Treatment of Endocrine Disorders of Childhood and Adolescence.* Springfield: Charles C Thomas.

PART FIVE

ASPECTS OF THE
ANALYTIC PROCESS

Chapter 9

THE OPENING PHASE OF CHILD ANALYSIS

Peter B. Neubauer, M.D.

The characteristics of the opening phase of analysis are not unique
to it, but represent the beginnings of complicated processes that continue throughout the treatment. We will emphasize establishing the
therapeutic alliance through interpretation of defense. Also we will
point to the role of educational methods, the preparation for analysis
in certain cases by the analyst becoming a primary object for the
patient, and the analyst's active attempts to win the child's interest in
the early days of child analysis. During the opening phase, as the
patient is learning the modus operandi of analysis, the analyst evaluates
the child's capacity to engage in treatment. The analyst assesses the
child's ability to experience and analyze early transference phenomena,
and decides whether a special preparatory phase or even a preliminary
non-analytic psychotherapy is required because of serious ego deviations. The characteristics and emphasis of the opening phase will vary
with the child's developmental stage and pathology.

Early in the history of child analysis the therapeutic process was
divided into various steps: the beginning phase, analysis proper, the
working-through period, and termination.

Some authors have attempted to subdivide the opening phase of
child analysis, and others have referred to this stage by different

terms. Thus, one can read papers on the initial phase of analysis, or the education period, or, as Anna Freud (1974) called it, the preparatory period.

The "initial phase" of analysis has been described for adults as well as children. Glover (1955) states that the opening phase "is determined less by the conditions of psychoanalysis than by the spontaneous reactions of the patient" (p. 19). Gitelson (1973) applies knowledge of child development and says the "first phase of analysis of adults is based on the symbiotic phase of the dyadic relationship" (p. 318) between mother and child (Mahler, Pine, and Bergman 1975). Spitz (1956), who also refers to the early mother-child relationship, asserts that while the analytic patient is in an anaclitic (dependent) position, the analyst maintains a "diatrophic" (caring) attitude (p. 260). Some understand the initial phase of analysis as a psychotherapeutic maneuver which leads to psychoanalysis proper.

EARLY CONCEPTS OF THE OPENING PHASE

As with so many other of the theoretical and technical propositions of analysis, the concept of the opening or initial phase has undergone a change. The resolution of conflict has always been a prime aim of child and adult analysis. In the beginning, however, emphasis was placed on the symbolic meaning of the conflict. Under the influence of the topographical point of view, the analyst attempted to reach preconscious and unconscious fantasies rather rapidly without the extensive analysis of defenses that is part of modern technique. The analyst attempted to win the patient's interest in this venture in the atmosphere of a positive transference. This was particularly true for children who do not come for treatment on their own volition, but rather at their parents' insistence and who did not subjectively suffer.

With the advent of the structural theory, the technique of analysis shifted from an emphasis on more or less direct interpretation of unconscious processes, to the interpretation of defense mechanisms, which then led to analysis of drive derivatives and fantasies. This substantial change affected the beginning of child analysis and the preparatory stage lost its earlier significance. Defense analysis, which could be undertaken from the beginning of treatment, resulted in the child engaging in the therapeutic process. Hence the analyst's interest shifted to establishing a therapeutic alliance with the child.

As Anna Freud (1974) stated, "What used to be effected by a prolonged introductory or preparatory phase of the treatment proper is now almost invariably brought about by the scrutiny and analysis of the patient's defensive mechanisms and maneuvers" (p. xii).

THE THERAPEUTIC ALLIANCE

The therapeutic alliance is not an instrument specific to the beginning phase. It is important throughout the analysis, and creates the milieu for the analytic work. Nor is the therapeutic alliance characteristic only of child analysis; it is also essential to the treatment of adults.

Zetzel (1956) introduced the term, thus permitting differentiation between the patient's relation to the analyst based on a transference neurosis, and those relations based on other qualities of the relationship. Greenson (1965) introduced the term "working alliance," which is "employed for designating the relatively nonneurotic, rational rapport which the patient has with his analyst" (Greenson 1965, p. 192). Kohut (1971) refers to this aspect of the relationship by the term *"realistic* bond" (p. 209).

There is extensive literature on the treatment alliance. Its definition seems to stress a working arrangement between the therapist and patient in which conscious and unconscious needs and wishes come to the aid of the therapeutic aim; it is an alliance to resolve internal conflicts. As Zetzel (1965) has pointed out, this alliance "initiates a new ego identification which, it is proposed, determines the nature, quality, and stability of the therapeutic alliance which may thus be defined as both an object relationship and an ego identification" (p. 48).

Anna Freud (1969) discusses this theme from the developmental point of view. She states, "the therapeutic alliance between analyst and patient is *not* carried by any of these earlier stages of object relationship, although all these earlier stages are material. The therapeutic alliance is based, I believe, on ego attitudes that go with later stages, namely, on self-observation, insight, give-and-take in object relationship, the willingness to make sacrifices. It is the oedipal relationship which offers those advantages" (p. 192).

All this implies a patient needs and wishes to form a positive relationship, and in spite of resistances and hostility, there are positive forces which come to the assistance of the analytic work. Thus, the child is able to form a new object relation that is meaningful. Technical questions arise about how one can establish and utilize this alliance. Some children are eager to establish such a relationship from the beginning of analysis. They may wish for it for reasons of dependence or to prove independence; their desire may be based on appropriate early trust or it may be an expression of a negative position. In any case, the child's inner psychological factors determine the relationship; the analyst's interventions alone do not create it.

There is no single procedure by which the analyst can abet the development of the therapeutic alliance. Some believe appropriate interpretive statements contribute to creating a therapeutic alliance and they consequently eliminate or at least shorten the opening phase of treatment. Others prefer to wait until the child has learned the analyst's attitude—his wish to help and understand, and about his nonpunitive or noncritical position.

To a certain extent, the analyst must teach the child about the analytic procedures, but for the most part learning occurs without didactic explanations. The analyst usually tells the patient that the treatment achieves its results through doctor and patient coming to understand the unconscious basis for the patient's symptoms or unhappiness. He may tell the patient that frankly revealing his thoughts and feelings will further this process. However, the child will learn how the treatment works mainly through participating in it and observing the analyst's modus operandi. From the start, the child will come to understand the analyst's helpful devotion to interpretations and his references to the way the patient deals with troubles. As he learns the analytic approach, he will accept the analyst's therapeutic activity and join him in the analytic adventure.

Certain children require special types of "education." Some children come from an environment in which little attention is paid to their feelings, or to their subjective world, and in which recognition of personal interests and wishes is absent. Under these circumstances, during the opening phase the analyst addresses himself to those aspects of the ego's self-observational capacities necessary to introduce the analysis. The task is to "educate" the child to know and express his feelings, and to help him realize that they deserve recognition.

Other children come from homes which give continuous gratification. These children may begin the analysis expecting their analyst will gratify their needs similarly. They may wish intimate contact, demand the analyst provide whatever they need, and behave as if the analyst were merely another instrument of gratification. To make his functions clear, the analyst must "educate" the patient and help him differentiate between therapist and parents. This may lead the child to acquire the degree of independence necessary for the therapeutic task.

However strong the therapeutic alliance may be, it is often interrupted during the analysis. Resistances may assert themselves and the negative transference may every so often win out. It has been stated (Novick and Kelly 1970) "that the intensification of internalized conflicts can lead to the use of externalizations, a defensive process which can overwhelm all the motives for maintaining a working alliance" (p. 245).

The nature of the child's difficulties (and the analyst's proclivities) will determine the degree to which an educational approach characterizes the opening phase of treatment. I must point out that one cannot easily assign such technical modifications to sharply delineated phases of treatment. In some cases they will continue to be operational throughout a large portion of the treatment.

THE INFORMATION ALLIANCE

The role of the parents is delineated in the consultation and early in the treatment. Optimally, the parents like and trust the analyst in whose hands they have placed their child, and antagonistic impulses that may interfere with the treatment are held in abeyance. The bond with the therapist for the sake of the child is important in sustaining the analysis even in times of stress.

The parents and child learn that the father and mother provide the analyst with the information and history necessary for the analyst to understand and help the patient more fully. An information alliance with the parents develops concomitant with the therapeutic alliance with the child. Once more, I emphasize that these developments early in the analysis continue, wane and are renewed throughout the analysis.

EDUCATIVE MEASURES

Most child analysts establish a relationship with the parents which rests primarily on the parents' gathering information for the analyst. This procedure often serves an educational function for the parents. Through observing their child and their interaction with him, they slowly gain knowledge of child rearing and an understanding of their child and his development. The questions the analyst asks, his interest in past and present family interaction and the significance he gives to certain events all have an orienting and guiding influence. The parents may perceive the analyst's attitudes and point of view and adopt his approach as they understand it.

Only rarely does the analyst actively educate the parents, a procedure that was necessary in the very early days of analysis when dynamic concepts were unknown to the general public. Anna Freud (1974) makes the point in her introduction to the first volume of her collected papers that when child analysis was first introduced, the analyst had to work "by himself," as neither teacher nor parents had sufficient information and understanding to support psychoanalytic treatment. At that time, a "psychological vacuum" made it necessary to carry out extensive educational functions in all cases.

At present, the analyst can generally rely on the parents' sophistication and provide a relatively small amount of information about the analytic procedure and the workings of the mind. However, some parents at times interfere with the analytic work to such an extent that the analyst must forcefully state what they must do to make the treatment viable. Most analysts dislike taking an authoritarian stance and prefer that discussion in a friendly and cooperative atmosphere clarify the problems that arise.

TRANSFERENCE

Another function of the opening phase is the evaluation of a child's capacity to establish and analyze transference experiences. We assume that a transference neurosis rarely occurs in children, but we do see some aspects of transference phenomena. The appearance of transference experience is based on the child's ability to differentiate between the primary object and later objects. This differentiation is essential for analytic work, for it is the basis of interpretation which relies on the capacity of the child to separate the past from the present. Ideally, early in the treatment, the child comes to recognize irrational feelings toward the therapist which he comes to understand as being derived from past feelings toward his parents. Displaced feelings from parents as they are perceived in the present occur continuously in the treatment of children.

THE PREPARATORY PERIOD

The widening scope of psychoanalysis imposes new demands on the analyst. Many patients can only be analyzed after a preparatory period. The therapist must decide not only whether the child is analyzable, but also whether preparation is required.

When the analyst does not try to actively win over the patient, as was the practice prior to present-day techniques, the differentiation between the representation of the real analyst and that of the analyst as a transference object is easier to establish. Many children are incapable of developing a transference. Some can do so only after a prolonged preparatory period.

Many young patients are taken into analysis suffering from various forms of ego disorders, developmental deviations, or disturbances based on intellectual and affect deprivations. These abnormalities are often intertwined with neurotic conflicts or symptoms. In treating these disorders, the analyst has to judge whether traditional psychoanalytic treatment can be applied effectively to correct the neurotic conflicts as well as preneurotic or non-neurotic deviations. This depends on the ability of the analyst to appropriately assess the various interacting forms of pathology at the beginning of the treatment.

A few examples can highlight these problems as they affect the opening phase of treatment.

Some children come to analysis without having developed appropriate object relations with a primary object; they have not established minimal object constancy. Under these circumstances, the analyst may become a primary object providing the child with continuity, understanding, and regularity during the psychoanalytic treatment. Often,

the true analytic process cannot be initiated until the child has sufficiently "developed" the capacity to establish an object relationship, i.e.,
until the treatment is experienced by the child as part of this relationship to the analyst. Under these circumstances, one will not observe
transference phenomena until this primary object relationship with the
analyst begins. After the analyst becomes the primary object, transferences *from* the analyst *to* others develop.

It has been suggested that in such cases a special form of treatment,
"Corrective Object Relations" (A. Alpert 1957, 1963), must precede
psychoanalytic treatment, and may even replace it. The therapist offers
himself to the child as a new object rather than as an interpreter of
intrapsychic conflict. Weil (1973) has observed that other types of ego
building will prepare children, ordinarily not suited for that therapy,
for analysis. Such preliminary treatment includes educational measures
and work which advances object relations. Consultation with the parents often involves advising them as to child rearing practices.

It is easy to decide that such treatment be instituted when the child's
deficiency in object relations is clearly in evidence, and his degree of
pathology is extensive. When the disturbance is less pronounced, or
when it is seen only in some areas of development, then psychoanalytic
treatment can be instituted. But under these conditions the analyst will
have to provide the ingredients which permit a belated object cathexis
and representation during the opening phase. Not until that has been
achieved can analysis proper occur.

A five-year-old boy came for analysis because he was fearful, undisciplined, and self-willed. From the beginning, he revealed preoccupations with dying, separation reaction, and fears stemming from
many levels of development. All of this was played out in actions
which included the analyst. When angry, the boy enacted a play in
which he attacked the analyst directly. When curious about sexual
functions he wanted to touch the analyst. When in need of comfort,
he wanted to be hugged. Direct gratification re-enactment in the
analysis was his preferred mode of function. For a long time, any
attempts to help him verbalize his thoughts or fantasies instead of
acting on them were ineffective. The analyst's statements about his
behavior led to more action, although at times the boy acted with
greater calm and restraint. He was not a hyperactive child; rather he

had to insist on mastery through doing. There were good reasons for his behavior and it was not too difficult to understand the mixture of predisposition and traumatic events which led to it. What I wish to stress is the effect this behavior had on the beginning of analytic treatment. The analyst had to be experienced as an "acting person"; only much later could he influence his young patient through verbal interchange.

Another group of children suffer from various forms of ego disorders. Their drive control may be insufficient, and they may experience excessive sensitivity to environmental stimuli as a result of threshold disturbances. Speech development may be delayed, and disturbances in the capacity to develop symbolic language impaired. Disorders in ego equipment, resulting in faulty ego functions, affect the child's sense of the outside world, his object-representations and self-representations as well as the narcissistic balance. These disorders are not primarily neurotic in nature, and while they do not result from conflict, they make conflict likely. Hence these children may develop neurotic disturbances which can be helped by psychoanalytic treatment.

A seven-and-a-half-year-old girl was taken into psychoanalytic treatment. From the beginning, she made cut-outs of people and inanimate objects which she used in her play. She enacted real situations: school activities, picnics with much food, and visits to private places. She never spoke about her life experiences or complained. Her affect was always even. The absence of family members in her play and the lonely retreats to her secret hideaway offered hints of an internal struggle which she wished to resolve. Fantasies and feelings were almost never directly expressed. At school and at home she showed the same matter-of-fact attitude that appeared in the analysis. Apparently she defended herself at home and in analysis by withdrawing from people, isolating her affect, and making use of repression, suppression, and denial. Attempts to point out her defensive needs, or to refer to events at home which may have disturbed her, were responded to with a thoughtful look or a short "yes" as she continued eagerly with her play. In the absence of complaints, feelings or fantasies, or responses to the analyst's "work," the beginning stage of analysis was deprived of its main instrument, interpretation.

Nor was it possible to create increased self-observation. Only slowly and over several months did the atmosphere of the analytic situation change her behavior. The child responded to the therapist's patient interaction and his commitment to verbalization with increasing trust and an identification with her therapist's attitude. Only then could interpretation become effective.

The characteristics of psychoanalytic treatment vary with the nature of each patient's personality. This imposes upon the analyst certain technical maneuvers which address themselves to the correction of underlying deviations. In children with severe ego defects, the variations in abnormalities are very great. It will tax the skill of the analyst to understand the interplay between various neurotic and non-neurotic disturbances, and to act appropriately.

Other children show little capacity for fantasy production, for the expression of preconscious material. Defending strongly against the expression of drive influence, these patients tend to be bound to concrete acts. When referring to their experiences, they adhere to reality. Only with great difficulty do they recognize feelings or subjective interests. With these children, the analyst's task is to help them overcome ego restrictions and the strength of their defenses. Only then is there sufficient freedom to explore preconscious and unconscious conflicts. Such restriction may be the result of neurotic and preneurotic disorders, due to conflicts on various developmental levels or due to insufficient stimulation. Here again we find that special characteristics affect the opening phase of treatment and require special technical steps so analysis proper can be undertaken.

The basic principle is clear. The initial analytic approach, as well as work in later phases, is determined by the personality structure of the individual patient. I do not refer to parameters, but to the analyst's adaptations to the child's needs, and the patient's response to the analysis. Patients view the analytic situation according to their needs, and take from analysis what they require. Sometimes the question arises as to what degree analysis in its traditional form is possible in work with children and whether treatment has become psychotherapy. Often enough, the opening phase succeeds in facilitating an advance in the child's development, so that his ego, superego, and drives are sufficiently mature for psychoanalytic intervention. This function differs greatly from the one which originally led to the recognition of a preparatory phase in analysis.

REFERENCES

Alpert, A. (1957). A special therapeutic technique for certain developmental disorders in prelatency children. *American Journal of Orthopsychiatry* 27:256–269.

———— (1963). A special therapeutic technique for prelatency children with a history of deficiency in maternal care. *American Journal of Orthopsychiatry* 33: 161–182.

Freud, A. (1974). *The Writings of Anna Freud, Vol. I 1922–1935: Introduction to Psychoanalysis. Lectures for Child Analysts and Teachers.* New York: International Universities Press.

———— (1968). *The Writings of Anna Freud, Vol. IV 1945–1956: Indications for Child Analysis and Other Papers.* New York: International Universities Press.

———— (1969). *The Writings of Anna Freud, Vol. V 1956–1965: Research at The Hampstead Child-Therapy Clinic and Other Papers.* New York: International Universities Press.

———— (1965). *The Writings of Anna Freud, Vol. VI 1965: Normality and Pathology in Childhood.* New York: International Universities Press.

Geleerd, E.R. (1967). *The Child Analyst at Work.* New York: International Universities Press.

Gitelson, M. (1973). *Psychoanalysis: Science and Profession.* New York: International Universities Press.

Glover, E. (1955). *The Technique of Psycho-Analysis.* New York: International Universities Press.

Greenson, R.R. (1965). The working alliance and the transference neurosis. *Psychoanalytic Quarterly* 34:155–181

Kohut, H. (1971). *The Analysis of the Self.* New York: International Universities Press.

Maenchen, A. (1970). On the technique of child analysis in relation to stages of development. *Psychoanalytic Study of the Child* 25:175–208.

Mahler, M.S., Pine, F., and Bergman, A. (1975). *The Psychological*

Birth of the Human Infant. Symbiosis and Individuation. New York: Basic Books.

Novick, J., and Kelly, K. (1970). Projection and externalization. *Psychoanalytic Study of the Child* 25:69–95.

Pearson, G.H.J., ed. (1968). *A Handbook of Child Psychoanalysis.* New York: Basic Books.

Spitz, R. (1956). Countertransference: comments on its varying role in the analytic situation. *Journal American Psychoanalytic Association* 4:256–265.

Weil, A.P. (1973). Ego strengthening prior to analysis. *Psychoanalytic Study of the Child* 28:487–301.

Zetzel, E.R. (1956). Current concepts of transference. *International Journal of Psycho-Analysis* 37:369–376.

———— (1965). The theory of therapy in relation to developmental model of the psychic apparatus. *International Journal of Psycho-Analysis* 46:39–52.

Chapter 10

TRANSFERENCE AND THE TRANSFERENCE
NEUROSIS IN CHILD ANALYSIS

Melvin A. Scharfman, M.D.

GENERAL CONSIDERATIONS

Transference has always held a central position in the clinical application and conceptualization of psychoanalysis. While in the context of
this paper it is neither necessary nor possible to extensively review the
analytic literature on transference, a few references to its usage may
help put the problem in some perspective in relation to child analysis.
Freud first wrote about transference in the "Studies in Hysteria" in
1893. By 1905, in "Fragment of an Analysis of a Case of Hysteria,"
he wrote:

> It may be safely said that during psycho-analytic treatment the for-
> mation of new symptoms is invariably stopped. But the productive
> powers of the neurosis are by no means extinguished; they are occu-
> pied in the creation of a special class of mental structures, for the
> most part unconscious, to which the name of "transferences" may be
> given. [p. 116]

Freud recognized that transference occurred, and knew that many of
the patients' experiences in relationship to the analyst were repetitions

of experiences with prior figures in their life. However, he felt transference was dependent on some aspect of the analyst which reminded the patient of someone in his past. In 1909, in "Five Lectures on Psychoanalysis," Freud stated:

> In every psycho-analytic treatment of a neurotic patient the strange phenomenon that is known as "transference" makes its appearance. The patient, that is to say, directs towards the physician a degree of affectionate feeling (mingled, often enough, with hostility) which is based on no real relation between them and which—as is shown by every detail of its emergence can only be traced back to old wishful fantasies of the patient's which have become unconscious. Thus the part of the patient's emotional life which he can no longer recall to memory is re-experienced by him in his relation to the physician; and it is only this re-experiencing in the "transference" that convinces him of the existence and of the power of these unconscious sexual impulses. [p. 51]

Freud formulated his ideas about transference more extensively in 1912, in *The Dynamics of Transference*.

> This struggle between the doctor and the patient, between intellect and instinctual life, between understanding and seeking to act, is played out almost exclusively in the phenomena of transference. It is on that field that the victory must be won—the victory whose expression is the permanent cure of the neurosis. It cannot be disputed that controlling the phenomena of transference presents the psychoanalyst with the greatest difficulties. But it should not be forgotten that it is precisely they that do us the inestimable service of making the patient's hidden and forgotten erotic impulses immediate and manifest. For when all is said and done, it is impossible to destroy anyone *in absentia* or *in effigie*. [p. 108]

He understood that patients seek to repeat their past in relationship to the analyst and to act upon it. This led first to the idea that transference was a resistance, and an interference with the analytic process. Freud then recognized the problem was to keep within the psychical sphere those impulses which the patient wanted to translate into behavior. In "Remembering, Repeating, and Working Through" (1914) he wrote:

> We render the compulsion harmless, and indeed useful, by giving it the right to assert itself in a definite field. We admit it into the transference as a playground in which it is allowed to expand in almost complete freedom and in which it is expected to display to us everything in the way of pathogenic instincts that is hidden in the patient's mind. Provided only that the patient shows compliance enough to respect the necessary conditions of the analysis, we regularly succeed in giving all the symptoms of the illness a new transference meaning and in replacing his ordinary neurosis by a "transference-neurosis" of which he can be cured by the therapeutic work. The transference thus creates an intermediate region between illness and real life through which the transition from the one to the other is made. The new condition has taken over all the features of the illness; but it represents an artificial illness which is at every point accessible to our intervention. It is a piece of real experience, but one which has been made possible by especially favorable conditions, and it is of a provisional nature. From the repetitive reactions which are exhibited in the transference we are led along the familiar paths to the awakening of the memories, which appear without difficulty, as it were after the resistance has been overcome. [p. 154]

This formulation clearly established the transference neurosis as the cornerstone of psychoanalytic treatment. At the same time, it created ambiguity and confusion regarding child analysis that have persisted to the present. One of Freud's major comments about the psychoanalytic treatment of children appears in the "New Introductory Lectures" (1933).

> We had no misgivings over applying analytic treatment to children who either exhibited unambiguous neurotic symptoms or who were on the road to an unfavorable development of character. The apprehension expressed by opponents of analysis that the child would be injured by it proved unfounded. What we gained from these undertakings was that we were able to confirm on the living subject what we had inferred (from historical documents, as it were) in the case

of adults. But the gain for the children was also very satisfactory. It turned out that a child is a very favorable subject for analytic therapy, the results are thorough and lasting. The technique of treatment worked out for adults must, of course, be largely altered for children. A child is psychologically a different object from an adult. As yet he possesses no super-ego, the method of free association does not carry far with him, transference (since the real parents are still on the spot) plays a different part. The internal resistances against which we struggle in adults are replaced for the most part in children by external difficulties. If the parents make themselves vehicles of the resistance, the aim of the analysis—and even the analysis itself—is often imperilled. Hence it is often necessary to combine with a child's analysis a certain amount of analytic influencing of his parents. On the other hand, the inevitable deviations of analyses of children from those of adults are diminished by the circumstance that some of our patients have retained so many infantile character traits that the analyst (once again adapting himself to his subject) cannot avoid making use with them of certain of the techniques of child-analysis. [p. 148]

Written almost a half century ago, these words are still pertinent. In the intervening decades, child analysis has become increasingly more widely applied, and yet questions continue to be raised by analysts about whether or not child analysis is really psychoanalytic treatment. The limitations of free association and the different part played by the development of the transference to which Freud alluded were the key arguments against viewing the analytic treatment of children as in any way analagous to the treatment of adults.

In an attempt to demonstrate the validity of the psychoanalytic process in children, a number of child analysts reported clinical cases which demonstrated extensive transference involvement, and several cases which indicated the development of the specific transference neurosis. The issue of determining whether or not a transference neurosis had developed appears in part to have been motivated by an attempt to draw a direct parallel to adult psychoanalysis, and to extrapolate what was held to be the central phenomenon in adult psychoanalysis into the child's analytic situation. Brody (1961), Fraiberg (1955, 1966), and Harley (1968) all describe the occurrence of transference neurosis in children. These children ranged in age from early latency to preadolescence. These reported cases would suggest that, at least in some children, a transference neurosis somewhat comparable to that of the adult may develop. While there are undoubtedly more cases than appear in the literature, the paucity of reported cases suggests that such a development is not very common in the analysis of children. Even in these reported cases, there are long stretches during which the transference neurosis does not appear to dominate the analytic process to the same extent one would see in the analysis of an suitable adult patient. Anna Freud (1926), who had asserted that transference neurosis was not possible in child analysis, modified her position some twenty years later (1946) when she stated that:

> One part of the child's neurosis is transformed into a transference neurosis as it happens in adult neurosis. Another part of the child's neurotic behavior remains grouped around the parent. [p. 70]

The need to draw a close parallel between the phenomena of adult psychoanalysis and those of child analysis appears to be unreasonable and unprofitable. Child analysts today would probably agree that the specific phenomenon of a transference neurosis is not an expectable or a necessary condition for a child analysis. On the other hand, child analysts do agree that a wide range of transference phenomena occur in the analysis of children. Which transference manifestations will predominate depends upon the developmental position of the child, and the maintenance of the analytic stance. These factors were discussed in panels held by the American Psychoanalytic Association in 1962 (Abbate 1964) and in 1965 (Van Dam 1966). The reports of these panels indicate there is no unaminity of agreement between child analysts about what constitutes the conditions for the development of transference, how development affects the capacity to experience transference reactions, and what constitutes a proper analytic stance in child analysis. Nevertheless, the panel reports provide useful clinical illustrations which demonstrate substantial areas of agreement. We will refer to these contributions later in the paper, when we discuss the capacity to develop transferences.

Kay (1971) has provided us with an excellent summary of the literature on transference and transference neurosis in child analysis. His paper was part of the work of a study group on transference in child analysis which examined transference phenomena from a developmental perspective.[1] The group correctly concluded that the nuances of transference phenomena in child analysis reflect the complexity of developmental progression and regression during any given stage. In any given phase there will be a fusion of varying degrees of different representations of the analyst based on the specific characteristics of that developmental phase, and on the specific nature of the child-analyst interaction at that point. To the child, the analyst will always represent the real object with whom he is interacting; an object with whom he repeats certain feelings and experiences that occurred earlier in his life, primarily in relationship to his parents; and an object who is pictured as similar to his parents in the present. As a new object, the analyst may become the focus of evolving libidinal or aggressive phase-specific developments that are not repetitions of early phenomena, but essentially new levels of organization. When this occurs, a new object representation of the analyst appears. As a new stage of development is achieved, the child views the analyst differently. Probably all of these configurations occur in the course of the analysis of any given child. The precise balance is significantly influenced by the developmental needs of the child in the context of his phase of organization.

Sandler, Kennedy, and Tyson (1975) confirmed the findings of Kay and the Downstate Child Study Group (Kanzer 1971). They suggest it is sometimes difficult to separate the transference from the real relationship with the analyst. They also suggest that one should not neglect either aspect; each aspect can be understood only in relation to the other. These authors categorize transference reactions as transference of habitual modes of relationship, transference of current relationship, transference of past experience, and transference neurosis but recognize that these are not always clearly delineated.

Their category of "transference predominantly of past experiences" seems closest to what would be considered transference by this author. They suggest certain authors may consider their category of transference of past experiences as the equivalent of transference neurosis. In that context they quote Anna Freud.

To me the difference between transference in children and in adults is the following: what the adult transfers and revives in the transference neurosis are object relationships of the past and relationships to a fantasy object, whereas the child, even in matters of the past, has this past relationship or fantasy firmly fixed to the persons of the parents. Therefore he has present-day objects (as opposed to past and fantasy objects) involved in his neurosis. The question then is—how far does the child transfer past relationships and fantasies *from the present-day objects of the analyst?* That is how I always saw the distinction. I think the child very rarely transfers everything in the analysis because the objects at home are still the more convenient ones, since they are still important to the child. I therefore think it is largely a matter of quantity, i.e. of *how much* is transferred. If one had an adult patient in a similar situation, almost all of his problems would very soon be grouped around the analyst, around such issues as the holidays of the analyst, the analyst's other patients. It would be comparatively unimportant for the adult patient's transference what he had been enacting at home. We call it a transference neurosis when, shall we say, three quarters of the patient's transference repetitions are now focused within the analysis. I do not think that the appearance of transference material in a young child's analysis diminishes in any way the interplay with his current objects at home, or rather the living out of the neurosis at home. Here I am speaking quantitatively, but I think that if we speak of qualitative differences we have to look at the difference between the real objects and fantasy objects in the child and the adult (p. 428).

In further discussing the question of transference neurosis, Sandler, Kennedy, and Tyson are in general agreement with the position stated in this article, and in earlier articles from the Downstate Child Psychoanalytic Study Group (Kanzer 1971). They maintain there is a need to examine transference concepts as they apply to child analysis in their own terms, rather than those derived from adult analysis only. These authors further state the need to view the material emerging in analysis from a number of perspectives. Specifically, they suggest the child analyst consider in his interpretations the relationship of the child to himself, to his parents, and to his internalized parents of the past, and choose the interpretation which is most pertinent at a given point. The analyst should be guided by the child's current feelings. In terms of the present paper, one would say that the child analyst chooses among reactions centering around himself as a new object, a real object, an object of displacement of feelings from the child's parents, and a transference object onto whom internalized representations of the past parents are projected.

THE CAPACITY TO DEVELOP TRANSFERENCE

Transference develops when repressed feelings originally directed toward the patient's parents or other significant figures of the past reappear with the analyst as their focus. There are certain minimal requirements for the capacity to develop transference feelings which can be utilized within the analytic situation in a productive manner. Settlage (Van Dam 1966) listed several criteria which he felt were necessary for the development of a utilizable transference. First, the child must have achieved object constancy, a development described as occurring between twenty-four and thirty-six months of age. A child who has attained object constancy has a stable internalized psychic representation of the nurturing object which is cathected with both libidinal and aggressive drive energy. This internal representation of a good parent will persist in the presence of frustration, or during the parent's physical absence. The achievement of object constancy results in the child's becoming less dependent upon the physical presence of the parental figure. At the same time, the child capable of object constancy can evoke past experiences which have been represented intrapsychically. This is a necessary condition if unconscious wishes of the past are to be displaced from the original object toward the analyst. Settlage also asserted object constancy is necessary for a child to establish a stable treatment relationship with his analyst.

Object constancy is not all that is required for the development of transference. Settlage maintained that for transference to develop, the child must have achieved some degree of ego autonomy, particularly the ego capacity for control and modulation of drive derivatives. This is necessary for the child to tolerate some degree of deprivation in the analytic situation, particularly lack of gratification of the transference wishes. Ego autonomy also decreases the need for motor discharge, with a concurrent greater capacity for representation on symbolic verbal levels.

Settlage does not mention certain other aspects of ego functions which could be added to this list of requirements for the development of usable transference manifestations. Some of these include the development of greater cognitive capacity, secondary process thinking, and reality testing. The advances in cognitive ability, which may deteriorate when the child is flooded with uncontrolled drive derivatives, enable the child to differentiate self and object and to discriminate between objects (as analyst and parent).

Ideally, to develop an analyzable transference, the child should be able to make the following distinctions:

1. Self-representation must be differentiated from object-representation. This requires the presence of a relatively stable self-representation rather than a fused parent-child representation.

2. Relatively stable object-representations of past and present parents must be differentiated from each other.

3. The analyst as a real person must be distinguished from the image of him based on displacement and projection of parental representations.

The child must be able to displace past representations of his parent onto the analyst while maintaining a realistic view in which the analyst is not confused with his parents. The child must be able to recognize the transference displacements from the parent, and know they derive from the past. Reality testing, self-object differentiation, and secondary process thinking must be present. No child—or adult—is capable of these difficult discriminations at the start of analysis. Only in the later stages of treatment is the ideal state, in which transference is fully appreciated, approached or achieved. Even then, it is frequently interfered with by regression. Transference, a normal but irrational state, is never fully dissolved.

To return to Settlage, he goes on to discuss the crystallization of the superego as a structural entity following an attempted solution of oedipal conflicts. This is another factor which facilitates the child's capacity to experience transference reactions. This structuralization, which includes a more stable internalization of parental values and standards, leads to further independence from the parents, and to an increased capacity to experience intrapsychic conflict. There are several ways the presence of a superego facilitates the development of analyzable transference. The child who is more independent of his parents feels somewhat freer to express affectionate or aggressive feelings towards the analyst. At the same time, the transference, which now includes displacement of those parental attitudes and values that contributed to the conflict, furthers therapeutic interests.

In a normal or neurotic child, these structural requirements—the achievement of object constancy, ego autonomy, and structuralization of the superego—are generally achieved before the child is five or six years old. On the other hand, the borderline or psychotic child, who is chronologically well into the period during which latency would ordinarily be present, may not have achieved sufficient stability of these psychic organizations. In spite of inner conflict, transferences of neurotic children can usually be analyzed. The borderline or psychotic child is deficient in this area. His transference reactions may involve confusion of self- and object-representations, extreme demands for gratification, and failures in reality testing.

The structuralizations described by Settlage are necessary for the development of transference. Further structuralization or other developments are then necessary for the development of a transference neurosis, especially one sustained over a long period in the analysis.

Transference neurosis has been defined in various ways. Some loosely use the term as a synonym for transference. Freud (1914) described it as the replacement of the patient's usual neurosis by an artificial illness centered around the person of the analyst. Symptoms disappear or diminish outside of the analysis, but the patient's conflicts reoccur with the analyst as their focus. Generally, however, in adult or child analysis, the symptoms remain even when the conflicts center around the analyst. Other forms of *transference neurosis,* such as those described by Greenson (1967) and Harley (1968, 1971), rarely appear in child analysis. A transference neurosis in which the analyst and analysis become central in the patient's life (Greenson 1967) is seen infrequently in children. Harley (1968, 1971) suggested that the occurrence of a *symptom* focused on the analyst, even when short-lived, signifies the presence of transference neurosis, and demonstrated such a situation in a child analysis. Fraiberg (1966) also described a circumscribed transference neurosis in a latency girl. Even when Harley's or Fraiberg's definitions are used, a transference neurosis is not often seen.

Clearly, the traditional concept of transference neurosis is an ideal. Most analysts agree that a transference neurosis does not always occur even in the analysis of adults. Certainly, it is rather rare in children. What is more important is that analyzable transferences do develop, and play an important role in a child analysis. The manner in which the analysis is conducted influences the extent to which this occurs.

ANALYTIC STANCE AND THE DEVELOPMENT OF TRANSFERENCE

The technique of analysis creates a climate which facilitates development of specific, observable, and analyzable transference reactions. Those factors which favor the analytic process also further the development of the transference.

The analytic situation provides a setting in which the patient expresses himself as freely and frankly as he can. The adult is asked to free associate and the child may be offered toys and other materials in an atmosphere that encourages free expression of thought in words and activity. There are as few limitations as possible. The child analyst may have to prevent his patient from actually injuring himself or his therapist, but this is rarely an issue with adults. The analyst pays attention to the derivatives of each of the psychic systems as they emerge. Interpretation, the basic technique in both child and adult analysis, is directed at defenses as they appear and impede the flow of material. As the analysis proceeds, appropriate interpretations of the manifestations of transferences play a significant part in the course of the treatment. Understanding the transferences and other displacements from the parents aids in the uncovering of disturbances in parent-child interaction, the lifting of repressions, and the removal of blocks to the completion of developmental processes and impediments to adequate functioning.

In adult analysis, the patient lies on the couch, relatively immobile and unable to see the analyst. This facilitates the development of the transference, its observability, and analyzability. Unable to see the analyst, the patient will imagine what he is like and attribute to him qualities derived from representations of the parents of his childhood. The analyst's neutral stance makes it possible to differentiate the fantasied picture of the analyst from what the patient actually perceives.

In child analysis, the situation is quite different. The patient faces the analyst, and watches his facial expression and movements. The analyst answers some questions and may reveal personal traits. Sometimes the analyst may offer a gift or accept a present. Under these circumstances, when transference reactions occur, the child can often easily justify them on the basis of his knowledge of the analyst himself.

Ideally, to preserve that degree of anonymity necessary for the analysis of the transference, the therapist should maintain an analytic stance which restricts his interventions to interpretations or preparations for interpretations. However, the child analyst runs the risk of interfering with the therapeutic alliance if he remains aloof. While the adult can accept the analyst's restrained behavior as necessary for treatment, the child may consider such behavior as strange, unfriendly, or hostile. The child cannot tolerate the degree of frustration and distance an adult can. The anger that emerges will often be unanalyzable, and interfere with the treatment.

The analyst must balance frustration against gratification to achieve an optimum state in which the child can participate in the analytic work. An excess in either direction will interfere with transference analysis, the therapeutic alliance, or both. What is of central importance in facilitating the emergence of the transference is maintaining a sufficiently analytic stance. Attention must be given to the therapeutic alliance with the child while at the same time avoiding unnecessary interventions which the child would interpret as the analyst's exerting a gratifying or restricting parental influence. As it is difficult for the analyst to achieve and maintain a proper posture, let us examine certain activities of the analyst in more detail to evaluate their influence on the treatment.

The analyst can easily participate as a real object in his interaction with the child through answering questions, engaging in physical contact, giving presents, etc. Early in an analytic situation such interventions may be necessary to encourage the development of the therapeutic alliance, but they should be kept to the necessary minimum. They impair the development of the transference. These interventions may be readily rationalized, especially by the inexperienced child analyst, as necessary to keep the child in treatment or to involve the child in the analytic work. Clearly, the child analyst must at times verbalize for the child, participate in play and answer certain questions. He may find some physical contact inevitable. In themselves, these interventions are not therapeutic, and should be engaged in only where they contribute to the ultimate therapeutic aims.

Play is an appropriate means of communication for the child. It should gradually be presented as an aid to understanding the child's difficulties. Physical contact may be comforting to the child and may alleviate anxiety, but the resultant absence of anxiety may interfere with the attempt to understand the nature of the child's discomfort. Some children are frightened by physical contact, and experience it as a seduction.

The analyst's speech can be very gratifying and necessary to sustain the child's interest. Verbalizations by the analyst are most effective where they deal constructively with the developmental limitations of the child. Putting things into words may help the child proceed with establishing secondary process thinking, and may help the child identify a particular object, urge, or feeling. But verbalizations' ultimate analytic use, interpretation, must be kept in mind.

Kay, in a more detailed description of the maintenance of the optimal frustration-gratification balance in chapter 11, correctly maintains there are hidden gratifications in the analytic situation, for example, working with the analyst, learning about oneself, and relief from illness. These gratifications nourish the therapeutic alliance.

The analyst may be tempted to behave like a parent and wish to feed, advise, or educate the child. These activities must be kept to a minimum as they interfere with demonstrating to the child that his view of the analyst as similar to his parents is based on transference.

Contact with the parents, both during the initial evaluation as well as in the course of the analysis, has been described as one of the factors which influence the development of the transference. Some authors have indicated that the analyst's contact with parents tends to fuse representation of the analyst and parent in the child's mind in such a way that the appearance of analyzable transference reactions are impeded. Most child analysts would acknowledge this as an interfering factor, but in view of the other developmental limitations, not a central one. (See chapter 13 on the Role of the Parents in Child Analysis.)

In the child analytic situation, the analyst presents himself as an object with whom the patient can interact and experience any thoughts and feelings he may have. The varying perceptions of the analyst are not limited by the analyst and are subject to analysis.

Having indicated these general considerations, we will consider some of the specific differences between prelatency, latency, and preadolescent children with regard to the role of transference in the analytic situation.

TRANSFERENCE IN PRELATENCY CHILDREN

From what has been said earlier concerning the degree of structuralization necessary to develop transference, it should be clear that most prelatency children have not fully achieved a level of maturity that allows for full transference development. Many prelatency children have not attained object constancy and differentiate self and object poorly. The secondary process thinking of prelatency children is not firmly established and verbalization is limited. Reality testing is not secure. Generally, the superego has not been firmly established. Difficulty with control and modulation of drives can interfere with cognitive functioning. Children this age are more dependent on their parents, and their parents are more available for direct experiencing and satisfaction of drive derivatives than is true of older children.

Transference reactions certainly may occur, but as a result of these factors, they are not sustained, and the child may not recognize them as such. When they occur, they are less likely to be utilized in the analytic situation, because the child may not understand the analyst's explanations of them. Nevertheless, the child analyst must be aware of the transference patterns, and differentiate true transference reactions from related phenomena—not always an easy matter (Lilleskov 1971). Particularly in the prelatency child a number of other reactions may be seen which resemble transference and yet are not. Frequently, the child displaces his emotional reactions in the present from his parents to the analyst. In addition, the analyst may be seen and reacted to as undifferentiated from the primary object. This occurs when the child has not yet achieved object constancy. The child may also react to the analyst as if he were a part of the child's self. For instance, superego aspects may be attributed to the analyst, particularly in children where internalization has not been securely established and externalization prevails. In addition, with all children, but perhaps more so with the prelatency child, the analyst may also be experienced as a new object around whom currently evolving, phase-specific drive derivatives can be organized. Experiencing the analyst as a new object occurs in all child analyses, but it is more frequent in situations where one of the child's parents is emotionally or physically absent. In such cases, the analyst may become the central figure around whom certain developmental conflicts are experienced and organized. For example, when one parent is absent, the analyst may become one of the figures in the evolving oedipal triangle. All of these situations make it difficult to know which of the child's many reactions constitute true transference reactions.

The child's use of the analyst as a means of communication in dramatic play during the analysis adds to the confusion. The analyst often plays roles the child assigns to him to demonstrate an internal conflict. In this process the child may conceive of him not only as playing out the role the child has designated, but may experience the analyst as if he really were the designated person, i.e., the child could say "you be a scary monster" and then experience the analyst as a scary monster. Thus, the dramatization becomes another vehicle for transference or displacement (Glenn, Kay, and Rosner 1971).

The prelatency child's emotional reactions to the analyst are not sustained. Nevertheless, they may be powerful, a result of the intensity of the child's drives at this age, and of the ego's relative incapacity to control and moderate the drive derivatives.

In the analysis of prelatency children transference reactions occur but are not prominent and clear-cut and they may not be the central focus of the analysis. The most common observable reactions are displacements of current conflictual involvements with the parents on to the analyst, and externalization in which the analyst represents varying ego or superego aspects of the child.

I have indicated the prelatency child's developmental difficulties experiencing transference reactions to a full degree, as well as the problems the child analyst has in discerning which specifically are transference reactions. It may now be necessary to emphasize that such reactions nevertheless do occur, and are an important part of the analysis of the prelatency child. They remain one of the main avenues for attaining access to some of the child's unconscious fantasies, and for providing material that may allow for fuller understanding of earlier areas of conflict. A clinical example will help to illustrate this. (Also see chapter 6, on prelatency analysis.) It will demonstrate that some degree of frustration of the child's wishes may lead to the elucidation of transference reactions.

CLINICAL ILLUSTRATION OF PRELATENCY TRANSFERENCES

Nancy was five years old and just beginning kindergarten when she was brought for evaluation by her parents. They were concerned because she had become increasingly fearful of going to school, and had missed half the classes that were held. For the two months previous to the consultation, she had become increasingly frightened when her parents told her they were going out in the evening, despite the fact that they always left her with a competent babysitter. On each occasion Nancy would demand they tell her where they were going to be, when they would come back, and even after obtaining this information, would insist they not go. If they did leave, Nancy would cry endlessly, and have tantrums at the time of their departure. Her parents first attempted to satisfy her wishes and stayed home, but they soon observed that the problem was becoming increasingly severe, rather than improving as they had hoped. When their own freedom to engage in social activity became seriously restricted, and Nancy's school difficulties persisted, they decided their daughter needed help.

From the initial history, it was clear Nancy had actually shown indications of a neurosis for about a year. Her first reaction of anxiety and then panic had occurred when she visited a friend's home and saw the child's parent in a wheelchair. She had become frightened, started to cry, and insisted on leaving. Subsequently, Nancy refused to return to that friend's home lest she see someone in a wheelchair. Her anxiety extended, and she became fearful whenever she saw any injured person. Within a few months, she began to cry hysterically and insist on leaving the room if she as much as saw someone wearing a Band-Aid. Several such reactions had occurred when she was out at a restaurant with her parents or visiting friends. During this period of time she had increasingly frequent nightmares. In response to Nancy's distress, her parents decided one or the other of them would sleep with her. On some occasions, they allowed her to sleep in their bed.

Nancy's fear of going to school had actually started when her teacher came to class with her arm in a sling. Nancy had become very frightened and wanted to leave school. Within a few days she felt panicky at the thought of going to school. Clearly, the phobia failed to bind her anxiety and had begun to spread. Her functioning became seriously impaired as more and more situations produced fear. She now suffered from a firmly established neurosis for which psychoanalytic treatment was indicated.

At the beginning of her treatment, Nancy openly discussed her fear, and said she wanted help. In her first few months of analysis it became clear she wanted the analyst to help her by telling her parents to limit their social life, and stay home with her at night. In addition, she felt the analyst should convince her parents she should not have to go to school. I attempted to explain to her I could not do those things. Instead, we would try to understand why she had such scary feelings; if we could accomplish that, maybe the other things wouldn't bother her. She reacted with anger and then with accusations that I didn't care about her and didn't want to help her. She told me how worried she was about bad things happening. Bad things might happen to one of her parents, especially when she was not with them. She also told me she was afraid when she heard her parents arguing, something she said occurred very frequently in their bedroom. She would become frightened someone might get hurt, usually her mother.

About this time Nancy began to ask an increasing number of questions about the analyst. She wanted to know where I went on weekends, what I liked to do, who lived in the house with me, whether I had children, whether I still had a wife, etc. On first view, this curiosity seemed to stem from displacement of her curiosity about the parents' intrusive sexual life, as well as from the natural, general curiosity typical of a child her age.

More specific manifestations of transference began to appear in response to a new request from Nancy. She wanted to know whether she could have something to eat when she came to the sessions. She insisted she was hungry, even though she usually had a snack at home just before her analytic hour. She especially wanted to know why I could not have any fruit in the office. She had specific fruits in mind, cherries or apples were preferred, but anything with seeds would be O.K. I suggested we play the "pretend game" and she tell me what would happen if I had those fruits in the office. She promptly said "I would swallow the seed." When I wondered what would happen after that, she told me, "You would be very excited, because the seed might start to grow inside me." As Nancy had already indicated some curiosity about pregnancy, I added that she must mean the seed would grow like a baby. She said yes, she would like to have a baby. She had always wanted a baby, but no one would give her one. Maybe if she could marry me, she could have a baby. Nancy consciously knew how babies were conceived as a result of her parents' explanations. However, derivatives of fantasies of oral impregnation appeared repeatedly in the next several sessions. She became more and more excited as she invented stories about gifts I would give her which somehow became babies. For instance, she told me that if I gave her a caterpillar, and she swallowed it, it would turn into a beautiful butterfly-baby. It seemed clear the forcefulness of oral impregnation fantasies had led to their dominance over any other information she had been given.

The next week Nancy was preoccupied with thoughts of babies and childbirth. She told me she was worried about her parents' having another baby. She did not like her brother who was somewhat more than two years younger than she. Through her play and verbalization, she revealed she envied and resented him. In fact, she hated all boys and would like to kill them. She said she thought her parents must like boys better, otherwise they would not have had a baby boy. She told me her father especially did not like little girls. Little girls were no good, she said as she pointed to her own breasts and genitals, because they had nothing up there or down there. If somebody liked her, he would give her a baby and then she could be a grown-up woman. If I didn't give her a baby, she would get very angry and she would bite me. She told me she could get so angry she would bite off my arm, my leg, or my penis. We were then able to see these angry thoughts expressed both her wish to have a baby by swallowing the seed, and her anger at being denied a baby. She told me she had wanted a baby long ago when mommy had one, but daddy didn't give her one. She began to become very coquettish and seductive in the sessions as she looked for evidence of her desirability. She wanted to know if I thought she looked pretty and whether I liked what she was wearing.

Interestingly enough, Nancy's oedipal attachment manifested itself in the analysis before it began to appear in her behavior with her father. Her envy, resentment, and disappointment in her father early in her life had compelled her to turn away from developing oedipal feelings toward him, and to regress to earlier levels of behavior. The fact that the baby born was a boy had further complicated her relationship with her father. He preferred boys, Nancy felt, and she resented that. Intense penis envy and resentment had developed along with feelings of her own inferiority, all of which had further estranged her from her father.

Some of this material appeared in the transference as jealousy of a young boy she sometimes met coming out of my office. She thought I must be nicer to him and give him presents. She had seen him fly a paper airplane as he left and decided I had given it to him. I could point out she felt as she had with her father and her brother, as if I preferred the boy to her. She angrily said I did, and then cried. After a while, Nancy said maybe I would still like her. Sometimes she thought her father liked her now, and she never believed that before.

When her ambivalence toward her father had become clarified, Nancy began to deal with some of her anger at her mother. We then learned some additional determinants of her fears of body injury. Her fears were not only reactions to her aggressive impulses against boys and her belief that her body was damaged as a punishment, they also derived from her anger toward her mother. On several occasions she dramatized a scene with puppets in which a woman was being brought out of a hospital in a wheelchair. I suggested she was trying to tell me her mother had been brought out of the hospital in a wheelchair following the birth of her brother, when Nancy and her father had gone to bring her mother home. She told me "No, it wasn't Mommy in a wheelchair, there was a man with bandages all over him. He was in a wheelchair." This helped to explain the precipitating phobic situation as related to her anger with her mother for going into the hospital and delivering her brother. She had missed her mother and worried her mother would not come back. Bandages and wheelchairs now represented her frightening aggressive wishes toward her mother, and her fear of being abandoned, left without a mother. It seemed Nancy had to establish some positive base in an oedipal attachment before she could deal with all of these concerns.

Her initial transference reactions also contained something more specific that we only learned about much later. The insistance of her oral impregnation fantasies had some relationship to reality experiences. On several occasions, about two years prior to the analysis, Nancy had shared her parents' bedroom. On at least two of those occasions she had observed fellatio. Her reaction in the transference revived her unconscious fantasies, and subsequently led to the appearance in consciousness of oral primal scene material.

This vignette does not provide very much feeling of the actual nature of the analytic process or of the wide range of materials covered. It should be clear that even insofar as the transference manifestations are concerned, this is but one thread, essentially isolated from the rest of the material. Hopefully it does illustrate the analyst in the position of being used as an object of displacement (the current curiosity about the parents' sexual activities), as a transference object (the revived wishes to have daddy's baby via oral incorporation and the subsequent disappointment and anger), as a new object (therapist and helper), and as a new object representation (the oedipal manifestations emerging in the analytic situation after some of the anger and disappointment had been worked through and before they could be reexperienced with the father). It is also possible to trace in more detail the nature of the transference including the reappearance in the transference of specific defenses.

Different representations of the analyst, as indicated earlier, will vary in the relative importance which any given one has in the analysis of a particular child. Transference manifestations would be interpreted as fully as possible in the course of the analysis, and displacements would be clarified and verbalized. When the analyst is utilized as the recipient of newly emerging or reemerging drive organizations of a given phase, it is less likely that this material can be subjected to interpretation. Rather, one hopes they will be taken from the analytic situation and be redirected toward the original object. In Nancy's case, as in all successful analyses, the analyst is seen not only as a transference object and displacement object, but also as a real person. The child recognizes his role as a partner in the therapeutic alliance—a friendly, helpful, insightful person whose interpretative activity will help her overcome her neurosis.

TRANSFERENCE IN THE LATENCY CHILD

There was a time when latency age children constituted an overwhelming majority of children in analysis. In recent years this has changed considerably, not only because of the increasing extensions of analytic work to younger children as well as to preadolescents and adolescents, but also because some of our views of latency age children have changed. Many of those children seen by analysts, who are chronologically in latency, do not show manifestations of a well-established latency process in psychological terms. To varying degrees they appear to show some of the characteristics of the prelatency child. They have not achieved a reasonable degree of ego autonomy, and structuralization of the superego is incomplete or faulty. With such children extensive use of dramatic play and less use of verbalization is likely, much like the prelatency child. The clinical manifestations of transference and the other representations of the analyst in such children is similar to the prelatency child. When one takes into analysis a child in whom latency is more firmly established, i.e., a child in middle or late latency, the clinical picture is very different. In latency there is a relative dominance of superego and ego functioning with respect to drive derivatives. Drive derivatives are much less manifest, especially early in the treatment. Drive derivatives, such as wishes, are less likely to be directly expressed either in play or verbalization. When they are, there is a great deal of restriction or modification due to the more complete repertoire of ego defenses. The latency child will continue to play, especially in early latency, but the nature of the play changes. Latency children tend to favor more structured play, and show more concern with rules and order. They are less likely to directly express aggressive or sexual wishes as openly in play. What appears is their expression in verbalized fantasies. These again show many modifications and elaborations due to the operation of varying phase specific defenses.

Superego formation results from more or less successful repression of oedipal feelings, but this is far from complete in the latency child. Guilt feelings and self-punitive acts appear in retribution for forbidden satisfactions. The superego restricts the more direct expression of many feelings, especially toward the parents. The child has a strong need to avoid the revival of such wishes when they begin to emerge into analysis. At times, affection toward the analyst—as a real, transference, or displacement figure—evokes guilt or provokes a conflict of loyalties which the analyst must point out. The child feels his affection for his therapist signifies faithlessness to his parents.

The latency child has a newly won and somewhat fragile control over drives, and some caution must be utilized in the treatment approach. The analyst first needs to consolidate a therapeutic alliance by varying technical means. Often, it is necessary to indicate to the child how the analysis can help him be more securely in control of his drives.

Because of his increased structuralization, in certain ways the latency child is much easier to deal with in the analytic situation. The analyst is not required to be a direct participant in play so often. Further, the latency child verbalizes more, generally manifests secondary process thinking, and is more likely to have clearly structured intrapsychic conflicts which lead the child to experience distress. Less hampered by his own activity, the analyst has more opportunity to be in the accustomed position of the adult analyst—that is, he can be free to observe and think about the child's productions. The relative dominance of the ego and superego provide the analyst with the opportunity to study and understand the operations of these organizations in great detail. The analyst is free to direct the major portion of his attention to such operations and to choose carefully timed, appropriate interventions. In approaching the treatment of the latency age patient, the analyst needs to recognize the child's need to maintain a defensive position. Many latency age children avoid talking about troublesome areas of feelings, and focus for many hours on mundane, everyday matters. Such behavior is particularly prominent in the early phases of the analysis. Fortunately, for the child analyst attempting to help the child approach and understand conflicts, these defensive positions are rarely so perfect that there are not occasional breakthroughs of the drive derivatives. Dreams offer a glimpse of the child's inner life. Latency-age children are more likely to report dreams, and these can be quite useful in the analysis. Initially there is difficulty in obtaining associations to the dreams from the child, but most children can learn to do this. Beginning as a game, they soon become interested in "figuring out" their dreams. Some latency-age children engage in telling long, complicated stories. These stories are somewhat modified expressions of the child's fantasies. Other clues occur in reports of television programs, books they have read, etc. Gradually, the child analyst will be able to piece together some understanding of the child's inner life, and will increasingly get indications of the form of transference the child is experiencing.

It is somewhat paradoxical that the latency-age child has more of the developmental requirements to experience transference reactions, yet guards against the revelations of these feelings as very dangerous. Defensive aspects of the transference—the transference includes the use of defenses against transferred drive derivatives—can be approached more easily than the id aspects. But here too, the analyst must interpret with caution. He does not want to interfere with the age-appropriate latency defenses that preserve adaptive and sublimated behavior. These also provide the control necessary in this developmental phase.

Transference interpretations proper are generally made slowly and with great care. Usually the oedipal transference is most strongly defended against, and preoedipal manifestations may be approached somewhat more readily. Some authors have described fairly extensive transference involvement in latency children. Detailed case descriptions have been provided by Fraiberg (1966) and Harley (1971). Fraiberg's 1966 paper is particularly interesting since it provides a follow-up of a girl who has been in analysis during latency, and who was again treated during adolescence. Both authors describe the development of transference neurosis in their child patients, and convincingly demonstrate extensive transference manifestations. Both also suggest oedipal transference issues are only slowly approached. Harley points out the first year of her young girl's analysis centered around her conflict with the preoedipal mother. Clinical material is presented to illustrate the development of transference reactions during this first year. They led to the recovery of memories centering around the birth of a younger sister when the patient was two years old. It was only during the second and third years of her analysis that oedipal material appeared more clearly in the transference, as part of a symptom which developed in relation to the analyst. In the context of this transference, repressed pregenital destructive components of the oedipal conflict, linked to traumatic events, were revived and could be analyzed when focused on the person of the analyst. Following this, the transference neurosis came to an end, and undistorted oedipal longings were able to achieve expression in relation to the original oedipal object. Harley suggested it was possibly the first time the child had been able to experience such expressions of affectionate feelings for her father. Fraiberg (1966) makes a similar point about the way certain feelings evolved in the transference are relived or re-experienced with the original object. She suggests this is related to the normal mode of childhood functioning—the translation of memories into actions. It also reflects the fact that the original objects are still available. She makes a further point that certain other material revived in the transference, specifically material that had been re-pressed, may be re-experienced only in the transference, without the need to seek any repetition with the original object. Fraiberg empha-sizes that full repression, that is, repression of the memory and of the libidinal aim involved, is a precondition for the development of a trans-ference which is more analogous to the adult transference neurosis. The availability of the original object is a factor which limits the intensity of the transference involvement. In most cases, it precludes the develop-ment of transference neurosis. The child lives with his parents who gratify him and frustrate him. This influences the intensity of his attach-ment to the analyst, whether he be a transference object, a real object, or a new object. As Anna Freud (1946) pointed out, the presence of the parents limits the strength of the child's reactions to the analyst. As his parents satisfy him, the child need not become involved with his thera-pist to the extent an adult patient would.

The child who is experiencing revived preoedipal longings in the transference may turn directly to the parent to gratify them. For exam-ple, the child may engage in a great deal of acting out the wish for bodily contact, if the parent allows such gratification. Where this occurs, the involvement with the analyst will be diluted, and the understanding of such wishes will be much more difficult. Some parents provide extensive gratification for their child, particularly if they have feelings of guilt about the fact that their child is in treatment. They may indulge their child or meet all of his demands. Such behavior must be dealt with in the analyst's contact with the parents.

Certain other factors may bring about intensified attachments to the analyst. When parents are not available for brief or prolonged periods, the child may turn more toward the analyst. Their absence may be brief and physical, as when they leave for vacations. At other times, it may be extended and based on either physical or emotional separations. Protracted illness, divorce, or separation may bring about physical separations. Depression and emotional unavailability cause the equiva-lent psychological absence. In such situations, the analyst, with whom the child spends so much time, may become the initial focus of an evolving libidinal level. An oedipal attachment could appear initially with the analyst and only subsequently with the parent. In this situation the analyst is perceived by the child as the object of that libidinal level before the parent is perceived at that level.

In spite of all of the many limiting factors, work with the transference is a most productive aspect of the analysis of latency children. (See chapter 7, on latency analysis.)

TRANSFERENCE IN PREADOLESCENCE

Psychoanalytic treatment of preadolescent youngsters has been viewed by many analysts as a rather high-risk venture, particularly when treatment is initiated during that developmental phase. Much of the knowledge we have about preadolescence has been obtained from the analysis of youngsters who enter treatment during latency, and whose analyses continue into preadolescence. On the other hand, there are a number of reports of analytic treatment of preadolescents. Kut (1953), Brody (1961), Fraiberg (1955), Harley (1970), and Maenchen (1970), among others, have discussed psychoanalytic treatment during this phase. Sandler, Kennedy, and Tyson (1975) also include references to preadolescent analysis. All of these contributions consider the role of transference during preadolescence. Only a very brief description can be given here of some of the developmental phenomena characteristic of preadolescence as they affect the analytic situation. (See chapter 8, on preadolescent analysis for further details.)

Preadolescence has generally been viewed as a phase during which the biological processes of prepuberty manifest themselves psychically by a quantitative increase in the drive derivatives and a relative fragility of the ego in relation to them. There is an increased indiscriminate cathexis of drive organizations which results in a recathexis of preoedipal and oedipal conflicts. The preadolescent youngster struggles against revived oedipal attachments, and also attempts to disavow the need for preoedipal gratifications from the parents. There is an attempt to move in the direction of greater independence of functioning—the beginning of the task which will occupy the adolescent years.

As part of intensified drive pressure and consequent bodily tensions, there is a greater need for motor discharge through activity. The preadolescent youngster, restless and driven, moves about particularly when he feels tense. This is one of the factors that can create difficulties in a psychoanalytic situation. The preadolescent youngster also has greater cognitive capacity and hence is better able to comprehend the nature of psychoanalysis. Able to intellectually grasp the nature of analytic work, he generally understands what is required, and attempts in some way to comply with these requirements. Although he can grasp the idea of free association, the fear of being flooded with sexual or aggressive feelings and revealing their content limits its use at this age. The preadolescent avoids play in the psychoanalytic situation because it is childish and potentially too revealing of his fantasy life. He therefore talks, but often does not free associate when he experiences increasing tension. Fearing he has revealed too much of his forbidden inner thoughts, he retreats from the analytic enterprise.

Brody (1961) has made some interesting points about the preadolescent's need for physical activity in relation to the development of transference in the psychoanalytic situation. It may be necessary for the preadolescent youngster to be allowed some physical activity within the session to make analysis possible. When such a youngster cannot expend and regulate his energies in physical activity, he will try to avoid deeper development of the treatment relationship. Preadolescents are able to speak more freely and engage in the analytic situation more fully if they are allowed to regulate themselves by a certain degree of bodily movement. Brody points out the youngster of this age who sits perfectly still, inhibited, and restricted during the session, is also likely to be silent. With a phase-specific safeguard or outlet of some body movement, the preadolescent youngster finds it easier to participate in the analysis and may show the capacity to develop a transference neurosis.

Brody mentions several developments she feels help the youngster in this regard. (1) The preadolescent is more independent of his parents and can have a more exclusive relationship with the analyst. (2) The youngster can be more objective about his parents and can choose more distant objects as heroes or villains. (3) Such youngsters show a higher degree of intellectual activity. This permits more abstract forms of communication and allows for less direct gratification. (4) Object choice, while still narcissistic, takes on a greater value than identification and makes it possible for symptoms to be focused on the person of the analyst. A preadolescent is capable of developing a transference, but tries to avoid revealing it. Tension in regard to the development of such feelings may be manifested in repetitive motor activities appearing in the analytic situation. Such activity may give the analyst a clue about when such feelings are too intense. The analyst must allow some regulation of these tensions by motor-activity, but must also be aware the motility can interfere with the development of an analyzable transference.

The preadolescent youngster may be frightened by the intensity of transference feelings. Some authors have suggested that when such feelings become focused on the analyst, the youngster will seek to break the bond between himself and the analyst in the same way he separates himself from his attachment to his parents. When the feelings toward the analyst are too strong, the youngster will provoke and attack his therapist, or even run away from treatment. Interpretations must be timely, appropriate, and properly dosed to be sure transference feelings do not become overwhelming. My own feeling is youngsters become most frightened if they develop overly intense, sexualized, oedipal transferences. These will be accentuated rather than relieved if the analyst interprets them as stemming from the parental object. (See Scharfman 1971 for a discussion of this technical problem in adolescence.) It is often better not to specifically interpret the origins of such feelings. Instead, the analyst should help the youngster understand the fear of their feelings as they relate to the analyst himself. A *crush* may serve a developmental need and can be tolerated as such. Anna Freud, in commenting on such a development in the analysis of an adolescent, described a *crush* on the analyst as a sudden, passionate involvement with a person who has been idealized. She correctly stated that it is experienced as a real relationship, and wondered if there is any possibility of demonstrating that such feeling is a repetition of feelings which originated in the past. Further, she doubted such an interpretation would diminish the intensity of the passionate feeling (Sandler, Kennedy, and Tyson 1975).

These considerations suggest that such affectionate feelings toward the analyst or others serve a developmental need which is phase-appropriate, and should not be subject to interpretation. Many of the other transference manifestations can be interpreted as they appear in the analysis. In fact, for many youngsters, the analysis of negative transference reactions, including pregenital fixations, leads to the appearance of a derivative of a positive oedipal attachment, i.e., a "crush," as a resumption of progressive development. This is particularly helpful when a youngster is moving in a direction that might lead to a perverse development in adulthood. If analysis can help him work through pregenital sado-masochistic fixations which would interfere with the development of heterosexual relationships in later adolescence, it will have accomplished a great deal. If necessary, those elements of the transference which may have remained unanalyzed may be able to be analyzed at some later time. Harley (1970) has written along these lines, as have I in an earlier communication (Scharfman 1976).

CLINICAL ILLUSTRATION OF PREADOLESCENT TRANSFERENCES

Bobby, a preadolescent boy with perverse behavior, started treatment at the age of eleven (for a more detailed case description of Bobby, see Scharfman 1976). He developed a highly sexualized and aggressivized preoedipal maternal transference through which we were able to understand much of his difficulties in his earlier life with his disturbed mother. Very little accurate historical information was available, so we had to reconstruct and understand his childhood through understanding the transference manifestations. Bobby's elaborate, intense, and almost paranoid transference feelings early in the analysis included ideas that I would put him in a mental hospital or give him electric shock treatments. Since I was licensed in medicine and surgery, he expressed the idea I might operate on him and cut off his penis. Bobby also wanted to know whether I had ever performed an abortion. This material led him to reveal accusations against his mother, including his thought that she had killed an earlier child.

Bobby's transference reactions were so intense he had difficulty differentiating me from his mother. This created a special technical problem working with this borderline youngster. At times, I had to do more than interpret within the transference. In this case testing reality was necessary for the development of an analyzable transference. Bobby's fears of me diminished when he realized I was not a menacing person, and that he displaced feelings from his mother to me.

After Bobby worked through some of his fear of his mother, he began to tell me secrets about her. Again, some of these appeared in the transference. Bobby wondered about what I did with his mother when she came to visit me, and reported thoughts that we did something sexual. He viewed me as someone who would be seduced, overpowered, and destroyed by his mother. He imagined he could not reveal secrets to me because I would inform his mother.

In the transference Bobby experienced me as a former lover of his mother, someone with whom she had an affair when Bobby was between four and seven years old. Bobby had often gone with his mother when she met her lover. While the couple made love in the bedroom, Bobby was left outside to play. When her lover died abruptly, Bobby was left with the thought she had destroyed him. This material was revealed first in the transference. The lover had been a central figure in what existed of Bobby's competitive oedipal strivings. His death brought Bobby's attempt to achieve a successful masculine identity to an end. He then regressed to a functional state dominated by his preoedipal perception of his mother as a powerful, destructive woman of whom he was terrified. He sought to please her in every way because of that fear. He felt he had to do exactly as she wished, or she would destroy him too. When these feelings were revived in the transference, they allowed Bobby a second chance to achieve a masculine identity. At first, he re-experienced the feelings of affection, guilt, and loss he had toward mother's boyfriend. He also re-experienced his feelings of competition and rivalry in the transference. Bobby began to show me how much he knew, and wanted to test my knowledge in different areas. He was going to be more successful than I. He would go to better schools, be a better athlete, and even be a better analyst.

As these feelings emerged, they gradually became more than a simple repetition of his earlier repressed oedipal feelings. These feelings now appeared in consciousness with greater intensity than they had earlier in his life. In addition, having reassured himself I was someone who could survive his mother's destructiveness, Bobby sought to identify with me. He felt his mother had destroyed all the other men in her life —an infant son, her husband, her lover, and her father. Before he could give up his regressed defensive position, Bobby had to make sure he had a chance to survive. Working through some of his preoedipal conflicts with his mother in transference enabled him to recapture the developmental position he had abandoned earlier, and resume progressive development. In that context, Bobby's relationship with me in the subsequent oedipal transference was more than a repetition of an earlier object relationship. He used me as a new object with whom he could engage in an oedipal struggle on a different level. Subsequent identification with me as a new object led to structural change.

This example demonstrates a few aspects of a much longer case report. It is presented primarily to illustrate a point mentioned earlier: the working through in the transference of preoedipal, sadomasochistic fixations may enable a preadolescent to move into an oedipal phase. He can then resume the normal developmental process with freedom to engage in developing heterosexual object relationships—one of the crucial tasks of adolescence. Working through even limited areas in analysis may allow that possibility in certain youngsters where the outcome might otherwise have been in jeopardy.

This brief example also illustrates several other points. Beginning in preadolescence with attempts to achieve independence from the parents, the search for new objects and new levels of relationships become a central goal, and is one which will persist through the adolescent years. This manifests itself in the analytic situation in the extent to which transference develops in its pure form—that is, as a repetition of an earlier object relationship. In a phase-appropriate manner, the preadolescent will also use the analyst as a new object in his attempt to achieve a new level of functioning. He will draw on the libidinal ties of the regressive aspects of the transference, but will also add to them. The analysis may thus serve to facilitate the resumption of progressive development, even though this particular use of the analyst may not be able to be analyzed at the time. In fact, interpretation might destroy the reparative process. However, if the analysis continues into late adolescence, it may be then possible to understand this aspect of the analysis.

This vignette may also serve as a departure point in discussing another aspect of transference in preadolescence. Bobby had great difficulties maintaining a mental representation of the analyst as separate from the transference representations. He could not experience the transference as an *as if* relationship. In his case, this was undoubtedly greatly intensified by his borderline functioning. However, it is something which may occur in a similar form in the treatment of many preadolescents or early adolescents.

As mentioned earlier, the quantitative increase in drive cathexis serves to weaken the ego in relationship to the drives. There are also many changes in the body which occur during preadolescence in response to hormonal and other biological shifts. These changes in the body, and consequently the body image, may also contribute to the ego's weakness. The body image, a basic component of self-representation and ego organization in general, is unstable and poorly perceived. Along with other factors, these alterations in self-representation contribute to a relative instability of ego organization during this period, and to a concomitant tendency to ego regression.

Transient ego regressions are quite normal during preadolescence. In the analytic situation, however, they may lead to difficulties in the patient's ability to differentiate the analyst as he actually is from the transference representation. This confusion of therapist and parent may be part of what makes certain transference feelings particularly difficult to manage for the preadolescent youngster. It can contribute to stormy periods or destruction of an analysis if they are not recognized and handled appropriately (Scharfman 1971).

CONCLUDING REMARKS

In a presentation such as this, it is obviously difficult to extrapolate considerations of transference in child analysis from more broad considerations of a given youngster in analysis; indeed, to do so would oversimplify the matter. The central thesis of this paper is that transference needs to be viewed in relationship to developmental process. All that can be hoped is that some indication of the range of different transference and related phenomena of a child's analysis, as well as their complex intermingling, has been communicated. There is clearly much we do not know about the range and relative balance of different representations of the analyst in different phases and about their technical applications. Child analysis itself, while focusing on broadening our understanding of developmental processes, is itself in the midst of developmental progress.

NOTE

1. The work of this study group, which consisted of faculty and advanced candidates of the Child Analysis Section of the Division of Psychoanalytic Education of the Downstate Medical Center, State University of New York, was reported in a number of articles in Kanzer (1971).

REFERENCES

Abbate, G. (1964). Panel report: child analysis at different developmental stages. *Journal of the American Psychoanalytic Association* 12: 135–150.

Brody, S. (1961). Some aspects of transference resistance in prepuberty. *Psychoanalytic Study of the Child* 16:251–275.

Fraiberg, S. (1955). Some considerations in the introduction to therapy in puberty. *Psychoanalytic Study of the Child* 10:264–286.

―――― (1966). Transference in latency. *Psychoanalytic Study of the Child* 21:213–237.

Freud, A. (1926). Introduction to the technique of child analysis. In *The Psychoanalytic Treatment of Children,* pp. 3–53. New York: International Universities Press, 1946.

―――― (1946). *The Psychoanalytic Treatment of Children.* New York: International Universities Press.

Freud, S. (1905). Fragment of an analysis of a case of hysteria. *Standard Edition* 7:3–122.

―――― (1909). Five lectures on psychoanalysis. *Standard Edition* 11.

―――― (1909a). Analysis of a phobia in a five-year-old-boy. *Standard Edition* 10:3–147.

―――― (1912). The dynamics of transference. *Standard Edition* 12: 99–108.

―――― (1914d). Remembering, repeating and working-through. *Standard Edition* 12:146–156.

―――― (1933). New introductory lectures on psycho-analysis. *Standard Edition* 22:1–182.

Glenn, J., Kay, P., and Rosner, H. (1971). Clinical illustrations of transference phenomena. In *The Unconscious Today,* ed. M. Kanzer, pp. 442–451. New York: International Universities Press.

Greenson, R. (1967). *The Technique and Practice of Psychoanalysis,* Vol. 1. New York: International Universities Press.

Harley, M. (1961). Panel report: resistance in child analysis. *Journal of the American Psychoanalytic Association* 9:548–562.

―――― (1968). The current status of the transference neurosis in child analysis. Paper read at Panel on the Current Status of Transference Neurosis, Annual Meeting of the American Psychoanalytic Association, Boston, May.

―――― (1970). On some problems of techniques in the analysis of early adolescents. *Psychoanalytic Study of the Child* 25:99–120.

―――― (1971). The analysis of a phobia in a latency child. In *The Unconscious Today,* ed. M. Kanzer, pp. 339–362. New York: International Universities Press.

Kanzer, M., ed. (1971). *The Unconscious Today.* Part V: Special Problems of Transference and Transference Neurosis, pp. 383–455. New York: International Universities Press.

Kay, P. (1971). A survey of recent contributions on transference and transference neurosis in child analysis. In *The Unconscious Today,* ed. M. Kanzer, pp. 386–399. New York: International Universities Press.

Kut, S. (1953). Changing patterns of transference. *Psychoanalytic Study of the Child* 8:355–381.

Lilleskov, R. (1971). Transference and transference neurosis in child analysis. In *The Unconscious Today,* ed. M. Kanzer, pp. 400–408. New York: International Universities Press.

Maenchen, A. (1970). On the technique of child analysis in relation to stages of development. *Psychoanalytic Study of the Child* 25:175–208.

Sandler, J., Kennedy, H., and Tyson, R.L. (1975). Discussions on transference. *Psychoanalytic Study of the Child* 30:409–441.

Scharfman, M.A. (1971). Transference phenomena in adolescent analysis. In *The Unconscious Today,* ed. M. Kanzer, pp. 386–399. New York: International Universities Press.

―――― (1976). Perverse development in a young boy. *Journal of the American Psychoanalytic Association* 24:499–524.

Van Dam, H. (1966) Panel report: Problems of transference in child analysis. *Journal of the American Psychoanalytic Association* 14:528–537.

Chapter 11

GIFTS, GRATIFICATION, AND FRUSTRATION IN

CHILD ANALYSIS

Paul Kay, M.D.

Perhaps no issue in child analysis is more pervasive than that of gratification and frustration. Every intervention of the analyst, be it a confrontation or interpretation, a restraint or a silence, affords a degree of pleasure or displeasure to both child and analyst. Many of the early child analysts overlooked the implications involved in gratifying their child patients. They provided them with gifts, food, candy, and other pleasures to make the analytic situation as enticing as possible. Many early analysts attempted to avoid frustrating their child patients to avoid provoking their anger.

In recent years, however, child analysts have come to recognize that children can tolerate more deprivation than had originally been thought. Such deprivation, in fact, may enhance the analytic process. Continuous evaluation of the total frustration-gratification balance in the analytic situation, as well as working to achieve the optimal balance necessary to advance the analytic process for both child and analyst, would seem to be more important than any one gratification or frustration for the child. This is the central point of this chapter.

Using the analysis of Bobby as a basis for discussion, I have reviewed my previous work on giving and receiving gifts (Kay 1967), a relatively simple form of the problem with which this chapter deals. Using the analyses of both Bobby and Danny, especially the latter, I have tried to demonstrate the numerous ways in which frustrations and gratifications manifest themselves in the analytic situation. With the help of Danny's analysis, I have tried to demonstrate the many ways the frustration-gratification balance influences the evolution of the therapeutic alliance and the transference. I have also tried to present the pleasures, irritations, and disappointments of the child analyst as he works with a particular child. Because child analysts often have difficulty in evaluating the frustrations and gratifications which they continuously, indeed inevitably, introduce into the analytic situation, constant scrutiny of the complex interaction between patient and analyst is necessary to assess the influence of the frustration-gratification balance in the analytic work.

DEFINITION OF GIFTS

The giving and receiving of gifts often poses difficult technical problems for the child analyst. Such transactions represent dramatic condensations of all the clinical and theoretical issues growing out of the underlying frustration-gratification pattern in every child analysis. For these reasons, and because the vignette of Bobby's analysis is focussed on gift-giving, a few words about the origin and definition of the word "gift" are in order.

According to Webster's Unabridged Dictionary (1965), the word *gift* is derived from the Anglo-Saxon *gifan,* to give. This word, in turn, is related to words associated with marriage. Gift is defined as the "act, right or power of giving or conferring . . . that which is given or bestowed . . . voluntarily transferred from one person to another without compensation . . . a natural quality or endowment regarded as conferred . . . talent . . . a bribe."

The foregoing definitions are remarkable in that, while hinting at complex and powerful currents of feeling associated with gifts, they succeed in omitting any direct reference to such feelings. Although their Anglo-Saxon roots suggest otherwise, these definitions seem to have debased the idea of a gift into an indifferent possession mechanically delivered by one person to another. The very essence of a gift is its humaneness as expressed in emotion, thought, and action. A gift, after all, is an excitement, an awesome event, a piece of magic in the middle of the day. Drenched with affection and other feelings, it seizes both giver and receiver, turns them upside down, and sets them aglow.

The psychoanalytic view of gifts helps to bring into focus and organize the rich and powerful currents of feeling and thought which gifts may represent and ignite in both giver and receiver. Abraham (1920, p. 342) for example, in the context of reviewing Freud's early ideas about the unconscious equation of love, mother's milk, feces, penis, and child with gifts, noted that in certain districts in Germany "suckling a child is called *Schenken* (to give, to pour)." *Schenken,* in general, connotes gift-giving in German. Since Freud and Abraham, analysts have repeatedly observed their analysands (as well as themselves) perceiving both associations and interpretations as gifts. In recent years, some analysts have come to regard gifts as transitional objects.

Ordinarily, gifts in child analysis are inanimate objects which the analyst or child may give to celebrate some traditional occasion such as the child's birthday or a special holiday. They are given with the expectation of pleasure by both giver and receiver. On these occasions the analyst may or may not use the gift to deliberately stimulate the child's interest in the analytic work. In their paper on gifts, Levin and Wermer (1966) use the term *gift* to refer "primarily . . . to articles which the child can possess, use, or consume" (p. 631) and its derivatives, such as a handshake or information.

GRATIFICATION AND FRUSTRATION

The foregoing views about gifts may serve as a useful starting point for appreciating the significance of gratification and frustration in general. A gift is only one example of a wide range of planned and unplanned gratifications possible in the analytic situation. Depending on the analyst's or child's perceptions, any inanimate object, activity, or experience in the analytic situation—including that of frustration—may be gratifying. Similarly, any experience may be perceived as a frustration. The child's world is essentially a pleasure-pain one, with very little neutral territory. Additionally, this neutral territory is apt to be subject to swift, sharp change into pleasure or pain. The analyst's world is different only in degree.

References to the issue of gratification and frustration in child analysis tend to overlook those which are built into the analytic situation and available to both child and analyst. Instead, they tend to overemphasize those which are planned and aimed at the child. A brief review of the intrinsic sources of gratification and frustration in the child analytic situation may serve to introduce and enrich the clinical and theoretical elucidation of this and related issues.

For many child analysts, the total analytic situation includes, to some degree, one or both parents. This is particularly true during the initial phase of the analysis of the young child, and for those children whose ego functioning is severely crippled. Parental sources of gratification may, at times, be crucial for the survival or success of the analysis. For example, as a result of the child starting analysis, his parents may alter their attitudes toward him. The child may experience considerable benign attention and concern from mother, father, and even from siblings. He may even feel for the first time that he is a very important, or even the most important, member of the family. The trip to and from sessions is apt to be especially gratifying if the child is alone with his mother, who may provide him with food, candy, and toys, as well as exclusive interest and warmth. The child may also experience a more subtle, but equally powerful pleasure derived from feeling approved by one or both parents for being in analysis. (The child may also recognize the adults' displeasure in having to sustain the analysis.)

The analyst may experience various significant narcissistic and professional gratifications from parental approval, cooperation, encouragement, and appreciation.

GRATIFICATIONS INHERENT IN THE ANALYTIC SITUATION

Gratifications for the child. The interaction between child and analyst may be highly gratifying to both participants. The child may enjoy the analyst for his real qualities as well as for his fantasied or transference qualities. The child, especially if he is lonely, derives gratification from the analyst's exclusive, consistent, and sustained attention. The analyst's unique combination of professional and personal qualities is apt to provide a powerful and unique experience for the child. By itself, this experience may enormously strengthen the child's self-esteem and functioning. The most remarkable qualities about the analyst's attention are its discipline and its aim of assisting the child's development. In comparison to most other kinds of attention which the child has experienced and may experience in the future, it is not exploitative.

Of even greater importance to the child is the gratification arising from working with the analyst on his problems. This shared work, based on various and changing forms of communication, inevitably accelerates the development of recently acquired basic ego functions. This is particularly true in the areas of perception, thought, speech, memory, and the control of feelings and impulses. These achievements usually lead to more complex ones. The child becomes capable of appreciating and testing reality, (the beginning of) abstract thinking, object constancy, and the organization and integration of knowledge about himself, others, and the inanimate world. These and other highly gratifying achievements pave the way for and are accompanied by the development of still more complex intellectual, social, esthetic, and creative capabilities. They provide new, discrete sources of pleasures for the child while reciprocally enhancing the development of both the basic ego functions and the analytic process.

One of the many discrete and more common sources of gratification arising out of the developmental gains stimulated by the therapeutic alliance is worth noting. Schowalter (1976, p. 433) speaks of the "invigorating sense of mastery and self-esteem" which a five-year-old boy experienced due partially to his ability to translate his affects into words. In general, any advance from primary to secondary process functioning may constitute a thrilling triumph for the child.

Many other gratifications arise out of the partnership with the analyst. There is a shared sense of adventurous exploration in exposing what is hidden, and solving awesome, dreadful, and tantalizing riddles. With the analyst's aid the child can translate into coherent, logical thought and speech what had been chaotic and wordless. These are exciting and momentous achievements for the child. The silent and invisible pleasure arising out of the child's enhanced capacity for trusting (as well as more effectively estimating the trustworthiness of) an adult as a result of this shared searching is of central importance. Furthermore, the partnership is rarely without the immediate, visible pleasure of at least some playfulness or humor, while pursuing the serious business at hand.

Gratifications from the real relationship to the analyst also depend to a considerable degree on the personal appeal which child and analyst have for each other, both spontaneously, and as a result of working together.[1] The experience of being liked by an adult, or of being a valuable source of understanding to one, may be crucial for both the initiation and the successful continuation of the analysis. The real relationship the child experiences with the analyst is possibly his first and probably his most illuminating bridge to the world outside of himself and his family. This provides the child with yet another important specific gratification. The analytic partnership, in this sense, could be viewed as a transitional experience with its mosaic of inner and outer realities, perceptions of the past, present and future realities and illusions, and its developmental gains. The whole enterprise of disciplined intimacy and mutuality with an adult who helps him to face and say what no one else can, while remaining respectfully comforting and protective, may well be a fantastically pleasing and stimulating experience to the child.

The results of successful analytic work lead quite directly to keenly felt gratifications for the child, especially those derived from symptomatic relief and insight. Less visible, but of great and enduring developmental significance, are those gratifications resulting from the child's increased ability to like and enjoy himself. The child becomes able to anticipate, prevent, or reduce real danger and failure, and to perform successfully in various situations. He can regulate his own self-esteem and sense of comfort, feel closer to his family, and make and keep friends.

The play and playfulness of the analytic work and atmosphere, long appreciated as sources of intrinsic gratification in the child analytic situation, deserve some elaboration because of their enormous developmental and transferential implications. Play and playfulness provide pervasive sensory (visual, tactile, auditory, and kinesthetic), affective, cognitive and motor experiences. To what extent do these reawaken in both child and analyst the residues of ancient experiences of the play and playfulness with themselves, their mother, or mothering figures in their infancy? Decisive gratifications, forever enmeshed with developmental achievements, had comprised those experiences. Might not the play and playfulness of the analytic situation continue to stimulate intrapsychic development in both child and analyst, as in the earliest play between mother and child, or indeed, between the child and himself?

Erikson (1972, pp. 132–133) speaks of "playfulness" and of the "interplay of inner resources" as an important opportunity for necessary experimentation. Playfulness allows the child a chance to restore and create a "leeway of mastery in a set of developments or circumstances" (p. 133). Referring to Spitz's concept of the dependence of intrapsychic growth on vision in the first months of life, Erikson states that the visual interplay between mother and child is the "primary facilitator" of the ego nucleus, the "ontogenetic basis of faith" (p. 135), and the beginning of a sense of mutuality. This visual interplay is but part of their affective interchange which, according to Spitz (1972), constitutes "fundamental education," and is the basis for all later development (p. 45). Ultimately, among other achievements, this fundamental education leads throughout childhood to imitation of and identification with the mother, thinking, a sense of identity and of responsibility for one's self, and a wish to learn and identify with others.

Vision, the "leading perceptual modality" for reality testing, adaptation, "organizing the surround," and registering all these experiences in "memory banks," provides the "indispensable prerequisite" for achieving "object constancy" (Spitz 1972, pp. 54–55). Vision plays a primary role in the internalization of conscience and fostering logical thinking (Spitz 1972, p. 58).

Tactile experiences of a playful nature are also of great developmental import in infancy. Murphy (1972), for example, notes that tongue play with nipple and food may increase the infant's cognitive awareness of himself, and bring about the first perception of the self (p. 122). Mother's "playful fingering" of the infant's body may not only contribute to the infant's "cognitive map" of himself, but also to the "sense of giving pleasure to others" (p. 122). Further, "active, mutual mother-baby play is a prerequisite for the development of the cognitive structuring which can carry play beyond primitive sensory-motor stages to a goal-oriented, symbolic, and constructive stage . . ." (p. 126).

Gratifications for the analyst. For the analyst, too, a wide range of discrete and diffuse gratifications of a professional and personal nature are available through the analytic partnership and the achievements to which it may lead. Professional gratifications include the successful analysis of a defense, the reconstruction of a fragment of the child's past or present life, and the repeated affirmation of his capacity for disciplined regression as part of the analytic process. Facilitating the child's development through helping him resolve his conflicts through interpretation, as well as through the work of the alliance, is apt to be the basic source of professional gratification.

The analyst may also experience certain discrete personal gratifications from working over the residues of his own problems, actively participating in the growing up of another person, and fulfilling altruistic aims. Some analysts may experience esthetic or creative gratification from the work as a whole, or from certain aspects of it. Bick (1962) has pointed to the gratifications stemming from "the intimate contact with the child's mind . . . the sense of privilege in being entrusted by the parents with their child . . ." (p. 329). Finally, receiving payment evokes a special kind of pleasure both professionally and personally which cannot be ignored.

FRUSTRATIONS INHERENT IN THE ANALYTIC SITUATION

Frustrations for the child. The built-in frustrations of the analytic situation are much more apt to be directly experienced and, therefore, much more prominent than the gratifications to both child and analyst. They hurt. For the child, they are apt to be due to the curb on impulse gratification and physical activity, as well those gratifications in his daily life, pathological and developmental, which the analysis forces him to give up or reduce. The analysis demands that the child be introspective, reflective, and organized in his perceiving, thinking, and speaking. As well, he is asked to recognize, think, and speak about painful feelings and thoughts to a strange adult. Perceiving and thinking with the detailed accuracy optimal for analytic work can be difficult enough for a child even without taking into account the effect of the primary process on those very functions. Perceiving and thinking analytically involves the extraordinary task of deliberately pursuing and holding onto primary process functioning to understand it through secondary process perception and thought. While such an achievement carries with it great pleasure and pride, the pleasure is gained only after much hard work and time.

The painful experiences confronting the child in the analytic situation are worth recalling in more detail. Analysis requires that the child see himself and his parents far more realistically than ever before or, perhaps, for the first time. Often, this is possible only to a limited degree. These experiences are linked to another group of very painful ones. I have in mind the weakening and discarding of defenses, especially those which may have been very gratifying. All the foregoing frustrations include smaller, discrete ones which result from the continuous pressure to consciously tolerate uncertainties, ambiguities, and ambivalences.

One of these ambiguities involves the analyst and the analytic experience as a whole. The child often comes to the analyst more or less consciously seeking a friend, a playmate, and a good parent, while vaguely and fearfully expecting an enemy. He finds a remarkably friendly, consistent, and understanding adult who often, however, seems to be or to feel like an enemy. While eagerly and innocently offering his heart, and his whole person, the child, for some time, gets nothing he can recognize and settle down with. He never does get a true playmate or parent. Instead, the child gets something vague and uncertain, something synthetic. Greenson (1967) speaks of adult analysis as a "painful, one-sided demeaning experience for the patient," although the analyst expects him to emerge from it as an "independent human being" (p. 278). This experience, magnified, occurs often enough to many child analysands.

Frustrations for the analyst. The frustrations of the analytic situation for the child analyst are well known and have been discussed in detail by Bornstein (1948) and other analysts. They arise primarily from the effect of the domination of the primary process on the child's functioning. The analyst attempts to quickly decipher the child's varied and fluctuating forms of communication, and to respond in an analytically productive way. This requires a unique blend of empathy, dispassionate concern, and insight. The analyst must be creatively attuned to the child's readiness to make use of the intended response, and this is apt to be the most common source of frustration. In work with children, the analyst is unable to think and speak in his usual adult fashion. He must be prepared for the sudden physical exertions or immobility demanded by the child's sudden and frequent changes in mood and behavior. The analyst's position must be maintained in the face of the child's impulsive, provocative behavior and his direct attacks on the analyst's self-esteem. These are but some of the common and formidable sources of frustration. Then there are frustrations confronting the analyst in his contact with the child's parents, because of their guilt and ambivalence toward both child and analyst.

Two highly variable, but potentially crucial frustrations for the analyst are of a personal nature and may stem from his wish to be both the child and the parent of the child he is treating. He may, for example, have to struggle with a powerful wish to prove he is a better parent than the one whom he is trying to help, while at the same time struggling with the less visible wish that the latter would take care of him.

THE THERAPEUTIC ALLIANCE

The analytic situation, then, teems with relentless streams of gratifications and frustrations, strong and weak, organized and frenzied, manufactured willy-nilly and continuously by both participants. At times the balance of these gratifications and frustrations tilts in favor of interpretive work and the formation of the therapeutic alliance. At other times, it tilts against them, depending on the use made of it by the child-analyst partnership. Consciously imposed gratifications or frustrations may disrupt or enrich this balance in either direction. Because this chapter will stress the importance of the relationship between gratification, frustration, and the therapeutic alliance, some elaboration of this bond is in order.

Child analysts generally view the therapeutic alliance as the mutual, conscious and unconscious commitment of both child and analyst to subject to analytic work the child's distress and the problems from which it springs. This commitment on the part of the child evolves by way of numerous temporary detours and reversals. From moment to moment, the child's commitment depends on his capabilities and defensive structure, the analytic situation, and his current life circumstances. The child's ability to regard the analyst realistically is crucial in determining his ability to enter into and maintain the alliance. These and other determinants are apt to be heavily influenced by the momentary gratification-frustration pattern. The foregoing statements also apply in principle to the analyst.

Schowalter (1976), in a recent statement on the complexity of the therapeutic alliance in child analysis, describes it as a bond which regardless of age "requires" the analysand to be able "to observe, understand, and communicate what is happening in the analytic situation, and relate this happening to his past experiences and to his analyst. The ability and willingness to speak and to listen are necessary to meet these criteria" (p. 433). He observes that "a few of the most common portions of this therapeutic alliance substructure would include positive transference, motivation, ability to form object relationships, reality testing, cognitive ability, defensive structure, and the idiosyncrasies of the analyst's particular style. Especially important in child analysis would be the analysand's . . . developmental abilities and the parent's relationship with the analyst" (p. 420). He stresses the "irrational" component of the therapeutic alliance, the difficulty in separating it from the transference, and his impression that it is only "relatively conflict free."

While stressing the nuclear importance of "accurate interpretation" in the evolution of the therapeutic alliance, Schowalter notes that the analyst's "dislike" of the parents or child, or an unresolved countertransference, may seriously impair its formation and effectiveness (p. 419). Although Schowalter appears to be skeptical about whether a therapeutic alliance actually exists in child analysis, the analytic vignette in his paper beautifully and convincingly demonstrates its existence.

Recently, Furer (1976, pp. 184–88) has introduced a concept of the therapeutic alliance in child analysis based partially on Mahler's concept of separation-individuation. Noting Geleerd's inability to find in child analytic work derivatives from the practicing and rapprochement subphases, Furer proposes that such derivatives can be found in the therapeutic alliance. He refers to the "various interactions between mother and child which become genetic forerunners of the nontransference-neurosis relation to the analyst" (p. 185). Empathy, "an example of the aim-inhibited refueling and sharing bridges between mother and child" (p. 185), which occurs during separation-individuation, is essential to the therapeutic alliance. The analyst becomes a mother substitute with whom the patient interacts in an empathic way. The analysand

tolerates frustration and is relatively impervious to pain, like the child
of the practicing subphase.

A BRIEF REVIEW OF THE LITERATURE ON
GRATIFICATION AND FRUSTRATION

In 1927, a few years after child analysis started, Melanie Klein (1948,
pp. 165–66), one of its founders, stated in her refreshingly forthright
way that the child analyst's

> activity is only apparent for even when he throws himself wholly into
> all the play-fantasies of the child, conforming to the models of repre-
> sentation peculiar to children, he is doing just the same as the analyst
> of adults who . . . also willingly follows the fantasy of his patients
> . . . beyond this I do not permit child patients any personal gratifica-
> tions, either in the form of presents or caresses or personal encoun-
> ters outside analysis . . . I keep . . . to the approved rules of adult
> analysis. What I give to the child patient is analytic help and relief,
> which he feels comparatively quickly. Beside this, in response to his
> trust in me, he can absolutely rely on perfect sincerity and honesty
> on my part towards him.

Melanie Klein did not subsequently alter her views.[2]
   About the same time, Anna Freud (1926), the other founder of child
analysis, stressed the need for an "introductory phase in child analysis
which follows its own rules . . . temporarily independent of analytical
theory and technique" in order to establish a "tie with the child which
would make him or her analysable"; she referred to the "paltry and
childish" methods of "enticement" which she used in that phase (p. 38).
By making herself "useful," "interesting," and even "indispensable" to
the child (p. 10) through various gratifications, educational measures,
alienation of the parents, and arousing the child's anxiety or guilt (pp.
11–13), she tried to induce in the child insight, the wish to be helped,
and confidence in herself. These achievements seemed necessary for the
analysis per se to begin.
   Four decades later, Anna Freud had changed certain of her views
(1945, 1946, 1965) toward child analysands—in particular towards

their defenses and the latter's accessibility to interpretation. Having long since given up the introductory phase and substituted for it the interpretation of defense, Anna Freud (1969, personal communication reported in Maenchen 1970, p. 179) urged the avoidance of direct instinctual gratification in play and in relation to the analyst. She also noted that the child's reactions to actual instinctual gratification during analytic sessions could easily be mistaken for a therapeutic alliance.

A few years prior to the publication of the foregoing statement, Levin and Wermer (1966) wrote the first paper dealing explicitly and systematically with the issue of gifts (and, to a lesser extent, other gratifications) in child analysis and psychotherapy. In it, they assert that if

in the psychoanalysis or psychotherapy of adult patients we provide direct information, offer specific advice, or give a 'gift' in any form, we would call such an action a 'parameter' of treatment. But in the psychoanalysis and psychotherapy of children, including most adolescents, we do not consider such a modification of the rule of abstinence to be a parameter, because we believe it to be part of standard procedure, which includes those measures used to establish a therapeutic alliance and a bond to the therapist that can endure the patient's resistance despite frequent reinforcement by parents and others. Furthermore, we recognize that in addition to the offerings of specific gifts at Christmas and on birthdays, 'giving' in one form or another usually takes place throughout the entire course of psychotherapy or psychoanalysis. . . . [pp. 630–631]

According to Levin and Wermer giving gifts "does not eradicate the state of therapeutic abstinence, since it does not yield a consistently high level of instinctual satisfaction" and "does not preclude the analysis of their transference implications" (p. 646). Furthermore, "the continuation of gift-giving may be necessary not only to maintain the therapeutic alliance but also to help the child acquire insight into his fears of giving and receiving, so that he can eventually master them . . ." (p. 647).

Levin and Wermer's position stands in direct contrast to that of Weiss, Anthony, Segal, and some other child analysts, whose position over the years has remained quite close to that of Melanie Klein. Weiss

(1964, p. 588)[3] wrote the first paper to focus on the application of the concept of the parameter to the issue of gratification and frustration in child analysis. He uses the term *parameter* to indicate all those gratifications and accommodations which the child's developmental status and circumstances (including, by implication, the child's psychopathology) call for to conduct an analysis as closely as possible to the classical technique used with adults. He states that "parameters of technique in child analysis are frequent and common, but for the most part they are ignored or assumed to be a necessary and unanalysable part of child analysis" (p. 588). Because they are deviations from classical technique and threaten the formation of a therapeutic alliance and transference neurosis, Weiss urges that they be used sparingly, and then analyzed and discarded as soon as possible.

Anthony's position (1964) is worth noting for its succinctness: "Gratification should be avoided, especially in the form of gifts and food. A non-gratifying environment may not enhance the rapport in the early phases of the treatment but . . . its consistent employment will do much to further the establishment of a genuine analytic situation and the subsequent development of transference" (p. 145).

Maenchen (1970, pp. 196–197), whose views on child analysis are essentially those of Anna Freud's, recently pointed out that in the analytic situation, "some sort of gratification is given, or taken, by every patient, child or adult, whether we consciously give it or not." The analytic situation "offers gratifications which are not planned, and their evaluation is not easy . . . gratification of impulses occurs in the freedom to express them in fantasy and play." This has a therapeutic value since "it makes it easier for the child to give up a wish and to accept unavoidable frustrations. Child analysis provides a controlled situation for play and fantasy, and makes use of it." She stresses the use of interpretation and token gratification in place of direct gratification of the child's demands wherever possible. More recently, Harley (1974, p. 604) and Furer (1976, p. 185), whose approaches are also similar to Anna Freud's, have explicitly urged the avoidance of gratification in child analysis.

Over the years, Anna Freud's thoughts about the issue of gratification in child analysis, and the thoughts of those influenced by her, clearly underwent a gradual and marked shift toward the position held by Melanie Klein. However, Levin and Wermer's views remain close to Anna Freud's early position, and demonstrate that the shift has not been universal. Where the shift has taken place, it has been accompanied by the cautious analysis of defense. This is in contrast to the analysis of symbols or drives which seems to dominate the approach of many Kleinians. Some child analysts influenced by Anna Freud assert that this type of interpretation may overstimulate the child's sexual and aggressive drives, and intensify his anxiety. As a result of such an interpretive approach, the child may experience considerable gratification in what is supposed to be a non-gratifying analytic situation.

CLINICAL ILLUSTRATION: BOBBY

In this and following sections, I will present fragments from the analyses of two boys, "Bobby"[4] and "Danny." The fragment about Bobby centers on his wish to give me a gift, my reaction to it, and the subsequent interaction between us. This incident occurred about a year after the analysis had started. He had developed a fairly strong, although diffuse, attachment to me which began to organize itself into an effective therapeutic alliance as we attempted to understand the meaning of his wish. The other fragment centers on Danny's persistent demands for gratification, mainly in the form of insisting I answer his questions and do things for him. It began in the consultative period before any attachment had developed between us.

The analysis of Bobby's attempt to give me a gift seems to make an especially good starting point for an elucidation of the underlying frustration-gratification issue precisely because, in this instance, it is the child who wants to do the gratifying. It points at the task of discerning and assessing the significance of just who is getting or receiving what gift or gratification, as well as the related tasks of using such wishes to facilitate the evolution of the therapeutic alliance and the transference.

Bobby started analysis at the age of ten with a history of stuttering, defiance, temper tantrums, and an inability to work in school or get along with adults and peers. He had to have his own way. He appeared to be preoccupied with either giving himself pleasure or avoiding anything which demanded disciplined effort. During the first few years of his life, Bobby had been reared largely by his mother and sister. Each of them had given him a great deal of pleasure through affection, food, play, toys, games, gifts, and close attention. These gratifications were alternated with withdrawing from Bobby because of individual and mutual preoccupations. Because of his father's work schedule, Bobby had had relatively little contact with him.

After the birth of his brother, when Bobby was two years old, his intense relationship to his mother became marred by frequent mutual provocation and quarrelling. Not only did his mother give much of her attention to the new baby, but she changed her attitude towards Bobby. She decided she had spoiled him, and now "lowered the boom." Bobby's stuttering and temper tantrums started about this time. Supposedly, Bobby wore his mother down through his defiance and his crying. The psychological loss of his gratifying mother was followed by her actual loss when he was eight years old. She was killed in an automobile accident about two years before the start of analysis. Bobby was said to have grieved for a few weeks.

To Bobby, his mother was a vivacious, fun-loving, giving woman. His father, a grim, constrained, and conscientious man was anxious to do well in his family life and work. He described his wife as domineering and moody. He remarried about a year and a half after her death. Bobby both welcomed and rejected the event. He experienced his father's remarriage as a loss of the father he had begun to know and enjoy for the first time and, in part, as the loss of a substitute for his dead mother. Despite these losses, Bobby liked his stepmother.

In the analysis, Bobby talked and moved about ceaselessly. He was moody, teasing, and demanding. He clowned and performed tricks. Bobby expressed complaints, and wishes of all kinds. He was involved in proving his superiority to his younger brother, as well as reacting to envy and jealousy of him. Along with sudden and brief explosions of glee, these behaviors constituted the generally chaotic world which he brought to my attention. Bobby's wishes, which were so powerful that their frustration was like "Chinese water torture," deserve elaboration. He was a sort of pleasure or fun addict who wanted limitless supplies of food, money, toys, free time, "fun," and magical powers. One series of wishes had to do with the fantasy of having babies inside him.

I responded to Bobby's frequent demands for food, candy, and other gratifications by attempting with occasional and limited success to use them to "find out," through the use of play and fantasy, why they were so important to him. He seemed to have little or no interest in finding out anything except how to enjoy himself. I never gave him food or candy. For a while, Bobby occasionally brought his own. He generally reacted to my frustrating him with anger or with pleasurable fantasies, games, clowning, magic tricks, jokes, riddles and dramatic play. These activities began to seem more and more like frenzied attempts to protect himself from unacceptable thoughts and feelings. My attempts to interpret these activities as defenses were unsuccessful.

Gradually Bobby began to talk about the death of his mother with increasing displays of feelings. Finally, he cried about it. He had missed her deeply and still did. He had a fantasy that she was "alive in heaven." As the months went by, we got to know a great deal about his struggle to deny her death, to control the pain which accompanied his memories of her, and to keep himself magically reunited with her. In addition to certain comforting fantasies, he had kept quite a few of her actual possessions as a means of keeping her alive and feeling close to her. Giving himself good feelings through actual or imagined gratification also seemed very important in helping him bear the pain of her absence.

Toward the end of the first year of the analysis, Bobby began to voice his hatred of our "work" and his wish for fun and play. He complained that like his father, I refused to play with him and only wanted to "work." He contrasted our situation with the fun which he had always enjoyed with his dead mother and still did, to some extent, with her sister. He began to compare me more and more with his father, stressing in detail our similarities and differences. Bobby became conscious of his father, stepmother, and myself as individuals. He made fun of some of the traits which he attributed to his father and me. He spoke of his desire to imitate and emulate those traits in us which he admired. He made some attempts in this direction.

Certain changes in Bobby's thinking came to his attention. He became acutely aware of the frequently vague, fragmentary, and disjointed character of his thoughts which he described as "galoshes in my head." The changes in his thinking became visible to him as he began to scrutinize his father's thinking as well as mine. Bobby enjoyed imitating as well as ridiculing our ways of thinking and speaking. He admired our ability to be logical and organized. He enjoyed trying to be "logical" and loved to use the word itself.

Bobby's curiosity about how things worked, which had always been lively, now became much stronger, more sustained, and better organized. For example, he began thinking about how various machines worked—such as the air conditioner in my office. He took an increasing interest in the way the analysis itself worked. For the first time Bobby began to make very brief, but deliberate and systematic attempts to understand his daily reactions and concerns. By this time, his restlessness and activities during the sessions had diminished. Bobby's activity, thinking and speech began to lose their chaotic quality, and take on organization, clarity, and continuity.

When the summer vacation approached, Bobby talked with some excitement about getting "someone" a "Father's Day present" (Father's Day had occurred a few days before). One day he brought a small paper bag containing a pipe. It was a "going away" and a "Father's Day" present. He had thought of getting me a fish for my fish tank, but had decided "a pipe doesn't die." Bobby urged me to accept the pipe and smoke it immediately. He said that while I was not really his father, I was like one.

I was touched by his offering and told him so. Smoking the pipe would be delightful, but, I reminded him, we had a special job to do here of finding out what things meant. Accepting the pipe was not the same thing as understanding why it was so important to him to give it to me. Bobby began to cry. He insisted I take the pipe. He denied having any special feelings about giving it to me, and he refused to discuss the gift any further. I asked him if he would agree to my placing the pipe in my desk drawer. We would keep trying to find out what the gift meant, but if he continued to feel as he does now, we would stop trying. I would then keep the pipe and smoke it. He accepted my suggestion and left appearing somewhat mollified.

In the next session, Bobby asserted that by smoking the pipe, I would think of him, and "remember" him. I told him that his idea sounded like the kind of "taking-in" idea which we had talked about in the past. (On several occasions, we had connected his taking-in of food and other pleasurable experiences with his reaction to his mother's death.) I added that smoking the pipe would be like my taking him into me so he would not feel we were separated during summer vacation. Bobby thought my smoking the pipe would make it unnecessary for us to "rejoin" during the summer. He began to cry. Again he asked me to take the pipe and smoke it. I replied that this was like asking me whether I would keep him with me or inside of me during the summer.

Bobby lost all control, and burst out crying. He was furious. He threatened to get very mad and throw things if I did not take the pipe. Sometimes, when he thinks of his mother, Bobby gets mad like this and wants to throw things. This is also how he feels when boys tease him. He threatened to take the pipe back.

This was Bobby's first outburst of frustration, anger, and tears in the analysis. It seemed to be a mild duplicate of the temper tantrums his father had described to me, but without the banging, kicking, and throwing of objects. I was moved as well as dismayed by both his outburst of feeling, and his persistent attempt to understand his reaction despite its severity. I told him I was very impressed by what he was saying, because it was as if my not taking the pipe was like losing his mother. As a result, it gave him the "atomic bomb feelings."

After calming down, Bobby said giving me the pipe was a very good solution to his problem, and if I took it he would have a good summer. I questioned his anger resulting from my not accepting the pipe on his terms. Perhaps he had to have his own way most of the time. Then he could avoid having "atomic bomb feelings" which so often led to trouble with other people. I added that Bobby had done a remarkable job in helping us to understand much of what this gift meant to him, but we had not yet found out why he was so angry about losing me and his mother. Bobby was annoyed and surprised. He denied that his mother had anything to do with his current reaction. He suggested I keep the pipe and smoke it if I wanted to during the summer. In the fall, we would decide what to do about it. Now he could have a good summer.

In the last session before summer vacation, Bobby again wanted to give me something. This time he quickly followed with a wish to get something from me. He would gladly accept a gift. He seemed relaxed and jovial. I did not offer him one. He left cheerfully after we wished each other a happy summer.

When Bobby returned in September, he asked me if I had smoked the pipe. He seemed to be in a good mood. I told him I had not. He wondered why he had been so upset before the vacation when I refused his pipe. He was no longer certain he wanted me to keep it, and didn't want to talk about it anymore.

Nevertheless, Bobby referred to the pipe again the following month in connection with the birth of his stepmother's baby.[5] Thoughts about the pipe had come to mind while he compared the baby's face with both mine and his. He especially noted the similarities between the baby's face and mine. Again Bobby alluded to the pipe as if it were a way of remembering me. He described the baby's behavior while she nursed and how he assisted in her care. Bobby recalled he had played with stuffed animals in early childhood. Bobby and the animals had taken turns feeding and caring for each other, like mother and child. Bobby and I discovered that the pipe he had wanted to give me represented a baby to him and the baby represented both of us.

As Christmas approached he again talked about gifts as he had the same time last year. Bobby wished his father would give him a gun, because he felt he was no longer a child who was interested in toys. Guns were for men. In the ensuing weeks, Bobby struggled to face and discuss his reactions to his penis and his masturbatory experiences.

DISCUSSION

1. The vignette above demonstrates some of the common meanings of a child's wish to give a gift, as well as some meanings of the gift itself. Consciously, Bobby's gift represented a going away present, affection, and gratitude toward me as a real person. Unconsciously, it represented a baby on the oedipal and preoedipal levels, and a means of remembering through oral incorporation. The data also suggests the pipe unconsciously represented mother, penis, the achievement of a sense of masculinity, and the wish to masturbate.

From the developmental point of view, Bobby's wish to give me a gift indicates the beginning of a shift from a narcissistic to a more realistic object relationship; from passivity to activity; from greed to generosity; and from bisexuality to masculinity and heterosexuality. The gift may be broadly viewed as a transitional object. It can also be considered an adaptation to his fear of the impending separation from me as dead mother, as father, and as myself. Bobby's wish to give me a gift represented an attempt to hold onto me both as myself and as transference figures. It was also an attempt to control the anxiety and rage provoked by these losses.

The following discussion deals primarily with the transference aspects of Bobby's wish to give me a gift. As the controlling, giving, and seductive mother, he wished to be impregnated by me as the analyst-father, and give me a baby. As a father, Bobby wished to give me, as the analyst-mother, a child. His wish to give me a gift also represented the wish to get one from me. His passive wishes towards me as the analyst-father seemed to constitute a transference resistance designed to protect him from the anxiety of facing the loss of his mother in the transference. Although the loss of the transference-mother was most prominent, Bobby also seemed to be reacting to the loss, through re-marriage, of his father of early childhood.

Coexistent with the transference aspects of Bobby's wish to give me a gift was the wish to participate in as well as the actual participation in the therapeutic alliance. This alliance was based partially on his perception of me as mother and father transference figures, and partially on his realistic perception of me.

2. Analysts may experience considerable inner conflict about giving and receiving gifts. This conflict, often unconscious, has probably manifested itself in scientific controversy about the propriety or usefulness of gifts. It is not surprising, then, that in reevaluating my original technical approach, I began to have doubts about my decision, as well as my implementation of analytic principles. To report the interweaving of rational considerations and countertransference reactions is rare in psychoanalytic literature. It is therefore with mixed feelings that I write this next section. I believe, however, that the publication of analysts' personal reactions to their work may clarify the significance and application of analytic principles.

Originally, I had interpreted Bobby's wish to give me a gift as one dominated by a resistance springing from his father transference. The developmental advance implied by his wish to give me a gift seemed outweighed by the probability that it represented an attempt to avoid facing the meaning of his leaving me for the summer. Therefore, I interpreted rather than gratified his wish.

However, later on, certain realizations gave rise to doubts. I realized that when there is a therapeutic alliance, or when the prospects of one are favorable, and when giving or accepting a gift may represent a significant developmental achievement, the analysis of associated conflict and transference reactions is still possible. I also realized that I had not, at the time, thought through the decision as carefully as I had believed. My decision may well have been based more on hunch and personal reactions than on rational grounds.

Another series of realizations was based directly on the work itself. For example, when Bobby announced his wish to give me a gift, and when he actually brought it to the session, according to my original notes, I had not given him much of a chance to express himself freely and spontaneously. Instead in both instances, I had intervened rather quickly with an interpretation, and an observation, suggesting that a personal element may have dominated my reaction. This personal element may also have shown itself in other ways. Consciously I had wanted to give Bobby as wide an opportunity as possible to come up with his own plan for solving the problem posed by his wish to give me a gift. Instead, I had quickly introduced my own. The actual situation and the transference being what they were, Bobby had no real option but to accept my arrangement almost as quickly as I had offered it.

The arrangement itself was somewhat misleading because while I took physical possession of the pipe (no small matter to a patient of any age), I frustrated his wish that I accept it on his terms. Bobby wanted me to smoke it and make it mine psychologically as well as physically. In effect I gratified his wish in one sense, while ambiguously frustrating him in another. Originally, I thought I had fully succeeded in frustrating Bobby's wish to give me the pipe. In fact, the frustration was partial. The decision to keep the pipe in my drawer and not smoke it was based on a desire to sufficiently frustrate Bobby so we could understand the meaning of the gift. At the same time I hoped to avoid frustrating him to such an extent that his anger would destroy the therapeutic alliance. (At any given moment, doubts about the optimal state of frustration-gratification balance in the analytic situation may stem partially from emotional or irrational elements which are apt to be unconscious.)

Another ambiguity in the arrangement I offered Bobby was in my failure to make clear at what point we would stop trying to understand the meaning of his gift, and I would accept it as he wanted me to. Ambiguity is inevitable, and at times useful in analytic work. The question becomes, how much is optimal.

My doubts were most stirred by the way I carried out my own arrangement. On two different occasions, while under great stress, Bobby asked me to take the pipe. Instead of accepting the pipe, as I had ambiguously promised to do, I interpreted both requests. I had violated my own arrangement. Ironically, I was getting my way, while interpreting his attempt to get his way. Bobby's rage at me had some real justification.

I tried to understand my doubts and my actual work with Bobby partially by reconstructing my state of mind during the analysis, especially during the gift episode. Bobby was one of the first children I analyzed. I recall being eager to do well with him. During his analysis, I was dimly aware of wishing to analyze him as rigorously as possible, as if he were an adult. I wanted to prove to myself and to certain teachers and colleagues that I could detect and interpret the most subtle transference resistance instead of confusing it with "reality." At the time, I recall having a certain scorn for "reality" as being unanalytic or antianalytic. I felt only work with "fantasy" represented "real analysis." I was also eager to show I could withstand the massive, unremitting coerciveness of an insatiable, demanding boy like Bobby.

I recall the impulsive element in what I initially thought was a deliberate and rational reaction to Bob's wish to give me a gift. The suddenness of his confrontation had jolted me. I was both delighted and confused. I recall, vaguely, a momentary struggle against the wish to accept the pipe as a sign of my analytic prowess, his gratitude and affection, and my wish to please him. I had come to like Bobby, and at times felt very sympathetic toward him because of the loss of his mother. I vaguely recall attempting to put aside my sympathy as if only an austere attitude would guarantee acceptable analytic work. I also wondered whether I had reacted to his demands as if they were a tyrranical seduction which I had to angrily oppose with equal tyranny by ambiguously refusing the gift.

Had I felt utterly free of all these concerns, I might have found a simple and direct way of sharing with Bobby the authentic dilemma with which his offer had confronted us. For example, I would have given him all the time he needed and desired to express his wish to give me the pipe. An arrangement could then have been worked out based on his own wishes and capabilities, as well as on our analytic aims. I would have tried to make our final arrangement as clear and precise as possible. Finally, I would have obeyed it unequivocally.

3. At the time of the arrangement, the gratification-frustration balance seemed to have favored the evolution of the therapeutic alliance

and transference. Bobby's major frustrations and gratifications seemed to revolve around the realistic and transferential aspects of the gift. How important were the gratifications arising out of our work to Bobby? They included his pleasure and pride in emulating his father and myself, in his self-discipline, and in the work itself. What ultimately allowed him to overcome the painful, real and transferential frustration I asked him to bear was the gratification of pleasing me, both as a real person, and as the parental figures I represented. Accepting or not accepting the pipe, while important, was not the primary issue. Aside from insight, it was giving Bobby, through our therapeutic alliance, an opportunity to experience both autonomy and mutuality in the analytic work facing us.

CLINICAL ILLUSTRATION: DANNY

The fragment of Danny's analytic experience reported in this section demonstrates the nature of the analyst's struggle to be flexible in his responses to a child's pressing demands, and to facilitate the development of the therapeutic alliance and the transference. I have tried to depict this flexibility mainly from the vantage point of the shifting network of frustrations and gratification which influence both child and analyst.

Danny, a handsome, bright, articulate ten-year-old boy, had been brought to me for analysis by his parents. According to them, he had a history of many difficulties. He frequently provoked the family (especially his mother), peers, and teachers to the point where they would scream at him, and ridicule and hit him. Danny seemed to have little interest in school or schoolwork. An aloof, manipulative boy who could charm adults when it suited him, he seemed never to have formed any real attachments inside or outside of his family. He had not called his parents "mom" and "dad" since early childhood. Bored and unhappy most of the time, Danny tended to concentrate on watching TV. He wet his bed often. On occasion, he soiled his pants and smeared his feces around the bathroom. Now and then he strutted about coquettishly in his mother's clothes. Other difficulties consisted of sporadic peculiarities in behavior and appearance.

Danny had two brothers, one of whom was his senior by two years, and the other his junior by four. Both, according to the parents, were growing up successfully and were a source of great pride and pleasure. Danny, they asserted, was the "rotten apple" who was disrupting an otherwise harmonious, loving family. Often he did not even seem to be a part of the family.

The father, an intelligent, conscientious, and successful businessman, was inclined to be pompous, taciturn, and rather cynical. He bitterly resented Danny's failure to give affection and conform to his notion of an obedient, loving child. He seemed to despise Danny. According to Danny's mother, her husband, like herself, at times lost control of his temper and attacked the children, especially Danny. Like her, Danny's father would then upbraid, and occasionally threaten the children with drastic punishments, or hit them. When very provoked by Danny, she or her husband would talk vaguely, but openly and angrily, about removing him from the family. When not angry, her husband appeared to be indifferent, withdrawn, or depressed.

By way of contrast, Danny's mother presented herself as a vivacious, bright, and responsible mother who enjoyed and indulged her children when she was not angry at them. During and after her pregnancy with Danny, she had felt overwhelmed. Her husband was rarely available for support. Danny's mother had to drive herself to the hospital when labor started, because her husband was asleep. She reared Danny with the help of several housekeepers, the first of whom stayed for five years. Danny apparently liked this housekeeper and the current one.

Danny's mother described her son as "placid" in early infancy, although a "dynamo" in utero and throughout his childhood. Both parents described their son as a "cold," "cantankerous," and destructive child. Danny's mother thought his general development and health had been normal. He had always wanted more milk. Bowel and bladder control were achieved by the age of three and a half. This was followed by sporadic regression in bladder control. Danny showed brief interest in and some talent for various artistic pursuits after the age of four.

During infancy, Danny wore a bar between his legs for about a month to correct an equinus varus. At about three, he had an adenoidectomy and tonsillectomy. His mother said he had been angry at the "hospital" and the "doctors," because on the day of his discharge he had had to wait a long time before she and her husband came to take him home. At his third birthday party, Danny ran to his room terrified when a hired magician appeared. About the time his brother was born, Danny began to harass his mother, touch her and various inanimate objects, and wet his bed. He became defiant at home and in school. His coldness and cantankerousness increased. He was said to have physically attacked at least one teacher early in his school career. He became accident prone.

Danny's mother recalled being irritable and depressed during his infancy. At the time she had gone "cold turkey" in an effort to give up an amphetamine habit she acquired while trying to lose weight. She had suffered from depressed and irritable moods since adolescence. She felt she had received considerable help with her symptoms from several years of psychotherapy. Some time after her treatment terminated, she asked her therapist to help Danny. He saw Danny once a week for several months on two different occasions in a modified, play-therapy type of treatment. The last period of treatment occurred about six months before Danny's parents consulted me.

During the consultation, which lasted several sessions, Danny briefly mentioned that he did things which angered his peers to the point of withdrawing from him, picking on him, or hitting him. Otherwise, Danny showed no awareness of any difficulty, and seemed to have no curiosity about why his parents brought him to me. For the most part, he seemed oblivious to his family, school life, and previous therapeutic experience. He ignored my attempt to bring this apparent obliviousness to his attention. With grudging reluctance Danny agreed to listen to my account of the reasons his parents gave for bringing him to see me. During and after my remarks, Danny remained silent.

During the consultation, Danny was generally controlling, irritable, demanding, and restless in his attitudes and behavior. At times he seemed imperious or contemptuous, especially when my responses to his demands did not suit him. Sometimes Danny seemed fearful that I would find out something about him of which I might disapprove. There were also moments when he was amiable and vivacious. In play, Danny was resourceful, creative, and thoughtful. He seemed concerned primarily with enjoying himself through questioning, tricking, or scaring me, and by playing out various fantasies directly with me, or through puppets.

Danny's questions were usually requests for suggestions about what he should do. Others were directed at my personal life, practice, and the office. I responded to his questions in several ways. To some, I responded by expressing the hope that we might use them as opportunities for finding out something important about his troubles. To questions which seemed developmentally or realistically appropriate, I replied factually and briefly. If Danny seemed very distressed, I responded immediately and directly unless I thought that an answer would threaten the consultative work. When I thought he was comfortable enough to tolerate the frustration, or when his question seemed predominantly manipulative or defensive, I remained silent. Occasionally, I attempted to interpret his questions according to the context. Not answering Danny's questions immediately made him angry or withdrawn.

Danny's dramatizations of his fantasies generally involved violence, robbery, and a doctor-patient relationship. He tended to put himself in the position of both the doctor or other authority, and of the person who was violent or did the stealing. When Danny played the role of the doctor, he encouraged me, as his patient, to talk about my troubles. As the patient in these enactments, I described as my difficulties those which were actually his. I based my description on direct observation and the history which his parents had given me. I indicated that these troubles might be due to various fears. My remarks seemed to fascinate, reassure, and trouble Danny.

When the consultation came to an end, I told him I thought he needed my help because of the way he provoked other children to mistreat him, and possibly for other problems he could not tell me about yet. I also briefly explained what the analytic procedure entailed in terms of expressing himself through speech and play, and adhering to a specific schedule. He was silent and appeared to be uninterested. Diagnostically, I thought of Danny as a borderline child who was closer to the neurotic end of the spectrum rather than the psychotic.

By this time, I felt Danny and I had begun to like and admire each other for certain qualities. His dramatizations suggested a craving for some sort of intimacy and mutuality with me. Danny's questioning indicated a wish to provoke me and a pleasure in doing so. However, it could also be viewed as an attempt to develop a relationship with me, and to find out what kind of an adult I was. Perhaps it was a primitive attempt to anticipate or prepare for a working partnership with me. Danny's single, brief acknowledgement of his compulsion to provoke his peers would be congruent with the foregoing considerations.

I found myself annoyed, at times, by his demanding, imperious behavior and manner. Danny seemed to experience frustration much of
the time when I would not accommodate him. His wish and ability to
dramatize, to involve me in these dramatizations, and his reactions to
them, suggested the possibility that sooner or later Danny might enter
into a gratifying and productive alliance. By the end of the consultation,
the balance of the gratification-frustration pattern favored the formation of a therapeutic alliance despite blatant signs of resistance.

During the first weeks of the analysis, Danny became increasingly
excited and irritable. His dramatizations, remarks, and play became
more diffuse and rather feverish. He had to be doing something. He did
not want to be interrupted. He hinted, not infrequently, that he was
bored and wished he were elsewhere. At times, Danny seemed anxious
and troubled. He often ordered me to be silent and not to "think." With
increasing delight, he began to harass and startle me more and more.
Once, when I called his attention to these tendencies, Danny laughed
suddenly and said, "I want to make you mad." He wanted to see what
I would do if I were "mad."

Danny intensified his questioning to the point where I experienced
it as an assault. I tried more often to gain an understanding of his
questioning through interpretation or by encouraging him to create a
dramatization based on them. Danny reacted to these unaccommodat-
ing interventions, especially interpretations, as he had during the consultative session, but more vehemently and with increasing boldness
and pleasure. At these and other times, he began to disparage and mock
me, call me "stupid" and curse me with obscenities.

Danny began to show increasing concern about losing control of
himself and provoking my disapproval. Several times, especially when
irritated with me for not accommodating him, he threw various objects
in my direction while indicating he was trying to control himself so he
would not hurt me. Once, Danny whirled his body about, made all
kinds of noises, and threw play equipment around the room. I told him
I did not want him to hurt himself, or me, or to damage the office. I
said I didn't like what he was doing, and I wanted to find out what was
troubling him. Danny stopped quite suddenly. He smiled sheepishly as
if he were relieved and embarrassed.

I added that he seemed very worried about being able to control
himself, and seemed to want me to help him to do it. I hoped he could

soon tell me about this so we could find out what it meant. Then he would have a chance to control himself. Danny busied himself with some toys as if he were ignoring me.

His response, however, represented the first indication of a wish and ability to deliberately give up a pathological gratification at my request. Was the loss balanced by the new gratification of pleasing me? Signs of friendliness and the ability to talk to me about himself were increasing. Once, for example, we were able to make use of his question about my favorite TV programs. I promised to watch television when I had the time so we could talk about the shows he enjoyed. Subsequently, we discussed those I had watched briefly. These were the first sustained, spontaneous, and coherent discussions about an important part of Danny's life. I enjoyed them, and apparently Danny did too.

In about the third week of the analysis, Danny's interest in girls' bodies and the anatomical differences between the sexes emerged briefly in the course of what appeared to be some casual doll play. This play quickly led to an enactment of the birth process, and his recollection of his younger brother's birth. During the next few sessions, Danny sporadically referred to his jealousy of his brother. He spoke about an old wish that his brother had never been born or would die, about his attempts to injure his brother in the past, and finally gave indications of his rage at his mother for having given birth. Danny spoke with some feeling, but in a very controlled, distant way. Suddenly, he seemed to lose all interest in this part of his life. He replaced it with his interest in Star Trek, his favorite TV program, which he often watched with his father, and which he now introduced into the analysis for the first time.

Once, while dramatizing a fantasy based on this program, Danny asked me what to do about the "control panel" on the space ship. The request was typical of those he had been throwing at me for some time and seemed entirely unnecessary. He appeared helpless and distressed. For the first time, in responding to such a request, I said that since I did not believe he really needed my help, I did not know how to answer him. I said that his request made no sense. Danny became irritated and mocked my speech. He complained I always said funny things. He called me "stupid." After a pause, I said he often asked me questions to which he seemed to know the answer. This was a puzzle. I could answer his question, I said, but felt we might learn something very important if I did not. I reminded Danny of what I had told him when treatment began—we were not here simply to play games and "talk," but to learn whatever we could about his troubles so we could get rid of them.

For the first time, he listened intently to my remarks. Instead of turning away in anger, he smiled shyly. Danny said he often asked his mother unnecessary questions. The other day he had felt no one in the family cared about him and got mad. He had asked his mother a lot of questions about what she was making for dinner that night, although he knew the answers. As Danny spoke, he set up the control board quickly and easily, and began a dramatization. In the play, a member of the crew attacked the monster after the monster had attacked the ship. The crew member's friend liked the monster, and protected him from being killed by his shipmate. Then he reassured the monster by talking with him about the situation. The session came to an end.

Danny seemed to be trying to tell me that his unnecessary questions represented an attack similar to the attacks he made on his mother when he felt ignored and frustrated by her. Apparently, the questions served as a substitute for a direct attack. Perhaps Danny's questioning originated out of his rage at his mother for giving birth to his younger brother, his jealousy of his brother, and his wish to understand this part of his life. Did Danny see himself as an attacking monster (like his mother), attacking me as the analyst-mother who had betrayed him? Did he also see himself as the child-monster attacked by the analyst-mother-monster?

Danny seemed, at any rate, to have perceived my response to his request as a friendly attempt to help him understand himself through thinking and talking instead of through feeling and action. He had begun to see me as a new, protective, and understanding adult who would not be tyrannized by his provocations, and who would not attack him or neglect him in favor of a rival. I was someone who would help him understand himself. His play suggests I might well have begun to appear as his first friend, in alliance with his emerging rational self to help control and understand the monster within him.

The Star Trek play was the one activity which he shared with his withdrawn, angry father. It had replaced the expression of his feelings and thoughts about his mother and brother. Did it therefore represent Danny's attempt to turn to me for love in the transference as he had towards his father in the past when he felt betrayed and frustrated by his mother? Possibly. Were Danny's perceptions of me as myself and as a transference figure so gratifying that, along with the gratification available through the token attacks in the play, they had allowed me to successfully frustrate his unnecessary demand for help and promote the formation of the therapeutic alliance? Probably. Possibly Danny's very early experiences of gratifying mutuality, trust, and learning with his mother and favorite housekeepers had been revived by our TV bond. The subsequent pleasant interactions were now silently contributing to the establishment of a working partnership.

Danny began the next session by blandly remarking that something had happened in school that day which he was going to put into the Star Trek play. While immersed in the play, he expelled some gas rectally. I was annoyed. I did not mention my annoyance, but referred vaguely to the odor. (Probably Danny had done this or something like it in school and could not talk about it directly.) About this time, a crew member who had been friendly to the monster explained in an affectionate and solicitous way that the other crew member, who had recently hurt the monster, had done so only because he had been frightened by him (the monster). The monster now indicated that he too had once been frightened. The monster and the crew member who attacked him were now getting medical attention.

A little later, Danny suddenly blurted out that he had to go to the bathroom. He ran out of the room. When he returned about five minutes later, he continued silently with his enactment, apparently oblivious to me. Suddenly, Danny seemed to lose interest in the play. After a while, I referred to his remark at the start of the session about something happening in school. He said one of the boys in his class had called him "the biggest faggot" in the class because he "sang" too much and for other reasons which he did not mention. Danny lay down on the floor and looked up at me. He was distressed, but was in a remarkably serious and reflective mood, one which I had not seen before. Some of his classmates called him a "weirdo." Everyone thought he had the "worst attitude" in the class, and did the least work. He indicated ruefully that this might be true. He could do well in some subjects, he added, but had trouble in math.

I was moved by Danny's demeanor and words. I said what had happened to him could hurt a lot, and I was very glad he could tell me about these problems, because I thought I might be able to help him with them. I added something about his need to make the children in school mad at him in the same way as he tried to provoke his mother and me. A little later, Danny vaguely talked about having a "lot of problems" to tell me about, but since we had all "year," he had time. This idea seemed to comfort him.

This was Danny's first deliberate and explicit acknowledgement of his wish and ability to tell me about his painful school problems, and the first clear intimation that he consciously wanted me to help him with them. This acknowledgement constituted the first indication of a conscious commitment to his increasingly realistic perception of analytic work. Along with the transference reaction we had analyzed in the previous session, it had followed my frustrating him.

By not allowing Danny to treat me like his mother, but as his analyst, had I reinforced his wish and ability to view and use me, as well as himself, realistically in the analytic situation? I had indicated that his helplessness meant something, and that I viewed him as competent for the analytic task and preferred him to do the same. For Danny, such a view probably meant that I considered him capable of self-control and of growing up. My frustration raised Danny's self-esteem, and reduced the pain of his frustration. At the same time, it had enhanced his ability to participate in the analytic work. The last episode of Danny's Star Trek play indicated his attempt to understand his need to attack as the result of a fear of being attacked. The play, as well as what followed, might be viewed as an externalization of the unconscious work involved in Danny's entry into a therapeutic alliance with me.

At this point Danny was ready to work on the gradual, explicit acknowledgement of his problems to himself and to me. He wanted to see my reaction, and was able, under certain circumstances, to accept a limited frustration from me. Danny's motivation included a wish to please me as a new friend and transference figure, and to a lesser degree, to understand the point of my frustrating him. The content of the Star Trek play and his mood during and after indicate the significance of the gratification which had followed the frustration I had asked him to bear. Analysis meant having a gratifying, understanding friend which was a rare commodity in the life of this friendless boy.

Danny seemed more excited, irritable, and demanding than usual in the following session. He said he had done something which I would not like. He would not tell me about it. He did not want me to talk either, especially in the funny way I did. Suddenly he asked if his mother had ever told me about his bed-wetting. I nodded. Well, he did not do it anymore! Just once in awhile. Did I know about bed-wetting? I told him I did, that I helped boys and girls with this problem and I would try to help him too. Danny seemed pleased. I was pleased he could finally share with me what appeared to be one of his major secrets, one he had held back since the beginning of our relationship.

Danny now seemed at a loss about what to do. He indicated he no longer wanted to talk about the bed-wetting. Could he talk about it in a play? But how? What did I think? Why didn't I tell him? Danny complained I never answered his questions. He was annoyed and impatient. I began to feel his distress. After a pause, when he seemed to be getting more and more irritable and could not come up with an idea, I said I would try to think of something. There was another pause. Danny brought up a few ideas only to discard them. He looked at me expectantly.

I suggested he invent a play in which someone does something which resembled bed-wetting. Danny was silent. Like losing control of himself in some way, I continued, after another pause. He seemed to relax. His face brightened up. He seemed to be thinking. Enthusiastically, Danny suggested he could have one of the crew in Star Trek play "beam down" to the planets. (He had often focused his play on this activity with great pleasure. It consisted of someone "shooting" a person with a special gun which energized him so he could be transported instantly through vast distances in space.) Danny now "beamed down" a member of the crew.

As he played, he touched his genital area occasionally. (He had done this in previous sessions, but not nearly as often or as openly as now.) For the first time, I drew Danny's attention to this activity near the end of the session. He seemed momentarily alarmed. Then he relaxed, smiled, and said shyly that the touching "felt good." The session ended as Danny continued with the play.

Danny's first acknowledgment of his bed-wetting, and his implied wish for my help in dealing with it, are further indications of his deepening involvement in the therapeutic alliance. However, prior to revealing his bed-wetting, Danny had indicated he had done something which I would dislike, and which he could not tell me about. The revelation about his bed-wetting, therefore, may have partially represented a seductive attempt to reduce his guilt feelings by being a good patient. Also, his revelation was partially a statement about the physiological equivalent of what he could not tell me. Did his enuresis, and the difficulties which he had mentioned in the previous session, represent, in part, symptomatic vehicles for anger directed primarily against his mother? Danny's angry demand that I tell him what to do, may have been aimed at reducing his guilt feelings by getting me to take symbolic responsibility for whatever it was he could not tell me. Presumably, it was an indirect expression of his anger at his mother.

Given the total analytic situation, I should have felt free to attempt to interpret Danny's demand for gratification before yielding to it. Our partnership was developing satisfactorily, and the pleasure and pride which his revelations afforded him were prominent. Still, I was concerned about Danny's mounting anger, anxiety, and possible loss of control. Had I reacted to my frustrating him two sessions before with guilt and with a wish to reduce it by accommodating him? Had I been affected by Danny's increasingly successful struggle to work with me and a desire to reward him? Quite likely. Danny's response, at any rate, was productive. For the first time, he could bring into the analytic situation signs of a possible masturbatory struggle organized around hatred of and longing for his mother. Probably Danny's bed-wetting and sado-masochistic behavior were also derivatives of this struggle.

Again in the next session he was quite troubled. Danny did not want to play "Star Trek" today. He indicated something "bad" had again happened which he could not tell me about. I was to say nothing. Danny became increasingly irritable. He vaguely referred to a conflict with his mother. Suddenly, imperiously, he demanded that I tell him what toys to bring to the session tomorrow! He reproached me scornfully for "thinking" instead of answering his question immediately. He did not want me to "help" him, but to tell him what toys to bring.

I felt a twinge of annoyance at his manner and was concerned about his irritability. I said I did think about his questions instead of merely answering them. Sometimes, like now for example, I did not understand them. I believed he could choose his own toys just as I believed the other day he knew how to set up the control board. I thought his question and his upset showed something very big was bothering him. He was trying to tell me about it, but was doing so indirectly, through his question. If only we could both puzzle out what it meant.

Danny almost shrieked with anger and frustration. He did not want me to help him find out anything. Why couldn't I just be an ordinary person and answer his question? After scolding and cursing me for several minutes, he suddenly said he had been very "fidgety" in the car on the way to my office. If he had had a toy he would have felt all right. This is why he wants me to tell him what to bring next time. I waited a few moments while Danny moved about aimlessly and seemed very distressed. Then I said, "If we could find out why you were 'fidgety' in the car in the first place, you might not need a toy tomorrow to feel alright." Again Danny demanded I tell him what toy to bring! Although he now seemed calmer, I felt his distress more sharply than before. I felt he needed some gratification to balance his frustration if the therapeutic alliance was to be maintained. Otherwise, Danny might find his anger unbearable, and disrupt our fragile partnership.

I offered him a "deal." Would he first try for a few more minutes to help us both find out why he had been so "fidgety" in the car? Then, if he still wanted me to suggest a toy for tomorrow, I would do so. Danny accepted the "deal." With an intensity which I had never seen in him before, he immediately told me for the first time, and in great detail, how he had to "touch" everything. He demonstrated this tendency by touching everything around him, including his body. The "touching" made him feel "good" and kept the "demon" away. No! There was no "demon"! I should forget what he said! Touching had something to do with being "fidgety." Also, touching his body was different from touching other things.

As Danny talked, he seemed to relax. He looked as if he felt cozy and conspiratorial. He liked to touch buttons and other things. This was particularly true when they made things happen at a distance, as in certain types of mechanical toys and household deveices. Danny liked playing with calculators. He had one at home. In the car, going to the session, he had enjoyed playing with the buttons on the dashboard, because they had reminded him of his calculator. His mother became angry and screamed at him for being "fidgety." He got mad and screamed back at her. Actually, Danny had been mad at her before they started out, because she had not given him enough time to pick out a toy for the trip. Furthermore, she had refused to tell him which toy to take.

I told Danny he had helped me very much to begin to understand his fidgetiness and touching. When he got angry at his mother, a fight took place inside of him. His mad feelings wanted him to hurt her, while his love feelings wanted to love and protect her. His fidgetiness was a way of controlling all these feelings. When the fidgetiness became too strong, he then had to touch things to control the fidgetiness. Sometimes, like today, the touching and fidgetiness got to the point where they got him into trouble with his mother. Danny seemed to be listening and thinking intently. Then he said, quietly, that he had done what he was supposed to do. Now I should tell him what toys to take.

I had been very impressed by Danny's self-discipline, his effort to cooperate, and his willingness to share more of his secret world with me despite his suffering. I felt rewarded and grateful. After expressing my appreciation for his waiting and for helping me to understand him, I carried out my half of our "deal." I suggested any toy which gave him a chance to press something, especially if it would make something else happen in another place, would be all right. I added that by now he had probably thought of something like this on his own. Danny immediately thought of Jack-in-the-Box and a few other toys, only to discard them immediately as choices.

He soon lost interest in choosing a toy, and instead began to eagerly elaborate on the idea of controlling something at a distance. He referred to various remote control devices such as the "beaming down" in Star Trek, and the opening and shutting of doors. He saw the power to perform these feats as magical, as well as scientific. It was a form of energy, like an invisible "ray." This could come from a thought as well as from a machine. Danny thought a lot about elevators. They go up and down as if by magic. The machinery responsible for their movement is invisible.

After Danny talked about this last idea for a while, I realized he was simultaneously defending himself against masturbation and was gratifying these masturbational impulses in a symbolic way. He seemed ready to begin to discuss his sexual feelings. I said some boys got "boners" just by having certain thoughts and feelings. He stared at me for a while, and then asked, "What is a 'boner'?" "When the penis gets hard," I answered. He seemed to think about my answer. He said sometimes his "dick" got "hard" and "stands up." Danny immediately shifted back to the idea of controlling things at a distance by an invisible force. If he could do that, he "would fight crime." No, he would not!

He would open up the "cabinets" (indicating the cabinets on the wall of the playroom, but probably meaning those in his kitchen) and eat the cookies inside. The session had now come to an end. Danny left in a friendly, good-humored mood.

Presumably, as the result of the "deal," I had helped Danny reveal what he had been unable to tell me in the beginning of the session through the use of a mutually agreed upon, limited, and controllable frustration. Danny's current anger at his mother, and at me as his transference mother, represented his reaction to various preoedipal and oedipal frustrations. For the moment, Danny's anger seemed due to my refusal to pick out a toy for him to play with in the car. Did this represent to him my refusal to approve of his wish to express his anger (and other feelings) directed toward his mother in the form of a mastur-batory substitute? Had Danny asked me, in effect, to help him fight what he regarded as his criminal feelings and actions, to take responsibility for them, in a sense, and offer him a substitute? Most likely. His resulting anger and pain could now be better appreciated.

Our "deal" was developmentally appropriate but later I wondered about its necessity. Our alliance had been progressing satisfactorily. Furthermore, Danny had begun to react productively to my initial frustration of his demand for assistance with a lessening of his anxiety. Nevertheless, reacting to his current distress and that of previous ses-sions, I had accommodated him. Was I again rewarding Danny for his participation in the work, as well as reducing my guilt feelings for hurting him? Had I felt threatened and intimidated as well as angered by his tyrannical outburst in the beginning of the session? As a result, had I been less able to assess his ability to tolerate a frustration? To reduce his guilt feelings for provoking his mother and for other reasons, had Danny again tried to seduce me through cooperation? Despite my doubts, the "deal" clearly pleased Danny and was a useful device. It enabled him to temper his anger and sufficiently relinquish his defense to reveal a distressing symptom, and to begin analyzing it.

After the "deal," I offered Danny two interpretations about his touching and his erections. I implied touching and the games he played defended against masturbatory activity, but did not explicitly describe these defenses. Nor did I tell him that his angry demand on me repre-sented an attempt to get from me what he had failed to get from his mother. These interpretations were to come later.

The growing therapeutic alliance was continually enriched by the growing network of gratifications and frustrations springing from our interaction. This made it possible for Danny and me to deliberately negotiate his demand for immediate gratification in such a way as to protect his autonomy and advance the analytic work in the face of his distress. The further evolution of the alliance is worth relating, because it clearly demonstrates some of its specific major enrichments, as well as the crucial narcissistic gratification it made available to Danny. This gratification seemed to strengthen the alliance all the more.

A couple of weeks after the last session Danny seemed unusually excited and restless. He walked about, climbed onto the table and chairs and jumped down. He touched things and talked a mile a minute. I worried he would hurt himself, but felt fascinated into silent impotence. Suddenly, Danny lay down on the toy chest and said quietly, "Tell me to slow down when I am like this so you can think."

He was very serious. In contrast to his usual imperious demand that I should not think or, in fact, interfere with him in any way, Danny now seemed to value my thinking and to want me to do it. At the same time, he showed his wish and ability to control himself, and gave me explicit permission to help him do so from now on. He seemed, then, to have internalized fundamental aims of the therapeutic alliance in regard to the control of feeling and action and the use of thought. Danny could tolerate and appreciate impulse restraint and frustration in the service of analytic understanding. Secondary process thinking had begun to triumph over primary process discharge. I was relieved, amazed, and delighted.

In a subsequent session, Danny told me he liked me to think about him, and liked to look at my face when I did. Also, he said he liked to come to sessions, because this was his only chance to talk about anything he wanted without anybody making fun of him. These two aspects of the alliance point up the special narcissistic gratifications it made available to Danny. My face had come to reveal to him his importance to me as a source of learning and pleasure. Hearing and seeing me, Danny could identify with me and acquire an analytic attitude. The visual element suggests the revival of memory traces of gratifying visual interplay (with developmental implications) between himself and his mother (and housekeeper) in infancy. His remarks also indicate the aim-inhibited libidinization of the thinking aspect of the alliance, a reflection perhaps of his liking me for liking him.

Then came a session in which Danny earnestly implored me to give him "advice," not "understanding" about a painful situation involving his older brother. He was, however, willing to talk about the situation instead of demanding and getting immediate advice. His talk led to an attempt to understand how the difficulty between his brother and him had arisen. This was the first time Danny had explicitly asked for help with an important problem of the moment, and the first time he could deliberately and easily put aside his demand for immediate gratification in favor of a cooperative attempt at understanding. His feeling of frustration seemed minimal. No "deal" was necessary.

Some weeks later Danny came to a session quite distressed. After trying to make a play out of a recent painful experience, he decided to talk directly about the trouble he so often had with his mother, his brothers, and other people. Why didn't people like him? Why did they call him names and ignore him? I referred to his provoking behavior at home, in school, and in the analytic situation. Danny asked, in a very serious way, what he could do about it. How could I help him?

In this instance, Danny had spontaneously shifted from the use of externalization and projection to the direct acknowledgement of his central, lifelong problem as he experienced it. Instead of only complaining about others, he was seriously acknowledging his troubles with people were due to something in him. Even more, Danny was ready to assume part of the responsibility for the resolution of the problem, along with a request for help in fulfilling that responsibility. Finally, he showed a direct and serious interest in understanding the nature of my contribution. The defensive aspects of his position seemed non-existent. He seemed to be getting sufficient gratification from the alliance itself so that gratification from dramatization per se had become superfluous.

Several months after this session, Danny wanted to go to the bathroom. Ordinarily, he would leave the room immediately or soon after announcing his intention. This time, he spontaneously and proudly controlled himself. Danny referred to the hope I had voiced at such times. I had asked him to try to control himself, if possible, for a while, and to talk about going to the bathroom to see what he might learn. Danny now revealed for the first time that sometimes he went to the bathroom because he had a "ball of fire" inside him, and wanted to "cool down." The "ball of fire" meant he was "mad" at me. At the moment, he was mad at me for saying things about stealing. His urge to go to the bathroom and his anger at me seemed to subside as he continued talking and playing. In this instance, Danny had achieved the internalization of another basic aim of the therapeutic alliance: the control of his bodily functions to understand their possible psychological significance. His pride in this achievement was obvious.

There is no way of knowing to what extent Danny was reacting to me as a transference figure whom he was eager to please and appease, and to what extent he was reacting to me as a real person. The frequent and wide fluctuations in his ability to participate in the therapeutic alliance for well over another year suggest the transference aspects of the alliance were probably quite large. These fluctuations may have also been due to a more immediate factor: Danny had difficulty stabilizing his various new internalizations.

DISCUSSION

Flexibility is one of the outstanding issues implicit in the foregoing account. Why did I gratify Danny immediately in one instance, refuse him in another, partially refuse him in a third, and make a "deal" with him in still another? I had responded immediately and favorably to Danny's request that I try to watch certain TV programs he liked, even though for the moment he was relaxed and friendly and might have tolerated a frustration. My accommodating response carried with it the potential danger of inviting him to control me, use me as a source of transferential gratifications and, in this way, intensify his already considerable resistance to the analysis. However, this request was his first explicit invitation to a friendly exchange which might evolve into a working relationship through direct communication in ordinary thought and speech—a dramatic change from his anxious, disruptive behavior. Also, Danny's request appeared to be developmentally appropriate, rather than manipulative or defensive. I experienced it as natural and spontaneous. Even so, it's possible that I had been seduced by the hope that accommodating Danny would lead to a gratifying respite from his harassment, his secrecy, and his repudiation of the analytic situation.

Our few TV talks, each of which lasted only a few minutes, became our first sustained, coherent, mutually interesting and gratifying exchange of words. These TV talks were also linked to his inner world, a world which clearly included his father, and therefore an indication of a possible father transference. Moreover, it gave Danny an opportunity to perceive me as someone real who could share and enjoy an important part of his real world. Danny could perceive me as someone like himself, from whom he could expect empathy. Our actual enjoyment of the TV talks seemed to demonstrate the validity of this perception. Given his chronic fear and distrust, his need to attack and to be attacked, his secrecy, and his ancient isolation even within his own family, this experience of mutuality, however brief, might have been momentous to Danny in strengthening his capability for becoming my analytic partner.

There is no way of demonstrating that our new TV bond led to the recollection of the birth of his brother and the emergence of other important aspects of his inner world which occurred soon afterwards. Still, the sequence cannot be ignored. The invitation into Danny's TV world and the communications which followed had begun to serve as the basis of the growing conviction in me that sooner or later we would be able to form a productive therapeutic alliance. This conviction was intensified by the professional and personal gratifications which I had already begun to experience in the analytic situation. It may well have played a significant background role in my ability to productively frustrate Danny's unnecessary request for assistance in "setting up" the control panel in the Star Trek play.

There were other background factors which probably favored our ability to use this frustration in an analytically useful way. I refer to the sustained approval and attentiveness which Danny's mother was giving him, more than he had ever experienced before—and perhaps, more than anyone else in the family had ever received. For me, Danny's mother's vigorous, steady support of the analysis visibly increased my basic conviction about succeeding with Danny in our analytic enterprise. Her attitude was a most welcome counterbalance to her husband's cynical attitude toward the analysis which tended to frustrate and discourage me. By this time, I had come to experience Danny's mother as an important part of the analytic situation, not only because of her open support, but also because of her detailed, frank reports.

In response to the frustration which I had asked Danny to bear, a mother transference emerged, coupled with the implied recognition of me as a new and different person. In addition, there was a demonstra-

tion of our ability to work together, a frank and detailed acknowledgement of his difficulties, and the clearly implied wish for the kind of help
I was offering. Whatever else was meant by lying on the floor as he
related his troubles, it indicated Danny's freedom to reveal his passivity
and helplessness to me, an unequivocal sign of trust.

My indication that I thought Danny did not need my help in "setting
up" the Star Trek panel control was the last, the most explicit, and most
useful of a series of previously unsuccessful attempts during the consultative phase to maintain a relatively abstinent atmosphere. Why it now
led to productive work is not entirely clear. Did the frustration of his
wish, coupled with his new perception of me, make its defensive purposes useless so that the underlying anger at his mother could emerge?
The frustration and its consequences offered an opportunity to realize
more or less consciously that we now had at our disposal a disciplined
vehicle for committed, purposeful understanding.

2. Flexibility results from the analyst's ability to use spontaneously
and, when necessary, suddenly, his perceptions of the immediate and
long-range gratification-frustration balance in the analytic situation.
The analyst must use these perceptions to help the child transform his
demand for a specific gratification into shared work aimed at determining whether the gratification is defensive, transferential, or realistic, i.e.,
useful. The analyst's ability to use his perceptions in this way depends
on his appreciation of the powerful developmental gratifications and
frustrations inherent in the analytic situation and available to both
analyst and analysand, his awareness of his irrational reactions, and his
ability to respond to them analytically.

Encouraging optimal autonomy as well as mutuality for both partners is an essential part of the work. The work, rather than the specific
gratification or frustration, is of primary importance because of its
profound analytic and developmental implications. It is this very work,
indeed, which offers crucial and matchless gratification. At the same
time, it helps to convince the child of the analyst's intention to help him,
while promoting the development of both child and analyst.

The proper balance of frustration and gratification enhances the
secondary process functioning so necessary for analytic work, while
making generous provision for the emergence of the primary process
thinking essential for communicating fantasies. The analysand is able

to identify with the analyst who objectively observes him while he, the patient, experiences inner emotional conflict. The proper balance of frustration and gratification also fosters reality testing and separation of self from object-representations. In differentiating himself from his parents and analyst as well as his analyst from his parents, the child can effectively participate in the analysis of transference reactions. An optimum gratification-frustration balance sets free for the analytic work more psychic energy for both child and analyst, and leads to strengthening of self-esteem, reducing the need for defenses and for substitute gratification.

SUMMARY

Frustration and gratification of a developmental, realistic, and pathological nature, planned as well as unplanned, inevitably pervade all analyses. This statement especially holds true for child analysis. What is crucial is the degree to which both analyst and child are able to achieve a balance of these frustrations and gratifications which is uniquely optimal for the evolution of a working partnership and transference. These achievements further the appearance of defenses, drive derivatives, memories and unconscious conflict. Failure to achieve such a balance may lead to an intensification of unanalyzable anger toward the analyst, or to a pleasant, non-analytic relationship. Realistic gratification is essential for the evolution of the therapeutic alliance and is readily available in the analytic situation. The patient enjoys emulating and pleasing his analyst. He finds joy in therapeutic accomplishment, mastery, and developmental achievement.

The analyst as well as the patient experiences frustration and gratification in the analytic situation. His emotional reactions to those experiences may interfere with or enhance his analytic judgment and position. They require, therefore, constant scrutiny. .

NOTES

1. Dickes (1975) has stressed the release of instinctual countercathectic energy following a successful interpretation in adult analysis.

Along with the improved ego functioning, the patient may experience affection as well as gratitude for the analyst's real assistance. This affection, aimed at the real analyst, in turn enhances the working relationship with the analyst (pp. 22, 23).

2. I have avoided the use of the terms *personal* or *instinctual* gratification in this chapter because they are too vague. Every gratification in the analytic situation is apt to be more or less "personal" and more or less "instinctual" to the child. Rather, I have viewed gratifications and frustrations in the analytic situation from the vantage point of their effect on the evolution of the therapeutic alliance, the transference, and the child's development.

3. In 1968, Weiss coauthored a paper with Fineberg, Kohrman, and Gelman which echoed these earlier views.

4. This is an abbreviation of a previously published paper (Kay 1967) supplemented by additional unpublished details.

5. What follows was omitted from the paper on which this account has been based.

REFERENCES

Abraham, K., (1920). Manifestations of the female castration complex. *Selected Papers on Psychoanalysis,* ed. E. Jones, trans. D. Byran and A. Strachey. Third Impression, London: Hogarth, (1948) pp. 338–369

Anthony, E.J. (1964). Panel: child analysis at different developmental stages. Reporter, G.M. Abbate. *Journal of the American Psychoanalytic Association* 12:135–150.

Bick, E. (1962). Symposium on child analysis, I: child analysis today, *International Journal Psycho-Analysis* 43:328–332; 342.

Bornstein, B. (1948). Emotional barriers in the understanding and treatment of young children. *American Journal of Orthopsychiatry* 18:691–697.

Dickes, R. (1975). The therapeutic relationship and alliance. *International Journal of Psychoanalytic Psychotherapy* 4:1–24.

Erikson, E.H. (1972). Play and Actuality. In *Play and Development,* ed. M.W. Piers. New York: W.W. Norton. pp. 127–167.

Freud, A. (1926). Introduction to the technique of the analysis of children. In *The Psychoanalytical Treatment of Children.* London: Imago. pp. 3–52

_____ (1945). Indications for child analysis. *Psychoanalytic Study of the Child* 1:127–149.

_____ (1946). *The Psycho-Analytical Treatment of Children,* Preface London: Imago, pp. ix-xii.

_____ (1965). *Normality and Pathology in Childhood.* New York: International Universities Press.

Furer, M.D. (1976). Panel: Current concepts of the psychoanalytic process. reporter, S.A. Morgenstern. *Journal of the American Psychoanalytic Association* 24:184–88

Greenson, R.R. (1967). *The Technique and Practice of Psychoanalysis.* New York: International Universities Press.

Harley, M. (1974). Panel: A comparison between adult and child analysis. Reporter, C.I. Feigelson. *Journal of the American Psychoanalytic Association* 22:603–11.

Kay, P., (1967). A boy's wish to give his analyst a gift. *Journal of the American Academy of Child Psychiatry* 6:38–50.

Klein, M., (1927). Symposium on child analysis. In *Contributions to Psychoanalysis.* London: Hogarth Press, pp. 152–184.

Levin, S., and Wermer, H., (1966). The significance of giving gifts to children in therapy. *Journal of the American Academy of Child Psychiatry* 5:630–52.

Maenchen, A. (1970). On the technique of child analysis in relation to stages of development. *Psychoanalytic Study of the Child* 25: 175–208.

Murphy, L.B. (1972). Infants' play and cognitive development, In *Play and Development,* ed. M. W. Piers. New York: W.W. Norton. pp. 119–126.

Schowalter, J.E. (1976). Therapeutic alliance and the role of speech in child analysis. *Psychoanalytic Study of the Child* 31:415–436.

Spitz, R.A. (1972). Fundamental education: the coherent object as a developmental model. In *Play and Development.* ed. M.W. Piers. New York: W.W. Norton. pp. 43–63.

Weiss, S. (1964). Parameters in child analysis. *Journal of the American Psychoanalytic Association* 12:587–599.

Weiss, S., Fineberg, H.H., Gelman, R.L., and Kohrman, R. (1968).

Technique of child analysis, Problems of the opening phase. *Journal of the American Academy of Child Psychiatry* 7:639–662.

Webster's New Twentieth Century Dictionary of the English Language (1965). Unabridged, 2nd ed. Cleveland and New York: World.

Chapter 12

DREAM ANALYSIS IN CHILD ANALYSIS

Ted E. Becker, M.D.

DREAM ANALYSIS AND DEVELOPMENTAL LEVEL

In child analysis, sustained free association is unavailable as a technique to reach the child's unconscious mental processes. Our inferences about the unconscious must come from observations of its derivatives in the child's general behavior, play, stories, drawings, fantasies, dreams, and the progression of associated activities during an analytic hour. Dreams offer the most direct access.

Free association is generally unavailable in all phases of childhood —from early childhood to early adolescence. The developmentally appropriate way a young child communicates is through action, not words. Discharge through action and primary process thinking, which we see in preoedipal children, should not be confused with goal-directed associations to a dream. The latency child's primary task is to develop defenses against incestuous wishes. Secondary process thinking is becoming consolidated. Free association would tend to undermine both of these, and is therefore rigorously avoided. Most preadolescents, much to their distress, are experiencing a preoedipal regression of some degree. Free association tends to move one further in the direction of regression and primary process thinking, and is not possible for the preadolescent. Most preadolescents, in fact, are so on guard that material is consciously withheld, and may only be revealed in adolescence. In early adolescence the upsurge of genital impulses brings a renewed struggle with incestuous wishes which must be defended against. During all of these periods the state of ego maturation and automatic defense against anxiety makes free association impossible.

There are exceptions. Certain children who possess superior intelligence and suffer from obsessional neuroses may be capable of episodes of free association. In certain cases, a special type of transference may permit periods of free association to a dream, as in the case of Martley described below. The borderline or psychotic child's speech may simulate free association when he is incapable of holding his flow of thought in check.

The technique of obtaining dream material in young patients depends on the characteristics of childhood, and varies with the child's developmental level. There are differences in the way children of different developmental stages communicate with us. In the young child, we learn from the child's play and other activities, as well as from information obtained during regular contacts with parents. As the child grows older, his verbal communications become more important than his activities. By early adolescence, the analyst usually avoids contact with his patient's parents, because such contacts conflict with the child's need for autonomy. As there are differences in the way a child can integrate our interventions at different ages, we modify our ways of communicating to facilitate the various modes of integration. The young child, in whom primary processes are still prominent, differs from the latency child, who presents his defenses to us. Our technique will take these differences into account. Whatever the differences may be in obtaining material from children, once we have obtained it, our technical interventions are essentially the same for all periods of childhood. Dream interpretation with children does not differ fundamentally from that with an adult.

PRELATENCY

In the prelatency child, primary process thinking is dominant and reality testing is poorly developed. Dreams may therefore be described as if they were real events. Questions like "Did you see those pictures at night when your eyes were closed?" may help the young patient distinguish them as dream images.

Dreams may appear dramatized as part of a young child's play. Fantasies, dreams and events of the day merge into one another. A parent's report that his child awoke frightened during the night may be a clue to the occurrence of a dream. If the child told his parent he saw a monster or some other frightening apparition, we may be sensitized to this fear if it appears in the child's productions during his analytic hour. "Mommie told me you had a dream about a monster last night. Can you tell me about it?" will often elicit the dream. A young child will usually tell us dreams if we ask about the pictures he saw at night when he was asleep. He may be reluctant to describe anxiety dreams, because relating them may revive the dream anxiety.

The following is an excerpt from a first diagnostic session with a six-year-old boy. Although he is six, the dream is typical of material one obtains from a younger child where primary process predominates. Dream, fantasy, nighttime, and daytime thoughts merge. Practically, it often does not matter in our analytic work whether we know what is dream and what is fantasy. However, the child's ability to differentiate one from the other may be of diagnostic value in assessing the development of secondary process thinking.

Justin's parents complained he suffered from fears of fire and dying. He had trouble falling asleep because of these fears, and would awaken with nightmares about fires, getting lost, animals attacking him and his parents, or a whale preventing him from getting back where he wanted to be. Justin loved a girl his age and talked about marrying her, where they would live, and the children they would have. He talked constantly, but his parents considered his conversation endless and meaningless, and had ceased listening.

He drew a picture of a room on fire, and then one of a monster. He told me, "The monster stuck his sword into a maiden—no, into the radiator and it got burned—no, into a plant and it broke off, and a leaf fell into the water and the alligator ate it up." My empathic response was, "Poor monster, what did he do to deserve such bad treatment? Were you ever afraid that such terrible things would happen to you?" He replied, "I was afraid my front would turn into my behind." "Where did you ever see such a thing as that?" I asked. The immediate reply was, "My mommie's front turned into her behind, and when I saw her again her penis was back." I sympathized with how frightening it was for him to think his front might turn into his behind, and that something might happen to his penis. This comment aroused Justin's castration anxiety; he then attempted to master his fear by becoming the aggressor. Justin shot me in the penis with the dart gun. He got under my chair and tried to attack me from below.

From the point of view of technique, it is worth mentioning that the affect of his fear of being wounded was the focus of this intervention. As Berta Bornstein (1950) repeatedly emphasized in her lectures, by dealing first with the child's affect, we will learn how he deals with his drives.

LATENCY

A prime developmental task of latency is to master oedipal and preoedipal impulses. Secondary process is in the ascendancy. With the development of the superego, guilt and a more stable defense system, there is a change in the character of the material a child presents. Unconscious material is defended against and disguised, except in children who have lagged behind in their emotional development. Even in the typical latency child, there are periodic breakthroughs of unconscious impulses. Mastery is not acquired all at once. Generally we must infer unconscious processes from the more disguised derivatives children of this age present. We may recognize the rise in the intensity of an impulse by the appearance or intensification of defensive behavior and attitudes. Play may become stereotyped and repetitive, and reveal little of unconscious impulses and a maximum of defense, for example, the infamous, endless game of checkers.

In latency and preadolescence the dream (and daydream) offers us the most direct access to the unconscious. (For further discussion of prelatency, latency, and preadolescence, see chapters 6, 7, and 8.)

THE REVIVAL OF ANXIETY
IN DREAM ANALYSIS IN TWO LATENCY CHILDREN

Dreams may come into the analysis of children spontaneously or we may have to ask about them. A child suffering from night terrors will present them with eagerness in the hope of receiving help. However, if the underlying wish becomes evident while talking about dreams, or the fright is reexperienced, the child may reveal his dream with greater reluctance or they may cease.

In the following case, the telling of the dream revealed to the child his death wishes, and his nightmares ceased.

Ralph, an eight-year-old boy, came into analysis because of night terrors which had been present as long as he could remember. They occurred almost nightly. He would awaken his nurse, who slept with her clothes on because she had to get up with him so regularly. The nurse and child did not "bother" the parents, who knew nothing of the nightmares. This attested to the parents' lack of involvement in the emotional life of their child. Only with the appearance of a serious school problem did Ralph's parents come to recognize the extent of his anxiety. He was then brought for analysis.

Ralph complained, "I always picture disasters." The nightly dreams involved earthquakes, fires, and plane crashes in which the parents were killed. Occasionally, he was involved as a rescuer. There was initial pressure to share these nightly tragedies with me, but within a week, and with no interpretation on my part, the death wishes involving his parents became evident to Ralph, and the nightmares ceased. He obviously longed to have a living mother who would relate to him. On some level, his mother was aware of this. "I wish Ralph had a blanket to take to bed with him," his mother commented. "He only takes those pencils and his toothbrush."

Over the following years of analysis, Ralph never again brought in dreams spontaneously, but only rarely, when I asked for them. In the first months the analytic material was an endless, repetitive, stereotyped game of checkers. In looking back, there had been an almost joking comment about "doing his parents in." Ralph made this comment before the nightmares ceased. It had been said so casually it seemed of little emotional importance. It was detached from any real affect. Repeated attempts were made to deal with Ralph's resistance. I pointed out to him that his nightmares had suddenly ceased after having been there "as long as he could remember." Another time, I suggested that the idea of "doing his parents in" each night must be very frightening. Ralph denied this, and also that he now dreamed at all. After several months of squeezing from the checker game whatever material there was about competition and rivalry with his brother, I told Ralph this checker game seemed to keep us from being able to find out anything about his troubles. I told him we would stop it. Ralph burst into tears. "My mother has never played a game with me in my life." When his mother heard this from him, she said, "Oh Dr. B., do I have to play a game with him?"

Here we can see how difficult it is for the child analyst to understand an action when the child does not verbally explain it. Through Ralph's objection to my suggestion that we call an end to our game playing, I came to see the significance of his behavior. Every day he guarded against his death wishes which were so evident in his nightmares by playing a game with me. In the game he lived out an unconscious fantasy of having his mother alive and playing with him. I was only aware of what seemed to be a defense responsible for a sterile analysis, and not the repeated gratification by me of his longing for his mother. When I interrupted the checker game, I interrupted his fantasy of a closeness with her. He was again faced with their separateness, his death wishes, and his overwhelming sadness.

From time to time I could elicit dreams by making comments about themes in his play. On one occasion Ralph built a city of blocks and bombarded it. He named the city and I recognized it as the very spot where his parents were on vacation. When I told him that it was a bit like his old nightmares, Ralph agreed. He told a dream, which had occurred the previous night, in which a city was bombed while his parents were there. In the dream, Ralph was involved in a rescue operation. He could now speak about his resentment about his parents going away from him.

This case may also tell us something about soliciting dreams in child analysis. If the dream itself is a symptom, as in this case, our query may elicit a defensive denial. If it is not a symptom, the dream may be something the child pays little attention to. In these instances, if we ask, he may tell us a dream.

In the following example, the recollection of a dream revived a dream anxiety in the session.

A seven-and-a-half-year-old boy, Joseph, had been in analysis for some time. His mother reported he had a nightmare the night before. In his session he drew, played, and talked about scary things. I asked if last night's scary dream was on his mind. Joseph hurled a block at me, and after a moment's pause, charged at me with feet and fists. The inner process, which we later understood, was that when I reminded him of the dream, he felt the original terror. Since I was the cause of his recollection, he attacked me with the block. Even before I moved, Joseph feared I would retaliate, and charged at me in self-defense, warding off the expected retaliation.

He then told me the dream: for him to be able to grow up, someone was dipping his leg into acid and it was dissolving.

Joseph suffered from severe dyslexia, poor muscular coordination, and an eye muscle imbalance which had required surgical correction. He perceived his difficulty as something wrong with his body, "an invisible handicap," that made him different from other children. They could read, write, engage in athletic skills, and in general grow and develop more easily than he—and without all kinds of special help. The dream expressed the wish his body would be changed so he could develop like other boys. However, this resulted in castration for his forbidden wishes for maturity. Simply asking about the dream had revived the anxiety, and set in motion his defensive attack.

ELICITING DREAMS AND ASSOCIATIONS

At one end of the spectrum are children who suffer from night terrors, want our help, and tell us their dreams. At the other end is the child who is brought to treatment because others think he should come, and not because he himself is suffering. This latter child will see no reason to report his dreams. In fact, it may never occur to him to mention them.

In an initial evaluation one will question a child about why he has come, or the reasons his parents have given him for coming. We ask how he felt about coming. We empathize with his discomfort over seeing a stranger, and not knowing what to expect. We identify ourselves as a person aware of and interested in how he feels, and not just how he behaves. In an initial evaluation we ask the child about any fears, worries, or dreams (good or bad) he has had recently, or had long ago. Most children will acknowledge they have had scary dreams at one time or another. If they are reluctant to tell them, a little encouragement will usually elicit the dream in great detail: "I bet you can remember if you try very hard" or "You have such a good memory for other things, I bet you can remember."

Once an analysis has begun, some children will tell us their dreams, probably because they perceived our interest during the initial contact. Other children will not report their dreams. We can proceed by analyzing the latency child's defenses with the hope that dreams will then appear. My experience has been that dreams are usually not excluded from the analysis by an unconscious defensive struggle, but rather that they are withheld as a part of a more conscious resistance. Even a child with a good therapeutic alliance may not spontaneously realize that dreams can be important in analytic work. If our relationship to the child is positive, and dreams do not appear, we must ask about them. "Any dreams lately?" We must make the child aware of the importance of dreams if we wish to have available this sounding of the forces in his unconscious. The aim of child analysis is to make unconscious processes conscious, and dreams (and fantasies) are the most direct access. If the child's relationship to us is not positive, asking him questions about dreams is futile, and should be avoided.

Once we have raised the question, "Any dreams lately?" we can expect a wide range of responses—from an acknowledgment of dreaming and reporting a dream, to the denial of dreaming and the appearance of defenses directed against our query. When Berta Bornstein's (1949) six-year-old patient, Frankie, was asked about his dreams, he insisted he never dreamed. Later in his analysis he added, "hardly ever."

If a child acknowledges dreaming and tells us a dream, we hope we can show him its usefulness and its relation to the rest of his life. If we can do this, we may have won his interest in dreams, and his cooperation in examining them. Anna Freud's (1946) comment to a child is a good place to begin: "No dream can make itself out of nothing; it must have fetched every bit from somewhere . . ." (p. 19). Or, put more simply, "Where do these pictures come from?" What we obtain when we raise such questions is predominantly day residue.

The following includes a first dream presented by a twelve-year-old boy, Martley, after about one month of analysis. He came into his session troubled and discouraged. He had flunked four tests and had wet his bed on several previous nights. "Maybe I was worried about the tests and wet my bed, but I don't know," he said. This child was asking for understanding. I had no understanding of his enuresis or his school failure at this time. There were no hints about significant unconscious fantasies. I told him, "Strange as it may sound, dreams can sometimes give us hints about what is worrying us, even when we have no ideas about it. They are about things that stay on our mind in the night, even after we have gone to sleep. Have you had any dreams these nights?" My relationship to this child was positive at this point and he was asking for help. It was an opportunity to introduce the notion of the usefulness of dreams. The circumstances were such that fruitful exploration was likely. Dreams subsequently played a major part in the analysis of this child.

Martley told me the following dream from the previous night:

A friend and I were on a boat and the owner was chasing us with a bloodhound. We were going from island to island in a motor boat. We stole a bucket. We bought two for the man and were given a third which we kept. He chased us down a path to a beach. There were twenty-five people with beach umbrellas. We hung under a coral cliff on the left, and the water was reaching up and smashing us against the wall. The man and dog did not find us and went away. We swam back to the boat and started up the ladder, I don't know why. The man was there. We acted like maintenance men and picked up a Coke can that had oil in it. He saw us and said, "You are the ones." We went back because we would get caught.

Martley spontaneously added his brother had had a nose-bleed during the night. He awoke to find his father in his brother's bed, and his brother in his mother's bed. He thought this occurred before the dream. There was an appreciable pause, and I asked, "Where did these pictures in your dream come from?"

"The science test I failed yesterday was on oceanography. There was a question about coral. I thought I knew it. I said, 'Old coral is destroyed by new coral.' The right answer is a star fish destroys the coral polyps." This wrong answer makes us suspect an unconscious, probably oedipal, fantasy was intruding.

I asked, "What about the buckets?"

"My brother and I played on the roof last night and stopped up the drain. In the dream I put the bucket under the spout and the rain stopped and the bucket did not overflow." This part of the dream about the buckets was not reported in the first telling of the dream. Also, the other boy is now identified as his brother.

I took this chance to introduce the idea of wish fulfillment, but without calling it that. "It sounds like after three wet nights you were hoping to catch the water and not wet the bed."

Martley laughed. "Yes. Last week I dreamed I was on deck with a blue shirt and brown pants watching the water skiers. Someone kept pushing me into the water. Then I was in a boat and going fishing, and someone pushed me in the water. I thought in my sleep, 'I think I'm going to wet the bed.' In the morning I had wet the bed. This is like figuring out a puzzle."

"I wonder where the stealing comes from, Martley?"

"I don't know."

"And your friend?"

"Oh, he and I went to Sam's house to make prank phone calls. Sam's parents were not there. My friend's parents were angry that we made prank calls. We called people saying we were selling Bibles or called the Chinese laundry complaining about an undershirt they had lost a year ago."

In trying to touch on possible stealing, wrongdoing, and fears of being chased, I suggested, "Maybe you were worried your friend's parents would find out and be angry."

A tentative "maybe" was Martley's reply. Then he was off on other material which appeared unrelated to the dream. As in the analysis of adults, when the material flows we follow it, and try to understand it. It had been a profitable introduction to the importance and relevance of dreams. Martley was pleased and surprised he could make connections.

As analysts, we can suspect the pursuing man is related to his father who had moved into his brother's bed during the night. We wonder about new coral that destroys old, which suggests oedipal competitiveness with his father. His relationship to his father, as well as the transference, was strongly positive. From Martley's developmental history, it was known that expressions of hostile feelings toward his father were virtually absent. We take note of Martley's question about the dream, "I don't know why we came back to the boat where the pursuing man was." As with an adult analysis, we keep all our speculations in mind, and do not share them with the child, or press him for associations. When his resistance began to rise and he drifted away from the dream, we followed him. We will remember that this drift occurred at the point where we were talking about some wrongdoings.

It was not for over a year that the children's forbidden games, parents finding them, oedipal competition, being pushed overboard, and other elements of the first dream and the dreams that came up as associations to it could be understood.

SOURCES OF INFORMATION THAT LEAD TO INTERPRETATION OF DREAMS

Early in this chapter I mentioned that children generally cannot free associate. However, a limited degree of association to elements of the manifest dream is possible. As seen in Martley's analysis, the child may respond to the analyst's questions about these elements, and some day residues may appear.

Some children seem to be better able to put dream images into drawings than into words. Even verbal children may choose to draw a dream after they have told it. In this way more detail is revealed. I do not ask a child to draw his dream, but wait to see his natural manner of presentation, which is in itself revealing. Some analysts may focus on dream material by writing down the manifest dream and associations for the child and collecting them as a child may do with drawings or stories.

Observation of the progression of associated activities and verbalization during the hour in which the dream was reported will help clarify its meaning. Of course, we also use our knowledge of the current state of the analysis to further our understanding. In addition, we know from our contact with the child's family the events and the emotional tone of the patient's outer life.

Finally, we possess knowledge of typical symbols. We may use these symbols to augment our interpretation or explanation if it helps clarify the meaning of a dream for a child. We do not make purely symbolic interpretations.

All of these sources of understanding a dream are illustrated in the case of Martley. I will continue to describe his dreams below. Once we attain an understanding of the dream from some or all of these sources, we use it no differently in child analysis than in the analysis of an adult.

INTEGRATING DREAM ANALYSIS INTO THE ANALYTIC PROCESS

Since the use of dreams is but one part of a child analysis, I cannot report dream material out of context. Parts of Martley's analysis that are not strictly related to dream analysis must be included or the process will be distorted and unreal. Dream interpretation integrated into the total treatment contributes greatly to the analysis of the child's defenses, conflicts, and drives.

Martley was twelve years old when he came for analysis. He came because of school failure, being bullied by classmates, severe rivalry with his younger brother, and enuresis. The dream reported above came after about one month of analysis.

During the three years of this ongoing analysis, dream material had been almost the only source of material revealing Martley's unconscious fantasies and conflicts. To an extent this was due to the fact that repression was one of his major defenses. Conversion symptoms occurred during the analysis when I aroused anxiety by an interpretation. Even then, Martley's feelings about me remained positive. With most children, when our interventions make them anxious, they react with some degree of hostility. Martley was not hostile in word, attitude, or action. Similarly, ambivalence to his father was hard to detect. His rivalry and aggression had, for the most part, succumbed to repression or was expressed in masochistic compliance.

We are familiar with this seeming conflict-free attitude in many enuretic boys. Martley told me the events of his daily life with friends and family more easily than most children. As with all children, his description of conflicts with peers or family often appeared in abbreviated ways or with significant omissions. Clarification of details occurred in weekly interviews with his parents.

The summer before commencing the second year of analysis, Martley spent a considerable period cruising on a sailboat in the Caribbean. For the first week he was afraid of going into the water. During the day, he complained of a variety of physical complaints, as he often did when he was anxious. At night, Martley would liven up and join in the fun. His father was aware of the anxious nature of this behavior. After a week on the boat he encouraged his son to go into the water to explore the coral reef. That night Martley suffered a night terror which he angrily denied when he was told about it the next morning. During the night he got up (he was frequently a sleepwalker), and while asleep shouted, "Get the spikes out of me, get the spikes out of me!" His father tried to speak to him in his sleep, but Martley could not be aroused. The next day, a cousin told Martley's father that Martley was afraid of him because he had been pressuring his son to overcome his fear and go into the water. In recounting these events, his father told me that two years before (one year before the first dream) his son had been on a coral reef in two feet of water. Martley had been terrified of stepping on a sea urchin and getting the spines in his feet. Indeed Martley's sister had once stepped on a sea urchin and underwent considerable pain having the spines removed. Martley's father rightly suspected this had something to do with Martley's fear of exploring the reef and with his nightmare, "Get the spikes out of me." On another occasion, when Martley and his father were swimming together in the ocean, Martley feared he would drown. His father shouted back to him he was only in three feet of water. The boy exclaimed, "But you are a hundred feet ahead of me."

Thus, more was understood about the first dream one year after it had occurred. The night his father had come to sleep in his brother's bed probably aroused feelings of being pursued and penetrated. The coral, through the sea urchins, brings us to Martley's fears of being penetrated by spikes. This fear surfaced in the night terror that had occurred during the summer. The night terror must have threatened to expose to Martley his passive, feminine, masochistic wishes and therefore had to be denied. The coral also leads us to Martley's desire to resist his passive wishes toward his father. On his oceanography test, Martley had made the mistake, "the new coral destroys the old coral polyps." Martley was constantly put into danger through his father's encouragment to master anxiety by doing what he feared. In the analysis, Martley would go along with a discussion without apparent discomfort until a vacant smile indicated "everything has gone black." This provided me with the first evidence of Martley's excessive anxiety. When this "blackout" passed, he would describe what had made him afraid. This was a transference repetition with me of an attitude so characteristic of his relationship to his father. Thus in the analysis Martley would immediately plunge in to discussing what had frightened him, in the same way he tried to please his father by attempting to actively master frightening situations. Only once did this attempt to master by telling me what had frightened him produce a second feeling of impending "blackout."

This is of special importance. The process of dream interpretation was aided by Martley's transference attitude of passive submission. Other pre- and early adolescent boys might have been less cooperative. Dream analysis was a way of trying to please me as he tried to please his father, even if it led to anxiety—with me a "blackout." This was fortunate because all relevant material came through work with dreams. It posed a problem because this transference attitude needed to be analyzed later. As will be seen in later material, this attitude had begun to shift and adolescent rebellion began to appear.

In Martley's first session after the summer he told me what he had been told of the night terror on the sailboat. He also told me the story about his sister stepping on the sea urchin, and his fears of exploring the reef even while wearing sneakers. We talked about the pressure his father put on him to do things he was afraid of. Martley assured me of his father's good intentions. An interpretation based purely on an understanding of symbols was not made. No mention was made of fears of sexual penetration. We do not interpret a symbol of sexual penetration when it is not in the context of more explicit sexual material or fantasies in the analysis. At this time, sexual material had not become a part of the analysis. Nevertheless, knowledge of symbols helped me to begin to understand something of Martley's passive homosexual wishes, something of his initial complaint of being bullied by other boys, and his now expressed feeling of being weaker than his father and his fear of competing with him in athletic ventures.

In the third year of Martley's analysis his parents divorced and his father quickly remarried. Martley was fourteen years and nine months old and was forming a relationship with a girl who already had a boyfriend. In a dream, Martley acted as if he knew nothing about racing cars. His rival was supposedly an expert in the sport, and in reality, he worked as a mechanic. In the dream Martley and his girlfriend were secretly building a racing car and practicing racing. The day came when the rival was challenged to a race and was overwhelmingly defeated and humiliated. In another scene there was a sign, "No Trespassing." The day residue was evident to Martley: his wish to beat his rival and the secret relationship which he had with the girl. The "No Trespassing" brought fears that the sixteen-year-old rival would come and attack him. These fears were more difficult for Martley to express. He tried to deny his fear by saying he would stand up to the boy. The competition with his peer was clear to him. What was not clear was his sense of triumph over his father after his parents' recent divorce. When his father moved out of the house, Martley withdrew from competition for the girl. On the other hand, his relationship with his mother began to improve for the first time. He sided with her against his father, and ridiculed his father both to his mother and to me.

While Martley's father and his bride were on a honeymoon cruise, Martley dreamed there was a party on a ship and that he jumped overboard. He added that the ship looked like a pirate ship from the back. Other siblings had gone on the cruise with his father. Martley denied any feelings of being left out. I told him it sounded as dangerous as that ship in his first dream. His manner of dealing with this dream fragment was of interest. He denied it was a pirate ship. I recalled that he had said it looked like one. Martley said, "Stop it," and acted as if I were teasing him, a behavior he had never shown before. This was the first time the sense of being bullied appeared in the transference. He could not recall his first dream. When I reminded him of it, Martley chided me that I had remembered it incorrectly. This challenging attitude paralleled increasing criticalness with me of his father's actions.

He retold the first dream in all of its detail. While telling about the man in the dream pursuing the two children, Martley interrupted himself to tell me of a bad coincidence that had happened with his eleven-year-old brother. His brother was about to kiss an eleven-year-old girl and at that moment his father called angrily from the other room, "Get the F . . . in here." Martley felt his brother interpreted this as being scolded for wanting to kiss his girl. The brothers talked and my patient reassured his brother that it was only a coincidence. "If you want girls to like you, you will have to stop chasing and hitting them," Martley said. To me he added, "That is what he thinks boys and girls are supposed to do. I used to think that too." In association to the two boys pursued by the man in the dream, we came to the child's view of sex —a boy chases and hits a girl. The younger brother confessed his fears of being teased if anyone found out he wanted to kiss a girl. He told Martley he was still embarrassed when he remembered that Martley had found him and a little girl undressed and under the covers looking at each other. This took place when Martley was nine and his brother was six. At the time, Martley had teased his brother.

Here Martley began to free associate for the first time. It occurred when he began to be able to show his aggression to me and to his father, and when his sexual feelings could be expressed. Probably at least two factors were involved. First, these affects were being freed by the analysis, and second, Martley was undergoing the psychic structural changes of adolescence.

When I asked Martley when *he* had been ashamed of *his* curiosity, he told me not to change the subject, because he had more to tell me about his little brother. He revealed that when he was eight years old he had been behind a couch with an eight-year-old girl. Her mother had come in saying, "Where are you? What are you doing?" They were exposing themselves to one another.

I reminded Martley of his own more recent guilt and embarrassment. A few weeks before Martley had held hands with a girl while driving in from the country. He told me he was worried a camp counselor who had been with him during the weekend would know about it and think it was wrong. Martley could not rest until he had discussed it with this older man. He had a generalized anxiety that it would be found out. There was guilt and embarrassment in telling me. He was confused that such a minor event could have been so upsetting. Now Martley and I began to understand the *manner* in which he had told me his pirate ship dream—his embarrassment, his feeling I was teasing him, and his initial denial that he could remember the dream. The analysis had revived

Martley's fear of being "found out" which was associated with his childhood "wrongdoings." This wrongdoing was far from his mind when he told me his first dream, after one month of analysis. At that time his interest in the dream waned with the mention of the wrongdoing. The oedipal wrongdoings, competition, and triumph were much closer to Martley's awareness. Telling the dream was associated with an affect that revealed an active conflict. We have thus returned to Martley's sense of wrongdoing in the first dream through an association to a fragment of the dream, "a man pursuing the two boys." These associations occurred three years after Martley had the dream.

Over the next week, Martley developed curiosity about what his father was doing with his new wife. Martley's enuresis had almost completely disappeared, but with his father's remarriage it occurred as a nightly event for two weeks. After the honeymoon, Martley and his brother spent a night with the newly married couple in their bedroom. Though Martley's father stated nothing improper had occurred, sexual fantasies about his father were stimulated. Martley acknowledged this, but did not describe his fantasies.

Martley's struggle with passivity in relation to his father became the center of his analysis as the summer approached. He had been increasingly resistant to his father's plans. Martley would comply, but in minor situations acted as if he had been mistreated and bullied. His father could not understand this behavior. Martley's enuresis, which had again disappeared, returned. He complained his father was a dare-devil who put him into danger and said his father would eventually kill himself. This idea distressed him. He told me his father had once been a racing car driver and quit because another driver was trying to provoke an accident to kill him. Now we were able to discuss his dream about car races and his desire to compete with and humiliate his father. This interpretation could only be accepted when it was accompanied by a statement of his loving feelings for his his father as well.

Martley came to a session in a fury because his father insisted Martley accompany him to a TV interview. Although his father had promised Martley would not have to appear on the program, Martley suspected his father might try to persuade him to appear. Still, he could not refuse to go; his father would not understand such defiance. Martley would go, and if made to appear on the program, would say, "You can make me come to the TV program, but you cannot make me stop wetting the bed!" Martley roared with laughter at this fantasy and at the expression he imagined on his father's face. "But I could never really do that to him."

His father had arranged an exciting trip into a wilderness area for the summer. Arrangements had been under way for months. Martley's father habitually made such arrangements without consulting anyone. At the last minute, Martley decided he would not go. He was tired of his father making arrangements without asking him.

"He is the original bully," Martley said.

"How long you have been struggling with these feelings, Martley. Remember the man in that first dream and the secret plans to defeat the racing car driver in your other dream? It is hard to let yourself know about such feelings when you love your father so much and know he would do anything for you."

Martley agreed.

His father was hurt and angry, but allowed Martley to to make his own decision. He arranged to have Martley flown into the wilderness rather than go by pack horse. (Martley had been afraid of horses for over a year. A horse had seized him by the pectoral muscle, lifted him into the air, and hurled him several feet against a tree.) After deliberation Martley agreed to go, but only with the understanding that he be consulted about future plans before they are made.

Martley's passive desires had yet to be dealt with.

Let me make a few concluding comments about the differences between dream analysis with Martley during preadolescence and early adolescence. In preadolescence, Martley would mention a dream, relate day residue, and then the material would be cut off. In adolescence, he could move ahead and tell of his wrongdoings. Material which was not repressed could be expressed in early adolescence, and could not be expressed in preadolescence. It is not infrequent that dreams, fantasies, and associated feelings of preadolescence are recalled and told only later, in adolescence.

DREAMS AND DEFENSE

As we have seen from the case presentation, manifest and latent contents of dreams help us understand patient's defenses. In addition, we learn from a child's mode of presentation something about his defense system. Martley told the same dream in different manners in two periods of his analysis. The second telling threatened to reveal his oedipal struggle, and mobilized denial and antagonism toward me.

Berta Bornstein's (1949) patient Frankie, even after acknowledging he dreamed, could not express his dreams directly. Frankie's dreams revealed passive, feminine wishes which were totally unacceptable to him. His dream content aroused such intense fear and resistance that at first he asserted that not he but God had produced the dream, and that the therapist, not Frankie, had dreamed it. Frankie described these dreams which the analyst supposedly was having. In a further defensive maneuver, Frankie stated that by turning on the light, he could end the dream at will. Turning passive into active was an important defense for Frankie. As passive wishes were analyzed and were not so strongly defended against, he could report his dreams as his own. The manner in which he reported his dreams monitored the strength of his defenses.

A nine-year-old girl, whose case was reported by Dr. Joseph Nieder, told her analyst when he asked about her nightmares, "If I tell you my bad dreams, will you get bad dreams?" This child's analysis was marked by a reluctance to talk or have her analyst talk. Her fear that her death wishes against her parents and siblings would come true if she spoke them was an important element in her pathology. For a long time, not to talk and not to allow talking was an important defensive maneuver.

SUMMARY

Although the fundamentals of dream interpretation are the same for all ages, the details of technique vary with the developmental level of the patient, and with other individual traits. The child analyst may have to take active steps to interest his patient in dreams and demonstrate their value.

A child is generally incapable of free association, and frequently cannot associate to elements of his dream. The child analyst, therefore, relies on the flow of material (both verbal expressions and activity) during the session in which the patient reports the dream, his knowledge of the current state of the analysis, information from the child's parents about the his life outside analysis, and the therapist's understanding of symbolism. Thus armed, the analyst can help the patient understand his dreams, and integrate those insights into the analytic work.

REFERENCES

Bornstein, B. (1949). The analysis of a phobic child: some problems of theory and technique in child analysis. *Psychoanalytic Study of the Child* 3/4:181–226.

Bornstein, B. (1950). Unpublished lectures on the technique of child analysis. *Archives of The New York Psychoanalytic Institute.*

Freud, A. (1946). *The Psycho-Analytical Treatment of Children.* London: Imago.

Freud, S. (1900). The interpretation of dreams. *Standard Edition* 4/5.

SUGGESTED READING

Blom, G. E. (1960). Panel report: the role of the dream in child analysis. *Journal of the American Psychoanalytic Association* 8:517–525.

Furman, E. (1962). Some features of the dream function of a severely disturbed young child. *Journal of the American Psychoanalytic Association* 10:258–270.

Harley, M. (1962). The role of the dream in the analysis of a latency child. *Journal of the American Psychoanalytic Association* 10:271–288.

Root, N. N. (1962). Some remarks on anxiety dreams in latency and adolescence. *Journal of the American Psychoanalytic Association* 10:303–322.

Chapter 13

THE CHILD ANALYST'S EMOTIONAL REACTIONS

TO HIS PATIENTS

Isidor Bernstein, M.D.

Jules Glenn, M.D.

The psychoanalyst brings to treatment a body of knowledge about the human psyche and an understanding of psychoanalytic method and process. He also brings himself as a human being with his own needs and incompletely resolved conflicts. Therefore, the therapist invariably develops irrational reactions to his patients. We will begin this chapter with a survey of those reactions common to all analyses, and then consider those specific to child analysis.

TYPES OF EMOTIONAL REACTIONS TO PATIENTS

The analyst's emotional responses to his patients have been categorized as "counter-transferences," but we prefer to classify[1] them as (1) counter-transferences, (2) transferences to the patient, (3) identification or counter-identification, (4) experiencing the patient as an extension of the analyst's self, and (5) reactions to the patient as a real person. This latter includes (a) empathic responses which can generate insight, (b) signal affects which can also be used adaptively, and (c) failure to achieve empathy due to differences in developmental levels between child and analyst.[2]

The reader should note that counter-transference is only one type of emotional reaction to patients. We will not only discuss counter-transference, but other types of emotional reactions as well. We will differentiate responses to children from reactions to parents. Inevitably there is an overlapping of categories which vary in degree of complexity.

Laplanche and Pontalis (1973) define counter-transference broadly as "the whole of the analyst's unconscious reactions to the individual analysand—especially to the analysand's own transference" (p. 92). Freud (1910) himself did not offer a full definition of counter-transference, but stated it "arises in him [the analyst] as a result of the patient's influence on his unconscious feelings" (p. 144). A justifiably narrow view of this phenomenon is that the analyst responds to the patient's transferences with unconscious transferences of his own. A male analyst, for example, may respond to a female patient's affectionate feelings, which stem from her infantile love for her father, with sexual feelings derived from his childhood attachment to his mother (Freud 1915). Or a child analyst may respond to a little boy's transferred antagonism as if the patient were a sibling the analyst had hated in childhood.

Counter-transference, thus narrowly defined, differs from the analyst's transference to the patient when he is not reacting to the patient's transference. For instance, the analyst may have transference reactions to his patient's appearance or behavior. In addition, an analyst may behave toward all patients as if they were infantile objects such as paternal or sibling rivals. This situation is quite different from counter-transference in response to a particular patient's specific transference. In such cases, the transference may be rigidly frozen and take the form of character traits with stereotyped behavior and attitudes. Counter-transferences and transferences include not only the displacement of drive-derivatives from infantile objects to contemporary objects, but also include other aspects of the personality, such as superego elements and defenses. Counter-transferences and transferences are deviations from the optimal neutral analytic stance.

Counter-transferences should also be differentiated from identification and counter-identification (Fliess 1953) in which the analyst responds to the patient by identifying with him. Identification with the patient is not uncommon in child analysis where the analyst develops relationships with both the child and his parents. Identifying with the child often occurs concomitant with the development of transferences to the child's parents, who are equated with the analyst's parents.

Counter-identification is a more complex phenomenon. The analyst reacts to the patient's identification with him by identifying with the patient. This involves a regression to a state in which self-representations and object-representations are poorly differentiated.

The analyst may experience the patient as an extension of himself in a variety of circumstances. A child analyst may unknowingly imagine himself to be the parent of his patient and view the child as a narcissistic extension of himself. This may interfere with analytic objectivity. In a more pathological form, the analyst may regress to a symbiotic phase, and feel as if he is fused with the patient as parent and child.

Reactive identifications can also occur. In these instances the analyst deals with a patient in an opposite manner from the original object. For example, the therapist may consciously or unconsciously behave benignly when the patient's parents were punitive.

Characteristically, the analyst also reacts affectively to the patient as a real person. When an adult provokes his analyst with barbed words, it is relatively easy for the analyst to keep this in perspective and attempt to understand the patient's behavior. However, in the midst of play when a child suddenly physically attacks the therapist, it is likely he will respond to the actual threat irrationally. Although the type of response will reflect transference feelings, desires to protect oneself or retaliate cannot be considered counter-transferences in their entirety. Counter-transferences are largely unconscious. These responses to the patient as a real object are quite conscious even when their reflex nature determines their occurrence. Nevertheless, the analyst should not complacently ignore his behavior; he should employ self-analysis here as he does with more patent counter-transferences, to ferret out the transference aspects. For instance, the analyst may be able to detect aggressive transference reactions toward his patient.

As the appearance of these constellations is inevitable, it has correctly been suggested that counter-transference, when it occurs, can and should be used to help the analyst understand his patient. There are those who injudiciously welcome overt counter-transference manifestations as clues to the patient's neurosis (Tower 1956, Little 1951). Some analysts hold an extreme position and insist responses are deposited in the analyst's psyche by the patient through projective identification. The analyst becomes the container of the patient's wishes (Bion 1963).

Counter-transference interferes with therapeutic activity, and the analyst should, but is not always able, to become aware of his affective state and discover the patient's provoking transferences which he will then be able to interpret.

Those who praise counter-transference confuse this phenomenon with empathy. Less intense feelings on the part of the analyst can be instrumental in creating empathy which is so essential to understanding patients (see Greenson 1960, Arlow and Beres 1974, Olden 1953, 1958). One may call these relatively faint emotions *signal affects* (Arlow and Beres 1974).

Alerted to his identification with the patient and his responses to the patient's real behavior or transferences, the analyst may use these as clues to understand his patient. The analyst will briefly imagine himself in the patient's situation, and through projection, surmise the patient's state of mind and feeling. There is, of course, danger that the projection will be inaccurate, that the guess will be incorrect. Hence the analyst who employs empathy as a guide must discipline himself so perception of reality prevails. He must select, as far as he can, only correct empathic responses and reject personal identifications and projections that have little or nothing to do with the patient himself. During an analysis, the therapist creates many hypotheses about his patient, many of which must be rejected. Sometimes a hypothesis, based on an empathic response, can be rejected only after an interpretation proves it erroneous or arid.

Signal affects arising from within the analyst may be used in a different way. The analyst, noting a faint suspicion that he is being attacked or a slight resentment, may step up his observations of his patient, and observe subtle aggressions or provocations that he might have otherwise missed. Similarly, signal affects of a libidinal nature may serve as clues. Again, conclusions should be confirmed and tempered by observation and reality testing.

The analyst may observe the appearance of an erotic or aggressive fantasy concomitant with a signal affect, or even isolated from emotions. These *signal fantasies* can be useful in directing the therapist's attention to his patient's behavior and communications.

EMOTIONAL REACTIONS IN CHILD ANALYSIS

Let us turn from generalizations to certain specifics of the child analytic situation.

The child analyst's reactions to family involvement. The child analyst, in contrast to the adult analyst, sees his patient's parents as well as the patient himself. He is in the middle of the family situation, and develops relationships with all of its members. The analyst's own oedipal involvements are often revived. As a result, he experiences an inner pressure to identify with his patient. As he accepts the child's evaluation of his parents, the analyst may lose sight of the reality of their role. Or he may so identify with his patient that he surrenders his analytic stance.

An analyst was treating a nine-year-old boy whose parents quarreled and drank a great deal. Frequently, the child's parents were late picking him up after his analytic appointment, and sometimes they failed to pick the child up altogether. The therapist shared the child's anxiety and became overly active in reassuring the child. The analyst had lost his parents early in life and had suffered a certain amount of both real and imagined neglect. He identified with his patient to a degree beyond that necessary to achieve empathic understanding.

Self-analysis and a knowledge of the parent as he actually is will counteract this tendency. In moderation, this type of identification can be used adaptively to understand the child.

The analyst, though knowing the parents, and appreciating their difficulties, and offering them tactful support, may acquire their attitudes and become unrealistic about his patient. He may feel obliged to achieve a quick cure for them, and become disappointed or angry if the child doesn't recover rapidly. The child may become a narcissistic object of the analyst who, like a parent, suffers too much with the child. He may employ pedagogical procedures that are unnecessary or better performed by the child's parents. If the analyst relies excessively on information about the child's behavior and his emotional state from parents, he may find his empathy with the child faulty because of the parents' distortions. In most cases, however, acquiring information from parents will clarify the child's productions in the analytic session.

The wish to be a child analyst frequently stems from the analyst's maternal identification and an unconscious wish to have a child. If a male analyst is conflicted about maternal identification, because of its female significance, he may find it difficult to react appropriately to the child. He may become too wary of warm feelings, or overcompensating, may become excessively mothering. A female analyst may become excessively attached to a child patient, particularly if she has no children of her own. If the analyst does have his or her own children, he or she may feel guilty about the attention, concern, and time given to the patient. This is particularly true if the patient is more charming and likeable than his own child or has similar problems. When the analyst's children grow up and leave home, his patients may serve as substitutes, thus complicating the analytic relationship.

Reactions to the child analytic situation. Adult patients lie on the couch and free associate with the analyst behind them. In contrast, the child patient faces the analyst, watches his activities, facial expressions, and other bodily responses, and provokes and directs many of the analyst's reactions.

The child analyst is not simply an observer and interpreter. He is required to participate in the treatment in a more physically active way than with adult patients. He must respond more rapidly to the active child. The analyst may carry out roles assigned to him by the child as part of the child's dramatizations and communication. He may play fantasy characters, draw pictures, and write stories at the child's request. The child analyst may have to protect himself from the child's attacks, and keep his patient from harming himself. It is difficult to engage in these activities, and at the same time evaluate the patient's conscious and unconscious state, his defenses and drives, and determine appropriate interventions. Faced with many alternatives which require quick decisions, at times the analyst is likely to express his own inner needs rather than recognize and react to the child's. He may at times act out rather than analytically react for the patient's benefit.

A child engaged the analyst in a competitive word game. In his excitement, the analyst became competitive, and with considerable satisfaction, reported how he had defeated the child. The analyst's behavior delayed the emergence of additional material related to competitive oedipal strivings.

Anthony (Abbate 1964, Casuso 1965) has suggested the child analyst can minimize his own confusion by remaining sedentary and relatively immobile, more like an analyst of adults, as he faces the child. This solution to the difficulties inherent in many child analyses may produce maladaptive behavior in the therapist. The analyst may keep the child from using appropriate means of communication. His understandable wish to keep a clear head may run against the child's need to have him actively participate. The child may react to the analyst's immobility as a model for himself, and interpret it as a prohibition against activity. As a result, the child may be prevented from dramatizing his fantasies in an age-appropriate manner. This may be especially true if the analyst, idealizing the adult model, feels that verbalization is essential to analysis, and play is of relatively minor importance. He may discourage the child from using the analyst to enact roles as a means of expression and communication.

The child analyst's intense need to behave like an analyst of adults may have an irrational basis. He may have fears of regression or release of impulses, and this may interfere with flexible adaptation of technique.

Reactions to the child's personality. Bornstein (1948) observed the analyst may fear the child who is unpredictable, narcissistic, and manifests highly charged emotions. The child's closeness to his unconscious may also pose a threat. Bornstein stated both doctor and patient may experience the therapeutic situation as a power struggle between the big and strong grown-up, and the small, weak child. In addition, the adult cannot rid himself of certain attitudes and concepts that are foreign to the child. The child's sense of time is limited; he conceives of the present and near future, but the past and distant future make little impression on him. We may add that if the analyst attempts to force the child to see connections between the past and present before the patient is ready, and he may never be, the child will be confused and rightfully feel the analyst doesn't understand him. Reconstructions must thus be made with caution.

Similarly, Bornstein continued, the child is confused by the adult's (including the analyst's) concerns about the future. Adults worry that the pathology they observe in the child may grow as the child does, or they may reassure themselves that the child is "going through a phase" and will outgrow his troubles. The child is bewildered by both these attitudes. When he suffers, he does so in the here and now. He often views judgments about the future as moral judgments and retreats from adults who make them.

The analyst must gear his responses to the level of the child's cognitive abilities. Freud (1909) observed that the child analyst must supply words for the patient more than the adult analyst needs to. In addition, the child analyst—more than the adult analyst—may have to synthesize and integrate the child's isolated productions to make them meaningful and useful. With continued analysis, children may be able to do more of this analytic work themselves. However, if the therapist adopts an overly passive attitude before the child is able to be active in this way, the analysis may not progress.

The failure of adults to develop empathy with children can be due to differences in the structure of their egos, including their cognitive abilities. It can also be due to differences in interests and experience. A fear of regression to childlike functioning may intensify the adult's inability to accurately re-experience infantile states. The adult may confuse the child as he actually is with a wishful concept of childhood. This may lead to a failure to appreciate the child's needs.

Fear of reexperiencing infantile conflicts, for example, those regarding masturbation with attendant castration anxiety, may press adults who identify with the child to avoid observing the manifestations of those conflicts. It may also cause the analyst to hesitate discussing evidence of the child's guilt and anxiety regarding masturbatory and othe sexual wishes.

A fearful, unpredictably aggressive three-and-a-half-year-old boy had two extremely disturbed parents. In his analysis, the analyst dealt comfortably with the child's separation anxiety. However, he reacted to material dealing with the child's castration anxiety, which stemmed from passive wishes towards the analyst, by pointing out the child's wish to be a baby. This difficulty dealing with the child's castration anxiety also reflected the analyst's own anxiety in reporting his first supervised case.

The child analyst must treat the patient according to his level of maturity, but he may have difficulty gauging the child's maturity. At times, the analyst may behave as if the child is a little adult, and use words and concepts beyond the patient's understanding. At other times, the analyst may underestimate the child's maturity. He may introduce unnecessary adult-child interactions that impede, rather than enhance, the analysis.

A typical problem regarding the degree of frustration a child can tolerate appears at traditional times for offering gifts (see Kay 1967). For the sake of the treatment, the analyst wishes to refrain from giving the child a present so abstinence can be maintained. In the past, most child analysts felt children would not be able to accept such an analytic arrangement. They thought the child would view his therapist as a mean, nongiving adult, and become angry with him. Analysis of such a reaction is possible in adult analysis, but it is not possible with a child who does not recognize the irrationality of his wishes. Earlier analysts thought if they failed to give a gift, unanalyzable fury would interfere with the *positive transference;* and an impasse would occur. (See chapter 2, on the general principles of child analysis, for a discussion of the therapeutic alliance.)

This line of thinking, which is often accurate, is supported by the child analyst's generosity, his desire to please his patient, and be loved by him. These characteristics may interfere with a correct evaluation of the propriety of a gift in particular cases. We now know many children are perfectly capable of differentiating the relatively abstinent analytic situation from other life situations where gifts are appropriate. Many children can tolerate the immediate frustration to achieve relief from their emotional disturbance through analysis. Hence, at present, there is a swing away from the relative gratification of previous child analytic technique, to a more abstinent procedure. Self-analysis and astute observation of the patient's state of mind are required to decide the optimal balance of gratification and frustration for any particular child. (See chapter 14, "Gifts, Gratification, and Frustration" by Paul Kay.)

We have indicated that the child's propensities to action affect the analyst. Bornstein (1948) has described a typical interaction in which the child actively, but subtly, provokes or attacks the analyst. The analyst then unknowingly withdraws from his patient, and the patient in turn continues the attack. Eventually, the patient takes the analyst's withdrawal to signify indifference and loses interest in the analytic process. At times, we may add, the child becomes antagonistic.

Children may be openly sexually seductive, and may want and bring about physical contact with the analyst, even genital contact. This obviously will threaten many child analysts. Some analysts will unknowingly respond with overt or disguised sexual reactions of their own; others will withdraw or become hostile. It requires tact and interpretation to utilize the child's sexual expressions. They are obvious communications and can be used for therapeutic purposes.

In the analysis of an attractive, tomboyish, little girl, the child analyst had no difficulty with many aspects of the analysis. He could work with her mother, who was competitive, domineering, and manipulative with him as well as with her husband and children. The analysis progressed satisfactorily as the analyst dealt first with the little girl's obvious penis envy. However, when the child became more mature, abandoned her wishes for a penis, and began to show unmistakable evidence of strong oedipal feelings directed toward the analyst, he repeatedly and erroneously interpreted this behavior as a power struggle. The source of difficulty was the analyst's defense against an inverted oedipal seduction. He was reluctant to comply with the child's request that they produce a book together. The literary creation represented a baby.

More disguised sexual expressions often create more difficulty for the analyst. The child's hostile or provoking behavior is often a manifestation of, as well as a defense against, sadomasochistic sexual behavior. Provocation may also be unconsciously intended to elicit punishment. The analyst, face to face with an attacking child who is hitting or kicking him or destroying furniture and toys, may be forced to stop the child's dangerous behavior when correct interpretation is not apparent or fails. If the analyst attempts to physically restrain the child, the patient will attain the physical contact he unconsciously wished, and sadomasochistic urges will be satisfied.

The child's regressed behavior encourages similar regression in the analyst who identifies with and empathizes with his patient. There is a danger, however, the regression in the service of therapy will get out of hand. For instance, the analyst's sadism may emerge, or the analyst, trying to avoid regression, may become aloof and unobservant.

The analyst may also identify with the child's magical expectations of cure. The parents may encourage the child to talk by assuring him this will result in the disappearance of his symptoms, for example enuresis. When this anticipated cure does not occur after a few sessions, the child will be disappointed. The analyst may share the child's disillusionment in the analyst's omnipotence.

The personality of the child analyst. It has long been recognized, although not made explicit, that the analyst of children and adolescents must possess certain qualities. In broad terms, these qualities have been characterized as "childlike" or "maternal." This includes a capacity for controlled regression in the service of the ego, an ability to comprehend nonverbal as well as verbal behavior, maternal and paternal caring attitudes, and a rather tolerant superego. All of these attributes present potential pitfalls.

The ability to participate in the child's play and other behavior (to be "childlike") can result in joining the child in defensive libidinization of the analysis. The outcome can be "play therapy." The goal of understanding and communicative interpretations is ignored. Similarly, playing the role of a parent may lead to protective, guiding, and prohibiting attitudes and behavior toward the child. However benign the analyst's intention, an enactment of an adoption fantasy is inimical to the real purpose of the analysis.

Unresolved conflicts and residues of infantile wishes may also color the analyst's attitudes. The wish to relive his childhood or adolescence, albeit in altered and improved form, directly or via the patient, can lead to vicarious gratifications. This will confuse both the analyst and the patient. The enactment of sibling rivalry, competition with the child's parents, or unconsciously encouraging the child to acting out is particularly compromising to the analytic stance.

A woman analyst tended to be impulsive, challenging toward authority figures, and mildly flirtatious. This analyst permitted an adolescent girl to cancel analytic sessions without fully discussing her reasons, to engage in rather promiscuous sexual behavior, and finally, to prematurely terminate the analysis by making arrangements to attend college out of town.

The analyst may be subjected to outside stresses that can influence his attitude toward his patient. The supervisory situation corresponds to an examination of the analytic candidate. The analyst is aware of his need to report to his supervisor, and this may revive examination anxieties with attendant fantasies of disapproval and punishment. Children and adolescents are realistically involved in examinations in their schoolwork. It is therefore quite possible for the analyst to find it difficult to deal objectively with their anxieties and uncover underlying fantasies.

Life circumstances may also have their impact. The analyst who is confronted with personal illness, or an illness or loss of a family member, will find it difficult to deal analytically with the child's concerns regarding illness or death.

An analyst reported that the loss of his own child had caused him to suspend his practice for several weeks. He notified his adult patients in an appropriate way. However, he found it necessary to reassure his younger patients that he was not ill. This was a reaction to his own feelings of loss. Among other determinants, the analyst experienced a need to protect his child patients from what he thought would be a traumatic experience for them.

Similarly, an analyst involved in marital difficulties will have trouble helping a child cope with real or imagined problems between his parents.

The above examples are illustrative of the type of difficulties an analyst might encounter as a result of unresolved conflicts reawakened during work with children and adolescents. If these conflicts are unconscious and the analyst is unaware of their existence, it is appropriate to ask how will he know they are interfering with his work. If the analyst is in supervision, the supervising analyst may be able to call this to his attention. Likewise, if he is still in personal analysis, it may appear there. Personal analysis is probably the most reliable place for some correlation to be made between counter-transference problems and the unconscious conflicts of the analyst. Finally, after a successful analysis, it is hoped the analyst is aware of those areas in his personality that are still vulnerable to regressive reactions under stress. This makes him alert to such signals as anxiety, boredom, or inappropriate interventions. The analyst could then review the situation, and hopefully, identify the particular problem which has been stirred up within him.

THE SIGNIFICANCE OF DEVELOPMENTAL LEVELS

Children at specific developmental levels stimulate particular emotional responses. The reader is referred to the chapters on prelatency, latency, and preadolescence for a fuller discussion of these periods. Here we will highlight some common problems.

The prelatency child is often creative, imaginative, and rather direct in his expression of drive derivatives. These traits make the analyst's work interesting and enjoyable; the analyst's appreciation of his patient is often great. Optimally, this stimulates the analytic work, but it may also impede it. The analyst may enjoy participating in the play so much he neglects to understand and interpret it. Or he will be so seduced by the child's id expressions that he neglects to see and interpret defensive aspects. And, of course, there is always the danger that the analyst will defensively avoid insight into the child's seductive play.

The relative lack of verbalization in prelatency children may distress some analysts. The child's use of speech and play in which primary process thinking dominates may confuse and disturb therapists who cannot sufficiently regress to understand the child.

A young child who clings to his parents and fears the analyst, who is a stranger, may inhibit the therapist. The analyst may find himself unable to be relaxed and flexible in the presence of the child's mother or father. He may become irritated at the child who appears to be preventing the analysis from proceeding by demanding his parents be included in the analytic situation. The therapist, adhering to the adult analytic model, prefers the dyadic relationship and resents the complications that a third party introduces.

A six-year-old child, who was hyperactive primarily because he feared his parents would desert him, threw paper about the play room. Alarmed by the loss of control the analytic situation permitted, the child called his mother into the room for reassurance. Although the analyst understood the situation well, he could not bring himself to make the proper interpretation in the mother's presence. The therapist believed such an interpretation would be a violation of confidentiality.

When the analyst feels comfortable in the mother's presence, treatment can procede.

An infantile, four-year-old boy insisted his mother stay with him in the play room, because he was afraid of strangers. He crawled onto his mother's lap and buried his head in her shoulder. He looked coyly at the analyst, and directed his mother to respond for him to the analyst's comments. The analyst accommodated his patient's wishes, and talked to the mother about the patient's interests and activities. After a while, the patient began to draw, one of the activities his mother had mentioned.

Latency children present typical problems which have to do with the two aspects of this developmental stage. Freud (1905) distinguished *ideal* latency from *interruptions* of latency. Normally, these two types of behavior alternate, but one may predominate for a long period of time. In ideal latency, sublimated activity prevails, and the child behaves in a compulsive way. During interruptions of latency, primitive impulses break through. The patient in the throes of an interruption of ideal latency is like the prelatency child in many ways. His play is interesting, and he may employ relatively unneutralized drive expressions. By contrast, the ideal latency child may bore the analyst with repetitive sublimated activity which affords limited access to fascinating, unconscious fantasies. The child may flip baseball cards endlessly, or insist on playing checkers or jacks. The bored analyst may find his attention to details blunted, and his capacity for understanding diminished. The analyst's patience may be taxed. He may be tempted to put an end to sublimated activity and get to the "real" material. Generally, cautious interpretations will keep the analytic process going and patience will be rewarded by further understanding of the child's conflicts and defenses. Aggressive attempts to break through the child's defenses may cause excessive anxiety. This can lead to an interruption of the analysis or interference with the child's sublimations.

A nine-year-old child desperately wanted to beat the analyst at checkers, and he insisted on playing week after week. However, the child continually missed opportunities to gain an advantage. Eventually, the analyst could interpret the child's inhibition of competitive urges.

The preadolescent typically disturbs the analyst by limiting the degree to which he confides in him. The preadolescent, faced with new and perplexing inner sensations, is not prepared to discuss these mysterious feelings with anybody. He cannot even face them himself. His communication with the analyst is cautious and restricted. Long pauses and nervous, aimless restlessness may annoy the therapist who wants to get on with the work. Irritation and a wish to provoke the patient into "cooperating" will impede the eventual development of an analytic process.

An eleven-year-old girl refused to talk about her physical development. She said she did not like boys looking at her. She told the analyst she wore two shirts and "would rather be flat." When the analyst told her she must feel uncomfortable about her bust development, she heatedly insisted he not use that word. She also declared she did not want to discuss such things with him. She preferred instead to obsess about whether she had cheated at school when she looked at another student's paper. At first the analyst attempted to understand the defenses. He soon observed his attempts at interpretation were experienced by the girl as pressure, indeed as attacks. He modified his approach. The patient helped him by suggesting, "Don't say anything, just listen." In the absence of pressure, she gradually revealed the reasons for her prudishness. She was concerned about "showing" because of a worry that menstruation, which she felt was imminent, would stain her clothes. Earlier in her life she had suffered from enuresis and felt humiliated by the stained sheets at camp and at home.

Another, smaller group of preadolescents, quite unlike those which we have just described, reveal a great deal about themselves and may even discuss their sexual wishes. However, most patients of this age try to keep their distance from the analyst and other adults. This enables them to further develop separation and individuation. Both preadolescents and adolescents are threatened by the sexual and aggressive feelings they have toward incestuous objects, and try to find nonincestuous replacements. If the patient views the analyst as a parent, the analyst may be subjected to irritating distance-keeping silence or criticism. The therapist may join the battle and protect himself from his counter-transference feelings toward the patient. If the child pictures the analyst as a mentor, things may proceed more smoothly.

The regressed behavior of many preadolescents stirs up animosity in many child analysts. The tendency to regress from oedipal to preoedipal strivings, and the prevalence of disorder and dirtiness based on anal fixations, may distress adults. For these reasons many believe analysis cannot be achieved in preadolescence. Not only do the patient's inner conflicts make him reluctant to communicate; the analyst may find the experience distasteful.

REACTIONS TO TERMINATION

As the analysis nears its end the child analyst begins to anticipate separation (Kohrman 1969). If the child has represented a real object for the analyst, the analyst may react with feelings of sadness or hostility. These feelings may be intensified if the child has become a transference object. The analyst may unconsciously delay ending treatment or avoid introducing the subject of termination. The analyst may also slip into a surrogate parental role. In his desire to protect both the child and the results of treatment, he may resort to counseling the child's parents, even when it is unnecessary. (See chapter 16, on termination.)

Often the child is more satisfied with the therapeutic outcome than his analyst. This reflects perfectionistic strivings and the adult's wish to provide a utopian existence for the child. Age-appropriate development makes it easier for a child to overlook residual symptoms or difficulties. The child isn't as interested as an adult in the future outlook.

NOTES

1. See also Kohrman et al. (1971) and Bernstein (1975) for discussions of classification. Kohrman et al. (1971), in a paper devoted to countertransference in child analysis, discuss many of the issues we will explore.

2. This list of emotional reactions is incomplete. As Dr. Alan Eisnitz suggested in a discussion of this article at the Psychoanalytic Association of New York on April 20, 1978, the analyst may, in addition, react emotionally to his own ignorance. He may become frustrated by and angry at the patient he does not fully comprehend. Students may be especially prone to this because they have not yet mastered psychoanalytic principles. As a further complication, an analytic candidate can become irritated because he believes he will fail to please his supervisor if he does not fully understand his patient.

Emotional reactions may also stem from situations that have little to do with the patient himself, for example, the analyst's residual positive or negative transferences to his own analyst, to his institute, supervisors, or to analysis itself.

REFERENCES

Abbate, G. M. (1964). Panel report: child analysis at different developmental stages. *Journal of the American Psychoanalytic Association* 12:135–150.

Beres, D., and Arlow, J. A. (1974). Fantasy and identification in empathy. *Psychoanalytic Quarterly* 43:26–50.

Bernstein, I. (1975). On the technique of child and adolescent analysis. *Journal of the American Psychoanalytic Association* 23:190–232.

Bion, W. R. (1963). *Elements of Psycho-Analysis.* New York: Basic Books.

Bornstein, B. (1948). Emotional barriers in the understanding and treatment of children. *American Journal of Orthopsychiatry* 18:691–697.

Casuso, G., Reporter (1965). Panel: The relationship between child analysis and the theory and practice of adult psychoanalysis. *Journal of the American Psychoanalytic Association* 13:159–171.

Fliess, R. (1953). Countertransference and counter-identification. *Journal of the American Psychoanalytic Association* 1:268–284.

Freud, S. (1905). Three essays on the theory of sexuality. *Standard Edition* 7:130–243.

———— (1909). Analysis of a phobia in a five-year-old boy. *Standard Edition* 10:5–149.

———— (1910). The future prospects of psycho-analytic therapy. *Standard Edition* 11:141–151.

———— (1915). Observations on transference-love. *Standard Edition* 12:159–171.

Greenson, R.R. (1960). Empathy and its vicissitudes. *International Journal of Psycho-Analysis* 41:418–424.

Kay, P. (1967). The boy's wish to give his analyst a gift. *Journal of the Academy of Child Psychiatry* 6:38–50.

Kohrman, R. (1969). Panel report: Problems of termination in child analysis. *Journal of the American Psychoanalytic Association* 17:191–205.

Kohrman, R., et al. (1971). Technique of child analysis: Problems of countertransference. *International Journal of Psycho-Analysis* 52:487–497.

Laplanche, J., and Pontalis, J. B. (1973). *The Language of Psycho-Analysis.* New York: W. W. Norton.

Little, M. (1951). Countertransference and the patient's response to it. *International Journal of Psycho-Analysis* 32:32–40.

Olden, C. (1953). On adult empathy with children. *Psychoanalytic Study of the Child* 8:111–126.

———— (1958). Notes on the development of empathy. *Psychoanalytic Study of the Child* 13:505–518.

Tower, L. E. (1956). Countertransferences. *Journal of the American Psychoanalytic Association* 4:224–255.

Chapter 14

THE ROLE OF THE PARENTS IN CHILD ANALYSIS

Jules Glenn, M.D.
Lawrence M. Sabot, M.D.
Isidor Bernstein, M.D.

PARENTS' MOTIVATION AND ATTITUDES

Children generally see analysts for consultation or treatment because their parents bring them. Typically, it is not the child who overtly suffers from his pathology, but his parent. The grown-ups observe the manifestations of the child's disability, and fearing that it will persist and take more serious forms, they want help for their son or daughter. The child is experienced as an extension of the parent who wants relief. This narcissistic configuration may be normal or it may involve extreme confusion of the parent's representation of himself and his child. The parent may empathically experience discomfort when his child is unhappy, or he may masochistically experience extreme agony when his child undergoes moderate suffering.

Parents also may be narcissistically disturbed by their offspring's pathology when the child hurts or embarrasses them through more or less direct attacks, or by creating disturbances in the community. Antisocial behavior may bring pressure on the parents to seek help for their child. In addition, school authorities may encourage parents to find a psychotherapist because some academic or social difficulty has been observed.

Whatever impels parents to seek an analytic consultation, they generally do so with caution. They may be optimistic about the consultant's ability to help, but may also fear he will be unable to. They may hope for a rapid resolution of the problem, but they may also expect a long and difficult therapy will be suggested. They may hope for advice that will end their difficulties, but worry lest the suggested alterations of behavior are beyond their capacity. They may feel confident that the analyst will be a kind, nonpunitive person, and nevertheless worry he will blame them for their child's disturbances. They may anticipate a deadly serious dissection of their destructive role in the etiology of their child's illness.

The expectation of blame may come from what the parents have heard is a frequent occurrence in treatment, but usually it is a product of projection as well. Parents often blame themselves or each other for their child's pathology. Many parents hope to raise a perfect child, one better than they. Having blamed their own parents for their deficiencies, they are distressed to find that, like their own parents, they have not succeeded. Bringing the child to an analyst may mean they have failed as parents. They attack themselves for the very faults they had criticized in their fathers and mothers. They fear the consultant will join them in this vendetta against parents. Or, the analyst may become a transference object. Like the parents' fathers and mothers, he is hated or loved and they expect hostility or affection from him.

Parents have many other fantasies; we will mention only a few. Some believe their child has reacted to their conscious or unconscious hostility (indeed, this may be true). Other parents experience their child's pathology as punishment for their forbidden libidinal or aggressive wishes. In these cases, a parent may unconsciously equate his child and his penis. Therefore, he imagines injury to his son or daughter is a punitive castration. This expectation may be especially prominent when libidinal attachment to the child is insufficiently neutralized and prohibited. Guilt may cause parents to believe their child is more seriously ill than he actually is.

The situation is complicated because grown-ups defend themselves against the painful affects produced by their child's sickness. Denial, for instance, leads some parents to hope and believe their child is perfectly well. Projection leads others to blame teachers or neighbors for any troubles. When repression appears, crucial aspects of the child's history may be forgotten.

Parents, then, come to the consultation with both trepidation and expectation. They hope their personal suffering will be ended by the analyst's help, and fear he will be unwilling or unable to provide relief.

THE ANALYTIC APPROACH TO THE PARENT-CHILD RELATIONSHIP

The analyst brings to the consultation a body of knowledge and experience that will help him keep the parent's role in proper focus. A complete survey of psychoanalytic (and other) findings about the normal development of the parent-child relationship and pathological outcomes is impossible here. A sketch of some of the important conceptions will be helpful in depicting the interrelations. The reader is also referred to chapter 17, in which Dr. Hellman describes some of the pathological interactions that simultaneous analyses of parents and children have revealed.

The infant is born with innate psychological apparatuses which may be immediately apparent or may manifest themselves as a child matures. Differences in activity levels (Fries and Woolf 1953), stimulus barriers (Bergman and Escalona 1949), and drive intensity (Alpert, Neubauer, and Weil 1956, Alpert and Bernstein 1964), for instance, will influence the child's development and his relationship with his parents. The complex interactions of innate and environmental factors as the child matures will determine his normal and pathological characteristics. Libidinal development through the oral, anal, phallic and later stages has a biological base and timetable. At the same time, the parents influence the form, content, and temporal appearance of these stages.

A degree of adult stimulation facilitates libidinal development, but while parents play a significant role, their role is not exclusive. The child will stimulate grown-ups to behave in ways that enhance his development. For instance, a child with a marked oral drive will cry vociferously until his mother responds appropriately and feeds him. Parents thus provide further oral stimulation, as well as gratification, and then a diminished need for stimulation. The overall, long-range effect may be an intensification of the oral drive or its attenuation, depending on the subtleties of the interaction. To cite another type of interaction, certain children with marked aggressive endowment may cry a great deal as part of their activity pattern. The cry may be interpreted by the parents as a plea for food, with consequent oral stimulation.

Mutual interaction between parents and child is also the key to ego development. The child of two or three months will respond to his mother with a social smile. This in turn stimulates her, and provides mutual libidinal gratification. It also furthers the child's ability to distinguish I from non-I (Spitz 1945) and sets the stage for further learning.

The parent or a parent-substitute must be available to the child for the optimal achievement of developmental milestones such as crawling, walking, and talking. But the child must possess the necessary biological apparatus (Spitz 1945, Provence and Lipton 1962) as well.

Psychopathology emerges out of mutual interactions between parent and child. Normally, children present clues to adults. These clues help parents understand and respond appropriately to their children. Mothers learn to differentiate hunger cries from those due to colic or other discomforts. In pathological development, the infant's clues are difficult to decipher and few or no parents are able to do so. Some parents are unable to react appropriately to clues that most adults would comprehend. Schizophrenic infants, for example, behave in such strange ways that the average mother cannot appropriately react to and care for her child. The child's tensions are insufficiently relieved, and the mother is unable to react in a way that stimulates development. The child's innate propensity for developmental arrest is reinforced. On the other hand, some mothers possess a remarkable faculty to respond adaptively to an atypical child.

Infants require protection from excessive stimulation which would otherwise traumatize them. However, the degree of stimulation necessary to cause trauma varies. A mother capable of preventing over-stimulation in one child may fail to provide a sufficient environmental barrier for a second, particularly sensitive infant (Bergman and Escalona 1949).

This same principle holds true regarding the stimulation necessary for optimal development. A quiet baby may fail to sufficiently stir his similarly quiet mother to satisfy his needs. But a second, hyperactive child might press the mother to provide him with optimal stimulation.

A different mother might respond to a hyperactive child maladaptively, and provide too much stimulation for that particular child (see Coleman, Kris, and Provence 1953).

Weil (1970), after reviewing child development research, stated, "the interaction between the infant's equipment and early experiential factors—an interaction that aggravates or attenuates initial tendencies—will lead, after a few weeks, to the emergence of a *basic core of fundamental trends* with which the infant enters the symbiotic phase" (see Mahler, Pine, and Bergman 1975, p. 442).

We have concentrated on early childhood, but the same principles apply throughout life. The nature of a child's oedipus complex will depend in part on preoedipal experiences (Silverman, Rees, and Neubauer 1975) which in turn are determined by biological and environmental forces. The intensity and content of the Oedipus complex will be further influenced by the strength of phallic drives in relation to pregenital urges as well as by the extent and type of parental stimulation. A structured superego arises as the child resolves his oedipus complex. This resolution will require limitations of the child's drive satisfaction by the environment, but the degree to which this is achieved will depend on the strength of the drives. The type of superego established will depend in part on the model the parents provide for internalization.

The sequential chain of interaction continues as the child enters latency, which requires adequate superego formation. Innate talent and capacity for neutralization will be supplemented by identification with parents, teachers, and other adults for the attainment of sublimations.

Parents may stimulate inner conflict in many ways. We will mention a few. Exceedingly strict adults may encourage excessively severe superegos, or they may promote sadomasochistic tendencies. Paradoxically, lax child rearing practices may have a similar effect: the child without parental control may find it necessary to construct his own strict ego ideal. Another pathological result of failing to appropriately restrain a child has been described by Johnson and Szurek (1952). They describe children with superego lacunae who carry out antisocial behavior unknowingly sanctioned by their parents. Children perceive and react to grown-ups' unconscious wishes (Burlingham 1935).

In evaluating the role of parents in a child's development, one must realize the traits which a child attributes to his father and mother are never identical with their actual characteristics. As we have noted in chapter 2, the libidinal stage of the child is prominent among the many factors which determine his representation of his parents. A child in the oral stage will view his parents differently from one in the anal or phallic phases.

Constitutional factors and parental influences are not the sole determinants of a child's development. Effects of the child's ordinal position in the family, twinship, adoption, or the presence of congenital defects are also potent. Childhood illnesses, death of parents, relatives and friends, seductions, and other traumatic incidents are among the many events that influence the child's personality. For the most part, these events are beyond the control of both the child and his parents. The fortuitous coincidence of several traumata, each relatively innocuous, may create an effect beyond the usual expectations.

This sketch of the child analyst's knowledge of the role of parent-child interaction is, of course, incomplete. However, it provides the reader with a background for understanding the analyst's approach to parents. He views the parent-child interaction not simply as one in which the adults influence the child, or cause his pathology, but as a truly mutual one. The child satisfies, stimulates, and provokes his parents. He is not merely a product molded by his environment. He is also an active force in determining his fate, whether it be normal or pathological.

THE ANALYST'S EMOTIONAL REACTIONS TO THE PARENTS

The analyst brings with him potentials for emotional reactions to his patient's parents. Many of these reactions can be classified as transferences. In addition, the analyst reacts to the real characteristics of the parents and may identify with them. The perceptive therapist recognizes these emotional responses as they appear, and utilizes signal transference affects and other reactions adaptively. He observes his responses when they are minimal and neutralized, rather than intense and uncontrolled.

Transference to the parents. Transference reactions to the parents, and identification with the child are extremely likely throughout the analytic process. During treatment sessions, the analyst looks at the world from the child's point of view, and tries to understand his patient's attitudes toward parents and other people. The analyst identifies with the patients as he empathically evokes memories of his own childhood relations with his parents (Olden 1953). Past antagonisms and affections toward his own parents, when they appear with minimal intensity, help the analyst to understand his patient's predicament and conflicts. Such feelings may become too intense, warp the analyst's judgment, and interfere with his analytic acuity. The analyst may experience transferences toward his patient's parents which interfere with his alliance with them. He may find himself blaming the child's parents, or in an attempt not to condemn them, the analyst may not notice their role in the pathogenesis of the child's illness. Sometimes, the child analyst, recalling feeling his parents failed him, searches for ways his patient's parents have failed. He may identify with the child who wishes to be loved or rescued by ideal parents, and become angry at the parents' failure. He may compete with the parents and try to take over their job. It has also been suggested (Ticho in Feigelson 1974) that an analyst's antagonism toward parents may be the result of a displacement of hostility toward his patient to the child's father or mother.

On the other hand, the analyst may react positively to the child's parents. He may wish his own parents had been aware of his problems and had been willing to seek help for him. Affection for his own parents can also be transferred to the patient's parents.

Reactions to the parents as real people. Most parents of children brought to analysts feel compassion for their child's distress, and are grateful for the analyst's conscientious and attentive care. They are willing to go to great lengths to help their child. Their predominant feelings are friendly, and their attitude is cooperative.

At the same time, they often come to the analyst burdened with guilt and fear. They may suspect or believe they have harmed their child. A belief that their child inherited defects from them or sustained birth injuries may reflect a conviction they have harmed their child. Parents may be angry at the child for causing them anxiety, shame, or guilt. If they displace antagonism to the analyst the parents may then confront him as a belligerent couple at the time of the consultation or during the course of the analysis. Sometimes the father or mother, frustrated by the analytic process, may lash out at the therapist. The causes of these feelings and behavior are often unconscious.

The analyst's reactions to parents' actual traits may include transference reactions, but they are not necessarily exclusively transferences. The analyst may identify with the parents in an empathic response and express his sympathy. He may find he is defending himself from a hostile barrage by reassuring them, or is excessively justifying the treatment, or is resorting to counter-attack. Analysts try to stem parental anxiety through the method they know best, interpretation, or through advice. We will discuss the disadvantages of treating and advising parents in a later section. At this point, we emphasize that the most helpful approach is one which is calm and communicates the analytic attitude. Careful fact finding and evaluation will allow the therapist to help the child through interpretation during his sessions.

At times, parents sabotage the analysis by keeping the child from sessions, provoking the child's resistance, or by providing misleading information to the analyst. When the analyst's work is interfered with by his patient, whether child or adult, he may react with irritation. However, his capacity for self-analysis, his devotion to understanding the patient, and his modulated therapeutic interest will generally enable him to maintain an analytic attitude. The analyst comprehends and interprets the patient's defenses, and recognizes resistance is a necessary aspect of treatment.

However, when interference is derived from parental activity the analyst may have greater difficulty maintaining his perspective. Transference hostility and concern for his patient's welfare may complement his irritation at the limitations placed on his effectiveness by parental impediments. When the therapist is aware of the nature and sources of his irritation, he will deal with it in a more objective manner.

Identification with real and idealized parents. We have already stated the child analyst identifies with real characteristics of the child's parents. When this leads to sympathy for their difficult position, the result can further the analyst's work. At times, however, the child analyst may become excessively uncomfortable as he identifies with parents who suffer and blame themselves, who attack and love their child, and who are disappointed and angry about their own parents' deficiencies. Parental feelings of failure and inadequacy may evoke similar feelings in the analyst and result in feelings of helplessness and confusion in the analyst. As Bornstein (1948) suggests, it's not surprising some child analysts feel terribly guilty when they do not achieve rapid resolutions of their patient's conflicts.

The child analyst who sees parents as neglectful, abusive, or abandoning will sometimes react by wishing to replace the "bad" parents. He may become forceful when he feels them weak, be directive when they flounder in their child rearing practices, and be kind when they are mean. Rescue fantasies in which the analyst identifies with an ideal parent replace a realistic analytic stance.

Blind spots may appear as the analyst struggles with conflicting feelings toward parent and child. Self-analysis is helpful to keep these to a minimum and to use emerging feelings to develop empathy.

CONSULTATION PROCEDURE

Ideally, the psychoanalytic consultation is a situation in which parents, imbued with strong desires to obtain help for their child, meet a knowledgeable analyst who possesses the capacity to use his previous experience as a person, a scientist, and healer to recommend the proper course to follow.

The evaluation requires detailed discussions with parents. A few analysts (Anthony quoted by Weiss 1964, Weiss 1964) recommend minimum contact with parents to avoid their distorting influence, but we believe this is unwise.

The consultant sees the parents initially for a variety of reasons. To determine the analyzability of the child, the analyst must ascertain the diagnosis, symptomatology, and developmental level of the child. He also needs to know whether and in what way the child has progressed and regressed in the past, as well as family and social background. The consultant discovers how the parents have reacted to the child and influenced him in the past, and must estimate their future behavior. He must decide if the parents are able to sustain the analysis, and if their behavior will support or discourage their child's progressions in development (see chapter 3 and Bernstein 1957, 1958). The consultant must, if possible, determine the parents' capacity to provide an environment in which development can be promoted after the child's arrests or inhibitions have been overcome. Both parents must be assessed. One parent may facilitate treatment even though the other impedes it.

A child is incapable of providing the details necessary for such an evaluation. Generally, he is not interested in his past, and does not possess the capacity to observe and remember the details of his past. He cannot recall his infancy, nor can he provide a running account of his more recent life. He cannot describe his parents' behavior or the events of his life fully because of his cognitive state and because of his age-appropriate propensity for denial. At best, the child will provide a history so distorted and with so many gaps that it is untrustworthy.

Even the parents' history will be incomplete and inaccurate to some extent. Contact with them after treatment starts is necessary for additional history. Some essential facts may never be provided by the parents. For instance, only the child will know his masturbatory practices and fantasies. These will emerge as the analysis proceeds. The child, not his parents, will be able to discuss his secrets. Although these secrets are vital to the eventual understanding of the child, the initial assessment does not require this material.

The consultant will also have to assist parents to prepare their child for his initial visit. With guidance, they are less likely to frighten their child. Instead, they will encourage him to talk frankly with the analyst, who will be introduced as a person capable of helping him. The parents need an understandable rationale, not a formula, to aid them in preparing their child. Usually, this is reached by a mutual exploration of the issues involved. The parents then conclude what makes most sense to tell the child. When asked what they would tell their child, parents sometimes come up with an excellent plan. In these instances, suggestions can be kept to a minimum. Parents cannot always follow an alien recommendation. They are more likely to successfully execute a plan that is at least partially their own. However, if the parents cannot arrive at a sensible plan for preparing their child, the consultant will have to provide one.

If the analyst recommends analysis (or some other form of treatment), he will have to discuss this with the parents. They will then decide whether to follow the analyst's advice. It will be necessary for them to evaluate the gains to be attained, and the burden in terms of time, emotional involvement, and money. Certainly the child cannot decide. The grown-up must act as an auxiliary ego from the outset.

An excellent consultative procedure is to allow the parent (or parents if both are present) to spend a session telling the story of his child's difficulties and successes in his own way. The analyst can encourage the father or mother by his sympathetic ear, and by questions that lead to further detail or clarification. In such a relatively unstructured interview, the consultant will be able to note the connections the parents spontaneously divulge. He will be able to guess what the child's illness means to each parent, the role each plays, and his reactions to the illness. The consultant will start to organize a picture of the child within the family as he observes and evaluates the quality of the parental interactions, and assesses their individual character structures. This is quite different from attempting to obtain a strictly chronological history.

In other interviews, the analyst can obtain the specific details of the child's development, symptomatology, and background the parents have inevitably omitted. He can also obtain an account of each of the parents' life experiences. Meeting with parents both alone and together provides an opportunity to learn details of their lives, and observe their interactions, thus providing further data for the evaluation.

With this information, the analyst is able to understand much more about the child than he could without knowing his environment and background.

The consultant will assess the parents' conflicts in relation to their conscious and unconscious attitudes toward their child. He will also assess difficulties that may arise during the course of the analysis, and whether an analysis should be undertaken. He will estimate the nature and strength of each parent's ego, superego, and drives, and the quality of his interactions with his child.

One must consider each parent's capacity for objectivity and empathy and the types of defenses he uses. The consultant will attempt to determine whether the parent has been able to maintain commitments to specific goals in the past. This will enable the consultant to decide if the parent can allow his child to remain in a lengthy and perhaps taxing therapeutic process. The analyst must also estimate the level of each parent's toleration for frustration, disappointment, and delay. The parent's sense of reality should be sufficiently intact so magical expectations are tempered and disappointment does not lead to an angry interruption of the analysis.

In evaluating the parent's superego, ideally one would expect the parent is not dishonest or overly manipulative with either the analyst or the child. A history of psychopathic behavior or questionable legal or financial dealings would argue against the recommendation of analysis, but would not completely rule it out.

If the adult lacks devotion to his child, as revealed by indifference, frequent abandonment, or abusive behavior, he probably will be unable to maintain a cooperative attitude during the analysis. A parent to whom monetary and materialistic considerations outweigh humanistic values may disparage the treatment and its aims.

At times, the analyst may find it so difficult to evaluate the parents' behavior (as well as the child's pathology) that a protracted period of assessment extending over many weeks or even months may be required. A working alliance with the parents as well as with the child is necessary for the treatment to succeed. The interaction between the parents and analyst during the consultation constitutes the start of the alliance.

Sometimes, the consultant may recommend that one or both parents enter treatment rather than the child. This may constitute a necessary step prior to the child's analysis or suffice in itself to maintain or improve the child's mental health.

THE POSITION OF THE PARENTS IN ANALYTIC TREATMENT

Let us proceed to a discussion of the types of relationship that develop once analysis is decided upon (see Burlingham 1935). The treatment centers on the child. Analytic results come about through interpretations by the therapist, and the development of an analytic process. The parent has an important, but secondary role. He bears the burden of arranging for the child to attend sessions regularly, and is responsible for paying for treatment. The parent acts as an alter ego for an immature child who is generally incapable of the judgments necessary for a successful and continuous analysis. The parent should be able to sustain analysis in the face of the patient's resistance. Adults in analysis are usually sufficiently tolerant of frustration and anxiety and cognizant of the future benefits that they will continue the analysis in the face of their resistance. A child, on the other hand, may be unable to bear the pain of the analysis or to keep the future in mind. The parent must provide the mature judgment to continue when the sick child cannot.

The parent himself has a difficult job. To maintain the child's confidence in the analyst, his parents' curiosity about the analysis is not satisfied. The analyst cannot reveal the child's communications. Parents' requests for advice about how to alter their own behavior to aid their child's recovery is usually thwarted. Instead, the parents are required to provide information to the analyst about the child's present circumstance and past experiences.

This task accentuates the parent's feeling that the analyst is a perpetually present observer of the family. He may picture the analyst as a benevolent onlooker, or as a severe, external superego figure who criticizes and establishes ideals for behavior. The frustrations and the time consumed bringing the child to and from the analyst's office and waiting for the child are bound to irritate the most devoted parents. In addition, guilty parents often feel the analyst is allied with the child against them. Parents often feel that they must surrender their child and their authority to the analyst.

Parents are sometimes jealous or envious of their child, who has the analyst's friendly ear and benefits from his interpretations. At times, parents wish analysis for themselves—especially as the child improves —and find limitations of time and money make this impossible. Such envy may appear even if the parent fears treatment himself and would not actually enter it.

The parent may have suffered from symptoms and entertained the idea of entering analysis prior to the start of their child's treatment. Or, the alteration of the balance of gratification and frustration within the family resulting from changes in the child may elicit parental symptomatology and personal distress.

Other difficulties are less easily observed. Bornstein (1948) has pointed out that parenthood serves to resolve remnants of the Oedipus complex through identification with one's parents and identifying one's children with one's parents. Deprived of their parental role, they seek other means, sometimes neurotic, of resolution. This too may impel them to wish treatment for themselves.

The child analyst may respond to a parent's wish for personal help by being tempted to act as his therapist, by desiring to be a sympathetic adviser, or by referring them for treatment. We will discuss these possibilities in later sections of this chapter.

CONTROVERSY REGARDING THE ANALYST-PARENT RELATIONSHIP

The parent occupies not one, but a complex of positions in the child analytic process. He initiates, sustains, and often ends the analysis. He supplements the child's ego in maintaining continuity of the treatment. He develops an information alliance with the analyst to provide data about the child's present situation and past experiences. The parent receives the analyst's suggestions about his conduct in relation to the analysis. At times, but not usually, the analyst advises the parent about child rearing. Frequently, parents seek support or help from the child's analyst for their own personal difficulties.

For dealing with parents, we will discuss various points of view and provide guidelines rather than provide rigid rules. While no fixed approach has met with universal acceptance, a general consensus has emerged from common clinical practice.

Generally there is continued contact between the analyst and the parents throughout treatment. There is disagreement about how frequently parents should be seen, if at all. We advocate seeing parents regularly, once a week under ordinary circumstances, at the start of the analysis and for a considerable time thereafter. Because analysis is often difficult for both parents and patient, the analyst must be available to lend the parents support when symptoms increase, persist, or after disappearing, return. Through regularly seeing parents, the analyst can help them understand the analytic process. The process goes on unobserved by parents even when, judged by external appearances, nothing is occurring or things are getting worse. We do not mean the analyst should reveal what the child has said or describe the patient's dynamics, but he can explain the process in general. Parents should understand the patient attains increasing insight as unconscious thoughts and affects become conscious. The analyst's refusal to reveal the child's secrets may disturb some parents. Here again, reassuring explanations are necessary to maintain the parents' cooperation in continuing the analysis.

Some analysts contend the analyst should see the parent as infrequently as possible (Weiss 1964).[1] According to this point of view, therapist-parent contact contaminates the analysis, obstructs the true development of a therapeutic alliance, and interferes with an analyzable transference and even a transference neurosis. The child may feel the treatment is for his parents, not for him. He may distrust the analyst and believe his secrets will be revealed. He may believe his fusion of analyst and parent is justified because they work together. Further, information about the child's present and past may mislead the analyst when parents distort the facts and see things from their own perspective and not their child's. If the analyst uses this distorted information in constructions, he may err seriously.

We disagree with the propositions of those opposed to frequent meetings of analyst and parents.[2] More often than not, we have observed that the therapeutic alliance is enhanced when the child learns his parents and analyst are working together on his behalf. The child should know meetings with the parents are held and should understand their purpose is to provide additional history and information. The child needs to appreciate the analyst's policy of not communicating to his parents anything discussed in sessions, and that he is entitled to know what his parents say, as long as no important parental confidence is betrayed. For the most part, children believe their parents and doctor when they say the analyst does not compromise his secrecy. In those few cases in which the child does not believe this, the analyst can refrain from seeing the parents. Preadolescents are more likely to be concerned about confidentiality than younger children.[3] (See chapter 8, on preadolescence.)

At times, parents confuse the analyst by providing unreliable or misleading information about the patient's past or present. The perspicacious therapist, however, can evaluate the data and avoid misinterpretations. If the analyst finds the parents confuse him too much, he can diminish his contact with them.

There is a distinct advantage to having accurate information about the events in the child's present life. Interpretations can be geared to include references to present actuality, as well as to the past. The analysis becomes more alive when defenses and fantasies are interpreted with regard to the reality of the day. Children, unfortunately, generally emphasize their inner life or concentrate on immediate reality, and provide little information about what is happening at home, at school, or elsewhere. When they do describe events, the full story often fails to emerge. Without information from the parent, the analysis becomes unbalanced. Fantasies may be explored without sufficient regard for the realities of the child's life.

As the informational alliance becomes established important data from the past as well as the present emerge. The parents recall things they had not remembered at the initial meetings. Errors and distortions of events can be corrected. The parents can ventilate and clarify their doubts, dissatisfactions, and concerns about the child and the analysis. Through obtaining a better picture of what is happening in the child's life, the analyst's clinical orientation and perspective become more accurate. Certain speech patterns or peculiarities in the child become understandable. The analyst's empathy with the child is improved. He is able to better understand how the child came to be disturbed. The analyst acquires a greater appreciation of the child's choice of defenses, adaptations, and interests. All this aids in making reconstructions. A knowledge of the child's development of object relations makes transference reactions more readily apparent. The analyst is able to better understand the subtleties of parental handling, interactions, attitudes, and conflicts. It becomes easier to distinguish between fact and fantasy in the child's statements. The analyst is aided in making more meaningful and accurate interpretations. He can more accurately evaluate changes in the child which occur as a result of the analysis.

It seems likely that at times seeing parents may produce some interference in the development of the transference. The fact the analyst meets with the parents outside the analytic situation makes his actuality palpable. The child's picture of him as a real person interferes with emerging transference images and with the patient's ability to distinguish transference aspects from the real analyst. The analyst's meeting with parents may convince the child his view of the analyst as a parent-like person is realistic. Nevertheless, in our opinion, these considerations alone are insufficient to prevent the development of a therapeutically utilizable transference; other determinants are of primary importance.

We believe intense and prolonged transferences rarely, if ever, appear in child analyses, because the child's cognitive development is immature. Further, the child is still involved with his parents. He lives with them, and they care for him and provide many of the gratifications he requires (A. Freud 1922-1970). In addition, the child analytic situation, in which the child sees and interacts with the analyst, is quite different from the adult analysis. The adult is more likely to develop an unrealistic picture of the analyst while he is lying on the couch with a minimum of stimulation. At times, the analyst's parent-like behavior—giving gifts or food to the child or providing pedagogical guidance to the adults—interferes with the analysis of the transference (see chapter 11, on gifts, gratification and frustration).

ADVICE AND EXPLANATIONS TO PARENTS

The analysis may be impeded if the child has realistic reasons to believe the therapist is not acting simply as an analytic interpreter, but as a therapist or adviser to his parents. If the child believes the analyst is a manipulator of his life, he may resent it, or encouraged by his parents, he may decide to rely on that method of help rather than seek to understand himself. Fantasies along these lines are analyzable, but their reality might interfere with the treatment. Nevertheless, explanations and advice are at times essential during the course of the analysis. The extent to which these are given is a matter of opinion and judgment.

Parents may not be aware of the analytic approach to resolving intrapsychic conflicts. Often, it is important for the therapist to provide them with an explanation. This can serve as a basis for understanding how analysis works: emphasis is on insight and restructuring of the personality rather than on symptomatic relief. If the child asks questions about his treatment or offers resistance his parents can then provide a more realistic statement and support the analytic approach. For instance, if a child complains about the analyst's relative silence or inactivity, parents unfamiliar with analytic procedure might become troubled. They might even echo the child's criticism. The knowledgeable parent, however, could furnish an adequate and supportive explanation. Of course, the analyst's explanation may not sufficiently reduce parental resistance to prevent the parents from undermining the analysis.

When parents become anxious about apparent worsening of behavior and symptoms, the analyst's reassuring explanations may enable them to better tolerate the difficulties. The analyst may inform parents that the analysis cannot be fully evaluated by the external behavior of the child. He may emphasize the importance of the process of intrapsychic change and assure them, without telling them details, that the analysis is proceeding as expected. For instance, if a previously inhibited child becomes rambunctious, messy, or defiant, this may reflect significant progress. Even temporarily regressive behavior can reflect positive changes.

During the consultation and in the opening phase, educative work may be necessary. It is necessary to advise parents about the need to report events in their child's present, daily life and recollections of the past. They may need to be asked to refrain from questioning the child about the analysis or using the analytic relationship in a threatening way to make the child behave.

It may be necessary to advise parents to preserve the analytic situation and its arrangements, or protect the welfare of the child.

For instance, if a parent grossly interferes with the analysis by leaving a small child alone in the waiting room before the patient has sufficient confidence in his surroundings, disruption of the analysis might result. The child might become so terrified at being deserted by the parent and the analyst that effective work becomes impossible.

A mother may ask the analyst whether she should bring her "sick" child to his session. To make an appropriate decision, the analyst must explore the realities of the situation. If the parent is tempted to bring a seriously ill child to his appointment, she may be expressing her hostility or revealing deficiencies in judgment. Under such circumstances, the therapist has no choice but to protect the child by telling the mother to keep him home. In such a case, not only would the child be harmed by his attendance, the patient may also resent the analyst's participation in parental negligence and lose trust in him.

A parent may bring a very sick child to his hour without consulting with the therapist.

Billy's mother brought him to the analyst's office after he injured his arm at camp. The analyst ascertained that the boy, who was in pain, resented not being cared for properly. Deciding the arm was probably fractured (it was), the analyst recommended the session be abbreviated so Billy could be examined by his pediatrician or an orthopedist.

Too much parental concern about physical illness may also impede the analysis and require the analyst's intervention. If a parent keeps a child from attending sessions because of minor illnesses, the analyst will have to advise that the patient keep his appointments. Otherwise, parental resistance to treatment may stimulate similar resistance in the child. A mother's worry about illness may appear in conjunction with other concerns.

Mrs. S. was terribly ashamed that her son, Johnny, was in analysis. She felt this to be a sign of her deficiency as a parent and insisted the family hide the fact from the maternal grandmother. When the grandmother visited—and at other times—Mrs. S. kept Johnny home because he had a slight sniffle. The therapist advised her that this interfered with treatment. In this case, the intensity of her resistance caused her to reject the advice, and eventually, to end the analysis prematurely.

At times a child will need his parents' permission before he can reveal certain concerns to the analyst. The patient may believe that his parents would object to the exposure of family secrets.

Eddie's parents quarreled at night believing their children were not listening. Eddie revealed his preoccupation with secrets by using pantomime instead of verbal communications during his sessions. The analyst learned from his mother that Eddie reacted to his parents' arguments by becoming anxious. He interfered with their fights by going to the bathroom or standing in their bedroom doorway. In his analytic hour, the patient reenacted aspects of his behavior at home by going to the toilet several times each session or by hiding himself under his raincoat. He also pressed the analyst to reveal family secrets of his own. Eddie was insistently curious about this. In such a situation, if interpretation does not enable the child to reveal and discuss the "family secrets," it may be necessary for the analyst to ask the parents to give the child verbal permission for frankness and honesty.

A child may refrain from verbalizing obscenities if he does not have his parents' permission. If this inhibition does not yield to analysis, the parents may be asked to give their consent so the patient can speak freely.

Generally, the analyst's advice should directly apply to the analytic setting. At times the analyst judges the child's environmental situation to be such that analytic work cannot succeed. At the very start of the treatment, the analyst may recommend changes in child rearing practices. On the other hand, he may wait until the analysis is in progress to ascertain if the parents can make the necessary corrective alterations. Once a patient sees his role in family difficulties, he will sometimes press his parents to change their behavior.

One analyst, during the consultation, recommended that the parents stop undressing in front of their eleven-year-old daughter who feared riding in an automobile. The new parental modesty had a beneficial effect. The child, relieved of perpetual excitement, became asymptomatic. Unfortunately, analysis then appeared unnecessary and plans for treatment were not considered. However, the girl needed therapy for related emotional difficulties, and later developed more serious character disturbances. This was manifested by her promiscuity and drug abuse. In retrospect, one can see in this case it would have been better to refrain from offering advice which was temporarily effective and thus precluded the much needed treatment.

Another analyst and his anxious patient worked together on the boy's feelings about his parents' frequent and blatant nudity. Eventually, the child effectively demanded that his parents clothe themselves properly. The analysis brought about a personality change that enabled the patient to alter his traumatic environment.

This does not mean one should never suggest changes in child rearing practices. There are times when analysis will not prove effective and the child will not improve unless the environment changes. If this is clearly the case, helpful suggestions are in order. For example, to overcome an analytic stalemate it may be necessary to advise parents to set expectable, reasonable limits for their child. The parent may permit excessive stimulation or traumatization, precluding possible resolution in the analysis. At times, the analysis may resolve a conflict but the original trauma may be repeated: a father may continue to beat his child or parents may not stop an older brother from attacking his younger sibling.

Parents often seek and welcome advice. Especially at the start of the analysis, they may expect a magical suggestion from an omniscient analyst will end the child's illness rapidly. If the analyst offers advice that fails, the parents, disillusioned and resentful, may terminate treatment. If the advice is effective, the gratified parental wishes may interfere with a more effective use of analysis. The parents may insist on more magical interventions and even tell the child of the doctor's powers. Patient and parents may then come to prefer manipulation to the more arduous task of analysis.

Parents are often unable to follow advice and become discouraged by their failures. Their propensities to pathogenic behavior may be deeply rooted in their personalities. In such cases, they cannot alter their behavior, and may not even wish to do so. Even when environmental change is vital to the analysis, the therapist must be reasonably confident that the parents are able successfully to follow his advice and he must be ready to support them if they fail. When the parents resentfully sabotage the analyst's suggestions greater difficulties may be in store. The parents may view the analyst as a toilet-training parent who is attempting to force them to do the right thing.

Environmental change can come about without advice. Struck by the destructiveness of their own behavior as they describe it in their weekly meetings with the analyst, parents sometimes decide to alter it. At other times, they respond to the analyst's unconscious facial expressions indicating his approval or opposition to some act. On some occasions the analyst may actually confront the parents with their inappropriate behavior.

Steven's parents took him to a toy store for a family outing, but did not purchase any of the many toys that appealed to him. They did not realize they were teasing him until the child's analyst pointed this out to them. As a result of the confrontation, his parents reflected on their behavior and modified it. They avoided other teasing behavior in the future.

Parents who are in treatment themselves may be stimulated by such a confrontation to discuss the significance of this pattern in their own therapy. Parental change occurs more effectively when the parents bring it about on their own or as a result of their personal analytic work rather than at the instigation of the child's analyst.

Often, analysis can proceed satisfactorily in the face of pathogenic parental behavior. In fact, such behavior may spur the child to talk about it. Were it to cease, the child's motivation to learn why he cannot cope with his parents' upsetting behavior may vanish.

Advice interferes with the analyst's neutral stance, and usually implies his values and ambitions for the patient. The child may object to the therapist's position and resentfully refuse to cooperate in the treatment. An undisciplined policy of regularly guiding parents in an attempt to provide an optimum environment is very likely to compromise the analysis.

Complex and contradictory problems develop when a crucial situation seems to require intervention. The following vignette illustrates the difficult decisions that may have to be made.

After about two years of analysis Mr. and Mrs. D. asked their son's psychoanalyst, Dr. G., whether they should arrange for their nine-year-old child, Bill, to have a circumcision. The patient, who had been brought for treatment for enuresis, no longer wet. A fear of being poisoned, which his parents had not known about, had improved markedly during the course of the analysis.

Mrs. D. had discovered a sore on her son's foreskin. She correctly surmised this was the result of masturbation. When she suggested a circumcision would prevent future sores, Bill responded enthusiastically. In the analysis, the patient came to realize he felt his uncircumcised penis was deficient. All his friends were circumcised and when they saw his genitals they made fun of him, saying he was a girl. To Bill, the foreskin was, as Nunberg (1949) described, a feminine structure akin to the vagina. Bill's preference for a small, clean, masculine penis rather than a larger, dirty one was reflected in his wish to have small, neat HO-gauge trains rather than big, dirty Lionel trains. Any fears he may have had of surgery required were not apparent. Castration anxiety was hidden behind the reassuring expectation that circumcision would make him masculine.

Dr. G. tried to evaluate the significance of any advice he might offer the parents, and the possible effects this might have on the analysis. He found his position difficult. There were several possible suggestions:

1. The parents could be advised there should be no operation.

2. They could be told to go ahead with the procedure.

3. They could be told to delay the decision until further analysis with the child and discussion with the parents had clarified matters.

4. The analyst could refuse to give advice directly, but could refer the parents to someone else for a recommendation.

The analyst's immediate impulse was to insist the operation not be performed, as it was a type of castration. He felt he would then be protecting his patient who would feel attacked and mutilated by the procedure. This was contrary to his patient's conscious feelings. Were Dr. G to make this suggestion to Mr. and Mrs. D., the boy would know of it and feel his therapist was depriving him of becoming more masculine. As far as Bill was concerned, the procedure would remove his femininity. On the other hand, were the analyst to agree the operation be done, he would be recommending surgery that was painful. The therapist believed Bill unconsciously conceived of the procedure as a punitive castration that would provide masochistic gratification.

There was much evidence for this view. Bill inhibited his urges to masturbate because he thought it wrong, and believed he would be punished for it. Rather than stimulate his penis, which was forbidden, he stroked his testicles, a displaced source of pleasure. Masochistically inclined, Bill would sometimes squeeze his testicles, producing pain. In his games he would act the victim, as well as the attacker. Eventually, a masochistic fantasy regarding the circumcision appeared: I will please my mother who wants me to have a painful castration.

Bill's mother was indeed quite eager for the operation. Apparently it represented a punishment for masturbation to her, but it was much more than that. Mrs. D. had recently undergone an abortion—a procedure she blamed on her husband. Her determination to hurt him manifested itself when, in a rage, she chased him about the house, knife in hand. In a session with the analyst, Mrs. D. described the planned circumcision while her husband cringed in his chair, seemingly protecting his genitals.

Although Dr. G. did not specifically recommend delay (which would have meant to Bill his analyst was interfering with his cherished operation), ongoing discussions with Mr. and Mrs. D. involved deferring the operation. During that time, Bill worked on his conflicting wishes and defenses. Dr. G. thought he had handled the situation well. He had not alienated Bill by proscribing surgery, hadn't threatened his patient by urging it, nor had he gratified Bill's masochistic desires. The analyst felt taking a stand for or against surgery would impede the analysis. If Bill objected to the analyst's position, his seemingly justified anger would keep him from open discussion. Had Dr. G. made any of the above suggestions, he would have gratified some irrational urge, and the abstinence necessary for analysis would have been abrogated.

Mrs. D. had previously reacted to Dr. G.'s relatively minor suggestions as if they were major criticisms. This also made the analyst hesitant to give advice. He feared she would regard any advice as an insult. Nevertheless, Mr. and Mrs. D. insisted on action. Dr. G. decided the only way to remain neutral was to suggest it was unwise for him to make the decision, and recommend Mr. and Mrs. D. see the consulting analyst who had referred them to him originally. To his surprise, the consultant discussed the issues with Mr. and Mrs. D., but refused to give definite advice. They returned to Dr. G. determined to get his advice.

Eventually, their talks revealed Bill's parents were unaware that circumcision involved pain. They transmitted the belief that the operation was innocuous to Bill. It soon became apparent, however, that unconsciously he knew the surgery would hurt. Mr. and Mrs. D. knew surgery would be performed under anesthesia and that cutting was involved. However, they did not think the incised penis would hurt after the operation. Even when the analyst expressed surprise at this belief, they adhered to it. Dr. G. recommended they consult a surgeon about this point of controversy. The surgeon could tell them if the operation would be painful. The suggestion involved a calculated risk: Dr. G. could not be certain what advice the surgeon would offer.

Meanwhile, Bill and his therapist discussed these problems during analytic sessions. Bill wanted the operation, and apprised by his parents that it would be painless, he had forgotten his original fears of the pain and danger. Eventually Bill realized a recent determinant of his fears of poisoning was the displacement of anxiety from the surgery to the anesthesia it entailed. He could be poisoned and killed by the drugs and the surgery. He became conscious that surgery represented punishment to him. Waiting had indeed been helpful to the analysis.

Mr. and Mrs. D. consulted a surgeon who confirmed that postoperative pain would occur. He also assured them Bill's health did not require a circumcision. The parents then decided against the procedure, and the analysis proceeded to a successful conclusion.

TREATMENT OF PARENTS

One of the purposes of seeing parents is to help maintain treatment even when the going is rough. The analyst offers parents emotional support. His encouraging, sympathetic attitude is quite different from the interpetive therapy used with analytic patients.

At times, the analyst may be tempted to use his most potent weapon, interpretation, to help parents endure their child's treatment, or to bring about behavioral change when it hampers the analysis. When advice fails, therapy for the parent may be indicated.

Parents may seek relief for their personal difficulties through involvement with their child's doctor. Complications may result if the analyst attempts to treat the parents himself. The child may harbor an oedipal fantasy that his analyst and his mother engage in intimacies. Through perceiving their special interaction, his oedipal fantasy may become unanalyzable. Similarly, the parent may find his wishes to compete with the child for the analyst's attentions actualized. If the analyst makes interpretations, the parents may develop more intense transference feelings toward him. These feelings lead to wishes to have their child fail while they succeed. Indeed, the parents may behave in such a way to make these wishes come true. Aggressive transferences mobilized by interpretation may create difficulties for the analysis which cannot be resolved. The analyst with two patients finds himself caught in a conflict of loyalties which compromises both treatments.

If the parents need treatment, they can be referred to a therapist for analysis or some other form of therapy. Often, this is a helpful way to aid parent and child break a deadlocked and destructive interaction. When parent and child are analyzed simultaneously, the child's prognosis improves. The parent then can be freed from the compulsion to gratify his own neurotic needs either through the child's emotional difficulties or through involvement with the child's analysis. The child will then be more able to focus on his own internal conflicts in his sessions. (See chapter 17, on simultaneous analysis.)

Although interpretations to parents are to be avoided, some extreme situations exist where the analyst must intervene with this powerful instrument. He must be sufficiently flexible so he can adapt his capabilities to the rare occasions which may require them.

Jimmy S. was doing rather well in analysis, but his parents' persistent fights at home threatened its complete success. Jimmy had come to treatment for enuresis which had disappeared with analysis. His fits of rage had a sadistic quality and also served masochistic aims. For instance, breaking a window was an attack on his parents which resulted in being punished by them. Eventually, Jimmy's identification with his fighting parents became the focus of the analysis.

Mr. and Mrs. S., despite their unreasonable squabbling, were extremely likable people. They and the analyst got along well. Their mutual respect enabled Mr. and Mrs. S. to endure the difficulties inherent in analysis, and to appreciate the sincerity of the interpretation eventually offered to them.

Jimmy's father and mother were narcissistic in that they would not compromise on their high principles. They berated themselves for being perfectionistic in their demands on Jimmy. As Mr. and Mrs. S.'s values did not always coincide, they frequently became extremely angry at each other when a stern code of behavior was violated. For example, Mr. S. might object to the exact words Mrs. S. used with a business associate at dinner. Mrs. S. might think her husband's treatment of her indicated a disrespect for women, which she objected to because it conflicted with her ideals. Their extremely civilized demeanor and the loftiness of their beliefs contrasted with the primitive rage that could appear. Their disagreements about issues on ethical grounds, and the extreme feelings involved, had them seriously consider divorce. Their fury reached a peak when Mr. S. poured gasoline on his wife, and was barely able to keep himself from lighting her with a match.

The seriousness of their behavior impressed them, but not sufficiently for them to return to therapy. Mrs. S. had recently called her therapist to discuss her fights with her husband. According to her, this therapist had been quite unsympathetic. He told her on the telephone she "had always been a bitch." She resolved not to return to him or to anyone else. Mr. S. had recently seen his former therapist for a number of visits. Mr. S.'s enuresis, which started after he had been injured in a fire five years previously, had responded to psychotherapy. He could not accept his therapist's recommendation that he enter analysis for treatment of the characterological problems that remained. He refused to see his doctor again.

Eventually, the child's analyst appealed to the couple's good sense with an interpretation that applied to both of them. He told them they were both wonderful individuals whom he respected as people and for their ideals. However, they attempted to achieve their ideals too rigidly and became intolerant of each other. They picked on each other for insignificant offenses. Each insisted the other be perfect even though both knew this was impossible. When one noticed imperfection in the other, he became furious.

The fruitlessness of their attitude became apparent to them, and surprisingly, their tolerance of each other increased and their fights diminished markedly. This not only had a beneficial effect on the parents; it also helped Jimmy's analysis. When he did not have to contend with actual fights at home, it was easier for him to relinquish his pathological identifications with his parents.

THE PARENT IN THE CONSULTATION ROOM

At times, especially in the analyses of younger children, a patient will refuse to leave the waiting room, or will only enter the consultation room or playroom if he's accompanied by his parent. (See chapter 6, on prelatency analysis, and Kolansky 1960, Schwarz 1950, McDevitt 1967.) The parent may implicitly or explicitly suggest she be present. An analogous situation may come about when a child returns to the waiting room during the course of a session. Most often these episodes take place in the beginning of an analysis, but they also occur later. The causes may vary and they are best considered in relation to the specific phase of analysis in which they occur.

At the outset of an analysis, observing the interaction between child and parent may facilitate understanding the possible sources of anxiety in the child and/or the parent. The parent may be anxious about bringing her child to a stranger. She may fear losing her authority, her closeness to her child, or her child's love. She may worry about being exposed as an inadequate or defective mother, or she may simply be curious about what goes on between analyst and child.

The child may react compliantly to his mother's conscious or unconscious wishes. Frequently, he is frightened because of separation or castration concerns, or by the reactivation of specific memories of prior traumata.

The analyst may deal with the situation by remaining alone in his office, seeing the child in the mother's presence in the consultation room, playroom, or waiting room; or by sending the mother out while he and the child remain together.

Sending the mother away is unwise because the analyst's neutrality is violated. The child will recognize the therapist has actively broken contact between him and his needed and loved mother, and will be realistically distrustful. With a young child in the opening phase of analysis, there are distinct advantages to meeting with mother and child together when the patient refuses to join the analyst in his office alone. This may be necessary for one session only or may continue for several weeks before the more usual analytic situation can evolve or resume. This may be an indispensible phase in the analysis, intricately involving the patient's core conflicts.

There are several advantages in seeing mother and child together. The mother's ability to understand and empathize with her child may be improved when she hears him talk about his troubles and observes the analyst's reactions. As the mother's sympathy grows, her cooperation in the analysis may be maintained or enhanced. Often, the mother in the consultation room can understand conflicts, precipitating events, or past determinants of the child's behavior that the analyst is at a loss to comprehend. She can then assist the analyst by supplying significant background information. In exceptional circumstances, she may provide a correct interpretation during the session or later on.

The parent can reinforce the analyst's specific interpretations, thereby assuring them of greater initial acceptance and aid in working through. Through her very presence as an ally of both child and analyst, the mother may reassure the patient she approves of the analytic process, and he need not worry about conflicting loyalties.

While we have emphasized the advantages of the mother's presence, difficulties may arise as well. The parent may become frightened by observing her child reveal his difficulties or by what the analyst says to him. The analyst may have to restrain himself, and not offer interpretations he would ordinarily make, to avoid upsetting her. At times, counter-transference, as well as reality factors, make the analyst uncomfortable. Additionally, the child may feel constrained by his mother's presence.

When a child refuses to enter the consultation room, or leaves it in the middle of a session it is usually due to regression following the appearance of anxiety induced in the course of the analytic work. Sometimes it reflects a change in the home situation. Whatever the cause, if the child does not return to the office after a short interval, it is common practice for the analyst to enter the waiting room and discuss the situation with the child there. Analytic understanding of the child, his age, his developmental stage, and the immediate precipitating cause of the behavior determines whether or not it is appropriate for the discussion to take place in the presence of the child's parent.

TERMINATION OF ANALYSIS

Throughout this chapter, we have discussed technical issues that arise during the consultation and various phases of the analysis. In this last section, we will concentrate on the final phase (Kohrman 1969).

The time and manner of termination is often influenced by parental reactions. Parents may end the analysis even when the therapist thinks it unwise. The totality of the family situation must always be considered when deciding when and how to terminate a child's analysis. Symptom removal, the end of a developmental arrest, and the child's appropriate movement into the next developmental phase are important factors that must be considered. The achievement of internal consolidation, the capacity for continued development, and the child's (as well as the parents') motivation at the time are other considerations. (See chapter 16, on the terminal phase.)

Often, parents rely on the analyst's judgment. However, sometimes parents press for termination. This is particularly apt to happen when presenting problems have disappeared or the burden of analysis has become too great for a variety of reasons, including the jealousy or resentment of other family members.

The analyst will discuss many of the factors determining the decision to terminate with the child's parents. He will need information from them to determine how the child is getting along outside of his sessions. When he suspects the child will need further help in the future, he will call this to the parents' attention. Sometimes, for instance, the advent of adolescence, with its characteristic increase of drives, will disrupt the balance of ego and id. Former symptoms may then reemerge or new difficulties may appear.

The parents may become alarmed at the reappearance of symptoms during the terminal phase. Explanations about patients' reactions to separation can be helpful. The parents' concerns about the child's responses to ending analysis may reflect the parents' concern about their ability to manage the child by themselves, or may simply be an expression of a feeling of loss of the analyst by the parents.

Near the end of analysis, parents sometimes ask questions about their child's future. How should the analyst deal with this? One approach is to fend off such questions. Supposedly, to do otherwise would be manipulative, nonanalytic, and ineffective. At the other extreme is a view expressed by some analysts who feel their patients' parents are inadequate to deal effectively with many life decisions. These analysts recommend environmental manipulation, such as educational guidance or advice in dealing with potentially harmful, seductive life situations. They believe this insures a more favorable outcome for future personality development. However, a middle approach seems to be most generally advocated: Possible solutions to problems posed by parents can be discussed. Trust is placed on the gains of analysis, the effects of ongoing, healthy developments, and the competency of the parents. Surrendering the analytic stance during the terminal phase could compromise the analysis of problems which arise with ending the treatment.

The terminal phase is the period in which previous gains can be consolidated and new insights achieved. The analyst must retain his analytic attitude from the start of the treatment to the end of the final session. In this way, the best possible analytic results can be attained, and the child's future welfare preserved.

NOTES

1. Anthony (1977) advocates flexibility in the practice of child analysis. He "treats every child . . . as a specific instance requiring specific decisions. . . ." Sometimes Anthony sees parents, and sometimes he does not. He asserts "that there are just as many problems connected with seeing parents . . . as with not seeing them. . . . [Seeing them] nearly always contaminates the analytic field . . . When I do not [see them], I have the inner feeling that I am working more analytically with the child . . ." (personal communication). Anthony's remarks should be understood in context. His sensitivity to the role of parents is reflected in the fine book on parenthood he has edited (Anthony and Benedek 1970).

2. Klein, who is sometimes said to advocate minimal contact with parents, actually wrote: "If we can succeed in establishing a good relationship with the child's parents and in being sure of their unconscious cooperation, we are in a position to obtain useful knowledge about the child's behavior outside analysis. . . . But if information . . . is only to be gotten from parents at the price of raising difficulties of another kind, then I prefer to do without it, since, although valuable, it is not absolutely essential" (Klein 1932, p. 48).

This statement is in essential agreement with our position, but tilts somewhat more toward avoidance of parental contact. We would add, in some cases, the analysis fails when the analyst does not see the parents for information in an attempt to avoid other difficulties.

3. When the child reaches adolescence, his need to exclude his parents is generally so great that continued contact with the parents is unwise.

REFERENCES

Alpert, A., and Bernstein, I. (1964). Dynamic determinants in oral fixation. *Psychoanalytic Study of the Child* 19:170–195.

Alpert, A., Neubauer, P. B., and Weil, A. P. (1956). Unusual variations in drive endowment. *Psychoanalytic Study of the Child* 11:125–163.

Anthony, E. J. (1977). Unpublished paper presented at the Association for Child Psychoanalysis. March, 1977

Anthony, E. J., and Benedek, T. (1970). *Parenthood: Its Psychology and Psychopathology.* Boston: Little, Brown.

Bergman, P., and Escalona, S. K. (1949). Unusual sensitivities in very young children. *Psychoanalytic Study of the Child* 3/4:333–352.

Bernstein, I. (1957). Panel report: indications and goals of child analysis as compared with child psychotherapy. *Journal of the American Psychoanalytic Association* 5:158–163.

—————— (1958). The importance of characteristics of parents in deciding on child analysis. *Journal of the American Psychoanalytic Association* 6:71–78.

—————— (1975). On the technique of child and adolescent analysis. *Journal of the American Psychoanalytic Association* 23:190–232.

Bornstein, B. (1948). Emotional barriers in the understanding and treatment of children. *American Journal of Orthopsychiatry* 18:691–697.

Burlingham, D. (1935). Child analysis and the mother. *Psychoanalytic Quarterly* 4:69–92.

—————— (1951). Present trends in handling the mother-child relationship during the therapeutic process. *Psychoanalytic Study of the Child* 6:31–37.

Burlingham, D., et al. (1955). Simultaneous analysis of mother and child. *Psychoanalytic Study of the Child* 10:165–186.

Coleman, R. W., Kris, E., and Provence, S. (1953). The study of variations of early parental attitudes: a preliminary report. *Psychoanalytic Study of the Child* 8:20–47.

Feigelson, C.I., Reporter (1974). Panel: a comparison between adult and child analysis. *Journal of the American Psychoanalytic Association* 22:603–611.

Freud, A. (1922–1970). *The Writings of Anna Freud.* Volumes 1–7. New York: International Universities Press.

———— (1960). Introduction to Katy Levy's paper on Simultaneous analysis of a mother and her adolescent daughter. *Psychoanalytic Study of the Child* 15:378–380.

Fries, M. E., and Woolf, P. J. (1953). Some hypotheses on the role of the congenital activity type in personality development. *Psychoanalytic Study of the Child* 8:48–62.

Geleerd, E. R. (1967). *The Child Analyst at Work.* New York: International Universities Press.

Greenacre, P. (1966). Problems of overidealization of the analyst and of the analysis: their manifestations in the transference and countertransference relationship. *Psychoanalytic Study of the Child* 21:193–212.

Hellman, I., Friedmann, O., and Shepheard, E. (1960). Simultaneous analysis of mother and child. *Psychoanalytic Study of the Child* 15:359–377.

Johnson, A. M., and Szurek, S. A. (1952). The genesis of antisocial acting out in children and adults. *Psychoanalytic Quarterly* 21:323–343.

Klein, M. (1932). *The Psycho-Analysis of Children.* London: Hogarth.

Kohrman, R., Reporter (1969). Panel: problems of termination in child analysis. *Journal of the American Psychoanalytic Association* 17:191–205.

Kolansky, H. (1960). Treatment of a three-year-old girl's severe infantile neurosis: stammering and insect phobia. *Psychoanalytic Study of the Child* 15:261–285.

Mahler, M.S., Pine, F., and Bergman, A. (1975). *The Psychological Birth of the Human Infant.* New York: Basic Books.

McDevitt, J. B. (1967). A separation problem in a three-year-old girl. In *The Child Analyst at Work,* ed. E. R. Geleerd, pp. 24–58. New York: International Universities Press.

Nunberg, H. (1949). *Problems of Bisexuality as Reflected in Circumcision.* London: Hogarth.

Olden, C. (1953). On adult empathy with children. *Psychoanalytic Study of the Child* 8:111–126.

Pearson, G.H.J., ed. (1968). *A Handbook of Child Psychoanalysis.* New York: Basic Books.

Provence, S., and Lipton, R. C. (1962). *Infants in Institutions.* New York: International Universities Press.

Schwarz, H. (1950). The mother in the consulting room. *Psychoanalytic Study of the Child* 5:343–357.

Silverman, M. A., Rees, K., and Neubauer, P. B. (1975). On a central psychic constellation. *Psychoanalytic Study of the Child* 30:127–157.

Spitz, R. A. (1945). Hospitalism. *Psychoanalytic Study of the Child* 1:53–74.

Van Dam, H. (1977). Unpublished presentation at the Association for Child Psychoanalysis, March.

Weil, A. P. (1970). The basic core. *Psychoanalytic Study of the Child* 25:442–460.

Weiss, S. (1964). Parameters in child analysis. *Journal of the American Psychoanalytic Association* 12:587–599.

Chapter 15

MELANIE KLEIN'S CONTRIBUTION TO CHILD

ANALYSIS: THEORY AND TECHNIQUE

Irma Pick
Hanna Segal, M.D.

THE BEGINNING

In "The Analysis of a Phobia in a Five-year-old Boy" (Little Hans), Freud (1909) refers to the fact that he himself had only one brief conversation with the boy. The general lines of treatment, based on the father's reported observations, were laid down by Freud, and carried out by the father.

The special knowledge by means of which he [the father] was able to interpret the remarks made by his five-year-old son was indispensable and without it the technical difficulties in the way of conducting a psychoanalysis upon so young a child would have been insuperable. It was only because the authority of a father and of a physician were united in a single person and because in him both the affectionate care and scientific interest were combined that it was possible in this one instance to apply the method to a use to which it would not otherwise have lent itself. [p. 5]

In his 1922 postscript to the paper, Freud (1909) wrote, "The publication of this first analysis of a child had caused a great stir and even greater consternation and a most evil future had been foretold for the poor little boy because he had been 'robbed of his innocence' at such a tender age and had been made the victim of a psychoanalysis" (p. 148).

In fact, in the intervening years, psychoanalysis had hardly explored the deeper layers of the unconscious in children, fearing that such exploration might be potentially dangerous. For example, Hug-Hellmuth (1921) wrote, "A proper analysis according to psychoanalytical principles can only be carried out after the seventh or eighth year. But even with children at this early age, the analyst must . . . turn aside from the usual routine and satisfy himself with partial results, where he thinks that the child might be intimidated by too powerful a stirring up of feelings and ideas, or that too high demands upon his powers of assimilation are being made, or that his soul is disturbed instead of freed" (p. 289).

Hug-Hellmuth took the view that interpretations should be given very sparingly; and although she occasionally used drawings and play as material, she did not develop this as a specific technique. In considering child analysis, Freud (1918) wrote, " . . . it cannot be very rich in material; too many words and thoughts have to be lent to the child and even so, the deeper strata may turn out to be impenetrable to consciousness. An analysis of a childhood disorder through the medium of recollection in an intellectually mature adult is free from these limitations" (pp. 8–9).

This was the climate in which Melanie Klein began her psychoanalytic play technique. Her first child patient, Fritz, age five and a half, was treated before 1920 and papers were written about the work in 1921 and 1923. Initially, Klein adopted the method Freud had used with Little Hans and thought it would be sufficient to influence the attitude of the child's mother. She suggested the mother encourage her child to freely discuss with her the many unspoken questions which were clearly impeding his intellectual development. This helped, but only partially. "It was soon decided that I should psychoanalyse him." With this decision, Kleinian child psychoanalysis began.

Melanie Klein (1955), in writing of the history and significance of her technique, says of Fritz's analysis: "I interpreted what I thought to be the most urgent in the material the child presented to me and found my interest focusing on his anxieties and the defences against them" (p. 4).

She describes her own consternation at the child's acute anxieties, but became convinced of the efficacy of her approach when, a few days later, she found that as a result of her interpretations the child's anxiety had been alleviated. Karl Abraham (1924), her mentor, supported her pursuit of her technique. He was to say, "The future of psychoanalysis lies in the play-technique" (p. xii).

The treatment was carried out in the child's home with his own toys. Klein found the child expressed his fantasies and anxieties mainly in play which she was then able to interpret. She discovered play corresponded to the free associations of adult. "I was also guided throughout by two other tenets of psychoanalysis established by Freud, which I have from the beginning regarded as fundamental; that the exploration of the unconscious is the main task of the psychoanalytic procedure and that the analysis of the transference is the means of achieving that aim" (p. 5).

TRANSFERENCE

The turning point of the history of psychoanalytic theory and technique came with the realization that the success of the method depended on the patient's readiness to accept interpretations. Often, it was discovered, these were opposed with unconscious resistances. Moreover, it was found patients developed intense feelings of love and hate toward the analyst. At first, Freud thought these factors were simply a hindrance. It was then recognized that these feelings and impulses were transferred from earlier relationships. They were not remembered, but relived and re-experienced in the relationship with the analyst. It was discovered that only insofar as these feelings and impulses were emotionally re-experienced and understood could real change in the patient be brought about. Indeed, what distinguishes psychoanalysis, both as a form of scientific investigation of the mind and as a form of treatment in adult neurotics, is the central importance attached to the role of the transference. All adult psychoanalysts agree on this point. However, in child analysis, two different viewpoints developed—one by Anna Freud, and the other by Melanie Klein.

Anna Freud (1926) was led to modify classical technique. In her view, children did not develop a transference neurosis. "Unlike the adult, the child is not prepared to produce a new edition, as it were, of the love relationships; the reason being that, to continue the metaphor, the original is not yet out of print" (p. 44). She believed negative tendencies directed toward the analyst were essentially inconvenient and should be reduced as soon as possible. "It is in their positive relationship to the analyst that truly valuable work will be done" (p. 41). Anna Freud therefore actively endeavored to gain the child's affection and cooperation. Her ideas about the weak egos of children led her to consider the analyst's role to be that of an educator.

Melanie Klein, on the other hand, started with the view that children can, and do, produce a transference neurosis. Transference situations arise if a method equivalent to adult analysis is employed. All educational measures are avoided and the transference is analyzed, particularly negative impulses directed toward the analyst. (In a different connection, by 1919, Abraham had shown that patients with a strong narcissistic character do not, as Freud had originally thought, fail to produce a transference. If one observes carefully, one can find evidence of a well-hidden negative transference.)

As early as 1925, Melanie Klein treated a very young child, Rita, aged two years, nine months. Rita suffered from night terrors and animal phobias. She was so ambivalent and so clinging to her mother that she could hardly be left alone. The analysis of so young a child was an entirely new experiment and was conducted in the child's home. When left alone with Klein in her nursery, Rita at once showed signs of what Klein took to be a negative transference. Rita was anxious, silent, and very soon asked to go out into the garden. Klein agreed, but instead of trying to soothe or distract her young patient, Klein interpreted her negative transference. From a few things Rita said, and the fact that she was less frightened when outside, Klein concluded Rita was particularly afraid of what the analyst might do when they were alone in the room. Rita linked her suspicion of Klein as a hostile stranger with her fear that a bad woman would attack her when she was alone at night. Further analysis of this and other anxieties enabled Klein to see that Rita's transference was not a fear of her mother in the present, nor indeed, of her actual experience of her mother now or in the past, but an introjected mother. This mother had treated Rita with far more sternness and cruelty than the real one had ever done. Transference occurred and developed on the basis of the child's projection on to the analyst of internal parental figures. Klein discovered even at two and a half, Rita's relation to the object already had a long history in which parental figures, based on projection and introjection, had been built up in the internal world. These figures form the basis of transference in the analysis of children and adults.

Klein's strict adherence to the analysis of transference enabled her to discover the very early origins of object relationships, and gave her access to what Freud had called the dim and shadowy area of the mind. She stressed that one could not observe the transference without establishing a proper analytic situation, and a proper analytic situation could not be established if one did not analyse the transference. As we know, in transference onto the analyst, the patient repeats earlier emotions and conflicts. It is our experience that we are able to fundamentally help the patient by taking his fantasies and anxieties back in our transference interpretations to where they originated—in infancy and in relation to his first objects. By re-experiencing early emotions and fantasies, and understanding them in relation to primal objects, the patient can revise these relations at their root, and thus, effectively diminish his anxieties.

PLAY TECHNIQUE

Rita's analysis was undertaken in her own home, and the child played with her own toys. During this treatment Melanie Klein concluded that analysis should not be carried out in a child's home. Even more important than the problem of maternal interference, Klein found transference can only be established and maintained if the patient is able to feel the consulting room or play room, indeed, the whole analysis, is something separate from his ordinary life. "For only under such conditions can he overcome his resistances against experiencing thoughts, feelings and desires, which are incompatible with convention, and in the case of children, felt to be in contrast to much of what they have been taught" (Klein 1955, p. 6).

In 1923, the analysis of an unresponsive, withdrawn child of seven caused Melanie Klein to decide to bring in a few small toys. She later (1932) wrote, "Play is the child's most important medium of expression. If we make use of this play technique, we soon find that the child brings as many associations to the separate elements of its play as adults do to the separate elements of their dreams. These separate play elements are indications to the trained observer; and as it plays, the child talks as well, and says all sorts of things which have the value of free associations" (p. 30).

Melanie Klein thought the child expressed his fantasies, wishes, and actual experiences in a symbolic way through play and games. In so doing, the child makes use of the same archaic and phylogenetic modes of expression, the same language as dreams. To correctly understand a child's play, it must be seen in relation to his whole behavior during the analytic hour. Klein stressed, as did Freud in discussing the understanding of dreams, we must not be content to pick out the meaning of separate symbols, but must take into consideration all the mechanisms and the method of representation. "The whole kaleidoscopic picture—often to all appearances quite meaningless, which children present to us in a single hour—the content of their games, the way in which they play, the means they use; the motives behind a change of game will yield up their meaning if we interpret them as we do dreams" (Klein 1932, p. 29).

Implicit and central to Melanie Klein's views on understanding the unconscious are the ideas discussed in detail as early as 1929 by Susan Isaacs (1948)—the mind is a whole. The higher functions do not act independently; the unconscious is not merely a vestigial or rudimentary part of the mind. It is the active organ in which mental processes function. No mental activity can take place without its operation, although much modification of its primary activities normally ensues before it determines thought and behaviour in an adult. The original primary mental activity has been called unconscious fantasy. There is no impulse, no instinctual urge which is not first experienced as unconscious fantasy. Even if a conscious thought and act are completely rational and appropriate, unconscious fantasy underlies it.

Although Freud himself made quite specific and similar statements about the unconscious, they have not been explicitly woven into the fabric of theory and technique in classical analysis. Some analysts intuitively understand that unconscious fantasy is ever-present and act on this. They always seek the unconscious content behind conscious acts and thoughts. However, many analysts do not, and when something appears to be rational or "objective," its connections with the unconscious remain unexplored. The danger is that these analysts see little in the patient's material, and do not recognize a transference situation unless it is expressed verbally and with direct reference to the analyst. In Kleinian analysis, with children and adults, the analyst's task is to discover and interpret the unconscious content which the patient is expressing at the moment, here and now in the session. The words may or may not be the form chosen for its expression. The patient may act out in various ways, as well as verbalize. It is the analyst's task to interpret to the patient the fantasy content behind his whole behavior so ultimately it may be more available for thought and verbal expression. The need to act out may lessen, and ultimately, the fantasy may be more fully expressed in words. Far from Freud's expectation that children's material is not rich, we find our difficulty is rather to disentangle from the wealth of material that which most urgently requires interpretation.

In Kleinian child analysis, through play and the child's other communications, the analyst aims at establishing contact with the child's unconscious fears and wishes. From the outset, the analyst tries to interpret the child's communications. Since interpretations relieve anxiety, the child's interest and cooperation is maintained.

THE PLAY TECHNIQUE SETTING

As in adult analysis, the child is ordinarily offered five fifty-minute sessions per week. Melanie Klein stressed every child should have his own individual box or drawer of toys. This forms part of the child's special and private relationship with the analyst. The material provided usually includes a set of small animal and human figures, small vehicles (cars, trains, airplanes, or boats), small containers, etc. The toys are small to make them easy to handle, and as nonspecific as possible to enable the child to endow them with properties from his fantasy world, rather than those of the toy manufacturer. For example, one would not include soldiers or cowboys, but would try to include figures of different sizes that would easily lend themselves to use as representation of children or adults. In addition, the child is ordinarily provided with paper, pencils, perhaps glue, cellotape, plasticene, string, and scissors. If possible, running water should be in the room, and cleaning-up brushes and cloths should be available.

The room is kept as simple and safe as possible. It is organized so the child is free to express a modicum of aggression without too much danger to himself or his surroundings. There should be a small table and chairs, an armchair, and a couch with cushions. The latter are often used by young children to express a variety of feelings and fantasies. As children progress in treatment, they may at times use the couch to lie down and free associate.

A very important part of the setting is the attitude of the psychoanalyst himself. Basically, this attitude should be similar to his attitude in adult analytic work. He should be friendly, impartially interested, and genuinely concerned to understand the patient's communications. At the beginning, the analyst might try to explain to the child something about analysis. "I will be seeing you for fifty minutes every day except Saturdays, Sundays, and holiday times. These will be toys for you to use when you are here. I would also like you to try to tell me about whatever is in your mind—dreams, thoughts, feelings, and so on, however silly or unpleasant they may feel to you. We will try to work together to understand about what makes you worried and unhappy." Naturally, the precise form of these introductory remarks will depend on the child's age and capacity to understand. In general, one trys to explain the toys are to be used in work with the analyst, rather than merely to "play with." This helps establish an atmosphere in which the analyst conveys to the child that analyst and patient are not here so much to "play" as to "work together" to understand the child's problems. In this way, the analyst assumes a "working" part of the child's ego is available which will be able to cooperate in the treatment. One might also tell the child he will be free to use the things in his own way, taking care not to say "you may do what you like here." It can be explained the toys in his drawer are only for him, and what takes place in his sessions will be exclusively between child and analyst. This gives the child an assurance about confidentiality.

From that point on, the analyst attempts to show the patient what is meant by trying to "understand" his problems. For example, if the child asks permission to use something, or says "what shall I play with," or seems to struggle with his inhibitions, the analyst would neither try to reassure him or guide him, but would take the anxiety expressed as a problem to be understood together. The child's anxiety would be acknowledged, and if any observation has been made that would help throw light on its nature, this is conveyed to him. If this is done successfully, the child will recognize and appreciate he is being given something "special." The next task might be to observe how the child reacts to what he is given: with pleasure, ambivalence, hostility, confirmation and endeavor to carry the exploration further, or with resistance and attempts to disrupt. These reactions can then be explored. In this way, the "setting" is very quickly established and understood by the child.

The whole setting of the analysis and the analyst's role as "interpreter" quickly becomes very important for the child, and comes to symbolize different early feelings. The child's attacks on the setting need to be understood. The capacity of the analyst to tolerate and manage this may constitute an important part of the child's treatment. In child analysis, the analyst may be faced with certain management problems ordinarily encountered only with psychotic patients in adult analysis. Particular attention needs to be paid to keep the setting as stable as possible. Experience shows children very quickly grasp the value and meaning of the analyst's interpretive function. When they demand noninterpretive behavior, this is often connected with an attack on their good object, the good internal feeding mother, and on the "good" or helpful part of themselves that knows that they require this understanding. Therefore, when one gives something else, be it a bit of reassurance or a present of one sort or another, it may be experienced as taking something else away—that which the child needs most, the food for thought to help him understand his problems. The child can obtain education or reassurance from others; it is the capacity to always try to understand that is offered uniquely by the analyst.

This is particularly important for students to grasp when treating severely or even minimally deprived children. There is often a determined attempt on the part of the child, and in the young analyst for his own reasons (be it competition with the parents, guilt about having had better mothering himself, identification with the deprived child, etc.) to make up for the deficiencies in the child's environment by taking on actual mothering functions. Of course, this arises in adult analysis, too. Nonetheless, perhaps both because of the child's vulnerability, and because of the analyst's vulnerability when early infantile identifications are aroused, the problem often seems particularly acute in the treatment of deprived children.

At times, the analyst needs considerable conviction and a secure relationship with his own internal objects to maintain the view that the most important experience of mothering he can give is to continue his efforts to understand what is being demanded, and put this into words for the child, rather than give second best by acceding to the actual demands. The moment the analyst embarks on actually taking over the role of a mother or father, this interferes with the process of observing and understanding the transference, and so deprives the child of what is potentially most valuable to him.

PROJECTIVE IDENTIFICATION, INTERPRETATION, AND THE ANALYST AS A CONTAINER

Recent developments of Melanie Klein's ideas, particularly an understanding of projective identification, have been elaborated by Bion (1962) and have focused attention on the question of the analyst's capacity to bear the patient's projections. Bion stresses much communication takes place by projective identification. The patient may feel omnipotently able to enter the analyst and take over his functions. At the same time, he may feel he evacuates into the analyst impulses or aspects of himself or of his internal objects he finds unbearable. Therefore, increasing attention is being given to the analyst's efforts to be sensitive to feelings which are aroused in him. If the analyst is able to "hold" them, these feelings may be scrutinized and thought about in an attempt to understand what the child is communicating.

I had the opportunity to supervise a student who commenced the treatment of an eight-year-old boy. The child, Robin, was described as poker faced, withdrawn, and unable to show a wide range of emotional reactions. At school, he was considered a loner and self-sufficient. After his birth, Robin was sent away from mother for twenty-four hours because of severe jaundice. When he returned, her milk had dried up. Apparently there were no difficulties with bottle feeding, but Robin did not give up his bottle until he was seven years old.

In treatment, the student experienced Robin as remote. She felt there were only brief moments in the session when she was able to get close to him. Robin frequently came late for sessions and prepared to leave early. When he was prepared to leave the session five minutes before it was to end, the student ended the session, feeling it would be unbearable to go on. During sessions, Robin appeared to be completely absorbed in his plasticene modelling or drawing, and the student felt very left out and helpless. He appeared very grown up and as though he could give her all sorts of information if he so wished. The student clearly felt herself in the position of a helpless child—needing information from him, waiting for him, or being rejected by him before the end of the session. It was possible to help her to see how Robin seemed to have grown very big, to have taken over the functions of a rather cold mother, and to have projected into the therapist his own impotent baby feelings, making her feel small. The feelings of being left out and wanting something from someone who wasn't available were unbearable to the child. At times, the student felt them to be unbearable too, as seen, for example, in her need to end the sessions early.

As work was done on these problems, Robin began to do more vivid drawings and to be more communicative about them. During the sixth week of his treatment, the therapist told him about her upcoming vacation. He appeared undisturbed and drew a picture of an idyllic country scene in which all was peaceful. It seemed to coincide with his apparently peaceful reaction to the news of her upcoming vacation. Robin indicated now, and on other occasions, that he felt they would be on this idyllic vacation together. In this way, the therapist's absence was not felt as loss, but as a time when they were ideally joined together. When the therapist suggested he was afraid of his anger about the upcoming separation, he said the grassy tufts in the vacation picture might be bombs. He then anxiously contradicted this, saying, "It really is grass."

Shortly thereafter, when the therapist reminded Robin of her vacation dates, he responded in an apparently sophisticated way, saying he knew she would be going with her family to America (she is American) and she would be sleeping with a man and going to a restaurant. Then Robin pointed to a picture which again began with an idyllic country scene, but now there was a boat departing (the analyst). In the sea, was an enormous whale with very large teeth and a huge tail, which was erupting into the landscape. It seemed that despite his apparently bland acceptance of the upcoming vacation, something huge was now erupting which was disturbing the peace. This whale with its biting teeth and menacing tail seemed to be a projection of his own biting and aggressive anal feelings into the father's penis (the man the therapist will be sleeping with during the vacation). Also it seemed to tell us something more about the way Robin's devouring greed and aggression "grew enormous" when he was in danger of being left. At this stage, he did not directly acknowledge the therapist's interpretations about his anger and anxiety about the upcoming vacation. However, he told his father he thought the therapist would die and not return. This, of course, was understandable in light of Robin's fantasy attacks on her.

In a later drawing, Robin produced a representation of a map of America in which the vacation boat was arriving. The continent was surrounded by menacing whales and sharks, and was filled with snakes, a lake of death, a blood forest, a volcano, a plethora of deadly and poisonous objects—representing dangerous fecal and urinary excrement. Robin's own internal volcano seemed to be erupting. However, while these drawings were vivid, he himself seemed to remain cut off. It slowly began to emerge that Robin saw himself as a star artist, whose drawings were much in demand. He felt his artistic productions were more significant than the therapist's interpretations. He ended a very elaborate and beautifully presented story (which he wrote when his therapist was away ill for a couple of days) with this conclusion: "The star fish is called a starfish because it is shaped like a star. It is poisonous and could kill somebody."

In the transference relationship it was becoming clearer Robin's view of himself as a loner and self-sufficient served as a defense against extreme fears of being left, as well. It also allowed him to maintain a view of himself as a "star" or an enormous whale. However, this defense made it more difficult for him to be available for help. His narcissistic manic defense covered up deadly and destructive or poisonous feelings which endangered his object and his capacity to be in touch with his need for help. Therefore, he was exposed not only to the loss of the external object (the therapist, standing for the mother going away), but his internal object was also destroyed, as well as the part of himself which was able to be in touch with his needs.

This problem was highlighted a few weeks later when the therapist made a technical error, which turned out to be instructive for both therapist and child. She had occasion to interpret Robin's rivalry with his father. Robin then paired animals together and insisted these pairs were the two of them together during the previous weekend. As though bringing further evidence in support of this claim, Robin said, "You *were* in my dream last night. You came to my school and then to my home—and then you went away." His therapist did not stay with and explore his feeling, and his first admission that despite his wish for them to be paired, his therapist had gone away. Instead, she became rather excited that Robin had brought a dream, told him how useful these were for analysis, and asked if he recalled any other dreams. Very quickly Robin said he did and told her another dream. He was going on an airplane to Africa. There was an elephant on the wing of the plane. The waiter asked him to capture the elephant with a net. He did, and gave it to the pilot. When they got to Africa, there was no cage for the elephant, so they gave it to the zookeeper.

It was not clear whether this was a dream or a story. However, it seemed to be an association to what had just taken place. When the therapist did not hold Robin's feelings about her going away, but instead encouraged him to be a "star" teller of dreams, he immediately grew enormous again—into an elephant. However, this elephant was extremely insecure—on the tip of a wing. Robin seemed to know that as a waiter (someone who has to wait), he must be caught and held. There must be a cage or a keeper for his feelings, otherwise they quickly grew into a mania which made him feel very insecure and frightened.

The emphasis in Kleinian child analysis is on a detailed following of the transference. At first, the therapist had to reach the child's feelings by being aware of and being able to use his feelings that were being projected into her, in order to bring Robin in touch with the nature of these projected feelings. With interpretation, Robin gradually showed his problems more clearly. An actual event, the therapist's upcoming vacation and their separation, was colored for Robin by the nature of his own angry responses, as well as his use of manic defenses. We begin to understand the apparent contradiction between his remoteness and his clinging to the bottle until he was seven. A child who denies his need for the object in the way Robin does, needs an object constantly present to maintain his view of himself as self-sufficient. The therapist needs to be able to contain the child's unbearable feelings. For example, Robin needed to feel there was a cage, something to hold him, to feel safe enough to be aware of his feelings about separation and to gain insight into them. This eight-year-old boy was in need of help to develop sufficient strength to tolerate or contain within himself the feelings aroused by separation. These feelings are like those a small infant may experience in the absence of the mother, including the manic defenses against biting teeth and the volcanic anal attacks which seemed to erupt in the face of loss. Robin could be helped to make contact with these infantile experiences and needs from which he had become so remote. The pressure he put on a young therapist (like his young mother) at times made it difficult for her to hold him.

The setting and the analyst's interpretive role within that setting can provide the patient with the experience of a containing object (Bion 1962) or the equivalent of what Winnicott (1965) has called the *good enough mother* (pp. 17–19). The Kleinian child analyst might differ from Winnicott in technique because of the conviction that an essential part of the holding experience resides in the analyst's function of observing the transference, and putting the child's feelings and experiences into words for him. This enables the child to internalize an object that helps him hold experiences in his mind. Kleinian analysts take the view that verbalizing, actually interpreting, is an essential part of child analytic technique.

The pressures on the analyst to move out of his interpretive role may take many different forms. For example, the adolescent, struggling as he does with the conflict between his child parts and growing-up parts, may try to get the analyst to be his collusive ally against restrictive parents. Or, the adolescent may so frighten the analyst by his capacity to act out his resurging sexual or aggressive feelings in a dangerous or self-destructive way, that he may try to force the analyst into the role of a sanctioning or forbidding parent. It is important that the analyst be aware of these dangers, and address himself to the patient's internal conflict. This necessitates making contact with the sane or mature parts of the adolescent which can cooperate with the analyst. Then, the analyst and patient together can try to understand the adolescent's infantile feelings and wishes, and his fears about his capacity to act out in dangerous ways. The adolescent is often confused about what constitutes omnipotence and what is genuine potency or strength. He requires the aid of the analyst's strength to enable him to face his conflicts, without mutual acting-out. Latency children use strong defenses against any experience of psychic reality. Great skill and patience is demanded of the analyst to tolerate the child's apparent indifference to the analysis, and in the face of this, to continue to minutely observe the child's behavior. For example, the child reading comics in the sessions may be projecting into the analyst his own rage at being left out of something.

At times, the child analyst also has the problem of coping with directly aggressive behavior. The child may flood the room or dangerously hurl something at the analyst. At least temporarily, this will prevent the analyst from interpreting as he intervenes to protect the room or himself. When the child makes persistent attacks of this sort, it is, of course, very difficult for the analyst to think, and she may, understandably, get angry. Again, it is important to sort out the child's behavior. He may be trying to provoke the analyst into playing the role of the harsh superego. Or the child may be making a sadistic urethral attack. The child may be evacuating into the analyst feelings of rage, literally giving the analyst his experience of what it feels like to be overwhelmed with rage, or flooded with anxiety. Sometimes, if understood, the very concreteness of these attacks may help throw light on the very primitive nature of the child's impulses, and the accompanying anxieties. It may reveal primitive attacks on the primal scene—the analyst's mind is experienced as the place where linking of thoughts takes place—the intercourse in the mind that produces the interpretation/baby. Or it may be a primitive attack on any possibility of the breast being able to link up with the baby's mouth. The patient may be like a screaming baby who fills his mother with so much confusion the food for thought cannot flow from the analyst or be received by the patient. In this way, the analyst can often gain access to early and often overwhelming anxieties and feelings.

Bion's developments of Melanie Klein's theories have had a considerable impact in elucidating some of these problems.

THE ANALYST'S RELATIONSHIP WITH THE CHILD'S PARENTS

In adult analysis (except perhaps in the treatment of psychotic patients), the patient ordinarily brings himself and is himself responsible for maintaining the continuity of the treatment. A child is brought to treatment by his parents, who are ultimately responsible for him and for maintaining the treatment. This presents an important complication in the child's treatment. The analyst has to consider the nature of his relationship to the parents as it may activate his own unresolved feelings towards his parents. For example, in the young student, one often detects competitiveness with the child's parents. The student needs to prove he can better understand the child, and given the chance, he would have been a better parent. Or the student may experience anxieties about alienating the child's affections. These feelings may complement the parents' own worst fears. Embarking on an analysis for their child is usually a very hard step for parents to take. Often they feel this represents an admission of failure, or they may fear the analyst is out to triumph over them, to beat them where they have failed, or to increase their guilt by adding his blame.

It is important that the analyst be aware of these feelings. It is usual to see the parents alone before commencing treatment, to hear in detail about the child's problems and their history. Also this give the parents a chance to meet the analyst to whom they are entrusting their child. Parents will often directly or indirectly express anxieties about the analysis. The analyst has the opportunity to acknowledge their anxiety and to convey that their roles are not in competition. The analyst is offering the child a quite different experience, one which would be inappropriate for the parents to give. We do not consider that the child's problems are due simply to his parents and we convey this. While we understand they blame themselves for their child's difficulties, we believe children have problems in their own right, for which they may require help. Although Melanie Klein wrote very little specifically about the analyst's relationship with parents, it is this fundamental attitude toward the child's problems that perhaps most influences our work with parents, and indeed, with the child himself. We need to convey to the parents by our attitude that we understand we are asking a great deal of them. We are asking them to understand the child's need to know his analysis is confidential and separate from his everyday life, and that further contact with his parents might interfere with treatment. This may be quite hard for the parents to bear, for their feelings of competitiveness or possessiveness, or their guilt, may make them feel they ought to be participating more directly in the treatment. It is necessary to assess each case, and to consider whether the parents are able to sustain the treatment without help, or whether they themselves require regular support. If this is required, it is preferable to arrange for them to communicate with a colleague, or perhaps a social worker, as too frequent contact between the child's analyst and his parents would cause a major disturbance in the analysis.

It is also important parents understand that undertaking a child analysis is a major and long-term commitment. In a moment of crisis or panic they may be ready to agree to anything in the hope of solving or dumping the problem. They may then come to resent the difficulties of getting the child to his daily sessions. We need to convey the seriousness of our own commitment to the treatment, and the importance we attach to maintaining the setting and its continuity. We need to be sure they understand that a quick relief of symptoms will not mean the child is cured, and will not be a cause for discontinuing treatment. Parents should be warned that there may be times when the child resists continuing treatment and must depend on his parents' support for the part of himself that does want to get well. It needs considerable tact on the analyst's part to gain the parents' cooperation, to indicate an availability if the parents are really worried or distressed about their child, and at the same time, to discourage interference in the treatment.

THE KLEINIAN POINT OF VIEW

As early as October 1923, Abraham wrote to Freud (1965), "I have something pleasant to report in the scientific field. In my work on Melancholia I have assumed the presence of an early depression in infancy as a prototype for later melancholia. In the last few months Melanie Klein has skillfully conducted the psychoanalysis of a three-year-old with good therapeutic results. This child presented a true picture of the basic depression that I postulated in close combination with oral erotism. The case offers amazing insight into the infantile instinctual life" (p. 339).

Melanie Klein's play technique became a tool with which new discoveries could be made. Her contributions to psychoanalytic theory stand out as a monumental achievement, the most important since Freud himself. Freud discovered the world of childhood through the analysis of adults. Melanie Klein, through the analysis of children, could confirm his theories by direct evidence, extend knowledge about childhood, and delve deeper into infancy. Understanding her technique with children requires knowledge of her basic views about infantile experience. These views very much influence the scope of observation of the Kleinian child analyst, and subsequently, the content of his interpretations.

Very early in her work, Melanie Klein became aware of the importance and variety of the child's early object relationships in fantasy and in reality, and of the richness of his unconscious fantasy. With her technique, she gained access to the patient's internal world and became aware of the complex and detailed way in which the child's external and internal world overlap and influence one another. She was able to formulate a coherent and detailed theory about the infant's earliest relationship to his mother, and about the very early roots of the Oedipus complex. Her work led her to believe that the origins of guilt and anxiety lay much earlier in childhood than Freud had believed. Fantasies referring to the infant's relationship to his mother's breast were responsible both for distortions of character in adults and for susceptibility to psychotic illnesses.

Melanie Klein took the view that the infant has an innate unconscious awareness of his mother. She said we know young animals at once turn to the mother and find their food from her. The human animal is not different in this respect, and instinctual knowledge is the basis for the infant's primal relation to his mother. She also thought a rudimentary ego exists and operates from birth onwards, and it has the important task of defending itself against anxiety. Klein considered the newborn baby experiences anxiety of a persecutory nature, both in the process of birth and in the adjustment to the postnatal situation. At first, the ego is largely lacking in cohesion and is dominated by splitting mechanisms. The young infant, without being able to grasp it intellectually, unconsciously experiences every discomfort as though it were inflicted on him by hostile forces. Conversely, if comfort is given (the warmth and the loving way he is held or the gratification of being fed) this process gives rise to happier feelings and is felt to come from good sources. This makes the infant's first loving relationship possible to at least part of an object—the mother's breast, or hands, or lap, etc.

The infant's discomfort is not a response to frustration, but is due to the infant's own internal forces. Melanie Klein developed Freud's concept of the death instinct and considered that the danger of being destroyed by the death instinct directed again at the self contributes to the splitting of impulses into good and bad. Klein also formulated the view that from birth onwards, some of the earliest activities of the ego are connected with the infant's earliest unconscious fantasies. Considered from this angle, introjection means the outer world, its impact, and the objects the infant encounters are not only experienced as external, but are taken in and experienced as part of his internal life. Projection means the infant not only evacuates stool, but also has a fantasy of being able to expel good and bad experience or parts of himself or his objects. This will influence the nature of the object he reintrojects. When the object is invested with love, the infant will feel he takes in a loving object, and when it is suffused with his own hate, he will experience it and take it in as bad and persecutory. From these earliest projections and introjections, an internal world is gradually built up. At first, it is dominated by a split in which the good objects and the good parts of the self are in some measure protected, since the aggression is directed away from them.

Thus, Melanie Klein took the view that the infant, from the outset, has powerful libidinal and destructive urges which are directed towards and experienced in relation to the mother, or a part of the mother. When the infant feels loving, he projects good feelings onto the breast, and is thus able to take in not only the actual milk, but also a picture or experience of a good and loving object. Conversely, when he is dominated by hatred or rage, these feelings, when projected, result in the reintrojection of a bad and frightening breast. He splits the breast into either ideally or wholly good, or totally bad and feared. When the infant does not have good enough experience, either because of the unsatisfactory nature of the object, or because he is excessively dominated by destructive feelings, especially greed and early envy, the building up of a good internal object is interfered with. While a great deal of work has been done on the infant's external experience, insufficient attention had been paid to the effect of the infant's internal impulses as a source of later difficulty. The excessively greedy child or the envious one (Klein, 1957) is never satisfied with what he gets, and therefore, does not have the experience of a good mother. Klein stressed the innate or constitutional factors present in the infant. She later postulated the idea of a primitive, early form of innate envy of the goodness of the mother's breast and its influence on the infant's internal experience of the external world, and indeed, on the actual capacity of the mother.

A responsive and appreciative baby may help the mother, whereas a grudging or resentful infant may affect her capacity to provide for him.

Freud viewed early infancy as a period of narcissism or non–object relatedness. Melanie Klein took the view that as object relations are present from the beginning, narcissistic patients do have relationships, but of a primitive and intense nature, dominated by hatred and destructiveness. These problems are accessible to psychoanalysis. Therefore, Melanie Klein and her followers have felt able to apply the classical Freudian technique to the treatment of psychotic and borderline psychotic patients, adult and child alike. Rosenfeld (1965), in particular, has made important further contributions in this area.

In normal development there is, from the beginning, a drive toward integration which increases with the growth of the ego. If the good internal object is established with relative security, it becomes the core of the developing ego. Even at best, though, the happy relationship with the mother and her breast is never undisturbed. Persecutory anxiety is bound to arise, and is at its height in the first months of life, emerging from the conflict between the life and death instincts. One of the many factors stimulating integration is that the splitting processes are never more than temporarily effective. The ego is driven to try to come to terms with the destructive impulses. Integration, when achieved, has the effect of mitigating hate by love, and in this way renders the destructive impulses less powerful. Melanie Klein considered this integrating process, which she termed the *depressive position,* ordinarily arises in the middle of the first year of the infant's life. Persecutory anxieties dominating the first months form what she termed the *paranoid-schizoid position.* However, integration is also difficult to accept. The coming together of the destructive and loving impulses, and the good and bad object, arouse anxieties that the destructive impulses may overwhelm the loving feelings, and endanger the good object and the good parts of the self. Klein maintained that integration can only take place step by step, and the security achieved is liable to be disturbed under internal and external pressure. This remains true throughout life. Full and permanent integration is never possible, because some polarity between life and death instincts always persist and remain the deepest source of conflict.

In the depressive position, the infant gradually becomes aware that the breast which he loves and which gratifies him is the same breast which he also hates when it frustrates him. With emotional growth, the infant's capacity for awareness of his own needs increases, as well as his capacity to recognize that the object also has needs of its own. In the paranoid-schizoid position, the infant's anxieties are essentially for his own survival. In the depressive position, the infant becomes capable of concern for the object, and of feelings of sorrow and anxiety about loss. He now links these feelings with his fears about the consequences of his own aggression, and an early sense of guilt arises.

It is impossible to do justice to these ideas in a few words. Melanie Klein was able to show in detail the very rich and complex nature of the infant's relationship first with his mother, and later with the other important figures in his life, such as his father and his siblings. The father is experienced by the young infant in a variety of ways. He is seen as a rival for mother's breast and her attention. The bad breast, later projected onto the father, is also seen as one of the earliest precursors of the harsh and primitive superego. On the other hand, when there is a good relationship to the mother, the loving feelings are also transferred to the father. In the depressive position, father is seen as an important complement to mother, and is needed by mother and child as a protector. All these attitudes were seen by Klein to form part of an early oedipal situation. They add variety and richness to the complexities of the early oedipal anxieties, which may be of a persecutory or depressive nature.

Melanie Klein's work with children and the findings she made had considerable influence on her technique with adult and child patients. The discoveries she made through child analysis, and the resulting theories, stressed the importance and speed of splitting mechanisms, and of projective and introjective processes, and the importance of the constant fluctuations in the state of mind of the patient. This led her to interpret more frequently than is usual in classical analysis. Step by step, Klein followed the splitting, projections, and introjections, and interpreted them to the patient. This detailed following of the patient's anxieties and his defenses against them in the transference enabled her to reach the deepest layers of the mind.

Treatment aims at aiding the patient to be less rooted in the paranoid-schizoid position, less dominated by splitting processes, and more firmly on the road to integration and an increased capacity for love and concern. During the process of the patient's transference onto the analyst of early parental imagos, the analyst's capacity to contain the patient's projections, and to talk to him about them gradually, enables the patient to have more insight into the nature of these impulses. As the patient can take in the analyst's understanding as good, his good internal object is strengthened, and helps him learn to deal with his destructive impulses. As he can do this and make more contructive efforts to preserve his good internal objects, persecutory anxiety and guilt lessens, and his trust in his good internal object and his own goodness will be strengthened.

Melanie Klein's findings have aroused considerable controversy in the world of psychoanalysis, but they cannot be ignored. They are as revolutionary in their impact as were Freud's earlier.

REFERENCES

Abraham, H.C., and Freud, E.L., eds. (1965) *A Psychoanalytic Dialogue. The Letters of Sigmund Freud and Karl Abraham. 1907–1926.* New York: Basic Books.

Abraham, K. (1919). A particular form of neurotic resistance against the psycho-analytic method. In *Selected Papers on Psycho-Analysis,* pp. 303–311. London: Hogarth Press (1927).

———(1924). A short study of the development of the libido, viewed in the light of mental disorders. In *Selected Papers on Psycho-Analysis,* pp. 418–501. London: Hogarth Press (1927).

Bion, W.R. (1962). *Learning from Experience.* London: Heinemann. Reprinted in W.R. Bion, *Seven Servants,* Jason Aronson, 1977.

Freud, A. (1926). The role of transference in the analysis of children. In *Introduction to Psycho-Analysis.* London: Hogarth Press. (1974).

Freud, S. (1909). Analysis of a phobia in a five-year-old boy. *Standard Edition* 10:5–149.

——— (1918). From the history of an infantile neurosis. *Standard Edition* 17:7–122.

Hug-Hellmuth, H. (1921). On the technique of child analysis. *International Journal of Psycho-Analysis* 2:287–305.

Isaacs, S. (1948). The nature and function of phantasy. *International Journal of Psycho-Analysis* 29:73–97.

Klein, M. (1921). Development of a child. In *Contributions to Psycho-Analysis.* London: Hogarth Press (1948).

_____ (1923) 1) The role of the school in the libidinal development, 2) Infant analysis. In *Contributions to Psycho-Analysis.* London: Hogarth Press, 1948.

_____ (1926). The psychological principles of infant analysis. In *Contributions to Psycho-Analysis.* London: Hogarth Press, 1948

_____ (1930). Importance of symbol-formation in the development of the ego. *International Journal of Psycho-Analysis* 11:24–39.

_____ (1932). Psychological foundations of child analysis. In *The Psycho-Analysis of Children.* London: Hogarth Press.

_____ (1955). The psycho-analytic play technique: its history and significance. In *New Directions in Psycho-Analysis,* ed. M. Klein, P. Heimann, and R.E. Money-Kyrle. London: Tavistock.

_____ (1957). *Envy and Gratitude.* London: Tavistock.

_____ (1961). *Narrative of a Child Analysis.* London: Hogarth Press.

Rosenbluth, D. (1970). Transference in child psychotherapy. *Journal of Child Psychotherapy* 2:72–87.

Rosenfeld, H.A. (1965). *Psychotic States.* London: Hogarth Press.

Segal, H. (1964). *Introduction to the Work of Melanie Klein.* London: Heinemann.

Winnicott, D.W. (1965). *The Family and Individual Development.* London: Tavistock.

Chapter 16

TERMINATION IN CHILD ANALYSIS

Samuel Abrams, M.D.

This paper is divided into three sections. The first contains a clinical description of the terminal phase of the analysis of a child. The second section describes the principles and practicalities of termination, utilizing the illustrative clinical material. The final section summarizes these issues in a more generalized form.

CLINICAL DESCRIPTION

"I dreamed that bubbles were coming out of the radiator."

Martin was eleven. He had been in analysis for five years. There was both curiosity and reflection in his simple declarative. He wondered, "How could bubbles come out of a radiator?"; he drew his dream. Perhaps the visual representation would help him figure it out.

The picture was not of an ordinary radiator. Instead, he drew a vent, specifically of a kind which was set flush in his bedroom wall. This was one part of an elaborate internal heating system which had been built into his large suburban home some years back.

His analysis was in its terminal phase. To a considerable degree, alliance had eclipsed submission, and the desire to understand had replaced mere compliance. The heating vent was one of a series of memories which we had gathered together over the years. For both of us, the image could call to mind the very beginning of treatment, since it had been a key which unlocked the first of many mysteries. Perhaps it was still serviceable as a code for this new dream.

Martin's parents were divorced when he was five. By the age of six-and-a-half he had yet to speak of it. Both parents felt quivers of concern. Martin's father was in analysis himself. He had discussed this phenomenon in his own treatment, and had come to recognize that a consultation was in order. Martin lived with his mother; she too agreed that some evaluation ought to take place. When Martin's mother and I met, she was knitting quietly in the waiting room. She started slightly when I walked in. "I almost lost a stitch," she said. "If I lost it because of you, I'd kill you." She delivered these lines in a playful and affable manner. I was amused. The unconscious significance of the remark, however, did not escape my attention.

I had seen her former husband twice, and he had given his version of their marital difficulties, and the divorce. Now she offered hers. The two views were not really so divergent. Each thought perhaps the other had not put enough effort into the marriage. Who knew exactly why passion had passed for both of them? In the second half of the twentieth century in America, both were aware that divorce had become more commonplace than marriage. The dissolution of their relationship was viewed as quite an ordinary, natural event, although there had been frequent quarrels.

With this stress on the ordinary, Martin's steadfast disavowal of the whole business stood out even more glaringly. He neither raised questions about the divorce, nor addressed comments to the noisy bouts. Why the silence? Martin's mother offered her explanation.

She had so carefully concealed matters, she said, that Martin was simply unaware of the existence of difficulties. By agreement, quarrels had been confined to the bedroom, precisely to spare the child distress or irritation. She understood Martin's silence as evidence of the competence of her practice of deception.

The mother spent five hours with me before I first met the patient himself. During that time her concerns faded. She supplied me with a great deal of information about her son and her own past life. It too had been tainted by parental disunity. She loved her son and wanted to help him. Her cooperativeness was to be enhanced even further by the following experience which occurred only a short while later.

In the course of one of her regular visits, a few months into the treatment, Martin's mother described certain bedtime difficulties. She recalled when Martin was little, he would rock back and forth in his crib, and sometimes injure his head by thumping it against the railings. Concerned that he might do some real damage, she would listen for the first sign of rocking and then rush to comfort him. I had been advised of the great distance between the two bedrooms, and wondered how she could hear such subtle sounds.

When Martin was very little, she explained, a new internal heating system had been built into the home. There were ducts penetrating the walls. Somehow they had been constructed so she could hear even the faintest of sounds coming from Martin's room as they funneled into his vent and out of hers.

My next question was natural; it even had a naive quality. "But if you could hear sounds from his room, couldn't he hear them from yours?—the quarrels? the discussions about divorce?"

Martin's mother stared for a moment. She shook her head. No, he could hear nothing. Perhaps the sound traveled only in one direction, she suggested. She wondered if that was possible. When she returned home, she experimented and brought the results of her research back to our next meeting. She stationed herself in her son's room, and asked someone to speak in a normal tone while seated in her bedroom. She could easily hear the voice. The original explanation offered to account for Martin's silence was obviously now invalid. Martin must have heard many things, and must have known many things. His silence was a serious disavowal after all.

Now, many years later, during the terminal phase of treatment, that vent was back. It had been a subject of discussion earlier, and by now it had become a symbol of a group of past experiences, and a mode of relating. Once the secret of the vent was unlocked, Martin engaged the divorce and the pain of loss and the dizzying effects of his confusion during that period of his life. He had resolved to say nothing, simply to try to be very good. When he was first brought to analysis, I encountered a charming little man, who was oddly without fear of contact with strangers, although he was quite disinclined to speak. Martin drew a good many pictures. He made up games for us to play. He grasped I was a "figuring-out-man" and recognized his drawings and games might be useful to help us both "figure out" his worries.

In time, this very good boy became a tyrant in the office. Crockery was smashed and furniture splintered. Reams of paper were used to create crude drawings of armed soldiers in brutal combat. Any attempt to bring up his parents' divorce, or to suggest the soldiers depicted a more private war, was encountered by a shouting retort. It was as if Martin's shouts could obliterate the facts. He vaulted about the room, sometimes in a daring manner, and occasionally inflicted minor scrapes or bruises in the process.

Months were devoted to the slow acknowledgement of the quarrels, the existence of a life in the parental bedroom, and to his unspeakably violent responses to all of it. At first, loyalty to both parents moved him to silence. Later, this justification for silence was replaced by the fear that acknowledgement would mean the end of all hope of a reconciliation and of his father's return. Ultimately, the silence reigned over Martin's murderous rage which he feared might erupt with uncontrollable force.

Martin felt he had reason to fear his rage. He had been a murderer of sorts. Before he was two, his parents travelled frequently. He was left behind with a caretaker, but he missed his mother and father. He especially missed his mother. He was not particularly verbal, but Martin found alternate routes to express his grievance about her absence. Once he smashed an expensive vase to the floor. On another occasion, he strangled his mother's pet parakeet.

It was not until the second year of his analysis that Martin permitted himself to recall that strangling. In more recent times, he had come to share his mother's love for all pets. The recollection of opening the bird's cage and grabbing it in his mother's absence made Martin shiver with pangs of guilt and regret.

"It was an accident. How could I do that? I didn't mean to do that." We came to recognize the simple formula he had devised: it was possible to hurt mother by hurting something she treasured.

As Martin grew older, this formula reached beyond the vase and the bird. During his third and fourth years, for example, Martin subjected himself to frequent injuries. He would rock so fervently in his bed that he bruised his forehead. He would fall and break a bone or tear a knee. He became the boy with multiple scars, and was a constant source of concern to everyone whenever he moved about. He often came perilously close to severe injuries. Martin's formula for assaultiveness extended: he hurt his mother by hurting something she treasured, and Martin was very much one of her treasures.

What we came to call his "falling business" at first, and his "hurting business" some time later, dominated a considerable portion of the midde period of the treatment. A variety of issues wove in and out of this central constellation. Three major areas outlined themselves. (1) Martin was having difficulties in school and his father was frantic about this: hurt yourself in school and thus hurt your father. (2) He became an "athletic daredevil": flirt with danger and incite your mother. (3) He came to inflict minor injuries on himself in my office, or would erupt into symptomatic excesses, or warn of imminent psychological collapse: stay sick and miserable and thereby injure your analyst. To observe the potential for a full-blown negative therapeutic reaction in a latency-age boy somehow struck me as quite remarkable at the time.

The analytic work made it evident that by the age of four-and-a-half Martin's "hurting business" had coalesced into a highly specific fantasy. The fantasy may have functioned as an organizer for many of his subsequent experiences. When it surfaced within the therapeutic setting, it was an exciting confirmation for both of us. It returned with the following recollection.

Martin remembered that when he was not yet five, he had become involved in a biblical story. He owned a recording of the story and played the drama over and over for a fairly long period of time. No one thought much about it. To the people around him, it didn't even seem likely he understood the tale. It was the story of Samson.

For Martin, Samson was a natural ideal. He was a hero who sacrificed himself for victory and for vengeance. The deceitful villainess proved to be naturally cast as well. Listening with childhood ears to the record, Martin heard her name incorrectly: the betrayer was not "Delilah" but "De-Liar." His mother frequently used concealment as a solution to encounters. The shorn locks of Samson turned out to have a kernel of personal truth as well. Martin always loved to repetitively twirl his hair. When he was little, he would often do so while eating. Sometimes the food would become hopelessly enmeshed within his twisted curls. His mother threatened to cut off a grimy lock if he continued his messy habit, and once or twice she carried out her threat.

Unconsciously, Martin synthesized the story's elements and readily identified with the biblical hero. The myth stated his adaptive stance with astonishing precision. We came to call this his "Samson business."

The unconscious fantasy gripped oedipal themes as well. His quest for manhood through growth and achievement had been hampered by implicit castration threats. Achievement had found the route of a masochistic triumph. The absolute control which he exercised over the certainty of his pains nurtured the narcissistic side of his nature as well.

With treatment, a different path of oedipality emerged. Initially, it appeared succinctly in the transference. "I want your patients. I want your wife." Martin outlined a diabolical plan. He would slip into my office, kill me, and skin me. He would put on my skin and everyone would think he was me. He could trick everyone—well, perhaps a few adult patients might see through it. With ebullience, Martin fashioned his plan. It was a creative fantasy, and pulled together the learned qualities of deception while graphically expressing the process of identification. Happily, in this oedipal solution, the aggression was turned outwards. Martin mused: wouldn't it be fun to take over his father's business when he grew up?

The dream of the bubbles and the radiator vent called all these events back for the two of us. The vent had been a conduit of secret information. Feelings of hate had surfaced and undergone a progressive transformation along with the progress of his analysis. Now, however, bubbles were coming out of the radiator. What was the latent content of these bubbles?

"I noticed something in the bathroom yesterday," Martin reported. "I had to go to the toilet and as I was peeing, I noticed how I could make bubbles."

A new grouping of memories fell in place ushered in by a sequence of imagined space trips. Martin, the astronaut, whirled in my desk chair preparing for lift-off. I was his Earth contact. He told me his adventures as he crashed down on Mars. He played with that word—it was a planet of mothers. He made trips to "Venus-Penis" and wired his reports back to Earth. Much of the truth of his parental relationship was reflected in these adventures. However, Martin stood adamant on one point throughout his communiques: there had been no parental intimacy. He had been encouraged to accept this myth. Martin must have known better; I reminded him of the secret conduit of the vent. At first he protested verbally. Then he shattered something in my office to express his protest more effectively. A few more splinters appeared on the edge of my desk. To further punctuate his protest, Martin, the astronaut, blasted off to a distant planet and switched off the radio contact between us.

No matter what else he accepted in the course of his treatment, Martin tried to hold strongly to the view of his parental abstinence. He insisted on this position throughout the middle years of his analysis. What could have been going on in the bedroom anyway?

Martin was now preadolescent. The feelings in his penis were different. He was more available for social contacts. An older girl tried to seduce him. He became frightened when she lay on top of him. His excitement surrendered to his fear and his penis became flaccid. Later, safely alone, he played with his penis, imagined touching the girl, and experienced a new sensation. It was a climactic kind of a feeling and Martin repeated it enthusiastically when he could. Although there was no ejaculation as yet, he spoke to me about the expected sticky stuff he had been hearing about from friends. It must be different from pee. Pee was dirty. Was it different, Martin wondered? He could not know what this new something would be like; he could only imagine it was like pee. With this idea, both of us realized a link had been established with the "bubbles" emerging from the radiator vent.

I told Martin he must have had some idea that a penis had something to do with sex for quite a long time. He could remember excited feelings even when he was very little. He probably decided that pee came out of the penis during sex, but pee was dirty for him. That made it even harder to imagine grown-ups making love. He could only imagine his mother was being peed on, that his father was making "bubbles" in her.

The reconstruction gave him pause. It was an idea that did not evoke a dramatic, immediate response. Instead, Martin became reflective. It was sensible. Why shouldn't he have been confused about such matters when he was little? It was nice not to be so mixed up anymore. The passions of adolescence might be more manageable now. His experiences with peers broadened, and a few months after this bit of work, the treatment came to an end.

The actual ending was not entirely without incident.

By that point in the treatment, Martin's parents had accepted the principle that the specific date of termination would be determined within the analytic setting itself. As soon as Martin and I agreed on a time, he betrayed his feelings about it with renewed excitement, provocativeness, challenges, and teasing of a kind which had become less frequent. He brought the news home to his parents. They were neither shocked nor dismayed. His discussions with them proved supportive; he was more available to their support now.

Certain practical matters concerning his fall school schedule made it seem a June ending would be reasonable. In spite of my own strong feelings that termination should ordinarily not take place at the threshhold of the natural summer separation, we arranged to stop in June. As the time approached, Martin spoke openly of the lost hope of his parents reuniting; he confessed how important I had become to him. He asked about returning some day if the need arose. When he felt reassured his "figuring-out" man would more than likely be available, it seemed to further buffer the potential loss.

Future events were to make me feel both regretful and relieved about the final days. I was regretful I had accepted a June date without pressing for the opportunity to observe the influence of the natural summer break. I was relieved our alliance was firm enough to be retrieved years later when a new need arose.

PRINCIPLES AND PRACTICAL GUIDELINES OF TERMINATION

Martin's analysis will provide the illustrative context within which to engage the issues of termination of the analyses of children. The major questions engaged will be the principles of termination and the practical guidelines that can be applied. In the course of dissecting these issues, other questions will surface. What similarities and differences exist between child and adult terminations? In considering terminations, what are some of the distinguishing features between an analysis and an analytically-oriented therapy? And finally, in what way is a *termination* to be differentiated from an *interruption?*

PRINCIPLES

When things are to be brought to an end, the claims of three parties to the child analytic contract have to be evaluated. The contract is an altogether strange one to begin with. There are many unarticulated clauses. Each of the three parties have expectations which he is either unwilling to talk about, or is unaware of entirely.

The first partner. One senior partner, the child patient, is frequently an unwilling participant. His unarticulated interest may be to get out of the whole thing altogether.

Martin wasn't so unwilling, as a matter of fact. At six-and-a-half, he was a lonely boy. Neither parent seemed to have much time to spend with him despite their affectionate feelings for him. Martin was hungry for personal contact, and found the frequent visits an opportunity to achieve an abiding friendship. Perhaps he might discover a replacement father or someone as stimulating as his mother who could play with him on a more regular basis.

The second partner. The second party to the treatment contract is the parents. Parents are strange junior partners. They usually initiate the enterprise, keep it going over some rough spots, financially support the whole business, yet rarely know precisely what's going on.

Martin's parents cooperated. They each came for their appointed visits. Father missed from time to time, ostensibly because of his work. Mother came regularly, and slipped into some of her own personal concerns once she felt more trustful. Their common goal was a well child, or at least a healthier one. Both were prepared to accept a physician's judgment as to exactly what "healthier" might entail. Their immediate concern was Martin's inability to openly talk about the collapse of the family unit. Later, when each could specify more concrete goals, Martin's father longed for better school performance while his mother hoped that her child might become less reckless. Generally speaking, the parents expected the analysis would assure a smoother life. Symptoms didn't seem to worry either the child or his parents. There were no phobias or fears or obsessions anyone knew about, at least not initially. When suffering finally surfaced, Martin didn't talk about it very much to his parents. The suffering of a child, unless it is outrageously manifest, is rarely an important motive for parents to initiate or to sustain a child analysis.

Martin had his secret goal: satisfaction of person-hunger. His parents each had their goals as well, specific ones and more general ones. What were the goals of the third party to the contract, the other senior partner, the analyst?

The third partner. The analyst who limits his practice to the treatment of adults has a sharply demarcated paradigm of treatment and termination. On paper it makes pleasant academic reading, although it may not proceed in just that way as frequently as one might hope.

Ideally, in a classical adult psychoanalysis, a recommendation for treatment is made for the relief of suffering arising out of a neurotic condition. The patient and physician agree on practical arrangements and enter on a special contract. The contract requires the patient to dedicate himself to attempt to "free associate," recognizing that the issues thus engaged will lead to a resolution of the chronic unrecognized conflicts which have given rise to his suffering. The analyst assures the patient of confidentiality and applies himself to "free-floating attention" so that he may assist with the work of clarifying and interpreting. In the course of this contract an unusual new artificial condition erupts—the "transference neurosis." Through this condition, the constellation of certain unrecognized childhood conflicts (the latent progenitors of the neurosis) comes to settle around the person of the analyst and invades the treatment setting. Concomitantly, there is a relief in the "outside" world while the neurotic organization is symbolically replayed on the field of the therapeutic interchange.

The affective involvements during this period can be quite intense. Suffering may be renewed and even intensified in the flux of feelings which erupt. The treatment alliance is under siege, but after some time (years, generally) the cooperative relationship fostered during the joint enterprise prevails. The "transference neurosis," this therapeutically induced necessary new edition of an infantile disorder, is resolved. Unconflicted love and work become possible. Somewhere in the course of the struggle between the transference and the alliance, the terminal phase of the treatment process asserts itself. No clear line, no specific moment may be discernible, although the beginning resolution of the transference neurosis is the recognizable landmark. Together, the analyst and the patient agree on the date when the work of the treatment will be formally brought to a conclusion. The patient leaves having achieved a loss of symptoms, a resolution of the underlying conflicts which had given rise to the various discomforts, and, perhaps most important of all, a new acquisition —the capacity for insight which remains available for future use. It is this acquisition which makes it less likely that he will require treatment in the future. Although new problems may arise which could require additional analytic work, when an adult analysis ends it usually does so without the expectation of further renewed contacts. [Abrams 1977]

For many reasons, the child analyst rarely finds himself confronting such a sharply defined process. From the outset, the patient-physician contract is complicated by the presence of a significant third party, the parents. Furthermore, "free association" is not a possible vehicle for a young child. Similarly, the analyst cannot slip quietly into free-floating attention. He is obliged to participate in play, dodge things, interact, and exchange comments with his young patient. At the same time, he trys to keep part of his head hovering in the atmosphere of the unconscious.

With adults, the beginning resolution of the transference neurosis introduces the terminal phase. It is a fine landmark with which to appraise the possibility of ending. The development of this special artificial condition requires, among other things, an enforcement of the abstinence of past infantile desires, along with the mobilization of a treatment alliance. Such activities on the part of the analyst allow unconscious parental representations to be deployed into the therapeutic interaction.

Children, however, have trouble dealing with these therapeutic postures. They are prone to categorize adults along fairly predictable stereotypes. Adults tell you what to do, they know better what's good for you, they possess the truth and pass it on. Sometimes, analysts are tempted to assume such traditional roles. Transferences and therapeutic alliances do not readily evolve out of that kind of stereotypic interaction.

Traditional role expectations is one encumbrance to the transference when doing work with children; a second arises out of natural, biological sources. Development entails a continuing push forwards. The child is propelled from the wellsprings of his endowment towards nutrients in the current environs with which to satisfy his phase requirements. Transference, on the other hand, is a derivative of the backward drift of mental life. Although a degree of abstinence might usually be expected to promote such a drift, the natural, persistent, progressive push may often overcome any regressive leaning.

As a result of such encumbrances to the emergence of customary landmarks which seem so reliable with adults, other guidelines must be found to systematize termination criteria with children. Such guidelines prove to be derivative of the very determinants which evoke the transference neurosis. The determinants are part of a complex psychological profile which may be clinically embraced by addressing four key questions.

Are the dynamic issues engaged? Have positive and negative oedipal matters been confronted and linked with specific references to the past? Are the preoedipal anlagen delineated?

With Martin, for example, the maternal side of his personality found expression with his own interests in pets—his "babies." From time to time, he brought his dog to his appointment and briefly established a family setting involving the three of us. Similarly, his search for manhood was reflected graphically in his Samson fantasy, and then more appropriately in his design to do me in and take my place. Preoedipal determinants manifested themselves as well. Rage against his mother's early absences and the reactive "hurting business" first made their appearance within the transference setting. In those early days, Martin could be quite responsive to the announcement of a session I would miss in the future.

Have specific drive-derivatives become manifest? The oedipus complex is not a cold drama. There is a crushing moan which any good stage oedipus must express at the instant of discovery. This epochal constellation contains passionate love, and it contains venomous destructiveness. Such feelings need to be represented in the treatment situation at one point or another. If symptoms erupt as a concomitant, that ought to surprise no one. In fact, in the course of engagement of this phase, Martin developed a transient eye tic, quite literally as a response to his sexual curiosity.

What is the direction of restructuring? After such genetic, dynamic, and energic considerations, the analyst must assess structure. Have more appropriate defenses evolved? Has emotional functioning showed signs of maturity? For example, are signal affects available or do massive explosive responses still predominate? There are lists of functions of the personality with which child analysts must familiarize themselves and more or less systematically tag as treatment goes on.

Has the resolution of past conflicts found a more fortunate pathway? It was a good sign when Martin surrendered his Samson model for something more on the order of a David.

The development and resolution of the transference neurosis is not a reliable, consistent sign in gauging the pace and determining the arrival of the terminal phase in the analysis of children. Consequently, the child analyst is forced to remind himself of the diverse components which go into fashioning that total process. It is his responsibility to see to it that each of these perspectives have found appropriate concrete representation in the course of the therapeutic experience.

If treatment ends before these criteria can be satisfied, the analysis should to be regarded as *interrupted* rather than *terminated.* Whenever any treatment is geared toward selective goals or when the analyst elects to channel the treatment along something less than what is implicit in all these points of view, then, strictly speaking, it is not an analysis but rather an analytically-oriented therapy. These comments are not meant to undermine either the wisdom of strategic interruptions or the role of many different therapies in childhood disorders. Under certain circumstances, a prudent abrupt ending proves to be a wise course of action, and in many conditions, psychotherapy is by far the preferred treatment modality.

And yet, even when these central criteria are satisfied, the child analyst's task is still not ended. More must be done, and at this point the adult paradigm loses its value as a model.

Something special is happening in a child which needs the closest of ongoing attention: the natural thrust toward growth and development. Therefore, one cannot end analytic treatment without having a certain degree of conviction that the progressive push is present and continuingly imposing its influence. One way the analyst may test this process is to carry the treatment into the beginning of the next phase of development before electing to bring it to an end. With Martin, therefore, it was not enough to redirect a damaged Oedipus and shore up latency. When it became evident that preadolescence was moving along satisfactorily on its own, the treatment could really close.

THE PRACTICALITIES OF TERMINATION

Practically speaking, the decision to terminate requires the agreement of all the parties to the contract. Martin was a little reluctant to leave. He could no longer remember exactly what he had initially wanted from treatment. I remembered. I knew his desire had not really been satisfied. He had neither found a new father, nor made a lifelong friend. However, he had negotiated a new kind of interaction with an adult, and through it, Martin had freed himself of a good many of his troubles. Fortunately, he had devised several ways of seizing nutrients for growth from his true father, and he was making real friends as well, more appropriate ones. What's more, he was feeling pretty good. Stopping was acceptable to him.

His parents were also agreeable. Whatever their hidden motives for bringing Martin, it was apparent to both that Martin was better off and seemed to be growing well. That was gratifying. His father still hoped for better school performance for his son. For her part, Martin's mother enjoyed the directions in which her son was moving. His affection, his sense of humor, and his amiableness pleased her. She was also gratified there was no awful breech between the two of them.

What of the analyst's practical requirements? Were they satisfied? Martin came to see me as an ally; I was his "figuring-out" partner. He had worked on a variety of important experiences and effectively used the medium of the relationship while doing so. Through it all, the alliance prevailed. He had become psychologically-minded and had acquired a certain degree of understanding akin to the adult counterpart of the process of insight. He became accustomed to trying to find out things by himself instead of simply complying with others. At the same time, Martin recognized things might go wrong in the future. He could come back again and talk with me, or maybe he could find someone else if I didn't happen to be available. His parents supported all of this. Progressive thrust prevailed. The contract seemed satisfied and the treatment could be ended.

The setting of the final date merits special attention. In general, once termination is expected within a reasonable period of time, the matter needs to be taken up explicitly with the different parties. Usually the analyst initiates such a discussion, but sometimes one of the other partners might do so during the time the analyst has been considering the possibility. It is always best if the first formal discussion occurs between doctor and patient. This raises the risk of the child running home to spring the news on his unprepared parents, and evoking a response from them in an endeavor to shield himself from his own reaction. Despite this possibility, the problems may be greater the other way around. Hence, as a rule, analyst and child first, analyst and parents thereafter. The child and parents may discuss it with one another whenever they choose to do so. If the child and the analyst have agreed on the wisdom of bringing the treatment to an end, generally the "junior partners" are able to cooperate in what is to come. On the other hand, no matter how great the accord between parents and analyst, a reluctant child who needs to extend the end of treatment retains absolute veto power. It is astonishing what disruptions, symptoms, and disagreeableness can emerge as expressions of reluctance.

A specific date ought to be delineated. Even a very young child can set down a written notation on the desk calendar. Such active participation, even if it involves simply underlining the expected day, is an important continuation of the child's recognition of himself as a cooperating partner, and not merely a helpless infant in the world of dominating adults. And if, while poised at the desk, the child elects a date somewhat earlier or later than what the analyst or parents had found preferable, every attempt should be made to honor the request, unless it is blatent acting out or an outrageous inconvenience. The inconvenience needs to be really outrageous to ignore the child's suggestion. Far too often, beginnings and endings are determined by quite arbitrary matters which leave little room for considering the interests of the children.

The school calendar is still another pernicious influence. Far too often, child treatment schedules get interwoven with school schedules. Consequently, there is an inclination to start analyses in September and end them in June. Much can be said about the value of helping a child separate analyses from his formal education. The analyst can use certain natural factors to facilitate such a differentiation. School holidays are noticeably different from treatment holidays; one may be sick enough to be absent from class, yet not so sick to miss the session. Also, the child's relationship to his teacher is palpably different from the one which evolves with his analyst. Therefore, in spite of the apparent convenience of a June termination, the need to sustain the established distinctions is yet another factor—albeit a minor one—that dictates against ending at the threshhold of a lengthy summer break.

The most important reasons for avoiding a June termination, however, involves substantive therapeutic issues. The "good-bye" feelings of ending may get buried in the excitement of vacation plans or in the anticipation of camp. The analytic engagement of the final loss may be blurred as a result. Issues, especially separation issues, crystallize at the point of parting. Personal convenience can never be a justifiable motive when matters of analytic process are at stake. Martin's June ending was an exception to my usual practice; later events only confirmed the wisdom of my customary approach.

The date ought to be set some months in advance. It should not be set so firmly that it excludes the possibility of an additional period of work if conditions warrant it, yet it should be sufficiently clear so it is recognized as definitely forthcoming. Between establishing the date and its actual occurrence, a symptomatic outcropping of the kind which Martin showed can generally be expected. Just as with adults, such symptoms often represent a form of protest over parting and afford an opportunity for further integrative work. Interpretation may precipitate fresh or renewed expressions of rage, responses to feelings of being deserted. The child may actively play the deserter rather than accept the role of the helpless "victim" of abandonment. Sadness and anxieties at the thought of being discarded frequently appear. Having parents at home to lean on, however, the child is less likely to react to the separation with the intensity of feeling so frequently seen with adults.

Under optimal conditions, this fantasy of desertion can be traced to specific antecedent experiences. The analysis of such transference reactions can fortify the therapeutic result. However, the analyst must also recognize that the child is losing a "real" as well as a transference object; some of the termination responses pertain to this "real" loss as well.

Parents may also react. They may become freshly indecisive. The imminent end may induce in them a more determined attempt to solicit advice or guidance or specific recommendations, however much they might have accepted the assigned junior partner role until this point. It is best if the earlier relationships can be sustained. However, the child analyst needs to keep the relationship to the parents positive enough to assure subsequent cooperation if there should be a need to return. To do so may require his offering some support or advice about this or that.

Sometimes the analyst feels tempted to offer advice to parents hoping to stabilize the child's environment and thereby forestall future relapses. This violation of his earlier commitment to interpretation and the mobilization of the analytic process as the chief instruments of the cure may appear justified on the grounds that the analysis is finished anyhow, so advice can no longer interfere with the basic contract. Two considerations ought to still that temptation. In the first place, it is unlikely parents who have chronically adhered to less than optimal practices would actually be able to implement any recommendations for change in response to an eleventh hour appeal. Secondly, a violation at the eleventh hour may cast a shadow on the possibility of the child's return for additional analytic work if the need does arise subsequently. While analysts have reported instances in which such an action has appeared justified, it would seem the pressures of silent counter-transference motives cannot always easily be excluded. In this, as in so many other circumstances, the analyst's self-awareness may prove to be the decisive factor. In any case, it is always most gratifying to discover there is no temptation to advise and no such action seems necessary; the child's progress itself is sustaining the termination.

Finally the child's parents ought to leave with the realization that even a completely successful analysis can never be an absolute immunity against every future contingency. Fate and biology are unpredictable. Although a child has been successfully ushered into a new phase and may have reasonably resolved the conflicts of the past, circumstance and endowment can still evoke new disturbances or even impart a shattering blow upon what appeared to be a thoroughly healed fracture point.

SUMMARY

This is an outline of the principles of termination and the practical aspects of ending analytic work with children.

I. Principles

A. The responsibility for establishing the criteria for termination falls almost entirely upon the analyst. Neither the child nor his parents can possibly understand the processes which are involved. If the decision to end is being pushed either by the child or the parents, it is more likely the analysis is being interrupted than terminated.

B. The development and resolution of the *transference neurosis* is not a reliable indicator with children because it rarely, if ever, evolves as it does with adults. However, the components of that neurosis are accessible in the analytic work with children. The dynamic past should be resurrected and played out in the treatment setting to a degree which assures conviction while certain key constellations are engaged. Energic matters ought to be activated. Structural and adaptive aspects inevitably become manifest.

C. Data appears which permits the analyst to demonstrate that the developmental process itself is freed from encumbrances and may be expected to move along.

II. Practicalities

A. All members of the partnership are more or less content. This rarely means the initial goals of the child and his parents are satisfied, but it always means the goals which the analyst originally conceptualized have been reached. Most often, they are goals which he may not have been able to articulate to his partners when they first visited.

B. A sense of alliance among the parties persists.

C. The date is set definitively between analyst and patient and the first negotiations concerning the end of treatment occurs between the two of them.

D. June is generally not the best month to stop. Important issues which are part of termination may too easily become buried in the excitement of vacation.

E. Everyone recognizes future circumstances may produce new troubles and another period of work may become necessary.

F. Finally, the pang of loss may not only be experienced by the child: parents and analyst may also detect some note of sadness in themselves.

REFERENCES

Abrams, S. (1977). Child psychoanalysis: termination. In *International Encyclopedia of Psychiatry, Psychology, Psychoanalysis, and Neurology,* ed. B.B. Wolman, vol. 3, pp. 132–136. New York: Aesculapius.

Firestein, S. K. (1974). Termination of psychoanalysis of adults: a review of the literature. *Journal of the American Psychoanalytic Association* 22:873–894.

Firestein, S.K. (1969). Panel report: problems of termination in the analysis of adults. *Journal of the American Psychoanalytic Association* 17:222–237.

Freud, A. (1965). *Normality and Pathology in Childhood: Assessments of Development.* New York: International Universities Press.

————(1968). Indications and contraindications for child analysis. *Psychoanalytic Study of the Child* 23:37–46.

Harley, M. (1961). Panel report: resistance in child analysis. *Journal of the American Psychoanalytic Association* 9:548–561.

Harley, M. (1971). The current status of transference neurosis in children. *Journal of the American Psychoanalytic Association* 19:26–40.

Hurn, H. T. (1970). Adolescent transference: a problem of the terminal phase of analysis. *Journal of the American Psychoanalytic Association* 18:342–357.

Kohrman, R., (1969). Panel report: problems of termination in childhood analysis. *Journal of the American Psychoanalytic Association* 17:191–205.

Robbins, W. (1975). Panel report: termination: problems and techniques. *Journal of the American Psychoanalytic Association* 23:166–176.

Van Dam, H., (1966). Panel report: problems of transference in child analysis. *Journal of the American Psychoanalytic Association* 14:528–537

Van Dam, H., Heinicke, C.M., and Shane, M. (1975). On termination in child analysis,. *Psychoanalytic Study of the Child* 30:443–474.

PART SIX

ADJUNCTS TO CHILD ANALYSIS

Chapter 17

SIMULTANEOUS ANALYSIS OF PARENT AND CHILD

Ilse Hellman, Ph.D.

In certain cases, treatment of the child does not proceed satisfactorily without simultaneous treatment of one or both parents.[1] This fact has been recognized by child analysts for many years and has led to the development of various techniques to deal with the problem. In child guidance practice, regular contact with one or both parents is maintained by a staff member, while the child's treatment is carried out by the psychiatrist or therapist in charge. The nature of the work done with parents ranges from discussing practical problems arising from the child's treatment, to psychotherapeutic intervention which aims at dealing with the parents' own disturbance. A great deal of literature on the various approaches within child guidance work has accumulated. However, a review of this literature is beyond the scope of the present discussion, which is confined to simultaneous psychoanalytic treatment of parent and child. The total number of simultaneous analysis cases that have been studied is small. This is not because of a lack of interest or awareness of the need for simultaneous analyses, but is essentially due to problems of availability of psychoanalysis in clinic settings, financial reasons, and the difficulties involved in publishing material referring to patients in private practice. Assessment of work carried out by simultaneous analysis is therefore confined to the small number of cases published, and to some unpublished cases which form part of the "Study on Simultaneous Analysis" carried out at the Hampstead Child Therapy Clinic, London.

THERAPEUTIC AIMS

One aim of simultaneous analysis has been to provide psychoanalytic treatment for parents and children who have been unresponsive to more superficial forms of treatment. In addition, simultaneous analysis attempts to provide the chance of successful treatment for children whose progress in analysis had been interfered with by the intensity and nature of his parent's pathology. In Anna Freud's words (1960): "Where the neurotic symptom, the conflict or the regression of a child is anchored not only in the young patient's own personality but held in place further by powerful emotional forces in the parent to whom the child is tied, the therapeutic action of analysis may well be slowed up or, in extreme cases, made impossible" (p. 379). If simultaneous treatment of the parent takes place: "The interpretations to the child [may] become effective, or . . . regressive libidinal positions given up in direct relation to the parent's relinquishing either a fixed pathological position of her own, or in other cases, relinquishing a pathological hold on the child" (p. 379).

Simultaneous analysis can also provide treatment for children whose parents feel disturbed by one or more aspects of treatment, or by changes in the child resulting from it.

Rachel's mother found it intolerable to feel her little girl's growing attachment to her analyst. She felt intense jealousy and interfered with the child's treatment by cancelling sessions, coming late, and ridiculing the analyst.

Rachel's mother reacted to changes in her child. When Rachel began to become active and aggressive as a result of treatment, instead of remaining passive and inhibited, her mother reacted with anger. She attempted to make her daughter submissive again, even though she realized Rachel was improving at her school work and in her relationships with other children.

In addition, parents are often fearful their children will divulge family secrets to the analyst. A full description of this situation and its destructive effect on the child's treatment was given by Dorothy Burlingham (1935) and has been confirmed in cases reported by other analysts. Gradual changes in the parent's feelings, fantasies, and conflicts concerning their child and their growing insight generally leads to an awareness of the nature of their interference with the child's ongoing development. Also, parents frequently become aware of the aspects of treatment which arouse their anxiety, jealousy, or other conflicting feelings. Such feelings frequently compel them to interfere with or even terminate their child's treatment.

RESEARCH AIMS

Clarification of developmental problems. The use of simultaneous analysis aims at clarifying a wide variety of developmental problems. The coordination of available material from concurrent analyses provides access to the unconscious meaning and motivation of parent-child interactions. This is needed for a fuller understanding of material from direct observation of manifest behavior between parent and child. Simultaneous analysis attempts to answer questions about the pathogenic effect of a parent's pathology on the child from birth, and throughout subsequent phases of development. Evidence is sought for the correctness or incorrectness of certain assumptions and is looked for in the material of both patients.

Understanding the interaction between parents and their children is of the highest importance during the period when the foundations of the personality are laid and the bases for mental illness are established. It continues to remain important as the child grows. As a child moves forward on the developmental scale, each step demands giving up former positions and gains, not only from the child, but from the parent too. It is only in the most healthy and normal cases that both parent and child wholly welcome progressive moves, and enjoy the child's increasing maturity and gradually increasing independence. More often, one or the other partner lags behind. The child is unable to free himself from fixations, or the parent clings to attitudes of protectiveness and mothering which are no longer justified.

In the worst cases, mother and child join forces in a regressive move. Such interlocking becomes particularly fateful at the onset of puberty. The simultaneous analyses of mothers and their adolescent children allow us to study the various ways in which individual adolescents strive to free themselves from infantile ties to their parents. While we receive no more than a dim impression of the parent's responses in cases where the adolescent alone is in treatment, simultaneous analysis enables us to trace each party's contribution to the success or failure of this developmental task.

Links between the parent's and child's pathologies. Simultaneous analysis aims at obtaining a clearer understanding of the relation between the parent's disturbance and the child's abnormal development. This is done by comparing details of their libidinal and aggressive feelings, fantasies, anxieties, and the nature of the defense mechanisms used by both parent and child. In this way, interferences with the child's progress are clarified.

Means of communication between parent and child. The pathways of unconscious communication through which various elements of the parent's pathology reach the child and affect it at various developmental stages were traced. Differentiation between preverbal, nonverbal, and verbal communication, and between fantasy expressed in action, or contained in the parent's mind, and the child's responses to the various ways communication reached him was established with considerable clarity in some areas, but remained diffuse in others.

Dorothy Burlingham (1955) clearly showed that in cases where a mother's fantasies lead to action, and her child was used to satisfy her own libidinal or aggressive needs, analysis was not able to free the child from the effect of his mother's interference. Had the mother's fantasies remained within her thoughts and feelings or had they been expressed verbally the outcome would have been different. In the case of Bobby, age three, analysis was able to free him from the effect of his mother's verbal communications. Although his fantasies had originated in his mother's unconscious, they had become Bobby's. They had undergone his elaborations, and had led to defenses. Therefore they could be dealt with analytically.

Clarification of concepts. Simultaneous analysis also aims at clarifying certain concepts which have been widely accepted and made use of in the past forty years. We are particularly interested in clarifying the tendency to make mothers responsible for a wide variety of childhood disturbances. This tendency has led to many pronouncements and to the use of global terms which are in need of differentiation. The great variety and subtlety of the ways in which various aspects of the mother's personality affect her child at different stages of development seemed in danger of oversimplification. Through simultaneous analysis, this danger has been counteracted as the complicated network of interaction can be traced. One of the concepts which tends to obscure deeper understanding is the much-used term *the rejecting mother.* The multiplicity of factors included in this term was demonstrated by Anna Freud (1955). All subsequent simultaneous analyses of mothers and children have given evidence of the complicated interplay of factors which become blurred when this concept is used. The term *overprotective mother,* though indicating one aspect visible to the observer, equally obscures the network of mutual responses which needs to be understood through analytic insight.

METHODS USED IN STUDIES OF SIMULTANEOUS ANALYSES

A variety of methods were used by different analysts in their research work.

The same analyst treating both mother and child. In her study of children suffering from ulcerative colitis, Melitta Sperling (1946) treated both mother and child herself in separate sessions. She felt it was preferable that the child did not know his mother was in treatment. This practice seems unwise, as it may interfere with the analyst's objective and neutral attitude toward both patients. Keeping secrets may also destroy the child's faith in his analyst's integrity. The child may suspect the therapist is treating his mother on the sly. Joyce McDougall (Lebovici and McDougall 1969) also treated both mother and son. However, the mother became her patient only after the boy had terminated his analysis, and had gone to boarding school in another country.

Different analysts treating mother and child. In the research project on simultaneous analysis carried out at the Hampstead Child-Therapy Clinic, London, all analyses of parents and children were carried out by two different analysts to reduce interference with normal analytic work to a minimum.

To study the material of both patients, a third analyst acted as coordinator. Analysts reported their material weekly to this coordinator. This method was introduced into the Hampstead Study by Dorothy Burlingham (1955) and was followed by the coordinators of all subsequent cases with one exception. Kata Levy (1960) analyzed a mother and also acted as coordinator in a case involving an adolescent girl.

In most cases, the analysts of parent and child did not communicate with each other, and the coordinator did not disclose material from the other patient to the reporting analyst. It was felt knowledge of the child's or parent's analysis might interfere with the analytic work. Acting as coordinator in two studies, Ilse Hellman (Hellman, Shepheard, and Friedmann 1960, Hellman, de Monchaux, and Ludowyk-Gyomroi 1961) used different methods for each. One study was carried out on the same lines as those generally adopted for the Hampstead Clinic Research. The patients' material was not communicated to the respective analysts. In the second study, the coordinator informed both analysts of the material or they were present while reports were given to the coordinator. Each analyst was free to discuss details of the material of both patients as it emerged. The purpose of this comparison of methods was an attempt to gain some insight into the helpful and detrimental aspects of knowledge of the parent's or child's material on each analyst's handling of his case.

At the conclusion of this study, both analysts felt their technique had not been different in spite of knowing the other patient's material. Interpretations were based only on their own patient's material and its transference implications. However, it became clear that the understanding of certain aspects of the child's material and increased certainty concerning differentiation between the child's fantasies and factual information were reached through knowledge of the mother's material. This referred especially to facts concerning the mother's sexual stimulation of her child. The child alluded to it in play and in symbolic form, but the fact that this was an ongoing experience had never been stated by the child.

In other cases as well, sexual experiences were left out by the child or referred to only in veiled form. In these cases, analysts were not informed of the parent's material, and the children did not refer to parental seductions as real experiences. This did not allow clear differentiation between reality and fantasy.

MAIN FINDINGS CONCERNING THE PATHOGENIC EFFECT OF THE PARENT ON THE CHILD

Detailed study of the psychoanalytic material of parents and children in concurrent analyses has clearly shown that simple conclusions about the effect of parental psychopathology on children are misleading. That a multiplicity of factors are involved has been impressively shown. Guidelines leading to a clarification of understanding these pathogenic effect have emerged from all cases, and have thrown light on the nature and degree of interference different elements of the parent's personality have on the child.

Interference with child's development. Approached from the developmental point of view, we can assess favorable and unfavorable conditions to which the child is exposed at each stage. A mother's symptom may contain features which provide her child with age-adequate experiences on one level, yet hinder normal progress on the next.

An example of this is found in mothers who experience intense anxiety when their child is not close to them physically. They either unconsciously feel the child as part of themselves, or need close contact to counteract hostility and guilt. These mothers' urge to hold and handle their child provides the young baby with the age-adequate experience of closeness to her. However, in the course of the first year, and increasingly from then on, this same baby experiences his mother's need for closeness more and more as an obstacle to the new developmental steps he is ready to take. The baby's need to move further from her, to explore his surroundings through increasing motor control, and to experience new objects, activities, and people can meet with his mother's continued attempts to extend the previous phase, when the child's need for closeness gave her the satisfaction she needed to keep her anxiety at a bearable level.

Mrs. A. frequently spoke of the "terrible experience" it was for her when her son became physically independent, and began to sit up and walk. She was compelled to push him back into the lying position and to prevent him from walking. His spontaneous change of position made her feel helpless and angry. His attempts to walk brought the feeling he was "walking away" from her, and rejecting her. Eric therefore had difficulty progressing past the practicing subphase of separation-individuation (Mahler, Pine, and Bergman 1975).

In these situations, conflicts are produced in the child between his active wishes, which may lead him to aggressive attempts to free himself from his mother's interference, and passive submission to her demands and prohibitions. Quick alternation of intense gratification and frustration experienced through the mother lays the foundation for a sado-masochistic relationship with her, with alternation of love, hate, and guilt as the pattern of their mutual interaction. Separation-individuation cannot take place normally. Such relationships are well known from direct observation of mothers and babies. However, the unconscious reasons different mothers need to use their children to deal with their own anxiety can only become known through their analysis. The child's reactions and his fears and fantasies in response to the use his mother made of him can only be gained from subsequent analysis through reconstruction and through his play and verbal communications, once he has reached the age when they become analyzable.

The situation described above was found in four cases studied at the Hampstead Child Therapy Clinic. In each case, the mother's ambivalence was the main reason for her need to keep the child close and well protected. These mothers were all guilty about a previous abortion, and wished to abort the child they subsequently were constantly concerned with.

In contrast to mothers compelled to keep their babies close to them, other cases were studied where mothers were unable to tolerate their babies' physical closeness, and had deprived them of this experience. Both types of disturbance belong to a category of mothers referred to by Anna Freud (1960). She points out that their illness interfered with their capacity for *effective mothering*. Without age-adequate need satisfaction, children of such mothers develop a wide range of disturbances.

The following material from the analysis of Mrs. Z. (Hellman, Schnurmann, and Todes 1970) can serve as illustration.

Mrs. Z. could not look at or hold her baby with pleasure. Feeling
Rachel suck her nipples was an ordeal. All Mrs. Z.'s attempts to feed
her baby were unsuccessful. She felt the baby was "sucking her dry,"
but simultaneously had fantasies she was starving Rachel. Therefore
Mrs. Z. was compelled to overfeed her daughter, causing her to be sick
frequently. Mrs. Z.'s mother had been unable to feed her, and this
played an important part in this mother's fantasies about her own
emptiness. Deprived of adequate mothering and feeding in this early
phase, the baby was exposed to painful experiences resulting from her
mother's guilt. The fear of starving her child led this mother to overfeed
her and this led to the child's digestive troubles. The foundation was
laid for Rachel's oral fixation. It played a central part in the disturbance
for which she was referred for analysis at the age of four. Rachel's
problems included excessive eating alternating with sickness, obesity,
and overdependence on her mother, to whom she was ambivalently
attached.

Obesity: a symptom in mother and child. Both mother and daughter
were addicted to food, and both were obese. It became clear from the
mother's material she was repeating with her daughter what she felt she
had been made to experience by her own mother. She thought of her
mother as a "food giver, not a love giver." Also, she felt her mother
was unable to love a female child. In her analysis, Rachel's mother
discovered with great guilt she too was a "food giver, not a love giver"
and that she could not love Rachel, because she was a girl. She was
compelled to make Rachel experience what she had. Unable to love her
daughter, she used food as a substitute. In Rachel's analysis, it became
possible to clarify the link between her eating compulsion and her use
of food as a substitute for mother's love. This was one important aspect
of her symptom of overeating.

In the mother's fantasies, food not only represented a substitute for
love. It also was a hostile weapon which she could use to harm the child,
making her sick, fat, and ugly. It had the twofold function of punishing
the child and ultimately punishing herself.

In Rachel's material, a clear division was seen between good, comforting food, standing for the love substitute, and bad, sick-making and

fattening food, representing the mother's hate. Rachel had to submit to eating "bad food" to retain her mother's approval, and to punish herself for hating her. A similar incapacity to handle and feed infants was found in other mothers in the Hampstead study. Eric's mother had unsuccessfully tried to abort him. When he was born, she felt she could not touch and hold him. However, she could not allow anyone else to look after him for any length of time because she felt guilty and jealous, particularly when her husband tried to comfort Eric.

Mother's fear of poisoning the child—child's fear of being poisoned. Mrs. A.'s guilt about her attempted abortion, and her continued death wishes were expressed in constant fears of poisoning her child with bad food. This persisted throughout his childhood, and played a central part in his life when he was referred for treatment at age eleven. Eric responded to his mother's fear of poisoning him by experiencing intense fears of being poisoned by her and by feeling sick. He gradually developed revenge fantasies, and would punish her by exaggerated sickness, and becoming unable to attend school. He forced his mother to stay home with him, and to buy luxury food which she could not afford.

In all the cases in which mothers experienced feelings of hostility and guilt in relation to their babies from birth, interference with feeding had led to symptom formation centering on food, and to a relationship in which ambivalence and distrust led to a prolonged dependence on the mother.

Abnormal concern with their children's digestion and defecation was found in all mothers whose anxieties about feeding were essentially based on their ambivalence. They constantly needed to ascertain that their death wishes did not come true by either starving the child or giving him bad food. Their attitudes toward cleanliness varied according to their own developments in the anal phase. In two cases, behavior based on unusually great undefended satisfaction in their children's defecation and urination was found.

Claudia's mother had been a bedwetter throughout her childhood and well into adolescence. She had been unable to train Claudia and showed no concern about her daughter's continued wetting. She derived pleasure from having the child in bed with her even though she wet. Her behavior made it plain to Claudia that her mother experienced sympathy with her when others in the household insisted on training her. Claudia's bed-wetting, which persisted into late adolescence, was partly a response to her mother's wish that Claudia would be just as she was as a child—stupid and infantile. Claudia's analysis showed her compliance with her mother's fantasy formed only part of the reason for her symptom. Claudia's own sexual anxieties and an early seduction by an uncle were responsible for Claudia's fantasy that she had nothing inside her to hold in the flow of urine. This long-lasting symptom led to intense experiences of shame and added to her self-devaluation, which also resulted from her pseudo-stupidity.

Bobby's mother also achieved satisfaction through participating in the process of her child's elimination. Toilet training had led to a complicated ritual between him and his mother. This was described in detail by Dorothy Burlingham (Burlingam, Goldberger, and Lussier 1955). Bobby's fears of emptiness if he let his feces go and fears of fullness if he held them in alternated. His mother had had similar fears in her own childhood, and had insisted on keeping her mother's attention during defecation. The analysis clearly showed Bobby's own fantasies were responsible for the conflict he experienced at the moment of defecation. However, his mother's attitude, combined with her own fantasies about her body content, united them in the daily ritual.

Cases in which the mother's reaction formation led to intense disgust and to an insistence on early cleanliness were studied by Melitta Sperling (1946). She analyzed mothers and children suffering from ulcerative colitis and found that one important factor in this illness was that it gave the mothers "legitimate" gratification of their repressed anal-erotic and anal-sadistic needs. The children responded with early intense reaction formation, and showed disgust at an unusually early age. However, their symptom gave both mother and child gratification through its messiness. Both joined in conscious disgust and unconscious gratification.

Premature sexual stimulation. Children used by their mothers from babyhood onwards as partners in sexual games display the effects of serious interference with all important aspects of normal development. Mrs. A. used Eric to relive the sexual experiences she had with her younger brother throughout her childhood. She had played the male role in these games, and stimulated her brother and penetrated his mouth with her tongue. She began this practice with Eric when he was a baby and discontinued it when he was twelve years old, after they had both been in analysis for over a year. Eric's symptom of vomiting was found to be related to these experiences, as well as to his fantasy of being poisoned, which he shared with his mother. The most damaging elements of his mother's stimulation arose from his states of excitation throughout the pregenital and phallic stages. Eric was forced into passivity during this stimulation. His latency development was hindered as a consequence. The pathological aspects of his preoedipal and oedipal relationship with his mother, who was felt to be an overwhelming, threatening figure, made his entry into puberty very difficult. He experienced the main developmental problems of adolescence in a highly pathological way.

Another mother initiated premature sexual stimulation in her baby's first year and continued until she had been in analysis for a considerable time. Mrs. Z. was compulsively concerned with her baby's masturbation. According to her, her daughter had masturbated intensely from the age of nine months. It was clear Mrs. Z. initiated her baby's first genital explorations, while she had watched intently and with mounting excitement. Mrs. Z. described reaching an orgasm-like experience and expected to see her child experience an orgasm too. Analysis clarified the link between the mother's own compulsive masturbation in childhood and the reenactment with Rachel. Mrs. Z. had denied being a girl, had been envious of her brother, and had played sexual games with him. Her disappointment that Rachel was a girl formed part of the hostility she experienced against her daughter. In the sexual play, Rachel partly represented Mrs. Z.'s brother. This denied Rachel was a girl. The mother played the male role in the fantasy. Rachel's response to her mother's persistent stimulation was enacted in her treatment sessions, and was brought into the transference through exhibitionistic masturbation and excitation.

In these cases, as well as in the study of Bobby and his mother by Dorothy Burlingham (Burlingham, Goldberger, and Lussier 1955), and Claudia and her mother by Ilse Hellman (Hellman, de Monchaux, and Ludowyk-Gyomroi 1961), the mothers' use of their children for sexual excitation and satisfaction led to long-lasting disturbances. In those cases where the child's treatment extended into puberty and adolescence, it became especially clear how the premature stimulation by the mother and the continued use of the children for sexual satisfaction had affected all important areas of their personalities.

The main conflicts of adolescence (A. Freud 1958) were intensified and the development toward a separate identity was difficult to attain even with long analyses. Libidinal and aggressive impulses were excessively heightened in response to the mother's changing behavior and the affective states accompanying it. The degree of anxiety arising from these experiences made the use of pathological defenses necessary. Sublimations were found to be severely disrupted through the libidinization and aggressivization of a variety of activities. Frustration tolerance was very poor and superego development was distorted as a result of the child's viewing the mother as a seductive, guilty partner who was also extremely threatening. Severe interference with normal oedipal development was found in all the cases studied. This was especially marked where the mothers used their children for sexual satisfaction from an early age. The children's approach to their fathers and the fathers' relationship to their children were disturbed by the mother's denigration of the father and her jealousy whenever the child showed signs of enjoying the father's company.

Eric's mother created a distorted picture of his father. She constantly ridiculed her husband's lack of education and emphasized he had lost a thumb and was therefore clumsy. This denigration of the father and her attempts to prevent a good relationship between him and the boy extended throughout Eric's childhood. Only after long analysis was he able to feel free enough to admit his love and admiration for his father. He was then able to see his father as the man he really was, and became able to identify and enjoy common interests with him.

Parents who are as disturbed as those included in the study of simultaneous analyses do not have marital relationships which allow their children to develop under conditions favorable for establishing a normal oedipal phase.

Marjorie Sprince (1962) described the case of Debby, whose father's close relationship to her was distorted by his pathology. His disturbance made him deeply concerned about her digestion. Both parents were closely involved with each other's and Debby's hypochondriacal fantasies about food and digestive illness. Forward moves in Debby's development were shortlived, and regression to oral and anal fixation points occurred again and again as these fixations were anchored in both the maternal and paternal relationship.

Divorce and illegitimacy were the cause of abnormal oedipal development in the other cases. Claudia's mother was promiscuous and unable to tell the child who her father was. Claudia maintained a close preoedipal attachment to her mother. In adolescence, her search for her fantasy father was acted out. Claudia became promiscuous as her mother had been, not merely due to identification, but as a result of other inner conflicts as well.

There had been severe interference with George's oedipal development. George's mother left the family after several extramarital relationships and abortions. The simultaneous treatment of seven-and-a-half-year-old George and his father was coordinated by Liselotte Frankl (1965). His father refused to allow a woman to join the household to look after George and his younger brother. This was based on his fantasy of wanting to be both a mother and father to his children. In his attempts to be close to George, he essentially made him a partner in his own depression and did not succeed in giving the child necessary care because of his ambivalence. The boy's fantasies evoked intense fears of his mother as a dangerous, destructive woman, and his aggressive wishes against her dominated his thoughts. Simultaneously, homosexual fears were expressed in the material of both father and son. Scenes of aggressive attacks took place which led to George's fantasies of taking up a woman's role with his father. Forward moves towards heterosexuality and the sublimations characteristic of latency emerged only slowly after both father and son had been in treatment for several years.

The child is used to fulfill mother's ambition. Parents' fantasies of achieving success which remain unfulfilled were found to govern their relationship to their child as he grew older, particularly when he reached school age. In two cases, the first signs of this attitude had become manifest by the onset of speech development.

Eric's and Rachel's mothers were concerned with their children's speech. They showed marked competitiveness with the achievements of other children of the same age, and spent a great deal of time talking and reading to their children. This had marked favorable results, and the children responded well to the amount of interest shown to them by their mothers. However, these mothers also put pressure on their children, and expressed anger and ridicule when their fantasies of outstanding success did not come true. These aspects by far outweighed the favorable effects, and created feelings of anxiety and hostility in the children. Pleasure and pride in their own achievements were interfered with, and self-esteem became uneven because of the extreme changes in their mothers' responses to them.

For Eric's and Rachel's mothers, speaking well had been important in their childhoods. This related to intense competition with older brothers and also meant they might fulfill a wish to reach higher cultural and special levels than the male members of their families. For Eric's mother, who competed with her husband in every possible way, this had an important meaning. Eric was felt to be a part of his mother, and his speech had to be like hers. This meant he should not speak like his father, who had a working class accent. Eric became able to speak well, but his verbal attacks against his mother alternated with a growing reluctance to talk to her at all. He found he could take revenge against her by attacking her with his great verbal skill, and by withholding communication. In addition, speaking badly, which meant being like his father, was used as a weapon against her.

Mrs. Z.'s use of Rachel to fulfill her own intellectual ambitions became marked in the later stages of her analysis. She deprived her child of any feeling that her school successes gave her pleasure, because Mrs. Z. was compelled to point out the negative aspects of Rachel's work. She also criticized the positive aspects which were never felt to be good enough.

The child represents the damaged aspect of the mother. In the analyses of David and his mother (Burlingham, Schnurmann, and Lantos 1958), much of the mother's approach to her son was based on the unconscious identification of him with aspects of herself she felt were abnormal and damaged. Analysis further showed she saw David as she imagined her own mother had seen her. She was constantly worried he was lonely and unhappy at school. His unusually intense fantasy life disturbed her. He was pale, thin, and spoke so faintly the teacher could not hear him. This description exactly fitted the mother when she was a child. She too had been pale, thin, anxious, spoke in a faint voice, and felt she was no good.

It appeared David felt and behaved as his mother expected him to. He developed an identification not only with his mother, but with her image of him which she conveyed in words and actions. Their communications by drawings and in fantasies about animals showed an unusually close understanding of one other. Her constant doubt of David's abilities prevented him from enjoying and fully developing them. She could never accept the reality of his successes and found it difficult to enjoy his growing independence.

Pseudo-stupidity: a symptom found in mother and daughter. Claudia's mother's unconscious need to force her child into her own childhood role was clear. This led to the impression they shared a symptom. While certain symptoms appear to be the same in mother and child, their different structures become apparent through analytic work. It becomes possible to differentiate between those elements of each patient's conflicts which led to symptom formation, and those mechanisms which interact and contribute to the need to maintain the symptom. Both mother and daughter had the symptom of pseudo-stupidity. It was clear each needed the denial and confusion in her own mind for defensive purposes. However, it was also possible to trace the mother's unconscious need to make her daughter relive her own role of the stupid child.

The mother's constant anxiety throughout childhood led her to play the role of the stupid girl in her family. This was the "safe role" in relation to her frightening mother and two older sisters. Her confusion, largely expressed in the use of nonsense words, protected her from expressing her hostility and envy, and against the dangers that might have resulted from it. The mother's symptom resulted from her confusion between the sexes, and from her displacement onto the intellectual field of a conviction she was damaged. Her blatant misuse of words and lack of knowledge of simple facts was used to display this damage— not only defensively—but to arouse interest and sympathy. Exhibiting her stupidity, misery, or poverty enabled her to receive kindness and sympathy from both her parents. The far-reaching use of the mechanism of denial was found to have a serious pathogenic effect.

Claudia's developing capacity to show curiosity made it possible to link her confusion and "stupidity" to her unknown father. The urgency of Claudia's curiosity, her fear of asking, and her distrust of what she was told showed the intensity of her conflict. It had a far-reaching inhibiting effect on her capacity to think and learn. The part her mother's disturbance played in this symptom was gradually clarified. This was the first and clearest link found in Claudia's far-reaching denial of reality, and her need to embellish and blur the facts of her own life. Claudia's analysis was very successful in this area. Her later school achievements, as well as her work attainments shown in a follow-up twenty years later, showed that analysis had been able to free her from "stupidity." It had originated in her mother's unconscious wish to keep her daughter dependent and closely linked to her through the shared symptom. The mother's confused thinking was also much improved through her treatment, and she became able to enjoy Claudia's intellectual achievements. Consciously, mothers aim to shield their children from experiencing the miseries of their own childhood. However, analysis shows their deep-rooted need to make their children repeat the fate of the devalued child they had felt themselves to be.

The damaging influence of a mother's rigid reaction formations is well known. It has a detrimental effect on the child, particularly in the anal phase, when cleanliness training becomes important. Two other defense mechanisms and their damaging effects have become especially clear in these studies.

Effects of defense mechanisms: the mother's denial of reality. If a mother's acceptance of external reality is disturbed, frequently these same areas remain unavailable to her child. Magical thinking, and the omnipotent denial the mother uses to avoid the intolerable facts of external and internal reality, are introjected by her child. He then operates with her mechanisms in these same areas, in the service of his own defenses. The child's attempts at reality testing are experienced by both mother and child as a danger. To the mother, the danger arises from the fear she will be forced to face the intolerable facts of reality through her child. To the child, reality testing and the acceptance of facts which are not in accordance with his mother's distorted picture brings the threat of loss of love, and his mother's hostility, guilt, and depression.

Effects of defense mechanisms: the mother's projections. Some mothers make extensive use of their children as objects of projection. Coleman, Kris, and Provence (1953) formulated that for such mothers, "the child has not become an individual; he remains a projective screen" (p. 27). These mothers cannot react to their children's needs and impulses on the basis of a perception of their children's internal situation. Instead, they respond in line with their own projections. The manifestations and changing needs of the child call up a succession of different infantile conflicts in the mother. As these become preconscious, they bring manifestations of the mother's own early anxieties, fantasies, and defenses. The child successively stands for these and for different early, conflicted objects in the mother's past. The persistent exposure to their mother's changing projections is severely damaging to a growing child. It interferes with establishing separateness from his mother, and differentiating between his own impulses and anxieties and hers.

THERAPEUTIC RESULTS

All mothers had come into treatment only after their children's analysts had indicated that their participation in the children's disturbance presented a serious obstacle to therapeutic success. Only Mr. N. had been in treatment previously. He had felt the need for help with his depression. None of the mothers had sought analysis to change or to gain insight into her own and her child's disturbance. In most of these mothers, guilt about their children's conditions led them to feel they must accept treatment. The therapeutic alliance was characterized by this situation and also by the fact that treatment was free. Therapeutic results were clearly influenced by these factors. Although insight was gained and favorable changes occurred, the parents, who did not seek analysis for their own sake, tended to develop a limited therapeutic alliance and achieved limited therapeutic goals. These parents' withdrawal from treatment indicated that their desire for treatment was based largely on guilt concerning their children's disturbance.

CONCLUSIONS

Further studies are needed. Ideally these should arise from analytic work with young women who come to or are in analysis with an awareness of their need for it. Under these circumstances, the child subsequently taken into treatment would have a better chance to benefit from changes in his mother and from insight she would gain through treatment. Ideally, preventive work should be done by promoting treatment for pregnant women who feel ambivalent about motherhood. Any analysis of a mother carried out after her child has become disturbed and has reached the age when he is analyzable cannot deal with the damage done to the baby during his first year. This has been demonstrated by cases in which the very capacity for mothering was interfered with, and in cases in which premature sexual stimulation took place.

This survey contains the main findings which emerged from the available material. The examples were chosen to illustrate what seemed to be the most typical effects parents' pathology has on their children. A large amount of material from both the parent's and the child's analysis seems to contain further aspects of more subtle pathological interactions. However, none of the authors found indications in the material clear enough to draw definite conclusions. Several coordinators expressed the wish that further research be carried out under planned conditions. Cases could then be chosen according to the pathology presented by either parent or child, or according to the type of developmental problem manifested by the child. Alternatively, attention could be focused primarily on preventive work; for this, young children would be selected as they reach the age of analyzability.

The present material has clarified areas in which treatment of a child without simultaneous treatment of the parent either would have failed or produced at most very limited therapeutic results. This study has also contributed to an awareness that inadequate need fulfillment in a child's earliest phases can lead to irreversible damage. In addition, the material contains ample proof of the severe pathogenic effect of premature sexual stimulation (see Greenacre 1952).

NOTE

1. The author wishes to express her thanks to Dorothy Burlingham, who was the originator of the Hampstead Study and whose encouragement and advice helped her throughout, and to Dr. Liselotte Frankl for the help she has given her.

REFERENCES

Burlingham, D. (1935). Child analysis and the mother. *Psychoanalytic Quarterly* 4:69–92.

Burlingham, D., Goldberger, A., and Lussier, A. (1955). Simultaneous analysis of mother and child. *Psychoanalytic Study of the Child* 10: 165–186.

Burlingham, D., Schnurmann, A., and Lantos, B. (1958). David and his mother (unpublished).

Coleman, R. W., Kris, E., and Provence, S. (1953). The study of variations of early parental attitudes: a preliminary report. *Psychoanalytic Study of the Child* 8:20–47.

Frankl, L. (1965). George and his father (unpublished).

Freud, A. (1960). Introduction to "Simultaneous analysis of a mother and her adolescent daughter," by K. Levy. *Psychoanalytic Study of the Child* 15:378–380.

––––––– (1958). Adolescence. *Psychoanalytic Study of the Child* 13: 255–78.

––––––– (1955). The rejecting mother. Lecture given to the Child Welfare League of America.

Greenacre, P. (1952). Pre-genital patterning. *International Journal of Psycho-Analysis* 33:410–415.

Hellman, I., Friedmann, O., and Shepheard, E. (1960). Simultaneous analysis of mother and child. *Psychoanalytic Study of the Child* 15: 359–77.

Hellman, I., de Monchaux, C., and Ludowyk-Gyomroi, E. (1961). Simultaneous analysis of a mother and her eleven-year old daughter (unpublished).

Hellman, I., Schnurmann, A., and Todes, C. (1970). Simultaneous analysis of a mother and her four-year-old daughter (unpublished).

Lebovici, S., and McDougall, J. (1969). *Dialogue with Sammy: A Psycho-Analytic Contribution to the Understanding of Child Psychosis.* Trans. J. McDougall. London: Hogarth.

Levy, K. (1960). Simultaneous analysis of a mother and her adolescent daughter. *Psychoanalytic Study the Child* 15:378–91.

Mahler, M.S., Pine, F., and Bergman, A. (1975). *The Psychological Birth of the Human Infant.* New York: Basic Books.

Sperling, M. (1946). Psychoanalytic study of ulcerative colitis in children. *Psychoanalytic Quarterly* 15:302–329.

Sprince, M.P. (1962). The development of a preoedipal partnership between an adolescent girl and her mother. *Psychoanalytic Study of the Child* 17:418–450.

Chapter 18

TUTORING: THE REMEDIATION OF COGNITIVE AND ACADEMIC DEFICITS BY INDIVIDUAL INSTRUCTION

Joseph Opperman

THE RANGE OF TUTORING SERVICES

Tutoring would hardly appear to need definition, let alone description. As a term, it is so easily apprehended, so self-illuminating, it seems to define itself. Still, it has yet to find its way into any comprehensive dictionary of psychological terms. In practice, however, tutoring has become a specific technique within the complex proliferation of educational specialties.

Further, tutoring is often the first recourse of the anxious parent for outside help when confronted by the child's apparently inexplicable school failure. The curious fact is that parents may be ready to enlist some mode of professional intervention for a child's academic difficulty, while at the same time denying his more obvious and alarming pathology. As considered here, the tutorial regime is a significant channel for the parent and child. Through it, they may become aware that the presenting learning problem may in fact signal an underlying emotional disturbance, or carry with it concomitant conflicts, indicating the need for a more direct therapeutic intervention.

There are varying gradations of sophistication and professionalism in tutoring. They range from the occasional short-term preparation of the well-integrated, optimally motivated student, who requires the services of a subject-expert tutor for a temporary and specific expedient, to a concerted, long-range remedial effort. The latter may span crucial stages of a child's life. It may extend into the conflict sphere, and the tutoring experience may act as a major psychological influence, either jointly and concurrently with psychoanalytic intervention, or quite independently.

Tutors are educational specialists in learning disability. They tend to cluster around two main theoretical foundations. They polarize around considerations of the significant etiological factors in the total learning history. One group tends to emphasize behavioral considerations, while the other emphasizes dynamic considerations. In approach and orientation, the behavioral remedial tutors relate learning disability to neurological, perceptual, and physiological factors. They seek discrete corrective approaches for such diagnostic entities as dyslexia, specific language disability, minimal brain damage, and developmental lags. This tutorial method stresses clearly circumscribed instruction, training-retraining, and such techniques as *patterning* when applied to the specific remediation of motor and coordination deficits.

At the other pole are educational specialists who attempt to specify the dynamics of the learning dysfunction as it relates to the child's total defensive structure. Where so determined, they tend to view a learning disability as a symptomatic inhibition resulting from emotional conflict. These different theoretical foundations with various eclectic assimilations branch out, and result in different tutorial techniques and approaches. In the long run, it is perhaps more fruitful to adopt the simple axiom that, more often than not, a learning failure is multidetermined. This is true even at an early age and certainly by the middle grades.

Beyond a simple definition of function—tutoring is the individualized remediation of cognitive and academic deficits—in actual practice, tutoring is a broad field encompassing diverse and significant educational approaches. This article will deal specifically with the tutorial situation as a vehicle for effecting significant learning functions in the ego of the child, and the techniques involved in this process. Tutoring is considered both as an adjunct to therapy and as a frontier of modern educational practice which extends toward the therapeutic sphere.

INDICATIONS FOR TUTORING

Often, tutoring provides the only strategic and timely therapeutic opportunity, or serves as a necessary forerunner in preparing the child for therapy when more direct psychological interventions are, for one reason or another, not immediately possible or advisable. It is essential, however, the tutor have a sensitive awareness of exactly what role and function he or she is fulfilling in the child's life, and to contain the tutorial situation clearly within those boundaries. This can best be done when the tutor is quite aware, through training and experience, of the differences between his educational function, and that of a psychoanalyst or psychotherapist who may intervene at a subsequent stage of the child's life or may be in the current picture simultaneously. When tutoring is conducted with an analytic orientation and discipline, which respects the limitation of the educational effort, as well as appreciates the channels it may open for symptom reversal and ego development, it may often be considered the intervention of choice.

There are specific conditions and indicators when tutoring alone offers special advantages in meeting the child's psychological and educational needs:

1. When there is massive denial by the parents, child, or both, of the psychogenesis of the learning dysfunction and its ramifications, and this precludes referral to an analyst or therapist.

2. When the child is capable of perceiving his deficiency in the learning area on a reality basis, is motivated to improve his capability to function academically, and the cognitive skills are comparatively conflict-free.

3. When the existing pathology or ego deficits would require an inordinately extended initial preparatory period for analysis, and the tutorial experience ultimately may serve the child as an introductory bridge to analysis.

4. When neurological deficits (perceptual anomalies, gross skill lags, dyslexia, and intellectual deficiency of one kind or another) open critical gaps in learning between the child and his acquisition of age-appropriate learning functions, and when a concerted, undiluted effort to advance his school skills must be made without delay.

Each of these categories will be amplified with illustrative case material. Here considered are the techniques of the tutor, and questions of structure and flexibility, goals, the relationship between child and tutor, and the relationship tutoring bears to the therapeutic model.

There are various levels of skill, analytic insight, and technical remedial experience that are brought to bear in the tutorial situation. Regardless of these levels, the optimal technique is one which adapts to the special, individual needs of the child. In the final measure, the tutor devises a curriculum uniquely adapted to the one child and to none other. What is easy, natural, and open with learning possibilities for one child may be constricting for another. The curriculum or task must be arrived at mutually, and this is true even when firm direction is required of the tutor. Examined in their underlying aspects, even these controlling measures are with the inner consent of the child, and his own will is operative in finding the optimal curriculum and learning activity.

When the tutor is sure of himself and has a good grasp of the circumstances of the child's life and the emotional fields of his experience, it is generally a good idea to let the child lead. It helps the child find a comfortable locus, it orients him in a controlled distance toward the tutor, and provides the fructifying groundwork for the child to give clues to his own needs and problems. A free-rein approach is especially desirable when previous learning experiences have been fraught with pain and frustration. Once the child has taken the initiative offered him, it is necessary to evolve together a comfortable but tight structure that makes clear the common goal toward which he and the tutor are embarked.

In all this, flexibility is the key—an alertness not only to individual differences but also to the differences in each child as he goes about living and learning. At times the tutorial structure must loosen sufficiently that the child may himself provide the most promising pathways for teaching him. In some instances, the situation is tightly controlled by the tutor. Such control will be exercised for children with attention and concentration difficulties or to counterbalance the openness of the analytic experience when the child is simultaneously in treatment. It is crucial for the child to learn something palpably needful to him, which he can carry away from the tutorial session. The overriding point in all technique is that the child experience the tutorial situation as meaningful. The tutor is responsible for making the experience an optimal part of the child's life, and for knowing the place it serves in his development. The child must become interested, involved, and absorbed. These are far-reaching goals for the tutor, and with some children he may have to settle for merely arousing attention—itself no unworthy accomplishment. In the long run, however, the tutoring situation must become important to the child or the game is lost and the enterprise hollow. Learning is an active process.

TUTOR-CHILD RELATIONSHIP

The tutorial situation is basically one of relationship. It is the conduit of communication for the remedial process, especially for the child with considerable impairment of academic skills. The dynamics of this relationship run all through the various aspects of tutoring, but it would be well to consider some salient factors of the psychological interaction between child and tutor.

The tutor cannot, or perhaps should not, expect a traditional preceptor-pupil relationship to unfold, with a compliant, docile, responsive pupil who regards the tutor as a consummate authority. This is especially so with children (and their parents, too) who have suffered a severe narcissistic wound as a result of learning impairment. It is well to remember that children and parents carry a stereotyped image and expectation of the tutor. In their view, the tutor will serve to impart instruction, and the tutee will passively (sometimes magically) receive and absorb it. Tutoring is often another thing given to the child, and the tutor may be seen as a hired acquisition or instrumentality. Under such conditions, parents may want a taskmaster, or a drill-sergeant relationship, out of the same constellation of circumstances that sends children to military school. It seldom works that way.

With the exception of many deprived and disadvantaged children who never experienced clear and consistent opportunities for instruction in disrupted homes and disorganized classrooms, learning-disabled children cannot sustain attention under such formalized structure. Nor, as a rule do children welcome being tutored; indeed, for some, it is painful. Structure is needed and, for the organically damaged child, is imperative. However, the structure required is different from the impersonalized stereotype described above.

The tutorial relationship is an involved, interactive process. The child comes to perceive the tutor as a constant, significant object, who responds to his needs for mastery in a conflict-free arena. The tutor, by making demands for learning within a relationship of acceptance and value affords the child protectiveness in finding realistic goals, and eventually opens avenues for independence and self-assertion. A child who learns to read after frustrating periods of failure and environmental struggle will perceive the tutorial experience as a palliative for the often-denied wounded narcissism of his past failure. Ideally, the tutor will aim for the child's sense of success, restored self-esteem, and pleasurable response to be transformed and differentiated from the *person* of the tutor, to the activity of learning. The object of the tutoring is to enable the child to function.

PARALLELS TO THE THERAPEUTIC MODEL

In many respects, the tutorial situation parallels technical aspects of the therapeutic model. However, it also differs from therapy in significant ways, particularly in its approach to the child. In its attempt at optimal closeness to the life of the child, and its attempt to understand the field of experience in which the child functions, tutoring differs little from therapy. However, children usually enter a tutorial situation with less anxiety, and on a practical level, they may be consciously willing to learn and cooperate. The tutor must see to it that the child is brought along in this stage of acceptance before significant achievement outcomes may be expected.

There are also practical considerations bearing on the relation of tutoring and therapy. When the child is concurrently in analytic treatment, it is essential the tutorial program does not interfere with the therapeutic work, but rather augment and widen it. The tutor will need to recognize his personal influences on the child within the range of permissiveness and the various displacements that may operate in the tutorial relationship. It may be advisable for the analyst and tutor to confer as needed, or on a periodic basis if the case admits of such collaborative exchange. Problems of confidentiality and consent, among others, must be surmounted.

TUTORING CONCURRENT WITH ANALYSIS

When tutoring and psychoanalysis are conducted simultaneously, the child can learn to distinguish domains of function along more or less discrete lines. However, some children have only a limited capacity for relationships, and thus may be unable to attach an appropriate level of significance to each relationship and experience. It may lead to a situation of a superfluity of helping functions—too many cooks. With frequent, cooperative exchange, conducted within the safeguards of confidentiality, but with the child's knowledge and agreement, tutor and analyst most often develop an avenue of professional communication, which widens the field of observation to both and always redounds to the child's benefit.

In the tutorial situation, resistance will usually take the form of a refusal to work or to cooperate in such technical matters as appointments and schedules. Through professional exchange between tutor and analyst, resistances appearing in one situation may be dispelled, warded off, or worked through in the other. As in the therapeutic situation, the tutor often becomes the displacement of the parents, with consequent difficulties when it is tinged with negativism and hostility.

Cues may appear in the analytic work that are of great value as material for learning, and sometimes leads to significant breakthroughs. For example, a young adolescent who had many gaps and confusions about family relationships and severe difficulty in spatial orientation began to construct a huge geneological chart with his tutor. The individual names and relationships were physically palpable, and could be manipulated and arranged until the total configuration was constructed. For children with organic disabilities, construction is an excellent means of finding structure and organization. The idea for this child's project grew out of the regular consultations between tutor and analyst, and the benign involvement of unusually cooperative parents. Consequently, in the treatment situation, there was an enrichment and productivity of material.

With such professional interchanges, the role of tutor and analyst is consistently clarified. Each practitioner is able to more clearly perceive a significant aspect of the child's world outside immediate purview. The tutorial experience may be seen by the analyst as an especially positive influence on the child's sense of mastery of his environment; while the tutor will be more readily alert to sense how this particular relationship and interaction with the child may have resonances in the therapeutic sphere.

Patterns which the child perceives in the tutorial sessions may be very valuable in the analysis. A stuttering patient learned from his tutor that he held his breath and "pushed down" as he spoke, thus preventing sounds from emerging. His analyst had not observed this pattern. Once therapist and patient became aware of this mode of speech, they could connect it with fantasies the patient had about pregnancy. The patient, in unconscious identification with his pregnant mother, wished to keep the rival baby from being born. The stuttering decreased markedly once this conflict was connected with the speech patterns.

Tutoring can further analysis, but the child may use it as an obstacle by splitting the transference. Through this mechanism he can evade analysis of his feelings toward the analyst. For instance, a child of eight, when angry at his analyst for a fantasied slight, started to concentrate on distasteful aspects of his tutor and attempted to provoke the tutor to behavior that would justify antagonism. Another patient, a boy of nine, unconsciously attempted to avoid forbidden friendly feelings toward his male analyst, and displaced these to his female tutor, on whom he developed a crush. In both these cases the displacement of feelings from analyst to tutor deterred analysis of the transference.

Splitting of the transference can be inadvertently fostered by behavior that leads to confusion of the mental representations of analyst and tutor. If the style of the tutor and analyst is similar, if the tutor interprets as does the analyst, the two may appear similar to the child. Excessive consultation between therapist and teacher may also facilitate the child's conceiving of them as similar.

TUTORIAL TECHNIQUES: ADJUSTING FOR INDIVIDUAL DIFFERENCES

Rules of procedure or technique in tutoring are of limited value in guiding the remedial process. Each case must be evaluated, and the relationship modified, according to the child's unique circumstances. The child will seek out and attach certain inner needs onto the tutor, who must be sensitive to this unconscious process so his response can meet those positive needs. Lying deeply hidden beneath the seemingly prosaic tasks of academic skills—reading, spelling, math, and so on— is a vast complex of emotional tones and psychological extensions.

Consider just a single strand or continuum—say, pleasure-pain, reward-punishment, indulgence-deprivation, gratification-limits. These are constantly operative in the tutorial relationship, as they are in all instructional modes, but the tutorial lends itself to differentiate individual differences to an exquisite degree. The tutor must know when to *feed* an answer and initiate and support, and when to withhold and frustrate to develop the child's independent mastery. He must know when and what kinds of gifts to present to the child—in exchange or at milestone events—and be aware that these offerings may be perceived as seductive blandishments, and of the subtle rivalries that may be aroused by them. Children often need proof of love, of the value in which they are held, and sometimes this takes concrete form. When the child is in analysis at the same time, he may be expected to test for limits, consistency, and competitiveness. He may compare tutor and analyst to ascertain who will give more. The tutor's generosity may then undermine the child's relation with his therapist.

Another situation that admits no hard-and-fast rule is the seemingly minute and commonplace matter of how long a child wishes to stay, or will be permitted to stay, in the bathroom. Sometimes the interrupted work remains tauntingly uncompleted. The response from the tutor of pressure, or some indulgence of infantile needs, will be modified according to the individual factors.

Some children require quid pro quo gratification before they are able to gather energy for attention and concentration. Others may test the tutor by trying to see how long and far the indulgence may be permitted. Overall, however, the relationship is most productive when the tutor is viewed as one who makes demands of the child within his capacity to fulfill them—that is, sets realistic goals for achievement— and as one who exercises and exerts controls from without, thus strengthening the child's command over his impulses and regressive tendencies. This may be done using the barest minimum of interpretation in an analytic sense, but interpretation should not be avoided or circumvented when the situation clearly demands it. Interpretations should be of the superficial clarifying type rather than deep explanations of drives and unconscious conflict.

Later case material may clarify this point, but an example may suffice here.

THE BOY WHO CONSIDERS HIMSELF "DUMB"

A sixteen-year-old boy of good intelligence had been able to achieve barely passing grades in junior high school, and now, in the tenth grade, was in danger of failing for the year. He was a strong, well-built youngster with an all-pervading interest in sports, in which he was able to excel as his academic performance fell. His drive as an athlete could be measured in contrast to the personality of the father, a passive, over-emotional, and slightly effeminized man.

When geometry and chemistry were added to the boy's course of study, his academic standing became critical. Tutoring began at this point. In sessions, he showed he was developing a self-image of being grossly inferior intellectually and socially.

Responding to this, and to his general tendency to self-derogation, the tutor remarked, "Why do you always want to think you're dumb, and then go about trying to prove it?" The boy seemed intrigued by this comment and said, "Geometry is too hard for me. I'm so far behind I don't even know what's going on in the classroom anymore. I haven't passed a test in weeks."

The tutor said, "Of course you can't pass a test if you don't study for it. Do you think it's magic or something?"

"My friends don't study, but they do okay."

"Oh, they study all right, but they're cool about it. You always seem ready to believe everyone is smarter than you. Now let's do this problem in slow motion, and see if you can get up the ladder one rung at a time."

The tutor was reassuring, encouraging, and instructive. In this instance, the boy's response and forward movement were immediate and steady. The boy began to hold his own academically, confirmed that his friends indeed did study and began to recognize that his own situation was far from hopeless. He needed desperately this evidence of his own intellectual adequacy, for at this point he was forming ideas of his future.

He was most eager to share his developing social experiences with someone, as well his uncertainty in that direction. He had always been inhibited in his relations with girls, but now he became more confident. He became more socially successful and experienced than a friend of his, a highly successful student, who now turned to him for guidance and instruction.

His parents were somewhat alarmed by his social interests, which were age-adequate and a positive reversal of his previous withdrawn pattern. In consultation with the parents the tutor was able to effect some liberalization of their attitude with a consequent lessening of their anxiety and gradual lessening of strictures.

There was a consequent two-fold spurt in adolescent development, intellectually and sexually. The boy was noticeably happier and more self-assured. This trend continued until tutoring was terminated shortly before the boy left for college, where he made a good record both academically and as an athlete. The difficulty of his poor identification was not interpreted, nor was it directly touched in the work. Parent conferences were reported and discussed, but the conscious and everyday derivatives presented in the tutorial were taken up and dealt with on a reality basis.

The reflection of feelings, rather than interpretation, is often desirable. Interpretation may involve entering a depth that will jeopardize the goal of a learning structure. Often the relationship can fulfill the objective of clearing resistances. For children who seethe with hostility toward parents and displace it to school, teachers, authority figures, and to learning in general, the tutor may be perceived as a special figure. During a period of acceptance and diminished resistance, the tutor may say, "Yes, I know you think she's unfair, and you're angry at her for failing you, but whatever you do, don't hurt yourself. Don't fail yourself. It's your education; don't regard it as though it belongs to your teachers to do with as they want."

The rationale here is to direct the anger so it serves the ego. Learning achievement is high on the scale of sublimations and unconscious retaliatory thrusts toward school performance are often self-defeating. An educator's intervention as mediator is often helpful without overt interpretation of the unconscious factors. The tutor may become an instrument to restore channels of communication between family members to replace acting-out signals. The tutor may also play an active role in management. Parents will often be open and grateful for suggestions to find more positive ways of relating to the child than through constant reminders of undone schoolwork. They are relieved to have the tutor assume responsibility for this aspect of their relationship.

THE PSYCHOLOGICAL FUNCTIONING OF THE TUTOR

The parameters of remedial education and psychoanalytic therapy connect and overlap as the tutor approaches the child. Certainly, tutoring is not mere reading-comprehension exercises. The tutor is a kind of "concentrated" educator. He exerts greater impact and influence extending over a longer period of time than the regular classroom teacher. Does he also exercise a psychological function in the child's life? If so, how is his function to be distinguished and differentiated from the psychotherapist's?

If the child solely needs instruction, and the tutor conceives his role as strictly limited to providing it, then a discrete demarcation of boundaries between the educator's function and the therapist's would seem quite clear. However, the functional field of the educator has broadened as understanding of the teacher's role in child development has deepened. The child, especially the adolescent, needs to find a conflict-free model in his strivings for mastery and independence.

When conditions are optimal and the groundwork correctly established, the tutor provides an essential psychological thrust toward this development—he may act as an ego ideal for the child at some crucial stage. The frequency and structure of the contact, and the very nature of the child's needs, make this identification process virtually inevitable. It is part of the operational field in a one-to-one tutorial conducted within a goal-oriented structure. It is ubiquitous and natural. When the tutor is aware of such unconscious identifications establishing themselves, they are never interpreted. Often, the child begins to take on the tutor's attitudes and values, and most desirably, the tutor's attitudes toward learning.

It is possible to theoretically differentiate the disciplines within a scientific scheme, and to establish domains of responsibility following recognized professional standards. However, in the life of the child, such gradations have no meaning. It is a matter of indifference to him whether the process is educational, therapeutic, or a little of both. An exception may be made in the case of sensitive minority groups and in parents whose denial defense is dominant, for whom therapy, in name or implication, may be threatening.

Several caveats must intrude at this point. The idealization of the tutor's role in meeting a child's emotional and psychological needs can often lead to superficial half-understandings. The teacher must not turn a classroom into group therapy in the name of preserving openness and freedom of discussion. Nor must the tutorial become an analytic hour. If that happens, it is at the educator's peril and most likely to the child's detriment, for these are enterprises easier to enter than to sustain, carry forward, and conclude with precision and control.

There is considerable difference between the insight derived from an educational process and the insight derived from interpretation, exploration, and introspection in the therapeutic field. Education speaks of the general, the universal, which the educator seeks to connect to the child. Therapy deals with the "I"—the special and unique "I"—from which the child makes developmental and cognitive connections to the outside world.

On a practical level, tutor and therapist carry out certain functions along parallel lines. For the child, both persons are readily available and often vital objects of displacements. Both are concerned with the age-appropriate coming into play of the ego functions. While therapist and tutor have these common goals, each approaches them differently. The therapist makes ego functions possible when normative educational pathways, including those of benign instruction, have not led to the expected mastery in cognition.

In meeting the special needs of children with learning impairments, carried out in a tutorial mode, an optimal balance must be sought between these two fructifying areas of competence. This vital combination of skills, derived from both education and psychology, circumscribes the field of cognitive remediation.

PREPARATION AND TRAINING FOR TUTORING

The specialized tutorial must meet the emotional needs of the learner. What follows describes the background of the tutor, who is qualified to work within this orientation, and provides an overview of the technique used in tutoring children within this mode.

Various degrees of sophistication and levels of training are to be found among remedial workers. The continuum ranges from those most comfortable with standardized reading materials—such as phonics workbooks, words in color, flash cards, and the like—to the open structure and individualized curriculum described in this article. The psychological dynamics of the one-to-one relationship are present whether the tutor is aware of them or not. This awareness should be used for the sake of the child's growth, without dislocating the benign sectors of the defensive structure.

The two or three times a week in which the tutor sees the child, like the formal, extrinsic elements in the therapeutic pattern, gives significance and connection to the learning effort. As the work proceeds, the child begins to view the tutor in a way peculiar to his own special needs. This perception is compelling and significant, and greatly determines the degree of success and response. It is vital that the tutor know what the child perceives of the tutoring sessions, and more importantly, of the tutor himself. Understanding how the relationship affects the child, the way the child exploits it for his own growth, and the needs the child attaches to it in his cognitive development are perhaps the most essential aspects of remedial technique.

Viewed in this context, what are the characteristics that identify the remedial tutor capable of working within the psychological framework? The readiness and capacity for grasping the dynamics, while simultaneously teaching have already been noted. A further characteristic of the tutor is his ability to observe the child while remaining a participant-observer. He is with it and aside from it simultaneously and continuously.

The tutor is able to observe best, to take note of the essentials, when learning with the child is a shared activity. The doing becomes an open arena of observation within a spontaneous atmosphere. A child may build an airport (learning to letter the names of airlines), make a model (reading the directions or not), build a puppet (and write a play to go with it), or talk, think, do a school assignment, or get down to work or out of it. The tutor's receptivity, as he partakes in the activity of learning, makes it possible for him to observe relevant and timely material as it emerges naturally in the learning process and, when significant opportunities arise, to recognize and seize the spontaneous breakthroughs.

A CHILD "WITHOUT TIME"

An eight-year-old with serious developmental lags, cognitive impairments, dyslexia, and other organic anomalies, but with better than average intelligence, told his tutor he did not know when his birthday was. "I think it's when the snow falls," he said. (It was in February.) In fact, all time sequences were confused in his mind—days of the week, months of the year, and clock reading. There seemed to be no fixed point to establish any sequence, and all previous attempts to memorize such series had always frustratingly drained away. The parents were sadly giving in to their fear the child was retarded, although the child himself had an essential strong streak of determination and will.

When he could not remember his birthday, the moment seemed right, a unique opportunity presented itself, and the tutor did something quite out of the ordinary. "Go where your mother is sitting outside, and ask her what day you were born. Remember it so you can tell me." The child went to his mother in the waiting room and returned with the information. It was written down and virtually absorbed, taken in, by the child. In this way, the day, the month, and the year could now become a fixed, orienting point.

This occurrence was fortuitous and unexpectedly fruitful. Thereafter, the door was opened many times between the mother in the waiting room and the tutor's office. What might have been an intrusive distraction became a revitalized tie between child and mother, which earlier had been infected by the massive narcissistic trauma for each of them. The pattern, "Go ask your mother," was the turning point in a previously pernicious trend. The child was able to ask for, receive, and retain discrete personal information. The interaction gave his mother a much-needed sense of participation to counter years of rejecting her "defective" child.

TUTORING, A REMEDIAL THERAPY

A tutorial approach engages and involves the parents. Of necessity, learning activity may evolve into "learning therapy," by seizing the advantage of the unique opportunity it presents for deep influences and symptom reversal. Psychological training for the tutor will enable him to sharpen intuitive understanding. At all times he must apprehend the meaning of the ego deficit within the configuration of the child's emotional life—cognition and feelings interact profoundly—and how the deficit colors the family relationship and the conflicts it gives rise to or intensifies.

The tutor who fulfills his task along these lines usually has had a combination of educational and psychological training. Optimally, this includes classroom teaching, academic training in psychology, a personal psychoanalysis, continuing participation in analytic study groups for teachers, and individual supervision of cases under careful psychoanalytic controls. Ideally, the tutor's background touches several disciplines. These, in combination, and when skillfully applied, establish a unique parameter that may be identified as remedial or learning psychotherapy.

The more the tutor knows about the child, the better able he is to arrive at an individualized curriculum. It is extremely important to observe the child in his actual learning situation. This is augmented by data from parents and the school, as well as psychological, neurological, and psychiatric evaluations. In time, all these contribute to creating a working atmosphere and pattern for each child which is unique to his needs.

FINDING THE OPTIMUM LEARNING ACTIVITY FOR EACH CHILD

No two cases are the same; each child presents fresh and challenging conditions, and the tutor invents highly individualized activities and materials to reach the child. The one-to-one relationship and open structure permit using whatever fresh experience is imprinted on the child's mind. It attempts to tie the emotional richness of the child's life to the cognitive milestones. This is not possible for the teacher in a group situation. A constant, consistent universe of experience is evolved by each child in an atmosphere of acceptance and exchange. While the intensity of this experience will vary from case to case, its significance for each child is quite profound. The tutor works with a full range of students—in age, talents, and diversity. His room contains many readily observable books which aid a child's motivation. It is always so astonishing and pleasurable for a third-grader, for example, to see the array of math texts with the grade numbers climbing higher and higher. Drawings on the wall, the activities in progress, and the momentos of children who have graduated are all part of this special environment. Each child optimally fits into a comfortable space and time, which he may claim as his own.

The child claims his time as a secure and constant object. He anticipates it on a regular, recurrent basis and it orients him structurally. For example, a nine-year-old, mildly retarded child stepped into the room, passed a child who was leaving, and said to himself and all the world, "It's David's turn now."

Cognitively damaged children like David need the opportunity to tie concrete experiences to emotionally satisfying object relations. For such children, the ability to fix ideas of time, space, and periodicity are significant milestones. They can be gained through step-by-step activity with the tutor, making use of as many body senses as possible. The child's relationship to his tutor gives the acquisition of these skills a human dimension and a depth. This is a fundamental aspect of the psychological approach to learning impairment and is a viable teaching method.

MOTIVATING THE CHILD

Standardized materials, however technically advanced, have limited value unless they increase the child's desire to learn. Teaching materials, such as drill materials in math or flash cards, which are devised and made by the child and tutor, are far superior. The child's motivation is the key to all technique. Motivation is also the essential factor in the psychoanalytic amelioration of a neurotic learning difficulty in which academic skills and achievement are inhibited by inner conflict.

The tutor best approaches the presenting problem operationally through the learning dysfunction, rather than by directly engaging the source of the symptom. Talking time is balanced with working time during the tutorial hour. The dialogue and exchange are held at the child's present reality level. The material is supplied by the child as he formulates his own course of study. Concentration is on the child's ego and his current learning problem. Again, the interpreting of unconscious material is minimal. Interpretation may be called for when the tutoring has come to a serious impasse or where its very continuation may be threatened. As noted above, rebellious, antiachieving adolescents must come to grips with the deeper sources of their acting out.

An eleven-year-old youngster was in the second year of his tutorial, which comprised his total schooling. He had been diagnosed schizophrenic, and had dyslexia and an especially severe handwriting difficulty, which originated both in emotional conflict and in an apparent lack of small motor coordination. He had been in a highly selective, independent school where he was unable to function. The one-to-one tutorial learning situation was the only one he could tolerate. At the time, he was not in treatment, although this was a goal of the tutorial. Further, it was hoped he would return to a more normal educational regime. He had been removed from his previous school because of his marked achievement lag, behavioral problems, and severe anxiety reactions.

In the tutorial, emphasis was placed on activities and projects tied to academic skills. He made striking gains both in cognition and in more appropriate behavior. Without any rational, observable cause, he then became increasingly resistant, unyielding, obstinate, and negative during the tutorial sessions. He became more and more agitated about his handwriting and clumsiness. Finally, he began to act this out by running from the room or hiding in a closet. One day, through the closed door behind which the boy was hiding, the tutor said to him, "I'm not your father. I'm me. And what we're doing is not your *homework.*" The obstacle disappeared from that session. Once the displacement had been refocused and oriented back to reality, the tutoring could proceed. It then went on with renewed vitality and responsiveness in the child. Such difficulties, once surmounted, unlock energy for genuine progress.

Sometimes, the child hears the tutor's words as an interpretation even though they were not intended to be. The remark may strike the child's unconscious and produce a sharp, ringing vibration. Once the relationship has become meaningful, the casual and natural communication of the tutor is used by the child and transformed for special, inner needs of growth. Sometimes this occurs with such force that it serves to unblock fixations or regressive behavior. Commonly a teacher learns from a former student that his casual comment was received in a way which had far-reaching consequences on the student's career.

THE NEUROTIC LEARNING DIFFICULTY

THE REMEDIAL APPROACH

The neurotic learning difficulty and the special methodology required in tutoring will be the focus of the discussion. Conflict areas are present in almost all learning disabilities, even where the disability is physiologically determined. Therefore, the term *neurotic learning dysfunction* is perhaps more descriptive of those cases in which learning failure is symptomatic. Usually it is part of an elaborate defensive structure.

In such instances, the treatment of choice is psychoanalysis or psychotherapy, as circumstances warrant. In the course of successful treatment, learning dysfunctions, as well as other symptoms, yield without the need for special remedial measures. In learning failure of neurotic origin, the activity of learning, achieving, or "knowing" may be highly charged with inner, usually sexualized meaning for the learner, and is thus inhibited. In such instances, tutoring in the sense of "extra help" to "catch up" is found to be of no avail. Often it exacerbates the problem when the whole tutoring collapses because of unconscious factors, and the child's sense of failure is again reinforced.

However, sometimes analytic treatment of such clear-cut neurotic learning disturbances may be foreclosed for one reason or another. For example, the child's anxiety and denial may be so overwhelming it precludes direct measures. Often when parents press for treatment, the child's resistance is compounded.

Parents may deny their own emotional involvement by seeking a purely external explanation for their child's learning dysfunction. "He's lazy," they may conclude. "He just won't work." Tutoring may then be the only viable alternative. It is then necessary to determine the kind of tutoring required for the child's problems and the most effective techniques to apply.

Parents sometimes believe all their child needs is to acquire that tired misnomer, *study habits.* They may blame the school and wish the tutor to instill these habits in a magical, instant process. Parents must then learn that their child's ingrained avoidance pattern is of an emotional nature and changing it is quite beyond the power of instruction per se. Teaching how to study is teaching how to be motivated. This is a psychological process.

The tutor will focus on the external problem—reading, low general achievement, whatever the presenting symptom appears to be—and often good progress is made. However, the basic, inner pathology remains unmodified. In many cases, significant by-products of tutoring come about, which open fresh pathways to future treatment. Often the tutor can educate parents and child about psychological treatment. Youngsters who had been threatened by and resistant to the idea of treatment may come to regard it differently.

This change in attitude is derived not so much from learning what therapy is or may lead to, as from the child's identification with his tutor. The child may take in the tutor's attitude toward the problems they face together. Often these problems are as diverse as math combinations or the question of whether the family should have a dog even though the mother is accepting, but reluctant. The tutor may often work at closer range to the life of the child than formal psychotherapy. Much time is given to shared, helping activity and the identification process occurs as a matter of the child's natural growth and forming of attachments.

Tutors are not interchangeable. An anxious child once asked at the beginning: "Will there be a substitute if you're not here?" The tutor's attitude, which the child perceives, is derived from many sources—his technique, his instructional style, his emotional tone and predilection, and his individual personality. These highly personalized facets vary from tutor to tutor. Yet a common element transcends these variables: The child recognizes the tutor's patience, acceptance, concern, interest, protectiveness, hopefulness and forward-looking, thoughtful planning.

Tutoring may be considered a holding operation in cases where the child is not immediately analyzable, or when his resistance is too great.

TUTORING AS PREPARATION FOR ANALYSIS:
THE BOY WHO DIDN'T CARE

A fourteen-year-old boy was referred for tutoring by a psychoanalyst who had his mother in treatment over a long period and who saw the youngster in consultation. The child had begun a precipitous downslide in all his schoolwork and was apathetic and uninterested in doing better. Although of superior intelligence, he preferred to remain in a school where little was demanded of him. He fiercely resisted treatment, but reluctantly accepted the need for academic improvement.

The tutorial was begun, as the lesser of two evils, two sessions a week of fifty minutes each. During the three years of tutoring, consultations between analyst and tutor were held regularly, and were known both to the child and his parents. When indicated, the tutor met with the child's parents with the child's consent.

What had looked like apathy and dullness in learning was the manifestation of a depression brought on by unresolved separation problems with the mother. The depression was further intensified by the onset of the mother's grave illness.

Little of the dynamic material was touched or opened directly in the tutorial. Rather, the initial period was an undiluted effort to reverse the critical pattern of school failure. Assignments were worked on together. The tutor leaned in the direction of feeding the child answers. The child gathered much energy during this phase by responding to the concerned and ready, helping attitude of his tutor. He would often feign a heavily dramatic hopelessness in the face of learning tasks. This was dispelled by patient encouragement and a refusal to assume and submit to the youngster's defeatist attitude of, "It's not worth it. I'm not worth it."

The child's grades improved, and his tutor encouraged him to attempt a more challenging school which was more commensurate with his ability and probable future direction. "Why should I?" the boy wanted to know. He'd simply have to work harder, and it wasn't worth it. The tutor did not give up the goal of upgrading the boy's schooling, and transmitted the idea the boy indeed was worth it and was valued.

The tutorial lasted until the boy graduated from secondary school. The relationship became meaningful and important to the child. He felt it was something he could count on. Further, the tutoring uncovered and encouraged a literary talent, which the depression had inhibited and which eventually provided satisfying sublimations. In the beginning, the boy was afraid to show his efforts, and his writing had to be nursed along. He used the tutor as a first reader, typist, proof editor, and finally as the keeper of his literary files.

The final goal in tutoring was most crucial—to again try to refer the boy for psychoanalysis. This time, the initiative came from the tutor. The suggestion was met with anger, resistance, fear of rejection, and a sense of betrayal. However, at this point his rage seemed more a demonstration of rebellion than assertion, a defense of his autonomy rather than overwhelming anxiety. At an earlier point, the tutor had told him, in simple truth, knowledge of one's inner life was perhaps the ultimate education to which all learning leads. The boy returned to this idea, romantically and idealistically, in finally accepting analysis.

In such cases, the tutorial is terminated gradually. It continued on a once-a-week basis for a few months while work with the analyst increased to four sessions a week. Later, when the transference was solidly established, the boy would periodically return to reclaim some of the poetry and stories he had left on deposit, in the secure knowledge it would be there when he wanted it, and also knowing he could be the one to leave and go forward with his life.

LIFE GAINS BEYOND "INSTRUCTION"

There are many other by-products of the tutoring experience. Academic success experiences resulting from the tutorial often enable the child to find less pernicious defenses than the inhibition of learning. As the case above illustrates, many children and parents need to be educated to accept referral for analysis following a preparatory stage of tutoring. If there has been strong resistance on the part of parents and child this is no easy task. Through the experiences shared in the tutorial, the tutor attempts to help them recognize another approach is needed to reach the source of the problem, of which the cognitive area is a single aspect. It is not logic that determines acceptance of treatment, but the child's emotional attachment to the tutor.

Sometimes further intervention is unnecessary. Where the timing and special circumstances of the tutorial are critical and its effect on the neurotic equilibrium is far reaching, at times no additional treatment is indicated. As the child gains in ego strengths, and cognitive deficits lessen, nonintellective areas are drawn along with the upward momentum of development. As by-products of the tutorial, and without direct confrontation of underlying material, the child may stop bed-wetting, cope more adequately with aggression and anxiety, and begin to deal symbolically and openly with reality problems instead of acting them out.

Often, opening a structured pathway of communication for a child, involving the flexible give and take inherent in the tutorial exchange, is precisely the emotional ingredient necessary to bring the child's potential strengths into operation. The lessons provide a facade or entryway for natural dynamic processes and self-balancing defenses to work at the service of the ego. The child identifies with the way the tutor looks at his problems. Parents also share in this process. Often this leads to a diminution of anxiety in the whole family picture and consequent improved relationships.

Although tutoring and the dynamics of the relationship may lead to these ego strengthenings, so that no further therapy is immediately indicated, basic conflicts may not be resolved. However, the child has gained a way of confronting difficulties, sometimes even a way of thinking, which serves him in good stead in later years. Individuals often graduate from a successful tutorial in childhood or adolescence into analytic help when the vicissitudes of life give rise to fresh tasks.

Tutoring children with neurotic learning dysfunctions must take account of the obstacles that keep them from learning. The tutor finds a way around the obstacles using conflict-free or acceptable channels. In time, the learning inhibition may shift and the defensive structure find realignment in a less pernicious and costly manner.

THE ORGANIC LEARNING DISABILITY

A REMEDIAL OVERVIEW

The organic child may also have neurotic components in his learning pattern. Teaching the organic child is not a question of removing or bypassing obstacles, but of adding pathways for intellectual and cognitive growth. The impoverished soil must be enriched with an infusion of nutrients.

However, basic tutorial technique is the same. The basic method of flexibility and openness applies to all learning impediments—emotional, neurological, or developmental, and is adapted to individual differences.

The organic child presents special challenges to the tutor. He must constantly and accurately measure the child's progress. Often, standardized tests are of limited value for this purpose. Tests with timed norms to measure academic achievement are limited in worth and may be misleading, for they have been validated with general populations. The development, learning outcome, and general prospects for organic children are often a wait-and-see proposition. The child's response to the tutoring is fundamental to such evaluation.

The limiting factors of the organic child's disability would seem more compelling than his growth prospects. But this is not always the case. The possibility for cognitive development in surprising directions is always present, and is encountered frequently. When this does occurs, the original ego deficits are so well covered it is sometime difficult to remember the basic flaw still exists.

A "HUB" TO TURN A "LEARNING WHEEL"

A nine-and-a-half-year-old boy had an IQ in the 75–80 range. With his tutor's encouragement the boy began to develop an interest in airports far beyond his grasp of other concepts. This interest had its origin among his earliest memories of saying good-bye at the airport terminal to his parents who traveled a good deal. This interest provided a hub of meaning around which a series of activities could revolve. It began with a rounded length of cardboard on which the child lettered "TOWER AIRPORT." Bit by bit a model was constructed—hangars, ticket counters, and a control tower—out of cardboard and magazine pictures. He also needed a toy store, a toilet, a restaurant, roads with signs, and a gasoline station. Over a period of a year, each day's activity was written down on a typewriter and was read back the next day. This established a considerable sight vocabulary.

This child had never accomplished learning numbers in their correct sequence. He could not count at all past ten. All the numbers after ten jumbled in confusion. He had difficulty sorting out whole and part processes, and organizing sequences of syllables and letters. Spatial orientation—left-right, up-down—was a major difficulty for him, and there were delays in various orders of skills and concepts. He had difficulty telling days of the week, months of the year, and clock time.

The airport became a revolving point for instruction. He began to count correctly in the following way. Playing the airport controller, he would say, "Airplane number one, come in, please." The tutor would reply, "Airplane number one, coming in." When the child made an error in sequence, the tutor would get on the radio and call the control tower, saying, for example, "This is number twelve. I'm supposed to come next." The child might then say, "Oh, I'm sorry, number twelve. You can come in now." Sometimes roles were exchanged. Arithmetic fundamentals became among this child's strongest skills. Over time he gained all the multiplication combinations ahead of most children in a normal class setting. Cognition is greatly enhanced when interwoven with emotional sources. Affective ties are just as powerful in organically impaired children as in normal children. Readiness and timing, as well as knowledge of the child's inner life, are essential to make use of such opportunities. This is one of the great advantages tutoring has over the average classroom situation.

REMEDIATING SPECIFIC DEFICIENCIES

The organic child calls for unusual and individualized strategies. He perceives the world with atypical orientations; workbooks and texts may be meaningless to him. Other instruction aids must be utilized.

For example, the tutor might go up and down in an elevator with the child pushing floor buttons and counting out responses to establish sensory-motor connections for number sequences. A six-year-old organic child for whom a rocket had a affective impact learned to sequence forward and backward using the rocket-launch countdown. Again, the tutor's sense of the child's total psychological field made it possible to capitalize on oblique but certain indicators of the child's own remediation. In a sense, each case of organic disability possesses an airport or a rocket, or, if not a *camino real,* perhaps a clear pathway to further development.

Organic cases often involve confusion of body coordination, left-right differentiation, and spatial orientation. Such difficulties are of fateful consequence in gaining academic skills. Persisting into the early grades, they are formidable roadblocks even to a child with superior intelligence. The child can become bewildered and discouraged. When such children add a column of figures, if the sum of the units column is 21, for instance, the child will invariably carry the 1 into the 10's column.

(Children with patterns of compulsive doubting may have similar difficulty.)

This particular "movement" in adding, mentally manipulating spatial elements, is opposite to the direction the child takes in reading. Organic children are vulnerable to perseverating this reading direction or the earlier, simpler pattern. In adding, the sum never exceeds the teens; they then learn always to carry 1, even though the column adds to 21 or 31. Such a child may persist in the error because he can do it "quicker" or simply because he wants to do it his way.

One finds similar patterns in children who are free of any neurological defects. The environment, in the home or through educational or social disruption, can impose barriers as formidable as perceptual-motor impairments. A young adolescent went from school to school without being able to establish the continuity of skills a good learning foundation requires. Whenever the school authority pointed out the youngster's severe underachievement and its underlying emotional basis, his mother would withdraw him and find another school. After so many changes and manipulations, the youngster was unable to find a rallying point to reverse his deeply ingrained arithmetic difficulty, which virtually aped the patterns in severe developmental lags.

For this child, the learning difficulty was a symptom of his problem; for the organic child, the deficit *is* his problem. For both children, the tutor's goal is to encourage cognition and development. His task, like the therapist's in many instances, is ego building. The tutor's function is to find an effective technique to open up and bring in the world.

ASSETS OF THE CHILD WITH EGO DEFICITS

The organic child brings an unusual and appealing asset to the tutoring experience. He is generally more open to help because his need is felt and conscious. If problems of anxiety and attention are overcome, the child may come with positive, almost eager, attitudes. He may understand his deficiency and his needs, although these have not always been verbalized. At some point, the child's atypical development, his difference, must be taken up openly with him in coordinated consultation with the parents. Otherwise, the impairment assumes a secret coloration with all its consequent overtones. The child is usually content to understand that he learns in a different way and has a different learning timetable than other children.

The child's willingness and interest, seized at a propitious time and reinforced by his desire to please, are enormous assets. The tutor is often rewarded by startling outcomes despite the physiological limits in the child's perception and intelligence. Children with learning deficits arising from environmental understimulation respond with similar receptivity.

Neurotic and schizophrenic children present complex and obscure connections between their inner life and their attempts to know and master. The tutor is cogently aware of crucially balanced defenses intervening in the learning process. The organic child, on the other hand, is often refreshingly uncomplicated and transparent. He senses the tutor as a benign ally and is glad to enlist him. Tutoring presents a fresh opportunity for him, and he is eager and cooperative. Narcissistic returns from such experiences are vital to the child and often are missing in his interaction with parents. The original narcissistic wound the parents suffered often tinges their relationship to the child in a way that denies an easy, accepting interaction. They may not truly enjoy their damaged child. The professional distance in the tutorial often provides a partial compensation, and provides the parents with a model for responding to the child and appreciating him.

IMPULSE CONTROL AND LEARNING

While the organic child has the assets of a readiness to be taught, is free of conflict, and almost intuitively senses his ego starvation, these children also may be quite unpredictable, because of their struggles with impulse control. The tutor should make the limits quite clear to the child: "You cannot hurt me, or yourself, or anything we use here for our work." The relationship with the tutor forms a channeling restraint. Goal-directed, productive activity also may neutralize energy otherwise frustratingly confined and impulsively discharged. The child may adopt a passive and obstinate reaction to the learning task. In time, this attitude can be deflected by mutually deciding on an acceptable activity or by exerting a patient, optimal demand on him.

Uncontrollable behavior outside the tutorial session is another matter. The child will often turn to the tutor for help by talking about his temper. Referral for medication or further psychiatric consultation take place at this stage. Teaching the child to deal acceptably with his impulses is a precondition for the growth of cognitive skills. For the organic child, his ability to learn anything represents a sense of mastery and control. The tutor, therefore, has an especially germane function in impulse control, a task he shares with the psychotherapist.

The child himself can give the tutor the image and metaphors to make the notion of controls and acceptable behavior concrete. A thirteen-year-old provided the tutor with such a hint that was profitably exploited. When this youngster lost his temper, and manically used provocative language and gestures, and destroyed objects, he said he found it hard to "cool down." He knew what a thermostat was on an air conditioner and on his house furnace. The idea of self-control was presented to him as an inner thermostat in his own mind, which he might be able to regulate. This idea also helped him accept medication more willingly, and there was a marked change in the frequency and duration of his temper outbursts. He needed a specific mental image, tied to prior experience, to afford a measure of autonomy over his impulses rather than extrinsic restraint. The image of the thermostat took—the child imbued it with relevance and meaning—after it had been discussed in the tutorial hour. He was able to internalize the concept based on his identification with the tutor and out of his need for inner regulation.

Such children are inordinately vulnerable to threat or what they imagine to be threatening. They need delicate, gentle, and understanding external controls. A single sign of impatience or irritation is interpreted as a signal of aggression or hostility. Any out of the ordinary interchange with the tutor may be distorted and misread as anger. As far as possible, the relationship should be maintained positively. However, a significant objective of the work is to gradually enable the child to tolerate and cope with limits and to help him understand that criticism does not mean rejection or lack of love. The tutor's attitude and tone reflect the genuine relationship. If the child senses the tutor's basic protectiveness, he will be able to take realistic appraisals of his behavior without sensing them as threats.

LETTING STRUCTURE FIT THE CHILD

Generally, organic children require a firm structure to provide concretization in dimensions of time, space, and objects to shore up infirm organizational capability. Limits and structure offer protectiveness and safety for such children.

A uniquely optimal structure will evolve out of a dialogue with the child. Finding a common ground is determined by alert appreciation of what learner and teacher bring to one another and by the subtleties of communication, especially in picking up cues.

Many of these points may be borne out in the case of an eight-year-old, mildly organic boy. He had good intelligence, and while he seemed to thrive in a tutorial regime, he was inattentive in school, dawdled over his work, and seldom completed it. His teacher was sometimes in a struggle over his seeming recalcitrance. However, the boy was so charming and innocent, he convinced his teacher there was no malice in not doing her assignments; he just couldn't organize them.

In the tutoring session, work was divided into digestible and apprehendable units, but he could not accomplish this in a group. He could start, but was soon sidetracked. In consultation with the classroom teacher and the school psychologist, the tutor suggested the boy be allowed to organize his time, work with a stopwatch, and provide his own direction. At the same time, his mother gave him a daily assignment book and a diary.

A sharp, positive change took place immediately. He worked diligently, with concentration, and even somewhat compulsively. His academic skills began to show significant growth. The stopwatch served to focus his attention and filtered out distractions. It was his self-regulator as he functioned with the tutor. The stopwatch made time into concrete, circumscribed, observable, physical units, and he was able to adapt it to serve a function his ego was unable to do unaided. Also, this youngster needed some special dispensation, something quite different, which could be openly discerned by the other children, because in fact he did learn differently. The stopwatch, a special privilege, was a concrete acknowledgment of that difference.

Later, at an appropriate stage, he gave up the stopwatch as more abstract internalizations replaced it. The stopwatch was absorbed, and its effect was irreversible. However, for another child, with a similar pattern of distractability, the stopwatch did not fit at all. For that child, the issue was on smaller goals, and more limited demands.

SPECIAL TUTORIAL METHODS FOR SPECIAL NEEDS

Organic children require atypical methods. A seemingly idiosyncratic device may be the fitting and comfortable one. The most effective educators seize creative moments and do not hesitate to improvise. Also, they must be careful attempting to dislodge a learning pattern an organic child has adopted. It may actually be accomplishing something vital for the child. It may appear as a regressive, infantile learning habit, like mouthing words while reading. In fact, these children need to move their lips or subvocalize, because their learning stages differ from the normal child's. They require a long intermediate stage to fix reading skills. They internalize the words in an attempt to hold and imprint meaning before it falls through their grasp without registering meaning. They also internalize the person who reads to them, teaches, directs, makes things plain, and opens the world. Therefore, attempting to make the child not say the words to himself, or keep his lips still while he reads, may operate virtually as a too-early weaning. The danger of reinforcing baby habits by allowing the vocalizing to persist is really quite minimal. The greater danger is that the child's frustration will be carried to hopelessness or rage in wanting to deny and cover up his difficulty in comprehending the material. The child's method, if he is making an effort to learn, is really the best.

Uncovering a suitable method is the product of an open and bold inventiveness. This combines some intuition informing an improvisational readiness. As in analysis, the child is given the lead as much as possible. The tutor can then appreciate and give weight to the dynamic factors within the instructional field. For example, the child will invariably give some cue to the tutor about wanting knowledge about sex, no matter what his level of understanding. If the six-year-old wants to know about "streaking" and the implication of danger to exposed body organs, he is asking for congruence and integration of his hypotheses, anxiety, and cognition. The tutor can deal with this curiosity at an instructional level, and be aware of its many psychological reverberations. For this reason, understanding with clarity, and in small doses, is the rule.

THE PARENTS' ROLE

The tutor must bear in mind that his intervention in the child's life, however significant it may be and whatever displacement it engenders, is temporary. This especially applies to cases where the child suddenly becomes productive after a period of obstinacy and struggle with the parents. Often the child had prolonged his deficits as to counter what he had felt as pressure and rejection, or had been clinging anxiously to receive his parents' reassurance. The child's response to the tutor may be felt by the parents as yet another blow to their already damaged narcissism. If possible, parents can be made to feel some investment of their own in the remedial process. This is true even if their contribution is to wait patiently on the sidelines and tolerate an unaccustomed noninvolvement in the child's schoolwork. The parents may actually want the remedial effort to fail to justify what they unconsciously feel is their own failure.

Parents and children, too, thrive best when the tutorial is carried on in an atmosphere of hopeful expectation. No promises or false hopes are given (although the parents may hear them anyway). However, any modicum of progress is met with shared gratification as a shared enterprise. Parents must be fed to enrich the child as well.

Some parents (usually the mother) have never been able to deal with the narcissistic injury the child's deficits signify in their unconscious. They therefore deny the child's severe organic limitations. On the other hand, children will be seen who, whatever other anomalies are present, are not mentally deficient, but whose parents (again, usually the mother) fear that this is what is wrong. (Fathers tend, more through denial than objective judgment, to correctly rule out retardation.)

In these situations, the tutor has a unique opportunity through his relatively early involvement, distance, and neutrality to provide parents with an optimal attitude consonant with each child's givens. The ideal attitude leads to an alliance with parents and children, fostering two-way identifications. The parents identify partially with the tutor's benignly realistic attitude toward the child's ego deficit.

Consideration of parents' needs can be made without violating the integrity of the special relationship between tutor and child. Parents feel as bewildered and helpless in the face of their child's learning disability, as they do when they enlist psychiatric help.

It is indispensible to the child's progress that an optimal distance be established for the parents' involvment in the learning process. The optimal distance varies with the particular circumstances. Sometimes it is necessary to wean the mother away from the child. For example, one mother implanted herself immediately outside the tutor's door at each session, and tried to catch stray words. Such a separation problem cannot be circumvented and must be dealt with through parent consultation.

The mother can sometimes become a significant element in the instructional field, as in the case of the child who left the tutorial session to ask his mother his birthdate and for similar information.

For depressed mothers, the tutoring experience may heal a part of that vital responsiveness, which the original narcissistic injury had contaminated. Something lost may be recovered.

Compulsive, highly functioning, ambitious fathers must deal with problems in their relationship with their sons, particularly sons who have cognitive deficits. Their spontaneity is lacking, and in its place is a simulated father-son interaction, characterized by caution and guardedness, a kind of reactive encapsulation of the wound. The relationship is cerebral, and lacks naturalness and ease. These fathers long for instruction about how to be less studied, less histrionically tense.

Sometimes the tutor can accomplish this through teaching by example. The tutor's criteria and posture toward the child's productions may become acceptable standards of achievement for these fathers. In this manner, they may allow themselves some measure of parental gratification. Respect for and identification with the tutor enhances this process.

ONE-TO-ONE, A LEARNING ENVIRONMENT

Cues for exploiting workable methods in tutoring cannot be programmed or planned but must be picked up when they happen. As in the therapeutic hour, nothing that happens is without significance, and nothing is thrown away haphazardly. Information is transmuted for learning — recycled to serve ego functions. What happens in tutoring is not random talk or activity in the sense of free association or play therapy. There is a circumscribed structure, a boundary, running from session to session, which the tutor fosters through a shared sense of instructional goals.

Spontaneity is a highly valued part of tutoring technique. The relationship should be formed through shared interests carried out on a common ground. Even the tedious and frustrating aspects of this activity will be most productive when conducted in a loving, accepting attitude. The learning activities may vary widely. They may lead to gardening, nature study, carpentry, electronics, model making, playwriting, poetry, or sculpture.

Somewhere short of the bizarre fantasies of children with ego deficits, and beyond the prosaic limitations of repetitive learning tasks, is a rich area open to discovery. True joy is experienced by a child who makes something, retains it in memory, and returns to find it physically confirming his mental picture. Children need to develop *idea constancy,* for too often the concepts they form do not have the enrichment of interlocking associations. Often they will begin their session making a beeline for the rocket, the ballerina, or the book of stories. These things have become emotionally invested, true mental objects. They have become constants to be counted on, they will not drain away as so often happens in their tangential experiences. Such objects are outgrowths of the child's unique structure; they are the child's true possessions.

In such a multimodal approach, with consideration for the dynamic processes, tutoring may make a significant impact in fostering ego functions. When the sessions involve continuity and importance, a clear and special learning environment will emerge. The session is a universe of experience the child claims for himself. Sessions with the tutor have an individual stamp, quality, and texture. The child experiences it as belonging to him, for in a sense, he has gained and achieved it for himself. It self-primes, stimulates and motivates more and more learning.

REFERENCES

Berlin, I.N., and Szurek, S. A., eds. (1965). *Learning and Its Disorders.* Palo Alto: Science and Behavior Books.

Bruner, J. S. (1966). *Toward a Theory of Instruction.* Cambridge, Mass.: Harvard University Press.

────── (1973). *Beyond the Information Given.* New York: W. W. Norton.

Clark, D. H., and Lesser, D. S., ed. (1965). *Emotional Disturbance and School Learning.* Chicago: Science Research Associates.

Cruickshank, W. M., and Hallahan, D. P., eds. (1975). *Perceptual and Learning Disabilities in Children.* Syracuse, N.Y.: Syracuse University Press.

de Hirsch, K. (1975). Language deficits in children with developmental lags. *Psychoanalytic Study of the Child* 30:95–126.

Ekstein, R., and Motto, R. L., ed. (1969). *From Learning for Love to Love of Learning.* New York: Brunner/Mazel.

Freud, A. (1936). *The Ego and the Mechanisms of Defense.* New York: International Universities Press, 1966.

Hagin, R., and Silber, A. (1977). Learning disability: definition, diagnosis, and prevention. *New York University Education Quarterly* 8: 2:9–15.

Hellmuth, J., ed. (1970, 1971). *Cognitive Studies: Volumes 1 and 2.* New York: Brunner/Mazel.

Kris, E. (1948). On psychoanalysis and education. *American Journal of Orthopsychiatry* 18: 622–635.

Johnson, D. J., and Myklebust, H. R. (1967). *Learning Disabilities; Educational Principles and Practices.* New York: Grune and Stratton.

Lerner, J. W. (1976). *Children with Learning Disabilities.* Boston: Houghton, Mifflin.

Rosner, J. (1975). *Helping Children Overcome Learning Difficulties.* New York: Walker.

Ross, A. O. (1976). *Psychological Aspects of Learning Disabilities and Reading Disorders.* New York: McGraw-Hill.

Sapir, S. G., and Nitzburg, A. C., eds. (1973). *Children with Learning Problems.* New York: Brunner/Mazel.

Weil, A. P. (1977). Learning disturbances: with special consideration of dyslexia. *Issues in Child Mental Health* 5:52–56.

Chapter 19

THE NURSERY SCHOOL AS AN ACCOMPANIMENT

TO PSYCHOANALYSIS

Elizabeth Daunton

FREUD'S THEORIES OF CHILD DEVELOPMENT

Freud, by charting the course of infantile sexual development (1905), illuminated the inner life of the young child. His observations and creative insights led him to trace sequentially the ways in which, from infancy, the child seeks drive satisfaction from his parents and his own body, according to his phase of libidinal development (oral, anal, phallic).

In the first decade of the century Freud's writings had important implications for parents and educators. In several papers (1907, 1908a, 1908b, 1909) he illustrated the vicissitudes of the libidinal drive and suggested ways in which these affected a child's ability to learn. In his introduction to "The Analysis of a Phobia in a Five-Year-Old Boy" (1909), Freud used a father's sensitive observations of his son to illustrate the component drive of curiosity, and the child's need to have his questions understood and answered by his parents. Freud concluded, from these and other observations, that the young child seeks answers to sexual questions not only to gratify himself and to reduce anxiety, but also to strengthen his sense of identity, and to increase his understanding of himself and his world. Freud therefore stressed the need for parents and educators to help young children by answering their questions truthfully and understandably.

Freud ended his discussion of the case of Little Hans by considering some general principles of education. "Hitherto education has only set itself the task of controlling, or, it would be more proper to say, of suppressing the instincts. The results have been by no means gratifying . . . Nor has anyone enquired by what means and at what cost the suppression of the inconvenient instincts has been achieved. Supposing now that we substitute another task for this one, and aim instead at making the individual capable of becoming a civilized and useful member of society with the least possible sacrifice of his own activity . . ." (p 146).[1]

The relationship of the libidinal drive to the process of sublimation was recognized by Freud as most significant for learning. He noted that historians of civilization had customarily regarded cultural achievements as "a diversion of sexual instinctual forces from sexual aims and their direction to new ones—a process which deserves the name of 'sublimation' " (1905, p. 178). Freud's unique contribution was to relate this same process to the development of the individual. At this time he saw the process of sublimation as beginning in the period of sexual latency of childhood. Subsequently (1908a), Freud again stressed the connection between the reaction formations of early latency and the process of sublimation. However, there was also a suggestion that the process begins at an earlier stage.[2]

In his study of Leonardo da Vinci (1910), Freud traced the sublimated "instinct for research" (p. 74), developed to an extraordinary degree in this man of genius, to its origins in the sexual curiosity of the phallic phase. Freud traced and compared most meaningfully three vicissitudes of the instinct which might follow "the wave of energetic sexual repression" (p. 79); neurotic inhibition, sexualization of thinking, and sublimation. According to the outcome of the process of repression, Freud suggested, a person's ability to think freely could be affected for a life time.

NEW APPROACHES TO THE EDUCATION OF
THE YOUNG CHILD

For educational theorists and teachers this period, too, was one of increased awareness of the child's curiosity and his ability to learn through active participation. Among creative educators, John Dewey (1902) and Maria Montessori (1909) were preeminent. While differing in some respects about educational principles and practice, both stressed that the child is only motivated to learn when the material is meaningfully related to his own experience—in the case of the young child, his experience as a member of a family.[3]

The preschool child's capacity for learning and social development was increasingly recognized by those who saw the process of learning as a continuum. In Montessori's work, first with retarded children and subsequently in the "Children's Houses" of Rome and Milan, she studied and trained her teachers to observe how the young child used his sensory apparatus, speech, and motility for learning and problem solving. The program was worked out both to meet the child's active interest in learning from two-and-a-half until entry into public school, and to help the parents support this interest.

These educators were not concerned with the sexual aspects of the young child's curiosity. However, they did stress that free curiosity is essential to productive learning. While Freud clarified the ways in which internal processes can inhibit learning, Dewey and Montessori drew attention to external interferences which stemmed from some traditional teaching methods, such as enforced passivity in the classroom, inappropriate material, and mass instruction.[4]

Before and during World War I, Montessori's educational theories and methods stirred much interest in Europe and the United States.[5] A charming letter written by Freud in 1917 to Maria Montessori showed that members of the analytic group in Vienna shared this interest. Plans had been made by Frau Schaxel to establish an institute in that city. In accepting Montessori's invitation to sign his name in support of an appeal for the foundation of the institute, Freud responded, "Since I have been preoccupied for years with the study of the child's psyche, I am in deep sympathy with your humanitarian and understanding endeavors and my daughter, who is an analytical pedagogue, considers herself one of your disciples" E. Freud (1960, pp. 319–20).

THE DEVELOPMENT OF CHILD ANALYSIS AND ITS RELATIONSHIP TO EDUCATION

The post war era saw the evolution of child analysis and increased opportunities for both the psychoanalytic study of child development and its application to the field of education. Important tasks of this time were to define the role of the child analyst, as it developed from a growing clinical experience, and to provide opportunities for cooperation between educators and analysts.

A review of the psychoanalytic literature of the previous six years published by Hug-Hellmuth (1920) speaks to the interest of psychoanalysts in both fields. The first paper on the technique of child analysis was published the following year (Hug-Hellmuth 1921).

Anna Freud's lectures on the Psychoanalytic Treatment of Children (1927) focused on those factors which were common to adult and child analysis, as well as those which differed because of the child's incomplete development and his dependence on parents and teachers.

In her paper, "Three Great Psychoanalytic Educators" (1969), Buxbaum discusses the significance of the appearance of three major works on psychoanalytic education between the years 1925 and 1930. The works were Bernfeld's *Sisyphus or the Limits of Education* (1925), Aichhorn's *Wayward Youth* (1925) and Anna Freud's *Psychoanalysis for Teachers and Parents* (1930). Buxbaum suggests the stimulus came from Freud's new books *Group Psychology and the Analysis of the Ego* (1921) and the *Ego and the Id* (1923). She draws attention to Freud's explanation of the way the superego and ego ideal are formed in childhood, as well as the way groups are formed by members' identification with the leader.

Various aspects of the child's dependence on the adults in his milieu were recognized; as well, there was increasing interest of teachers in understanding the behavior of children in the classroom. This promoted fruitful interaction between child analysts and teachers in Vienna, lasting until the disruptions of the Anschluss in 1938 (A. Freud 1946, 1974; Furman chapter 5). The value of this cooperation had been officially recognized in 1929 when the school inspectorate of Vienna commissioned Anna Freud to give her series of lectures on *psychoanalysis* to the teachers of the Children's Centers. Subsequently, she held a regular seminar for nursery school teachers with Dorothy Burlingham. The *Zeitschrift fur Psychoanalytische Padogogik,* first published in 1926, provided a forum for child analysts to communicate their clinical findings, and for analytically oriented teachers to share their observations of children in the classroom.

It was during this period that Montessori classes were established in Vienna and provided some of the centers of cooperation between educators and child analysts. While Montessori's stress on motivated activity as a mainspring to learning was fully appreciated, psychoanalytic study of the various developmental phases led to a questioning of some of her theories and adaptation of her methods. In considering Montessori principles and methods, Buxbaum (1932) stresses the importance for learning both of the child's identification with the teacher and the instinctual roots of his interests. She also clarifies the role of fantasy, showing it can help the young child to master reality, particularly the painful reality of his oedipal relationships.[6]

The relationship between child analysis and education was viewed in a different light by Melanie Klein, who also began her work as child analyst in the post war period. While appreciating the influence of the school in the child's development (1923), Klein's main focus of interest was in delineating the analyst's role in contrast to the educator's (1927). This differentiation also aroused keen interest among other members of the British Psychoanalytic Society (Isaacs 1933). Susan Isaacs, already a psychoanalyst when she became director of the Malting House School, was active in transmitting psychoanalytic principles in practical terms to interested parents and teachers (1929).

Burlingham's experience with analytically trained teachers in Vienna made her keenly aware of difficulties they might encounter in the classroom and in their contacts with parents. She also recognized, however, their unusual educational assets. Burlingham concluded her article, "Problems Confronting the Psychoanalytic Educator" (1937) by describing for the first time how teachers could contribute to preparing a child for treatment. They could use their observations to clarify a child's areas of difficulty for both parents and child, and explain how these could be helped by analysis.

In reviewing this period of cooperative work between analysts and educators, Anna Freud noted that "the extensive work done in psychoanalysis applied to education had in time its welcome repercussions on the therapeutic analysis of children" (1946 p. 11). Changes in technique had become possible because of the increased understanding and support among educators. These observations were complemented by those of Hoffer (1945) who noted that changes in psychoanalytic theory had permitted increased cooperation between analysts and teachers. This could proceed more favorably when "psychoanalysis progressed from a psychology of instincts to one of personality" (p. 303) and when use could be made of these newer views on ego and superego development.

Anna Freud (1946) has described the developments in analytic education after 1938. Members of the analytic community, who had been forced to leave Vienna, had continued their work in conjunction with colleagues in Holland, England, and the United States. Nursery schools, based on analytic principles, had been established in Boston, Detroit, and Los Angeles. The directors of the Vienna nursery, now resident in London, had founded the Hampstead nurseries which served the needs of children in war-time.[7] The residential nursery for emotionally disturbed children at Westerham, directed by Ruth Thomas, was based on the same principles.[8] While conditions were unfavorable for analytic treatment of children at this time, research based on daily observation of nursery children continued (Freud and Burlingham 1944a, 1944b). In this context, their observations concerning the relationships formed by the children with their nursery school teachers are of special interest (1944b).

THE COOPERATIVE WORK OF THE CHILD ANALYST AND THE NURSERY SCHOOL TEACHER

In the past thirty years there has been a great impetus in nursery school education in the United States. Stemming from observations and concern for individual children, there has been growing interest and expertise among teachers in understanding normal child development and its deviations. This interest has led to establishing programs in a number of centers in which analysts offer courses in child development, both normal and pathological, as well as provide consultation services for nursery school teachers. Some centers, including the Reiss Davies Study Center, Los Angeles, and the Center for Research in Child Development, Cleveland, have developed curriculum courses for teachers; until recently this had been a relatively neglected field (Ekstein and Motto 1969, Ekstein 1969). During this period a number of therapeutic nursery schools and kindergartens have been established, as well as centers which provided both nursery school education and opportunities for treatment for some students (see chapter 5).

There has been increased recognition during this period of the teacher's contribution in helping a child with tasks of mastery. This has stemmed from a fuller understanding of the lines of development (A. Freud 1965), and of the role of verbalization (A. Katan 1961). When she understands the stages of the child's developmental progress, the teacher can help him more effectively in the areas of separation, peer relationships, bodily functioning, and in meeting new experiences. The young child needs the adult's verbal help in comprehending his outer world, including the events of his daily life, and also his inner feelings. As Katan explains, "verbalization leads to an increase in the controlling function of the ego over affects and drives." Also, "verbalization leads to the integrating process, which in turn results in reality testing" (1961 p. 185). Archer and Hosley (1969) have described the application of these ideas in the classroom. They have also been discussed by Edgecumbe (1975). The teacher's ability to clarify outer reality and inner feelings can contribute positively to a child's ego identifications and superego formation. For example, John, a five-year-old, masked his anxiety by outbursts of excitement in the classroom. At times, when the teacher could see reasons for this, she suggested John had more reason to be worried than excited. As John began to show more ability to recognize and express worries, the teacher would respond to his excitement by asking him to stop and think what was causing his behavior. John showed he had begun to identify with and internalize his teacher's expectations when he could sometimes curb his own excitement and give an explanation of his concerns, such as his father's absence or the illness of his dog.

Where cooperative programs for teachers and child analysts already exist, they pave the way for the particular cooperation which contributes positively to a child's treatment. The settings of a therapeutic nursery school or of a nursery school in a treatment center provide many advantages in this respect.[9] The contribution of the nursery school to assessment and diagnosis has been discussed by A. Katan (1959) and E. Furman (chapter 5). The nursery school's role in treatment through the parent has been described by E. Furman (1957, 1969). The focus here is on the contribution of the teacher in preparing parents and child for the child's analysis, on the ways in which treatment can be supported in the school setting, and on the nature of the cooperation between teacher and therapist during the child's analysis. These topics have been carefully considered by Oppenheimer (1969), whose discussion is based on material from twenty-four analytic cases. Treatment of the child in the classroom setting has been discussed by Kliman (1972) and Ronald and Kliman (1970).

THE CONTRIBUTION OF THE NURSERY SCHOOL–KINDERGARTEN TO PREPARATION FOR TREATMENT

In some instances, family circumstances make it impossible for a child to begin analysis outside the school setting.[10] Among these are cases where for health reasons, transportation problems, or other family commitments, the parents would be unable to bring a child for daily treatment.

Mary, who entered nursery school at age four, had severe arrests in ego functioning and object relationships. When plans for her treatment were being considered, Mary's mother developed a serious illness requiring several hospitalizations. Mary's treatment was postponed until her mother's illness was in remission. Because of the mother's condition, and the travelling distances involved for the family, the analyst went daily to see Mary at the nursery school building. Mary remained an extra year in the kindergarten at this school to continue her treatment.

Addie's mother died when she was nearly four; she was then raised by her grandparents who also had the care of Addie's two younger sisters.[11] The grandparents were warm and effective parental figures. The grandmother took the initiative of seeking treatment for Addie. She was concerned by the child's tendency to stiff necks, disobedience, withdrawal at school, and confusion over her mother's death. Because of the grandparents' health problems and their limited income, it was essential Addie's treatment take place in the day care center. Her treatment began at age five. After her entry to public school, Addie's analyst continued to see her at the center until treatment was completed.

When she has an established relationship with a child and his parents, the teacher can help significantly in a number of ways in the preparation for treatment.

Teacher's work with parents. As Burlingham (1937) and Oppenheimer (1969) have indicated, the teacher may take the initiative in drawing the parents' attention to difficulties in the child which interfere with his development. This is painful for them, because it affects both their parental self-esteem and their own views of the child. However, they may come to terms with the teacher's assessment on the basis of their concern for the child, which they see is shared by the teacher.

Mark, a four-year-old, had a conflictual relationship with his classmates in nursery school. He had good ideas and wanted to include other children in his play. However, he scared and annoyed them by his unpredictable hitting. At home, Mark preferred solitary activities and had few playmates so his difficulties were less obvious to his parents. When his teacher discussed Mark's hitting trouble with them, they were appropriately distressed and understood this as one indication of his need for treatment.

Four-year-old Jim alternately charmed his teachers by his wise sayings and sympathetic comments, and provoked them by his wild excitement and omnipotent expectations. Sharing adult attention was most difficult for Jim. His teachers noticed that while he was creative himself, he related to other children mainly by imitation.

Jim's parents had greatly enjoyed his advanced development. He was the apple of his mother's eye and she had devoted herself wholly to his care. During a very difficult pregnancy in his third year, his mother could not carry out her usual activities with Jim, but spent much time reading to him. The pregnancy ended tragically when his mother gave birth prematurely to a baby who died soon after. Previously the mother had kept close verbal contact with Jim. In her distress, she had been unable to discuss the death of the baby with him meaningfully. Later, with help from a therapist, she was able to do so.

During Jim's first months in school, it was noticed his mother helped him with controls by requests and suggestions, rather than by increased expectations of him. Jim was therefore very dependent on his mother for controls. His father tended to be more impulsive with his son; he could be easygoing or at times severe.

It was especially hard for this mother to share her son's upbringing with others. Initially, she saw his difficulties as due to his teacher's unreal expectations of him, or the influence of other children. A number of visits made by both parents to the classroom, and the opportunity to discuss their doubts with both therapist and teachers, helped convince them Jim's difficulties were his own, and seriously interfered with his development. Jim began analysis a year before entering elementary school where he made a good adjustment.

When parents are already concerned about their child's problems, the teacher may be able to clarify or confirm his difficulties from her own observations, and support the parents in seeking treatment for the child.

Jenny, who was nearly five when she entered school, could be a warm and friendly child. However, she reacted to inner conflicts and outer frustrations with rages. She berated her parents and playmates, and could not listen to reason or accept help in gaining control. She warded off superego conflicts by externalization—the other person was always to blame. It was not long before Jenny's difficulties became obvious to both teachers and classmates. Her mother was relieved to have her own recognition of Jenny's troubles supported by the teachers. Previously, she had felt frustrated by her pediatrician's reassuring response when she had discussed the child's difficult behavior with him. Subsequently, Jenny's parents took the initiative in seeking analysis for her.

Peter was a boy who had suffered many losses. The most painful had occurred when he was one-and-a-half: at this time, his father decided to leave the family and live in another city. His teacher noted that Peter, at age five, was a boy with low self-esteem, easily upset by failure, and seemed to suppress anger when corrected. She further observed he was developing an armored attitude of, "I don't care," to protect himself from feelings. In a conference the teacher shared her observations with Peter's mother who said she also had noticed, with growing concern, the same difficulties in Peter at home. These observations shared by teacher and parent contributed to the mother's decision to obtain treatment for her son.

The teachers were helpful to the mother in another respect. Peter was to have treatment with a different therapist from the one who had previously worked with her. This involved a difficult change for the mother. She found it hard to express anger about the change to either therapist, but showed it in an unusual disregard of school policy. The teachers recognized the transition must be difficult and helped his mother explain to Peter that her upset feelings related to the separation and were not caused by disappointment in him.

The teacher's work with the child. The teacher can enhance the self-perceiving function of the child in two ways especially. She can help him become more aware of difficulties so they become less ego syntonic. This may require she understand some of his defenses. The teacher can also appreciate the child's strengths and increase his own pleasure in them.

In Mark's case, his teacher recognized his wish to make friends and his good ideas in play. She pointed out his hitting trouble prevented other children from enjoying his ideas and wishing to play with him. As a result, Mark became more aware and unhappy about not being able to control his hitting. When his mother then explained treatment could help him with this trouble, Mark listened intently and appeared relieved.

As the teachers questioned the way Jenny blamed them or her classmates when she was unhappy, Jenny became more embarrassed by her outbursts. Her classmates were also helpfully candid in their disapproval of her rages. Jenny became interested in a classmate who was in treatment and told her mother she wished she had someone to talk with. When her mother asked whether there was something she especially wanted help with, Jenny replied sadly, "It's my school troubles."

Peter, on the other hand, felt acutely anxious, rather than relieved, at the suggestion of treatment. After his mother had shared with him her wish he would have help with the many hurt feelings hidden behind his "I don't care" talk, Peter began to complain of stomach aches before coming to school. He seemed embarrassed by his contacts with teachers, as though he felt he had such terrible problems extreme measures had to be taken.

Following a discussion with the therapist, his teacher clarified that having treatment did not mean he had trouble learning or managing in school; he was doing well. His troubles came from his sad feelings about his father, and from not feeling good about himself as a person. Some days later, Peter had difficulty separating from his mother at school. After she left, his affect seemed to change and he walked about with a transparent grin. One day he drew his teacher's attention to this, asking if he did not look like "the happiest little boy you have ever seen?" His teacher replied she thought he was trying very hard to look happy on the outside, but she also thought he must be feeling quite different on the inside.

In the week before treatment began, Peter acknowledged his anxiety and used his teacher's help in mastery. Noticing he was greatly preoccupied at lunch time, his teacher asked Peter what he was thinking about. He got up and whispered to her, "tell the kids I'll be talking with Mrs. M. about my unhappy troubles, and I don't like it, and I want my mommy to come with me."

THE NURSERY SCHOOL'S SUPPORT OF PARENTS DURING THE CHILD'S TREATMENT

A young child with difficulties severe enough to warrant analysis often taxes his parents' funds of emotional and physical energy. The child's attendance in school not only provides respite for the parent and a chance to recoup these energies, but the opportunity, with the teacher's help, to view the child differently in a more objective setting. This distancing can promote both a more empathic and a more realistic relationship with the child.

The teacher's interest and concern about family experiences as they affect both parents and child can be of great support. Those who work with young children become keenly aware of the frequent crises, and difficult and painful life situations with which children and their parents are faced. During the course of a child's analysis, parents and child may have to contend with family illness, divorce, bereavement, financial crises, or a combination of these. Any of these experiences can impose almost overwhelming burdens on parents. For most, it is a relief both to have their own concerns appreciated by the teachers, and to know the child's concerns will be understood and recognized. There are, however, times when the parents' preoccupation, guilt, and tendency to deny or isolate make them unaware of the impact of family events on their child. Then it is often the child who lets the teacher know of these events and conveys the way they affect him.

The teacher's shared observations bring to parents aspects of their child's behavior of which they had been unaware. Sometimes these may refer to the mastery of a skill or a new developmental step. At other times, there will be concern with aspects of the child's behavior which reflect interferences with his functioning. The parents may be unaware of these because home and school make different demands on the child, or because previously they had been able to deny the child's difficulties or to regard them as unimportant. In either case, the teacher presents the child to the parents in a more realistic light, and aspects of his personality which would have remained isolated from their thinking become more available in their work with the child's analyst.

Tom had attended nursery school for seven months before beginning analysis at age four-and-a-half. He had many hospitalizations during his first two years caused by asthma and other respiratory problems. Currently, his asthma often caused interrupted sleep for himself and his parents, and during the day his demanding and withholding behavior often led to friction between him and his mother. The father was supportive of his wife and son, but family pressures were increased by the demands of his work which involved regular trips away from home.

It was a relief and support for the mother to be able to share her concerns and frustration with the teachers about Tom's asthma and his difficult behavior. They could confirm he was provocative at times from their own experience. By discussing their own observations with the mother, they could help her be more aware of connections between some of Tom's coughing and wheezing spells, and his missing affects. For instance, his spells seemed to occur in school when Tom spoke of his father going out of town, when he had to take part in an activity he disliked, or when he was unable to hold his own with another child.

The teachers recognized with the parents that in many areas such as imaginative play, problem solving, and verbal skills, Tom functioned exceptionally well. They could also point out he could not make full use of his skills because his rigidity, and his need to dominate and exclude interfered with his relationships. Tom's eating restriction and fears of water were more apparent at school than at home.

The mother became pregnant shortly before Tom's analysis began. She had a most worrying, difficult pregnancy with a serious possibility of miscarriage. She had to enter the hospital at short notice in her fifth and seventh months. The teachers continued to give support to both parents. Since it would have been impossible for the parents to consistently bring Tom to his treatment appointments, a teacher brought him throughout his stay at nursery school. While the parents were aware of some of Tom's concerns at this time, others were overlooked or denied. A teacher learned Tom had seen his mother bleeding and brought this to her attention so she could discuss it with him.

WAYS IN WHICH THE NURSERY SCHOOL HELPS
THE CHILD DURING TREATMENT

The prelatency child needs the support of open communication and agreement on educational goals between parent and analyst to integrate his experience (Buxbaum 1954, Oppenheimer 1969). A period of preliminary work with the parents of young children is therefore often crucial for treatment. This process of integration is also helped when the teacher understands the analytic goals, and the child's reactions to treatment, and when there is agreement between teacher and analyst concerning educational aims.

The main areas in which a teacher can help the child in treatment are in providing a climate of support, in promoting sublimations, in holding up realistic expectations, and showing the child how to meet them. These expectations refer to all aspects of ego functioning, including the acquisition of inner controls and relating to adults and peers. The teacher helps the child to be aware of his changing capacities in these areas. In many cases, there are opportunities for the teacher to show the child how restrictions or inhibitions, which are apparent in school, cause him to lose out in pleasure and mastery.

It is helpful to all nursery school children when teachers are informed about the reality events of their life and in tune with their feelings. A child's treatment is one of these realities. A familiar teacher can be most supportive when a child is faced with anxiety at the beginning of treatment, during absences of the therapist, or when conflicts experienced in the treatment are shown in the classroom. At times the teacher may merely observe this behavior; at others she may respond verbally. When his behavior constitutes an interference for the child or his classmates, she can help him distinguish between the classroom and treatment situations.

The teacher's recognition of conflict and adjustment to treatment. Tom's therapist had an office in a different building from his nursery school. Initially, Tom showed his fear of his therapist by procrastination, and dawdling in dressing to leave school for his appointment. The teacher who accompanied him sympathetically suggested his slowness showed his worry about treatment. Gradually, Tom could admit this instead of dawdling. At the same time, the content of his fears became apparent in treatment. He was afraid he would be physically overwhelmed, and made to stay in the therapist's office, as he had been earlier when he was confined in the hospital.

Peter's analyst had phoned his teacher to say she would not be able to keep her appointment with Peter. She arranged to come later in the morning. The teacher noted Peter turned "purple with anger" when she told him about the change, but he smiled and tried to say it was all right. A few weeks after Peter began treatment, his teacher observed "several times Peter has commented on another child's behavior or feelings in such a way that one recognizes his analytic experience." For example, when Anne was frantically asking questions at lunch Peter said, "I guess she's worried about that trip her father and mother are going to take."

Steven's mother died suddenly three months before he entered nursery school at age four. During his analysis, his father, at the therapist's suggestion, discussed the circumstances of the mother's death with his son. The father let the teachers know about his talk with Steven. They noticed a change in Steven's behavior at school. Previously rather quiet, he now repeatedly asked them "why?" about many aspects of school life and was not satisfied with the answers. The teachers shared this observation with Steven's therapist. When, through the analytic work, Steven began to integrate his painful feelings about his mother's death, his pressing "why" questions ceased in the classroom.

Help with sublimations and mastery of tasks. Without treatment, some children cannot learn, play, or engage in other sublimated activities because insufficient neutralized energy is available. In these cases, an important aim of treatment is to free this energy. When this can be accomplished, it is of utmost value that teachers can help the child to channel the freed energy and to take the necessary steps in active mastery of tasks.

When Roger came to nursery school at age four he could sometimes talk meaningfully with a teacher; at other times he talked indistinctly, whispered, or became lost in fantasy. Roger could not use teacher help in learning a task, share his teachers with other children, or enjoy their company. His chosen companion was a teddy bear. Sometimes Roger mothered his bear, at others it was a source of excitement for him. When Roger came without his bear, he spent long periods inert on the floor and was often unable to respond to the teacher's approaches.

Roger was his parents' first child; his mother felt conflicted between the demands made on her by the baby and by her husband who was beginning a new career. There were several changes of home during Roger's first one and a half years, and his mother continued to work part-time until he was three and a half. She had felt Roger was unresponsive as a baby, in contrast to her second son, who was born when Roger was two. Roger had not yet begun to talk; it seemed speech had not been sufficiently libidinized by the mother. After his brother's birth, Roger had frequent tantrums and regressed in his precariously gained toilet training. When his brother could walk, Roger frequently hit him and imitated him in many ways. When Roger began nursery school, his mother was again pregnant. She rested frequently, and because she felt so frustrated in her relationship with Roger, she became more withdrawn from him.

In the early weeks of treatment, begun when Roger was four and a half, his analyst verbalized his sad and angry feelings about his mother's pregnancy and his sister's birth, which recalled earlier painful separations from mother. The analyst also interpreted his defensive identifications with his brother by regression, and with his mother in her passivity and withdrawal, as ways of warding off his feelings.

Within several weeks his teachers noticed changes in Roger which enabled them to relate to him differently, and to help him move forward in several areas, especially sublimation. The most basic changes were an increased activity, a wish and ability to communicate verbally, and more tolerance of frustration. One of Roger's teachers observed:

Much more of his conversations now are around concrete situations and facts so he sounds more normal than we have ever heard him at school. . . . Furthermore, he has not shown his anger once by lying inert on the floor and refusing to move when it is time to dress, or when he doesn't get a chair the right height. In fact, now when there is not a high chair available, he will express a desire for one, and then proceed to sit comfortably on a low chair without further comment.

With this freer, happier Roger, has come an increased awareness of other children and a desire to play with them . . . With the creative media he has shown marked improvement. He used to make just scribbles with the brown crayon, now he will draw trucks, cars and houses. These figures can be recognized without Roger telling us what they are.

At music Roger would often just sit in the corner by himself and refuse to participate in the activities. Now, however, most often he will join in with the group game or rhythms and add considerably to the group.

We have done little with Roger to prepare him for kindergarten, because up to now it was so difficult to reach him through talking or showing him how to do anything. However, with his marked improvement, we shall start now to help him learn to take turns, tie his shoes, and do some of the other skills required of a school child.

Steven's mother died while plans were being made for him to begin nursery school at age four, so he needed special help from his teachers. It was most important they help him maintain a positive memory of his mother through talking about her and recalling she had chosen his school for him.

Some aspects of Steven's relationship with his mother had been conflictual. However, mother and son had enjoyed several activities together, especially story telling, reading, and drawing. The teachers also fostered these activities, recognizing their meaning for Steven.

His interest in books was significant in another way. Many of the books he sought out in school and took to his treatment were concerned with mothering and loss. The stories helped Steven to begin and continue mourning for his mother.

During his two years in nursery school and kindergarten, Steven's wish to have drawings made for him and to be read to changed gradually, with the teachers' encouragement, into a pleasure in mastering these activities for himself. Because of their libidinization by the mother, which was maintained by the teachers, all aspects of learning could become sublimated for Steven. He later did exceptionally well in elementary school.

Help with reality testing and inner controls. Five-year-old Charles was a boy with very uneven development. Exceptionally bright, he had low frustration tolerance and control over his libidinal and aggressive drives. He cried at group time because it was so hard to wait for his turn to speak. Charles also warded off feelings of low self-esteem by grandiose talk, intellectualization, and denial. He felt inadequate in acquiring physical skills like swinging and bike riding and avoided them.

Charles's parents had expected little of him in the way of self-control, partly because of their great anxiety about his health. He had been prone to respiratory illnesses and high fevers since infancy, and had made many emergency trips to the hospital and experienced a long hospital stay at the age of two. The parents had been helped to have more realistic expectations of Charles and to be less tolerant of his defensive behavior.

During his analysis, the teachers helped Charles to distinguish between satisfactory and inadequate work in the classroom and to stick with tasks he found difficult. They continued with a program of helping him step by step to master playground skills. They discussed with him that his avoidance of certain activities, like baseball, came from lack of confidence, rather than, as he claimed, already knowing how to play.

The most demanding effort required of the teachers was in helping Charles gain control of his own behavior. When he acted disruptively in the classroom he was asked to leave the group. The teacher discussed with him his need to work on controlling himself instead of expecting grown-ups to manage this for him.

Charles had reason to be concerned about many events in his life, including a move to a new home and his father's prolonged work trips. While sympathetic about his home troubles, his teacher asked him to keep these at home, rather than let them spoil his school day. She also requested he take his worries to treatment rather than show them in school.

At first Charles responded teasingly to his teacher's request asking, "What shall I carry my worries in?" and it took much patient work before he took her requests seriously.

When he left for public school, Charles had made some progress in self-control, but his biggest gain was in accepting responsibility for his own behavior. One day when his father met him at school he told him, "I've had three days in a row with no time out—today's report is a short one, Dad, because it's been a good day."

COOPERATION BETWEEN TEACHER AND ANALYST DURING TREATMENT—THE VALUE OF TEACHER OBSERVATIONS

Teachers have opportunities to see the child in a variety of daily situations which differ from those of home. Sometimes they notice conflictual behavior which proves to be displaced from a family relationship. They also see a wider range of behavior than the analyst can usually observe in the treatment hour. Through her long term relationship with the child, the teacher also observes aspects of behavior which reflect dynamic changes. She can therefore bring difficulties or progressive steps to the analyst's attention, which would otherwise escape notice. In describing classroom behavior, a teacher may also provide a meaningful context or added dimension to conflicts which were already apparent to the analyst. Both kinds of observation can stimulate the analyst's reflections, increase his understanding of the patient, and challenge his thinking about how to best share this understanding with his patient.

Tom's analyst learned from his teachers he was unable to enter the small swimming pool at the school with the other children. She could then ask Tom what worried him about the pool. He shared his fear of being splashed, especially on the face. It was learned from Tom's mother that during some of his high fevers, he had been very much upset when being bathed in cool water. Tom revealed his feelings of helplessness and his fear his mother would not lift him out of the bathtub when he talked about these cold baths. This anxiety about his mother's intentions subsequently proved to be a most important theme in his treatment.

Before Tom's oedipal conflicts were apparent in his treatment material or in his home behavior, the teachers noticed his habit of setting up play situations so he had a companion, while a third child was excluded. The teachers shared their observation both with Tom and with his analyst. His analyst then discussed with him the passive into active mechanism which children sometimes use so they won't be the one to have "a horrible left out feeling." She could also wonder with Tom when children were most likely to have that feeling. His oedipal feelings then emerged in fantasy play in treatment, as well as in protests at home about his parents' shared activities.

The teachers observed that while Tom had previously shown pleasure in other children's loss of control, he had now become disapproving, and pointed out his own behavior in a superior way to the teachers. The observation raised an important question for the analyst, whether Tom's disapproval represented a normal step in his superego development or whether it indicated a defense in formation which would alienate him from his own impulses and feelings. Having formulated the question, she could later conclude from the analytic material that Tom's behavior represented a defensive externalization.

His teachers' description of Charles' out of control behavior proved helpful to the work of the analysis. When Charles repeatedly challenged the teachers to control him, they expected him to be more responsible for himself. However, there were times when he acted as though his whole body was beyond his control. He could not sit still for short periods, kicked the tables, and snatched papers from the wall. His analyst recognized this behavior reflected Charles' attempts to deal with his masturbation conflicts. Since he felt he could not control his masturbation, he expected others to do it for him.

THE ANALYST'S SUPPORT OF THE TEACHERS' WORK

Conferences between teachers and analyst give both the opportunity to look at all aspects of the child's personality and to follow him along the lines of development. They also allow recognition of various aspects of the teacher's work, including some of the inherent difficulties.

Analysts who work with nursery school teachers come to appreciate the many demands on their patience and skills. Teachers have to pursue their goal of helping each student take the necessary educational steps.

They also have to deal with children who are disruptive or whose defenses interfere with classroom activities and their own progress in various ways. By contrast, the analyst's task is less physically and emotionally demanding, and it is well for this to be recognized.

There are times when teachers feel responsible for a child's difficulties and blame themselves for his arrests and lack of progress. A child's behavior may induce his teachers to treat him as an exception. An understanding of the genetic roots of his difficulties, as well as knowledge of his present home life, helps teachers be more objective.

There is much to be gained, too, when analysts share with teachers their understanding of a child's defensive behavior in the classroom. These clarifications can free the teacher to approach the child in a different way. Their understanding of Charles' use of externalization and Jim's defensive omnipotence, for example, enabled them to make appropriate demands of the boy, and to help each feel more responsible for his own behavior.

During his mother's pregnancy, Tom became controlling to an annoying degree with both teachers and classmates. It was helpful to his teachers to understand that Tom's determined attempts to take charge of school events warded off feelings of helplessness about life at home. He was painfully aware of his mother's fear she would miscarry and he had been very frightened by her sudden hospitalizations.

In Roger's case, his teachers had felt both responsible and frustrated when he lay inert on the floor and they were unable to reach him in his withdrawal. Their recognition that he warded off both anger and feelings of loneliness by identifying with his pregnant mother, enabled them to approach him differently. While sympathizing with his feelings about home, they felt less need to coax him out of his passivity. Instead, they pointed out how much fun and learning he was missing by this behavior.

NOTES

1. Freud's postscript to the case of Little Hans shows that his views on education as well as treatment had been widely misunderstood. "The publication of this first analysis of a child had caused a great stir and even greater indignation, and a most evil future had been foretold for

the poor little boy, because he had been 'robbed of his innocence' at such a tender age and had been made the victim of a psychoanalysis" (1922, p. 148).

2. See Freud's discussion (1908a, p. 171) of the transformation of anal erotism as a result of education.

3. Margaret and Rachel McMillan, pioneers in the nursery school movement in Britain, also appreciated the crucial importance of family relationships in the young child's development. They emphasized that the child's sense of his own identity is rooted in the family and encouraged teachers to observe and foster the child's relationship with his parents. Their work was a stimulus to the beginning of nursery school education in the United States (Braun 1966).

4. Among many illustrations of such interferences Montessori gives the following poignant example. She was observing the efforts of a two-and-a-half-year-old boy whose view of some floating toys was obstructed by his classmates. Unsuccessful in forcing his way to the front, he spotted a little chair. He moved toward it, "his face illuminated with hope—at that moment the teacher seized him—in her arms and lifting him up—said 'Come, poor little one, you shall see too' " (1909, p. 92).

5. E. Plank (1966) notes that in the United States at least eight books were published on the Montessori method between 1912 and 1915.

6. I wish to thank Miss Thesi Bergmann for her translation of this paper.

7. This was a day nursery for toddlers, founded and maintained by Dr. Edith Jackson, and administered by Anna Freud in conjunction with Dorothy Burlingham and the pediatrician, Dr. Josephine Stross.

8. This nursery was administered by the National Council for Mental Health on behalf of the Ministry of Health, Great Britain.

9. The case of Addie, described below, is an example of cooperative work between grandparents, teachers, and analyst in a different setting.

10. I am very grateful to Lois Archer, Program Director of Hanna Perkins Nursery School and Kindergarten, and to the following teachers for sharing their observations with me: Mary Anderson, Joanne Blair, Patricia Church, Susan Cobb, Carolyn Ede, Elizabeth Edmondstone, Alice Frum, Marjorie Gates, Helen Kaufman, Sandra Redmond, Pamela Rowland, Judy Shepherd, and Mary Jo Thoman. I wish to thank also these child analysts associated with the School and the

Cleveland Center for Research in Child Development: Marion Barnes, Elizabeth Fleming, Mary H. Flumerfelt, Erna Furman, Robert Furman, M.D., Myron W. Goldman, Jean Kushleika, Beverley Ord, and Arthur Rosenbaum, M.D.

11. Addie's case has been reported by Goldman in *A Child's Parent Dies* (1974).

REFERENCES

Aichhorn, A. (1925). *Wayward Youth.* Vienna: International Psychoanalytic Press.

Archer, L., and Hosley, E. (1969). Educational program. In *The Therapeutic Nursery School,* ed. R. Furman and A. Katan, pp. 21–63. New York: International Universities Press.

Bernfeld, S. (1925). *Sisyphus, or the Limits of Education.* Vienna: International Psychoanalytic Press.

Braun, S. (1966). Nursery education for disadvantaged children: an historical review. In *Montessori in Perspective,* pp. 7–23. Washington, D.C.: National Association for the Education of Young Children.

Burlingham, D. (1937). Problems confronting the psychoanalytic educator. In *Psychoanalytic Studies of the Sighted and the Blind,* pp. 71–79. New York: International Universities Press.

Buxbaum, E. (1932). Analytische Bemerkungen zur Montessori-Methode. *Zeitschrift für Psychoanalytische Pädagogik* 7/8:324–333.

———— (1954). Technique of child therapy. *Psychoanalytic Study of the Child* 9:297–333.

———— (1969). Three great psychoanalytic educators. In *Learning for Love to Love of Learning: Essays on Psychoanalysis and Education,* ed. R. Ekstein and R. L. Motto, pp. 28–35. New York: Brunner/Mazel.

Dewey, J. (1902). *The Child and the Curriculum.* Chicago; University of Chicago Press.

Edgcumbe, R. (1975). The border between therapy and education. In *Studies in Child Psychoanalysis Pure and Applied: The Scientific Proceedings of the Twentieth Anniversary Celebrations of the Hampstead Child Therapy Course and Clinic,* pp. 133–147. New Haven: Yale University Press.

Ekstein, R. (1969). Psychoanalytic notes on the function of the curriculum. In *Learning for Love to Love of Learning: Essays on Psychoanalysis and Education,* ed. R. Ekstein and R. L. Motto, pp. 47–57. New York: Brunner/Mazel.

Ekstein, R., and Motto, R. (1969). Psychoanalysis and education: an historical account. In *Learning for Love to Love of Learning: Essays on Psychoanalysis and Education,* ed. R. Ekstein and R. Motto, pp. 3–24. New York: Brunner/Mazel.

Freud, A. (1930). *Psychoanalysis for Teachers and Parents.* New York: Emerson Books.

———— (1946). Preface to *The Psychoanalytical Treatment of Children* (English Edition). London: Imago.

———— (1963). The concept of developmental lines. *Psychoanalytic Study of the Child* 18:245–265.

———— (1974). *The Writings of Anna Freud,* Vol. I. 1922–1935. New York: International Universities Press.

Freud, A., and Burlingham, D. (1944). *War and Children,* ed. P. Lehrman. New York: International Universities Press.

———— (1944). *Infants Without Families.* New York: International Universities Press.

Freud, E. L., ed. (1960). *Letters of Sigmund Freud.* New York: Basic Books.

Freud, S. (1905). Three essays on the theory of sexuality. *Standard Edition* 7:130–243.

———— (1907). The sexual enlightenment of children. *Standard Edition* 9:131–139.

———— (1908a). Character and anal erotism. *Standard Edition* 9:169–175.

———— (1908b). On the sexual theories of children. *Standard Edition* 9:209–226.

———— (1909). Analysis of a phobia in a five-year-old boy. *Standard Edition* 10:5–149.

———— (1910). Leonardo da Vinci and a memory of his childhood. *Standard Edition* 11:63–137.

———— (1921). Group psychology and the analysis of the ego. *Standard Edition* 18:69–143.

———— (1923). The ego and the id. *Standard Edition* 19:12–66.

Furman, E. (1957). Treatment of under-fives by way of parents. *Psychoanalytic Study of the Child* 12:250–262.

———— (1969). Treatment via the mother. *The Therapeutic Nursery School,* ed. R. Furman and A. Katan, pp. 64–123. New York: International Universities Press.

Hoffer, W. (1945). Psychoanalytic education. *Psychoanalytic Study of the Child* 1:293–307.

Hug-Hellmuth, H. (1920). Childhood psychology and education. *International Journal of Psycho-Analysis* 1:316–323.

———— (1921). On the technique of child analysis. *International Journal of Psycho-Analysis* 2:287–305.

Isaacs, S. (1929). *The Nursery Years.* London: George Routledge and Sons.

———— (1930). *Intellectual Growth in Young Children.* London: George Routledge and Sons.

———— (1946). The relation between the processes of education and psychoanalysis. In *Social Development in Young Children,* pp. 403–413. London: George Routledge and Sons.

Katan, A. (1959). The nursery school as a diagnostic help to the child guidance clinic. *Psychoanalytic Study of the Child* 14:250–264.

———— (1961). Some thoughts about the role of verbalization in early childhood. *Psychoanalytic Study of the Child* 16:184–188.

Klein, M. (1923). The role of the school and the libidinal development of the child. In *Contributions to Psychoanalysis 1921–1945,* pp. 68–86. London: Hogarth Press.

———— (1927). Symposium on child analysis. In *Contributions to Child Analysis 1921–1945,* pp. 152–184. London: Hogarth Press.

Kliman, G. (1972). Analyst in the nursery: an application of child analytic techniques in a therapeutic nursery—a schematic description. Presented at New York Council on Child Psychiatry.

Montessori, M. (1909). *The Montessori Method: Scientific Pedagogy as Applied to Child Education in "The Children's Houses."* Trans. Anne E. George. Introduction by J. McV. Hunt. New York: Schocken, 1964.

Oppenheimer, R. (1969). The role of the nursery school with the children who received direct treatment. In *The Therapeutic Nursery School,* ed. R. Furman and A. Katan, pp. 274–292. New York: International Universities Press.

Ronald, D., and Kliman, G. (1970). The unique function of the teacher in an experimental therapeutic nursery school. Presented at the American Association of Psychiatric Clinics for Children Meeting, Philadelphia.

PART SEVEN

A SPECIAL SITUATION

Chapter 20

SPECIAL PROBLEMS IN THE PSYCHOANALYSIS OF

ADOPTED CHILDREN

Herbert Wieder, M.D.

Although many authors have written about the influence of adoption on personality development (Schechter 1960, Reeves 1971, Peller 1963, McWhinnie 1969, Goodman 1963, Frish 1964, Clothier 1943), reports of its influence on psychoanalytic treatment have been minimal. The 1966 panel on adoption at the American Psychoanalytic Association (Schechter 1967) included a description of the analysis of only one adopted child.[1] Consequently, we lack the insights into adoption problems that the microscope of analytic therapy provides. Recently, Daunton (1973) described the opening phase of the analysis of an encopretic child who was an adoptee, but the author of this unpublished paper limited the scope of her observations on adoptees. Glenn (1974), using analytic insights derived from his own experience and supplemented by data from the literature and his colleagues, applied psychoanalytic formulations to the plays of Edward Albee, who is an adopted child (see also Blum 1969). Noting both adaptative and maladaptive consequences, Glenn (1974) states, "Being adopted . . . does influence personality development and, if the child becomes an artist, the resultant fantasies may reveal themselves in his creative products. Moreover, the adopted child's wishes and defenses may serve as the well-spring for his artistic activity" (p. 413).

In other articles (Wieder 1977a,b) I have reported in detail the clinical observations and theoretical conclusions derived from the psychoanalytic treatment of adoptees. This presentation extends the horizons of those papers to reach conclusions about appropriate treatment technique.

There are many kinds of adoptions. (1) A child may be relinquished by his biological parents at birth or within a few weeks after birth, and be adopted at that time. (2) The child may spend months or years in foundling or foster homes before adoption. (3) A step-parent may adopt a child after the death of one parent and the remarriage of the other, or as a sequel to divorce. (4) In some adoptions the biological parents were married, but in others they were not. (5) There are also mixed ethnic adoptions in which a parent of one ethnic group adopts a child of another, for example, Vietnamese children adopted by Caucasians. (6) In unusual circumstances an adult may be adopted. (7) Recently, single adults of either sex have adopted children. (8) An adopted infant may be anatomically or physiologically flawed. The term *adoption* or *adoptee* therefore may designate a variety of relationships which differ from each other sociologically and psychologically.

Various types of adoption influence the child differently. The child who is shuttled from one foster home or institution to another will be affected by the actual loss of objects, which a child adopted at birth will not experience. This report relies on data derived from studies of physically normal people adopted at birth or shortly thereafter, who had an unbroken relationship to their adoptive parents, and in addition, had been told of their adoption before the age of three. These criteria, which would be considered optimal circumstances, were utilized to study the effect of knowing one is adopted (Wieder 1977a) independently of real, or actual memories of a relinquishment.

ADOPTION AS A SPECIAL INFLUENCE

The adopted child carries a much greater risk of developing an emotional disturbance than a bloodkin child (Schechter 1960, Bohman 1970). Although only two percent of the population is adopted, the incidence of adoptees of all types in the psychiatric patient population ranges from fifteen to thirty percent (McWhinnie 1969, Goodman 1963,

Child Adoption Research Committee 1951). The paucity of clinical studies of the special problems adoption imposes on treatment is surprising in view of these statistics, and the wide professional interest in these children.

The term *special* is itself ambiguous. That any patient or family has its own personal, and therefore special, reality is axiomatic. However, certain classes of patients, of which the adoptee is one, have substantively different realities which are central to their very existence and profoundly influence their development and personality formation. The reality of the adopted child involves a disruption of the biological matrix of family structure, and encompasses particular attempts at repair. For these reasons, the lives of adoptees and their families have been viewed as experiments in nature.

The people in adoptive families manifest all of the different personality types and symptomatology classified in the psychiatric nomenclature. They also demonstrate many similarities in configurations of conscious and unconscious preoccupations, fantasies, strivings, and defenses. These similarities set them apart from the nonadoptive population, and are derivatives of the defenses and adaptations evoked by the emotional issues and reactions in an adoption.

The term *special* may be applied to those adaptation-defense reactions motivated by the need to adopt or be adopted. The nature of the lives of adoptees and adoptive parents results in characteristic fantasies. The special problems of treatment eventuate from the projection of these fantasies into the therapeutic relationship, where their genesis is recapitulated in the transference.

Difficulties in the treatment of these children often involve the parents who simultaneously exert facilitating influences. The dynamics of the parents' personalities, and their relationship to each other and the child, are as influential in the decisions to initiate and maintain treatment as the symptomatology of the child (Bernstein 1958). The parents' defensive fantasies and attitudes contribute to resistances in any child's treatment.

Adoptive parents and adoptees influence each other's special defensive-adaptive responses. As with all families, their problems are mutually interwoven. For clarity we will first consider the parental and then the child's contributions to the special problems of treatment.

ADOPTION AS EXPERIENCED BY ADOPTIVE PARENTS

The attitudes of adopting parents and their adopted children are so intertwined it is difficult to separate them. Nevertheless, in this and following sections, I will attempt to concentrate first on the parents' experience and conceptualization of adoption. Although emphasis will be placed on the pathologic consequences and resistances, the reader will realize there are many useful, adaptive, and healthy consequences as well.

The prospect of psychiatric consultation or treatment is more anxiety laden in adoptive families than in bloodkin families. The adoptive parents' special fantasies and fears underlie this exaggerated feeling of threat.

Even after many years, adoptive parents experience their relationship to, and possession of, the child as tentative and endangered. An adopting mother frequently tends to be oversolicitous to the baby and intolerant of its active strivings toward separation-individuation (Mahler 1968). In this regard, these mothers are not overtly different from many bloodkin mothers who encourage dependency and passivity. Though fed from many sources, the adoptive mother's oversolicitous behavior particularly reflects her defense against a special, fearful fantasy of losing the child. As revealed below, an inability to allow separateness is often the first clue.

In the adoptive mother's description of her overindulgence of Jeannie as a baby, she also portrayed herself as fearful of separating herself from her child, or having her child separate from her. She made herself a willing playmate, thus undermining Jeannie's attempts to play with other children. "We spent all our time together." She expressed her fear Jeannie would abandon her in hate if she were angered. Placating the child and keeping her happy underlay the mother's inordinate fear to either apply reasonable and necessary frustration and discipline or permit distancing and separation.

Pete's adoptive mother described herself as oversolicitous and overindulgent. She had always resented and opposed any situation that separated her child from her. When Pete was a baby, she had almost succeeded in isolating him from the adoptive father. She confessed her inability to deny Pete any satisfactions from babyhood on. She couldn't bear to have him cry "and grow up feeling he wasn't loved or wanted. I lived in fear he might someday want to find his real mother." Treatment of Pete had been advised from his fifth year, but his mother could not permit treatment until, at age fifteen, "he was too tied" to her, and in danger of failing out of school. If treatment were to be initiated, she insisted at first, she had to be able to determine the frequency of his visits.

Adoptive parents fear the revival of memories and reminders of the circumstances impelling the need to adopt. During a consultation, as parents supply the necessary developmental history of the child, their defenses against remembering often weaken, unleashing previously controlled affects and fantasies. Jeannie's parents are representative of many adopting parents.

Extremely uneasy about seeking psychiatric help, Jeannie's parents delayed the process until, at age seven, Jeannie was unmanageable at school. They supplied her history in an informative and detailed account of her growth and development. Only late in the session did they hesitantly reveal Jeannie had been adopted at birth. Though joyful at receiving the baby, the adoption also contained a painful and personally bitter element. For the mother, the need to adopt, like the need for treatment, was associated to her self-image of personal failure. The idea of being a "parent failure," symbolized by having a child with problems, was grafted onto her self-image of being a biological failure as well. The mother could not control her tears in talking about her "shame of barrenness." Both parents hated to be reminded of their procreative history, because of the associated affect of shame.

Acquisition of someone else's child, unconsciously experienced as a theft, motivates the formation of distressing fantasies. Contributing to the parents' dread of losing the child, two typical fantasies appear regularly. The baby will be taken away from them as a retaliatory punishment for having stolen the baby, or the baby will hate them, abandon them, and seek to return to the inherently preferred biological parent. The fear and guilt represented in these attitudes and fantasies show how adoptive parents always feel as if they are under scrutiny and subject to accusations of unworthiness. Giving the consultant a history is often equated with confessing guilt. Prior to the adoption, parents underwent the agony of legal, and social investigation to determine whether they were fit or unfit to be parents. To some extent this endows their ideas with an aura of realism.

Jeannie's adoptive mother would play make-believe games with her. One was introduced by the mother to make Jeannie feel "like a princess, wanted, special, and important," and contained a royalty theme. The mother didn't recall the content other than that a child-princess lived in a world of make believe. Mother was the queen, and Jeannie the princess. When Jeannie introduced a wicked witch into the scenario, the mother thought, "This is me!" She became frightened and guilty, and stopped the game.

Jeannie's treatment revealed the bad mother-witch in her fantasy was a fantasy image of the abandoning, biological mother. The adoptive mother, however, interpreted the bad witch as herself, quite contrary to Jeannie's idea of her. The material suggested that fantasies akin to the classic Family Romance (Freud 1909) were activated in the mother, and projectively misinterpreted in the child. Later discussions confirmed the mother felt guilt about possessing Jeannie, "for keeping a mother and daughter apart." In time, the mother revealed her fear I'd find her to be a bad mother and recommend Jeannie's return to her "real" mother. She had feared the agency would do this prior to the adoption.

Albert's adoptive parents feared "bringing things out that are best not talked about." This related to the adoptive mother's fear "Albert would hate us for having taken him from his real mother." Albert had been told his biological mother had died, "so he wouldn't ever want to search for her."

In spontaneous speech, Jeannie's and Albert's mothers, like many adoptive mothers, refer to the biological mother as "*the* mother" or "real" mother. Society refers to the nurturing, or adoptive, mother as "real" also. The confusion in the adoptive parents' and adoptees' minds is that "real" refers to "blood." In social or psychological usage "real" refers to nurture as well. The analyst's suspicion that the adoptive mother imagines her child to be indissolubly bound "by blood" to the biological mother, is frequently confirmed when the adoptive mother states this fantasy explicitly.

The belief that a mother and child are biologically inseparable makes the knowledge that a mother can give up a child, emotionally unbelievable. Therefore adoption is often fantasized as a violent rupture of the bond, perpetrated by the adopter, who then feels guilty.

The fantasy of this indissoluble bond is not limited to adopting parents. All of us carry unconscious residues of the relationship to the mother during symbiosis (Mahler 1969). The sense of literally and physically belonging to the mother is part of the symbiotic child's illusion. When a bloodkin child intellectually learns of his biological mutuality, later known as the "blood tie" to the mother, the sense of belonging to and having possession of each other which was established through nurturing is reenforced.

The conscious knowledge that they didn't "make the baby" is a realistic contribution to the adoptive parents' thoughts that the child isn't really theirs. The knowledge of the actual biological history undermines the emotional truth that nurturing produces an indissoluble bond.

Threatened by their belief they will be punished for separating the biological mother and her child, adoptive parents defend themselves by producing compensatory fantasies. Frequently, the parents proclaim and try to enact the fantasy, "We are a *natural* family."

Often adoptive parents do not mention the fact of adoption while consulting about problems they are having with the child. When the fact is revealed, it is often accompanied by, "But that has no bearing on the problem." They need to deny the adoption and all circumstances surrounding it. The wish to supply the illusion of biological unity is often clearly apparent. "If we are a natural family we have nothing to fear and all the reasons for an adoption never existed" is the message. Of course, many adoptive parents are aware of their special circumstance and do not hide it from the consultant. Indeed, they may worry excessively about the impact of adoption on the child.

The fantasy of being a natural family is continually undermined by everyday reminders of the absent biological relationship and by the knowledge of being adoptive, not biological, parents. All of my patients have referred to their obvious lack of mutual family features. Children look for physical similarities between themselves and their parents in their ongoing definition of themselves in a family group. To have mother's eyes or daddy's nose is an important confirmation of belonging. A parallel process goes on in parents who see themselves and their parents mirrored in the physical qualities of the child, reproducing the "blood-line." In bloodkin families, confirmation of biological mutuality is re-enforced daily. Adoptive parents do not have that experience. Instead they are reminded of the absence of biological mutuality and the associated affects of guilt, shame, and fear.

Consultation or treatment assaults their defenses, because it is necessary to be honest and candid about matters which both the adoptive parents and the adopted child have found to be fraught with fear, shame, guilt, and confusion. A dominant fear of adoptive parents is of losing the child's love or even the relationship itself. The adoptee's basic concern is losing his adoptive mother. Mother and child reactively cling to each other when they feel threatened. Anything that seems to either party as a coming between them is repulsed. Treatment is often viewed as such a threat.

Pete felt allied to me and protected from engulfment by his adoptive mother. At the time, he recognized the implication that he might therefore become separated from her and grow up. The mother also sensed his attachment to me. "He doesn't like to miss sessions." Although she was consciously approving, she felt threatened. With Pete's collusion, she attempted to interfere with treatment. Pete might miss a session because she was late or forgot to pick him up. I discussed this with her, and she was able to desist. Though reassured his relationship with me would not be cut off by his mother, Pete was angered that his own manipulations to have her interfere were exposed and thwarted. His anxious concern about whom to depend on was diminished by his fantasy that I was now stronger than his mother. "If she listened to you, then you must be boss. I must be good or you, like my mother, could send me away." I now represented the savior-adoptive mother to the child who was reacting to his adoptive mother as if she were the bad, abandoning, biological mother.

Adoptive parents often focus on the adopted child's hostile, rejecting behavior toward them. This both stimulates and is an illusory confirmation of their fears of being unloved, failures, and abandoned. At such times, adoptive parents seem unable to recognize and trust in the permanence and reliability of the attachment established through nurture that the adoptee manifests in his ambivalence.

In adolescence, the phase-specific tasks of disengagement from parents accentuate the fears of both the adolescent and the parent. The ubiquitous adolescent search for the nonincestuous object may, as a seeming paradox, include the adoptee's wish to find his biological parents. The presence of this wish is viewed by adoptive parents as justifying their fears.

In summary, from the moment adoptive parents are confronted by a need for therapeutic help, the adoption motifs are revived and, it seems to them, reenacted. Their need to deny painful affects of shame and guilt, their fearful fantasies of losing the child, and their need to protect their family structure contribute to their special reasons for resistance.

ADOPTION AS EXPERIENCED BY THE CHILD

Adoptees suffer the same conflicts, crises, and disturbances that affect bloodkin children, but perhaps more so. In another paper (Wieder 1977a), I demonstrated that knowing one is adopted acts as a forceful and pathogenic influence on preschool age childrens' personality and ego development. This knowledge is a psychological burden other children are spared. In addition, the experience of being an adopted child also elicits defensive-adaptive responses. As we have noted, the adoptee grows up in a special milieu. All of the tensions and conflicts of the adopting parents—their personalities, their special reactions to barrenness, their motives for and expectations from the adoption which express themselves verbally and nonverbally—influence the child. The experiences of the baby prior to adoption, his constitution, knowledge, and experiences are woven into fantasies and thought processes giving a special cast to the psychology of the adoptee.

Only their ideation and thought contents objectively distinguish adoptees from bloodkin children and make them special or unique. Until the story of adoption has been communicated and becomes part of his memories and fantasies, the adopted child who had been immediately placed as a neonate is indistinguishable from a bloodkin.

Fear and confusion characterized my patients' initial early childhood reactions to being told of their adoption. The information had contributed a reenforcing quality of actuality to the illusion of pre-existing, ubiquitous fears of loss of object and love. The stories they were told about adoption were transformed into fearful fantasies about the actuality of an abandonment. Defenses then had to be mobilized to stem separation anxiety.

Their histories revealed that after the adoptive parents told them the details about their adoptions, the children became confused, frightened, and disorganized. They often turned away from their parents and refused to listen to their explanations. Denial was supplemented by the mechanisms of reversal and displacement as the child actively rejected the adoptive mother upon being told he had been given up by another mother. In time, the child reworked and revised the adoption stories in unsuccessful attempts to control the anxiety engendered by them. Threaded through all phases of development, the fragments, themes, and distortions of the adoption data were both products of and further stimulants to anxiety. As a mode of mastery, a tendency toward repetitive reenactment of fantasies derived from the adoption data also eventuated. A prominent focus of defense was against conscious recall of the realistic history of their relinquishment.

Each came to believe they had been "gotten rid of," and left to die because they were bad, damaged, or disgusting, and were later rescued by a savior mother. Reminders of their actual history evoked hatred of the biological mother, as well as shame and fear. Denial or isolation of information then limited what they could know intellectually, and denial of related affects limited what could be felt consciously. As the child's defenses against the pain associated with adoption were applied to other areas of his life, a more generalized disturbance developed. Denials established an estrangement between what could be generally known and the degree of affect considered tolerable or admissible. Disturbances in learning and relationships ensued. Denial as a principal defense severely affected reality testing, cognitive functioning, and object relationships.

The child's relationship to the adoptive mother became his model toward other persons. A conscious attitude of anger and hostility, accompanied by rejecting behavior, masked and defended against the yearning to be loved and to love. Because the adoptive mother was ambivalently and confusedly viewed as an all-powerful savior who will get rid of a child who is bad, the child had difficulty trusting her and others who come to represent her.

Pete described his awe and fear of his adoptive mother. Without her presence, in fact or fantasy, he felt powerless. He must not anger her or she might get rid of him, leaving him helpless to face life. He looked upon her as a savior and contradictorally as an abandoner.

These polarities reflect the many confused and contradictory ideas and images, along with heightened ambivalence, eventuating from adoptees' conflicts. Relationships have become dangerous to them, because they imply potential abandonment by a hateful object, or engulfment by a "savior." Their "reject before you're rejected" attitude defends against these fearful consequences by turning passive experiences into activity. All of my patients viewed their adoptive parents as saviors, total submission to whom was imperative to insure survival.

The adopted child's vacillating, ambivalent, overtly hostile, and covertly compliant behavior transmits and generates a quality of instability and dissatisfaction. In this behavior they also reflect their confusion about the meaning of adoption as a process. They become uncertain about what the word itself means. Illogical ideas arise. The child starts to believe that the adopting mother is the abandoning mother, and that the term *adoption* means *abandonment.*

Pete made a slip of the tongue. While talking about how lucky he was to have been adopted, he said, "If I hadn't been given away—no, I mean if I hadn't been adopted, I'd be in worse shape."

The idea that adoption can mean abandonment contains a truth, for adoption is a two step process. A giving away is followed by a taking in. Other terms, such as *mother, father,* and *parents* are also used in a confusing manner by adoptees.

I have found in listening to adoptees that they do not identify parents according to adoption jargon as "real," "true," or "original." At times they use the term *mother* to signify the biological mother. At other times, they use the word to refer to the adoptive mother. If asked for clarification, they will then use phrases such as "the one who bore me" or "the one who raised me." If older and more sophisticated, they may refer to their biological, adoptive or birth parent. In spontaneous speech, the term mother is used interchangeably for each. This manner of speaking reflects the child's confused mental representations of his parents, and enhances special disturbances in reality testing and style of thought. These grow out of the knowledge that two sets of parents exist, but in actuality, the child experiences only one set. Hateful feelings from fantasies about the absent, unreachable, biological parents are displaced to the adoptive parents. Both adoptees and adopters become confused and threatened when the child directs these feelings to the adoptive parent. This behavior may reappear in the transference which activates the abandonment theme of adoption.

Jim's relationship to me had a friendly and positive quality which he tended to suppress. Although he revealed a strong working alliance, he insisted he felt "no relationship" to me. He recognized distress if an appointment was cancelled, was always prompt, and was afraid to complain because I might take offense and not see him anymore. His fear of abandonment was always in evidence. As his positive feelings became more apparent to him, he became restive. He acknowledged that the friendly atmosphere paradoxically frightened him.

When I said he seemed to want to reject me precisely because he was experiencing friendly feelings and wishes, he said, "I had a fantasy of moving into your apartment building. Then I could practically live here. At first it seemed like a great idea, but then I began to wonder if that meant I really depended on you, and I got scared." Rejection of the one he wanted—analyst, adoptive mother—represented a defense against both engulfment and abandonment contained in the thought, "You have to be good or you're gotten rid of."

His overtly rejecting attitude hid an inner compliance. He continually tried to be a "good boy" to protect himself against abandonment. The analysis of the transference demonstrated the presence of positive feelings and the fear of an engulfing dependence on the nurturing object. His normal, conscious wish for a relationship with a person he wanted was derived from primitive, oral, ambivalent wishes that aroused his fear of losing that person. This fear in turn motivated the defensive rejecting behavior toward the adoptive mother or, in the transference, me.

Fantasies representing themes about adoption are discernible from the beginning of treatment.

A patient had seen another doctor prior to seeing me. He commented, "The first doctor didn't care about me. He made me feel like I was nothing and I hated him. I want to be here, this is better. It makes me think of things I don't like to think about, but it helps me." We learned in the treatment that the first doctor represented the abandoning, biological parent, and I symbolized the nurturing adoptive one.

In discussing his transfer to me from another therapist, another patient said, "Dr. A. probably sent me away because I did something wrong." This thought related to a long held belief that his biological mother "got rid of me because I was no good." He also expressed anger at his parents for "taking me from Dr. A. and giving me to you." He wasn't sure to whom his anger should be directed and was confused about "who gave me away or was I taken." His thinking always went to "mother" as the target of his anger, but he wasn't sure which "mother."

Although adoptees often claim they are not consciously preoccupied with thoughts about their adoptive status, everyday experience contradicts them.

Jeannie claimed she never thought about adoption. However, in her associations to daily school or treatment experiences, adoption themes were barely disguised. I knew from her history that Jeannie's disruptive behavior had led to her placement in a "special class" where she remained through the third grade. In that year she had been allowed to spend time in the "regular class," hopefully to permit reentry into fourth grade regular classes.

In the opening sessions, she played school and talked about her class. I realized I was not sure at all times to which class she was referring. I told her I knew she had two classes, a regular one and a special one. "This is confusing to me, perhaps it's confusing to you," I said. Her next remarks indicated how the thoughts about school and teacher were the vehicle for the adoption theme. "I don't know why the regular teacher sent me away. I hate her for that. I didn't do anything wrong, but she said I had. Anyway, I like special class, it's great. You can do anything you want to, and don't have to do what regular kids do."

She revealed her concerns about being in two classes simultaneously. "The special teacher says I can't stay in special class either unless I'm good. So I try. The only thing I don't like about being in special class, is it makes me feel different. If I was in regular class, I wouldn't feel like I was bad."

When I suggested having two classes can be as confusing and upsetting as having two mothers, she responded, "I don't want to hear about adoption. I know I had other parents." This was immediately followed with a disavowal: "I never had other parents—well I know I did, but I don't want to think about it, it makes me so angry I could break down this house." Whenever adoption was mentioned directly, Jeannie would react with anger and cling more to her adoptive mother. Adoption and her fantasies about it aroused separation fears.

THE PROBLEM IN TREATMENT

Both parent and child share fears of loss of object and love, although their reasons differ. They also share a readiness to believe their fearful fantasies which contain distorted elements of reality from their life histories. To them, fantasy is not just imagination; it contains actuality and a feeling of probability. Extensive use of denial, fantasy formation, and phobic avoidance are characteristic and principal defenses of both parent and child.

We find ourselves confronted by concerned parents who consciously want to help their child, but who are afraid of losing him by being exposed as kidnappers or failures, or by the child's abandonment of them for his biological parents. These parents endow the therapist with severe, judgmental, and punitive motives. On the other hand, the child has an exaggerated dependency on the savior, adoptive parent. He fears abandonment by that parent to the therapist who may represent both the abandoning, biological parent and the rescuing, adopting parent. The therapist and the adoptive parent are alternately and unconsciously experienced as the hated, abandoning, biological parent. The parent and child cling to each other to ward off the danger to their relationship, and the fantasized punitive, engulfing analyst. Elements from the treatment situation are often experienced as realistic recapitulations of historical elements. Therefore, transference experiences may be felt as too real, especially in those patients whose reality testing is unstable. The fantasy "we are a normal family" is constantly threatened with disillusionment as the topic of adoption enters the clinical work.

The parents' attitude of denial is revealed in their remark "adoption has nothing to do with" their child's problems and often this is echoed by therapists. To a nonadoptee society, adoption connotes only a humane, nurturing, "taking in"—a healing process—and it is not viewed as a trauma. Society defensively minimizes the traumatic implications of reproductive barrenness and abandonment, which the members of the adoptive situation verbalize.

The topic and events of adoption stir up powerful emotions and unconscious defenses associated with fantasies of abandonment. Therapists are not immune to this reaction, and may insist the adoptee's developmental reactions are occasioned with trauma other than the knowledge they are adopted. There is truth in this. Adopted children have other problems as well, and attitudes about their adoptive status may even represent a defense against anxiety from other sources. However, the adoption theme does run through the child's life, and influences his development. By organizing the various developmental states in special ways, adoption influences the developmental process.

My data unequivocally demonstrated the knowledge of adoption itself is traumatic. Fulfillment of the need to be adopted or to adopt initiates chronic stress trauma (Kris 1956). Although adoption is intended to mend the biological rift in the life of each member of an adoptive family, it fails to do this to a significant degree. For as adoption alleviates the difficulties, it simultaneously introduces a special reality with which the family must cope.

THE WORKING ALLIANCE WITH THE PARENTS

Part of the task of the child analyst is "to keep the child's parents in a favorable attitude toward the analysis . . . To maintain the sympathy and cooperation of the parents throughout the entire analysis is a difficult and trying problem; and yet if one does not succeed in this, the analysis moves inevitably to an abrupt and premature interruption" (Burlingham 1935 p. 69).

Circumstances have not changed since Burlingham wrote the above in 1935. One potential source of failure for the therapist is his underestimation of the traumatic aspects of the adoptive situation. Empathizing with the adoptive parents' special fears enables the therapist to more quickly recognize their manifestations and deal with them tactfully. From the time of the consultation and throughout the course of the child's analysis, the parents will recount to the analyst details of the patient's life. The process of disclosing the history of the adoption and its sequelae will weaken defenses and evoke anxiety. Consequently, the analyst must be prepared to take a more psychotherapeutic stance with the mother than conventional child analytic procedure suggests.

The situation is somewhat eased if the mother is, or has been, in treatment herself. The untreated mother cannot help but react with denial, avoidance, and withdrawal. It will be the task of the therapist to help the mother recognize and cope more realistically with her stress. With the option of referring the mother to someone else, or seeing her himself, the child's therapist frequently does best to choose the latter course. The child's analyst should work with her in a supportive noninterpretive capacity until she is able to tolerate the illusory separation from, or loss of, the child that treatment implies.

The usual analytic procedures of engaging the latency-age or younger child's mother only as an historian, or of not seeing the parents of early and middle adolescents frequently or at all, will be intolerable to most adoptive mothers. At some point, the child will experience the analyst as the powerful, adoptive, savior-mother in the transference, and will unleash more hostility to the adoptive parent who is now irrationally experienced as the abandoning, hated, biological mother. The transference picture changes frequently, and when the analyst becomes the hated, abandoning, biological mother, the child will cling to his adoptive mother, who will encourage this return to her to the detriment of treatment.

More time must elapse and discussion occur with the mother until she can permit working alliances to develop between analyst and child on the one hand, and analyst and herself on the other. Then she will develop a capacity to reveal painful and defended history. She must be helped to allow the child to suffer, be angry, and distant, and not withdraw the child from treatment, or overprotect him from necessary developmental tasks.

Some may consider the work done with the parent nonanalytic contamination. It is an alteration in the child's milieu occasioned by the analyst's intervention. But, without it, frequently no analytic work will be possible with the child. We may consider a modification of procedure as appropriate to or dictated by the developmental or psychodynamic position of the child (Maenchen 1970).

Most often, the mother can be helped with discussions of her special fantasies, and offered realistic reassurances. When the mother's anxieties diminish, the therapeutic work with the child may proceed. The parent's need for the natural family fantasy contains an amalgam of all the defensive attitudes. Slow, patient, and tactful discussion of the irrationality of this fantasy, its meaning, and its counterproductive quality, can strengthen the parents' conviction in the durability of the bond established by nurture. Interpretations of the unconscious contents should be avoided. Parents should be helped to accept that theirs is not a natural family in the sense they would have wanted it, but that it approximates it in many important ways.

This becomes an important issue as the latency child becomes adolescent. When he openly expresses curiosity about his biological heritage, the child arouses alarm in his adoptive parent. The wish for data about their biological parents is, I find, generally present in adoptees. However, the actual search for the biological parents is less common. Though my patients have expressed the wish that the circumstances impelling adoption had not existed, none wanted to realistically or actually replace their adoptive parents as "parents."

Bloodkin children also leave and reject parents, find other objects and relationships, but retain realistic bonds of attachment and belonging. If the adopted adolescent's wish and search could be viewed by the parent as an expression of becoming more mature, and if more confidence in the nurturing bond prevailed, then some of the alarm and furor could be dispelled. I believe adoptees in their teens should be allowed to know more about their biological past, and if it arises they should be encouraged by the adopting parents to pursue their wish, and investigate their past with a minimum of guilt.

EGO DEFICITS

There is a final, technical point about the order in which the patient's problems should be approached. The rich and interesting fantasy life and the unusual psychodynamics will be seductively attractive to the therapist. However, their clarification should not necessarily be the initial therapeutic focus. In accordance with the basic principles of psychoanalytic technique, the analyst should first direct his attention to surface manifestations, especially the affect and defenses of the patient, before fully interpreting his fantasies.

The analyst may be tempted to prematurely deal with the adoption fantasies because they are often preoccupations of the adoptee. In many cases, these derivatives deserve early consideration. However, not infrequently ego deficits that evolve from the conflicts generated by adoption, as well as other sources, require attention and correction before the fantasies can be interpreted.

The children I have seen suffer from ego disturbances of varying severity. Sometimes the constitutional basis for these difficulties impress the analyst as primary. In other cases, the ego deficits result from an extensive use of denial to defend against anxiety from conflicts about adoption. The use of denial extends into other areas of the patient's life, with resultant difficulties in reality testing and the ability to learn. If the child believes learning about his biological parents is forbidden, all learning can become threatening. In addition, learning may also undo a denial, and reexpose the child to the warded-off hatred associated to fantasies of the abandoning, biological mother. Schoolwork becomes difficult.

These deficits, when present, will influence the technique from the beginning. Although the attraction to the fantasies may be strong, attention should first be directed at improving reality testing by concentrating on the way the child experiences reality. The patient may not be able to recognize the unrealistic nature of his appraisal of the analyst. Only after prolonged contact will the child be able to appreciate the therapist as a real person different from his parents, and hence able to analyze the transference.

Identification with the analyst and his reality orientation may further the child's reality testing and his ability to learn. At times, the analyst may refer the child for special educational measures to help overcome academic difficulties.

Another related disturbance in ego function one often encounters in adopted children is hyperactivity at home or in school. Again, although constitutional factors may seem predominant, the influence of intrapsychic conflict may be crucial. Sometimes the child may resort to active running from his adoptive parents as a defense against experiencing a passive being left or to actively escape from the adoptive parents whom the child imagines to be evil.

Adoptive parents frequently fear their child's anger or disapproval, and fail to exert controls, prohibitions, and discipline. Superego deficiencies may result from this evasion, as well as from the child's idea that he need not obey adults who are not really his parents. Frequently, the superego and ego deficits will require scrutiny before fantasies can be analyzed.

Ideally the entire personality structure will eventually be analyzed. The relationship of adoption fantasies which are products of ego-id-superego interactions, will be understood in conjunction with other fantasies, ego defenses, and deficits.

NOTES

1. This analysis, although summarized in the panel report (Schechter 1967), has not been otherwise published.

REFERENCES

Barnes, M. J. (1953). The working through process in dealing with anxiety around adoption. *American Journal of Orthopsychiatry* 23: 605–620.

Bernard, V. W. (1953). Application of psychoanalytic concepts to adoption agency practice. In *Psychoanalysis and Social Work,* ed.

Marcel Heiman, pp. 169–209. New York: International Universities Press.

Bernstein, I. (1958). The importance of characteristics of the parents in deciding on child analysis. *Journal of the American Psychoanalytic Association* 6:71–78.

Blos, P. (1963). The concept of acting out in relation to the adolescent process. *Journal of the American Academy of Child Psychiatry* 2: 118–143.

Blum, H.P. (1969). A psychoanalytic view of *Who's Afraid of Virginia Woolf? Journal of the American Psychoanalytic Association* 17:888–903.

Bohman, M. (1970). *Adopted Children and Their Families.* Stockholm: Proprius.

Burlingham, D.T. (1935). Child analysis and the mother. *Psychoanalytic Quarterly* 4:69–92.

Child Adoption Research Committee (1951). A Follow Up Study of Adoptive Families. New York: Child Adop. Committee, March 25.

Clothier, F. (1943). The psychology of the adopted child. *Mental Hygeine* 27:222–230.

Daunton, E. (1973). The opening phase of treatment in an adopted child with a symptom of encopresis. Presented at Association for Child Psychoanalysis, April 7, Ann Arbor.

Freud, S. (1909). Family romances. *Standard Edition* 9:235–241.

Frish, M. (1964). Identity problems and confused conception of the genetic ego in adopted children during adolescence. *Acta Paediatrica Psychiatria* 21:6–11.

Glenn, J. (1974). The adoption theme in Edward Albee's "Tiny Alice" and "The American Dream" *Psychoanalytic Study of the Child* 29: 413–429.

Goodman, J.D. et al. (1963). Adopted children brought to psychiatric clinic. *Archives of General Psychiatry* 9:451–456

Kris, E. (1956). Recovery of childhood memories in psychoanalysis. *Psychoanalytic Study of the Child* 11:54–88

Mahler, M. (1968). *On Human Symbiosis and Vicissitudes of Individuation, Vol 1: Infantile Psychosis.* New York: International Universities Press.

McWhinnie, A.M. (1969). The adopted child in adolescence. In *Adoles-*

cence: Psychosocial Perspectives, ed. G. Caplan and S. Lebovici, pp. 133–142. New York: Basic Books.

Maenchen, A. (1970). On the technique of child analysis in relation to stages of development. *Psychoanalytic Study of the Child* 25:175–208.

Mitchell, H. McK. (1944). Adopted children as patients of a mental hygiene clinic. *Smith College Studies in Social Work* 15:122.

Peller, L. (1963). Further comments on adoption. *Bulletin of the Philadelphia Association for Psychoanalysis* 13:1–14.

Reeves, A.C. (1971). Children with surrogate parents: cases seen in analytic therapy and an etiological hypothesis. *Journal of Medical Psychology,* 44:155–171.

Schechter, M.D. (1960). Observations on adopted children. *Archives of General Psychiatry* 3:21–32.

_____ Reporter (1967). Panel: Psychoanalytic theory as it relates to adoption. *Journal of the American Psychoanalytic Association* 15:695–708.

Wieder, H. (1977a). On being told of adoption. *Psychoanalytic Quarterly* 46:1–22.

_____ (1977b). The family romance fantasies of adopted children. *Psychoanalytic Quarterly* 46:185–200.

_____ (1978). On when and whether to disclose about adoption. *Journal of the American Psychoanalytic Association.* In press.

PART EIGHT

APPLICATIONS OF THE
PRINCIPLES OF CHILD ANALYSIS

Chapter 21

APPLICATION OF PSYCHOANALYTIC PRINCIPLES
TO TREATMENT AND PREVENTION IN INFANCY

Sally Provence, M.D.

In an earlier paper (Provence 1972) on psychoanalysis and the treatment of psychological disorders of infancy, I dealt mainly with the importance of careful diagnostic work, some ways of organizing observational and interview data to facilitate treatment, and some of the characteristics of a therapeutic environment for infants. In the current presentation, the focus will be on the application of psychoanalytic principles to the prevention and treatment of such problems.

For many years, psychoanalytic theory has been an important part of infant care, and many of its propositions have influenced the general child care advice given to parents and parent surrogates. It has also influenced the practice of agencies and of individuals whose work it is to assist parents when an infant's development is threatened, or to develop alternative plans for his care if, for any reason, his parents are unable to provide for him.

This paper will address two factors: (1) the ideas derived from psychoanalysis which have the most immediate applicability to the tasks of child rearing and the alleviation of problems of infancy, and (2) the most common settings and situations in which professionals directly or indirectly participate in planning for infants in the United States.

THE IMPORTANCE OF THE FAMILY

I will begin by assuming the family remains the setting of choice for rearing infants in this country, though I realize some will question this. That some families are noxious and destructive for infants, that some are unable to provide a healthy child rearing environment in today's complex and stressful world, that many need assistance on a scale not now available, that our current methods of helping are too little and often too late, I accept as reality. However, these factors do not, it seems to me, argue against the probability that a family unit is likely to remain the most important and constructive place in which to rear children, given the high value we continue to place upon individual development and upon resourcefulness and creativity. Increasingly there may be family groups of nonrelatives in which the members assume roles and make abiding commitments to one another of sufficient strength and continuity that they are able to function well as child rearing environments. Such groups would simulate a family in the protectiveness, dynamic importance of its members to each other, and the support systems for adults and children provided by a well-functioning, traditional family.

PSYCHOANALYTIC IDEAS APPLICABLE TO CHILD REARING AND THE ALLEVIATION OF PROBLEMS

It is impossible to mention more than a few of the ways in which psychoanalytic theory, practice, and thought influence current attitudes toward and practices involved in infant care. The following selection makes no claim to completeness. Several ideas have been included which appear to have been either the most influential or of the most obvious relevance to the treatment of developmental problems of infants in the first two years of life.

The central role of object relations. Perhaps the most influential proposition in psychoanalytic developmental psychology for the prevention and treatment of problems of infancy is the unique importance of the child's relationship to others. These relationships influence the child's development as an individual, and as a member of a society and a culture. A belief in the importance of forming a close relationship with a specific maternal figure early in life, and of the continuity and quality of that relationship stands at the center of recommendations about how best to provide for an infant's developmental needs. There are several dimensions of this concept. The mother-child relationship is both biological and social. Mutual adaptation of mother and infant is not only an indicator, but probably a necessary precondition for optimizing the relationship. Those important influences which we call by the general term *experience* in infancy are mediated primarily through the mother, and come about in close association with her care of the infant. The development of stable and abiding relationships with people stems from and is colored by the nature of the child's experiences with people (including both his mother and father) in his early years. This fact has guided many of our recommendations about child rearing.

In the translation of theory into practice, a commitment to the importance of the object relationship has a powerful influence in specific therapeutic situations. For example, it determines the decision to assign mainly one nurse to care for an infant who has been hospitalized because he has failed to thrive, or to keep to a very small number those who are caregivers for young children in day care. It is the most important guiding principle in many activities of counselling, educating, and treating parents to support and enhance the parent-child relationship. It also underlies decisions to train therapists who can work with disturbed infants directly, fulfilling a role that includes both the nurturing skills of a parent, and the observing and healing talents of a psychotherapist.

The child comes to his understanding of the world of inanimate objects through his relationships with people. The cathexis of toys and other playthings by the infant and the ability to involve himself in playful activity is closely linked with the quality and quantity of maternal care (Provence and Ritvo 1961). Playful activity—playful social interaction, as well as play with toys—is one of the characteristics of healthy infants; the inability to play is a danger sign. Moreover, helping the infant to play is a well-established activity of parents and therapists. It is both a conventional and productive way of interacting with an infant. There is no doubt that most infants can best be helped to play by those with whom they have a personal relationship. Disturbed or deprived infants will need an opportunity to develop such a relationship before they can engage themselves in beneficial play. Implications for planning are obvious: a familiar adult is more successful than a stranger; a person who can appropriately meet the infant's bodily and emotional needs is in the best position to help him play.

Innate and experiential factors as codeterminants of development. This concept includes a wide variety of propositions either derived from or congenial with psychoanalytic theory. The developmental process comes about through the interaction of the innate and experiential, and the process cannot be defined or understood except as interactional. Many psychoanalytic theoreticians, clinicians, and observers have contributed data supporting this view. Benjamin's 1961 paper is a particularly helpful contribution. Included in the concept of innate factors is maturation. Maturation is defined as a progressive and dynamic unfolding process dictated primarily by intrinsic factors (genetic and constitutional), and taking place according to a biological timetable. It encompasses differentiation and organization of functions, as well as emergence and growth. The concept of the gradual differentiation of the psychic and somatic systems out of a relatively undifferentiated state helps one understand empirical data about the tendency of infants toward global, rather than localized responses. Infants are prone to respond to psychologically stressful experiences with somatic symptoms and/or with delays or disturbances in several aspects of development rather than only one or two.

Each individual child has a unique ego constitution, and the autonomous functions of the ego emerge in relation to it. In addition, there are variations in drive endowment. These two concepts are heuristically valuable propositions which serve as guides both to understanding deficits in the child's development, and to the formation of treatment plans. Furthermore, when some one of the somatic apparatuses which underlie such autonomous functions of the ego as motility, visual and auditory perception, intelligence, or speech are found to be impaired, it is important that remedial action be taken as early in life as possible. This will optimize the child's ego development, and is a practical issue of considerable importance.

While the importance of innate and experiential factors is entirely familiar to psychoanalysts, and is generally accepted by most child specialists, the carryover into practice is often quite neglected. Such an approach is essential to comprehensive diagnostic work which must address both biological and psychological factors. Moreover, such diagnosis cannot be successfully carried out without the cooperation of professionals with a variety of skills. At times the psychoanalyst will require the assistance of a geneticist, a neurologist, a general pediatrician, an endocrinologist, and other specialists. Conversely, when these professionals are responsible for diagnosis, they will need the skills of the psychoanalyst or other mental health professionals if accurate diagnoses are to be made. The analyst and the child's physician must be able to talk to each other if their work in the child's behalf is to succeed.

The phase concept. The phase concept, so familiar to analysts, encompasses the characteristics and organization of the psychic life during particular libidinal phases. It also includes the idea of characteristic developmental tasks to be accomplished during particular phases, as well as phase-specific vulnerabilities. The phase concept most commonly influences infant specialists by its emphasis on supporting a favorable parent-child relationship, protecting the child from discontinuity of care, and alleviating problems engendered by separation, deprivation, or inadequate nurturing. Developmental needs are translated into child care practices which have the greatest likelihood of meeting those needs. Efforts have been made by infant specialists to conceptualize and plan nurturing environments for very young children, emphasizing the settings and experiences that ought to be provided. Another application of knowledge about developmental phases results in an emphasis on protection from traumatic experiences during periods of particular vulnerability. Perhaps the most frequently acknowledged example of an influence on practice has to do with protecting the child from excessive anxiety in accordance with his phase of development.

Learning as a crucial aspect of the ego's task of adaptation. Many years ago, Hartmann (1939) pointed out that the human child has very little instinctual equipment to enable him to survive, adapt to, and master his *average expectable environment.* He must acquire many of his adaptation processes through learning. This emphasis on learning is translated into considerations about what experiences are appropriate for a particular child; what frequency, intensity, and timing are likely to facilitate learning; what kind of encounters with specific people will enhance development, etc. Specific plans are developed from the diagnostic data.

Balance between frustration and gratification, pleasure and pain. Some degree of frustration for the infant is not only inevitable, but desirable to enhance the development of his personality. The question becomes, what is a favorable balance between frustration and gratification? In the abstract, we cannot answer this question. In clinical practice, we encounter most often those infants who have endured a larger measure of frustration and pain than is good for them, although an occasional infant is seen whose development has been interfered with because of excessive gratification. As a valid and clinically useful guideline, the care, socialization, and training which support infant development should contain a large component of experiences of gratification and pleasure and only a small component of frustration and deprivation. In practice it is usually possible to counsel parents or others caring for infants about how best to try to achieve such a balance in their day-by-day interactions.

The concept of parenthood as a developmental process. This includes knowledge about the crisis of becoming a parent and the adaptation it requires. There are individual differences both in an individual's readiness for parenthood and his capacity to adapt. As well, the infant's characteristics and his changing developmental needs and style affect parental attitudes and behavior. Social and psychological supports are needed for parenthood. It is not always easy, even for skilled professionals, to understand the adult in his role as a parent. A professional's training may lead him to focus mainly on the adult as an individual. This assessment must be enlarged to include his characteristics as a parent of a child of a particular age and his functioning as a family member. In the absence of such an assessment, one will fail to understand some of the influences which may be brought to bear on the infant, either to enhance or impede his development. This is especially important since most parents bring only the infant not themselves, as the patient. Along with its gratifications, child rearing is a difficult task and most parents of infants are in need of a support system. The supports, psychological and tangible, must come from their own families, from professionals, or from some other community resource if they are to develop well as parents and nurture their infants in a healthy way in a complex and often high-pressured society.

The power of unconscious influences. The idea that parents are under powerful unconscious influences is not a widely accepted operational concept among those who take care of the very young. Parents can be articulate, well-intentioned, and in their own way, conscientious. At the same time, they can be quite inadequate and frankly noxious as parents for a particular child. This is often incomprehensible to workers in settings in which infants are brought for care or treatment. The acceptance of this idea not only makes one's evaluation of the infant's problem more sensitive and comprehensive. It also is an important determinant of the way a therapeutic program for children is designed. This includes decisions about who the therapist will be, what the program's goals for the child are, and what kind of help the parents need to resolve their problems in caring for the child. Failing to appreciate the influence of unconscious factors is seen most often when advice is given ("play with your baby"; "just relax when you feed him"; "don't worry about his spitting up") and parents cannot follow it. Many infant care specialists need assistance from psychoanalytically oriented clinicians to observe and influence the contradictions between the parent's conscious intent and his behavior. Such awareness is important both to provide more effective treatment of the mother and infant, and to assess the need for referring a parent for additional psychological treatment.

THERAPEUTIC INTERVENTION IN INFANCY: A CLINICAL ILLUSTRATION

The following report is of a critical situation in the life of an infant which was alleviated through therapy. It involved both the baby and her parents. Although the situation presented is less severe than many, I have chosen this particular example because it so vividly illustrates many of the points made above.

Mary L. was eleven months old when a consultation was sought as part of a workup in the hospital pediatric ward. She had been admitted on her pediatrician's advice because of her parent's concern—which the pediatrician shared—about her delayed physical growth and recurrent episodes of vomiting. An extensive medical workup had not identified a physical reason for her symptoms. After a week in the hospital, her weight remained about the same. Her mother, who was present when the psychoanalyst consultant first came to see Mary, was distraught that no diagnosis had been made, and feared her child would "waste away and die" if something was not done soon. The consultant described Mary in his notes as "a big-eyed, sober-faced infant who looked apprehensive and began to cry weakly when I approached. I turned my gaze from her to her mother as we talked. Soon Mary stopped crying and began to suck her tongue. I took a small toy from my pocket and held it out toward her, while still talking with her mother. Mary looked interested in the toy, and while her fingers and hands made tentative grasping movements, she did not approach and grasp the toy. She did not creep on all fours, pull to stand, nor get herself into a sitting position, though she could sit with good trunk support when placed." Over the next three days, several interviews with both parents were conducted. Mary was observed in her parents' presence, when she was alone, and with her nurses. In the interviews Mary's parents revealed they had felt very much under stress in their personal lives since before the baby's birth. Mrs. L., an intelligent, attractive young woman of twenty-two, had just begun work on a graduate degree when she became pregnant. Her husband, age twenty-three, was also in graduate school. Both stated that the pregnancy had come at a bad time for them. Nonetheless, they decided not to seek an abortion and felt they would be able to manage somehow. Mary was born prematurely, weighing four-and-a-half pounds. She was kept in the hospital for three weeks after her mother returned home. While the pediatrician did not think the infant was in grave danger, Mary did have some respiratory difficulty and gained weight slowly. Mrs. L. was apprehensive about the baby's condition and could hardly bear to visit her in the premature nursery. When the infant, then described as healthy, was discharged home, the young couple felt uncertain about their ability to take care of her and they had no relatives nearby to help them. Mrs. L.'s apprehensiveness about her infant heightened when her husband's visiting mother talked about the resemblance of Mary's eyes to her own firstborn child who had died of a urinary tract anomaly at age nine months. Mary's mother abandoned her intention to breast feed, and there was trouble finding a formula the infant would take well. The baby was irritable and the mother had difficulty comforting her. As her anxiety about Mary's survival continued, she also felt angry at the child who had so disrupted her life, and had, she was convinced, little chance to grow up. Mary's mother was conscientious in carrying out the basic physical care of her infant, but was only minimally able to enjoy her through cuddling or talking, and was often not psychologically available to the baby. Feedings were rarely pleasurable for either parent or baby, and vomiting, which occurred fairly often, repelled and upset the mother. The nurses on the ward found the baby both pathetic and frustrating. They had much sympathy for the articulate, worried young parents and were concerned about the infant's fragility and failure to improve.

The first stage of the therapeutic plan arranged for the infant to remain in the hospital until substantial improvement was seen. The number of hospital personnel involved with the child was reduced. One main nurse was assigned as the infant's principal therapist. Reducing the stress in Mary's feeding situation was the first therapeutic objective. Other immediate goals included activating the infant through interactions around her bath and other situations, and encouraging Mary to play with toys, through playing for and with her. Mrs. L. was asked to live-in, but was relieved of major responsibility for child care for a few days. It was hoped that gradually she could take over the care of her infant, with the staff ready to assist as needed. In addition, Mrs. L. and her husband were to meet with the clinical social worker to discuss some of their problems, especially those regarding child care.

Therapeutic efforts began while we were obtaining the history and developing plans. Mary was moved into our research unit where it was possible to assign one nurse as her major caregiver. Temporarily, and with the parents' agreement and understanding, we asked them to spend time with Mary, but did not involve them in her care. The nurse-therapist, an experienced, skillful, and warm person, was able to accept both the infant and parents. One of her prime tasks involved the feeding situation. The nurse-therapist spent a great deal of time adapting to the baby's alternating frantic eagerness for food and avoidance of it. At first, Mary was fed in her room while alone with her nurse. Extraneous stimuli were markedly diminished. During the hour the feedings took place, the nurse talked to the baby. When Mary's attention waned, the nurse patiently waited for her to regain interest in the food. Gradually, over several days, she induced Mary to touch the food or to hold a spoon or bread crust.

The baby's bath time quickly became a major social occasion. The nurse was able to be gentle, and respected the baby's sensitivity, but she also stimulated the baby to be active. Mary soon began to splash in her bath. Sitting in the warm water, well supported by her nurse, Mary began to play with bath toys. As she was dried and dressed, her nurse continued to talk with her and was always alert for the child's response. Mary gradually became more expressive and socially responsive. The increased cathexis of toys, motor activity, and social exchanges was gratifying to both staff and parents.

During the first days, the infant's social contacts were largely restricted to and defined by her main nurse-caregiver, a second, substitute nurse, and Mary's parents. After a week, the parents' wish to spend a long weekend together away from home and infant care responsibilities was supported by the staff. By that time, Mary's parents had developed enough confidence in the hospital staff and the consultant to allow themselves to enjoy a brief vacation. The baby seemed comfortable with her nurse-therapist and the staff felt Mary would tolerate her parents' absence without mishap.

Over the next three weeks, Mary began to show more pleasure and satisfaction in eating. She became more actively interested in getting her hands into her food and in finger feeding. While she continued to cry irritably and forlornly at times, obviously from some unhappy tension state, these episodes diminished markedly. She smiled more and vocalized both responsively and spontaneously. Mary began to ask for social contact through spontaneous smiling, calling, and reaching toward others. Her increased animation and her upsurge of physical activity, as well as her weight gain, changed her appearance dramatically. Her mother began to express a tentative optimism about the outcome. With the sensitive and skillful assistance of the nurse, Mrs. L. could handle the baby and interact with her in a much more supportive and enjoyable way. Sessions with the social worker helped the parents be in close touch with the methods and goals of the treatment plan. They had the opportunity to discuss the difficulties of the past months, and to make plans for the baby's return home. During the last week of Mary's hospitalization her parents, primarily her mother, resumed care of the baby with increasing confidence and success. The nurse-therapist was available to assist when needed and saw

Mary often, but stayed in the background most of the time. The parents let the staff know when they felt ready to take Mary home. They knew they could rely on the staff for future assistance if they needed it. A period of crisis for parents and infant had been resolved successfully. The mother-infant relationship improved as did the baby's development and growth. One could not say there would be no further difficulty. Mary was probably less robust psychologically than one would have wished. Nevertheless, her object relationships were progressing and her tension and withdrawal had been lessened. In addition, Mary's parents had learned they could be helped with the problems and stresses of their lives.

SETTINGS AND SITUATIONS IN WHICH INFANTS AT RISK ARE SEEN AND CAN BE HELPED

There are several common situations in which plans for programs for the care, protection, and treatment of infants come up most often. Some of these deal with infants who are biologically vulnerable to deviational development, and who therefore need an optimizing environment in which to grow and develop. Other situations involve children who can be said to be at risk because of their life situation. Primarily these infants are without families who are prepared to nurture them in a reasonably adequate manner. Several settings and situations will be described briefly because of the frequency with which they are employed, and because an examination of these experiences shows the importance and influence of some of the guiding principles of psychoanalysis.

The child in his biological family. Many families of young children are ill equipped, unless given considerable assistance, for the multiple, complex, and often arduous tasks of child rearing. It is of central importance to assist individual parents in negotiating the psychological and adaptational crisis of parenthood, and to help them cope with a reasonable degree of success and pleasure. Providing such services over a period of time would strengthen the families of many children and prevent their decompensation. It would also permit recognizing those individuals who are trying to function as parents, but have no possibility of success. In such case, alternate plans could be developed for the infant before substantial damage occurs. Such a program of services would require developing a staff of physicians and other workers with an understanding of the early years, of what promotes or interferes with developmental process, and of what enables parents to function well.

The primary health care system. A primary health care system can become perhaps the single most important avenue through which mental health principles, including knowledge from psychoanalysis, can be translated into practices which enhance the development of infants. The physicians, nurses, and other health workers who function in clinics, child health conferences, offices, and other health agencies are usually the first persons to whom parents turn when there is a problem with their child. A disorder in infancy which ultimately proves to be due to psychological factors may present itself as a bodily symptom such as vomiting, or diarrhea. Or it may present itself as a problem in eating, sleeping, or physical growth, or as a delay in normal motor development, or social and speech functioning. In addition, a disturbance in an infant's affective expression or his capacity to play may bring a parent to seek professional help. Psychoanalytic principles are least often applied in these settings. However, there is an enormous potential for their use if such principles can be translated into practices that influence health care. Without an operational knowledge of the unconscious influences which are important determinants of parental behavior and of what they communicate to their infant, the physician or nurse may be mystified by an articulate and well-intentioned parent. If diagnosticians are not aware of the frequency of somatic manifestations of psychological difficulty, their study and treatment may be directed in an ineffective way. Moreover, infants may be incorrectly diagnosed as mentally retarded, brain damaged, aphasic, or with some other biological handicap when in fact the disorder stems from inadequate nurturing. It can be argued that what is needed is more training for primary physicians, nurses, and other health workers. However, I am convinced that favorable change requires that mental health professionals join the primary health care staff, and not simply be available as consultants.

The infant in the hospital. At the present time sick infants are treated at home as much as possible, and this possibility has increased enormously with newer methods of treating physical disease. Nevertheless, there are many times when the hospitalization of an infant becomes necessary either for diagnosis or treatment. Perhaps the most important policies designed to protect the infant's mental health are those which are intended to minimize separation from his mother or other emotionally important adults. This maintains the continuity of affectionate care by specifically important individuals. Arrangements such as rooming-in and frequent visits are essential. It is also important that the number of adults providing care and treatment for the hospitalized child be kept to a minimum.

Day care arrangements. Recognizing the importance of the child's relationships, of continuity of care, and of supporting his relationships and images of family members has an important influence on planning day care centers. It dictates, for example, that there be an adequate number of adults to take care of the developmental needs of infants and toddlers. It should also be recognized that the age at which an infant enters a day care center will strongly influence the way the experience will affect him. The length of time a child spends at the center each day is another relevant consideration, because the younger the child, the more he needs frequent contacts with emotionally important individuals who support and sustain him. The child should not be away from his parents for a longer period than he can tolerate. Guiding principles of child care, anchored in the propositions and concepts presented earlier, translate into practice through attaching the infant to a smaller, rather than larger, number of caregivers during his time in the center. In addition opportunities should be created and sponsored for the parent to be with his child at the center as frequently as possible.

For an infant, the learning environment includes many transactions with people who take care of his body and are interested in him as a social being. In day care, as in other settings, selecting staff suited to work with infants is crucially important to promoting a growth experience. The learning environment should be in accord with the developmental needs of infants and toddlers.

Adoption. The adoption of infants has developed as one solution to two of society's situations—infants without parents and adults who desire children. Perhaps the most conspicuous change in the policy of adoption agencies in the past fifteen to twenty years has been the increased trend toward placement during the early weeks of life. This practice is based on a belief in the importance of forming a close relationship with a specific maternal figure early in life and in the importance of continuity of care. Implicitly, it acknowledges that adoption at infancy is most likely to facilitate establishing bonds of love between the child and his adoptive parents, and enables them to make the child their own more quickly. This, in turn, furthers optimal development. The earlier practice of delaying placement of infants until their developmental status could be reliably measured and a prediction made about their intelligence has been largely abandoned. However, some unfortunate delays are recurring because of emphasis on the rights of unwed fathers. During the time required for the necessary legal process, the urgency of the infant's earliest psychological needs are usually overlooked to his detriment.

Foster home care. Thousands of the nation's children live in foster homes, including many infants. Finding foster parents capable of supporting the child's developmental needs is no easy task. However, understanding human behavior and motivation influences the approach of selecting foster parents. Most agencies involved in foster care aim at avoiding multiple placements and frequent changes in placement. Continuity of affectionate care from a parent surrogate is recognized as being of great importance if the child cannot receive such care from his biological parent.

Group residential care. In this country institutional care for infants has diminished in large part because of an acceptance of the proposition that an infant needs to form a primary attachment to a maternal figure who provides the major part of his care. Under these conditions, the infant gradually extends his world and benefits from relationships to other adults and to children. However, group residential care continues to exist. Sometimes this is by design. Programs are created by those who believe it is possible to provide adequate care for infants in groups. At other times, group care is used by default, for example, when a child's biological family is unable to care for him and a substitute family cannot be found. As long as there is the necessity for such care, for whatever reasons, certain questions are relevant. Will primary attachments to specific individuals be sponsored, and if so, will the group residential setting be staffed in such a way to allow this to occur? What are the qualifications of a person chosen as a caregiver for infants? Will workers be encouraged to form close attachments to infants or will this be discouraged? A number of recommendations about what that environment (primarily the human environment) should provide to promote infant development were defined in an earlier publication (Provence 1967).

Child custody issues. With increasing frequency and seriousness, issues about child custody are being raised. Many of the important issues involved for children have been discussed by Goldstein, Freud, and Solnit in *Beyond The Best Interests of The Child* (1973). This book provides a fine example of how psychoanalytic principles can be utilized to influence the decision-making processes of the courts. For it is their responsibility to decide what is in the best interest of the child, or as these authors prefer, what is the least detrimental alternative. The child under two is less likely to be shuttled back and forth between parents and other relatives than are older children. In the decision to separate or divorce the issue of who will be responsible for infant care frequently comes up. Understanding psychoanalytic developmental psychology views of the child's developmental needs is of paramount importance. It is remarkable how often one encounters parents who, with the best intentions, fail to recognize that a series of people trained in the care of infants, however competent, cannot provide the continuity of affectionate interest and care required for adequate development.

One always hopes that prevention of problems, at least of severe and disabling problems, is possible. In spite of the existence of considerable knowledge about what favorably influences infant development, we have not been very effective in applying it. We would accomplish a great deal if we were willing to develop and support, on a large scale, those services which would translate knowledge into practice. Some of the avenues through which this could occur have been mentioned. Some are supportive, and some are remedial. Early recognition of the problems of infants, children, and parents in danger could lead to the alleviation of much suffering and psychological disability. In such an effort, the application of knowledge from psychoanalysis would continue to be of vital importance.

REFERENCES

Benjamin, J.D. (1961). The innate and the experiential in development. In *Lectures on Experimental Psychiatry,* ed. H.W. Brosin, pp. 19–42. Pittsburgh: University of Pittsburgh Press.

Ferholt, J., and Provence, S. (1976). Diagnosis and treatment of an infant with psychophysiological vomiting. *Psychoanalytic Study of the Child* 31:439–460.

Goldstein, J., Freud, A., and Solnit, A.J. (1973). *Beyond the Best Interests of the Child.* New York: The Free Press.

Hartmann, H. (1939). *Ego Psychology and the Problem of Adaptation.* New York: International Universities Press, 1958.

Provence, S. (1967). *A Guide for the Care of Infants in Groups.* New York: Child Welfare League of America.

Provence, S. (1972). Psychoanalysis and the treatment of psychological disorders of infancy. In *A Handbook of Child Psychoanalysis: Research, Theory and Practice,* ed. B. Wolman, pp. 191–220. New York: Van Nostrand Reinhold Company.

Provence, S., Naylor, A., and Patterson, J. (1977). *The Challenge of Daycare.* New Haven: Yale University Press.

Provence, S., and Ritvo, S. (1961). Effects of deprivation on institutional children: disturbances in development of relationship to inanimate objects. *Psychoanalytic Study of the Child* 16:189–205.

Chapter 22

AN ANALYTICALLY ORIENTED APPROACH TO THE

DIAGNOSTIC EVALUATION

John A. Sours, M.D.

The structure of the diagnostic evaluation is essentially the same whether the child enters analysis, psychotherapy, tutoring, receives some other modality of help, or requires no treatment at all (see also chapters 3, 4 and 5 on evaluation). The consultant must recognize that his evaluation may further treatment, if it is necessary, or interfere with it. He must establish a relationship with child and parents that will provide him the information he needs to advise them as to the proper course, and to help them take that advice.

Although the opening phase of insight-oriented therapy is generally regarded as commencing with the completion of the diagnostic workup and the treatment agreement, it really begins with the referring phone call and the initial arrangements for the first consultation hour. Strictly speaking, the opening phase is the beginning of the treatment process in which an attempt is made to foster the therapeutic alliance, anticipate interfering factors, lay the groundwork for a working, informational relationship with the parents, anticipate the transference potential, and indicate that as much as possible treatment is to be a verbal communication. In child treatment, the opening phase is often the child's first experience of separation from his mother; for the prelatency child this separation is often a convoluted part of the first month or so of treatment. The beginnings of a positive transference and a therapeutic alliance are in the opening phase of treatment. Successful initiation of treatment requires proper handling of parent and child during the evaluation. In addition, the consultation provides the information that allows the consultant to determine the nature of the pathology and the optimal treatment.

THE INITIAL CONTACT WITH THE CHILD'S PARENTS

The child therapist immediately finds himself in a multiangular relationship when he receives a phone call from the parent of a child to be seen in consultation. The therapist's first question to himself is usually an attempt to identify the referring party. In 90 percent of cases, it is the mother who calls either because she is most interested in the consultation, or because this task has been delegated to her by the child's father. Occasionally, calls for treatment may be made by the child's social worker, who has been looking after the family, or by a guardian. Some referral occurs on the basis of social contacts. Occasionally the parent's own therapist may make the initial call. Parents' friends may also make contact, hoping to make it easier for the child's parents to call the therapist. Such friends often have a child in treatment with the therapist, or may have relatives who do. Consultations may also be initiated by school teachers or guidance personnel, tutors, or learning disability therapists. Parents will occasionally call for consultation and clearly refuse to indicate how the therapist's name was learned.

When the mother calls, she frequently encounters a telephone answering service which is apt to be gruff, mispronounce her name, or ignore her. This immediately prejudices her attitude toward the therapist and his style of operation. A malfunctioning or impersonal telephone answering machine that taxes the mother's frustration level may also color her view of the therapist. Over the phone, the mother usually will attempt to focus on her child's problems by indicating difficulties in school behavior and performance. Isolated symptoms, like bed-wetting, nightmares, and separation anxiety, are often cited. Divorced mothers are very apt to concentrate on the what they assume to be effects of the divorce on the child. For example, a divorced mother may indicate alarm for her five-year-old boy. Every time the father calls, the boy plays with his penis while speaking on the telephone. The mother can be reluctant to disclose who referred her and resent the therapist pursuing this point because of her concern that he may have a priority of referring sources. In speaking with the mother it is important to learn the age of the child and his name. It is also important to assume nothing from the mother's initial remarks over the telephone. When the mother inquires about whether the consultant has time for her child, invariably she also means time for treatment if it is necessary. It is seldom that the therapist or clinic can guarantee treatment time. It is important that this be indicated. Oftentimes the mother will not indicate whether her spouse will accompany her to the first session. It is better not to pursue this because the whole question of her relationship to her husband should emerge spontaneously in the first consultation hour. It is important to signify that the initial meeting with the parent is for information and history gathering, and the child's presence is unnecessary. A mother may suggest that she prepare a chronological history of the child's development, as well as a chronicle of the family on both sides. This type of data gathering may be helpful, but one must be wary lest it drain away from the first consultation hour and set an unhappy style for further meetings. Many parents, aware of family therapy, assume the entire family should come for the first visit. It is useful to tell the mother over the telephone that you will help her prepare the child for his consultation. When giving the mother her first appointment hour, one should reiterate the time of the hour and the office address. Often her anxiety will make her forget and this will lead to confusion and embarrassment.

Fathers who call for appointments for their children are usually widowers, divorced, or uncertain of their spouse's competence in the matter. Or else the father is a mental health professional looking for a consultation for his child. There are some instances in which a father will call because of his increasing concern for his child in the face of his inability to communicate with his wife. Often the father's reason for the referral is superficial, simplistic, and obscured by denial. I am reminded of a referral on which the father called indicating that he felt his son was much too hesitant and timorous. According to his father, this was manifested by his faulty golf swing. The father was a professional golfer who had done badly that year and projected his concerns onto the child. In the first consultation, fathers are apt to be more critical of the consultant than mothers. Many ask for professional credentials, academic affiliations, and move quickly into a competitive stance which hides their fear that the therapist will supplant them. Occasionally the father appears for the first hour, and discloses he is divorced and a practicing homosexual. He may be genuinely and realistically concerned about his son's difficulties. However, he may also worry that the boy's heterosexual child therapist will take umbrage to him and attempt to alienate his son. In arranging consultations with fathers it is important that time be tactfully considered lest the father feel the therapist regards himself as more important and entitled to chose a convenient time in his own busy schedule.

Parents will occasionally ask whether psychological testing should be done before both they and their child are seen. Frequently they are concerned about minimal brain damage (MBD) or psychosis. Sometimes we encounter child therapists who, concerned they may miss subtle variations of MBD, acquiesce to the parents' request for premature testing. This is an unwise practice because psychological testing should be ordered for clarification of specific diagnostic, dynamic, and structural issues elucidated during the course of the consultation. Psychological testing is comparable to ordering a specific series of x-rays in medicine in order to clarify a diagnostic problem. There is always the danger that the testing psychologist will increase the child's resistances to consultation and treatment. The psychologist may choose to meet with the parents after the test session and take it upon himself to make diagnostic, if not therapeutic, recommendations.

Parents will often inquire on the telephone how many times it will be necessary to see the therapist before the child is seen. It is important to let them know it may be necessary to see them several times to obtain a proper developmental history. Extensive diagnostic interviewing of the parents—beyond two or three sessions—heightens the chances of the parent developing a transference. In addition, the therapist may react to the patient with a regressive counter-identification with one of his parents. The latter is especially true in working with adolescents. The mother is usually the best source of the developmental history, which the consultant may not obtain until the third or fourth parental session. One should not, however, exclude the father, if he is interested in coming after the first parental hour. Parents may suggest the child's caretaker, be she grandmother or maid, is a better historian and want the consultant to see her. Frequently the parents are correct, but if such a person is seen she should be reassured that the child's problems will not be blamed on her. There are occasions when grandparents want to meet with the consultant or therapist. This should be permitted only if the parents suggest and support the idea. It is a delicate matter, especially when the grandparents are financially supporting the treatment and insist on meeting the therapist to assess their investment.

Both parents may blame themselves for their child's condition and fear that the consultant will blame them too. Often they fear that he will take the side of the other parent. This is especially frequent when the parents are separated or contemplating divorce. (See chapter 14, on the role of the parent in child analysis.) When taking a history, the consultant should be aware of these parental concerns.

How much developmental history one needs before meeting the child depends on the clinical problem and the complexity of the parental situation. One should keep in mind, however, that the initial developmental history is always incomplete and sometimes erroneous. When faced with their shame and guilt, all parents, whether they know it or not, are inaccurate. Their own repression, screen memories, and scotomatization also work against a reconstruction. Only during the course of treatment is the correct development history revealed and then usually through the transference. Some corroboration by the parents is possible.

The parents should be told, if insight-oriented treatment is necessary, that the therapist will be meeting regularly with the mother and, if possible, the father in order to keep abreast of developments at home and to obtain a better understanding of the child. The initial developmental history is a chronological growth map which points out in rough outline the effects of stresses and strains on development. Important external events in the child's life and the ongoing developmental history of the parents is also determined. How the parents negotiated their own development in their twenties and thirties is useful in understanding the child's past milieu. The parent will usually want to provide information from schools, psychological tests, past consultations, and pediatric reports. It is better to forgo perusing this information until the child has been seen thoroughly in consultation. One can indicate to the parents that the therapist would like to take a fresh look before he is biased by past opinions, even though they have been provided by the most competent people. A call to the child's teacher, school psychologist, or therapist before the child has been evaluated is also premature. In the first hour the parents will sometimes request a tutor be engaged immediately if the child has a learning disability. I prefer to wait until I have evaluated the child and then help parents find a tutor able to work with the therapist without the inclination to function as an auxiliary analyst.

Psychological testing should also be postponed until the child has been thoroughly evaluated.[1] Then, if indicated, testing can be done in a collaborative manner. The therapist and psychologist coordinate their efforts in an attempt to attain specific information about the child's affective, cognitive, and intellectual functioning. The child and his parents should be prepared for testing. They may each have preconceived notions about psychological tests. The child should not be tested if there is any danger of harming the future therapeutic alliance or if there is a danger of flooding the child's ego with anxiety. A referral to a child neurologist concurrently with psychological testing is premature. At this point, such extratherapeutic contacts can affect the potential transference and jeopardize the therapeutic alliance.

In helping parents prepare their child for his first consultation, it is important to let them express what they feel will be the most acceptable and meaningful reason for the child. The parents' desire to conceal the fact that the therapist is a physician or a clinical psychologist must always be avoided. Parents may want to emphasize a specific symptom as a reason of referral, but it is better for them to identify for the child his emotional pain. In preparing preschool children, one must take particular care to insure the child he will not be subjected to a painful medical examination and will not be unduly separated from his mother. It is best to indicate to the parents that the child will be seen for the entire session and they will not be included. For those children where separation anxiety can be anticipated it is helpful to let the parents know the therapist will assist them in easing the child's entry into the consultation room. If the mother insists the child will not come in without her, the therapist can acknowledge a willingness to accommodate this arrangement, while at the same time reassuring her one is often surprised by the ease with which a child can enter a consultation room. It is important to reassure the parents that after the child has been seen, they will again meet with the therapist to discuss his findings and make appropriate plans. Emphasis here is on the informational alliance with the parents.

In preparing parents for the consultation and the possibility of treatment, one should keep in mind the parents' motivation for the child's treatment counterbalances their psychopathology unless the latter is strongly destructive to the child (Bernstein 1958). When the pathology interferes with the consultation and it is apparent treatment will be seriously jeopardized, then the possibility of the parents' own treatment, either individually or as a couple, should be considered. However, if possible, this discussion should be postponed until the end of the consultation. Likewise, it is important to discuss during the consultation treatment schedule, fees, charging practices for missed sessions and vacations, etc., and to deal with these issues directly. However, the therapist should not discuss these issues too early in the consultation, before the evaluation is completed and the treatment plan presented, because the parents may feel they are being rushed into an unbreakable contract which will be binding for some years.

For the consultation of the adolescent patient, an entirely different procedure is followed. When the parent calls for the consultation, the mother is told it is usually preferable that the adolescent be seen first. On the telephone an attempt should be made to obtain some idea of the presenting problem. If the adolescent is in earshot of the parent at the time of the telephone call, it is best that the therapist speak to him then, introduce himself, and give the teenager the appointment and any necessary directions to the office. The parents are told the therapist will be in touch with them to obtain background history and to discuss their teenager's situation. When the adolescent is seen in consultation, the therapist must mention at an appropriate point that in his experience parents want to meet with the therapist to know what he is like and to determine if the teenager is in good hands. The teenager is then reassured that strict rules of confidentiality are followed, especially for adolescent patients. The teenager should know in advance about the meeting between his parents and the therapist and should be given a full disclosure of what was discussed and what his parents said. Evaluating and treating the preadolescent—the child between latency and early adolescence—requires even more tact and foresight. The preadoles-

cent is quick to revolt, be resistant to the development of transference, and be fearful of loss of controls and his sense of narcissistic
self-sufficiency (Harley 1974).

ARRIVAL OF THE CHILD FOR THE FIRST
CONSULTATION SESSION

The preschool child is most apt to clutch and cling to the mother.
The opening phase of the treatment of a preschooler always requires
more thought and patience. Sometimes we are surprised to see the
preschooler gleefully run into the consultation room and make an
inspection of the toys and items in the playroom. Many preschool
children display an avid curiosity for the therapist as a new person in
his life. For those children initially reluctant, it is helpful if the therapist
warmly distracts the child from his mother and does not linger in the
waiting room. Chatting with parents does not help a reluctant preschooler. If the child absolutely refuses, he can be reassured the door
will be left ajar. If all these approaches fail, the mother should then be
invited into the office. Encouraging the mother to read a newspaper or
magazine may calm both mother and the child. Such tactical approaches should be discussed with the parents before the first visit of
the preschooler—or any child who may not have achieved object constancy.

There is no point asking the preschooler why he has come to see the
therapist. Observing his play, making comments which encourage play,
and watching his overall motor-effective behavior is most important.
One should never be surprised if the preschooler's mother suddenly
bursts into the session to check on the child. One should usually not
interpret in front of the mother unless the comment is for the mother
and does not make the child more tense. At the end of the hour the
mother's reunion with the child is often informative. Her anxious questions of what happened, and her need to question and reassure the child,
should be noted as well as the child's reactions.

Oedipal and latency children are usually brought to their first session
by their mother. Occasionally the father will bring the child if the hour
is convenient for him. Separation is usually not difficult for children in
this age range. The child's behavior in the waiting room should be

observed. Whether he reads magazines, talks to people, or plays with a child waiting for another therapist is important.

In the first hour, let the child decide where he wants to sit. Encouraging him to go into the playroom may offend him. If he chooses the playroom, one should not mention specific materials or an activity he should do. Let him first talk and see what he wants to discuss. The materials provided for the child should be simple enough to elicit communications—free expressions of wishes, feelings, and thoughts. (Pearson's Handbook [1968] and Maenchen's paper [1970] provide good discussions of play materials.) The material of the first session or two may be entirely irrelevant to what seems to be the child's problem. At the end of the first hour, the child should know the therapist will see him again, because it is important he understands whatever trouble and pain he has.

In the first consultation hour with the preadolescent or adolescent one should guard against treating the patient as a small child. If the teenager is over sixteen, it is not advisable to use his first name because "overfriendliness" can unsettle the teenager. In the first hour with the teenager it is most important that the therapist quickly identify his affect and thereby assure the patient he has some understanding of his anguish and pain. The contemporary adolescent has simultaneous contrasting feelings which disrupt the self. The therapist must also display an interest in helping him work out his difficulties without involving the teenager's parents.

During consultation hours the therapist thinks about the child in categories referred to in the mental status examination. His approach is not methodological and procedural. It is a way of seeing and thinking about the child and his behavior. He carefully follows the child's motor behavior, play, and affects. Questions are asked only to clarify what the child is doing. They are kept at a minimum. (In some ways, the child consultant is like the experienced British diagnostician who stands alertly by the patient's bedside observing everything about him before deciding if he requires further examination.) The child is not encouraged to do any specific thing in the session. This free-floating observational approach is hardly novel to adult assessment. One does not push a piece of paper in front of an adult patient and ask him to write serial sevens and draw human figures. When this kind of intervention occurs in child therapy, the therapist's anxiety about the openendedness of the consultation is apparent. One is reminded of Ferenczi's first consultation with Arphad. "I gave him some paper and a pencil and he immediately drew a cock (not unskillfully). Then I got him to tell me the story about the cock, but he was already bored and wanted to get back to his toys. Direct psychoanalytic investigation was therefore impossible, and I had to confine myself to getting a lady who was interested in the child and, being a neighbor and friend of the family, could watch him for hours at a time, to note down his curious remarks and gestures." Ferenczi (1913) displayed his unfamiliarity with children in this consultation. He did not realize that Arphad was not able to free-associate like an adult and that information about the child's neurotic disturbances could come only through free play.

The entire mental status can be done by observation, a kind of free-floating attention, following the child's affect and only asking questions which resonate with the child's affects. This is the activity involved in the assessment of the child: general appearance, motility, coordination, speech, intelligence, thinking and perception, emotional reaction, manner of relating, fantasies, dreams, and character of play (Goodman and Sours 1967). The assessment presupposes the knowledge of childhood psychopathology and its common ground with adult psychopathology (Freeman 1974, Flappan and Neubauer 1975).

We will not consider the range of diagnostic possibilities in children in this chapter, which emphasizes procedural and dynamic matters. The consultant should be alert to diagnostic considerations and decide whether the child suffers from distress due to normal or pathological developmental conflicts, developmental arrests or lags, neurosis, schizophrenia, a borderline condition, brain damage, cognitive defects, reactions to environmental stress, etc. However the consultant must not simply view the child in terms of categories which are oversimplified statements of overlapping conditions. He must evaluate the patient's entire personality and interaction with those about him.

The question of neurological impairment and damage must be pursued if it is suggested by findings of the mental status, the developmental history, school reports, or the child's general appearance. Expressive and receptive language disturbances, apraxia, reading disability, poor fine-motor coordination, poor balance, dysdiadockokinesia, clumsiness, tremor, and strabismus, and choreiform and athetoid movement are significant hard findings and call for pediatric neurological consultation.

On the other hand, soft neurological signs are elusive, slight, variable, and not clearly associated with neuroanatomical lesions. These include hyperactivity (high activity level, incessant and driven activity, flight of ideas, garrulousness, and no cognitive focus), poor concentration and slowed attention, learning problems, impulsivity, low frustration tolerance, resistance to social demands, dependence, introversion, emotional lability, and irritability. None is specifically neurological; all can be mimicked by emotional disorders. If the child consultant expects to treat the child, it is best that he not examine the child in the traditional neurological approach. It is preferable that he do a "play" neurological examination during the course of the mental status (Goodman and Sours 1967). An adequate neurological appraisal can be done without a reflex hammer and pin.[2] (Neurologists at the National Hospital, Queen's Square, aptly demonstrate this fact by their subtle observational approach.) If the consultant is still uncertain about soft signs, his level of neurological competence then calls for a neurological consultation and, quite possibly, psychoneurological testing (Siegel 1975).

In evaluating a child's history, past psychological testing, pediatric reports, and school appraisals, the child consultant must always question the evidence for any reported minimal brain damage (MBD). Especially among paramedical and educational people, the MBD diagnosis, now an umbrella term,[3] refers to a variety of developmental and neurological disturbances. Many of these disturbances require differential diagnostic experience and sophistication and more than an acquaintance with childhood psychopathology and genetic-structural development (Schrag and Divoky 1975). Occasionally a trial period of psychological treatment is necessary to form a proper diagnosis and treatment plan.

END OF THE DIAGNOSTIC CONSULTATION WITH THE CHILD

It is always difficult to know how much to tell the child about his difficulties. However, one should indicate to the child an awareness that his pain leads to some specific difficulties. If the therapist plans to see the child for treatment, this information should be given him. If he is to be referred to a colleague, it is essential he be told this and encouraged to explore his feeling that he is being rejected. The reason for the

referral should be explained to the child. If the child is to be seen in
treatment by the consultant, it is not necessary to discuss the frequency
of sessions at this time. This matter must first be discussed with the
child's parents. It is important to have an idea of what the child's
schedule is, including commitments to play, lessons, tutors, and other
afterschool activities. The therapist should tell the child he will have
a discussion with his parents next. Adolescents and preadolescents
must be reassured completely of confidentiality. With younger children,
where it is necessary that parents have an ongoing understanding of the
child, strict confidentiality is neither appropriate nor helpful except in
matters of sexuality, fantasies, and "secrets." In fact, the myth of
complete confidentiality is often perpetuated in child psychiatry and
expressed by the attitude that parents are hostile and destructive to the
child and must be kept at arm's length if treatment is to proceed
successfully. It is necessary to educate parents to the nuances of the
child's problems if the parents are to understand him and bring about
some change in themselves to sufficiently facilitate the child's development. This approach is in lieu of advising parents on what they must
do to help the child without giving them an understanding of him. To
give advice to parents is unrealistic when we know from adult therapy
that such advice is not effective and, in fact, is met with intense resistances. From child practice, we know that when a sexual seduction by
a parent occurs, the therapist is tempted to take a stand against the
parent's action. We also know a parent will seldom accept this kind of
recommendation. In such instances, frequently the parent's seductive
activities then become covert.

It is useful for the therapist to try to anticipate his countertransference liability for each case. Bornstein (1948) and Kohrman (1971) have
discussed the enormous possibilities for countertransference problems
in treating children and adolescents. The therapist should also consider
his attitude toward the child's parents: is he identifying with them, confusing them with his own parents or his analyst, or competing with them
or trying to rescue the child?

In formulating the case before meeting with the parents, the child
therapist should review his historical material and the consultative play
sessions. He should use a mental status schema and his own version of
a metapsychological assessment to draw together his observations and
impressions of the child. Silverman and Ross's coordinated diagnostic

profile in the Wolman Handbook (1972) illustrates the need for simplicity. In looking at these data it is helpful to keep in mind the child's developmental lines, the sequences of the libidinal phases, the mode of aggression, ego defenses and responses, sucking and weaning and eating behavior, the child's attitude toward cleanliness, his feelings about sharing possessions of the body with the mother. With an adolescent one should view independence and self-determination, the child's egocentric view of the world, and all erotic play, and transitional object activity (A. Freud 1965). The developmental profile is also a very useful way of collating data and integrating one's thoughts about the child.

Diagnostic criteria (Nagera 1963) also include libidinal and aggressive drive development, ego and superego assessment, regression and fixation which point to the level of the child's dynamic and structural conflict, the nature of the regression, the degree of internalization conflict, the level of language, the capacity of the child to form a therapeutic alliance (particularly in the preschool age range), his dependency on primary objects, his use of the analyst as a primary object, the quantity and quality of the transference that can be expected, and the degree to which one can anticipate aggressiveness. This overall assessment is done as part of the diagnostic formulation. Although Nagera's full assessment is useful for research, it is too cumbersome to be of general use in practice. A therapist should be familiar with the full assessment so he can adapt it to his own style and particular needs in both diagnosis and periodic assessments of children during treatment.

ARRANGEMENTS FOR TREATMENT

In first arranging treatment it is important to delineate for the parents the child's dynamic disturbances, and to formulate it in language that it is comprehensible to them. Since the therapist's overall initial formulation is tentative it should be kept to himself, ready for emendation and change as treatment progresses and material unfolds. It is also vital the parents understand what comprises treatment for a child of that age—whether it is play therapy, a combination of play and verbal therapy, or for the late adolescent, therapy or analysis. The mother of a young child, particularly if she is a symbiotic mother, will want to know what the therapist can offer her child that she cannot provide herself. In fact, she may even raise the question of why her love is "not enough" . . . "why (she) cannot play as well as you with the child," etc. Frequently the parents will inquire how they will know when the end of treatment is approaching and what they can expect will be the duration of the treatment. It is helpful to compare the child with the adult, indicating that treatment is usually not as long as with adults, although one cannot always be certain. In any case, the goal of treatment is not simply symptom removal, but the restoration of the child to his expected developmental path. It should be made clear to the parents that the formulation of the child is not complete and finished. You will be learning more about the child as treatment progresses. Your relationship with them is primarily informational, and they will share with you (below the preadolescent child) information helpful to them and that they should change nothing abruptly in their relationship with the child or in his environment lest they "muddy the waters" for the therapist. Even though visits with the parents will be arranged, they should be encouraged to call the therapist if they feel he should know something immediately. The parents should understand the therapist cannot work in a vacuum. From the transference the therapist will get clues about developmental and traumatogenic events and situations and will want to ask the parents additional historical questions. As affective changes occur in the treatment, the child's memory is apt to expand, and he will be able to provide more genetic material. This can be contrasted with the developmental data provided by the parents (Kennedy 1972).

At this point consultations with psychologists, language therapists, or child neurologists may be made if they are necessary.[4] It is essential the parent know exactly the indication and what can be expected. The child will also need to be prepared. Particularly he will need to understand that this consultation is not in any respect a substitute for treatment, but is an ancillary procedure for learning more about his difficulties. The parents may want to know about the advisability of putting the child into a sports group, karate lessons, an afterschool play group, etc., as a way of fostering his development. Here specific consideration for each child is essential. As I have indicated above, the range of possible therapies is large (see chapter 23). The consultant must recommend the appropriate treatment for the particular child. Many child therapists find it difficult to recommend intensive treatment because they are afraid of frightening the parents and making them resistive. The therapist must be convinced himself of its advisability and efficacy before he can convince the parents.

Sometimes when analysis is indicated, but the parents cannot accept it, it is better to start intensive therapy on a two- to three-times-a-week basis and then allow both parents and child to become comfortable with that frequency. At an appropriate time, when the child's conflicts become clear to the parents, his need for intensity manifests itself, and a therapeutic alliance is formed, increasing the frequency is more acceptable. I do not feel the child's school should be contacted about treatment unless it is necessary because of the child's academic difficulty or to arrange his schedule.

A fee schedule must be established. The therapist's position about charging for missed sessions should be stated at this time, but only if the therapist feels he knows the parents well and has a firm relationship with them. Charging for missed sessions, when it is not possible to fill the vacant session with a consultation or parent visit, can sometimes be more tactfully explained once the child is in treatment and has missed a session. By that time the parents know the therapist; and he feels more comfortable discussing financial matters with the parents. If referral to another therapist is necessary because of schedule, the parents should understand the reason for the referral and not be left with a sense of rejection and a feeling the therapist does not like their child. It is essential this referral be made to the therapist with his full knowledge of the initial consultation. Otherwise the parents' feeling that they are starting over will become real.

NOTES

1. Editor's note: Postponement is a far from universal procedure. See note 4.

2. Editor's note: Many psychiatrists avoid doing a neurological examination themselves if they think the child may enter psychological treatment. The child might misunderstand the procedures and conceive of the physical contact as part of psychotherapy. He might feel seduced or attacked and then fear further contact with the therapist.

3. Some alternative terms have been used to describe MBD. They are

not, however, all synonymous for MBD. There is, for example, a difference between minimal brain damage, an organic condition, and func-
tional disorders such as maturational lag or developmental imbalance
and dyslexia. Hyperactivity may be due to cerebral dysinhibition or
simply anxiety or excitement. These alternative terms are: The Strauss
Syndrome, The Brain-Injured Child, The Hyperactive Child, Minimal
Brain Injury, Minimal Brain Dysfunction, The Brain Damaged Child,
Minimal Neurologic Handicap, The Hyperkinetic Child, Dyslexia,
Chronic Brain Syndrome, The Perceptually Handicapped Child, The
Perceptually Disabled Child, The Dysfunctioning Child, Development
Imbalance, Maturational Lag, Central Nervous System Dysfunction,
The Child with Cognitive Defects, and Neurophysiologic Immaturity
(Clements 1966).

4. Editor's note: Many consultants prefer referring the child for
psychological tests, special studies of cognitive style and abilities, physical examinations (including neurological studies), when necessary, earlier in the consultation. The consultant can then integrate the findings
of these examinations with the historical and direct observational data
in making the evaluation. Treatment plans can best be made after doing
these studies.

REFERENCES

Bernstein, I. (1958) The importance of characteristics of parents in
    deciding on child analysis. *Journal of the American Psychoanalytic
    Association* 6:71–78.
Bornstein, B. (1948). Emotional barriers in the understanding and
    treatment of young children. *American Journal of Orthopsychiatry*
    18:691–697.
Clements, S.D. (1966). *Minimal Brain Dysfunction in Children.*
    NINDB Monograph No. 3, U.S. Department of Health, Education
    and Welfare.
Ferenczi, S. (1913). A little Chanticleer. In *Sex in Psycho-Analysis,* pp.
    204–213. New York: Dover.
Flappan, D., and Neubauer, P.B. (1975). *Assessment of Early Child
    Development.* New York: Jason Aronson.
Freeman, T. (1974). Childhood psychopathology and psychotic

phenomena in adults. *British Journal of Psychiatry* 124:556–563.

Freud, A. (1965) *Normality and Pathology in Childhood.* New York: International Universities Press.

Goodman, J.D., and Sours, J.A. (1967). *The Child Mental Status Examination.* New York: Basic Books.

Harley, M., ed. (1974). *The Analyst and the Adolescent at Work.* New York: Quadrangle.

Kennedy, H.E. (1972) Problems in reconstruction in child analysis. *Psychoanalytic Study of the Child* 26:386–402.

Kohrman, R., Fineberg, H.H., Gelman, R.C., and Weiss, S. (1971). Technique of child analysis: problems in counter-transference. *International Journal of Psycho-Analysis* 52:487–497.

Maenchen, A. (1970). On the technique of child analysis in relation to stages of development. *Psychoanalytic Study of the Child* 25:175–208.

Nagera, H. (1963) The developmental profile: notes on some practical considerations regarding its use. *Psychoanalytic Study of the Child* 18:511–540.

Pearson, G.H.J. (1968). *A Handbook of Child Psychoanalysis.* New York: Basic Books.

Schrag, P., and Divoky, D. (1975). *The Myth of the Hyperactive Child.* New York: Pantheon.

Siegel, M.G. (1975). Psychological testing. In *Personality Development and Deviation,* ed. G.H. Wiedeman, pp. 456–486. New York: International Universities Press.

Wolman, B.B., ed. (1972) *Handbook of Child Psychoanalysis.* New York: Van Nostrand Reinhold.

Chapter 23

THE APPLICATION OF CHILD ANALYTIC

PRINCIPLES TO FORMS OF CHILD PSYCHOTHERAPY

John A. Sours, M.D.

For a number of reasons child psychotherapy has been comparatively neglected over the years. The responsibility for helping children with emotional problems was initially invested in educators whose efforts were to foster controls and facilitate mastery and achievement. Only after World War I were psychoanalytic concepts made available to educators. From a small group of Viennese teachers emerged a theory and a technique of child analysis which was conceptually consolidated before World War II.

Outside of child analysis, the main therapeutic thrust remained with educators and pediatricians. After 1945, various forms of child psychotherapies began. Most were time-limited, focused play therapies and directive, manipulative therapies. Great hope was placed in casework efforts with the expectation that education of parents would eventually be therapeutic and prophylactic for children. The problem-solving orientation of casework, however, was disappointing. Eventually family therapy developed, drawing its inspiration from the facts and theories developed by psychoanalysis and from the sociology of small groups.

In the last decade child analysis has gained an increasing acceptance as a treatment modality rather than just a body of knowledge of human behavior, interesting and valuable to theorists of the mind (A. Freud

1971). However, there has been no advance in psychoanalytic child psychotherapy as great as the achievements in the 1940s in adult psychiatry when techniques of psychotherapy were studied and refined by adult analysts. During the recent exfoliation of adult treatments, nothing comparable occurred in child treatment. Over twenty years ago, Buxbaum (1954) called for research in the application of treatment techniques to the spectrum of childhood psychopathology. "When we know which technique is best suited for which particular disturbance, we will be able to make optimum use of the constructive ideas of child therapy produced under the influence of psychoanalysis" (1954, p. 297).

To a great extent, child analysis has contributed to the understanding of children and techniques of treating them because it exposes a therapist to an intense experience. It is comparable to that of a supervised adult analytic treatment where there is a rich fluidity in the triadic situation, both between and among the patient, analyst, and supervisor (Malcove 1975). The child's parents heighten the therapist's emotional reactions and overall awareness, and to some degree provide developmental information useful for analytic reconstruction. Material in child analysis is clearer and less derivative than in adult work once the child's modes of communication are understood. Transference manifestations, fantasies, dreams, and responses to strains and traumas are readily encountered. The immaturity of the child's ego and superego, and the pressure of his instinctual drives make treatment a dynamic experience for the therapist. This is especially true if the theoretical and technical approach to treatment is based on an understanding of infantile sexuality and psychosexual development. With increasing experience in child analysis, theory becomes less Cartesian and more clinically appreciated. Furthermore, theories of human development and of the mind, when viewed through the everyday experiences of the child analyst, are alive, exciting, and applicable to clinical experiences and phenomena. In understanding that theory does not precede clinical fact, the child analyst is able to closely study techniques and tactical maneuvers in all child treatments. Child analytic concepts help the child psychotherapist map his course and explore the rugged terrain of therapeutic intervention. Through the child analytic experience, the therapist obtains a fuller appreciation of actual childhood events, adultomorphized memories of childhood, the family romance, screen memories, and the highly personalized myths of childhood.

We classify treatment of children as indirect and direct therapies. In the former the child is helped through alterations in his environment, predominantly his family. In direct therapies the child himself is seen. Often the two modes of intervention are used concomitantly.

We have examined child analysis as a form of direct child therapy in preceding sections of this book. In this chapter we will concentrate on psychoanalytically oriented psychotherapy, a form of interpretive treatment based on analytic understanding. This treatment, which may be a diluted form of prolonged, open-ended intensive treatment, may also be less intense and briefer. It usually aims at dealing with basic personality structure. Other child therapies attack specific immediate problems rather than attempt personality alteration, or use specific and limited modes of intervention. Often the techniques of the various child therapies derive from child analysis. In addition, psychoanalytic knowledge can help understand the modes of action of treatments that arose independently of analysis.

INDIRECT THERAPIES

Indirect treatments do not involve the child per se. They take place through the parents by encouraging them to change the child's environment, urging them to seek treatment for themselves, or by seeing the parents for marital therapy or to help them to communicate with their child. These therapies are based on psychoanalytic observations that the child's neurosis may result from or be reinforced by maladaptive parental behavior. Often if the adults can change, the child will get better. Sophisticated clinicians are aware of the complex interaction between parent and child, and of the persistence of neurotic unconscious conflicts even after the environment has changed. They are cognizant of the fact that the child, as well as the parents, is instrumental in the etiology of his disorder (see chapters 14 and 17).

We find a variety of indirect treatments (Allen 1946, Hartman and Hurn 1958, Krug and Stuart 1953) have been used with children. These include attitude therapy (Levy 1937), family therapies (Szurek 1942), the well-established casework techniques (Coleman 1949, Hamilton 1947), and the more recently organized parent effectiveness therapies and crisis intervention.

DIRECT THERAPIES

In direct therapies, the child himself is seen by and interacts with the therapist. This category includes child analysis, psychoanalytically oriented psychotherapy and other forms of therapy.

Child analysis. In the last decade child analysis has become increasingly used in the intensive treatment of children. It has been said that it is the only intensive treatment for children (Bernstein 1975). In large part the increased utilization of child analysis is a result of the widening interest in early human development and preoedipal pathology (A. Freud 1946, 1965) which facilitates the scope of indications. The predominant type of child analysis is Freudian in this country (Sterba 1959), but there are Jungian and Kleinian (see chapter 15) groups in various parts of the United States.

Child analysis relies principly on interpretation for its effectiveness. It proceeds from the surface to the depth, analyzing resistances and defenses before id content to allow interpretation to move freely between id and ego. It offers the person of the analyst as a transference object for the revival and interpretation of unconscious fantasies and attitudes. Impulses are analyzed as far as possible in a state of frustration to keep them from being acted out and gratified. Relief of tension doesn't come from catharsis, but from lifting material from primary thought process to secondary thought process. Like adult analysis, child analysis turns id into ego content (A. Freud 1965). Defenses are altered, and energy freed for adaptive uses.

Analysis is the treatment of choice for permanent, neurotic symptomatology and regression if the child's future development is endangered or his emotional development has been compromised. It is indicated when, against a background of object constancy and ego and id balances, there is neurotic interference with libidinal development which reduces the strength of libido to overcome neurotic regression and fixation. It is also indicated when there is neurotic, quantitative, and qualitative interference with ego development. Analysis is often of value in cases where object constancy has not been achieved, the child is too immature to internalize, an intrasystemic or intersystemic imbalance exists, no regulatory stability or neurophysiological balance holds, and the child seems predisposed to anxiety, frustration intolerance, omnipotence, and pathological aggression. Careful assessment of each child is required to determine the optimal therapeutic approach. In order for the child to benefit from analysis he must be sufficiently intelligent and have sufficient potential for psychological mindedness to understand the analyst's interpretations. He must also be able to tolerate the relative abstinence that analysis requires. At times a trial analysis is necessary to make this decision, or a period of time in therapy or in nursery school is needed to permit ego building. Other considerations include whether the child's parents' motivation for treatment transcends pathogenic aspects of their pathology, whether at least one parent will be able to support the analysis, whether the parents can accept the child's improvement and whether travel, schedule, finances and other logistics of four to five visits a week will block parental cooperation (see chapter 3).

Child psychoanalytic psychotherapy. The structure and techniques of this treatment are similar to the psychoanalytically oriented therapy of adults. It is derived from psychoanalysis and will be described in comparison to analysis.

Unlike analysis, in which the patient sees the therapist four or five times a week, the child in this treatment has only two—or at most three —sessions a week. The goals of psychoanalysis are ambitious—reconstructing the personality so that the balance and nature of ego, id and superego change. The goals of child psychoanalytic psychotherapy, while more modest, are palpable and significant. They are primarily symptom resolution, behavioral modification, some degree of structural personality change and the return of the child to normal developmental thrusts.

The difference in frequency of visits is significant in achieving these aims. Only with the sustained work and intensity of interaction that four or five visits a week allow, can the more ambitious program be achieved. In psychoanalysis, the scope of the work is wide, while in psychotherapy the exploration is more focal. In analysis, the transferences and other displacements are analyzed as fully as possible; both past and present are taken into account. In therapy there is greater emphasis on understanding current interactions outside of the therapeutic relationship and on inner conflicts. The focus is usually on the child's life situation and central conflicts insofar as they can be ascertained. In therapy, time, the patient's capacities and the joint goals of child and therapist limit the degree of exploration.

The patient's means of expression are similar in both analysis and psychotherapy. With prelatency and latency children, play and speech are the modes of communication. Teenagers usually use speech alone and may be capable of a modified free association technique. The techniques of psychotherapy include interpretation used closely in conjunction with verbalization, clarification, manipulative changes in attitude, abreaction, suggestion and reassurance of a new trusted object, as well as the corrective emotional experience of a new object. With younger children, therapy attempts to facilitate the developmental continuum of action games, play, fantasies, words, and symbolic functions. The child therapist helps a child find more appropriate defense mechanisms and establish adaptive mechanisms. The child's easy accessibility to genetic-dynamic aspects of character and symptoms enables the therapist to get closer to infantile development. Therapy facilitates the work of defenses against drives, allows partial discharge of drive derivatives, and weakens drive pressures.

Generally, in child psychotherapy, the patient has sessions less frequently than in analysis. (Supportive therapy in which insight is not encouraged usually requires fewer sessions—perhaps one a week—than psychoanalytically oriented therapy which depends on the achievement of insight.) When the treatment is not analysis, the therapist generally avoids meeting with the child more than twice (or at most three) times a week for a number of reasons. First, children selected for psychotherapy usually do not benefit from the greater frequency. Their psychological mindedness is limited, and the extra sessions do not generate more understanding. In addition, many children selected for psychotherapy are threatened by the greater contact with the therapist, and retreat from him. Others settle into the treatment too comfortably without then finding out about themselves. They thrive on the dependent position, and cannot use interpretation to become more independent. Perhaps more perilous, some children who are not suited for analysis but can benefit from therapy regress excessively when the frequency is greater. Unconscious fantasies may become conscious, compelling, and uncontrollable.

Other warnings derive from analytic experiences. Interpreting drives prematurely may cause enormous difficulties for the child. Therefore, the therapist should defer interpretation of unstructured wishes until sufficient work with defenses has preceded it. Pointing out early in the treatment the child's desire to take an oedipal position, kill an oedipal object, or take revenge for abandonment, may result in intensification of defenses. At times a child may consider drive interpretation outright permission to act out. He may feel egged on and give vent to his aggressive or libidinal impulses in a maladaptive way.

Encouraging the child to suppress symptoms may lead to strengthening phobic responses. The therapist may become the phobic object, and the patient may become most reluctant to enter the treatment situation. Participation in child play for the purpose of cathartic release, when it does not lead to lack of control, may encourage repression and momentarily decrease symptomatology through discharge of instinctual tension. Improvement is usually a palliative and temporary, but may be useful in helping child and family over a crisis. However, a false hope may be provided as the conflict between ego and id remains and may erupt once more. The limits of this technical approach was known to Freud in 1895. Devaluing the child's conflict may for the moment reassure the child; it consoles and encourages the ego, but, on the other hand, it tends to scotomize the conflict. Such a maneuver implies a critical attitude toward the child's symptomatology. Encouraging the child to transcend his difficulties through mature, controlled behavior is a command to the ego to surrender to the superego and reality demands.

In psychoanalytically oriented child therapy rather than use suppressive measures, we hope for ego change and modifications. Interpretive activity is directed to themes reflected by the child's play activity. As therapists, we focus on warded-off conflicts in an attempt to bring them into consciousness.

Insight oriented child treatment—whether analysis or analytically oriented psychotherapy—utilizes *interpretations* of a *defense*. There is a careful perusal of resistance, affect, and transference and sometimes even transference neurosis. Interpretation first aims at the defense against warded-off affects before conflicts are interpreted. Treatment is aimed at understanding and working through these areas. Metatheory is given a secondary role, primarily useful for explication of clinical data and direction of the treatment process. The child therapist guards against the psychological fallacy of reductionism: attributing behavior at a later phase of development to unresolved conflict from a previous epoch. An anxiously negotiated separation-individuation in toddlerhood with anxiety in the rapproachment subphase does not explain post-toddler development and pathology which has both added to and modified earlier fixations and deviations. Construction must proceed slowly behind defense analysis as a means of working through distortions, condensations, and displacements to which memory is vulnerable.

In general, discussion of ego resistance should precede that of id content. Repression, denial, isolation, and externalization must be identified, lifted, or sufficiently bypassed to permit the experience of painful affect. The treatment is from surface to depth, from the motor level to fantasy, and then eventually to verbal expression and representation. In the more psychoanalytic treatments, it is helpful to encourage the child to use the therapist as a transference object. Even though the therapist is a real object to the child, it is possible, with certain children in treatment situations of sufficient intensity, to interpret transference manifestations, provided the child has attained object constancy. We find in child treatment the transference is more aggressive than libidinal, especially in the young child. Impulses are best understood in a state of frustration, and an effort is made to avoid undue gratification of a child. Every possible effort is made to foster a therapeutic alliance and to use the therapist as a new object. Even more so in child than adult psychotherapy, countertransference responses must constantly be avoided. Too often the therapist identifies with the child, particularly the latency child, in attempting to provide the child with a good emotional experience in treatment. The child's lack of motivation for therapy can mobilize aggressive feelings in the therapist. The child's activity can disturb the therapist's attention and push him into activity of his own. The therapist may become intolerant of the child's anxiety, feel compelled to reassure him, and fail to see oedipal conflicts.

Even though interpretation is the primary tool of analysis, the patient responds to other aspects of the analytic situation, particularly those that focus on his special needs and offer satisfaction. Identification with the analyst is central to this process and is a facilitating therapeutic activity. It helps the patient develop inner structures, modifies defenses, strengthens the ego, makes appropriate adjustments in the superego—"tuning" the superego to instinctual needs—and fosters neutralization of energy. The same occurs during the therapeutic process of psychotherapy, where introjection of and identification with the therapist attenuates the patient's sense of emptiness. In both analysis and therapy, the child uses the therapist as a real object, from whom he learns adaptive styles of behavior, thought and work, without the therapist's consciously and actively teaching these. Especially for children whose parents have not been an auxiliary ego to their development, the analyst is an auxiliary ego who helps the patient modulate his emotional responses, adjust his frustration tolerance, and control impulsivity. These facets of the treatment process heighten the patient's ability to use adults, outside of treatment and the home, constructively and adaptively. The results of working through this developmental arrest is most conspicuous in the child's receptivity to learning from teachers. Primary deficiencies in learning, however, are best dealt with through tutoring.

Settlage and Spielman (1975) have observed that in the analysis of children with primary faulty structural development, certain factors that are generally overlooked in the analysis of neurotics become prominent. In the treatment of faulty structural development, the interactional aspect of the therapeutic process is very much in the foreground. The child's lack of adequate structure, ego autonomy, and self-regulation requires the empathic participation of the analyst as a temporary auxiliary ego. This participation helps the patient maintain emotional equilibrium and keep impulses and anxiety within bounds so the therapeutic process can proceed. The analyst satisfies needs the patient has not had satisfied in development. Indeed, through the analyst's participation as an auxiliary ego, the patient may develop more adequate structures. The patient may identify with the analyst as a real person and learn adaptive modulation, control, compromise, and appropriate social behavior instead of being at the mercy of his sudden impulses. As Settlage and Spielman suggest, these factors are important to the analysis of children with faulty structure, and may also play a significant role in the skillful psychotherapy of such patients. Not only can the therapist be available to the child through identification, but he can also consciously teach the patient more effective defensive maneuvers and adaptive styles.

With children up to the midlatency ages, it is essential parents be regularly seen to increase their understanding of the child's behavior and pathology. Only in this way will the parents be able to change their own attitudes and interactions with the child. Direct advice to parents is seldom effective, particularly early in treatment, unless the parents' attitude toward the child is empathic and their understanding is sufficient to enable them to interact meaningfully with the child. The therapist must guard against giving "wild" advice which is simply acting out his unconscious motivations. Direct prohibition to the parent, specifically in matters of sexuality and seduction, is not effective and may be disruptive to therapy. Furthermore, encouraging parents to alter an attitude toward their child early in treatment is frequently confusing to the child, as well as to the therapist because the child's interactional patterns, behavior, and defenses can shift.

Furman (1957) has advocated treating children under five through the mother. Using a method similar to Freud's analysis of Little Hans (1909), the therapist sees the child's parents and discusses with them the child's behavior, conflicts, and fantasies. The therapist then suggests interpretations which the parents can offer the child. In a discussion of this method during a panel on prelatency analysis (Olch 1971), Kestenberg stated the procedure would be very difficult or impossible without auxiliary information about the child. She noted that this treatment is carried out in a superb nursery school, the Hanna Perkins School in Cleveland, where such data are available. At the panel, Glenn and Van Dam (Olch 1971) each cautioned that the parents may, after the treatment is over, continue to interpret to the child, and this may have pathological consequences. The child may react with intense hostility to the parents' comments and institute excessive and maladaptive defenses, or the child may believe the interpreting parent is urging him to carry out acts which are usually forbidden. Further, the child may think the parent can read his mind, and is a powerful omniscient being. This can interfere with normal separation-individuation.

INDICATIONS FOR CHILD PSYCHOANALYTICALLY ORIENTED PSYCHOTHERAPY

In general, neurotic conflicts which do not seriously interfere with libidinal or ego development can be treated with one of a variety of psychotherapies. If the balance between wishes and repressive forces of the ego is not upset, internalization of conflict is minimal, and there is a preponderance of external conflict, the effectiveness of psychotherapy is greater than when these factors are absent. If there is a preponderance of internalized conflict, in general, psychoanalysis is indicated. Children with internalized neurotic difficulties who are not potentially psychologically minded, or whose general intelligence is lower than what analysis requires, should be treated by a psychotherapy in the range of supportive to expressive. Children with neurotic symptomatology and imbalances, structural ego defects and deviations, and preverbal disturbance and failures in individuation-separation frequently need a more structured treatment which is best provided by psychotherapy. Children with blatant psychotic, perceptual, and cognitive defects cannot be treated with psychoanalysis, particularly if boundaries of ego and self fragment under aggression in unstructured situations. Psychotherapy is indicated if the child is in a developmental phase that makes analysis difficult. For many preadolescents, analysis is not possible because their defensive organization is too rigid.

Analysis is generally not indicated if the child is in serious enough difficulty in his community to make his environment not supportive enough for analytic work.

Parental psychopathology is also a factor in the choice of treatment. Parents whose own pathology is rigid and unrelentingly damaging to the child cannot be expected to make an understanding and effective rapprochement with the child. Often, in this situation, it is necessary to put the child into psychoanalysis with the view of not only working through his internalized conflict, but also desensitizing the child to his unchanging, noxious environment.

There are children whose parents cannot cooperate in the arrangements of the analysis, who cannot be counted on to bring the child at the frequency required for analysis. In addition, there are parents who cannot tolerate their child's analysis because of their own neurotic pathology. If both parents are psychotic—particularly if they are paranoid and delusional about the child, analyst, or treatment—analysis is not likely to succeed. There are circumstances where psychoanalysis is indicated because of an early trauma which the child has strongly defended himself against through denial and maladaptive character formation. An example is a child who has never seen one of his parents and has been raised by the remaining parent or adopting parents. Whenever faced with trauma and strain, he attempts to deny any separation, object loss, and psychic pain. Psychotherapy is not likely to result in a defensive shift sufficient to allow this child contact with the repressed affects surrounding traumatic early events.

The goals of psychotherapy are limited and restricting. Aside from the other quantitative and qualitative factors affecting the progress and depth of treatment, the frequency of sessions determine the extent of defensive, structural, and adaptive changes (Heinicke 1965). Intensity permits a new integration, better balance of defenses, dominance of the most progressive libidinal phase with sublimation and neutralization, capacity for wider affective expression including humor, less primitive superego responses, and heightened self-esteem. Once or twice weekly therapy does not allow this degree of integration and adaptation. Problems of aggression and masochism, for example, resist resolution in a low-frequency treatment. The child psychotherapist is not usually able to work out problems of passivity and intense negative oedipal yearnings and cannot provide the child with an intensive working-through process. The termination phase of child psychotherapy is usually not long or intense enough to permit a recrudescence of initial symptomatology and allow the child to again experience his yearnings for a lost object.

Treatment of the preschool child with a developmental interference (rigid feedings, toilet training, or prolonged separations) is usually directed to the parents through counselling or family therapy. Gross external environmental infringements on the unfolding of a child's development do not warrant treatment of the child. The same is true of developmental conflicts created by phase-appropriate environmental demands or the child's arrival at a certain maturational level which resonates phase-specific conflicts. If a developmental interference is transformed into a disabling developmental conflict by ill-timed or traumatic environmental demands, then more than counselling or family therapy is needed for the parents. Appropriate individual treatment of the father or mother is then indicated. Individual treatment is also indicated for a parent who cannot tolerate a particular developmental conflict or symptom, because it brings to the parent old anxieties. For example, a parent who traumatically interferes with a preoedipal child's masturbatory needs establishes a developmental interference which is then transformed into a developmental conflict, because of incipient phallic-oedipal maturation and structualization. Optimally, psychotherapy of the parent will achieve this aim relatively quickly, if the child can benefit. There are times, however, when the length of treatment precludes immediate aid and other measures are necessary as well.

Developmental conflicts, reflected as mild behavior disorders, fears, and other symptom-formations, are apt to be transitory. The child will find a solution through reaction-formation, sublimation, equilibration of structures, or formation of a character trait from a component instinct. If the intensity of the conflict is strong, drive and ego development asynchronous, or external factors unmodifiable, the ego resorts to rigid defense reorganization which results in a monosymptomatic neurosis, and leads, if not resolved, into neurotic conflict with bombardment by pregenital discharge. With the formation of psychic structures in the oedipal phase, the conflict becomes intersystemic and internalized.

With the conflicts of the Oedipus complex as precipitating cause and the neurotic symptomatology explained by the classical formula of danger, anxiety, permanent regression to fixation points, rejection of reactivated pregenital impulses, defense, compromise formation, the infantile neurosis not only comes nearest to the corresponding adult disturbances in metapsychological identity, they also offer the analyst a role within treatment which is similar to the one he has with adults. [A. Freud 1965, p. 219]

Psychotherapy may be necessary for preoedipal children who suddenly develop monosymptomatic neurotic problems like sleep refusal, stool retention, anorexia, and specific fears. These are isolated, symptomatic, developmental conflicts that do not interfere with overall function. Many of these children require their mother's approval for their thoughts and feelings. For their ego to weather the conflict, the child needs the support and protection of his parent. At times, instructing the mother on how to relate to the child is helpful (Furman 1957). In therapy with the mother present, the child is able to express himself through the therapist, clarify feelings, reduce anxiety, open up drive activity, and avoid pathogenic defenses. Therapy establishes an equilibrium between the child's ego and the parent. Bornstein (1935), Bonnard (1950), Burlingham (1951), and Fraiberg (1952) have described these treatments. Some of these young children with developmental conflicts, however, turn out to have either more serious disturbances in separation-individualization or internalized conflicts, and these require more therapy or analysis.

Another group of preoedipal children for whom psychotherapy is sufficient is preschoolers with habit disturbances in eating, sleeping, toilet training, and discipline—mostly related to a lack of parental instruction and environmental structuring. A similar group of young children is those preschoolers who act out thinly disguised parental wishes. Therapy, in conjunction with guidance of the parents, may suffice with young children. With both groups in later development, when the diagnosis is impulsive behavior disorder or sociopathic behavior, more intensive therapy or analysis is required because of an initially neurotic determinant or residual traumatic psychopathology and identifications.

Other nonneurotic disturbances do not lend themselves to typical insight improvement. Clarification of frightening affects and internal and external dangers only floods the ego with anxiety and hinders secondary process thinking. Borderline to psychotic children require an individualized therapy, aimed first at strengthening the ego through reassurance, corrective experience, and educative measures. Once structuralization has advanced, modified interpretation of defenses, transference, and resistances can be done. Likewise, children with defects in libidinal development—deprivations in object relations and symbiotic problems—present the therapist with technical difficulties. Interpretation of transference manifestations usually do not bring about change unless there has been traumatic or neurotic arrest in development. Because of early deprivation in object relations, a new emotional experience is required to further libidinal development and prepare the way for later interpretation through verbalization and clarification.

When normal development appears to be jeopardized by a recent trauma, therapy is the treatment indicated (Buxbaum 1946). Many of these children have sustained a loss, often a parent from a divorce. Providing the child with an abreactive clarification of his experience may prevent transient symptoms from derailing future development. When the trauma becomes deeply repressed or reactivates an old fixation, then analysis is usually required.

PSYCHOTHERAPY AS PREPARATION FOR ANALYSIS

A form of psychotherapy was once suggested as preparation for child analysis. A. Freud (1946) recommended a *preparatory analysis* for children to bring out his sense of suffering, show him his problem with impulse control, make the analyst useful and interesting, fostering confidence in the analyst, and turn the decision for analysis more toward the child. With increasing understanding of ego defenses and transference manifestations in children, Bornstein (1949) suggested defense analysis and isolation of painful affect in lieu of a preparatory phase. In 1952, however, Sylvester recommended a preparatory phase before analysis for borderline children who rely on primitive, nonverbal modes of interaction, have little facility at mastery, and are not able to separate from the mother. Psychotherapeutic techniques aimed at increasing ego strengths and educational measures were part of the therapist's activity. Weil (1973) extended this concept in her formulation of a *new preparatory phase* for ego consolidation and balancing of internal forces. Because of multiple imbalances between ego and drive endowment within the ego (separation-individuation, inadequate defense organization, etc.), between libido and aggression predominant and between hostile and nonhostile aggression, presignal anxiety is excessive as an aftermath of early unrelieved tension, undampened by protective sensitivity thresholds and respondent mothering. The lack of object constancy, fear of object loss, diffuse presignal anxiety, and maladaptive defense organization contraindicates analysis and makes these preschool children ideal candidates for an ego strengthening psychotherapy coordinated with special tutorial help.

A similar psychotherapeutic approach was suggested by Furman (1957) for prelatency children. This approach utilizes a therapeutic nursery school for ego-strengthening and at the same time starts the child in intensive therapy as a preparation for later analysis (see chapter 19).

CHILD PSYCHOTHERAPY WITH LIMITED GOALS OR LIMITED TECHNIQUES

Many children do not require open-ended interpretive treatment, but need a more focal goal-directed therapy. For others, interpretive treatment is the optimal approach, but circumstances, including parental motivation, make it impossible.

A variety of treatments has emerged to meet the needs of patients who can benefit from limited forms. For instance, children with relatively healthy personality structures who have experienced serious traumata can be helped by treatment aimed at mastery of the traumatic situation. Such focal treatment techniques will be selected because they fit the child's problem.

Sometimes the treatment chosen will depend on the interests of the therapist. A talented clinician with a particular bent can be of great help to a child who needs the treatment he is particularly adept at. However, if a therapist follows his own interests rather than select treatment appropriate to the child and his family, the outcome will be detrimental.

As we will see, many of the techniques used in focal therapy are also used in child analysis, where they serve as but one of many forms of communication and expression. Children in analysis frequently make use of dramatic play or puppetry, for instance. Other types of play, like preplanned, like dramatizations planned by the therapist on subjects he thinks are important, are avoided in analysis because they interfere with a spontaneous analytic process. Treatment with limited goals often provides limited technical approaches and limited opportunities for the child.

In this section, I will survey the many treatments with limited goals and techniques. Because children love to play and can both communicate and solve problems through this means, many treatments focus on play techniques (Amster 1943, Ginott and Lebo 1963, Schaefer 1977). They have included active, passive, release, and structured play, as well as free play (Woltmann 1955). In addition, a great many specific technical approaches to child therapy have been reported: word pictures (Lowenfeld 1939), finger painting (Arlow and Kadis 1946), clay modeling (Bender 1952), puppetry (Woltmann 1951), abstract and graphic art (Bender 1952), water play (Hartley, Frank, and Goldenson 1952), use of food (Haworth and Keller 1962), checkers (Loomis 1957), free art expression (Naumburg 1947), and mud and clay (Woltmann 1950). However, many advocates of these play techniques suggest that a specific technique be used in child therapy, either for the entire therapy or a particular phase. This leaves the child out of the decision and blocks the movement of the material.

Basic techniques in child therapies are suggestion, abreaction, manipulation, clarification, reassurance, and corrective emotional experience with the new object, as well as interpretation. Child treatment operations include the production, utilization, and assimilation of the child's material, as well as the reorientation and adaptive adjustment of the patient. Analysis depends primarily on interpretation for its effectiveness. Other factors, incidental to analysis per se, are the major components of other forms of child treatment. These therapeutic factors include identification with the therapist (often making the patient feel more complete because of his contact with the therapist), giving up symptoms out of love for the therapist, educational intervention by the therapist, and alterations of the patient's milieu. Because contact is less intense in therapy, the therapist has less access to information and is not as able to make correct interpretations. His interpretations may be incomplete, inexact, or incorrect (Glover 1931). The transference cannot be fully interpreted because it is muted. Nevertheless, the limited interpretations may relieve symptoms; the therapist's words may ring of magic for the patient, and give him a sense of sharing with a powerful person. The therapist must keep in mind this potent factor in the treatment, and be careful it does not exceed its therapeutic usefulness.

Review of the various child therapy techniques reveals specific goals, technical operations, and psychopathology (Moustakas 1952). For example, Solomon (Haworth 1964) advocates the use of a single doll in active play treatment. The therapist selects a doll which he considers to be symbolic of the patient's major conflict. The child then selects a doll in response to the therapist's, and they play out the dynamic theme. Presumably, this allows the therapist to make appropriate comments about the play activity and its symbolic meaning to the child. This treatment approach purports to foster abreaction, abort stereotypic play, permit thematic change, enhance productivity, foster verbal communication, increase the range of consciousness, and decrease anxiety. Solomon recommended active play for a specific symptom or situation, like car sickness or fear of the dark and thunder. It has also been employed for children with phobias and diffuse anxieties. The technical approach requires the therapist to be familiar with the child's basic conflicts to enable him to manipulate the play in terms of the child's needs. Child analysts know this degree of understanding is seldom attained during the consultation period, and frequently such understanding is not possible until the child has been in treatment for a period of time. For example, the child's individual responses to separation object loss, triadic object relations, and castration fantasies cannot be determined simply by initial evaluation and the beginnings of treatment.

Release therapy, a form of active play, was advocated by Levy (1939) for the treatment of the sequelae of traumata. He suggested its usefulness for specific frightening and upsetting events and experiences such as the birth of a sibling, the breakup of a family, and death. He indicates its usefulness in short-term treatment of the child who has at least one family member supportive of his treatment. Its effectiveness, he believes, comes from simple release of drives and feelings. As in other forms of repetitious play, the child gradually acquires active mastery of traumata. (This will be discussed later when therapeutic play is reviewed.)

Hambridge's concepts of structural play (1955) are similar to those of active play. This play activity is thought to facilitate independent, creative, free play, test the significance of specific symbols and themes, permit abreaction, and allow for mastery of anxiety through a corrective emotional experience. Structuring play along the lines of sibling rivalry, peer interaction, punishment by elders, separation experiences, discovery of genital differences, primal scene experiences, dramatization of dreams, birth of siblings, etc., implies a deep understanding of the child. The weakness of this treatment operation lies in the same fallacy of active play: the treatment presupposes an extensive knowledge of the child which is not possible in the consultative assessment. Furthermore, testing out a dynamic hypothesis through structured play is apt to increase the child's resistance and obscure the ongoing theme of therapy.

Bender's view of play, largely influenced by her interest in perceptual problems, led her to use puppets in therapy (1952). Materials are selected by the child to permit him to elaborate the content and function of his fantasies. As the main element of play therapy, puppet play is questionable because there are few children who are capable of or willing to persist in this style of play therapy. On the other hand, it is the rare child in treatment, whether psychoanalytic or psychotherapeutic, who will not occasionally use puppet play.

In 1947 Axline advanced a theory of nondirective, unstructured play based on the hypothesis that given the opportunity, a child becomes more mature and positive in his attitude toward his world. Nondirective free play is essentially client-oriented, and is based on the assumption that the child has both a given growth impulse and the ability to solve his own problems. The child is given complete acceptance and permission with the belief he is capable of self-determination. Of course, impulsive children who require restraint will not benefit from overly permissive free play.

Nondirective treatment of children is derived from Rogers's non-directed treatment of adults (1966). The client is encouraged to talk freely, but a minimum of interpretation is used. The therapist often paraphrases what the client has said. This echoing may serve as a narcissistic gratification, as described by Kohut (1971, 1977) in his discussion of the mirror transference. The patient, finding his thoughts emphatically reflected by the therapist, may recover under the influence of an infantile fantasy that he has united with a powerful parent-like figure.

Play activity fostering therapeutic communication through mutual story telling is another approach to child treatment. The therapist reconstructs the child's story and feeds it back to the child who, according to Gardner (1971), recognizes the symbolic content, overcomes the problem through understanding, or is desensitized to it. The therapist takes a very active role in the manipulation and interpretation of the story material. The treatment relies heavily on the release of aggression with the aim of modifying oedipal tension and increasing self-esteem. Like any active, structured therapy, the technique is naive because it presupposes the therapist's intimate familiarity with the child's core conflicts. It is only feasible to make up a story for a patient at the end of treatment, as a way of assembling an easily understood "reconstruction." Furthermore, by leading the material, even if he were familiar with the child's basic conflicts, the therapist does not permit the child to expand ego awareness. Such an active approach to child therapy permits the flow of countertransference feelings and responses into the child's material. This further beclouds the whole therapeutic process.

Play, which combines wish with resistance and defense, is rich material for therapeutic activity (Greenacre 1959). There are basically three indications for structured play. It is extremely useful in short-term therapy for children who are anticipating trauma or have recently experienced trauma with uncertain psychological sequelae. For instance, children who face extensive dental or surgical procedures or have experienced a death of a loved one may benefit by a circumscribed period of play in which the child is able to play out his fantasies and tensions. This approach is most useful in hospitals and institutions. It is also useful in diagnostic assessment and beginning therapy of young, latency girls who have been molested or raped. It is effective in understanding the extent of psychic trauma and the degree to which earlier conflicts and fixations have been reactivated by a sexual trauma.

Another form of therapeutic play is free, spontaneous play (Peller 1954). This play varies enormously from day to day, from patient to patient, and from age to age. This type of play is free, spontaneous, and unstructured (Ekstein and Friedman 1957). Whatever the therapist says or does in play is done to foster the play. Usually he does not interpretively respond to it or play beyond the child's level. This play may be repetitive and reflects a traumatic experience or a masturbation fantasy. Repetitious play often serves to help the child master the effects of trauma. He attempts to become the active master rather than the passive victim. A child who has been or will be operated upon may play he is the surgeon rather than the helpless patient. Here identification with the aggressor is utilized as a defense. In addition, by initiating the traumatic play himself, the child attempts to master the anxiety. The play also relieves his tension and provides various gratifications. The play may involve aggressive and counteraggressive activities, masochistic defeats, attempts at object recovery and removal, maneuvers which foster identification, and provide activity to overcome passivity, affectionate yearnings, and wishes to be beaten. The presence of a nonpunitive therapist will ease superego demands and permit these gratifying activities.

Another variety of play often encountered in the course of child analysis and therapy is dramatization. This involves a creative use of play materials which recreate a family constellation and affective situations. Over the course of a number of sessions, an oedipal girl's play with the doll house may clearly reveal the intensity of her oedipal wishes, as well as the frustrations and disappointments associated with this phase of development. Dramatization is an ego-dominated play, remarkable for its structure and control. In some ways, dramatization play is like a Greek chorus. It instructs the patient-therapist-audience. Dramatization is not the same as acting out, but it may involve the therapist in undue direct action and this would necessitate interpretation.

In the case of any therapeutic play activity, it is usually wise to avoid interpretation of the play. Interpretation frequently frightens the child when he recognizes the deeper meaning of his activity. It then stops the play and works against the child's utilization of it as a sublimatory activity. Therapeutic play, however, should be stopped by direct prohibition or through interpretations if it is dangerous to the child or therapist or allows direct sexual gratification. Otherwise, the play activity should not be disturbed by the therapist's comments. Play itself has an ego-enriching and adaptive value (Alexander 1953, Erikson 1940, Simmel 1948, Waelder 1933, Winnicott 1971). Symbolic realization (Sechehaye 1951), in which the therapist joins a psychotic patient in gratifying bizarre wishes symbolically, does not appear to have any useful therapeutic value per se. However such gratification may help establish a relationship which can lead to a therapeutic process.

There is also a range of therapies for children, from commonsense supportive, expressive-supportive, to intensive-expressive (modified parametric analysis). Some children require ego-building through an expressive-supportive therapy before embarking on analysis. Others can go no further than an intensive-expressive therapy with intermittent analysis of transference and primitive defenses. Supportive-expressive therapy can also be used for children who, because of unfavorable life circumstances, need an essential adaptation, and therefore, only partial defensive modification. We also see the opposite situation: children who are traumatized by parents' pathology or life circumstances and require desensitization to the parents and a new adaptive balance of impulse and defense. Other children, particularly prelatency patients with developmental conflicts, need only a supportive therapy and environmental manipulation to buttress defenses, clarify feelings, and abreact painful affect. Play therapy for anticipated trauma offers a child much the same.

With the recent interest in minimal brain damage dysfunction (MBD) (Clements 1966, Schrag and Divoky 1975) and pharmacotherapies for reducing hyperactivity and improving learning, we now have what might be called neurotherapy. This is a form of drug therapy for hyperactivity and cognitive-attentional deficiencies. It is combined with educational and tutorial assistance for the child with a crippling learning disability, as well as with a modicum of supportive therapy and guidance for the parents. Individual child therapy and parental guidance supplement medication in helping the child control his impulses and achieving gratification without any adaptive side effects.

Behavioral modification techniques (Yates 1975) are also used with children. It is specifically used for disorders of eating (anorexia nervosa), simple bed wetting, and monosymptomatic and multiple tics. Utilizing the principles of operant conditioning, the adult rewards the child when he surrenders his symptoms and/or punishes him when he retains it. At best, such treatment stimulates parents or their surrogates to perform the normal parental role of encouraging appropriate values and behavior. At its worst, the child is provided with an artificial and inhuman environment or is subjected to sadomasochistic gratifications.

Proponents of these techniques tend to believe the conditioning is mechanical in nature, and neglect the fact that a new interpersonal relationship with the therapist is formed or the child's interaction with his parents is enhanced. Increased gratification from these relationships, superego modification and ego strengthening are important therapeutic modalities. When a formerly inconsistent parent becomes predictable, the child benefits.

Group psychotherapy has a long history in child therapy. It has been used mostly with latency age children. Slavson (1945, 1950) used activity groups for this age range as did Redl (1945) in his formulation for this age group. Abroad, Foulkes and Anthony (1957) introduced play group therapy which encompassed both group discussion and activity. Inhibited children unable to get along with peers may benefit from group interaction. Other children who have difficulty talking to an adult therapist may do so in the group setting. In interpretive group therapy, the children join the leader in interpretation. Wild analysis, vicious attacks on group members or group denial may emerge. Accurate interpretations may be more effective when another child makes them.

CONCLUSION

Child psychoanalysis is effective treatment for many disturbances. However, there are conditions and circumstances in which it is not indicated. In this chapter, I have described numerous other psychological treatments, and differentiated these from analysis. I have paid particular attention to the interface between psychoanalysis and psychoanalytically oriented therapy, and attempted to sharpen the boundaries.

The principles of psychoanalysis have influenced the development and raison d'être of many forms of child therapy. These principles can also help us understand the effectiveness and deficiencies of forms of treatment which developed independently of analysis.

REFERENCES

Adams, P. L. (1974). *A Primer of Child Psychotherapy.* Boston: Little, Brown.

Aichhorn, A. (1935). *Wayward Youth.* New York: Viking.

Alexander, F. S. (1953). A panel discussion on diagnosis and therapy through play. *New York Academy of Science,* 15:99–101.

—————— (1954). Psychoanalysis and psychotherapy. *Journal of the American Psychoanalytic Association* 2:722–733.

—————— (1958). A contribution to the theory of play. *Psychoanalytic Quarterly* 27:175–93.

Allen, F. H. (1942). *Psychotherapy with Children.* New York: Norton, pp. 45–86, 122–164.

—————— (1946). Combined psychotherapy with children and parents. In *Modern Trends in Child Psychiatry,* ed. N. D. C. Lewis, and B. L. Pacella, pp. 257–263. New York: International Universities Press.

Amster, F. (1943). Different uses of play in treatment of young children, *American Journal of Orthopsychiatry* 13:62–68.

Arlow, J., and Kadis, A. (1946). Finger painting in the psychotherapy of children. *American Journal of Orthopsychiatry* 16:134–146.

Arthur, S. A. (1952). A comparison of the techniques employed in psychotherapy and psychoanalysis of children. *American Journal of Orthopsychiatry* 22:484–498.

Axline, V. M. (1947). *Play Therapy: The Inner Dynamics of Childhood.* New York: Houghton-Mifflin.

Bender, E. (1952), Clay modeling as a projective technique. In *Child Psychiatric Techniques,* pp. 221–237 Springfield, Ill.: Charles C Thomas.

Bender, L., and Woltmann, A. A. (1936), The use of puppet shows as a psychotherapeutic method for behavior problems in children. *American Journal of Orthopsychiatry* 6:341–354.

Berman, E. M., and Lief, H. I. (1975), Marital therapy from a psychiatric perspective: an overview, *American Journal of Psychiatry* 132: 583–590.

Berne, E. (1961), *Transactional Analysis in Psychotherapy: A System, Individual and Social Psychiatry.* New York: Grove.

Bernstein, I. (1958), The importance of characteristics of the parents in deciding on child analysis, *Journal of the American Psychoanalytic Association,* 6:71–78.

———— (1975). On the technique of child & adolescent analysis, *Journal of the American Psychoanalytic Association* 23:190–232.

Bibring, E. (1954). Psychoanalysis and the dynamic psychotherapies, *Journal of the American Psychoanalytic Association* 2:745–770.

Bloomfield, H. H., Cain, M. P., and Jaffee, D. T. (1975). *TM: Discovering Inner Energy and Overcoming Stress.* New York: Delacorte.

Bonnard, A. (1960). The mother as therapist in a case of obsessional neurosis. *Psychoanalytic Study of the Child* 5:391–408.

Bornstein, B. (1945), Clinical notes on child analysis. *Psychoanalytic Study of the Child* 1:151–166.

———— (1948). Emotional barriers in the understanding and treatment of children. *American Journal of Orthopsychiatry* 18:691–697.

———— (1949). The analysis of a phobic child: some problems of theory and technique in child analysis, *Psychoanalytic Study of the Child* 3/4:181–226.

———— (1935). Phobia in a two-and-a-half-year-old child, *Psychoanalytic Quarterly* 4:93–119.

Boss, J. (1963). *Psychoanalysis and Daseinsanalysis.* New York: Basic Books.

Boyer, L., and Giovacchini, D. (1967). *Psychoanalytic Treatment of Characterological and Schizophrenic Disorders.* New York: Jason Aronson.

Breuer, J. and Freud, S. (1893). Studies on hysteria. *Standard Edition* 2:1–306.

Broyard, A. (1975). Book review. *New York Times,* October 23, 1975.

Burlingham, D. T. (1951). Present trends in handling the mother-child relationship during the therapeutic process. *Psychoanalytic Study of the Child* 6:31–37.

Buxbaum, E. (1946). Psychotherapy and psychoanalysis in the treatment of children. *Nervous Child,* 5:115–126.

———— (1954). Technique of child therapy: a critical evaluation. *Psychoanalytic Study of the Child* 9:297–333.

Chess, S. A. (1959). *An Introduction to Child Psychiatry.* Grune and Stratton.

Clements, S. D. (1966). *Minimal Brain Dysfunction in Children.* NINDB Monograph No. 3, U.S. Department of Health, Education, and Welfare, pp. 9–10.

Coleman, J. (1949). Distinguishing between psychotherapy and casework. *Journal of Social Casework* 30:219–224.

Corsini, R., ed. (1973). *Current Psychotherapies.* Chicago, Ill.: F. E. Peacock.

Ekstein, R., and Friedman, S. (1957). The function of acting out, play action, and play acting in the psychotherapeutic process. *Journal of the American Psychoanalytic Association* 5:581–629.

Eissler, K. R. (1953). The effects of the structure of the ego on psychoanalytic technique. *Journal of the American Psychoanalytic Association* 1:104–145.

Erikson, E. H. (1940). Studies in the interpretation of play: I. Clinical observations of play disruption in young children. *Genetic Psychology Monographs* 22:557–651.

Ezriel, H. (1952). Notes on psychoanalytic group therapy: II. Interpretation and research. *Psychiatry* 15:119–126.

Ezios, R. (1974). Implications of physiological feedback training. In *The Nature of Human Consciousness,* ed. R. E. Ornsteing, pp. 376–386. New York: Viking.

Ferenczi, S. (1913). A little Chanticleer. In *Sex in Psycho-Analysis,* pp. 204–213. New York: Dover, 1956.

Flappan, D., and Neubauer, P. (1975). *Assessment of Early Child Development.* New York: Jason Aronson.

Fieldsteel, N. D. (1974). Family therapy-individual therapy: a false dichotomy. In *Group Therapy,* ed. L. Wolberg and M. Aronson, pp. 45–56. New York: Stratton, 1974.

Finch, S. (1960). *Fundamentals of Child Psychiatry.* New York: Norton.

First, E. (1975). The new wave in psychiatry. *New York Review of Books,* Feb. 20, 1975, p. 8.

Foulkes, S. H., and Anthony, E. J. (1957). *Group Psychotherapy.* London: Penguin Books.

Fraiberg, S. (1952). A critical neurosis in a two-and-a-half year-old girl. *Psychoanalytic Study of the Child* 7:173–215.

Framo, J. L., ed. (1972). *Family Interaction.* New York: Springer.

Freeman, T. (1974). Childhood psychopathology and psychotic phenomena in adults. *British Journal of Psychiatry* 124:556–563.

Freud, A. (1945). Indications for child analysis. *Psychoanalytic Study of the Child* 1:127–150.

———— (1946). *The Psychoanalytical Treatment of Children.* New York: Schocken.

———— (1954). The widening scope of indications for psychoanalysis (discussion). *Journal of the American Psychoanalytic Association* 2:607–620.

———— (1965). *Normality and Pathology in Childhood.* New York: International Universities Press.

———— (1971). *The Writings of Anna Freud, Vol. VII, 1966–1970: Problems of Psychoanalytic Training, Diagnosis and The Technique of Therapy.* New York: International Universities Press.

Freud, S. (1909). Analysis of a phobia in a five-year-old boy. *Standard Edition* 10:3–152.

———— (1919), Lines of advance in psycho-analytic therapy. *Standard Edition* 17:167–168.

Fromm-Reichmann, F. (1954). Psycho-analysis and general dynamic conceptions of theory and of therapy: differences and similarities. *Journal of the American Psychoanalytic Association* 2:711–721.

Furman, E. (1957). Treatment of under-fives by way of parents. *Psychoanalytic Study of the Child* 12:250–262.

Gardner, R. A. (1971). *Therapeutic Communication with Children.* New York: Jason Aronson.

Geleerd, E. R., ed. (1967). *The Child Analyst at Work.* New York: International Universities Press.

Gill, J. (1951). Ego psychology and psychotherapy. *Psychoanalytic Quarterly* 20:62–71.

_____ (1954). Psychoanalysis and exploratory psychotherapy. *Journal of the American Psychoanalytic Association* 2:771–797.

Ginott, H. G., and Lebo, D. (1963). Most and least used play therapy limits. *Journal of Genetic Psychology* 103:153–159.

Glover, E. (1931). The therapeutic effect of inexact interpretation: a contribution to the theory of suggestion. *International Journal of Psycho-Analysis* 12:397–411.

_____ (1945). Examination of the Klein system of child psychology. *Psychoanalytic Study of the Child* 1:75–118.

_____ (1955). *The Technique of Psychoanalysis.* New York: International Universities Press.

Goodman, J. D., and Sours, J. A. (1967). *The Child Mental Status Examination.* New York: Basic Books.

Green, A. (1975). The analyst symbolization and absence in the analytic setting (on changes in analytic practice and analytic experience). *International Journal of Psycho-Analysis* 56:1–22.

Greenacre, P. (1959). Play in relation to creative imagination. *Psychoanalytic Study of the Child* 14:61–80.

Greenson, R. P. (1967), *The Technique and Practice of Psychoanalysis,* Vol. 1. New York: International Universities Press.

Haley, J., and Hoffman, L., eds. (1967). *Techniques of Family Therapy.* New York: Basic Books.

Hambridge, F. (1955). Structured play therapy. *American Journal of Orthopsychiatry* 25:601–617.

Hamilton, G. (1947). *Psychotherapy in Child Guidance.* New York: Columbia University Press.

Harley, J., ed. (1974). *The Adolescent and Analyst at Work.* New York: Quadrangle.

Hartley, R., Frank, L., and Goldenson, R. (1952). The benefits of water play. In *Understanding Children's Play.* Columbia Univ. Press.

Hartman, N. M., and Hurn, P. A. (1958). Collaboration as a therapeutic tool. *Social Casework* 39:459–463.

Hatcher, C., and Himelstein, P., eds. (1975). *Handbook of Gestalt Therapy.* New York: Jason Aronson.

Haworth, M. J., and Keller, M. (1962). The use of food in therapy. *Journal of the American Academy of Child Psychiatry* 1:548–63.

Haworth, M. R., ed. (1964). *Child Psychotherapy.* New York: Basic Books.

Heinickle, C. M., et al. (1965). Frequency of psychotherapeutic sessions as a factor affecting the child's developmental status. *Psychoanalytic Study of the Child* 20:42–98.

Horney, K. (1939). *New Ways in Psychoanalysis.* New York: W.W. Norton.

Horowitz, M. (1975). Discussion group on new therapies. American Psychoanalytic Association meeting, May 1975, Los Angeles, California.

Janov, A. (1970). *The Primal Scream: Primal Therapy: The Cure For Neurosis.* New York: Dell.

Jung, C. G. (1954). *The Development of Personality.* New York: Pantheon.

———— (1968). *Analytical Psychology: Its Theory and Practice.* New York: Pantheon.

Kaplan, H. S. (1974). *The New Sex Therapy.* New York: Brunner/Mazel.

Kennedy, H. (1972), Problems in reconstruction in child analysis. *Psychoanalytic Study of the Child* 26:386–402.

Kernberg, O., et al. (1972). Psychotherapy and psychoanalysis. *Bulletin of the Menninger Clinic* 36:3–276.

Klein, M. (1954). *The Psychoanalysis of Children.* London: Hogarth Press.

———— (1955). The psychoanalytic play technique. *American Journal of Orthopsychiatry* 25:223–237.

———— (1960). *Narrative of a Child Analysis.* New York: Basic Books.

Kohut, H. (1971). *The Analysis of the Self.* New York: International Universities Press.

———— (1977). *The Restoration of the Self.* New York: International Universities Press.

Korman, R., Fineberg, H. H., Gelman, R. C., and Weiss, S. (1971). Technique of child analysis problems in counter-transference. *International Journal of Psychoanalysis* 52:487–497.

Kramer, C. H. (1968). *The Relationship between Child and Family Psychopathology: A Suggested Extension of Psychoanalytic Theory and Technique.* Chicago: The Family Institute of Chicago.

Krug, O., and Stuart, B. L. (1956). Collaborative treatment of mother and boy with fecal retention, soiling and school phobia. In *Case Studies of Childhood Emotional Disabilities, Vol. II,* ed. G. Gardner, pp. 1–29. New York: American Orthopsychiatric Association.

Langs, R. (1974). *The Technique of Psychoanalytic Psychotherapy, Vols. I & II.* New York: Jason Aronson.

Levy, D. (1937). Attitude therapy. *American Journal of Orthopsychiatry* 7:103–113.

———— (1939). Release therapy. *American Journal of Orthopsychiatry* 9:713–736.

Lippman, H. S. (1956). *Treatment of the Child in Emotional Conflict.* New York: McGraw-Hill.

Loomis, E. A. (1957). The use of checkers in handling certain resistances in child therapy and child analysis. *Journal of the American Psychoanalytic Association* 5:130–135.

Loew, C. A., Grayson, H., and Loew, G. H., eds. (1975). *Three Psychotherapies: A Clinical Comparison.* New York: Brunner/Mazel.

Lowen, A. (1967). *The Betrayal of the Body.* New York: Collier.

Lowenfeld, M. (1939). The world pictures of children. *British Journal of Medical Psychology* 18:65–101.

Maenchen, A. (1970). On the technique of child analysis in relation to stages of development. *Psychoanalytic Study of the Child* 25:175–208.

Machover, K. (1951). *Personality Projection in the Drawing of the Human Figure.* Springfield, Ill.: Charles C Thomas, 1952.

Malcove, L. (1975). The analytic situation: toward a view of the supervisory experience. In press.

Masters, W. H., and Johnson, V. E. (1966). *Human Sexual Response.* Boston: Little, Brown.

May, R., et al. (1958), *Existence.* New York: Basic Books.

Moustakas, C. E. (1952). *Children in Play Therapy.* New York: McGraw-Hill.

Nagera, H. (1963). The developmental profile: notes on some practical considerations regarding its use. *Psychoanalytic Study of the Child* 18:511–540.

———— (1966). *Early Childhood Disturbances, The Infantile Neurosis, and the Adulthood Disturbances.* Monograph No. 2, *Psychoanalytic Study of the Child.* New York: International Universities Press.

Naumburg, M. (1947). *Studies of the "Free" Art Expression of Behavior Problem Children and Adolescents as a Means of Diagnosis and Therapy.* Nervous and Mental Diseases Monograph 71.

Olch, G. (1971). Panel report: technical problems in the analyses of the preoedipal and preschool child. *Journal of the American Psychoanalytic Association* 19:543–51.

Pearson, G.H.J. (1968). *A Handbook of Child Psychoanalysis.* New York: Basic Books.

———— (1974–1975). What is psychotherapy? Proceedings of the 9th International Congress of Psychotherapy, Oslo 1973. *Psychotherapy and Psychosomatics* 24 (4–6) and 25 (1–6).

Peller, L. (1954). Libidinal phases, ego development and play. *Psychoanalytic Study of the Child* 9:178–198.

Rambert, M. L. (1949). The use of drawings as a method of child psychoanalysis. In *Children in Conflict.* New York: International Universities Press.

Rangell, L. (1954). Similarities and differences between psychoanalysis and dynamic psychotherapy. *Journal of the American Psychoanalytic Association* 2:734–744.

Rank, O. (1945). *Will Therapy.* New York: Knopf.

Redl, F. (1945). The psychology of gang formation and the treatment of juvenile delinquents. *Psychoanalytic Study of the Child* 1:367–377.

Reich, W. (1949), *Character Analysis.* New York: Orgone Institute Press.

Rogers, C. R. (1966). Client-centered therapy. In *American Handbook of Psychiatry, vol. III,* ed. S. Arieti, pp. 183–200. New York: Basic Books.

Rycroft, C. (1975). Freud and the imagination. *New York Review of Books,* April 3, 1975, p. 26.

Schaefer, C. E., ed. (1977). *Therapeutic Use of Child's Play.* New York: Jason Aronson.

Schrag, P., and Divoky, D. (1975), *The Myth of the Hyperactive Child.* New York: Pantheon.

Sechehaye, M. A. (1951). *Symbolic Realization.* New York: International Universities Press.

Segal, H. (1964). *Introduction to the Work of Melanie Klein.* New York: Basic Books.

Siegel, M. G. (1975). Psychological testing. In *Personality Development and Deviation,* ed. C. H. Wiedeman, pp. 456–486. New York: International Universities Press.

Simmel, E. (1948). The 'Doctor Game', illness, and the profession of medicine. In *Psychoanalytic Readers, Vol. 1,* ed. R. Fliess, pp. 291–206. New York: International Universities Press.

Slavson, S. R. (1945). Group therapy with children. In *Modern Trends in Child Psychiatry.* ed. Nolan Lewis, and B. Pacella. New York: International Universities Press.

——— (1950). *Analytic Group Psychotherapy with Children, Adolescents and Adults.* New York: Columbia University Press.

Smirnoff, V. (1968). *The Scope of Child Analysis.* New York: International Universities Press.

Smith, A. (1975). *Powers of Mind.* New York: Random House.

Sterba, E. (1959). Child analysis. In *Readings in Psychoanalytic Psychology,* ed. M. Levitt, pp. 287–310. New York: Appleton-Century-Crofts.

Stone, L. (1954). Psychoanalysis and brief psychotherapy. *Psychoanalytic Quarterly* 20:215–236.

Strupp, H., and Bergen, A. (1969). *Research in Individual Psychotherapy.* Chevy Chase, Md.: National Institute of Mental Health.

Sullivan, H. S. (1953). *The Interpersonal Theory of Psychiatry.* New York: Norton.

Szurek, S., et al. (1942). Collaborative psychiatric therapy of parent-child problems. *American Journal of Orthopsychiatry* 12:511–520.

Tarachow, S. (1963). *An Introduction to Psychotherapy.* New York: International Universities Press.

Toffler, A. (1975). Beyond depression, *Esquire,* February, p. 53.

Tymchuk, A. J. (1975). *Behavior Modification with Children: A Clinical Training Manual.* Springfield, Ill.: Charles C Thomas.

Waelder, R. (1933). The psychoanalytic theory of play. *Psychoanalytic Quarterly* 2:54–61.

Wallerstein, R. S., and Robbin, L. L. (1956). Further notes on design and concepts. In: The psychotherapy research project of the Menninger Foundation. Second Report. *Bulletin of the Menninger Clinic* 22:119–125.

——— (1972). Transactional psychotherapy: critique of a viewpoint.

In *Psychotherapy & Psychoanalysis,* ed. R. S. Wallerstein. New York: International Universities Press, 1975.

Weinreb, J., ed. (1960). *Recent Developments in Psychoanalytic Child Therapy.* New York: International Universities Press.

Winnicott, D. W. (1971). *Playing and Reality.* New York: Basic Books.

Witmer, H. L. (1946). *Psychiatric Interviews with Children.* New York: Commonwealth Fund.

Wolman, B. B., ed. (1972). *Handbook of Child Psychoanalysis.* New York: Van Nostrand.

———— (1975). *The Therapist's Handbook.* New York: Van Nostrand.

Woltmann, A. G. (1950). Mud and clay, their functions as developmental aids and as media of projection, In *Personality—Symposium on Topical Issues,* ed. W. Wolff, pp. 35–50. New York: Grune and Stratton.

———— (1951). The use of puppetry as a projective method in therapy. In *An Introduction to Projective Techniques and Other Devices for Understanding the Dynamics of Human Behavior,* ed. H. H. Anderson and G. L. Anderson, pp. 606–638. New York: Prentice-Hall.

———— (1955). Concepts of play therapy techniques. *American Journal of Orthopsychiatry* 25:771–783.

Wynne, L. C. (1965). Some indications and contraindications of explatory family therapy. In *Intensive Family Therapy: Theoretical and Practical Aspects, with Special Reference to Schizophrenia.* ed. I. Boszormenyi-Nagy and J. Framo, pp. 289–322. New York: Harper.

Yates, A. J. (1975). *Theory and Practice in Behavior Therapy.* New York: John Wiley.

Chapter 24

PSYCHOANALYTICALLY ORIENTED

PSYCHOTHERAPY OF PSYCHOTIC CHILDREN

by

Rudolf Ekstein, Ph.D.

and

Elaine Caruth, Ph.D., Beatrice Cooper, M.S., Seymour W. Friedman, M.D., Peter D. Landres, M.D., Joel Liebowitz, Ph.D., Thor Nelson, Ph.D.

The pioneering psychiatrists who originally studied psychotic conditions focused on the diagnosis, etiology, and when their conceptualizations permitted sufficient optimism, the treatment of severely disturbed adult patients. Only later was childhood schizophrenia recognized as an entity which in the past had been frequently misdiagnosed. Even now many psychiatrists find it difficult to label a child schizophrenic because they maintain a pessimistic attitude regarding outcome, and hence categorize even some extremely disturbed patients as *borderline, atypical* or *emotionally disturbed.* In this chapter we will concentrate on clearly psychotic children while recognizing that some of the dynamic and structural configuration and treatment approaches apply to borderline patients who do not become overtly psychotic (Knight 1953).

Kraepelin (1919) emphasized the diagnosis and classification of adult dementia praecox, and Bleuler (1911) was interested in the thought and affect disorders of these patients (whom he called schizophrenic) and

Editor's note: The therapeutic methods described in this chapter were developed to a great extent at the Reiss-Davis Child Study Center where the authors worked together. Since the article was requested the direction of the Center has changed, and there is no longer a Childhood Psychosis Project.

the *process* of the disease. Both were pessimistic about the prognosis of the illness with or without treatment. So too was Freud (1911), although he provided dynamic and structural concepts that could be utilized in developing psychotherapeutic measures (Freud 1911, 1924a, 1924b). What appears manifestly as different etiological views concerning the cause of the illness reflects later conclusions about the cause of the cure.

In her pioneering studies Bender (1942, 1947, 1956) described the characteristics of childhood schizophrenia. She emphasized the constitutional and neurological bases for the disorder, and advocated electroconvulsive treatment as well as a modicum of psychotherapy. Kanner (Kanner 1942, 1944, 1954, Eisenberg and Kanner 1956) was known for his rather static approach to the definition and delineation of childhood autism, and concurred with Bender in suggesting educational treatment techniques. Szurek (Szurek and Berlin 1956), Rank (1949), and Bettelheim (1956, 1967) emphasized psychological causality and advocated psychotherapy. Mahler's careful studies of autism, symbiosis, separation-individuation, and object constancy in normal children clarified the autistic and symbiotic mechanisms of schizophrenic youngsters and adults. The contributions of Bettelheim and his collaborators concerning the therapeutic environment and modes of hospitalization have had tremendous impact on our own conceptualizations.

The therapeutic measures to be described in this chapter were developed at the Reiss-Davis Child Study Center, and were influenced by previous research of Ekstein and his coworkers at the Southard School in Topeka, Kansas.

The section concerned with etiology and diagnosis was contributed by Seymour W. Friedman. He stresses that diagnosis should be considered a process, not merely a label, and that it is an integral part of treatment. Thus, a correct diagnostic process is a reflection of the treatment to follow, and is in fact a trial treatment.

Joel Liebowitz and Thor Nelson are concerned with psychological testing of psychotic and borderline children. They not only test in the initial stage of treatment, but view the function of psychology as a permanent, continuing task of the treatment team as we retest during different treatment phases. Thus, their work is not merely a measuring instrument, but is integrated into the total treatment process.

The work contributed by Elaine Caruth and Rudolf Ekstein is a review of different analytic treatment techniques that have been useful in work with psychotic children.

Work with these children cannot be done unless one works with the parents as well. The section contributed by Beatrice Cooper, the social work colleague on the treatment team, deals with this function.

Finally, Peter Landres reports on the need for the understanding and use of support systems such as schools, sensitive teachers, boarding homes, day treatment centers, and hospitals.

While each of the contributions has been prepared by different authors, all contributors share a similar view. Through collaborative work we have tried to form a *treatment team* integrating the various functions which slowly lead us to arrive at similar conclusions. In this sense, each section was prepared by all. However, the division of labor mirrors the fact that we have not yet succeeded fully in developing the synthesis at which we aimed. Nevertheless, the aim was synthesis. Whatever fragmentation remains indicates the difficulty of the work. The fragmentation of the task is caused sometimes by the mind of the fragmented child, sometimes by the fragmented family, and sometimes by the fragmented society. Realizing this task is far from complete, we submit these ideas for colleagues and students, hoping they will join in the quest for knowledge, better techniques, and the strengthening of hope.

ETIOLOGY AND DIAGNOSIS IN CHILDHOOD PSYCHOSIS

Biological and clinical sciences confronted with the responsibility and challenge of understanding and mastering the global chaos, confusion and bewilderment that characterize the lives of psychotic children and their families, have utilized numerous theoretical approaches to the etiology of this disorder. Through ceaseless efforts to explain and understand, these sciences hope to master and control this still enigmatic human mental illness through the use of reliable and predictable therapeutic procedures. The cause, they believe, will be the key to the cure of psychosis.

Scientists—and this includes biologists who seek a physical or physiological basis for the disorder, as well as clinicians and psychotherapists who study psychological and interpersonal processes—have developed a variety of theoretical approaches to etiology, diagnosis, and treatment. These theories vary in sophistication and validity.

Laboratory scientists seek discrete causes of the patient's pain to relieve it. They suggest specific physiological dysfunctions explain complicated psychological states. In this way, they essentially agree with the patient who attributes his difficulties to a cause he conceives as being outside of himself. Patients and their families understandably attempt to determine the etiology of the psychosis in an effort to rid themselves of the offending source of the chaos in their lives, and to restore peace and order. As we will see, the individual's personal theory—or myth —of etiology will determine the procedure he chooses to rid himself of pain.

In contrast to those who seek a discrete explanation for psychoses, we who represent a humanistic approach see etiology in terms of the complex events that led to the present disturbance. Through understanding the development of the psychosis, the therapist can determine what processes can be instituted to change the painful illness, rather than remove the "causal" factors. Etiological factors are not seen as static, discrete causes, but rather as a constellation of interacting events between internal and external forces that, in a constantly changing process of development, seek an equilibrium. Cause leads to effect which in turn becomes cause for further change that, once initiated, makes the distinction between cause and effects meaningless; they become two aspects of a unified process (Ekstein et al. 1971, 1975).

We are reminded here of Mahler's conception of the development of the human infant. An undifferentiated mass is present at the beginning of human life. The fetus and mother, and after birth, the infant and mother form a somato-psychic unity. The baby is totally dependent on his mother. Constitution and environment, nature and nurture, although they do conflict, are essentially complementary. The infant is vulnerable, and susceptible to traumatic experiences, while the mother is capable of protecting her child, and preventing excessive traumata (Bergman and Escalona 1949). In the case of the schizophrenic child, heredity or other biological variations may make the infant more vulnerable than most, but this potential alone does not determine the outcome. The parent may act to diminish or augment the degree of disturbance by protecting the child or failing to do so. A cycle may then develop in which mutual interaction causes further disability.

Bettelheim (1956, 1967), whose approach is somewhat different, emphasizes the mother's traumatization of the ubiquitous, constitutionally sound child whose innate capacity for mastery and influence over the environment must be confirmed, supported, and fulfilled in the mother's reinforcing responsiveness.

By contrast, the purely biological approach postulates physical, physiological, or chemical disorders which cause psychosis. The complex family-child reactions to the biological deviance are ignored. Once the etiology is determined, the treatment consists of removing the more or less discrete biological cause of the painful situation, supposedly curing the disturbance. Medication may be prescribed to alter the chemical cause. Electric shock treatment may be instituted to change the patho-physiological state. By ignoring the complicated interactions we have postulated above, the biological treatment may actually become part of the pathological processes. The psychotic child's characteristic, incomprehensible, unpredictable explosions of violence and regressions to intolerable states of primitive helplessness and dependence provoke counterreactions consisting of violent rejections and attacks. Biological treatment may serve as a disguised assault. Therapist and parent may insist the child change his behavior or be removed from the family so he no longer causes so much distress to those around him.

Contributions of Bender, Kanner, Bettelheim, and Mahler. Bender (1942, 1947, 1956) is an outstanding authoritative clinician and researcher who views childhood schizophrenia as a constitutional, biological illness. According to her, it is a well-recognized syndrome with characteristic disorders in every area of functioning of the personality, and it is based on an organic dysfunction akin to an encepholopathy. In a later modified view of the etiology and pathogenesis of this disorder, Bender conceives of childhood schizophrenia as a result of a combination of inherited tendencies, and noxious and traumatic events, intrauterine or paranatal, resulting in a global disorganization in the patterning of all functions which are seen as embryonic immaturities or maturational lags. Bender traces the origin of the childhood schizophrenic syndrome to the dysfunction of the fetal and immature vestibular system which interferes with the more complete differentiation and maturation of the perceptual motor system and results in a retention of a primitive plastic pattern of tone in all muscle and tissues. Bender further identifies the primary symptomatology of this syndrome as a lack of patterning, maturational lags, and plasticity in the areas of behavioral, homeostatic, motility, perceptual, ideational, and interpersonal functions. She considers anxiety, which is a core problem of schizophrenia, to arise secondarily from a failure in differentiation and patterning in perception of internal, i.e., somatic and visceral sensations, as well as external perception, and in the failure to experience reality. This view of the etiology consistently and logically led to a prescription for medical, biological procedures as a basis for treatment. It justified the use of convulsive therapy and various psychotropic drugs as the primary form of treatment aimed at dealing with the underlying biological somatic pathology.

Kanner (1942, 1944, 1954), in his differentiation and identification of infantile autism as a special entity in the larger group of infantile psychoses, related the etiology of this illness to an "innate inability, an autistic disturbance of affective contact." He also cited emotionally cold, refrigerated, rejecting, although frequently highly intelligent and intellectual parents as a major causative factor.

Constitutional, hereditary, and other predisposing factors have been emphasized by other authors as etiological determinants of this psychotic illness. Researchers have postulated an inherent deficiency in the child's ability to relate or to accept mothering. This innate vulnerability is present at the beginning of the child's life, and is a hereditary or constitutional anlage, an inherently deficient tension-regulating apparatus. Bergman and Escalona (1949) have described unusual sensitivities and perceptual distortions resulting from an inadequate stimulus barrier, so ordinary stimuli could prove overwhelming to these children.

In contrast to those who regard brain dysfunction and related biological and constitutional factors as the single cause of the schizophrenic illness or of its more specialized or related form of infantile autism, there are those who have held equally strong views in defense of the environmental and psychogenic, to the exclusion of biological and constitutional factors. In this area of etiological determinants, the mother-child relationship in the early neonatal period has been primarily implicated. This created the unfortunate controversy over the presence or absence of the schizophrenic mother and the concomitant pejorative tendency to blame the parent. This has muddled the real meaning of the role of the mother and her mothering function in relation to the development of the child's schizophrenic illness. Introducing these emotional issues obscured scientific attempts to understand and assess the role and function of the mother in relation to the pathogenic process. Most certainly, incompetent or deficient mothering could play a significant role in the development of childhood emotional and developmental disorders. However, parental inadequacy could not be proved the sole cause of this global illness. Similarly, a specific brain dysfunction, even if scientifically and clinically validated and confirmed, cannot account for the total clinical picture of childhood schizophrenia. Nevertheless, some studies have demonstrated that certain qualities and configurations of the mother-child relationship are more frequently and clearly associated with childhood schizophrenia and infantile autism than others.

Bettelheim (1967), an eloquent and passionate spokesman for the psychogenic etiology of infantile and childhood autism, has not openly involved himself in the controversy between constitution and environment. He contends that the basic flaw in infants who later become autistic is not a defect in their central nervous system, but consists of the absence of an age-appropriate personality structure through which they experience and deal with the world. The controversy over nature versus nurture, genetic endowment versus the impact of environment, becomes irrelevant in light of the well-accepted view that constitution itself is not a final, unchanging entity, nor a biological unchanging structure with a predetermined function. Rather constitution is a process in which the outcome of all inherited function is determined by the interaction of the genetic material and the environment in which the organism develops. It is the peculiar, special pathogenic interaction between the infant and his nurturing, emotional, parental environment during periods of special sensitivity that Bettelheim is convinced is destructive to the developing self of the child. The critical periods for earliest human infantile and childhood personality development are between the ages of six to nine months, and again from eighteen months to two years. Bettelheim claims seeds are sown during these periods which ultimately, perhaps inevitably, result in the formation of infantile or childhood autism.

Bettelheim, although identifying his views on the etiology and pathogenesis of this illness with psychoanalytic theory and scientific philosophy, takes distinct exception to what he regards as the classical psychoanalytic view of the basic primary helpless, passive, dependent position and attitude of the infant. He insists from the time of its birth, the human being is basically active in his attitude, aspirations, and efforts to master his own fate and to influence his nurturing and caring environment. Dependent in reality upon his parents or substitutes for his physical existence, the infant nevertheless does not feel and recognize this actuality. Inside and outside are confused as the baby experiences selfness. Bettelheim sees the golden age of the human infant as one in which he wishes to act on his own and, through his act of mastery, influences the giver to give to him, even if his aspirations to master his own fate are at the sacrifice of his oneness with the all-giving mother.

Bettelheim (1956) equates the dehumanizing impact of the catastrophic experience of the survivor of a Nazi German concentration camp with the etiology of infantile autism. In that extreme situation, the entrapped victim was convinced he could not escape by his own efforts and that what he did would not alter his ability to master his fate. The resulting dehumanization, isolation, and sense of inescapable futility is, according to Bettelheim, similar to what takes place in the autistic child. He too develops inner feelings of complete impotence about making himself felt and recognized as an autonomous, masterful self by the persons in his external world from whom he receives no emotional response and no verification of his active, striving, influencing self. Repeated failure of parents to recognize and confirm the child's innate capacity to make his primordial selfness and needs known, and repeated failure to master his environment, lead the child to stop trying. He turns his back on his parents and the world, and withdraws to within a self that has lost the desire to reach out, relate to, or even recognize the external world, that is, to the pathological state of infantile autism.

In optimal development of the self, the infant views the world as mainly satisfying and good because he receives good care at all times, to a great extent resulting from his own activities such as reaching, sucking, and smiling. Experiencing frustration and lack of control over the world before a feeling of command is established, and experiencing the world as basically frustrating before being convinced of its satisfying nature and essential goodness, results in the reappearance of frustration and failure when the child later starts to function independently. Bettelheim states that the essential autistic anlage "is the conviction that one's own efforts have no power to influence the world because of the earlier conviction that the world is insensitive to one's reactions." This anlage he attributed to the catastrophic, destructive effects upon the infant's innate sense of mastery of destructive, deficient, insensitive parenting by mother and father.

Mahler (1952, 1968) regards the nature-nurture issue in the etiology of childhood psychosis as moot. However, she strongly holds to the view that in the primary etiology of autistic and symbiotic child psychosis is an inborn, constitutional, and probably hereditary primary core defect. The child is unable to meaningfully perceive and therefore utilize the catalyzing mothering agent to maintain homeostasis. Conceivably, this primary defect could be acquired very early—in the first few days or weeks of extrauterine life. In conceptualizing childhood psychosis within the framework of psychoanalytic theory, Mahler derived supportive data from observations of normal children and parents in a nursery school setting, as well as from intensive therapy of psychotic children. Observations of normal development and relatively minor deviations led her to formulate in greater detail the autistic beginnings of human development and further stages of separation-individuation which she had postulated as the basis of her studies of schizophrenic children (see chapter 6, on prelatency analysis, for some of the details of normal development; see also Mahler, Pine, and Bergman 1975). Observations of normal families then permitted refinements in conceptualizations regarding psychosis.

Tracing its genesis and natural history from pathological deviations, Mahler formulated her theory of child psychosis on the basis of two crucial, key concepts. These concepts, *symbiosis* and *separation-individuation*, underlie both normal and pathological development.

Without further elaborating upon Mahler's brilliant formulation and conceptualization of the vicissitudes, stages, and processes of self and personality development from the beginning of life we would point to her emphasis on the significance of the role of the mother in the etiology and pathogenesis of psychotic illness.

In the case of child psychosis, Mahler expressed her belief that the core disturbance lay in the child's inability to perceive the mother as a nourishing, protecting, and supporting agent for his state of comfort and inner homeostasis, and for coping with the adaptive, integrating, and synthesizing task of mediating and integrating internal and external stimuli. The child is unable to view his mother as separate from himself, and is therefore unable to use her for these functions and psychological purposes. This core disturbance prevents the gradual disengagement of the developing self from the maternal object in the process of separation-individuation and prevents the development of normal psychological object constancy. Inability to successfully progress through the subphases of separation-individuation ends in failure to attain either a solid sense of reality, or a sense of individual entity and identity.

Mahler believes the primary, ultimate, and basic etiology of psychosis in children, the *cause of illness* so to speak, lies in a pathological disturbance of the *mothering principle,* or *mothering agent.* This stands for the perception of, and seeming acceptance of, the relieving ministrations that come from the human mothering partner in the symbiosis, and is experienced by the infant as pleasurable need satisfactions from the world (or the therapist in the later corrective therapeutic process). Mahler implies the primary etiology may have derived from some active pathogenic agent within the child himself, and hence could be seen as a constitutional defect or constitutional mediating factor which gives direction to the developmental process. Ultimately, this leads to the outcome which we know as childhood psychosis. She also implies the etiology of the illness is not a specific event or agent, but rather a pathogenic process leading to a disturbed outcome of an otherwise normal mental process.

Mahler views the mothering principle as the primordial substance and area out of which human development subsequently occurs. This undifferentiated mass makes its presence known from the beginning of human life in fetal intrauterine existence in the form of a somato-psychic dual unity between mother and the new form of life. In the beginning, this life is totally dependent upon his mother for existence until separation and individuation occurs as part of the normal course of events. This view implies a defect or deviation took place in the process of normal and expected development either within the child or within the mother's capacity to provide adequate and appropriate nurturing and responsiveness. The process is seen to include both mother and infant, one or the other. From the very beginning, what eventually becomes a symbiosis was a somato-psychic dual unity in which there was no separateness of parts. Each part plays its own part in this unity. It exists and survives as a process and a function rather than as an entity.

Mahler contends her own research observations do not support theories implicating the mother exclusively or even primarily as a schizophrenic agent. Rather, Mahler prefers to approach the problem of constitution and environment, nature and nurture, not as a conflict between them or as one having exclusive influence, but rather in terms of a complementary series, that is, as a matter of relative strength of influence that each factor exerts unbalanced by the corrective influence of the other.

Clinical illustration of a psychoanalytically oriented approach. We will concentrate on our own psychoanalytic, process-oriented, developmental approach to the etiology and diagnosis of childhood schizophrenia (including autism). We will not discuss other psychotic disturbances such as manic-depressive psychosis, which rarely occurs in children, or organic brain disorders. We will demonstrate our approach through the use of clinical material describing Robby and his parents. We will attempt to discover what the illness consists of, how and why it comes into being, and for what motives, reasons, and meaning. Optimally this is done best in a collaborative process within an integrated research treatment and supervision design (Ekstein et al. 1971).

Mr. and Mrs. A. came to the psychiatrist because their four-and-a-half-year-old psychotic child, Robby, was tearing up their house and their lives. They described their son as a wild little animal. His constant chaotic, aimless dashing about, striking out, tearing, clawing, and hurling of himself and objects around him had disrupted the entire family. The parents' sense of harmony and autonomy had all but vanished as they tried desperately, but unsuccessfully, to control and communicate with their child. In desperation, they had even tried to lock Robby in his room, but he had removed the doorknob and hinges from the door that contained him, as well as from other doors. Distressed and helpless, they blamed the child's destructiveness for their intolerable state. In their minds they established an etiology for and diagnosis of their problems: their destructive child was the cause. They asked, "How do we get rid of this painful situation? We are helplessly trapped, and we need your help to rid us of our suffering and free us from our nightmarish existence."

The mother offered her elaborations of the etiology. She explained her child was very unhappy. She believed if she could do and provide everything he demanded to make him happy, he would be good and not have the urge to tear up their home. The child had acquired a special meaning for his mother. He was living proof she had failed as the all-giving, all-fulfilling mother. She had not created a perfect life for her son, just as her own mother, who had temporarily abandoned her in infancy, had failed to produce an ideal existence for her.

The father said, "The child is destroying our life and we cannot stop him, we cannot control him. No matter how much I punish him and threaten to send him away, I cannot make him do what I want." The father revealed that his own feelings of helplessness, rage, and guilt arose out of a sense of having failed to create the perfect child. This occurred even before he became infuriated at Robby for the child's extreme behavior. The father had felt rage and guilt when he had been unable to fulfill his own father's angry demands that he be a perfect child. These feelings left Mr. A. incompetently paralyzed vis-à-vis Robby. He could not love his son without hate, could not let go of him because of guilt, and could not live with him in peace because of his intense hate.

Through his behavior (translated into psychodynamic language), the child was saying: I have nothing inside me to make me feel alive, human, safe, and protected. I don't feel my parents are with me, so I have to look for them and find them outside of me in everything around me. Anything I can grab hold of I have to tear away and hold onto, because symbolically everything is my parents. What my parents see as destroying them and their home is rather my search for them, my attempt to hold onto them. If they say I'm wild and uncontrolled, I say I have a reason, an etiological theory for this: My mother propelled me into the world prematurely, before I was ready to deal with the world. I possess an inadequately developed nervous system and ego which fail to provide me with controls to stop the impulse to tear up the house and destroy our lives. I have no one inside me to give me the power to regulate and control my impulses. I have nothing inside me to give me a feeling of being complete and competent, and to make me feel I am good and able to do the right thing. I have to possess and control all the doorknobs so I can control the door my parents used to lock me away from them literally and figuratively. I will now take control over all doorknobs so my parents have no power to lock me up, and leave me alone, deserted, and abandoned. In this way I will remove the cause, the etiology, of my fear of being abandoned and separated from them. If I have the doorknobs, I also have mother, and I have myself. My mother did not give me a complete somato-psychic organization, but I will make my own and have complete autistic control over my survival. Besides, I am as bad as my parents feel they are. They think they can only produce bad things like me.

After years of treatment Robby had achieved some degree of individuation and separation and formulated a more sophisticated version of his etiology. He now believed he was ill because he had been conceived by his father's bad sperm and his mother had delivered him prematurely after she fell in the snow. He described the changes that had occurred in him during treatment as having led to a new Robby whom he now assessed as potentially all good, all powerful, and as an idea in God's mind. In this way Robby created a new etiological myth which simultaneously carried within it a new diagnosis, a new prognosis, and a new prescription for treatment. Robby had moved from his original, physiological, causal conception of his illness as a somatic, bodily defect and badness to a more sophisticated, psychological, etiological concept of his illness. Now his illness was defined as the delusion of being reunited in perfect, symbiotic union with a perfect God, without which he became ill but which when created becomes his treatment. According to Robby's prescribed treatment, the perfect symbiosis with the perfect Being would make him perfect too. By substituting the perfect surrogate for the original, defective parent, Robby maintained his static notions of a discrete cause that can be externally dealt with by getting rid of it and replacing it with a better cause. The parent surrogate in the form of God was now viewed as the "cause of the cure," as well as a part of his current self-evaluation and diagnosis.

Robby was a small, handsome, yet delicate child. In his first diagnostic hour, he appeared poised and intensely alert like an animal. He almost seemed to be sniffing out a danger he felt to be all around him. He quickly dashed away from his mother into the consulting room. He took the room in with a glance and began to quickly explore everything available. He went through the toys and discarded everything he touched as if he were not truly in contact with the inanimate things or with the therapist.

The therapist acknowledged Robby's need to look over everything in this strange place. He said Robby wasn't sure what he could do or was supposed to do. The therapist spoke of finding out together what Robby would like to do and why he had come here to see the therapist. Robby instantly dashed to the door of the waiting room and loudly slammed it shut, closing out his mother. What Robby was unable to express in verbal language he forcefully acted out through very determined behavior. The examiner now observed that they were together, just the two of them, and that he could understand Robby's constant activity. He said it must be very like the way Robby felt, always going, always running, and always in motion, as if motion were the only way to escape from his inner danger. However, he added there was no real escape in this helter-skelter activity. Almost as if to validate this all-enveloping danger, a sudden sound of rushing air from the ventilator led the child to retreat in terror. Robby huddled up within himself as if to escape from the intolerable sounds, and then dashed wildly out of the office in a trance-like panic. He slowly recovered after returning to the office with the therapist.

After his therapy started with the same psychiatrist, Robby brought in a doorknob from home. He began to organize all his therapy sessions around a search for one after another of these magical, fetish-like symbols of his need to control contact with his mother. He also needed to escape from her. One hour, after removing the knobs from the doors in his usual way, Robby, suddenly possessed by a need to urinate, darted into the hall, and halted at the closed door of the public toilet. When he entered the restroom he stopped short at the sight of a man urinating, and he tried to observe the man's genitals. The man turned away abruptly, and told Robby to get away. The therapist reassured Robby he would have his chance to urinate like the man, and eventually Robby did so with an expression of great pleasure. Then he explored the other cubicles for other men whom he might observe urinating. Suddenly he raced to the door and removed the doorknob. The therapist said he could see Robby wanted to control the door so they could be alone and keep everyone else out, but "now it's time to go back to our office. That's our place." Robby was asked to put the doorknob back so they could open the door. He did not protest, and immediately replaced the knob. However, neither Robby nor the therapist could open the door because the knob had been damaged. When doctor and patient realized they could not open the door from the inside, Robby became restless and anxious. The therapist tried to open the door a number of times, but failed. He said it looked as if they could not open the door themselves and would have to call for help. Robby became increasingly anxious and the therapist assured him, "We will find a way to get out." He knocked on the door and called. Someone heard their plea, and opened the door. Robby dashed back to the office. The therapist was now quite late for his next appointment. He trailed behind and greeted Robby's mother and his next patient in the waiting room. The mother's quizzical, humorous glance seemed to express her recognition that the therapist had been as inadequate in his helping role with Robby as she and her husband had been. The therapist's next patient, an adult woman, seemed puzzled as she listened to the therapist's explanation. The therapist felt sheepish and embarrassed, and carried these feelings into this new situation, just as Robby's parents felt their chaotic life with Robby intruded into the totality of their life space. The therapist continued to feel embarrassed and helpless in the next hour. He wondered how Robby's parents had been able to survive so long.

In this therapy hour with Robby, as in every psychotherapy session with a psychotic child, we see in condensed form the many components of the patient's personality and his relationship to the world that constitutes his life space. Robby's constricted life centers around doorknobs and their multitude of meanings. His thinking is dominated by primary processes, primitive impulses, and wishes for symbiotic union. The therapist's office and the therapist himself became external representations of Robby's inner symbiotic world from which the patient attempts to escape. Impelled by a fear of losing control, which specifically focused on a physiological need to urinate, Robby entered the locked public toilet. When he encountered an obstacle to his urgent need to urinate, he replaced his frustration and anxiety with an inquisitive, intrusive, and fascinating exploration of a stranger's genitals and his act of urination. Robby succeeded in delaying urination and then worried he may not be able to carry out the act like the man in the toilet. After urinating successfully and thereby achieving autonomy over his body, Robby looked for additional adventures and new situations to master.

However, Robby's increased independence felt dangerous to him, and he attempted to protect his symbiosis with his therapist by taking possession of the doorknob. To his dismay, the patient impulsively damaged the knob and deprived himself of the means to retreat from his inner symbiotic world and to return to his mother in the real world.

Robby and the therapist were just as unable to extricate themselves from the concretized and restricted life space of the toilet as the boy and his parents are to successfully execute reality-oriented, purposive, productive actions. Like the parents, the therapist had to call for outside help to extricate Robby and himself from the entrapping, symbolically externalized symbiosis.

The symbiotic, psychotic child derives a delusional sense of omnipotence from his imagined union with the mother without whom he cannot survive. Although Robby is impotent in reality, within the symbiosis he can maintain a delusional, autistic, omnipotent control over his world. Through the knob, he symbolically holds the world in his hands and reduces it to a concrete state of constriction and smallness he can control. Mastering it, he can allow access to those whom he accepts, but keep out all those he regards as dangerous. His fantasy world, his life space represented by the doorknob, becomes a whole world both inside and outside of himself. Robby thus recreates the world as he imagines it, and combines perceptions from the autistic and symbiotic stages. The world belongs to him alone or to him and his mother with whom he feels fused.

The doorknob acquires a host of meanings, many of which are symbolic. Through it he can keep his mother—whom it represents—and control his impulses. Through it also he can provoke the external world and make real his feeling that symbiotic union with mother is dangerous. The doorknob is a deanimated object the child creates to protect himself. External objects are so terrifying the psychotic child must defend himself from the animate world by making it lifeless. (We differ here with Von Monakow [quoted by Mahler 1968] who believes the psychotic child is constitutionally incapable of differentiating the animate from the inanimate.)

In addition, Robby can use the knob as a higher-level tool to reach into the world as a separate person. With it he can try to separate himself from his parents when separation insures his safety from an engulfing symbiosis. His parents have used the door both to lock him out of their lives and to permit him access to their protection and care. Now he controls the instrument of separation and intimacy.

The knob is a substitute for Robby's own impulse control and for his nervous system apparatus which he regards as incomplete and defective. It is also the indispensable and only means available to Robby, who has no spoken language, to communicate with the therapist and his mother. The therapist, by understanding the meaning of the doorknob, has access to the internal knob that opens the locked door of the child's inner world. Through the doorknob, Robby tells his mother of his great need for her and his desperate fear of being closed out by her. This signal language elicits his mother's response, if not her understanding.

Eitiology, diagnosis, and treatment are thus fused in one situation. The etiology is the failure of the normal symbiosis to function according to the mothering principle postulated by Mahler. The diagnosis is determined by observing the state of helpless, interlocking symbiosis between Robby and his parents. Robby has failed to acquire normal impulse control and the normal capacity to accept mothering and help from his parents. This configuration was confirmed in the psychotic transference.

To more fully understand the genesis of Robby's illness, we must consider the child's meaning to his parents in relation to their past, their unresolved conflicts and unfulfilled aspirations, and to their fantasies about themselves, both as the children of their own parents, and as the parents of their own child.

Mrs. A.'s father deserted her mother and her older siblings before she was born. Her mother felt she could keep the older children at home, and provide for them through full-time, exhausting work. However, she felt it was necessary to turn her newborn infant over to a foster mother until she was able to take care of her some years later. As a child, Mrs. A. missed knowing her father and in fantasy longed to be his special, adored, and idolized little girl. She remained attached to the fantasy of restoring her father. She acted out this fantasy in subsequent relationships with her husband and Robby. She imagined she was indispensable to their life and emotional security, and indeed attempted to create such a relationship with Robby. Unconsciously she imagined she had found the longed-for, adored father who needed her so much he would never leave her. This enabled her to deny the pervasive feelings of abandonment which had dominated her development. Mrs. A. wished for an

undifferentiated state of oceanic bliss in which she and her loved one
constituted a world of her own making. She would never be alone.
Instead of creating this longed-for, satisfying symbiosis with Robby, she
could only construct a symbiotic relationship in which both child and
mother felt imprisoned. The mother's irresistible, all-consuming attempts to gratify Robby's every libidinal impulse and keep him from
feeling abandoned frustrated his healthy ego needs. He could not become independent, endure frustration, or modulate drive derivatives.

Mr. A. had felt isolated and like an outsider in relation to his own
parents. To him they always seemed to stand together and support each
other against him. He had looked to his father to be his friend and
rescuer in his severe conflicts with his mother. Instead, his father had
always seemed to take his mother's side. Mr. A. found himself hating
both his parents and feeling hated by them. His father had been an
autocratic, perfectionistic disciplinarian who was in complete control
over the family's life. He had been intolerant of any weakness, misdeed,
or inefficiency. Faced with his father's demands, Mr. A. felt he could
never do anything right, and could never gain his father's approval as
a capable and competent person. As the father of a disturbed child, Mr.
A. was completely unable to control his son's life and impulses. His own
feelings that he was ineffectual, a failure, and the object of his own
father's anger and contempt, became accentuated. He became furious
at Robby who, as a result of projection and displacement, became his
own bad self as well as his hating, controlling, demeaning father.

Summary. In this clinical illustration we see the complex development
of interrelationships between the psychotic child and his parents which
comprise the etiology of the disorder. A causal continuity exists not
only between the interacting child and his father and mother, but also
between these adults and their parents.

In schizophrenic children the complex genesis leads to a developmental arrest. The patient remains fixated predominantly in the autistic or
symbiotic stage. He may regress and advance from one to the other in
his defensive or adaptive attempts at maintaining an equilibrium. The
child is subject to uncontrolled, unneutralized, aggressive outbursts
when inevitable frustration occurs. These outbursts lead to overwhelming panic lest he destroy the world about him—those he loves—and
himself. Cautious advances to more mature behavior and libidinal

stages cause anxiety and regression. Deficient ego development is characterized by a predominance of primary process thinking, poor reality testing, failures of neutralization, and the use of primitive defenses.

The parents both instigate and are caught in their child's pathology. Cause and effect become fused and interrelated.

Views of the etiology of psychosis in which discrete causes are isolated appear naive and unrealistic when one observes the complex interactions. Treatment cannot consist simply of removing the cause. Help can come only from a realignment of forces within the family and within each member of the family. This is achieved through emotionally potent insight laboriously attained through the family's interrelationships with members of the therapeutic team working in close collaboration.

PSYCHOLOGICAL EVALUATION

The Project on Childhood Psychosis at the Reiss-Davis Child Study Center embodies a team approach to the evaluation and treatment of seriously emotionally disturbed children on an out-patient basis. In the evaluation process itself, representatives of the various disciplines—psychiatry, psychology, and social work—blend their skills and unique approaches to arrive at an understanding of a particular child and his social context. Each discipline brings its own expertise to the evaluation procedure. The contribution of the clinical psychologist is based largely on his expertise with psychological tests. A psychological evaluation brings a child into a standardized situation and presents him with standard tasks. The test findings then lend themselves to a comparative analysis and allow an objective evaluation of the child's mode of reacting.

We in the Project on Childhood Psychosis regard psychological testing as a way of evaluating a child's ego functioning. We do not use tests differently than one would with normal or neurotic children. If one views mental functioning as a continuum from normalcy to psychosis, we are primarily concerned with one end of the continuum, that is, with testing borderline and psychotic children. However, we have found that one is not assessing something unique in the basic personality structure when working with such children. In our experience we have found psychotic and borderline children do not possess psychological conflicts so unique that they are not seen in normal and neurotic children. Rather, it is the organization of the psychic structure and the way in which the psychotic child deals and copes with himself and the world about him that constitutes his uniqueness. Our testing is aimed at identifying that particular uniqueness.

We consider psychological testing to consist of more than the administration of various tests and the scoring of the obtained responses. The testing session itself—from the time the psychologist greets the child until the child leaves the session—constitutes a task for the child. How he meets and deals with this task is of considerable importance. Everything that occurs within the testing session constitutes test data. Some of the more traditional parameters include the child's relationship with the examiner, the way he approaches the tasks themselves, and the way he copes with the test situation. All of this constitutes clinical data. We believe the clinical data that comes out of the relationship built around the testing situation provides a structure within which to view the data coming from the test responses. Often it is the subtle gesture, the roll of the eyes, the stereotyped mannerisms, and other behavioral cues which provide an understanding of the meaning of a particular response. For example, a fourteen-year-old boy greets the examiner with a sweaty handshake and an anxious hello. Once inside the consulting room, he anxiously handles one object after another. With a rush of words and in a staccato-like voice, he attempts to reassure himself he is safe by stating over and over again how much he likes the room and the objects in it. However, tension builds, and the boy begins to mutter, "It's melted, it's melted." When asked about this, he could only relate in words and action that "it" had fallen to earth. Further probing elicited the comment that his cat had melted from the roof of his house. The session was obviously a heated one for this youngster. When one looks at this piece of behavior, it is in striking contrast to the youngster who is equally anxious, but whose ego is able to bind the anxiety with more appropriate defenses. We look at testing as a process and not as a static collecting of data. Therefore this piece of behavior is as diagnostically important as any formal test reply. We do not view testing as something performed in a vacuum, nor do we view test responses as an end in and of themselves. Such restrictions would only make our task of evaluating and understanding borderline children more difficult.

The psychological evaluation needs to be relevant—it needs to have a specific purpose. Certain questions must be established which the testing is designed to help answer. For example, in our situation, it is not enough for the psychologist to provide a differential diagnosis. Almost all the children seen in this setting are seriously emotionally disturbed, and fall within the borderline or psychotic range. Rather, we are concerned with delineating the nature of the disturbance of the ego functions of the child. We address ourselves to certain specific issues. One of the most important of these is whether or not the child can benefit from treatment methods employed by us—intensive, long-term, psychoanalytically oriented psychotherapy on an out-patient basis. For this reason it is important the psychologist evaluate the child's ability to form a relationship, and the nature of this relationship. As the testing session proceeds, comments which may be more or less interpretive in nature may be made to evaluate the child's reaction. Is the child able to make use of the examiner or is his relationship to the examiner characterized by an autistic quality, in which the examiner is regarded as an extension of the child? In this context, shifts in the interaction between the psychologist and the child are also important. At one moment is the child more, or less, in contact? Is the relationship consistently inappropriate, or are there moments when this is more so than otherwise? More often than not, there is no dramatic shift in the child's manner of relating. Rather there are subtle, moment-to-moment alterations to which we try to be sensitive. On occasion, however, this shift may be quite dramatic. For example, one eight-year-old boy had been referred because of his odd behavior. Intelligence testing had been completed and his reaction to some of the projective tests was within reasonable limits. However, a seemingly innocent comment brought a dramatic shift to an otherwise calm youngster. While talking about his father, the child was asked if he was ever punished by him. At the mention of the word "punished," the child literally jumped from his chair. Tears welled forth as if a dam had been opened and the child was overcome. He fidgeted anxiously in his chair and soon began to moan and then to sob bitterly. No amount of effort on the part of the psychologist seemed to help him regain control. The session had to be terminated. On his return a few days later, the child's odd gestures were all there in full panorama. His language was more obviously peculiar, and his associations more obviously odd. It was as if he had tried to hold himself together, but when the dam was opened, all effort to keep things under control had been abandoned. It simply was too taxing and the pathology flowed forth. We are also concerned with other relevant issues, such as appropriate schooling, living arrangements, and other realistic considerations, depending upon the circumstances of the particular situation before us.

The psychologist uses a variety of tests in an attempt to reach an overall assessment of the child's functioning. Each test has a specific purpose, but it is the total testing battery which presents the best overview of the child. Traditionally psychological tests are viewed in terms of their degree of structure, or the degree to which they allow a person to exercise freedom in developing the form and content of his response. Paper and pencil personality inventories which require a yes or no response are highly structured and offer little room for the individuality of the person to emerge. Such tests have been little use in understanding borderline psychotic children. All of our tests require an examiner-subject interaction. All of our tests may be considered *projective tests,* because they offer the child an opportunity to express himself. The size of this arena varies with the particular test. However, even those tests which are relatively structured and allow only single response provide valuable information if the clinician is sensitive to the process which eventuates in the final response. For example, often a relatively structured task, such as a sentence completion item, reveals a whole area for further exploration. For example, a fourteen-year-old girl replied to the statement "Sometimes I think . . ." by stating, "I am a goose, but not really, except that goose makes me think of loose, which feels good so I laugh." Here one can see the ego's fainthearted effort to insert reality (". . . but not really . . ."), but the primary process is too strong and wins out. Nevertheless, the appearance of the ego, no matter how weak, is an important consideration. Again, we are not simply concerned with identifying the language as bizarre. Rather we are concerned with the nature of the idiosyncrasy. In what way is the child disturbed? This question is the starting point of further exploration and the search for further meaning into the process of the illness. If anything symbolizes our work, it is the view that all is process. We are concerned with the unfolding of the psyche, not with the mere existence of pathology.

The individual intelligence test provides us with information about the patient's intellectual functioning and potential. In addition, we consider it a projective test, although a relatively structured one. We glean replies for their richness. Nothing is simply answered; everything is a potential source of understanding. Sometimes the bizarreness of a reply is so apparent it cannot help but be noticed. For example, one nine-year-old boy was asked what he would do if he lost one of his friends' toys. He answered, "Kill him. Get him. Grab him by the throat." On the surface, the question seems innocent enough. For this child it elicited a full expression of his pathology. While we can see this child has extremely poor impulse control, his response is but the beginning of our detective story. We look at the data like so many clues, and piece together a picture of the psyche—the ebb and flow of impulse and defense. Even when we come to some understanding of the process itself, it remains an initial hypothesis ready to be altered and modified as more data is understood.

The Rorschach is one of the least structured psychological tests. It consists of ten cards, each with an inkblot design. The subject is given considerably less structure by this test than by most other tests used in the battery. Therefore there is a greater potential to observe the child's struggle between impulse and defense, and as a consequence, in the borderline and psychotic child, one is apt to see a greater degree of disturbed thinking. For example, one eight-year-old child looked at a Rorschach card containing the color red. While this is but a small part of the card, it consumed this child's total interest. As one so often sees with the severely disturbed child, the blot itself served only as a jumping-off point for the emergence of his preoccupying fantasies and impulses. The child is unable to respond to the reality of the blot as his impulses pour forth. For example, this particular child responded in the following way, "Oh. Murder. Murder on the Orient Express. (He giggles.) It's murder. I can't stand blood, really." Obviously, the child's reply is less than appropriate. But, more importantly for our purpose, we look at such aspects as the ebb and flow of the disturbance. Does the thinking remain disturbed when the child copes with aggressive fantasies? Is the functioning more intact when other material is expressed? Is it in the context of certain fantasies that regression is under the sway of impulse rather than in the service of the ego? What is the child's behavioral functioning as the response is revealed? Is he detached from the affect or overwhelmed by it? These and other questions continually occupy our attention as we listen to the child's responses to the various Rorschach cards.

We will not describe all of the psychological tests and procedures utilized by us. Each clinician develops his own familiarity with tests useful for him in understanding and organizing data. The tests themselves are simply ways to obtain understanding of the child. Material from a Rorschach is not necessarily deeper or more profound than material gathered from other tasks. Our model implies that all tests reflect the process of the psychological functioning, although some tasks are more effective than others in revealing the inner psychological organization of the child.

The data obtained from the testing is best understood within the context of a theoretical framework. Ours is a psychoanalytic point of view. As such, we pay particular attention to the child's ego functioning. It is our belief one can gain a full measure of understanding of the psychotic process through such observation.

The psychotic child experiences difficulties in self-object separations, object constancy, loss of ego boundaries between inner and outer reality, and the nature of the splitting process. All these factors are important considerations in gaining an understanding of a particular child. In our testing, we do not attempt to gain data along specific dimensions. Our purpose is not to identify the presence or absence of such phenomena, but to describe how they operate in the child's psychic life while he is in the testing situation.

PSYCHOANALYTIC PSYCHOTHERAPY

Theodore Reik once suggested psychoanalysts cannot be trained, but rather they are born. We do not share his pessimism concerning the training of clinicians. Nevertheless, when we observe clinicians who work with psychotic or borderline children, we usually see them as people who, although they have received thorough training, also have some added gift, some special capacity for empathy, or some personal experience which has driven them to those deep commitments necessary to treat psychotic children. We are often puzzled whether these clinicians can be trained or whether we might just by chance discover those who have a special natural gift, a deep humanism, and a total commitment to be involved in those most difficult treatment processes. Often these processes are experienced as hopeless, and cause the clinician to fluctuate between hope and despair, but they are also seen as a vital challenge.

It is difficult to speak about a philosophy of treatment which so often seems to be based on faith rather than on a final theoretical answer. Nevertheless, it seems necessary to develop a treatment philosophy, and a guide which attempts to lead the therapist towards improved techniques. We have tried to develop such a basic treatment model below.

In the literature today, clinical reports seldom present a completed treatment process. Instead they give rather fragmentary aspects and excerpts without elucidating an underlying treatment philosophy. What can be inferred however is a philosophy that implies the treatment of neurotic children is basically different from the treatment of psychotic children. We seek to present a treatment philosophy and a treatment model in which the psychotic child and the neurotic child can be dealt with similarly, but not identically. One of Freud's basic contributions was developing and defining the differences between neurosis and psychosis while maintaining a single conceptual framework of psychopathology.

A treatment model. We will first present a graphic model of the treatment process derived from classical analytic procedure, but applicable to any kind of patient. Later it will be necessary to introduce particular modifications for particular kinds of patients. When we speak of a scientific model we are speaking neither of a replica in the sense of a miniature model car, nor are we speaking of a model that is a pure ideal. However, there are elements of idealization and replication in what we mean. A scientific model is designed to provide a frame of reference through which a tremendous amount of clinical material or observational data can be utilized to make predictions. If the model permits us to make predictions about what will come or postdictions about the past, and if these can be confirmed by the ordinary scientific methods of verification, we can say this model teaches something about internal relationships of observational facts. The model permits us to think about a variety of data in a way that will reconcile these data. In other words, the essential features hidden within a wealth of data are somehow made visible through the model. Our present model of the treatment process is derived from the viewpoint of classical analysis. This may subsequently be replaced with a different model from a different point of view.

The original model of the treatment process, and the precursor of the one to be presented, was described fifteen years ago (Ekstein 1956) at a time when interpretive intervention was still seen as something emanating from outside the treatment process. Consequently the analyst and what happens to him was omitted from the model. However today we recognize treatment also involves an interaction, even though the interaction is a very unique one and the essential process is an intrapsychic one. Psychotherapy is considered not merely an interpersonal process, an interactional process, or a communication process: To understand the intrapsychic process of psychotherapeutic change one must also understand the impact of extrapsychic processes upon it during the period of change.

The reference points and lines of the graphic model on page 673 allow the assimilation of information regarding (1) the state of mind of the therapist, (2) the state of mind of the patient, (3) the interaction between the therapist and patient, and (4) the impact of the therapist and the patient upon the world. This last issue is most important in working with psychotic children and is of lesser impact with more mildly disturbed children (Ekstein, Wallerstein and Mandelbaum 1956).

Referring to the model below, the *basic observational data* consists of the *interpretive process,* which is the primary activity of the analyst, and the *free associative process,* which is the primary activity of the patient. The process of communication between the patient and therapist is set up under conditions which are unlike a social relationship. These conditions dictate a different set of rules with a different focus and a different function for both patient and therapist, even though both share the same long-range purpose: intrapsychic change in the patient, and the restoration of psychic functioning on an age-appropriate level.

Let us now describe the treatment process as depicted in this model. At the start of treatment, the patient can be described in terms of his symptomatology and aspects of his personality. He possesses an unrealized regressive potential and an unrealized maturational potential. At the start of treatment the therapist can be described in terms of his incomplete diagnostic picture of the patient and in terms of the potential insight and skill that cannot be fully utilized at the start.

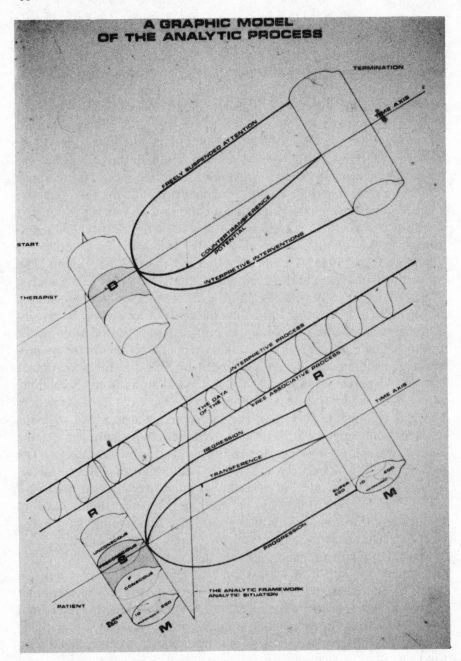

Both patient and therapist have certain rules to follow; in psychoanalytic treatment the therapeutic contract defines the activities of the analyst as well as the patient. Basic rules govern both; the patient's task is to attempt to talk freely, and the therapist's is to attempt to listen freely. Thus, the *free associations* of the patient are met by the *freely suspended attention* of the therapist which is focused on understanding and later interpreting such elements as transference, adaptive and defensive mechanisms, regressive behavior, and unconscious communication. The therapist participates in a process to help the patient become aware of unconscious defenses, conflicts, and feelings. The therapist thus has a dual function. There are elements paralleling the regressive and progressive elements of the therapeutic process in the patient. The therapist's capacity to regress in the service of the professional ego is utilized in the function of listening freely. This has been described by Theodore Reik (1948). He vividly discussed the metaphoric thinking, the pictorial images, and the intrusive thoughts that occur to the analyst when he listens freely with his "third ear." This adaptive regression of the therapist is bound and limited by the goals of treatment. It remains in the service of interpretive work, not in the service of meeting the therapist's own needs. It is a regression tamed and sublimated by professional training. His freely suspended attention is for a particular purpose. Nevertheless we might roughly parallel the doctor's listening as a regressive functioning comparable to the patient's free association, which is also in the service of the therapeutic purpose. As well, the therapist's interpreting is the progressive functioning comparable to the patient observing himself as the result of a mild split in the ego. The patient's ego is split between a regressive functioning in which he allows himself to free associate, but nevertheless must be controlled. He is still able to observe the difference between transference and the reality feelings and thus his potential for progressive functioning is furthered by the development of insight.

Continuing with the model, we see the transference development of the patient is matched by a *countertransference potential* of the therapist. The countertransference potential must remain in the service of treatment through identification which helps the patient, rather than through overidentification which compels the analyst to act out with his patient. We differentiate between empathy, which is controlled, and a full-blown, uncontrolled countertransference (see also Bernstein and

Glenn chapter 13). There may be a fine line between these two phenomena.

Returning to the diagram, note that the patient's free associations are met by the therapist's interpretive interventions. The rules for patient and therapist are like mirror images of one another. They are very similar: neither can act as they would in an ordinary social situation, and the rules define all behavior within the analytic situation. The patient must reveal his needs, but not act them out. The therapist must check his needs, but not repress them. He utilizes them in the service of understanding instead of allowing them to deteriorate into counter-transference reactions. The analyst uses his empathy to supplement and stimulate his intellectual and theoretical understanding of his patient and the treatment process; he plans and controls his interpretations.

Modifications in the treatment model. When working with children and schizophrenics, it is almost impossible to maintain a classical analytic framework at least with regard to externals. The child does not free associate. He does not understand and cannot comply with the rules of adult analysis. The schizophrenic has difficulty containing his impulses, separating himself from his environment, evaluating reality, and comprehending as well. He extracts from the therapeutic situation elements that meet his special requirements. The model we have described as the classic analytic conception must be adapted to the unique problems of treating childhood schizophrenia because of his unique personality structure.

Supplementing the topographic model of the personality (Freud 1900) with the structural model (Freud 1923) helps us conceptualize the personality structure of the schizophrenic. The topographic model focuses on conscious and unconscious mental processes, and is particularly adequate to describe certain clinical phenomena typical of schizophrenia. Drive derivatives and fantasies that are ordinarily unconscious, may be active and conscious in psychotic patients. Pandora's box opens and hate, greed, and other forbidden impulses and desires burst forth. Certain clinical maneuvers can function to "put the lid on." However, we do not consider these to be adequate therapy. Rather they are manipulations which lead to so-called *reconstitution*—an untreated, covered-up disease process, much like a carcinoma that must be left to its malignant course within the patient.

The structural model of the personality portrays the psychic organization in terms of id, ego, and superego structures which are best described in terms of the functions and processes (Beres 1965). The metaphor of Pandora's Box no longer applies. Symptoms comprise both the impulse formation and the defense against the impulse formation. The wish and the reality testing capacities, the impulsivity and the delay functions are all expressed through the symptom. Such a model permits the recognition of the quasi-adaptive resolution of a conflict represented in symptom formation. Such a model recognizes conflict can take place on any level of the organization because there are functional relationships between the different aspects of the personality structure. However all these relationships can take place at different levels of the personality organization which is perceived as a hierarchy of structures.

Many contemporary analysts combine these two models. Id, ego, and superego functions may all be represented at various levels of consciousness. These various levels of consciousness may perhaps best be construed as different layers of psychic organization which form a hierarchy from an undifferentiated archaic phase. Latent dispositions can be found in this phase which will later develop into the organizers of more complex structures within the personality. Such an integrated model permits a more refined and subtle description of the specific ego deviations from which psychotic children suffer.

Psychotics use of the therapeutic situation. The characteristics and needs of borderline and psychotic children lead them to seek help through features of the treatment relationship that other patients use to a lesser extent or not at all. The analytically oriented therapist, aware of his patient's special requirements, meets these needs.

The psychotic patient often feels incomplete and uses contact with the therapist to complete himself. A fantasized introjection or other means of identification makes the patient feel more comfortable for the period he retains the image of the therapist and keeps contact with him. In addition, attaining such identification may be a step toward a more permanent structural change within the patient.

The patient's mechanisms of defense and adaptation are primitive, and involve fantasized fusion with the therapist. Through treatment, the patient may become capable of using more mature forms of identification, and be able to differentiate himself from the objects around him.

He may advance past autistic and symbiotic functioning as he undergoes separation-individuation. However, maturity and a sense of separateness produce anxiety and loneliness. The child regresses to the use of autistic and symbiotic mechanisms. Experiencing fusion during the symbiotic state may result in fears of engulfment. This may in turn lead to an autistic retreat, which is itself regressive, adaptive, and frightening. Attempts to separate once more appear, only to create anxiety.

The therapist can help the psychotic or borderline child in his quest for maturity first by understanding his patient. He must be able to follow his patient's progress and retreat along tortuous and confusing pathways. The therapist must attempt to adjust to the child's use of language, play with metaphor, play development, and his capacity for object relations. The therapist's playfulness and language should reflect the child's.

The therapist must be able to empathize with his patient. Through identifying and understanding, he can talk to his patient in the child's own language. This allows the patient to feel understood. The satisfaction of a secure and non-threatening contact can further the child's steps to maturity. The child may experience this contact as being fed and supported by a kind, parental—often a primitive maternal—figure.

Interpretations can help the child understand and weather anxious periods. Labeling bodily sensations and urges can help him control and tolerate them. Identifying defenses may help strengthen them when they are adaptive and aid the patient in dispensing with them when they fail to resolve conflict.

In addition, the therapist is available—even offers himself for identification. Through this identification the child can acquire reality testing, secondary process thinking, and the use of more mature defensive and adaptive mechanisms. For example he can acquire impulse control which is so necessary for him to achieve greater health. The child's superego, previously primitive and often a mere superego precursor, can become more mature and effective. Preoedipal impulses can become less intense and oedipal urges more stable and less distorted.

The progressive movement is slow and indirect. Before mature mechanisms can be acquired, the psychotic or borderline child will use primitive devices and the therapist will offer himself as a primitive part-object from the past. Only when the familiar but perilous archaic road is made relatively safe can the child use it for more mature ventures.

Clinical illustration. To illustrate these concepts clinically we will present material from a therapeutic session with Theresa, a schizophrenic adolescent girl who has been in treatment approximately four years (see Ekstein 1963 for further details). The following excerpt from her initial psychological test report describes some of the features that will be revealed in the treatment hour to be discussed:

> Theresa is a psychotic youngster who shows a massive hysterical overlay in her personality structure. The psychological test picture is of a girl who is fending off open psychosis through becoming like a nine-year-old girl. She is simple-minded, withdraws any libidinal investment from the outside world, and remains close to, and wallowing in, fantasies of the latency period in which she found herself most protected and happy. Yet, despite these massive efforts to protect herself, Theresa is a fearful youngster whose fearfulness assumes panic proportions. Her terrifying fantasies become so vivid to her that she finds only sporadic protection and support from these kinds of defensive maneuvers. Basically she appears to be a labile, strongly affect-charged young person, who lives extensively and richly in fantasy. In her thinking, reality is readily pushed aside in favor of autistically preferred frames of reference. Added to this is a borderline personality flirting on the fringe of delusionary and hallucinatory ideation. Theresa reaches out intensively to all objects and persons for stability, but this outreach is made on the level of a much younger child.

For most of the treatment hour Theresa functioned on a marginal level, but still within the limits of what would be described as predominantly *secondary process functioning.* She seems capable of dealing with tasks and assuming responsibility for what she is doing. She is preoccupied with the usual problems of living, but careful examination reveals an infantile outlook. However, when the pressure from material she wants and yet fears to talk about becomes stronger her level of functioning changes. Theresa desperately tries to cling to discussing "something nice" to avoid being overwhelmed by a flood of archaic material. She then starts to talk about "The Creature." This delusional introject, a kind of substitute superego organization, helps her to attempt to maintain an optimal level of ego function. Theresa calls on the Creature to aid her in organizing her functioning in much the same way a normal person may conjure up the image of the police to sustain and strengthen his determination to avoid committing a minor traffic violation. However, this substitute or precursor of the superego is not experienced as an inner part of her, but rather as an external factor in the environment. It helps her to maintain some level of integration as she continues to deal with the archaic material flooding her.

In this hour the Creature appears to strengthen Theresa's determination to talk nicely and avoid the influx of primitive fantasies and primary process thinking. The struggle between her wish to communicate and her desire to avoid communicating what is not "nice" interferes with the process of communication. The struggle between the regressive and progressive forces within her leads to paralysis. There is a progressive breakdown in her ego organization, and consequently a breakdown in the superego structure with which she attempts to maintain inner control. As the flood of disruptive material becomes more primitive and archaic, more primitive and archaic means are needed to counter it. Low-grade defenses are used to ward off low-grade, primitive impulse derivatives.

A relationship exists between the Creature and the therapist. The Creature must be considered an auxiliary helper, somewhat like a mother. Theresa created it to help and guide her, and it contains both benevolent and punitive features. The Creature poses as her protector by defending against the expression of bad thoughts and helping her to not become paralyzed by them. When Theresa becomes angry at herself because of her own feelings, she imagines she had angered the Creature who then brings about a paralysis. As long as she can function on a "nice level" (as an immature little girl), the Creature permits her to continue functioning on a nonpsychotic level. However, when the pressure of instinctual forces threatens, the Creature becomes the aggressor and Theresa freezes to avoid the inner danger. To avoid danger the Creature creates a virtual paralysis of advanced ego organizations, and concomitantly, a regression takes place to the very archaic level from which the danger originally emanated.

In part the Creature originated as a disguised representation of the therapist. The patient, eager to control her flooding impulses, used the analyst as a new, protective, and restrictive mother. She created the Creature in the therapist's image. Theresa introjected his representation, and then, projecting, used it as an external, controlling, superego substitute. As long as the Creature-therapist was used adaptively to support reality testing, secondary processes, and healthy restraint, the therapist did not need to interpret its qualities of frustration and anger. When the Creature itself became a threatening figure, and a regressive archaic expression of uncontrolled id forces, the therapist intervened. He interpreted the loss of control, and supported the adaptive use of both Creature and analyst.

The fatal flaw. In developing other aspects of our integrated model of treatment, we must consider the nature of object relations in the schizophrenic child, particularly the autistic and symbiotic positions.

To borrow an insight from one of these patients (who are in fact the source of all our insights), we deal specifically with problems of the *fatal flaw*. This is the clinical derivative of the underlying basic deficit in object relations and ego development in such patients. A hospitalized, adolescent youngster, suffering from a schizophrenic character disorder, observed that the other patients, as crazy as they were, would have ordinarily been able to make outstanding contributions in their various fields. However, they all seemed to possess a single flaw which prevented them from functioning outside the institution and making use of their talents. In part this observation was a projection of an insight into his own condition. A puncture in his megalomanic armor permitted this youngster to recognize he was still ill, and despite his many talents, a *fatal flaw* still existed in his own psychic organization which interfered with his functioning.

This fatal flaw is a deficit in the psychic structure which drives the individual mercilessly and repetitiously towards destruction. It has long been recognized in the literature of the theatre and mythology. Writers like Chekhov, Ibsen, Tennessee Williams, and Arthur Miller have dramatized the internal drama in such people. *The Glass Menagerie* (Williams 1945), for example, describes a young woman's retreat into an inner world puppetted with introjects from the past—the glass menagerie—and her withdrawal from the outer world peopled with frightening, terrifying extrojects projected outward.

Early analytic understanding of such basic personality deficits tended to be limited to interpretations around unresolved oedipal conflicts and the variety of resulting manifestations. Early analytic writings considered schizophrenia the result of an inverted position of an unresolved oedipal conflict. With the expanding developments in ego psychology and a deepening understanding of structural aspects of the psychic organization, the fatal flaw, particularly in psychosis, can be understood in reference to the nature of the early mother-child matrix, and in reference to how the nurturing experiences in these very early pre-oedipal stages influence ego development.

An interpretation of the mythological tale of Achilles provides visual images which permit an understanding of these concepts in allegorical terms.

Achilles' mother, Thetis, was a woman whose fears, ambitions, and desires for her baby can easily be identified as "what every woman wants." Achilles, like all the heroes of the Trojan Wars, was predestined to die in the struggle to attain the mother imago in the form of Helen. We refer here not to the myth's oedipal implications, but to the underlying struggle against the overwhelming feelings of a destructive death-like fusion with the mother, and the autistic-like isolation following separation from the symbiotic mother.

Thetis is a sea nymph, and her oceanic feelings of omnipotence and knowledge about birth are therefore legitimate. She knew her son must become a hero to meet her own and the culture's expectations. She wished to protect him from the dangers of battle and make him invulnerable. Thetis took Achilles to the River Styx, a river which separated the world of the living from the world of the dead *(the world of secondary process from the world of primary process)*. The river could give magic invulnerability and yet inevitably, since its banks also touched on the world of *reality testing,* it did not have complete magic to give. Thetis is described as careless because she dips Achilles into the river holding him by one heel, and thus creating his vulnerable spot. *We suggest this description of Thetis as careless is the prototype of today's professional paranoia toward parents.* We view the Achilles heel, the one vulnerable spot, as the inevitable result of the human infant's prolonged dependency on his mother. If one must be held to become invincible, then the invincibility is itself a result of this original dependence. The inevitable flaw is the result of any system of child rearing. Kubie (1936) has observed we will always find an infantile neurosis no matter whom we analyze, or how healthy they appear. The child rearing process itself leaves residues of the original dependency because the source of dependency, the infant's tie to his mother, is also the tool through which the dependency must ultimately be resolved. This flaw exists in sickness and in health. However, there are differences in the nature of the flaw. It may be adapted to and utilized in the service of progressive, forward moving development or it may become a destructive, regressive force in the personality.

Achilles' mother once dressed him as a beautiful girl with long hair so he wouldn't be detected by Ulysses' messengers who sought him because of his fighting prowess. Ulysses, however, was not fooled by this maiden who did not play with trinkets like the other maidens, but rather fingered daggers and swords, and Ulysses persuaded Achilles to go to battle. Thetis was then driven by her ambition for her son to become a hero and fulfill the masculine role. She acquired the best armor she could for her son from Hephaestus, but Thetis could not protect Achilles' vulnerable heel.

Going beyond the immediate metaphor, we might say that this mother couldn't let her son find an identity of his own. She vacillated between holding him back, forcing him into a helpless, feminine role and prolonged dependency on her, and at the same time pushed him towards fulfilling a heroic, masculine role. This helped create Achilles' fatal flaw. His psychic organization was incapable of resolving the conflicts over separation and individuation. The mother-child nurturing experience may help the young baby grow strong and fulfill himself or may only nurture the mother, and fulfill her own megalomanic wishes for success through her child. In the healthy child, the love of his mother and his desire to be protected by her is nevertheless outweighed by his hate of dependency, and his active desire to climb toward a mature, independent identity.

The influence of the early preoedipal situation on object relations has only recently been elaborated and refined, although its influence is essentially implicit in early *instinct theory*. Instincts are described as "object seeking"; they have an aim and a mode of discharge. Behind this terminology are the precursors of insights into ego psychology and early object relations. *Three Contributions* (Freud 1906) describes psychological development in terms of both process and structure. It describes how the growth processes of change and development modify structure, and at the same time, are limited by structure. When we talk about a mode of discharge, we have the beginnings of ego psychology, in which ego functions are described in terms of the object, as well as biological aim. However, these earlier descriptions of objects tended to emphasize their part-object qualities, and their sexual gratification potentials, such as the breast, genitals, and erotogenic zones. These early descriptions of objects view them almost as deanimated fragments paralleling the automation-like early description of instincts. At that time instincts were defined in a way that tended to reify them in concretistic fashion rather than recognize them as explanatory concepts.

In our attempt to describe object relations from both a genetic and a functional standpoint, we hope to understand the basic flaw which the schizophrenic child brings to us in treatment. Referring to our model, it is essential we understand the child's basic deficit in object relations to understand and make appropriate use of the ensuing transference and countertransference configurations and their implications.

Clinical illustration of the fatal flaw. When the following clinical situation occurred, Billy's schizophrenic character and thought disorder were, as yet, invisible. Years later reevaluation enabled us to see the seeds of more serious pathology within this early material. Also, at the time we did not have a full picture of the child's mother. She had presented only the resourceful, competent, ambitious side of herself and her desire to be a good parent. We were unaware of her personal disturbances and her pathological relationship with her son.

In this fragment of a therapeutic session, Billy, an eleven-year-old boy, is playfully acting out the role of a rescued hero. He is relating his tale on the radio to an invisible audience, to be understood as the mother. The therapist is the assigned announcer in and of this play. The boy had always acted out his fantasy of wishing to be rescued by his mother, who like Thetis rescued her son while driving him into dangerous situations. In his play the patient describes sailing into an atomic explosion. Being alone will not only result in a violent explosive destruction, but it will also lead to being rescued from the danger by his mother.

In retrospect, one can see the child's internal struggle. He utilized the therapist as a deanimated object who could introduce him to the mother (the audience) before whom he exhibited his narcissistic prowess. What at the time appeared to be neurotic dramatization was in reality a psychotic play acting.

Billy fluctuated between perilous situations. Being alone and autistically oriented is dangerous and can lead to explosions. He must attempt to unite with his mother, but this is also dangerous and can result in similar destruction. He must therefore detach himself from objects and revert to autism. The play contains the theme that he can never get beyond the autistic position and join his object. The transference too can be understood as a repetition of early narcissistic positions. He uses the therapist as an extension of himself, while at the same time warding off the symbiotic threat of union.

Kanner described autistic children (Kanner 1942, 1944, 1954, Eisenberg and Kanner 1956), and Mahler (Mahler 1952, 1968, Mahler and Furer 1960) provided us with the understanding that the autistic and symbiotic positions of the psychotic child are not static. The child progresses into the symbiotic stage only to regress to autistic functioning if that becomes too frightening. Mahler (Mahler, Pine and Bergman 1975) observed children normally go through an autistic stage lasting about two months and then enter the symbiotic stage. This stage continues until they are about five months old but symbiotic features persist beyond that age. In the autistic stage the child's perception of the external world is minimal. In the symbiotic stage the child perceives the outer world to a greater extent, but still conceives of his mother and himself as an encapsulated unit. Self- and object-representations are poorly differentiated. Autistic children are arrested primarily in the autistic stage, but they may progress into the symbiotic stage. If this is found to be dangerous, they regress to autism. Children with symbiotic psychosis are either arrested in that stage of development or have regressed to it. Under the influence of anxiety as separation-individuation proceeds they may regress further to autistic functioning. Regression to autism can thus be a defense. When this regression is partial and occurs in conjunction with more mature mechanisms, it can also serve as a step toward individuation. The child retreats and advances as he attempts to avoid feelings of fusion with his mother. The negativism of the secondarily autistic child is not the simple indifference of the infant in the autistic stage. It is negativism in the service of independence—like the one-year-old who says "no" to assert his autonomy.

Although Mahler makes clear that the autistic stage is a normal developmental phase in all children, she does not preclude the possibility that childhood schizophrenia has a physiopathological etiological component.

Prior to Mahler, Klein (1960) and particularly Fairbairn (1954) described the lack of differentiation of self and object in terms of object relations theory. If the breast is insufficient to satisfy the child it is hated, but since the infant also perceives the breast as a part of the self, the self is hated too. Both breast and self are split into a good and a bad part.

Ekstein and associations have utilized Mahler's insights (Mahler and Elkisch 1953, Mahler and Furer 1960) primarily in reference to application to techniques of therapy and understanding of transference issues. The therapist's awareness and understanding of his patient's inner flaws increases his skill and the safety of the treatment process. Just as the work of the sculptor needs to account and adjust the inner flaws of the marble, the therapist must recognize his patients' defective and sturdy areas.

At the age of fifteen and a half our patient was hospitalized in an effort to separate him from his parents, particularly from his mother. Also, Billy had begun to act out the self-destructive fantasies he had had since he was eleven. After two days in the hospital, he told his mother he was writing a book with his therapist. In fact, the book was only a paragraph. At the decisive moment of this paragraph the boy could not complete it, and his writing drifted off into nothingness.

I walked down an early morning road and saw the rain and heard the chattering of squirrels. The thickets of thorns and briars hid them and the early morning colors clung to my eyes as a filter which only could see the rain and the moss like mists. Step lively, now; and don't think of her white sheets and the ivy-covered brick buildings of the city. To rest in her arms was worth all the wind and the autumned colors that shrouded the crescent landscape and that pull in my body now. I feel like an autumn leaf in this freedom of a wilderness and this hinterland is my life now; and my tired feet will vouch for that. So beautiful and detached from the mother tree, isn't that the story of an autumn leaf as it sails a crooked sea of . . .

In this prose poem we recognize the expression of the danger of separation from mother, i.e., of metaphorically becoming an autumn leaf drifting like a crooked leaf in the freedom of a wilderness. Billy describes his absolute dependence on his mother. It is frightening because it takes away all his self-initiative. When he does face freedom, he only has chaotic impulses. His capacity for work or love is of a symbiotic nature. This is not the symbiosis of a permanently regressed child who can only think through the other; this boy has fluctuating periods when he is able to observe quite insightfully both his own and his mother's psychic functioning. He fits Knight's (1953) description of the borderline patient who has isolated islands of more mature ego functioning, but is frequently reduced to a more regressed position (the autumn leaf). He is either attached symbiotically to his mother (the tree) or else is detached to drift autistically in a destructive, impulsive manner (sail a crooked sea). Thus, although we can see manifestations of many other developmental features the boy's poem aptly describes the autistic-symbiotic struggle.

Just prior to his hospitalization, in his last attempt at social adjustment—a kind of quasi-identification with and attempt to surpass his father who is a successful entertainer—Billy tried to produce a movie with a group of peers. The boy dressed as a Beatle and was a guitar player. The group planned to purchase camera equipment to produce this film. The therapist wholeheartedly supported the venture though he cautioned perhaps the group should develop the plot before they bought equipment.

The plot involves an adolescent, black boy caught in a struggle over segregation. This boy is lonely and his only attachment is to a little girl doll he has loved and kept with him from childhood. He retains the doll even though he realizes he should give up this remnant of his past and look for a real object. Then a beautiful white girl and he fall in love. She wants him to discard the doll for her, and he relegates it to the gutter. However, the world of white people destroys their alliance and he returns to the gutter to search for his lost doll. The story stops here because the boy knows he will not be able to recover the doll, his lost childhood. Since he cannot have the white girl, the mature love object of adult life, he wanders aimlessly searching the streets.

This story shows another aspect of Billy's object relations. He attempts to deanimate, to make a doll out of a real life object and thus master the object or the self. In the story, the doll and the white girl both represent features of his mother. Even though the plot is disguised as an adaptive revolutionary social plot, it is not future-directed. It merely hides his underlying psychosis. The white girl stands for the tabooed genital aspects of his oedipal conflict inasmuch as there are aspects of his personality which have reached the level of genital activity. Shortly before being hospitalized he had impregnated a girl friend. In the plot he describes his reaching out for the real object—the white girl—and his inability to "touch" it. He reaches out for the doll, the symbol of the early mother-child matrix, but makes this early mother into a puppet who is only capable of doing his bidding. She has no separate internal structure of her own—just like the inner chaos of the boy himself. The boy is torn between returning to the chaos of his symbiotic fusion with the mother-doll, where one or the other is made into a puppet, and the chaos of searching for, but never reaching, the forbidden, inaccessible oedipal object—a level of object relationship with an independent separate person, something of which he is not yet capable.

The boy's ego is so organized that he can only passively observe the internal struggle with panic and admiration (Wexler 1969), his ego cannot do anything about it. He has no more power to act than we do when we observe a movie and would like to change the plot. The struggle of the little black boy is observed and described by a bright, perceptive child whose intact intelligence can only observe helplessly what goes on within him.

Introjection, incorporation, and identification. Introjective, incorporating and identificatory processes are the main mechanisms through which a new position is brought about and maintained in the development of object relations. In "Life and the Dialogue," Spitz (1963) discusses the issue of when and how the child discovers his mother is not merely like Harlow's wire monkey mother, but is truly alive. Through this discovery, the child's previous experience of life as a quasi-monologue is modified and he enters into a dialogue with his mother. In work with schizophrenic children we are dealing with precursors of the *monologue* and the *dialogue*. The precursor of the monologue is equated with impulses which must be immediately gratified.

The precursor of the dialogue is the interaction with the part-object, the breast, with which the infant must learn to *negotiate*.

These issues refer to the very beginning of object relations and are the central problem in schizophrenia, where a true dialogue is never fully achieved. In the schizophrenic position an attempt is made to restore a world in which there is no need for the dialogue, and where the object remains deanimated and the reign of impulses may be restored. In both the autistic and symbiotic positions, impulses run wild, ego controls are frozen or unavailable, and objects are deanimated or fused with, become part of the self. Anarchy reigns in this world where there is no commander because the capacity for maintaining even part-introjects is not yet available. Treatment aims at restoring the capacity for maintaining introjects as stable representations in the absence of the object. In the language of Melanie Klein (1960), this period is a world of part-objects—a world which cannot be maintained by the child if part-objects are not present, a world which cannot be integrated or synthesized into a whole person. It is an introjected world of part-impressions which are never integrated or synthesized. Instead, people are like puppets, and are seen only in terms of one trait. These part-objects are of an either/or nature. Either they are all-giving or all-hating, but in both instances they are all-dangerous. The all-giving, positive objects present the danger of symbiosis and the loss of the identity, while the all-hating objects present the danger of destruction through rejection and abandonment. The autistic position may be understood as a defense against the dangers of symbiotic fusion and the loss of identity, while the symbiotic position may be understood as a defense against the autistic isolation created by a hostile, rejecting mother. These are early or psychotic equivalents of the love-dependency versus independence-isolation dichotomy.

In healthy development, object relations are brought about through processes that range from very primitive to more advanced ones. The final process of identification may be considered the end point of a continuum ranging from a very primitive kind of imitation of external behavior (referred to in its earliest instance as *fascination*) through incorporatory introjective mechanisms to a more mature identificatory process. The dialogue begins when the child discovers demands in the environment can be met by imitative responses such as smiling. Gradually the child develops the capacity for *incorporation*. This is a crude mechanism in which there is no conceptualization, and no language. There is only the capacity to experience through a physiological response. The child can only take in and eat up outside stimulus. This is his only literal experience of the world.

With increasing complexity of structure, this mode of taking in gradually becomes more discriminating about what is taken in and what is spit out. It is the prototype experience of what is good and what is bad, what is self and is nonself. Introjective mechanisms are then developed in relation to part-objects, for example, the positive breast and the poisonous breast. As these part-objects are synthesized into integrated objects with both positive and negative aspects, the child becomes capable of true identificatory mechanisms. Mature identification presupposes the capacity for language. There is a tremendous difference between the precursors of mature identification prior to the acquisition of language and the type of identification possible once language is available. To illustrate how differences in age make differences in the ways in which a basically identical conflict can be experienced and described, we might refer to the patient described previously. At the age of eleven Billy pictured the autistic and symbiotic struggle in a fantasy play in which he sailed into an atomic explosion when alone on the ocean. At the age of fifteen in his poetry, the boy describes the same conflict in terms of "the beautiful and detached leaf floating away on a crooked sea." Different ideational capacities have been called upon to describe identical, underlying conflicts. The development of mature object relations, and the progression from the monologue to the dialogue, depend upon a parallel development from the use of primitive mechanisms, incorporation and introjection, to the use of the more mature mechanism of identification.

In describing the processes of identification it is important to specify and understand not only how but what is identified with. In certain instances we may use primitive mechanisms in the service of more advanced functions. For example, Wexler (1969) has described an actress who, in an attempt to "live herself into" the world of the Chinese children she was to portray, lived with and watched them. She felt as if she were actually swallowing something at the moment she finally experienced the empathy she had sought. Kris (1952) has described certain literary and artistic experiences as regressions in the service of the ego. These experiences are flexible, reversible, and under the control of the observing, critical ego. The content of the identification may be primitive and close to imitative devices, or it may require advanced functioning. For example, a student analyst may acquire many of the simple, external characteristics of his supervisor, or he may identify with his complex and sophisticated ideas.

Finally, what may look like a mature identification may reflect a breakdown in personality organization. An individual's personality may be determined by a fusion experience with the other person. Identity is given up as the patient returns to a symbiotic position.

In Elaine's efforts to imitate Christ, and to be like Him, she became Him (Ekstein and Wright 1964). She lost the capacity for distance devices through which she was attempting to imitate Christ, and instead could only fuse with Him. However, this destroyed her own identity, and she had to turn against this evil as well. At times she became homicidal. Since she had lost the capacity to differentiate between self and object, her attacks on others involved suicidal intent.

Frequently psychotic children deal with their incapacity to identify in an ordinary way through the use of psychological "crutches." Artificial distance devices are used to help protect the child against fusion experiences. Elaine did not have advanced identificatory processes available to her. Nor did she possess artificial distancing devices such as the use of space or time fantasies through which she could have placed some distance between herself and the conflict.

Advanced mechanisms of identification involve a balance between a taking in and a putting out, between projection and identification and introjection. Mature identification may utilize projective identification. This is a rather primitive mechanism insofar as it involves a recognition that the other individual has something in them that is also in us. Introjective identification, which is based on the recognition that there is something in the other we want in us, may also be used. Advanced capacity for identification, involving both projection as well as introjection, however, presupposes the availability of synthetic functions, for without them we can only experience part objects as well as part self-representations, as is the case if only projection is available. For example we see only the denied hate in them but do not recognize it in ourselves, nor recognize anything else in them. Normal identification is like normal osmosis. It is a two-way process resulting in the capacity to understand what goes on in others as well as in ourselves. When it is one-sided, as in the deanimation we have described, the patient says, "I can only identify with you in a certain way, since I am not like you."

Wexler refers to this problem when he asserts that these schizophrenic patients can only experience the therapist by introjecting him. To contact them, he says, the therapist must feed himself to his patients. This feeding should not be merely symbolic, such as when we give a patient a pictures of ourself, or offer him an apple (instead of the breast) as suggested by Sechehaye (1951). We believe it is more correct to suggest we may regard treatment as a metaphorical feeding, but there should be no concrete prescription to that effect. There is a difference between concrete feeding and symbolical gratification.

The main part of this section dealt with a proposed model for treatment which we found helpful in the treatment of psychotic children. We want to emphasize that this model was developed in a somewhat playful way. In speaking about play, we speak about a serious undertaking, the play with thoughts and models—the attempt to identify with the kinds of thoughts children have and the adaptation of our thinking to their thinking so we can identify with them and help them build a bridge towards us—thus *they* can identify with us.

In previous publications, we have written about other identificatory devices, such as attempting to adjust to the child's language, his play with metaphor and simile, his indirect way of talking, and his different stage of language and play development.

It is perhaps essential to know that we are identified with a rather skeptical hopefulness. While we believe treatment is possible, we have no final answers. The treatment model above is offered as a tool for the reader to work and play with and to see whether it is useful for and acceptable to his own style of working, and his own conceptualizations.

WORK WITH PARENTS

Work with the parents of psychotic children not only protects the child's treatment, it also becomes an integral part of the treatment process. It is a vital support system and helps synthesize the different treatment modalities comprising the complex therapeutic situation. A previous communication (Ekstein, Friedman, Caruth, and Cooper 1976) stressed the optimal treatment plan for a schizophrenic child should be derived from a full evaluation of his total intrapsychic and interpersonal structure and functioning.

Although each child's treatment requires a different kind of structure, schizophrenic children and their families generally present similar organizations. The schizophrenic child and his environment frequently form an almost undifferentiated unit in which parent and child supplement each other's symbiotic needs. The relative lack of stable differentiation within the individual child's psychic organization interacts with an environment that also lacks differentiation. The child confuses himself with his parent who, in turn, is uncertain about where he ends and his child begins. Each may look to the other to reconstitute or restore himself.

Both parent and child often confuse self-representation and object-representation. What is within the child becomes fused with what is without. In effect, differentiation dissolves and fusion is re-established. Internal conflict does not remain internal. Instead, it is observed in the struggle between the patient and his environment. Not only does the child project; the environment appears to confirm the reality of his most frightening and dreadful projections. The external world seems to reflect, mirror, or resonate his inner reality.

The child may stimulate such behavior. If the child succeeds in provoking the objects in his outer world to echo the archaic, unstable, introjects of his inner world, he confirms their validity.

The treatment philosophy developed at the Reiss-Davis Clinic emphasizes individual work with parents as well as children. This is necessary to help parents understand the options available to them and enable them to make appropriate and stable choices as they attempt to cope with the bewildering relationship with their psychotic child. Our focus is on how they can function in relation to the current problems they are having with their child, rather than on their past mistakes.

A relatively stable parent may be pulled into a regressive, symbiotic relationship by prolonged, close contact with a schizophrenic child. However, all too often we find the parents themselves have previously failed to achieve an integrated and well-functioning personality. In either case, the treatment plan requires they support and participate in a difficult, demanding, and draining therapy for long periods of time. Special help is needed if they are to succeed.

In addition, the child frequently requires special schooling and/or additional persons to enter his home to supplement parenting. We have come to realize the importance of helping parents accept and work with private nurses, occupational therapists, educational therapists, etc., while the child is at home, in a day hospital, a full-time hospital or a special school.

The very nature of childhood schizophrenia frequently makes contact with those support systems essential when the child requires new objects as he moves away from maternal symbiosis. Trained personnel can serve as new objects who avoid reestablishing the symbiosis which the child may seek to establish with his extrafamilial environment as well. The therapeutic design must be integrated and the therapists and their allies—parents, teachers, and nurses—must work together to withstand the child's antitherapeutic attempts.

These sick children all too frequently succeed in seducing the agencies working with the family to participate in their illness rather than to counter it. Even psychiatrists, social workers, substitute parents, and school personnel may succumb. In his desperate need to assume omnipotent control over his external environment, the child may destroy the capacity of his environment to feed his starving potential for normal living. The child attempts to get the environment to feed the pathology, and become part-objects that are the image of the illness itself, and thus sustain the helpless, nihilistic, autistic core. Not only therapists, but the total therapeutic environment must withstand the onslaught against its integrative capacity to provide a comprehensive, calm, and unified program. The child's therapist, the parent's therapist–social worker, and all other personnel must remain united in their mutuality of goals even as they retain autonomy over their respective functions. They must remain whole objects capable of sharing a purpose while simultaneously retaining individuality of function. Restoration of the capacity for inner choice and freedom to function remains the primary goal.

Clinical illustration. An extended excerpt from the casework therapy with a mother will serve to illustrate many of the problems outlined. Mrs. A. was an extremely disturbed woman whose paranoid thinking interfered with her ability to rear her child and to participate in the treatment process. Although such serious pathology is not uncommon in the parents we treat, the reader will realize many of the fathers and mothers of schizophrenic children are neurotic rather than psychotic. Many, as we have described, find themselves compelled to react to their child's vexing disturbance quite differently than to their normal or neurotic offspring.

The seriousness of the pathology of parents like Mrs. A. appears to demand intensive therapy, but we often find the parents can accept only treatment on a less frequent basis. At the same time, in the case of Mrs. A. (and many others), simple supportive measures would not suffice. She could not benefit from reassuring explanations of her child's pathology as some parents can.

Barbara A. was a withdrawn and uncommunicative five-year-old schizophrenic child whose parents desperately wanted to help both to cure her and to cope with her while she was ill. Despite Mrs. A.'s premonition her daughter was seriously ill, she could not accept treatment until three exhaustive consultations in three reputable psychiatric, medical, and academic facilities were completed. The family was referred to the Reiss-Davis Clinic where Barbara was engaged in three sessions of psychotherapy each week. Her parents were seen in individual interviews with the social worker.

Mrs. A., a basically intelligent, well-educated woman, was terribly insecure. Despite previous psychiatric treatment for phobias, she remained poorly organized and felt life was desperately meaningless and hopeless. She could not provide her daughter with sufficient maternal warmth, and attributed this to having failed to receive love from her own mother, whom she came to hate. Mrs. A. could not bear to engage in play with Barbara because the bizarre quality of her daughter's fantasies frightened her. Identifying with her disturbed child when close to her, the mother recoiled from contact, and estranged herself from her daughter. Any close contact led the mother to feel the child to be a sick extension of herself, and this threatened her with the possible appearance of delusional, archaic thinking. She feared she would become furious at her daughter and hurt her. When Barbara tried to communicate with her mother, Mrs. A. had to retreat.

In this interaction we can see a persistance of an early, undifferentiated, symbiotic union between mother and child. It was a union the mother had to avoid because of the anxiety it generated in her. We could predict that as the child grew more mature, the mother would be unable to respond with gratifying parenting.

Mr. A. was somewhat stronger than his wife and could tolerate Barbara's needs. He became a substitute maternal figure from the very beginning of the child's life. The father's later acceptance of his daughter's fairy-tale-like fantasies and story-telling made Mrs. A. jealous and reenforced her strong disapproval of Barbara's ideation. The father assumed the role of the provider-feeder and protected his daughter from the mother whom he saw as a sick person whose aggression had to be restricted. He seemed to have the capacity to provide the child with a nurturing figure she could cathect, and thus counteracted the mother's toxic influence. Barbara was pulled between two diametrically opposed systems of parental approval and disapproval. The early undifferentiated mother-child alliance created a mixture of omnipotence and lack of power. The child had the inner potential to cry, and to reach out to touch her mother, but her mother was unable to react to this signal and provide a satisfying response.

Mr. A's position was complicated. He blamed his wife for his daughter's psychosis and felt neglected himself. He became affectionate toward his daughter whom he felt was more responsive than his wife and, more capable of allowing him to meet her needs. He could not find a satisfactory balance of distance and intimacy with the members of his family. He tried to desensitize himself, and numb himself to the problems the therapeutic situation tended to make him face and feel. Hence, he isolated himself from the program; he attended his sessions each week, but he remained aloof.

Mrs. A., on the other hand, while struggling against the treatment, participated more fully. However, from the very beginning she behaved irrationally toward the social worker. Mrs. A. was demanding, negativistic, and raging. She attacked the social worker with abandon. This behavior directed her feelings of antagonism away from Barbara and she slowly began to be more available to her child, although in a tentative and hesitating manner. Nevertheless, this was sufficient to somewhat diminish the threatening incestuous feelings Barbara had for her father while she was able to retain his representation as a caring person.

The struggle portrayed in the seeking out of the therapist-social worker, only to resist and run away, reveals the level and the pathology of the interpersonal relationship. Fear of fusion was so overwhelming they avoided the reality, preferring the longing for the object to the object itself. The struggle is repeated in the generations.

Mrs. A.'s attacks on her social worker had another paradoxical affect. It made her feel more alive and effective. This was true outside treatment as well. Mrs. A. became more alive when she was hostile to people. She fought those she thought could be verbally intimidated, but whom she could not harm. She also felt more like a person when she experienced the possibility of separation.

The clinic came to symbolize a repository for psychosis. "Craziness" was brought to the clinic where it was maintained and valued, and the mother made the most of this in the transference relationship with the social worker. Through denigrating the social worker, Mrs. A. expressed her negative, murderous feelings toward her own mother whom she felt had prevented her successful development and growth.

In addition to syphoning destructive emotions and redirecting them away from her child, the clinic treatment served to inhibit maladaptive behavior. Mrs. A. needed the social worker's support to restrict her use of the child as an extension of herself. Similarly, Mrs. A. used the social worker as a deterrent when she felt compelled to overwhelm doctors with descriptions of her hypochondriacal fears. Without the social worker she would inundate her physicians with details of psychosomatic symptoms, her fear of dying, and her unrealistic belief she was going through early menopause.

As a reaction to her own anxiety about menopause, Mrs. A. started to fear her six-year-old child was about to menstruate. This delusional concern reflected her wish for help with her maturing daughter.

At the same time that Mrs. A. voraciously sought treatment, she tried to dilute it with demands for marriage counseling. She was relieved when the social worker would not be side-tracked by this request and held to the weekly, individual sessions.

Nevertheless, during one period both parents were seen conjointly to discuss specific issues. At this time, Mrs. A's anxiety was so severe hospitalizing her was considered. Mr. A. was strengthened through treatment to accept that his wife, as well as his child, might need more intense individual therapy, not necessarily to prevent complete breakdown, but for positive reasons. Mrs. A. needed help to maintain herself as an adult rather than as a demanding, angry, unsatisfied child. Despite these insights, Mrs. A. continued to be seen once a week. The treatment enabled her to become more mature, but regressions continued to occur.

Mrs. A. was encouraged to "do her own thing," and return to the professional activity in which she had been trained, but had relinquished. Being able to resume her professional role was a reflection of her increased maturity. It had a beneficial affect on Barbara's development as the mother's part-time work provided the family with additional funds to provide for a mother substitute. It also enabled the mother to find satisfactions outside of the home so she became less involved in sadomasochistic battles with her husband and daughter. Mrs. A. often withheld information about improved relationships with members of her family. This reflected her continued fear of maturity, and her need to remain infantile. Separation and individuation occurred slowly and uncertainly.

The parents' therapy can be a valuable source of information with which the clinic team may gauge the child's pathology and improvement, as well as changes in family interaction. Although at this time Mrs. A. described improvement only reluctantly, information obtained from her indicated positive development in Barbara's fantasy life. Barbara described elaborate stories entitled "The Forgives and the Forgets" to her father who helped her illustrate her tales. In one version two men fought over the affections of one woman. After intense and prolonged combat, the heroine accepted the love of both suitors although she married only one. In another story, two dogs fought for the love of one puppy. The social worker, aware of the child's fantasies, could better conceptualize Barbara's conflicts and their relation to her mother's disturbances. Barbara's stories, despite the triangular love relations, depicted a preoedipal child's attempts to resolve dilemmas resulting from being caught between her battling mother and father. (But perhaps a background oedipal patterning could be lessened as well.)

The social worker faced Mrs. A.'s intense feeling in the case work relationship. Her countertransference reactions helped her understand Barbara's reactions to her mother and the inevitable confusion the child experienced.

Mrs. A.'s paranoid ideation became more apparent in her interaction with the social worker. Projecting her own feelings of unworthiness, she became overtly antagonistic and denigrated the therapist's professional identity. She felt persecuted by the social worker and often stamped out of her office feeling violated. By such separations from her fantasied persecutor, she avoided harming her. On one occasion, her fury became out of control, and Mrs. A. lunged out of her seat threatening to strangle the social worker. An appropriate interpretation (that if she destroyed the social worker, she would lose the one person she needed, a person to hate) resulted in Mrs. A's gaining control. Mrs. A. hated her social worker, loved her, and wanted to protect her all at the same time. She relied on her for help and assistance.

A triangle now developed in the mother's relationship within the clinic. She felt the social worker was a dangerous person who prevented her from talking to the director of the project whom she did not know, but had endowed with benevolent powers. He could, she felt, save her from the persecutory social workers. However, she also felt he was weak and ineffective because he acceded to the social worker's evaluation.

As with Barbara, the punitive aspects of Mrs. A's fantasies were clear. The social worker represented her dangerous mother with whom she wanted to fuse. She represented the bad mother, while the project director acquired the idealized aspects of the preoedipal mother. This splitting was accompanied by an ability to maintain a pathological relationship with the social worker. Thus, the social worker became a hated person to whom she was chained.

Concomitantly there were glimmers of a more mature, healthier, ideation. The project director was the ideal father from whom the social worker-mother keeps her. The punitive aspects prevailed. Mrs. A. tried to avoid a longed-for but dangerous fusion with her mother-image. She turned her love to hate, and projecting it, felt attacked by her social worker. The weak distinction between self-representation and object-representation made for the rapid and confusing intermeshing of primitive identifications and projections.

Discussion. This extended excerpt from case work with Mrs. A. illustrates a number of basic principles:

1. Work with parents protects the treatment, but it also does more —it is essential to the alteration of the child's environment and the vital support system that helps synthesize the different treatment modalities.

2. Case work with parents helps the therapeutic team understand the child's pathology and the complex interaction between all the family members.

3. As this interaction is of etiological significance and supports the child's pathology, the understanding obtained through case work will aid the therapist to resolve difficulties in the course of individual therapy.

4. If the parents continue to support the child's pathology, the treatment will be impeded. The understanding acquired through case work will be used to help the parent with his difficulties and thus further the child's improvement.

5. The child reacts to his parents and also provokes responses in them that confirm the child's fantasies and convince him of the truth of his projections.

6. The social worker attains understanding of the parent-child interaction by identifying parental pathology as revealed in his work with them. The parents' descriptions of their background and rearing, their present fantasies, wishes and defenses, and their habitual interactions are important sources of insight. In addition, observation of the parents in the case work situation (including ascertaining transference reactions) is extremely helpful. The social worker's countertransferences can indicate how the child responds to the adults in his environment.

7. Armed with insight, the social worker can help the parent resolve his inner conflicts, attain greater maturity, and achieve more adaptive gratifications. This will enable the parent to become more available to the child as a mature object and to participate less in the child's psychotic ideation. When necessary, the social worker will help the parents accept valuable additional help for the child from support systems. Special schooling, hospitalization, and the presence of parent substitutes in the home may be vital parts of the therapeutic design.

8. Flexibility is essential. Although generally (as in the case of Mr. and Mrs. A.) a relatively fixed format is adhered to (in which the mother and father were seen weekly); at times conjoint interviews are employed.

DAY TREATMENT, RESIDENTIAL TREATMENT AND HOSPITALIZATION

While we have stressed the individual approach to the treatment of severely disturbed children, we have come to recognize the advantages of individualized milieu therapeutic approaches in many instances. There are times when therapy alone (parental included) fails to bring about a diminution of destructive symptoms or acting out. The family or community may not be able to tolerate the child's pathology. Therapy may also fail to bring about a progressive change. In such cases, additional facilities may be necessary. We refer to all additional efforts as *support systems.* They support both the individual treatment and the family in treatment.

In this section we will discuss certain support systems: day treatment, residential treatment, and hospitalization.

Writers have approached the use of such facilities in different ways depending on the nature of their understanding of the disorder and the curative process.

Noshpitz (1976) asserts removing a child from his home makes him available for individual psychotherapy, which is the central therapeutic endeavor. In residential treatment centers the staff collaborates to establish an environment which orders the child's life in the service of wholeness. "Wholeness means the marshaling, interweaving, and integrating of a wide variety of therapeutic modalities around a central conception of patient need" (p. 81).

Bettelheim (1950), on the other hand, believes seriously disturbed children do not fit into pretreatment environments. Rather their treatment environment must be tailored to fit them. Formal therapy is not a major aspect of this treatment. Bettelheim believes the cause of illness is the parent's emotional rejection of their child. His basic treatment design is to counter the affective deprivation of mechanical, deanimate, parental care through continuous, affectionate, animate, pleasurable exchanges with people in the therapeutic milieu.

He also emphasizes the child's need for experimentation with, and exploration of, pleasurable body functions, and his need for expressions of drive-based activities which have been inhibited at home and can never be achieved by the child in his original environment. Although Bettelheim does not emphasize formal individual therapy, he does stress the use of a "continuously maintained one-to-one relationship within a therapeutic milieu."

Describing the nature of adult actions within this milieu, he states they "always maintained spontaneous within the indications set by the psychological reality of the individual child. This was the spirit in which every child received such gratification as his instinctual and defensive needs dictated at any given moment."

Redl (Redl and Wineman 1951), developed his concept of *milieu therapy* and attempted to show the extension of psychoanalytic therapeutic principles into every aspect of the child's treatment process. He observed that the attitudes of the institution personnel toward the children's activity and educational programs, and toward rules and regulations, are of the utmost importance in helping or impeding the patient's progress.

As we have noted, we believe the treatment of psychotic children must center on individual treatment of the child which is carried out in conjunction with individual work with his parents. We maintain the therapeutic task begins with the contact between therapist and patient and extends from this therapeutic process into the therapeutic milieu. The child develops a relationship with the therapist which is based on his attachments and retreats from his parents. The patient's feelings of communion and fusion lead to both involvement with his therapist and fears of this involvement. The severely disturbed child clings to a fragmented and distorted inner image of the early relationship to his parents or other objects, and fears new relationships which would change them. When the child enters day treatment, residential treatment, or is hospitalized he tries to recreate the relationship he had with his parents and therapists. The reactions of the personnel are crucial to his recovery. The child has an opportunity to find new, mature objects with whom he may, with the help of individual therapy, develop more mature object relationships. At the very least, a support system provides alternate opportunities for involvements and learning for the severely disturbed child. Character changes resulting from the new relationship may facilitate learning. Here we include educational achievements and the development of sublimations which enable the child to use his drives in an adaptive manner.

Entering a therapeutic milieu away from home activates specific problems and creates new opportunities for solutions. When a child enters a day treatment center, he resides at home, and hence separates and unites with parents and center personnel each day. Reactions to these experiences and the communion-fusion experiences can be seen in psychotherapy and in the therapeutic milieu. The child may achieve increased tolerance for the necessary separations and, at the same time, his parents may experience and master separation anxiety. Parent and child may also come to reunite in healthier ways.

Residential treatment and hospitalization involve more permanent separation. This often leads to a diminution of communion-fusion related symptoms. Not infrequently this is accompanied by separation anxiety and symptomatic attempts to master this, such as autistic withdrawal.

Ideally, the initiation of treatment in a residential or hospital setting allows for indefinite continuation of all established personal relationships. Optimally the child's individual therapy should continue and so should his contacts with educators, parents, and other important persons and things in his environment. Unfortunately, hospitalization often follows a negative response by the child and/or parent to a diagnostic or therapeutic intervention. The child, who dreads fusion with his therapist, loses him, and symptoms of feared fusion are replaced by symptoms of feared separation.

In all of these settings—day treatment centers, residential treatment center, or hospitals—the function of personnel is limited by the degree to which the severely disturbed child acknowledges them. Defensive patterns for dealing with fear of new relationships should therefore be treated as they occur, as well as be interpreted in individual therapy. Contacts around the child's spontaneous activities should be encouraged. All psychological patterns which interfere with spontaneous activity need to have their intrapsychic sources recognized and understood, and personnel in the milieu should be able to respond appropriately. Fusion-communion, separation, clinging to old object images, and aggressive expressions of destructive fears are all different in purpose, and therefore, must be treated accordingly. Activities and educational processes only become meaningful after contact with personnel can be maintained. As change occurs, parental treatment is vital to avoid negative parental defensive patterns.

Personnel continuity over many years is essential, because severely disturbed children tolerate losses poorly and need long-term object relations for ego growth and to develop object relations for both ego growth and for the development of object constancy. The continuity increases the ego's ability to experience separations and reunions, distance and closeness. The increasing ability of the ego to rely on continuity permits object-related conflicts to be relived and worked through both in psychotherapy and in the treatment milieu. The combination of working through and support permits the ego more attachment to and dependency on personnel. Out of the continuing interaction, new ego functions can develop or be freed from destructive conflicts. Among these new functions are body image functions, object-directed expressions of psychosexual (psychosocial) development, time sense, thinking prior to action functions (repression-suppression of action), increasing frustration tolerance functions, memory functions, and reality-testing functions. Imitations and incorporations become identifications and enhance the development of new ego functions. New adaptations and defenses begin to appear. Displacement defenses permit deflection of drive and emotional expression to permit the appearance of previously destructive elements in a more neutral way and to allow the maintenance of interpersonnel relationships. This option of deflection away from key object relationship allows the emergence of multiple and diversified interests and activities. At the same time, the ego is subject to regressions and distortions so the total picture is highly variable. The supporting systems of the milieu provide emotional support and cognitive experience. They provide support for the ego while also acting as models for the new functions of the ego. Eventually, when separations and reunions are sustained without regression, the ego can function, to varying degrees, without support, and to the same varying degrees, object constancy can be said to have been achieved.

CLOSING STATEMENT

Although committed to clinical research, we have found when faced with the task of treating psychotic children that formal research is most difficult. One is forced to move very slowly. This area of research in psychiatry and psychoanalysis is not usually supported by the community or by social and governmental agencies. One who deals in this area of research is not only a pioneer, but an unsupported and sometimes suspect investigator.

When seeking support for such work we have found we are frequently questioned about its worth. Parents, schools, the community, and those with opposing viewpoints within the field itself have suggested that such an investment of strength for so few is not worth the time and effort. Therefore, a certain amount of hostility is involved in treating such children. How can the therapist and/or the research team defend itself and at the same time feel worthy in this work? One must develop sustaining power. There are no guarantees of a predictable, safe outcome, of high income, or of clearcut technique or success. Erikson (1950) has pointed out frequently the psychotic child and his mother lack *sending power*. We who treat such children also lack it. Only through clinical research can such a treatment situation be sustained. Indeed, there is always the necessity to search for more understanding of the treatment process of such patients. The diagnostically oriented research person often seeks the final truth. We advocate a search to set the patient free from the illness and therefore advocate that clinical research be built into the treatment model. It should be aimed specifically at developing techniques for facilitating the treatment. This nonobjective research is an integral part of the work itself. It is an attitude which must be based on faith—perhaps that type of faith implied in Stefan Zweig's book, *Mental Healers* (1933), which emphasizes the value of healing. Gertrude Schwing (1954) has expressed this same attitude succinctly in her book, *A Way to the Soul of the Mentally Ill.* The commitment, devotion, and involvement necessary to treat such patients requires a kind of faith in one's own worthiness as a therapist. Through sensing this the therapist makes no demands on the patient to be worthwhile.

There are many treatment islands which need communication bridges from one to the others to learn from each other. This chapter is meant to aid in this task.

REFERENCES

Bender, L. (1942). Childhood schizophrenia. *Nervous Child* 1:138–140.
_____ (1947). Childhood schizophrenia. *American Journal of Orthopsychiatry* 17:40–56.

———— (1956). Schizophrenia in childhood—its recognition, description and treatment. *American Journal Orthopsychiatry* 26:499–506.

Bergman, P., and Escalona, S.K. (1949). Unusual sensitivities in very young children *Psychoanalytic Study of the Child* 3/4:333–352.

Bettelheim, B. (1956). Schizophrenia as a reaction to extreme situations. *American Journal Orthopsychiatry* 26:507–518.

Bettelheim, B. (1967). *The Empty Fortress: Infantile Autism and the Birth of the Self.* New York: Free Press.

———— (1950). *Love Is Not Enough.* Glencoe, Ill.: Free Press.

Bettelheim, B., and Sylvester, E. (1948). A therapeutic milieu. *American Journal Orthopsychiatry* 18:191–206.

Beres, D. (1965). Structure and function in psycho-analysis. *International Journal Psychoanalysis* 46:53–63.

Bernfeld, S. (1928). Uber faszination (concerning fascination). *Imago* 14:76–87.

Bleuler, E. (1911). *Dementia Praecox or The Group of Schizophrenias,* Zinkin J. trans. New York: International Universities Press, 1950.

Eisenberg, L., and Kanner, L. (1956). Early infantile autism. *American Journal of Orthopsychiatry* 26:556–566.

Ekstein, R. (1956). Psychoanalytic techniques. In *Progress in Clinical Psychology,* Vol. II. ed. D. Brower and L. E. Abt, pp. 79–97. New York: Grune and Stratton.

———— (1963). The opening gambit in psychotherapeutic work with a severely disturbed adolescent girl. *American Journal of Orthopsychiatry* 33:862–871.

Ekstein, R., Bryant, K., and Friedman, S. W. (1958). Childhood schizophrenia and allied conditions. In *Schizophrenia,* ed. L. Bellak and P.K. Benedict, pp. 555–693. New York: Logos Press.

Ekstein, R., Friedman, S. W., Caruth, E., and Cooper, B. (1976). Reflections on the need for a working alliance with environmental support systems. In *In Search of Love and Competence,* ed. R. Ekstein, pp. 241–252. Los Angeles: The Reiss-Davis Child Study Center.

Ekstein, R., Wallerstein, J., and Mandelbaum, A. (1956). Countertransference in residential treatment of children: Treatment failure in a child with a symbiotic psychosis. *Psychoanalytic Study of the Child* 11:303–311.

Ekstein, R. and Wright, D. G. (1964). The space child—ten years later. *Forest Hospital Publications* (Des Plaines, Ill.) 2:36–47.

Ekstein, R., et al. (1971). *The Challenge: Despair and Hope in the Conquest of Inner Space.* New York: Brunner/Mazel.

Ekstein, R., et al. (1975) Panel Program. Silver Anniversary Scientific Program, Reiss-Davis Child Study Center.

Erikson, E. (1950). *Childhood and Society.* New York: W.W. Norton

Fairbairn, W.D. (1954). *An Object-Relations Theory of the Personality.* New York: Basic Books.

Freud, S. (1900). The interpretation of dreams. *Standard Edition* 4/5.

———— (1906). Three essays on the theory of sexuality. *Standard Edition* 7:130–243.

———— (1911). Psycho-analytic notes on an autobiographical account of a case of paranoia. *Standard Edition* 12:9–82.

———— (1923). The ego and the id. *Standard Edition* 19:12–66.

———— (1924a). Neurosis and psychosis. *Standard Edition,* 19:149–156.

———— (1924b). The loss of reality in neurosis and psychosis. *Standard Edition* 19:183–187.

Kanner, L. (1942). Autistic disturbances of affective contact. *Nervous Child* 2:217–250.

———— (1944). Early infantile autism. *Journal of Pediatrics* 25:211–217.

———— (1954). Childhood schizophrenia (Round Table, 1953): Discussion. *American Journal Orthopsychiatry* 24:528–562.

Klein, M. (1960). *Psycho-Analysis of Children.* New York: Grove Press.

Knight, R.P. (1953). Borderline states. In *Psychoanalytic Psychiatry and Psychology,* ed. R.P. Knight and C.R. Friedman, pp 97–109. New York: International Universities Press.

Kraepelin, E. (1919). *Dementia Praecox and Paraphrenia.*

Kris, E. (1952). *Psychoanalytic Explorations in Art.* New York: International Universities Press.

Kubie, L. S. (1936). The normal neuroses of childhood. *Child Study* 13:195–198.

Mahler, M. S. (1952). On child psychosis and schizophrenia: autistic and symbiotic infantile psychoses. *Psychoanalytic Study of the Child* 7:286–305.

_____ (1968). *On Human Symbiosis and the Vicissitudes of Individuation.* New York: International Universities Press.

Mahler, M. S., and Elkisch, P. (1953). Some observations on disturbances of the ego and in a case of infantile psychosis. *Psychoanalytic Study of the Child* 8:252–261.

Mahler, M.S. and Furer, M. (1960). Observations on research regarding the "symbiotic syndrome" of the infantile psychosis. *Psychoanalytic Quarterly* 29:317–327.

Mahler, M. S., Pine, F., and Bergman, A. (1975). *The Psychological Birth of the Human Infant.* New York: Basic Books.

Noshpitz, J.D. (1976). The therapeutic aspect of residential treatment. *Journal of the Philadelphia Association for Psychoanalysis* 3:71–84.

Rank, B. (1949). Adaptation of the psychoanalytic technique for the treatment of young children with atypical development. *American Journal of Orthopsychiatry* 19:130–139.

Redl, F. and Wineman, D. (1951), *Children Who Hate.* Glencoe, Illinois: The Free Press.

Reik, T. (1948). *Listening with the Third Ear: The Inner Experience of a Psychoanalyst.* New York: Farrar, Straus.

Schwing, G. (1954). *A Way to the Soul of the Mentally Ill,* trans. and intro. Ekstein R. and Hall B. New York: International Universities Press.

Sechehaye, M. A. (1951). *Symbolic Realization.* New York: International Universities Press.

Spitz, R. (1963). Life and the dialogue. In *Counterpoint: Libidinal Object and Subject,* ed. Herbert S. Gaskill. New York: International Universities Press.

Szurek, S. A., and Berlin, I. N. (1956). Elements of psychotherapeutics with the schizophrenic child and his parents. *Psychiatry* 19:1–9.

Wexler, M. (1969). Personal Communication.

Williams, T. (1945). *The Glass Menagerie.* New York: Random House.

Zweig, S. (1933). *Mental Healers.* Trans. Eden and Cedar Paul. New York: Viking.

Chapter 25

THE TEACHING OF CHILD PSYCHOANALYSIS IN
THE UNITED STATES

John J. Francis, M.D.

EARLY HISTORY

Child psychoanalysis, like adult psychoanalysis, has its origins in the research and theories of Sigmund Freud. From his study of adult patients and his own self-analysis, as well as from the contributions of the colleagues who joined him, a body of knowledge concerning the special problems and treatment of childhood neurosis began to develop (Freud, S. 1938, p. 144). The 1909 publication of Freud's "Analysis of a Phobia in a Five-Year-Old Boy" is usually designated as the beginning of child analysis. The well-known case of "Little Hans," whose analysis Freud conducted through correspondence and occasional direct discussion with the child's father, was probably the first psychoanalytic approach to childhood mental illness.

Somewhat later in the United States, child guidance clinics were set up as a result of the pioneer studies of delinquent children conducted by Dr. William Healy (Rexford 1962, Lewin and Ross 1960, Smirnoff 1966). Methods for dealing with mentally ill children in these clinics bore a similarity to Freud's approach in the analysis of Little Hans. These clinics, and the growth of the child guidance movement in general, exerted a major influence on the development of child psychiatry as a specialty field in medical practice.

By 1920, child psychoanalysis began to be defined as a form of treatment distinct from adult psychoanalysis. At this time Hermine Hug-Helmuth (1921) was a leading figure in propounding definitive concepts of child therapy. Using play as a bridge for conducting the treatment of latency children, she formulated specific theories and techniques for psychoanalytic work with children.

In Vienna in the 1920s, Anna Freud (1930) began to combine her knowledge and experience as a nursery school and kindergarten teacher with her understanding of psychoanalytic theory and practice. She undertook the analysis of several children on an individual basis. She also conducted a training program for teachers, emphasizing the application of psychoanalytic principles to teaching practices. Through this work with young teachers, a child guidance center similar to those developed in the United States was established in association with the Vienna Psychoanalytic Institute. This center served the purposes of training and research, and also provided needed treatment for troubled children from the Vienna slums. The success of the clinic and the skill and sensitivity of Anna Freud as a teacher, aroused the interest of several candidates in the Vienna Institute of Psychoanalysis in work with children. Actually, the child psychoanalytic training program and the Anna Freud school of child psychoanalysis date their beginnings to 1926 when, at the suggestion of Anna Freud, two of her students began to meet regularly with her to present cases. Thus, the first seminar in psychoanalysis was established. The three cases presented in this first seminar were Anna Freud's patient with an anxiety neurosis, Editha Sterba's delinquent boy, and Jenny Waelder-Hall's case of night terror. Interest in the seminar spread throughout the Vienna Institute and more members requested permission to join the meetings. Individuals concerned with teacher training, and later child psychiatrists and child guidance workers from the United States sought training in Vienna under the tutelage of Anna Freud and her colleagues. The pressure to enlarge the group became so great that two additional seminars, one chaired by Marianne Kris and Editha Sterba, and the other by Jenny Waelder-Hall and Berta Bornstein, were established, primarily for beginning students. Many of the theories of the defenses included in Anna Freud's (1936) *The Ego and the Mechanisms of Defense* were derived from and tested in these seminars. Waelder-Hall's (1930) classical paper on the analysis of a case of night terror, as well as a remarkable collection of case reports by child analysts published in *The Psychoanalytic Quarterly* in 1935, grew out of the presentations at these seminars (Angel, B. Bornstein, S. Bornstein, Buxbaum, Poertl, and Sterba).

During this early period, the child psychoanalytic training program was ill-defined, and consisted primarily of supervision of child cases which were begun only after a candidate had conducted two adult cases under supervision. The length of time required for attendance at seminars, and the conduct of supervised analyses was not yet established. However, most of the candidates continued to attend the seminars long after graduation. Since at that time literature on child analyses was almost nonexistent, there were no required reading lists or courses in literature. Developing the theory and technique for child analysis was a major focus of the clinical work. As the program progressed, Anna Freud's seminar concentrated primarily on clinical problems.

Psychoanalysis of adolescents was also being attempted in Vienna. Some of the analysts involved in the child seminars were working with patients from age thirteen into adulthood. In general, the adolescent analyses were conducted in a manner similar to the treatment of adults. Use of the couch was an accepted aspect of the treatment. The results with adolescents proved to be successful in many instances (Waelder-Hall 1975).

In Berlin at about the same time, Melanie Klein was developing her school of psychoanalysis along somewhat different lines. (Since the Kleinian school is discussed fully in another chapter in this book, no description of it will be offered here.)

The growing threat of the Nazi regime, and the subsequent political developments in Europe, caused the dispersal of the group of gifted scientists who had gathered around Sigmund Freud and Anna Freud in Vienna. They scattered to many parts of the Allied world, but most of them remained dedicated to the teaching, practice, and study of psychoanalysis. Although both Sigmund Freud and his daughter Anna settled in London and continued their work there, many of the men and women associated with psychoanalysis came to the United States. Because of their devotion to psychoanalysis as a form of treatment, and as a method for the study of human psychology, and because of their wisdom and skill as teachers, they attracted enthusiastic followers in the field of child psychiatry and from the child guidance centers already in existence throughout the country. The majority of Viennese-trained child analysts settled in the large eastern cities of the United States. Groups of eager young students gathered around them to learn the new concepts of and approaches to the treatment of children. Thus, by the end of World War II, child analysis and the training for treatment of child mental illness was a recognized specialty within the field of psychiatry in the United States.

DEVELOPMENTS IN THE UNITED STATES

In 1948 when a new version of "The Standards for Training of Physicians in Psychoanalysis" was published by the Board on Professional Standards of the American Psychoanalytic Association, child analysis was listed as the eighth of nine subjects in the required curriculum. Although many advances had been made in the theory and technique of child analysis, many problems still remained in relation to training programs. Many of these problems have continued to plague the field of child analysis to the present time.

Lewin and Ross (1960), in their study of psychoanalytic training, included a review of the training required for work with children. They noted that the requirement of child analysis was taken seriously by relatively few training institutes. They found institutes did not follow the suggested curriculums in general, and unless child analysts were members of a particular institute, no course of study in child analysis was offered. In most of the institutes in the United States, child analysis was more or less an isolated stepchild of adult analysis. This isolation continued in spite of great enthusiasm for analysis of children among candidates and among professionals in allied fields, and in spite of the fact that in many institutes, the most highly regarded teachers were often child analysts from the Vienna Institute.

Since its first publication in 1948, the *Psychoanalytic Study of the Child* had been recognized as perhaps the most important annual in the field of psychoanalysis. Nevertheless, Dr. Sara Bonnett, in her 1959 study of child analytic training and practice in the United States, found that only four of the fourteen institutes offered formal child analytic training programs (see Addendum I). Little child analysis was being practiced even by those strongly identified with the field and in considerable demand as teachers and consultants because of their work in child analysis (Rexford 1962). The reasons for this paradox were manifold. The well trained teachers and supervisors of child analysis were located in several large centers, and a few others were scattered throughout the country. No clear definition of child analysis, either as a body of knowledge or as a technical method, had been firmly developed. Child analysis was confused both with child psychiatry and with child guidance. During this early period many influential people argued there was no essential difference between these three disciplines. Some of this confusion still persists, although remarkable progress has been made in recent years.

In this country, child psychoanalysis was developed primarily among child psychiatrists. Many of the analysts working with children were established child psychiatrists active in the departments of psychiatry in various medical schools. Many of the workers in the field were involved in child guidance clinics, and in small communities; they were part of a team of physicians who worked in public health clinics. They frequently saw patients in these clinics once a week or less, on visits from the larger communities where they resided and were associated with the psychoanalytic institutes. The demands made by various clinical facilities, staffed by psychiatrists, social workers, and psychologists eager to learn about analysis from experienced child analysts, tended to drain time and energy from institute programs for training child analysts. The demand in the analytic institutes for the child analysts' increasing participation in programs related to adult work played a similar role in diverting the energies of the child analytic group away from the practice and teaching of child analysis.

Another factor, which in a subtle way probably retarded the development of child analytic training, was noted by Lewin and Ross (1960). For those seeking training in child analysis, the 1948 Standards for Training required certain additional electives to the usual required courses. These electives included not only courses in child analysis, but courses dealing with nonpsychoanalytic techniques for the treatment of children. This inclusion suggests that even on the committee setting the standards there were members with doubts about child analysis as a form of treatment distinct from psychotherapy. Even today some analysts will ask the question, "Is child analysis really analysis?" Such uncertainty about the nature of child analysis is reflected in the fact that the largest case loads of child analytic cases were those of lay analysts trained abroad or trained unofficially in the United States. Also, at the 1950 meeting of the American Psychoanalytic Association in Detroit, the case presented to Anna Freud for discussion was of an analysis conducted by a lay analyst.

During the decade of the 1950s several developments in the area of training for child analysis stimulated interest and focused attention on child analytic education. These developments included:

1. The appointment of a Committee on Child Analysis by the Board on Professional Standards of the American Psychoanalytic Association to formulate the minimal requirements for a training program in child analysis.

2. The site visits conducted by Lewin and Ross which culminated in publication of "Psychoanalytic Education in the United States."

3. The recommendation of the Committee on Child Analysis that all candidates be required to attend a course in child development and a clinical seminar on child analysis.

4. The charge to the Committee by the Board that minimal training standards in child analysis be determined and that these standards be based primarily on the training programs then in existence in Boston, Chicago, New York, and Philadelphia. During the 1965 Mid-Winter meeting of the American Psychoanalytic Association, Dr. Maurice Friend and his colleagues of the Division of Psychoanalytic Education of the Downstate Medical Center, State University of New York delivered a report to the Committee on Child Analysis. The methods and problems of establishing a well-structured child training program were described in detail. This report played a significant part in furthering interest in child psychoanalytic training.

In their publication, Lewin and Ross (1960) pointed to the questions and concerns of many analysts about the relationship between child analysis and adult analysis. Although some of the issues have been resolved, some remain. Many analysts believe that because so many parameters are required in child analysis, work with children varies a very great degree in technique from adult work. Many adult analysts do not consider work with children to constitute a "real" analysis because of the many deviations from the classical approach. Therefore, they feel child work represents a special field within psychoanalysis and should not be part of the analyst's original training. In their view, candidates should receive thorough training in adult analysis before being exposed to child analysis. This conviction has often led candidates to focus on adult work and postpone or lose interest in working with children and adolescents. Since graduation and membership in an analytic society depended upon completion of adult training, many promising child analysts were lost by the wayside. By the time adult analytic training was completed, many candidates were too old or too involved in psychoanalytic practices to undertake a new and difficult program of training for child analysis. Of course, these attitudes varied in different institutes. However, the major focus in every institute was on adult training. This is still true today.

The loss of promising child analysts to the adult field was overcome in some groups when the candidate was inspired by an especially stimulating, charismatic child analyst. In some instances the dedication and interest of the candidate in child work sustained him through the long and arduous training period. Some of the most effective child psychoanalytic programs owe their existence to this kind of devoted individual.

In some institutes, development of child programs has been hampered by a kind of self-imposed isolation of the "child group" from the main body of adult analysis. Perhaps because of a need to establish themselves as specialists, some child analysts kept aloof from the institute in general. All too often, the child committees have tended to function as education committees, and have insisted on the right to make all decisions including those usually made by curriculum committees, faculty committees, education committees, and at times even executive committees. This problem tended to occur especially in institutes when one individual was particularly brilliant and forceful.

A STUDY OF CHILD ANALYSIS

Existing child analysis training programs. In 1966 the Committee on Child Analysis of the American Psychoanalytic Association undertook a lengthy project. Its major purpose was to implement the accreditation of established child training programs. Not only did members of the

Committee discuss procedures at great length, but the advice of officers and committee chairmen of the Board of Professional Standards was sought and accepted. As a result of these intensive discussions, subcommittees of two members each were formed. These subcommittees would review the child analytic training program of each institute to determine whether that program met the minimal requirements for acceptance. To make this determination, the subcommittee planned to review in detail the history, course of study, graduation requirements, curricula vitae of supervising and teaching child analysts, the relation of the child program to its own institute, and any other data pertinent to the decision to approve and accept the program. Though the committee members felt a site visit to each institute would be desirable, this was not economically feasible. The committee agreed that consultation with local chairmen of education and child committees, members of faculties, and candidates would be another valuable means of gaining a clear picture of each institute's program. Thus the committee emphasized the need to collect data, to clarify any areas of confusion, and to understand specific institute problems before the subcommittee would submit a final report to the full Committee on Child Analysis.

To initiate the evaluation procedure, the Committee agreed to send each institute a form with a covering letter inviting it to request approval of its child analysis training program through correspondence with the Chairman and Secretary of the Board on Professional Standards and the Chairman of the Committee on Child Analysis. It was suggested that descriptive information about the structure of the child analytic program, the course of study, the requirements for graduation, and the faculty should be included with the request for approval. The information would be considered by the Committee on Child Analysis in order to respond with a useful evaluation of the request for approval. Under unusual conditions, the Committee would request permission from the Chairman of the Board on Professional Standards to make a site visit. Recognizing there would be wide variations in the child analytic training programs of different institutes, the Committee decided that if a program was functioning adequately, if it was in the process of strengthening problem areas to attain the minimal requirements, and if the quality of training was such that competent child analysts were being graduated, the existing program would be recommended to the Board on Professional Standards for approval. The Committee on Child Analysis believed that by gaining experience through the review and evaluation of the various programs, the Committee's ability to be helpful, especially to the weaker programs, would increase. The Committee felt this help could be offered without invading the provinces of the local institutes. The philosophy of the Committee and the Board was that this work should serve as an aid to individual institutes rather than operate as a policing function. At the start, flexibility was considered essential. The approach had to be tailored to each situation, yet structured sufficiently to assure that the standards of the American Psychoanalytic Association be met.

Developing programs. The function of the Committee on Child Analysis in regard to institutes developing child analytic programs would be to circulate the minimal standards, the procedures for application, and other literature regarding child analytic programs, but it would make no direct solicitation of applications from the institutes. The Committee also decided that the enabling committees for developing new programs, also consisting of two members appointed by the Chairman of the Committee on Child Analysis, would be more active and function in a way similar to that of the Committee on New Training Facilities. These subcommittees would be more exacting in their requirements that a new child training facility meet the required standards of a child psychoanalytic training program. The Committee intended that the enabling subcommittee would function more actively in consultation and supervision of the development of a new program. The Committees' activities would include a careful evaluation of the curriculum, of each supervisor, of each teaching analyst, and of each candidate. The Committee would require candidates be given a course of study and clinical experience assuring them of a comprehensive exposure to child psychoanalytic knowledge and orientation. At least one site visit would be made by the enabling subcommittee before recommendation for approval be submitted to the Child Committee of the American Psychoanalytic Association. Here too, however, the Committee noted that some flexibility would be necessary. The Committee recognized that sensitivity to special situations would be essential in relation to the developing program and also to the position of the child psychoanalytic program in its own institute and to that institute's relationship with the American Psychoanalytic Association.

SOME NOTABLE FINDINGS IN THE SUBCOMMITTEE
REPORTS

The study of child analytic training programs revealed a great variety in programs existed among institutes throughout the United States. The data gathered by the various subcommittees should be made available to a group of unbiased researchers of various orientations with the aim of publishing its findings. Such a publication would give psychoanalytic educators in this country a complete picture of the status of education in child analysis as it was in 1972 when the last established program was approved. Some of this data has already been studied by the Committee on Child Analysis. However, the more complete these studies can be, the more the science of child psychoanalysis will benefit.

Some of the general findings of the six-year study can be reported here. The Committees found institutes varied in many aspects and to a great degree not only in philosophy, theory, practice, technique, but even in the concept of child analysis. Great differences existed even though most of the senior child analysts had been trained primarily in the Anna Freud school of child analysis. The influence of the Kleinian school was minimal and was evident only in institutes with teachers trained in the British Psychoanalytic Institute, some areas of continental Europe, or who had come to the United States from South America. As was true in Vienna in the early thirties, in many institutes clinical work (supervision, continuous case seminars, and clinical conferences in that order) was considered the most important portion of the child analyst's training. Almost every institute did include the literature of child analysis, which has become voluminous. Most programs had required reading lists, reading seminars, and postgraduate study groups for this purpose. Some institutes had well organized programs which stressed hours, courses of study, didactic material, and emphasized these areas as much as clinical work. Others offered the candidate only minimal exposure to both clinical and course work.

In almost every institute courses on child development were offered early in the candidate's training. Most of these courses had been included as part of the curriculum in the mid-fifties when meetings with institute representatives began. In general these child development courses were well conceived in both content and mode of presentation. They were usually a requirement for all candidates. There was some variation among different institutes in major focus. Some institutes presented approaches other than the psychoanalytic approach. Interest in the work of Spitz (1957, 1965), Escalona (1968), Mahler (1968), and the Hampstead index was widespread. Piaget had not yet become popular and was offered only in rare instances. The concepts of Erikson (1950, 1959) were studied in some institutes more than in others. Another course offered in many institutes and required of all candidates in some was observation of infants and/or young children in nurseries, nursery schools, and kindergartens. This course was required most often in institutes located near centers for training child psychiatrists. There was a great variation in this course; the quality and content depended largely on the interests and ability of the teachers. In most institutes attendance at case seminars was required for two or more years. However, candidates usually attended for longer periods. As was true in Vienna many years ago, it was not unusual to find analysts who had graduated some years before still attending child seminars. In general, the child analytic graduate tends to maintain contacts with his colleagues by attending seminars long after graduation. Clinical conferences were held less frequently and considered less important than the new minimal standards indicate is desirable.

Prior to 1961 the average number of supervised cases was two. The age and sex of the case seemed to be based more on availability and interest of the candidate or supervisor than on other considerations. Since only one supervising child analyst was usually available in any area, few candidates had worked with more than one supervisor. However, members of the Child Committee were surprised and gratified to learn how many dedicated candidates travelled long distances to gain experience with additional supervisors. This burden was assumed without complaint, and some students used visiting teachers to supplement local supervision. In the Baltimore-D.C. Institute, for example, several candidates commuted to Philadelphia and New York for supervision; several were able to use Selma Fraiberg as a supervisor when she visited Baltimore. She came to the Institute initially to teach a course on child development and was appointed a supervisor when the Institute was granted a waiver for such appointment by the American Psychoanalytic Association. This was the first such waiver granted to an institute for a lay child analyst of the younger generation. Various other means for securing second and third supervisors were used. A unique method was devised by Dr. Margaret S. Mahler for the Philadelphia Psychoanalytic Institute. She supervised the supervisor. This method consisted of appointing a promising young graduate, who had not yet met the requirements for appointment as a full child supervisor, to the position of associate supervisor. His supervisory work was then supervised at intervals by Dr. Mahler. This method proved successful in this Institute and elsewhere. It has been picturesquely called "piggyback" supervision.

Negative findings. Some negative aspects in child analytic training were noted as a result of this project. These are of interest both historically and also from the standpoint of improving psychoanalytic education.

1. Erik Erikson's (Lewin and Ross 1960) ambitious attempt to define the characteristics of child analysis and child analytic technique met with little success. Although much progress was made through establishing the Association for Child Psychoanalysis in 1965, the review of training programs in 1972 revealed great differences still exist. The question "What is child analysis?" is as yet largely unanswered (Eidelberg 1968).

2. The Committee frequently found the child analytic training program in an institute was dominated by one analyst. This was sometimes a European trained analyst with a great deal of knowledge and skill, with several dedicated students who analyzed children under his supervision and followed his technique. Much of the time his technique was competent and the work of the analysts he trained of high quality. However, frequently the work deviated from the theory and technique developed by Anna Freud and her group. Over the years, as experience had increased knowledge and sharpened technique, the Anna Freud group had learned many parameters used in child analysis earlier were unnecessary and at times slowed the progress of the analysis. In some institutes these new findings were not taken into account and technical interventions of a psychotherapeutic type were used. As a result, mistakes in approach and technique were transferred from one person to another and repeated over and over again. Also, because some older analysts worked in isolation, they became inflexible and rigid regarding the practice of child analysis. Occasionally, younger analysts found it necessary to leave a particular area to broaden their knowledge and experience. In some instances when training was dominated by an analyst more on the basis of his personality than his ability, the results proved to be tragic for promising young people.

3. In some institutes so much confusion existed with child psychotherapy that the techniques of child psychoanalysis could not always be recognized as such. In these instances, the teacher or teachers had little or no training or experience in analysis themselves. However, because a teacher was analytically oriented, he had accepted the designation "child analyst" when he moved to a new area where no other child analysts were located. For those working in his department, his approach became "child analysis." This problem was a most difficult one for the Committee. Various methods of modifying the situation were tried. None were very successful. The programs, however, were accepted. The members of the Committee on Child Analysis felt a great uneasiness. However, it was hoped that by maintaining contact with such a program and working with the situation over a period of time, the Committee on Child Analysis could bring about desired changes gradually. One method of approach was to suggest to the local institute that teachers from other areas be given visiting appointments. This plan at least offered some of the students exposure to different approaches and theoretical concepts.

4. Because candidates for child analysis were older and already graduates of the adult program, supervision of child analytic candidates tended to be less consistent, detailed, careful, and prolonged than in adult programs. These students were anxious to learn and were well grounded in analytic technique. They could quickly make the transition from working with adults to working with children. For these reasons less emphasis on supervision was not regarded by the Committee as necessarily detrimental. However, a spelling-out of the training standards in child analysis was expected to correct deficiencies in supervisory practices.

5. In some institutes the presentation of a case at a continuous case seminar was considered an equivalent of supervision. Though this was sometimes done with younger candidates, for the most part, it served as a substitute for a candidate's second or third case and seemed to be most effective with a good supervisor and a good candidate. It gave the other members of the seminar, most of whom were advanced in their training, an opportunity to follow the work with a patient and to understand the thinking both of the analyst and the supervisor about the material as it emerged. In general the Committee felt this was unacceptable as a substitute for supervision. However, some members

felt institutes might experiment further with this procedure because in some situations it offered a valuable learning experience.

6. A significant deficiency was noted in the widespread absence of experience or training in analysis of adolescents in most institutes. This was due largely to the paucity of teachers trained in the treatment of adolescents. In addition, for reasons yet unknown, little interest in analytic involvement with adolescents seemed to exist. Several subcommittees reported to the Committee on Child Analysis comments from members of various institutes indicating analysis of adolescents was considered impossible.

7. In almost all institutes there was a gradual dropping off of the number of applicants for training in child analysis, as well as a decrease in the number of patients available for treatment. This seems to be a national problem. A search for the underlying causes should be made not only by those involved in the training of child analysts, but also by educators in psychoanalysis in general. Analysts who complete training with no exposure to child analysis are deprived of a useful experience. If children with analyzable problems are being treated by other methods, they are not receiving the treatment they need.[1]

TRAINING STANDARDS

The ideal child analytic training program, like the ideal psychoanalytic institute, has not yet been developed. The training standards formulated by the American Psychoanalytic Association are fairly general, especially as regards didactic seminars. The standards established in 1966 were revised in 1978. Insistence upon meeting these standards has been applied in a flexible fashion because of different problems facing each institute. Psychoanalytic education in the United States and elsewhere is not uniform at the present time and it is unlikely that it can ever be completely so. However, the establishment of criteria for certification of child and adolescent analysts in 1978 may lead to greater uniformity. There are certain essentials without which a training program cannot accomplish its goal of graduating adequately trained analysts, who can treat patients competently. In child analysis, as in adult analysis, the essence of training lies in the personal analysis. Beyond the personal analysis, each candidate must be assured of careful, regular, and competent supervision. The supervision must include a significant number of patients with a variety of disorders. Different age groups and both sexes should be treated over a long enough period of time to allow the analytic process to be effective in alleviating the disorder for which analysis was undertaken. In addition, the candidate should experience a termination phase as an essential part of understanding and working with the analytic process.

Official standards for training require at least three cases. This seems to be an absolute minimum for most candidates. Attendance at continuous case seminars for at least three years is another essential aspect of a candidate's training. Seminars and clinical conferences offer the candidate an opportunity to broaden his experience, to learn from the experiences of others, and to share in a group learning process. Exposure to courses in theory, technique, and other aspects of psychoanalysis is equally important, for in treatment, theory cannot be separated from practice. Each complements the other. The content and number of didactic seminars, and the portion of the student's time devoted to them are still a matter for discussion, study, and experiment in many institutes. Seminars on child development, special theory related to children, and seminars on the theory of psychoanalytic technique with children at various ages and stages of development would seem to be essential to any adequate training program. This would also apply to training in the analysis of adolescents, an area in which our knowledge and understanding have increased markedly in recent years (see Addendum II).

THE CORE CURRICULUM

Child analysts have studied the curriculum in psychoanalysis on the basis of what is called a *core curriculum*. This concept is based on studies done by Mahler (1967), Lustman (1967), Kolansky (1971), and others. The objective of this curriculum is to integrate topics which are taught in both adult and child programs and make them available to candidates in both divisions. The goals of this effort are to shorten the amount of time required to complete the psychoanalytic course of study and to avoid duplication, with the recognition that adult and child analysis involves many identical psychological issues. Several variations of the core curriculum have been established in institutes throughout the United States with varying degrees of success. One question still at issue is whether every candidate should be required to treat a child in analysis.

Probably the most significant study and complete outline of a core curriculum was developed by Commission IX, Child Analysis, of the Conference on Psychoanalytic Education and Research of the American Psychoanalytic Association (Settlage et al. 1974). The concept of a core curriculum is based on the proposition that psychoanalysis, as a method of understanding and treating neuroses, has reached maturity which requires a shift of emphasis within the overall conceptual framework. Though the conceptual framework of the past—the psychoanalytic treatment of the neuroses—would continue to be central in training, it is no longer considered adequate as an exclusive frame of reference for understanding and evaluating both advances in theory and emerging adaptations of analytic methods. The essential theme of the Commission report was that the developmental orientation provides a needed broadening of the frame of reference. In this orientation, psychoanalytic theory and treatment of neuroses assumes its deserved position of prominence on an expanding continuum of theories of pathological formations and of psychoanalytic modalities for their treatment. The authors felt these changes were necessary because of theoretical and technical advances associated with two complementary and overlapping trends. First there has been a move into observational studies of psychic development in the first years of life. In addition, the widening scope of psychoanalysis as a clinical and theoretical instrument for understanding and treating forms of psychopathology more severe than neuroses has been noted. The work takes into account the findings of Anna Freud (1965), Erik Erikson (1950, 1959), Piaget in Flavell (1963), Spitz (1957, 1965), Mahler (1968), Mahler, Pine and Berman (1975) and many others, and includes the development of the individual from birth throughout life. All aspects of the education and training of a candidate are included in this framework, and the report offers a detailed outline of a comprehensive curriculum for the training of psychoanalysts. There are many constructive suggestions and recommendations in this material. However, some proposals raise questions which call for additional discussion and study. In general, the report is a monumental work which will serve as a stimulus for much rethinking and reevaluation of the whole field of psychoanalytic education for some time to come (see Addendum III).

LAY ANALYSIS

The complex problem of training lay analysts has been a matter of serious study in child analysis. On a limited basis a number of gifted, nonmedical child analysts have been educated in the United States outside of recognized psychoanalytic institutes and without the approval of the American Psychoanalytic Association.[2] A number of these lay analysts have contributed significantly to the field of child psychoanalysis. This extrainstitute child psychoanalytic training has been conducted by various individuals over the past twenty-five years, sometimes with the knowledge of some members of the American Psychoanalytic Association who raised no objection. Freud's views on lay analysis are well known and much of this training was conducted by able child analysts who shared his views. Many senior child analysts have felt the training of lay child analysts was absolutely essential. They regard it as a practical solution for dealing with the lengthy training period for adult analysis which has discouraged so many medical analysts from undertaking the additional lengthy programs to qualify for child analysis. These lay trainees were interested in child analysis primarily, and though they were given enough contact with the analysis of adults to give them grounding in psychoanalysis, for the most part, they have concentrated on the practice of child analysis. In 1971 a number of lay analysts were voted full membership in the American Psychoanalytic Association and in their local societies, giving them status equal to other members of the Association. Obviously these individuals were carefully selected by their teachers for training and have had outstanding professional careers. Many now occupy respected positions in American psychoanalysis. The quality and productivity of these nonmedical analysts, who were trained under such difficult conditions, argue favorably for the acceptance of selected lay analysts for training, especially in the field of child analysis. Their accomplishments should influence the resolution of the controversial issue of nonmedical training.

The question of lay analysis has been a subject of repeated discussion in American psychoanalysis and in the American Psychoanalytic Association. The problems involved are complex and as yet unresolved. The training of lay analysts at present is approved as training for research. To offer clinical training to a nonmedical trainee requires a waiver from the Board on Professional Standards for each individual. The training of lay analysts in Europe has been less of a problem. Trainees who graduate from the Hampstead Program in England are designated as "child therapists." Many have come to this country and have proven to be competent child analysts. Child therapy training programs in Clevelend and elsewhere are patterned after the Hampstead program. Training in child analysis without experience with adults, though proposed and carried out by the Dutch Psychoanalytic Society, has been rejected in this country. Most psychoanalytic educators still consider a thorough grounding in the analysis of adults essential. Many institutes have modified their programs to permit experience with children earlier in a candidate's training. In most instances this modification has been successful.

THE RELATIONSHIP OF CHILD AND ADULT ANALYSIS

Questions about the relationship of child analysis to adult analysis abound in psychoanalytic literature and are raised repeatedly during professional meetings. Essentially these questions address the degrees of similarity and difference, how each form of analysis contributes to the other, and how each serves to increase knowledge of psychoanalytic psychology, theory, and technique. From its inception child analysis has broadened our knowledge of theory and added to technical skills. It may be useful to recall the significant contributions the analysis of children has afforded to psychoanalysis in general (Feigelson 1973).

I have already recounted how Anna Freud (1936) herself and Lewin and Ross (1960) credited the data, clarity of expression, and clear demonstration of the defenses to her work with children. Anna Freud's young patients demonstrated repeatedly the defenses delineated in her classic monograph. Particularly, the defenses against affects were revealed most clearly by child patients.

The analysis of children has demonstrated the causes of various kinds of symptomatology with a clarity and directness rarely available from the analysis of adults with its necessary reconstructions. Jenny Waelder-Hall's (1930) "Case of Night Terror" is an excellent example of this clarity. The patient, Anton, demonstrated that his illness had developed from oedipally rooted anxiety about his aggressiveness towards his father. He revealed how, in his child's mind, he had arrived at the conclusion that the tachycardia he experienced with sexual excitement was due to damage arising from sexual games. A remark of his father's that "Such games make one sick" had contributed to Anton's development of the symptom. As Waelder-Hall (1935) states, "It seems that child analysis shows us quite generally the psychic processes in statu nascendi and perhaps allows us a direct view of the process of development of a neurotic formation" (p. 274). Child analysis has contributed to the field of psychosomatic medicine by helping us to understand the connection between the mental process and its affect and the expression of the feeling by the body itself. Since the discharge of a feeling in the body is the child's primary method of handling affect one can frequently see, while working with children, a physical symptom when an affect would be expected to occur. An example of this is a little girl of four who had to be removed from her two-year-old brother's room because she was striking him. When she had gained sufficient control after crying, she said to her mother, "My stomach says you don't love me." Such observations are commonplace for the child analyst in his daily work. Knowledge of the fantasy life of an adult patient which the analyst recovers only after long and patient effort, and usually by means of reconstructions, is more directly available to the child analyst. The belief in magic, the power of wishes, the identity of thought and deed, the infantile fantasies of beating, oral impregnation, and anal birth, are directly expressed by children.

Recent observational studies of infants and children have served to confirm many of Freud's theories about the earliest transformations and shifts he was able to reconstruct in his analyses of adults (Erikson 1950, Escalona 1968, Kohut 1971, Mahler 1968, Piaget in Flavell 1963, Provence in Wolman 1972, Spitz 1957 and 1965, and Smirnoff 1966). These observations have clarified many aspects of the pregenital phases and made it possible for us to use our psychoanalytic understanding more effectively in the treatment of disturbances arising from the earliest periods of life.

Insight and understanding of the child's mode of thinking and feeling gained from analysis of children has aided immeasurably in the development of technique for the analysis of adults. From analytic work with children we have learned defense analysis. We have learned how to speak to the defensive side in a way that has meaning for the patient and will be effective, and the necessity for making complete interpretations and thus prevent the arousal of the need for additional defenses, increased resistance, acting out, or turning away from analysis with a negative transference reaction. A child will respond immediately and directly if an intervention is off the mark, timing is wrong, or both aspects of a conflict are not acknowledged and his narcissism protected. We have gleaned from child analysis how important the recognition of the presence of affects is and how useful a naming of the feeling can be in aiding progression of the analytic work.

Work with children keeps us more in tune with nonverbal communications, aids us in the correct choice of words, and the formulation of a communication to the patient. Some analysts maintain child analysis has taught us how to communicate with the child in the adult. Many analysts have noted from work with children, we see more clearly that the patient in analysis presents a composite of present reality and past reality. In essence, this is the important part of the analytic concept of working with the past in the present.

In light of the above it would seem to logically follow that institutes should offer all candidates in training for analysis of adults the opportunity to have the personal experience of analyzing a child under supervision and possibly an adolescent as well. This has been proposed by many competent psychoanalytic educators both in this country and abroad. In most institutes there have been individuals who have successfully taken one child case under supervision and have found the experience extremely rewarding. It has helped them gain a degree of understanding and technical skill in adult analysis much greater than would have resulted had they had only the adult training. Attempts to analyze children by other adult analysts have failed badly, and at times have been tragic experiences for both the analyst and the patient. It seems that some analysts, though quite sensitive and skillful in work with adults, are afraid of children and lack talent in this work.

Some analysts still maintain that some aspects of child technique—play, activity, lack of use of the couch and free association, and differences in transference—all are parameters which modify the technique to such a degree that the fundamentals of psychoanalytic technique are lacking. To these analysts, child and adolescent analysis represent a treatment modality which is not truly analytic.

Most institutes as well as the American Psychoanalytic Association have come to accept as integral parts of analytic training courses that include child development, psychopathology of childhood and adolescence, and basic techniques of child and adolescent analysis, as well as attendance at seminars and clinical conferences on analysis of children and adolescents for all candidates in the institute. Whether every candidate could or should analyze a child or adolescent under supervision is a question to be answered in the future.

SUMMARY

Psychoanalytic education has come a long way since that evening in Vienna many years ago when Anna Freud, with two students, established the first psychoanalytic continuous case seminar. At the present time (1976) in the United States there are eighteen approved training programs in child analysis and four institutes with child analytic training programs in various stages of development. All of these programs are based on the standards developed by the American Psychoanalytic Association. The goal is to offer candidates in child analysis a training consistent with our present knowledge and understanding of the field. In addition, contributions from training programs from other parts of the world are being incorporated in our approach to analytic education.

Training in child and adolescent analysis has evolved through many phases of growth. It is now established in the institutes along with training in the analysis of adults. Literature on child analysis is extensive and includes valuable information not only about the psychoanalytic treatment and understanding of children and adolescents, but also of adults. Much research has broadened our knowledge of the development, learning, and adaptation of children from birth to adulthood. Further development of psychoanalytic education and the integration of child and adult psychoanalytic training continue to offer new areas for further exploration (Sullivan in Wolman 1972).

ADDENDUM I

Institutes of the American Psychoanalytic Association with approved training programs in child psychoanalysis (September 1, 1976).

1. Baltimore-District of Columbia Institute for Psychoanalysis
2. Boston Psychoanalytic Society and Institute, Inc.
3. Chicago Institute for Psychoanalysis
4. Columbia University Psychoanalytic Clinic for Training and Research
5. The Cleveland Psychoanalytic Institute
6. Downstate Medical Center, Division of Psychoanalytic Education, State University of New York, College of Medicine at New York City
7. Institute of the Philadelphia Association for Psychoanalysis
8. Los Angeles Psychoanalytic Society and Institute
9. New Orleans Psychoanalytic Institute, Inc.
10. New York Psychoanalytic Institute
11. Philadelphia Psychoanalytic Institute
12. Pittsburgh Psychoanalytic Institute, School of Medicine, The University of Pittsburgh
13. San Francisco Psychoanalytic Institute
14. Seattle Psychoanalytic Institute
15. Southern California Psychoanalytic Institute
16. Topeka Institute for Psychoanalysis
17. Washington Psychoanalytic Institute
18. Western New England Institute for Psychoanalysis

Institutes with developing child analysis training programs

1. St. Louis Psychoanalytic Institute
2. University of North Carolina-Duke University Psychoanalytic Training Program
3. Michigan Psychoanalytic Institute
4. Denver Institute for Psychoanalysis, University of Colorado, School of Medicine

ADDENDUM II

The following is a reproduction of a portion of "Training Standards in Child and Adolescent Psychoanalysis" published by the American Psychoanalytic Association Board on Professional Standards, Stanley Goodman, Chairman (1978):

Requirements for Admission to the Child and Adolescent Psychoanalysis Training Program of an Accredited Institute

1. An applicant for admission shall be an active candidate or graduate of an accredited Institute.

2. Prior to his training, or during child and adolescent training, the candidate shall have gained considerable familiarity with the psychology, development, and diagnosis of normal and pathological conditions in children. This experience may be acquired through training in child psychiatry or effectively supervised experiences with children in a variety of settings as, for example, pediatric services, schools, day care nurseries, or through other means devised by the individual Institute.

Requirements for the Completion of Training in Child and Adolescent Psychoanalysis

A candidate in child and adolescent analysis, regardless of his status otherwise, whether a member of a Psychoanalytic Society, a graduate of an Institute, or a regular candidate, must fulfill all the requirements of the child and adolescent analysis training program. In order to graduate from the program he should already have graduated, or simultaneously be graduating, from the adult training program.

It is clear that training in the psychoanalysis of children and adolescents at various stages of their development requires special additional didactic courses and seminars, and supervision beyond the regular courses required for training in adult analysis.

1. Didactic Seminars. The curriculum in adult analysis, according to the Board's recommendation, includes courses in child and adolescent development. Candidates in child and adolescent analysis shall have additional courses in the psychopathology of children and adolescents, and the theory and technique of child and adolescent analysis, including the basic literature of child and adolescent analysis. They shall also be required to demonstrate a thorough knowledge of the developmental

sequences and characteristics of childhood and adolescence, including both theoretical and clinical aspects.

2. Continuous Case Seminars. Continuous case seminars in child and adolescent analysis shall be attended for at least three years. It has been found that clinical supervised work is enhanced by concomitant attendance at, and presentation in, the continuous case seminars. Therefore, it is highly recommended that these be attended until supervision is concluded and graduation from the child and adolescent division has taken place.

3. Supervision. Candidates in child and adolescent analysis shall be required to do sufficient clinical work, under supervision, to demonstrate satisfactory competence in the analysis of children and adolescents. Experience over the years has shown that the attainment of such competence requires that the child and adolescent analysis candidate shall:

a. Analyze at least two children and one adolescent under supervision, one of whom must be a latency child, and one of whom must be an adolescent whose analysis is begun when the patient is already in some phase of adolescence. . . . It is preferable that the third case be a prelatency child. Both sexes should be included. The conditions necessary for conducting child and adolescent analysis require that the frequency of sessions be no fewer than four times a week.

b. Have worked with at least two but preferably three supervisors.

c. The candidate should be supervised on a weekly basis with at least one case (usually the first). The frequency of supervision on the remaining cases shall be determined by the candidate and supervisor. At least one case should be supervised up to and through the termination phase of the analysis. In general, a minimum of one hundred and fifty hours for the total supervisory experience with the three cases is desirable, with a reasonable distribution of supervision among the three. In all instances, however, the primary goal is for the candidate to achieve and demonstrate analytic competence.

ADDENDUM III

Proposed developmental core curriculum reproduced from Position Paper, The American Psychoanalytic Association Conference on Psychoanalytic Education, Training and Research, Commission IX (Settl-age et al. 1974, pp. 50–61).

First Year (192 hours)

I. THEORY

Metapsychology (2 semesters)

The course on metapsychology presents the basis for contemporary theory. Beginning with Freud's early view on infantile sexuality, phases of instinctual development, the topographic theory, and early views on defense, the course will continue with development, revisions in meta-psychology, early concepts of narcissism, aggression, psychic energy, sadism, masochism, anxiety and conflict, and conclude with early struc-tural theory.

Readings in Theory (2 semesters)

The readings are selected for the purpose of complementing the course on metapsychology. Ideally, the same instructor will teach both the metapsychology, or a portion of it, and the correlated readings.

Introduction to Theory of Dreams (1 semester)

Freud's *Interpretation of Dreams* will be studied with emphasis on chapter seven.

II. *Human Development* (2 semesters)

In the first year, this course will cover development from the neonatal phase through the latency phase. Discussions of theory and literature are correlated with direct observation of newborn infants, older infants, toddlers, nursery school children, and early elementary school age children. The relevance of observed behavior to the psychoanalytic theory of instincts and ego development is still under debate. The value of direct observation in understanding human growth and development is incontestable, however.

Over the first and second years of the curriculum, this course is to span the entire life cycle. It will convey an understanding not only of the details of psychic development, but also of the nature of developmental processes. In order to highlight the interplay between bio-physiological and psychological development, the course will include pertinent information about physical growth and development and the anatomical and physiologic changes taking place in the successive stages. The importance of this is notably illustrated by puberty, the climacterium, or senescence.

Direct observation of development should be carried out in conjunction with this course, but with careful planning in the interest of conservation of time and of assuring that the observations are integrated with the didactically taught content.

While the scheduling of development courses has in the past differed in different institutes, its central importance suggests that it be placed in the first year and continued in the second year, if necessary. Since knowledge of all of the stages of development is relevant from the outset of a given adult analysis, the course should advisedly not be carried beyond the first two years.

III. Psychopathology
Freud's Case Histories (1 semester)

The five case histories will be studied with the aim of correlating clinical material with Freud's early concepts of pathologic formation.

Assessment of Analyzability (1 semester)

The criteria for analyzability of adults, children, and adolescents will be studied on the basis of metapsychological assessment of level of development in drive, ego, and object relationship. The ability to assess a patient at a given age is sharpened by comparison with the issues at a different age.

Consideration should be given to having the candidates attend conferences in conjunction with the institute clinic, perhaps periodically throughout the span of training. Also, an account of the assessment period should be given for each of the cases presented in the Continuous Case Seminars. This course could be the basis for selection of the first supervised case, and might appropriately involve participation of the supervisor(s).

IV. Technique
Principles of the Psychoanalytic Method and Technique (1 semester)

This course will be concerned primarily with the basic principles and the beginning of an analysis. Consideration will be given to therapeutic alliance, development of the transference neurosis, clinical use of dreams, the therapeutic attitudes and posture of the analyst, and the rationale for variations in technical approaches based on the ego development of the patient.

V. *Clinical Case Conferences—Adults, Adolescents, and Children* or *Continuous Case Seminar—*Adult (2 semesters)

Selection of a beginning case or cases will place emphasis on the opening phase of the analysis.

Second Year (192 hours)

The beginning of second year course work should be correlated with the beginning of the first supervised analytic case. In this model curriculum the first case is an adult patient with a classical neurosis. Some Institutes permit selected candidates to have a child as a first case, but there is not enough experience with this approach to suggest it offers any advantage to the candidate in basic training. The advantage for the candidate in child analytic training has been the opportunity to get started earlier in treating children, thus shortening the often unduly prolonged training of the child analyst. In the model core curriculum the child analytic training requires no more than one extra year of required course work, and supervised work with children and adolescents can potentially begin parallel with the second adult case. The need for taking a child case first to save time is thus obviated.

I. *Theory—Metapsychology* (2 semesters)

This course will study structural theory in depth, concentrating on ego psychology and including correlation with recent contributions from experimental work in biology, psychology, ethology. Readings will be woven into the fabric of the course.

II. *Human Development* (2 semesters)

In this year, the course will cover development from adolescence through old age with continuing study of phase-specific developmental tasks, crises, conflicts, and interaction of the individual and his environment.

III. *Psychopathology from the Developmental Viewpoint* (2 semesters)

This course will present basic concepts of psychopathology. It embodies the approach outlined under Basic Education, and thus will be weighted on the developmental, rather than the nosological side, emphasizing psychogenetics and psychodynamics, and studying pathological formations as vicissitudes of development. It would include consideration of developmental disturbances and developmental deviations, as well as the elements of neuroses, psychoses, and the in-between pathologies. It will include pertinent reading, and the concepts will be amply illustrated by clinical vignettes.

IV. Technique
Adult Analysis (1 semester)

Continuing from the first-year course on technique, this course will focus on the traditional technique of analysis of adults in the middle and later phases of the analysis.

Introduction to Child Analysis (1 semester)

Because of its overlap with the course on adult technique, this course should be taught by an experienced child analyst also experienced in the analysis of adults. As was the case in the course on assessment of analyzability, the distinctions and comparisons of analysis during different age periods, so helpful for learning, can thus be drawn side-by-side.

The course will present the concepts and principles of child analysis and include the following: a résumé of the history of child analysis with emphasis on the changes which have occurred in the last twenty years; the initial consultation sessions with parents and child; assessment; preparation of child and parents for analysis; the role of the parents; the opening phase; adaptation of technique to different developmental levels; therapeutic alliance; transference; resistance; reconstruction; and dreams.

Reading will be integrated with the course, and include both contemporary and the classic early papers, the latter serving the important purpose of highlighting the changes which have occurred in the theory and technique of child analysis, and the concepts of enduring value.

V. *Continuous Case Seminar—Adult* (2 semesters)
   Continuous Case Seminar—Child (2 semesters)

These seminars will ideally be scheduled on alternate weeks throughout the year.

Optimally, in the child case seminar, a prelatency age child should be presented in alternation with a latency age child. In the third year adolescent case seminar, an early-phase adolescent would be similarly alternated with a later-phase adolescent. Cases of both sexes would be represented in both seminars. The seminars should be viewed as vehicles for explorations beyond the material of the particular case under discussion—that is, for the inclusion of references to other patients, adults as well as children and adolescents, and for references to the literature from adult as well as child analysis. Experience demonstrates that the candidates quickly emulate this method and take the initiative in referring to their own adult and child cases and relevant papers, a tendency clearly to be fostered.

Also optimally, one of the two cases in the child seminar should be presented by an advanced candidate or recent graduate, so that the seminar participants may gain a sense of the richness and depth of which child analysis is capable in the hands of a more experienced analyst.

Third Year (160 hours)

The beginning of course work in the third year should be correlated with beginning a child case by those candidates who elect training in child analysis. For other candidates, the supervised analysis of a child, although encouraged, is elective and its timing can be decided flexibly depending on the status of the individual candidate.

I. Theory—*Metapsychology* (2 semesters)

In keeping with the concept of spiral progression, this course will review earlier presented theoretical concepts in the light of the candidate's actual analytic work with patients, will elaborate on already taught concepts, and will take up new and emerging concepts.

II. *Psychopathology from the Nosologic Viewpoint* (2 semesters)

Psychopathology will here be presented in terms of the classical view of syndromes, but these in the light of current ego psychology and developmental concepts. The discussed syndromes will include neuroses, narcissistic disorders, borderline states, character disorders, psychosomatic illness, and psychoses in adults and children.

III. Technique
Adult Analysis (1 semester)

This course (a) will discuss technical issues in the use of dreams in adult analysis, also drawing comparisons from the analysis of adolescents and children, and (b) will discuss the technical issues involved in the psychoanalytic treatment of patients with more than neurotic psychopathology.

Introduction to Adolescent Analysis (1 semester)

This course should be taught by an experienced child analyst also experienced in the analysis of adults. Distinctions and comparisons to analysis with adults and with younger children can thus be drawn.

The concepts and principles of adolescent analysis will be presented, including: differing views on the analyzability of adolescents; the role of parents as contrasted with their role in child analysis; initial contact with the adolescent; analyzability; special problems of technique with the younger adolescent; the approach to the college student as a late adolescent; preparation for analysis; phase-specific areas of vulnerability and resistances in boys and girls; transference; and criteria for and handling of termination. Reading will be integrated within the course.

V. *Continuous Case Seminar—Adult* (2 semesters)
  Continuous Case Seminar—Adolescent (2 semesters)

These seminars will ideally be scheduled on alternate weeks throughout the year.

Fourth Year (96 hours)

IV. Technique
  Advanced Technique (1 semester)
  Clinical Case Conferences on Technique (1 semester)

These courses jointly have the aim of reviewing and pulling together the technical considerations and issues presented in the earlier technique courses, in terms of both concepts and application. Clinical cases will be used as a vehicle for comparison among not only adult, adolescent, and child cases, but among neurotic and more serious disorders.

V. *Continuous Case Seminar—Adult* (2 semesters)
  Continuous Case Seminar—Either Child or Adolescent (2 semesters)

The candidate in training in child and adolescent analysis will take both the child and adolescent seminars. Because of this requirement, he may have less inclination toward elective courses than the candidate in adult analysis only.

VI. *Electives*

Electives are by definition optional and their format and duration are flexible. They will vary from year to year and consist of courses or study groups offered on the basis of interest among faculty and candidates.

Fifth Year and Beyond

V. *Continuous Case Seminars* (2 semesters)

Attendance at continuous case seminars is required until the candidate is approved for unsupervised work. The candidate in adult analysis will attend the adult seminar, but may elect the child or adolescent seminar. The candidate in child analysis will attend both the child and adolescent seminars.

VI. *Electives*

These will continue to be offered to candidates and recent graduates.

NOTES

1. The foregoing has been primarily based on the Reports of the Committee on Child Analysis to the Board of Professional Standards from 1965 to 1973 by the Chairmen during this period, Drs. Albert J. Solnit and Calvin F. Settlage.

2. In Europe lay child analysts were trained prior to the establishment of institutes and as part of institutes' training.

REFERENCES

Angel (Katan), A. (1935). From the analysis of a bedwetter. *Psychoanalytic Quarterly* 4:120–134.

Bornstein, B. (1935). Phobia in a two-and-one-half-year-old child. *Psychoanalytic Quarterly* 4:93–119.

Bornstein, S. (1935). A child analysis. *Psychoanalytic Quarterly* 4: 190–225.

Buxbaum, E. (1935). Exhibitionistic onanism in a ten-year-old boy. *Psychoanalytic Quarterly* 4:161–189.

Eidelberg, L., ed. (1968). *Encyclopedia of Psychoanalysis,* pp. 67–70. New York: The Free Press.

Erikson, E. H. (1950). *Childhood and Society.* New York: W. W. Norton.

———— (1959). *Identity and the Life Cycle.* New York: International Universities Press.

Escalona, S. K. (1968). *The Roots of Individuality.* Chicago: Aldine Publishing

Feigelson, C. I. (1973). Panel Report: a comparison between adult and child analysis. *Journal of the American Psychoanalytic Association* 22:603–611, 1974.

Flavell, J. H. (1963). *The Developmental Psychology of Jean Piaget.* New York: Van Nostrand Reinhold.

Freud, A. (1930). *Psychoanalysis for Teachers and Parents.* New York: Emerson Books.

––––––– (1936). *The Ego and the Mechanisms of Defense.* New York: International Universities Press.

––––––– (1946). *The Psychoanalytical Treatment of Children.* London: Imago.

––––––– (1963). The concept of developmental lines, *Psychoanalytic Study of the Child* 18:245–265.

––––––– (1965). *Normality and Pathology in Childhood.* New York: International Universities Press.

Freud, S. (1909). Analysis of a phobia in a five-year-old boy. *Standard Edition* 10:5–149.

––––––– (1938). An outline of psychoanalysis. *Standard Edition* 23: 141–207.

Hug-Hellmuth, H. (1921). On the technique of child-analysis *International Journal of Psychoanalysis* 2:287–305.

Kohut, H. (1971). *The Analysis of the Self.* New York: International Universities Press.

Kolansky, H. (1971). Some reflections on a psychoanalytic core curriculum. *Bulletin of the Philadelphia Association for Psychoanalysis* 21: 59–69.

Lewin, B. D., and Ross, H. (1960). *Psychoanalytic Education in the United States.* New York: W. W. Norton.

Lustman, S. L. (1967). The meaning and purpose of curriculum planning. *Journal of the American Psychoanalytic Association* 15:- 862–875.

Mahler, M. S. (1967). Child development and the curriculum. *Journal of the American Psychoanalytic Association* 15:876–886.

––––––– (1968). *On Human Symbiosis and the Vicissitudes of Individuation.* New York: International Universities Press.

Mahler, M.S., Pine, F., and Bergman, A. (1975). *The Psychological Birth of the Human Infant.* New York: Basic Books.

Pearson, G. H. J., ed. (1968). *A Handbook of Child Psychoanalysis.* New York: Basic Books.

Poertl, A. (1935). Profound disturbances in the nutritional and excretory habits of a four-and-one-half-year-old boy: their analytic treatment in a school setting. *Psychoanalytic Quarterly* 4:25–36.

Rexford, E. N. (1962). Child psychiatry and child analysis in the United States today. *Journal of the American Academy of Child Psychiatry* 1:365–384.

Settlage, C. F., et al. (1974). The American Psychoanalytic Association Conference on Psychoanalytic Education and Research. Commission IX.

Smirnoff, V. (1966). *The Scope of Child Analysis.* New York: International Universities Press. 1971.

Spitz, R. A. (1957). *No and Yes—On the Genesis of Human Communication.* New York: International Universities Press.

_____ (1965). *The First Year of Life.* New York: International Universities Press.

Sterba, E. (1935). Excerpt from the analysis of a dog phobia. *Psychoanalytic Quarterly* 4:135–160.

Waelder-Hall, J. (1930). The analysis of a case of night terror. *Psychoanalytic Study of the Child* 2:189–227, 1946.

_____ (1935). Structure of a case of pavor nocturnus. *Bulletin of the Philadelphia Association for Psychoanalysis* 20:267–275, 1970.

_____ (1975). Personal Communication.

Wolman, B. B., ed. (1972). *Handbook of Child Psychoanalysis.* New York: Van Nostrand Reinhold.

CONTRIBUTORS

Jules Glenn, M.D.
Clinical Associate Professor of Psychiatry, Training and Supervising Analyst, and former Chairman of the Child Analysis Section, Division of Psychoanalytic Education, Downstate Medical Center, State University of New York
Editorial Board, *Journal of the American Psychoanalytic Association*

Melvin A. Scharfman, M.D.
Clinical Professor of Psychiatry, Training and Supervising Analyst, and Chairman of the Child Analysis Section, Division of Psychoanalytic Education, Downstate Medical Center, State University of New York
Director, Pride of Judea Children's Services, Queens, N.Y.
Attending Psychiatrist, Long Island Jewish–Hillside Medical Center

Samuel Abrams, M.D.
Clinical Associate Professor of Psychiatry, Training and Supervising Analyst in Child and Adult Analysis, and Chairman of the Education Committee, Division of Psychoanalytic Education, Downstate Medical Center, State University of New York
Chairman of the Committee on Psychoanalytic Education, American Psychoanalytic Association

Former Chairman of the Program Committee of the Association for Child
Psychoanalysis

Ted E. Becker, M.D.

Training and Supervising Analyst, and Chairman of the Child Analysis
Committee, New York Psychoanalytic Institute

Isidor Bernstein, M.D.

Clinical Associate Professor of Psychiatry, and Supervising Child Analyst
at the Division of Psychoanalytic Education, Downstate Medical
Center, State University of New York
Training and Supervising Analyst, New York Psychoanalytic Institute
Lecturer and Supervising Child Analyst, Columbia University Psycho-
analytic Center for Research and Training, College of Physicians and
Surgeons

L.J. Byerly, M.D.

Clinical Assistant Professor of Child Psychiatry, Medical College of
Pennsylvania
Chief of Psychiatry, West Jersey Hospital, Camden, N.J.
Faculty, Philadelphia Psychoanalytic Institute

Elaine Caruth, Ph.D.

Associate Clinical Professor, Department of Psychiatry (Child), University
of California at Los Angeles School of Medicine
Senior Faculty and Supervisor, Los Angeles Institute for Psychoanalytic
Studies
Member, Association for Child Psychoanalysis

Beatrice Cooper, M.A.

Clinical Associate and Social Work Supervisor in Child Psychiatry at the
University of California at Los Angeles Neuropsychiatric Institute
Department of Child Psychiatry
Formerly Senior Psychiatric Social Worker, Childhood Psychosis Project,
Reiss-Davis Child Study Center

Elizabeth Daunton

Associate Professor in Child Therapy, Department of Psychiatry, School
of Medicine of Case Western Reserve University

Member of the Center for Research in Child Development, Cleveland, Ohio

Consultant to Kindergarten of Hanna Perkins Therapeutic Nursery School and Kindergarten, Cleveland, Ohio

Rudolf Ekstein, Ph.D.

Clinical Professor of Medical Psychology, University of California at Los Angeles

Training and Supervising Analyst, Los Angeles Psychoanalytic Society and Institute, and the Southern California Psychoanalytic Society and Institute

John J. Francis, M.D.

Associate Clinical Professor of Child Health and Development and Psychiatry and Behavioral Sciences, George Washington University School of Medicine

Training and Supervising Analyst, and Co-chairman of the Committee on Child Analysis, Baltimore–District of Columbia Psychoanalytic Institute

Past President, Baltimore Psychoanalytic Society.

Co-editor of *Masturbation from Infancy to Senescence*

Seymour W. Friedman, M.D.

Senior Faculty, Los Angeles Psychoanalytic Society and Institute.

Member, Association for Child Psychoanalysis

Supervisor of Psychotherapy, Reiss-Davis Child Study Center

Formerly Director, Clinical Services and Research Associate, Childhood Psychosis Project, Reiss-Davis Child Study Center

Erna Furman

Assistant Clinical Professor in Child Therapy, Case Western Reserve University School of Medicine Department of Psychiatry

Faculty member, Cleveland Psychoanalytic Institute

Faculty member, Cleveland Center for Research in Child Development

Consultant, Day Nursery Association–Center for Human Services

Staff Member, Hanna Perkins Nursery School and Kindergarten

Ilse Hellman, Ph.D

Training and Supervising Analyst and Chairman of the Education Committee, British Psycho-Analytic Institute

Member of the Training Committee and Chairman of the Adolescent Study Group, Hampstead Child-Therapy Clinic

Paul Kay, M.D.

Clinical Associate Professor of Psychiatry, and member of the faculty of the Child Analytic Section, Division of Psychoanalytic Education, Downstate Medical Center, State University of New York

Instructor in Psychiatry, Long Island Jewish–Hillside Medical Center

Selma Kramer, M.D.

Professor and Head of Section of Child Psychiatry, Medical College of Pennsylvania

Training and Supervising Analyst, and Chairman of the Child Analysis Program, Philadelphia Psychoanalytic Institute

Chairman of the Committee on Child and Adolescent Analysis of the American Psychoanalytic Association

Peter D. Landres, M.D.

Director, Psychiatry Department, Reiss-Davis Child Study Center

Lecturer, Center for Early Education

Member, Los Angeles Psychoanalytic Society and Institute

Joel M. Liebowitz, Ph.D.

Diplomate in Clinical Psychology

Formerly Supervisor of post-doctoral fellows, and Research Associate, Childhood Psychosis Project at Reiss-Davis Child Study Center

Thor Nelson, Ph.D.

Presently in full-time private practice

Former Research Associate, Child Psychosis Project, Reiss-Davis Child Study Center

Former Associate Professor, California State University, Los Angeles

Former Director, Child and Adolescent Program, Resthaven Psychiatric Hospital and Community Mental Health Center

Peter B. Neubauer, M.D.

Clinical Professor of Psychiatry, Training and Supervising Analyst, and former Chairman of the Child Analysis Section, Division of Psychoana-

lytic Education, Downstate Medical Center, State University of New
York

Director, Child Development Center, New York, N.Y.

John Turner Lecturer, Columbia University Psychoanalytic Center for
Research and Training, College of Physicians and Surgeons

Former President, Association for Child Psychoanalysis

Secretary General of the International Association of Child Psychiatry and
Allied Professions

Joseph Opperman

Member of the American Psychological Association

Member of the Association for Child Psychoanalysis

Formerly Staff Consultant, Caroline Zachry Institute for Human
Development, and the Educational Institute for Learning and Research

Irma Pick

Supervisor of Child Therapists, Tavistock Clinic

Supervisor of psychoanalytic trainees at British Psychoanalytic Society

Sally Provence, M.D.

Professor of Pediatrics, Yale University Child Study Center, New Haven

Special Member, Western New England Psychoanalytic Society

Member, Association for Child Psychoanalysis

Lawrence M. Sabot, M.D.

Clinical Assistant Professor of Psychiatry, and Training and Supervising
Division of Psychoanalytic Education, Downstate Medical Center,
State University of New York

Qualified Child and Adolescent Analyst, New York Psychoanalytic
Institute

Albert M. Sax, M.D.

Assistant Lecturer, and Supervising Analyst in Child and Adolescent
Analysis, New York Psychoanalytic Institute

Hanna Segal, M.B., Ch.B., F.R.C. Psych.

Member of and Training Analyst at the British Psychoanalytic Society

Visiting Professor of the Freud Memorial Chair, University College, London, 1977–1978

Author of *Introduction to the Work of Melanie Klein*

Martin A. Silverman, M.D.

Clinical Assistant Professor of Psychiatry, and Secretary of the Child Analysis Section, Division of Psychoanalytic Education, Downstate Medical Center, State University of New York

Senior Research Psychiatrist, Child Development Center, New York, N.Y.

Adjunct Professor of Communication Science and Disorders, Montclair State College, Upper Montclair, N.J.

Editorial Board, *Psychoanalytic Quarterly*

John A. Sours, M.D.

Clinical Assistant Professor of Psychiatry, and Training and Supervising Analyst, Columbia University Psychoanalytic Center for Research and Training, College of Physicians and Surgeons

Associate Instructor for Child and Adolescent Analysis, New York Psychoanalytic Institute

Herbert Wieder, M.D.

Supervisor, Child and Adolescent Psychiatric Training Program, and Physician-in-charge, Adoption Study Center, Brookdale Hospital Medical Center, Brooklyn, N.Y.

Qualified Child and Adolescent Analyst, New York Psychoanalytic Institute

INDEX